CONTENTS

FOREWORD

The Treaty establishing a Constitution for Europe fundamentally changes the structure and nature of the Union, since it establishes a new European Union. It is the successor to the existing European Union and replaces the two current principal treaties of the Union, the Treaty establishing the European Union and the Treaty establishing the European Community, and incorporates and gives binding legal force to the Charter of Fundamental Rights.

The Treaty is an uneasy compromise and reflects the tension arising from the conflicting interests of the small and large states, the balance between the social, economic and environmental policies, which together represent the three principal objectives of the Union, and the two principal views in which direction the European Union might go: that of the inter-governmental view of separate nation states acting in a free market and that of the European Union being a single entity operating under the principles of a European social market with the Member States having a sub-ordinate role.

This new European Treaty comes very soon after the Treaty of Nice, which was signed on 26 February 2001 and only came into force on 1 February 2003, once the ratification process had been completed.

The Treaty of Nice was intended to prepare the Union for enlargement. In the event, the issues proved to be too contentious to resolve and the resulting Treaty was an uneasy compromise that did not satisfy anyone and a declaration was attached to the Treaty which prepared the way for a Convention to be formed to consider these issues.

The Convention quickly developed beyond the initial remit of considering whether a Constitution might be appropriate and what its content might be to actually preparing a constitution.

In a speech to the College of Europe in Bruges on 2 October 2002, Valery Giscard d'Estaing, the President of the Convention said:

> *"The Laeken decision to convene this Convention ... is the recognition that the Union has reached a major turning-point in its history, and that it must therefore rethink, readjust and – in part – reinvent the system, and propose a New Europe."*

> *"I see [the Union] as being a Union of European States closely co-ordinating their policies and administering certain common competences, along federal lines."*

Although the word *'federal'* in Article I-1 has been removed, this is largely cosmetic and the words used in its place, *'the Community way'* indicates that the intention of greater integration is still implicit in the Treaty.

In addition, Valery Giscard d'Estaing said that the simplification of the current treaties would lead to a *"new single document, inevitably erasing the former texts and calling for its ratification as a whole"*. This demonstrates the very different nature of the Constitutional Treaty to the Single European Act and the Treaties of Maastricht, Amsterdam and Nice, since each of these in turn modified the preceding treaties without repealing them. If a Member State had not ratified these earlier treaties, they would not have become law and the Union and the Community would have reverted back to the previous situation.

As with the previous European treaties, all of the Member States must ratify the Treaty before it can come into force. In the ratification process that takes place within the national parliaments, the Treaty can only be accepted or rejected as a whole and amendments cannot be made to parts of the text.

The aim of this book is to identify the principal important areas in the Treaty and to help the reader to interpret the provisions of the Treaty.

This is the fifth book by the BMDF on the European Treaties and follows the same layout as the previous ones.

The analysis is in the front of the book [pages in Roman numerals]:

- There are summaries on the background the Treaties and some notes on the text of the Treaty, to explain the layout and the annotations that the BMDF has added to the text;

- The main part of the analysis covers the principal issues and key points in the Treaty and the changes to the legislative procedure;

- there is a summary of the changes in the voting by the Council from unanimity to qualified majority voting and a summary of the areas that are still under unanimity;

- the additional papers include the Laeken Declaration, two speeches given at the time of the signing of the Treaty, and the report by the Presidency of the Convention to the European Council on 18 July 2003.

The complete text of the Treaty, together with all of the Protocols and Declarations is shown in pages on Arabic numerals.

In addition, the BMDF has prepared:

- two sets of Tables of Equivalences to enable the reader to trace individual Articles from the existing Treaties to the corresponding Article in the Constitution, and to show the change in numbering from the draft Constitution to the final text;

- a fourteen-page comprehensive index to the Treaty.

BACKGROUND TO THE CONSTITUTION

The Treaty establishing the Constitution developed from a general agreement within the European institutions that the legislation and the institutional arrangements that had been drawn up under the existing European Treaties have become increasingly incapable of allowing the Union to function. In particular, the arrangements for qualified majority voting in the Council agreed in the Treaty of Nice, did not resolve the concerns over the ability of the European institutions to be able to operate after enlargement. The initial treaties were drafted in 1957 to accommodate a European Community of six Member States and were not designed to accommodate twenty-five countries.

Currently, there are three major Treaties forming the primary law of the European Union: the Treaty on European Union (TEU), introduced by the Maastricht Treaty, the Treaty establishing the European Community (TEC) and the Treaty establishing the European Atomic Energy Community. A fourth Treaty, the Treaty establishing the European Coal and Steel Community, expired on 1 July 2002. In addition to the three principal Treaties, there have been a number of acts and treaties that have supplemented and amended these major treaties, including the four accession treaties. These amending treaties and acts are listed in Protocol No. 33 attached to the new Treaty. All of these treaties and acts are repealed by the Constitution (Article IV-437).

The Treaty of Amsterdam began the process towards preparing the Union for enlargement, by including a Protocol containing provisions for the size of the Commission and the weighting of votes in the Council, which included the concept of dual majority (i.e. votes and size of population in each Member State). The Protocol did not contain any details on these provisions and also included a provision that at least one year before the membership of the European Union enlarges to 20, there would be another inter-governmental conference.

In the negotiations leading up to the Treaty of Amsterdam, the issue of enlargement was addressed but no conclusion could be reached. A protocol was agreed on the size of the Commission and the modification of the voting in the Council. In addition, a declaration was attached to the Treaty by Belgium, France and Italy, stating that they considered that the Treaty of Amsterdam did not properly address the changes of the institutions for enlargement. This view formed the basis of the discussions at the successive inter-governmental conferences leading up to the Treaty of Nice.

The issues left in Amsterdam were reconsidered at Nice and the Nice Treaty attempted to prepare and adjust the operations of the Community institutions for enlargement. Nice was an uncomfortable compromise which satisfied none of the Member States and it was recognised that the Treaty would not prepare the Union for enlargement. it was agreed that there should be a further Treaty to resolve the problems of enlargement on the institutions of the Union. A Declaration was attached to the Treaty of Nice instigating the process that continued with the Laeken Declaration in December 2001 and the Convention on the future of Europe and culminated in the agreement of the new Constitutional Treaty on 18 July 2004.

The review of the future of the Union was intended to cover the following major points, as stated in the Declaration attached to the Treaty of Nice:

- how to establish and monitor a more precise delimitation of powers between the European Union and the Member States, reflecting the principle of subsidiarity;

- the status of the Charter of Fundamental Rights of the European Union, proclaimed in Nice, in accordance with the conclusions of the European Council in Cologne;

- a simplification of the Treaties with a view to making them clearer and better understood without changing their meaning;

- the role of national parliaments in the European architecture.

The Laeken Declaration arranged for the Convention on the future of the European Union to be formed to review these points and to reach a conclusion that would in turn be the basis for discussion by the heads of government to produce a new Treaty. The Convention was formed in March 2002. After eighteen months of discussion, the text of the concluding draft Constitutional Treaty was presented by the Convention to the European Council on 18 July 2003. There was then a review by the European Union's Legal experts, which was followed by the Inter-Governmental Conference under the Italian Presidency.

The text had a number of irreconcilable issues in it, principally a dispute between France and Germany on the one hand, and Spain and Poland on the other, over the distribution of the number of weighted votes in the Council, and in December 2003 it was agreed by the Heads of Government that the issues were so difficult to resolve that the discussions on the Constitution should be stopped.

The Irish Government took over the Presidency of the European Council in January 2004 and decided to attempt to reinstate the negotiations. They were successful in reconciling the concerns of the Member States and on 18 June 2004, the Treaty was agreed in Brussels. The formal signing took place on 29 October 2004 in Rome, which reflected a certain symmetry, in that the Constitution represents the start of a new European Union, and Rome had been the place where the first Treaty of Rome had been signed in 1957, to establish the European Economic Community. The expectation is that the Constitution will be ratified in the next two years and come into force on 1 November 2006 (Article IV-447).

Ratification and entry into force of the Constitution

The procedure of ratification of the Treaty follows the approach of the existing Treaties, in that each Member State ratified the Treaty under its own constitutional methods. There has been one modification, where if after two years of the signing of the Treaty, two-thirds of the Member States have ratified the Constitution,and the remaining Member States have difficulties in ratification, the matter will be passed to the European Council (Article IV-443(4)). This provision suggests that the European Council would attempt to reach a compromise, by introducing derogations and additional Protocols or Declarations to ensure that all the Member States would be able to ratify the Constitution.

At the end of October 2004, eleven countries had announced that they either would or would be likely to hold a referendum on the Constitution. These countries are Belgium, the Czech Republic, Denmark, France, Ireland, Luxembourg, The Netherlands, Poland, Portugal, Spain and The United Kingdom. In the case of the United Kingdom, the date of the referendum has not yet been set, though it is likely to be in the spring of 2006.

Since so many countries have declared that they will hold a referendum, there is a large possibility that in at least one country, the Constitution will not be ratified. In that event, the Constitution cannot come into effect. There are a number of possible outcomes:

i. second (or more) attempts are made at ratification in the States concerned. This would perhaps apply to the smaller countries, but in a large country, where the first result had been emphatic, a second referendum would be unlikely;

ii. the Treaty is discarded and the European Union continues with the existing Treaties. Given the political effort and time that has been expended, it is unlikely that this would be tolerated and attempts to continue the process would be soon made after any failure of ratification;

iii. renegotiation of the Constitutional Treaty;

iv. partial entry into force of the Constitution by a small number of countries under the terms of the existing 'enhanced co-operation' provisions;

v. implementation of some of the provisions of the Treaty by some of the Member States, with individual opt-outs being negotiated by the countries. This would follow the precedence set in the Maastricht Treaty for the UK with the opt-outs from EMU and the Social Chapter;

vi. individual withdrawal of a Member State, either at its own request or through forcible departure, at the behest of the other countries. This would be a final resort if one country prevented the others from implementing the Constitution.

Development of the provisions of the European Treaties

The competences of the European Union have developed over time, from the first Treaty of Rome in 1957, which was essentially a Treaty concerned with the economic aspects of the European Community, to the much more clearly-defined political ambitions of the later Treaties that amended the Treaty of Rome, as described in the first two paragraphs of the Laeken Declaration. The new Treaty develops this process further by repealing the current European legislation and establishing a Constitution.

The Treaty of Rome

The Treaty of Rome, signed in 1957, established the European Economic Community and was the second of the three treaties establishing the European Communities. The others being the Treaty establishing the Coal and Steel Community (now no longer in force) and the Treaty establishing the European Atomic Energy Community

The Treaty of Rome laid down the overall structure together with the principal terms and initial provisions for the economic community, including the development of the internal market and the common agricultural policy, and the structure of the Community institutions. In this treaty, the concept of qualified majority voting was introduced, although the majority of areas were under unanimity. There were provisions drawn up in this Treaty that would pass to qualified majority voting from unanimity after an initial period lasting until 31 December 1971.

The Treaty of Rome introduced:
- the legal personality of the Community;
- the four fundamental freedoms of the Community (freedom of movement of services, capital and workers and the freedom of establishment);
- a customs union - elimination of restrictions on trade, including quotas;
- competition policy and taxation, state aid and anti-dumping provisions;
- harmonisation of laws to create the common market;
- economic policy - general requirement of the Member States to operate and co-ordinate, and treat their economic policy as a common concern;
- common commercial policy;
- the role of the European Parliament was restricted to consent and opinion.
- budget provisions;
- the process of the revision and ratification of the Treaties.

The Single European Act

The Single European Act came into force on 1 July 1987 and had as its main purpose the speeding-up the process of the introduction of the Common Market   the aim to formally change areas under unanimous voting to that of qualified majority, these changes following the terms as laid down in the Treaty of Rome for the time-scale of change-over.

This Treaty was essentially brought about owing to the Luxembourg Compromise of 1966, which required the Community to take into account an individual member state's concerns that its vital national interests would be damaged if a certain policy were adopted. Under this agreement, little progress in the formation of the internal market was made and changes to the voting system to allow qualified majority voting was considered vital to improve the decision-making to enable the common market to develop.

Another aspect of the Single European Act was the introduction of the concept of a common foreign policy, termed 'European co-operation in the sphere of foreign policy' and was the forerunner of the provisions introduced by the Maastricht Treaty. In the Single European Act, the emphasis was placed on the Member States so that they will endeavour to implement a foreign policy and give due consideration to other Member States. They would ensure that common principles and objectives are gradually developed. The role of the Community institutions was restricted to being informed.

The Treaty extended qualified majority voting to eight areas that had been stated in the Treaty of Rome that these should change from unanimity to qualified majority after the end of the initial period on 31 December 1971 (by the time of the Single European Act, it was already sixteen years after this should have happened). In addition, four other areas were introduced with qualified majority voting and the Treaty provided for the European Parliament to have an increased role in decision-making.

The Treaty also introduced measures concerning:

- the harmonisation of legislation concerned with the functioning of the Internal Market was changed to qualified majority voting;
- environment;
- research and technological research;
- the Court of First Instance, to assist the Court of Justice;
- the concept of economic and monetary union. This was drafted in general terms and the text stated that the Member States should co-operate to ensure the convergence of economic and monetary policies necessary for the further development of the Community (Article 20.1 SEA).

The Maastricht Treaty

The Maastricht Treaty came into force in 1992; it introduced the concept of the European Union and the Treaty on European Union and reinforced the irreversibility of the progress to 'ever-closer' union. The Treaty introduced the concept of the three pillars, of the Economic Community, the Common Foreign and Security Policy, and Justice and Home Affairs. In the case of the last two areas, the role of the Court of Justice was clearly defined and restricted.

The most important aspect of the Treaty establishing the European Community were the introduction of the provisions for the introduction of the Single Currency. In addition, the voting process for co-decision was introduced. Finally, a small but important change was to remove the word Economic from the title, indicating the fundamental change in the Community's approach to the Treaty and the ideals of the European Union as a whole. Importantly, it did not give legal personality to the Union.

- the Treaty introduced more social provisions, including the 'Social Chapter', from which the UK Government gained an opt-out;
- establishment of 'citizenship of the Union' to enjoy the rights confirmed by the Treaty and be subject to the duties imposed thereby;
- strengthening economic and social cohesion by structural and other aid to the poorer EC countries;
- widening the scope of the competence of the European Communities into new areas, such as education, public health, culture, consumer protection, trans-European networks, industry and development co-operation;
- introducing the concepts of subsidiarity and proportionality into the Treaties;
- the Treaty repealed the provisions of the Single European Act concerned with foreign policy and introduced the Common Foreign and Security Policy, with an increased role of the Union to implement a common policy, with clearly defined objectives, and a defined role for the European Council, although the area still remained essentially an inter-governmental one;
- the environment given greater prominence in all EC acts and became the third principal objective of the European Community, with the economic and social objectives.
- the concept of co-decision with the Council acting with the European Parliament to pass acts of the Community, hence increasing the role of the European Parliament.
- 30 Articles were moved or introduced subject to qualified majority voting.

The Treaty of Amsterdam

The Treaty of Amsterdam came into force in 1997. The aim of the Treaty was to prepare the Union for enlargement and to develop the decision-making of the Community institutions through the extension of co-decision and strengthening the involvement of the European Parliament and introducing more qualified majority voting

The Treaty introduced:

- the concepts of the fundamental principles of the European Union: liberty, democracy, respect for human rights and fundamental freedoms and the rule of law;
- moved the provisions concerned with asylum and immigration from the TEU, and therefore inter-governmental in nature, to the TEC, and therefore justiciable by the Court of Justice, though there were qualifications to the extent of the role of the Court of Justice, and a passerelle clause

was introduced to allow the Council to change the method of voting from unanimity to qualified majority voting after five years from the date of entry into force of the Treaty;

- incorporation of the Schengen *acquis* into the Treaties, through a Protocol, the UK secured an opt-out from this;
- change of name of 'Justice and Home Affairs' to 'Police and Judicial co-operation in Criminal Matters', following the guidance of the European Council meeting in Vienna to develop a single geographical area of freedom, security and justice.
- introduced the concept of closer co-operation into the TEU, which was open to all Member States;
- the concepts of subsidiarity and proportionality were developed by the introduction of a Protocol;
- Social policy was developed, through the inclusion of the Social Chapter in the main text of the Treaty, as the UK had given up its opt-out;
- the Articles of the Treaty on European Union and the Treaty establishing the European Community were renumbered and twenty-four areas were moved to qualified majority voting from unanimity.

The Treaty of Nice

The Treaty of Nice continued the process of preparation of the Union for enlargement started at Amsterdam, including dealing with areas that had not been concluded at Amsterdam. These were the size and composition of the Commission, the reweighting of votes in the Council and the possible extension of qualified majority voting. Some of the other areas changed by the Treaty were:

- forty-six articles were either moved to, or were introduced into the Treaty subject to qualified majority voting from unanimity;
- closer co-operation was renamed as enhanced co-operation and extended to cover the common foreign and security policy;
- the common commercial policy was extended to intellectual property;
- Eurojust was incorporated into the treaties;
- judicial panels attached to the Court of Justice were introduced in order to free up the main courts for more important cases.

The Draft Treaty establishing The European Union (draft Spinelli Treaty)

This draft Treaty is otherwise known as the Spinelli Treaty, named after the Italian socialist MEP Altiero Spinelli, who is regarded as one of the principal architects of the European Union, to the extent that one of the buildings of the European Parliament in Brussels is named after him. This draft treaty is arguably one of the most influential documents concerned with the development of the European Union.

It was drafted in 1984 and was presented to the European Parliament, where it was overwhelmingly passed on 14 February 1984, by 237 votes for, 32 against and 34 abstentions. Although it never became law, as the Council did not approve it, it did form the basis of the negotiations of the Single European Act in 1986 and it had considerable influence on the Maastricht Treaty of 1992. Most of the ideas and principles have now been included in the Treaty on European Union and the Treaty establishing the European Community.

The provisions of the Spinelli Treaty which have been included in the current Treaties mainly concern:
- the creation of the European Union and Union citizenship;
- the principle of subsidiarity;
- the institutionalisation of the European Council;
- the investiture of the Commission by the European Parliament;
- the principle of legislative co-decision between the European Parliament and the Council;
- co-operation in foreign and security policy and justice and home affairs;
- the European monetary system;
- social, health, environment, consumer, culture, and development aid policies;
- the multi-annual programming of expenditure.

The main provisions which had not been included concern:

- revision of the Treaty through the use of the co-decision procedure;
- abolition of unanimity in the Council (Article 23 of the Spinelli Treaty provided for abolition of the veto within ten years);
- the designation of Commission members by the Commission President;
- the Council being composed of ministers entrusted with the Union's affairs;
- the suspension of the rights of Member States in the event of serious and permanent violation of the Treaty provisions (this is partially covered by Article 7 TEU);
- the Union's shared competence in the area of energy;
- financial autonomy of the Union;
- the introduction of a hierarchy of Union legislation (basic law, laws, budgetary laws, regulations and decisions);
- the Union having exclusive competence over competition policy.

It is very noticeable that the majority of these provisions have now been introduced by the Treaty establishing the Constitution, in particular, the shared competence in energy (Article I-14 and III-256), the hierarchy of laws (Article I-33) and the continuing process of the introduction of co-decision (now termed the 'ordinary legislative procedure' in the Constitution). Competition policy is partially covered by Articles I-12 and III-177, where the Union will provide the arrangements for the Member States to co-ordinate their economic policies.

The Treaty establishing the Constitution

The principal intention of the Constitution is to prepare and re-design the European institutions for enlargement, while not affecting the *acquis communautaire* of the European Union. In addition, the opportunity has been taken to codify and consolidate the disparate parts of the European legislation into a single document, including two principal Treaties, the Treaty on European Union and the Treaty establishing the European Community, and the five Treaties of Accession and repeals the existing Treaties.

Under the Constitution:

- all of the existing Treaties are repealed and replaced by the Constitution;
- the Constitution forms the basis of a new European Union and replaces the existing European Union;
- gives legal personality to the Union;
- states that the Constitution and European Union law has primacy over the Member States;
- gives the Charter of Fundamental Rights legal status;
- draws together into two Protocols all of the Treaties of Accession, including the recent accession of the ten new Member States;
- includes the explanations to the Charter of Fundamental Rights as a Declaration;
- introduces a Union Minister for Foreign Affairs;
- introduces an appointed President of the European Council, who will be in post for two-and-a-half years;
- defines the areas of exclusive competence of the Union and the areas of shared competence with the Member States;
- redefines the co-decision process as the 'ordinary legislative procedure' and terms other methods of voting in the Council as 'special legislative procedures'.
- extends qualified majority voting under the ordinary legislative procedure (co-decision) to forty-four areas, of which nineteen are new areas. Sixteen areas are extended to qualified majority voting in the Council through the special legislative procedures, with five new areas.

NOTES ON THE TEXT

Structure of the Treaty

The text of the Treaty in this book is taken from CIG 87/2/04 REV 2, published on 29 October 2004, The text of the Protocols is drawn from CIG 87/04 ADD 1 REV 1, published on 13 October 2004 and the Final Act and Declarations are drawn from CIG 87/04 ADD 1 REV 2, published on 25 October 2004. These are the final versions of the Treaty and were used in the formal signing of the Treaty on 29 October 2004.

The Treaty has eight sections. The first five, the Preamble and Parts I to IV represent the main text of the Treaty. The other sections are the Protocols, the Declarations and the Final Act.

Preamble	lays out the philosophical aspirations of the treaty and of the Union;
Part I	contains the text of the Constitution and lays out the general principles under which the Union will operate;
Part II	contains the text of the Charter of Fundamental rights;
Part III	contains the detailed provisions of the policies and functioning of the Union, including the voting mechanisms and the implementation of the principles in Part I;
Part IV	contains the general provisions, including the ratification and revision procedures;
Protocols	these provide detailed provisions on specific areas that have been more generally described in the main text of the Treaty. There are thirty-six and they are integral to the Treaty and are legally binding. These include details on the involvement of the national Parliaments and the role of subsidiarity;
Declarations	these give supporting statements and interpretation to the provisions in the main text of the Treaty and in the Protocols. There are fifty Declarations and they are attached to the Treaty but are not legally binding. They give a clear indication of the political will behind the statements. One of the more important declarations describes the explanations to the Charter of Fundamental Rights.
Final Act	this Act states that the Member States have signed and thus formally adopted the Treaty establishing the Constitution together with the associated Protocols and Declarations.

In addition, there are two Annexes attached to the Treaty. Annex I lists the products that come under the provisions of the common agricultural and fisheries policies in Articles III-226. Annex II lists the non-European overseas countries and territories that have special relationships with some of the Member States and are subject to the provisions of the Treaty in Articles III-286 to III-291. The Annexes are shown after Part IV.

Background to the final Text

The Treaty establishing the Constitution has undergone a series of changes and amendments from the initial draft drawn up by the Convention to the final text signed by the Heads of Government on 29 October 2004.

The Convention was given eighteen months to complete its tasks. It spent fifteen months discussing the text of the Constitution in Part I and the Charter of Fundamental Rights in Part II, leaving only three months to discuss Parts III and IV. As a result, there are a number of anomalies in the text of Part III, including obsolete articles such as Articles III-167(2) and III-243, on German reunification, and Article III-215 on "paid holiday schemes". In the final version of the Constitution, the legal experts have made some adjustments to the wording of Articles III-167(2) and III-243, so that they may be repealed five years after the entry into force of the Constitution.

Once the Convention had completed its work and presented the signed draft text to the European Council on 18 July 2003, it was agreed that a working party of legal experts should review the draft, to consider any anomalies in the wording and in particular to ensure that the texts of the Treaty in all of the official languages agreed with one another.

The legal experts were not in a position to be able to modify the technical details of the text, as this is reserved for the Heads of Government. The major changes which they made included a paragraph added to the Preamble stating that the Heads of State wish to ensure the continuity of the *acquis communautaire*, the movement of the article on the symbols of the Union to Part I of the Treaty from Part IV, to give the symbols more prominence, the redrafting of the existing Protocols to reflect the changes introduced by the Constitution and a major rewriting of the Protocol on the role of national governments to include a definition of draft European legislative acts and the procedure of the forwarding of information to the national parliaments from the European institutions

In the negotiations under both the Italian and the Irish Presidencies, there were a large number of changes to the Convention text, culminating in the European Council meeting in June 2004 when the Treaty was agreed, subject to a final review by the Working Party of legal experts. This review also renumbered the articles of the main text of the Treaty.

Numbering of the Articles

In the initial drafts of the Constitution, each Part of the Treaty was numbered separately and this has led to confusion in identifying particular articles. In addition, the Group of Legal Experts made a number of changes to the draft texts and as a result, there were gaps in the sequence of the numbering of the articles.

In the March 2004 meeting of the European Council, it was decided to simplify the numbering and to number the articles consecutively throughout the main text of the Treaty.

The final numbering of the Treaty has been completed during the final revisions of the Treaty in preparation of the signing on 29 October 2004 and **this revised numbering system is used throughout this book**.

Each Article has been numbered with consecutive Arabic numbers, with the appropriate number of each Part attached to the Article number.

	Original Numbers	Revised Numbers
Part I	I-1 to I-59	I-1 to I-60
Part II	II-1 to II-54	II-61 to II-114
Part III	III-1 to III-342	III-115 to III-436
Part IV	IV-1 to IV-10	IV-437 to IV-448

A detailed set of Tables of Equivalences to compare the original and the revised numbering of the Articles in the Constitution have been prepared by the BMDF and are shown at the back of this book.

Annotations in the Text

In Parts I, III and IV, the articles in the official text of the Treaty do not have any references to the old article numbers from the current Treaties. Where appropriate, the BMDF has included references to these old articles to show the origin of the articles in Parts I, III and IV. New articles introduced by the Constitutional Treaty are indicated as such.

The references are shown after the article number i.e. Article III-121 *(new)*; Article III-122 *(ex Article 32 TEC)*. In particular cases, such as Article I-14(2), ex-article numbers are shown against individual provisions i.e. - Tourism *(new)*; - Environment *(ex Article 174 TEC)*.

The ex-article numbers refer to the article numbers in the Treaty on European Union (TEU) and the Treaty establishing the European Community (TEC), as renumbered by the Treaty of Amsterdam and included in the consolidated treaties as modified by the Treaty of Nice.

The new Treaty extensively rewrites and reorders the articles from the earlier Treaties, and so in some cases the references to the old article numbers can only give an indication of their origin. This particularly applies to Part I of the Treaty and to the areas in Part III concerning 'Freedom, Security and Justice' (starting at Article III-257) and 'The Union's External Action' (starting at Article III-292).

In Economic and Monetary Policy, Article III-197(2) defines the provisions that do not apply to the United Kingdom, owing to the opt-out from the Euro. BMDF notes are attached at the end of each individual article or provision to indicate the articles that do not apply to the UK.

The United Kingdom has an opt-out in the areas of border controls, asylum and immigration judicial co-operation in civil matters and police co-operation; the opt-out is described in two Protocols (Protocols 18 and 19). BMDF notes are attached at the end of each individual article or provision in the main text of the Treaty to indicate where the opt-out applies.

Under the terms of Protocol number 34, on the transitional provisions relating to the institutions and bodies of the Union, the voting arrangements in the Council described in Article I-25 do not come into effect until 1 November 2009, as this will be the start of the first period of office of the Commission and the European Parliament after the entry into force of the Constitution. In order to highlight these provisions, BMDF notes are attached to the relevant articles in Parts I and III.

Tables of Equivalences

The BMDF has prepared two sets of Tables of Equivalences. The first set enables the reader to trace articles from the current two main treaties (the TEU and the TEC) to the Constitution. There are four columns in the tables showing changes to the numbering of each article: the original numbering used in the Treaty of Rome to the Maastricht Treaty, the new numbering in the Treaties of Amsterdam and Nice, the initial numbering used in the Draft Constitution and the fourth column shows the revised numbering in the final text of the Constitution.

The second set of Tables shows the comparatives of the original and the revised numbering of the articles in the Constitution. This has been prepared to enable the reader to trace numbers in other publications, including debates in the Houses of Parliament, which have used the original numbering when referring to articles in the new Treaty.

General Index

A fourteen-page subject index has been included, prepared by the BMDF, covering all parts of the Constitution and the principal Protocols and Declarations attached to the Treaty. In addition, there is an Index for the Protocols on page 125 and an index for the Declarations on page 233.

Sources and References

The analysis and the text of the Treaty have been prepared using a number of different documents.

1.   The base document is the Final Report by the Convention to the European Council (CONV 850/03) dated 18 July 2003, which is referred to in this BMDF book as either the Convention Draft or the 'Giscard' Draft.

2.   The following documents have been used in the BMDF preparation of the text:

*   CIG 87/2/04 REV 2. 'Treaty establishing a Constitution for Europe'; Brussels, 29 October 2004.

*   CIG 87/04 ADD 1 REV 1. 'Protocols and Annexes I and II annexed to the Treaty establishing a Constitution for Europe '; Brussels, 13 October 2004.

*   CIG 87/04 ADD 2 REV 2. 'Declarations to be annexed to the Final Act of the Intergovernmental Conference and the Final Act'; Brussels, 25 October 2004.

3.   Reference has also been made to the following Convention and IGC documents:

*   The Draft Treaty establishing a Constitution for Europe, The European Convention, Brussels CONV 850/03, dated 18 July 2003;

*   CIG 50/03. 'Editorial and legal adjustments to the draft Treaty; Brussels, 25 November 2003 (26.11), and the associated corrigenda;

*   CIG 50/03 ADD 1. 'Editorial and legal adjustments to the Protocols of the draft Treaty; Brussels 25 November 2003 (26.11), and the associated corrigenda;

*   CIG 50/03 ADD 2. 'Editorial and legal adjustments to the Protocols of the draft Treaty; Brussels 30 April 2004 (07.05), and the associated corrigenda;

*   CIG 50/03 ADD 3. 'Declarations attached to the Final Act of the IGC; Brussels 13 May 2004 (14.05) and the associated corrigenda;

*   CIG 81/04 PRESID 23. 'Meeting of Heads of State or Government, Brussels, 17/18 June 2004'; Brussels, 16 June 2004.

*   CIG 85/04 PRESID 27. 'Meeting of Heads of State or Government, Brussels, 17/18 June 2004'; Brussels, 18 June 2004.

*   CIG 86/04. 'Provisional consolidated version of the draft Treaty establishing a Constitution for Europe'; Brussels, 25 June 2004.

*   CIG 86/04 ADD 1. 'Provisional consolidated version of the Protocols annexed to the draft Treaty establishing a Constitution for Europe and of Annexes I and II'; Brussels, 28 June 2004.

*   CIG 86/04 ADD 2. 'Provisional consolidated version of the Declarations to be annexed to the Final Act of the Intergovernmental Conference'; Brussels, 25 June 2004, and the associated corrigenda.

*   CIG 87/04. 'Treaty establishing a Constitution for Europe'; Brussels, 6 August 2004, and the associated corrigendum.

*   CIG 87/1/04 REV 1. 'Treaty establishing a Constitution for Europe'; Brussels, 13 August 2004.

*   CIG 87/04 ADD 1. 'Protocols and Annexes I and II annexed to the Treaty establishing a Constitution for Europe '; Brussels, 6 August 2004, and the associated corrigendum.

*   CIG 87/04 ADD 2. 'Declarations to be annexed to the Final Act of the Intergovernmental Conference'; Brussels, 6 August 2004, and the associated corrigenda.

4.   Reference has also been made to the following UK Government documents:

*   'The Draft Constitutional Treaty for the European Union', FCO Cm 5897, August 2003.

*   'A Constitutional Treaty for the EU: the British approach to the Intergovernmental Conference 2003', FCO Cm 5934, September 2003.

*   'Prospects for the EU in 2004', FCO Cm 6174, April 2004.

*   'White Paper on the Treaty establishing a Constitution for Europe', FCO Cm 6309, September 2004.

PRINCIPAL ISSUES AND KEY POINTS

Nature of a Constitution

A Constitution could be described as a legal document defining the framework of how a state is organised and how the divisions of sovereign powers are regulated. Hence, it is the body of fundamental principles and rules of a state from which stem the duties and powers of the government and the duties and rights of the people.

In the United Kingdom, the constitution is based on statute, common law and convention and, as there is no formal draft, it is considered to be unwritten; as a result, it may be modified from time to time by act of Parliament. In the United States, the constitution cannot ordinarily be modified, except through such processes described in the constitution itself.

The Constitution of the European Union represents the primary law of the Union and can be modified by amendments to the Treaty by the processes laid down in the Treaty [Article IV-443].

The 'Three Pillars' and Consolidation of the Treaties

One of the purposes of the Constitution has been to consolidate all of the existing legislation into a single document and to combine the TEU and the TEC. This has been done with the exception of the Treaty establishing the European Atomic Energy Community, which has been left as a separate treaty.

Under the existing TEU and TEC treaties, the Union has a 'three Pillar' structure, comprising the European Community, Common Foreign and Security Policy and Justice and Home Affairs [now termed police and judicial co-operation]. The second and third pillars are included in the Treaty on European Union and are principally based on intergovernmental agreements, while the provisions in the European Community are judiciable under the Court of Justice, as are certain parts of police co-operation (rulings on guidelines and on visas, asylum and immigration). The role of the Court of Justice is restricted in relation to the second and third pillars, and Article 46 TEU defines the extent of the powers of the Court.

The three-pillar structure was not explicitly stated as such in the text of the TEU or the TEC, but it was a general interpretation of the Treaties agreed at Maastricht. Under the Constitutional Treaty, the pillar system has been removed and the three policies have been consolidated into a unified text. The whole of the Treaty becomes justiciable under the Court of Justice, with certain exceptions in the foreign and security policy and police and judicial co-operation.

Ratification, entry into force and revision of the Constitution (Articles IV-443 and IV-447)

Each Member State has to ratify the Treaty in order for it to become law (Article IV-447). It is intended that the ratification process should take two years from the date of signature, through the ratification processes of each country. This will either take the form of a parliamentary system or by referendum. The Treaty should enter into force on 1 November 2006, or failing that, the first day of the second month after the last Member State has ratified the Treaty.

However, there is an additional qualification in the Treaty, that if two years after the signature of the Treaty, four-fifths of the Member States have ratified the Treaty and one or more Member States have difficulties, the matter will be referred to the European Council. (Article IV-443(4)) A Declaration to this effect (Declaration no. 30) is attached to the Treaty, which repeats the provision in the text of the Treaty.

In theory, this provision has no effect as in order for it to become law, the Treaty has to be ratified; this article is therefore a statement of intent, indicating the political will to ensure that the Treaty will pass into law.

Preamble

The Preamble at the beginning of the Treaty serves to describe, in general terms, the aspirations for the Constitution. The Preamble for this Treaty is very different in structure and emphasis to those of the previous European treaties, where introductory Resolutions and Affirmations by the

Heads of State reflected the issues agreed. Although it is not binding, the Preamble is important in that it is intended to express the clear common political will among the contracting parties and to define the intentions of the Union.

The first draft was written by Giscard d'Estaing in October 2003 after the Treaty had been formulated by the Convention and included, in Greek, a quotation by the Greek historian Thucydides (c. 460-399 B.C.).

In the final version of the Treaty, this quotation has been removed and an additional paragraph has been added stating that the *acquis communautaire* will continue. The term "ever closer union" in the third paragraph of the Preamble, which had been included in an early draft, has been redrafted to read "united ever more closely".

Primacy of Union law (Article I-6)

The principle of European law having primacy of over that of the Member States was established by a Court of Justice case, *Costa v. ENEL*, Case 6/64. The ruling by the Court concerned the provisions of the European Community and stated that the Member States and individuals are bound by Community law and in addition, Community law must be applied by the national courts.

When the Treaty of European Union was introduced by the Maastricht Treaty in 1992, nearly twenty years after the Court's ruling, the extent of the Court's authority was clearly defined and the Union had an inter-governmental structure. In several Member States, the national courts have queried the extent of European law over national law, and the conclusions of these courts have been that European law only has force because the Member States confer that authority.

This article in the Constitution removes any ambivalence and formally extends the primacy of law from Community law to cover European Union law. This establishes the concept that European Union law has primacy over that of the Member States in both international and internal law, that is the national law inside the Member States themselves. In addition, the Article is explicit in stating that the Constitution itself will have primacy over the law of the Member States. In the current Treaties, it is not stated that the provisions of the Treaties, which make up the primary law of the Union, do have primacy.

Legal personality (Article I-7)

Under the current treaties, the Union does not have legal personality while the separate Communities (the European Community and the Atomic Energy Community) do; as a result, the Union has been unable to act in its own right and has only been able to act through the Community institutions and the jurisdiction of the Court of Justice is restricted under Article 46 TEU to certain areas.

The reasons for giving legal personality to the Union is ostensibly to enable it to act in making international agreements, for example under Article I-13 and Articles III-323 to III-326, but this is not defined or limited as such in the Constitutional Treaty and therefore has wider implications. Currently, the Union has not had a budget of its own and has depended on that of the Community (e.g. in the Common Foreign and Security Policy). In the Constitutional Treaty, the Union will have its own budget, allowing it to become independent from the Member States.

Symbols of the Union (Article 1-8)

Symbols of the Union have been introduced into the Treaty, including the definition of the flag, the anthem, the motto and the public holiday. In addition, it is stated that the currency of the Union will be the euro, even though there are only twelve countries that are currently members of the euro out of the twenty-five Member States of the Union. The expectation is that all the Member States will in time join the euro.

The date of the public holiday, 9 May, commemorates the date in 1950 when Robert Schumann, the then French Foreign Minister, gave a speech describing plans for France and Germany to pool their coal and steel production; this led to the formation of the European Coal and Steel Community in 1951and the European Community in 1957.

Competence (Articles I-11 to I-18)

The Constitution explicitly lays out the extent of the competence, or powers, of the Union, which the Member States have conferred to it. Where there is exclusive competence, only the Union can act, and the Member States can only act where the Union gives them the authority. The areas of exclusive competence, such as conservation of marine biological resources, have been defined in the judgements of the Court of Justice but have not been laid out in the Treaties until now.

Social and employment policies (Articles and (3)) and the common foreign and security policy (Article I-12(4)) will be co-ordinated by the Union, which will have the competence to define and implement guidelines for these areas.

The Member States will co-ordinate their economic policies (Articles I-12(3) and Article I-15), but the Union will have the competence to define guidelines and the arrangements for co-ordination. The Union has exclusive competence over the monetary policy of the Member States in the euro. The text of the Treaty has been altered from the earlier drafts, where the Union would co-ordinate the economic policy of the Member States, and the changes to the text reflect the concerns of the national governments that they should be able to preserve their ability to conduct their own economic policy.

Shared competencies (Article I-14)

The addition of areas of '*shared competence*' (Articles I-12 and I-14) to those in which the Union has exclusive competence (Article I-13) widens the powers of the Union. The term '*shared*' is misleading as Member States can only exercise their competence when and to the extent '*that the Union has not exercised or has decided to cease exercising the competence*'. Member States have to respect the primacy of European law and cannot enact laws that conflict with existing European law and principles.

The phrase, '*the Union ... has decided to cease exercising the competence*' is the only mention in the Treaty of the concept that part of the *acqui*s, or competences, might be returned to the Member States. There is no explanation of the mechanism for this procedure, therefore the European Council would act under the general provisions to decide by unanimity.

Flexibility (Article I-18)

This Article derives from Article 308 TEC and has not in itself changed. The flexibility of the clause is more to do with competence and implied powers of the Union, rather than the flexibility of either the interpretation of the Treaty articles or the flexibility of Member States to opt in or out of the provisions.

Flexibility in the European Union means more that there is a pragmatic method to solve any irreconcilable opinions between the Member States, and allowing certain countries to opt-out of various Union projects, such as the Single Currency and border control co-ordination in the Schengen *acquis*. It is expected that these derogations are temporary, and that all Member States will join EMU and Schengen and indeed the Constitution (Article I-8) states that the currency of the Union is the euro.

The principal aspects of flexibility in the Treaty are the enhanced co-operation provisions (Articles I-44 and III-416 to III-423). These provisions can only be applied where there is no exclusive competence. There are no separate rules for the area of freedom, security and justice.

The intention of the Constitution was that Part I would be able to stand-alone and be read as a single document without any reference being needed to the other parts. However, enhanced co-operation is sufficiently complicated that the provisions in Part III have to be referred to in order to understand the application of the provisions in Part I.

Although the enhanced co-operation provisions have been in the Treaties since the Treaty of Amsterdam, they have not yet been implemented. They have tended to have been used as a mechanism to encourage Member States to negotiate any difficulties they have had over certain policies, rather than a principled disagreement. This might change, with the concerns over the process of ratification of the Constitution and in specific policy areas, such as corporate taxation.

European Council (Article I-21 and III-341)

The articles describing the role of the European Council have been more clearly defined and the Union Minister for Foreign Affairs is included as a member. In a new provision, a member of the European Council may act on behalf of one other member as well as himself and any abstentions will not prevent the Council from adopting a measure either by unanimity or by a simple majority.

The Treaty provides for specific tasks of the European Council, where it will define the strategic interests and objectives of the Union in the foreign and security policy, (Articles III-293, III-295 and III-300) and in justice and home affairs (Article III-258).

European Council President (Article I-22)

The system in the current Treaties provides for equal rotation of the presidency every six months among the Member States, which in an enlarged Union would mean that each country would have the presidency once every 12½ years. Under the terms of the Constitution, the President of the European Council will be elected by the European Council by qualified majority and will have a term of two and a half years. However, there is great concern in the smaller States that the larger countries will vote in their chosen candidate and the smaller countries will not have a President.

A clause in the earlier drafts of the Treaty specifically excluded the President of the Commission from becoming the President of the European Council. However, this clause has been removed from the final draft, and there is nothing in the text of the Treaty to prevent the President of the Commission also becoming the President of the European Council.

There has been a late change of title to 'President' from 'Chair', which had been used in the earlier drafts. The term 'chair' had been used to satisfy the British, since the term 'President' has certain implications of governance.

The President of the European Council is may convene an extraordinary meeting of the European Council to define the strategic policy of the Union in foreign and security policy (Article III-295).

Commission (Article I-26)

The responsibilities of the Commission have been laid out for the first time in the treaties and these include:

i.   the promotion of the general interest of the Union, to take appropriate initiatives to that end, ensuring the application of the Constitution, and Union law under the control of the Court of Justice, and the exercise of co-ordinating, executive and management functions;

ii   the sole right to initiate and prepare proposals for Union legislative acts, except in specific cases;

iii.   the initiation of the Union's annual and multi-annual programmes and execution of the budget and programme management;

iv.   representing the Union in external relations, except for the Common Foreign and Security Policy.

The Commission has been given new powers in the Constitution, so that it may impose competition regulations concerning the detailed rules for agreements that are exceptions to the general prohibitions and that improve trade (Article III-165(3)). In the Treaty establishing the European Community, the Commission could only make proposals in this area.

Selection and number of Commissioners (Article I-26)

Under the current treaties, there are either one or two Commissioners from each Member State, with two Commissioners being drawn from the larger States. Under proposals in the draft Constitution, from 1 November 2009 the numbers would have been restricted to fifteen voting members, consisting of the President, the Union Minister for Foreign Affairs and thirteen others with one Commissioner per Member State. In addition, there would have been a new group of commissioners, who would be non-voting and appointed from the remaining Member States. This system provoked a great deal of criticism from the Member States during the IGC and a compromise was reached. The structure of the Commission has been altered to reflect the interests of all the Member States, and there will be a transitional period before the numbers of the Commission are reduced.

In the final text, there will one Commissioner from each Member State for the first Commission to be appointed after the Constitution has entered into force, so this will be for the five-year period starting on 1 November 2009.

In the second and successive periods of office (starting on 1 November 2014), the Commission will be reduced a total number of members corresponding to two-thirds of the number of Member States, including the President and the Union Minister for Foreign Affairs. With the current number of Member States, the total number of Commissioners will be 19, with 17 coming from the Member States. The Commissioners will be selected on a strict rotational basis. This has raised concerns that the abilities of the European Commissioners will vary markedly and this will potentially cause problems in the operation of the Commission.

Union Minister for Foreign Affairs (Article I-28)

The Union Minister will be appointed by the European Council, acting by qualified majority, and will conduct the Union's common foreign policy. There is a potential conflict in the position, as the Minister will be both a Vice-President of the Commission and at the same time be answerable to the Council. In addition, there is concern that the title of Minister suggests that the Union has a government, of which the Union Minister is a member.

The Foreign Minister will be assisted by a secretariat, created by the Constitution, the European External Action Service, composed of staff from the national diplomatic services as well as staff from the Commission and the Council (Article III-296(3)). Its role will be to assist the Union Minister for Foreign Affairs and to provide the staff in the Union's delegation in third countries and to international organisations. This gives an indication that the Union intends to establish a separate body that is the equivalent to the Foreign Office.

New Legislative structure (Article I-33 to I-36)

Two new forms of legislative acts are introduced, European laws and European framework laws, and these form the principal method of legislation of the Union, while directives will no longer exist. The system of co-decision has been renamed the 'ordinary legislative procedure' and is intended to be the standard method of enacting legislation in the Union. Co-decision or the ordinary legislative procedure comprises of the Commission making proposals and the Council and the European Parliament liaising together to pass the legislation. A more detailed analysis of this is shown in the chapter on legislative procedures.

The Union's External Action (Article I-40 to I-41 and Articles III-292 to III-329)

This area, corresponding to the first pillar in the existing Treaties, has been extensively rewritten and the principles are shown in Article I-40. The emphasis has changed: under the current provisions, the Common Foreign and Security Policy **might** lead to a common defence (Article 17 TEU and Article 2 TEU). In Article I-41(2) the Policy **will** lead to a common defence.

External action includes the common foreign and security policy, the common security and defence policy, the common commercial policy and international agreements, where through its newly acquired legal personality, the Union will be able to conclude agreements with third countries.

The Court of Justice does not have jurisdiction over this area and the limitations on its actions are defined in Article III-376.

A European Defence Agency is introduced, to be involved with defence capabilities development, research, acquisition and armaments (Articles I-41(3) and III-311, and Protocol no. 23)).

The concept of permanent structured co-operation for Member States that have the appropriate capability is introduced (Articles I-41(6) and III-312, and Protocol no. 23). The intention is that the structured co-operation will take effect by 2007, with combat units available within a period of 5 to 30 days and sustained for at least 120 days. The Member States involved are expected to harmonise their defence as much as possible, while remaining autonomous.

The Constitution introduces solidarity (mutual defence) clauses, where if a Member State suffers a terrorist attack or a major disaster, the other Member States will be obliged to come to its assistance (Article I-43 and Article III-329).

Area of freedom, Security and Justice (Article I-42 and Articles III-257 to III-277)

This area is the successor to the provisions under the heading of 'Justice and Home Affairs' introduced by the Maastricht Treaty and modified by the Treaty of Amsterdam. The whole policy has been extensively redrafted

The term 'area of freedom, security and justice' was introduced into the text of the Treaties by the Treaty of Amsterdam. At the European Council meeting in Tampere in 1999, the principles of the area of freedom, security and justice were developed to give more structure and to include the roles of Europol and Eurojust, and establish a European Police College for senior law enforcement officials.

The intention is to consolidate all of the disparate parts of the provisions spread throughout the Treaties into a single co-ordinated policy for the whole of the geographical area of the European Union. This follows from the policy of removing the internal borders within the European Union, to allow the freedom of movement for European citizens throughout the European Union.

The policy areas include external border controls, asylum and immigration, cross-border crime including money laundering and taxation matters, and a genuine European area of justice, including the mutual recognition of judicial decisions. The external border control matters include the provisions of the Schengen *acquis*.

The policy also includes the provisions of the Charter of Fundamental Rights, to ensure the right of freedom of movement and security of individuals within the borders of the European Union.

Under Article III-377, the jurisdiction of the Court of Justice will not extend to review the operations of national police forces or the actions by Member States with regard to internal security.

At present, this area is one of the three pillars and is generally inter-governmental, and the Court of Justice has a limited jurisdiction. In the Treaty of Amsterdam, the areas of asylum and immigration were removed from the inter-governmental procedures to the European Community, and so came under the jurisdiction of the European Court (with a limited amount of inter-governmental co-operation and voting in the Council by unanimity). Under the new Treaty, this area comes under the authority of the Community method of legislation and the area, including the provisions on Eurojust and Europol, is justiciable by the Court of Justice. There is an exception to this, in that the Court has no jurisdiction to review the validity or proportionality of operations carries out by the police or other law-enforcement services of a Member State or the safeguarding of internal security (Article III-377).

National parliaments will be involved in this area, in judicial co-operation in criminal matters and police co-operation (Articles III-270 to III-277) and they will be able to review proposed legislation under the terms of the Protocol on Subsidiarity (Protocol no.2).

Member States have the use of an 'emergency brake' in judicial co-operation in criminal matters, concerning mutual recognition of judgements and criminal offences, so that the Member State is able to oppose a draft framework law and the matter will be passed to the European Council for further discussion (Articles III-270(3) and III-271(3)).

Enhanced Co-operation (Article I-44 and Articles III-416 to III-423)

The concept of enhanced co-operation provides the opportunity of a small group of Member States to act together more closely in a particular area than the rest of the Member States. The minimum number of States that can be involved is nine, or one-third of the number of Member States.

The provisions for enhanced co-operation were introduced in the Treaty of Amsterdam and then given more depth and detail in the Treaty of Nice. The provisions have not been extensively changed in the Constitution, though they have been redrafted and there has been one significant change.

Member States that wish to join in with an arrangement under enhanced co-operation have to demonstrate to the Commission that they are willing and able to fulfil the conditions of entry (Article III-418). This means that Member States can be excluded from the opportunity to participate in the enhanced co-operation.

Since the Union institutions are involved, legislation relating to enhanced co-operation becomes Union law and will be justiciable in the Court of Justice.

Democratic Principles (Articles I-45 to I-47)

The Constitution formalises a number of principles under which the Union will operate and are effectively rights of the individual citizen. As a result, they have links to the Charter of Fundamental Rights, particularly Title III and Title V of the Charter on equality and citizens' rights. The principles are democratic equality, representative democracy and participatory democracy and are in addition to the concepts of subsidiarity and proportionality.

The principle of participatory democracy enables citizens and representative associations to have the opportunity to explain their views on any area of Union policy. In Article I-47(4), there is provision for individuals to petition the Commission to make proposals on any Union policy. In order that this can take place, there has to be at least one million people involved from a significant number of Member States. The Constitution does not give any details on how this might operate, but European laws will be used to define the terms. This could be used by a single-issue pressure group, on an area such as the environment, to initiate legislation.

The Union's Resources (Article I-54)

The Union's method of financing the budget comes from taxes and duties, termed own resources. Included in this is VAT and the UK negotiated a rebate in the 1980s. Currently, the whole of the area is under unanimity, but the Constitution will enable the Council to act by qualified majority in laying down the method of procedure in Article I-54(4) and this could enable the council to withdraw the UK rebate.

Voluntary withdrawal from the Union (Article I-60)

Any Member State may decide to withdraw from the Union and the process of withdrawal would be expected to take up to two years. At the moment, Member States are in theory able to withdraw under the terms of the Vienna Convention on the Law of Treaties of 27 January 1980.

The new provisions appear to make the process of withdrawing from the Union a difficult process and would involve a complicated combination of national law, European law, and international law, together with a lengthy negotiation period. The process of withdrawal would itself need a Treaty to define the terms of both the separation and the new relationship.

Under the terms of the Article, the Council is able to act by qualified majority on the conditions of the agreement with the Member State leaving the Union. There are no provisions laid down on how the negotiations for withdrawal would take place and over what time-period, or what the nature of the relationship would be after withdrawal. In addition, there are no provisions for withdrawal from the Single Currency in the Article.

Charter of Fundamental Rights (Part II)

The concepts in the Charter have been drawn from the European Treaties (particularly Article 6 TEU, which concern discrimination, fundamental freedoms and the obligations of the Member States to their citizens), rulings by the European Court of Justice and the European Convention of Human Rights of 1950.

The principle of fundamental rights was introduced into the formal treaty structure in the Maastricht Treaty of 1992, where Article 6(2) TEU, now Article I-9, stated that 'the Union shall respect fundamental rights.' The intention is that the Charter should apply primarily to the institutions and bodies of the Union, and to the Member States when they are applying Union law (Article II-111).

In 1999, the European Council of Cologne agreed to establish a Charter and the presidents of the European Parliament, the Council and the Commission proclaimed the Charter at Nice on 7 December 2000. At this stage, the Charter did not have legal status and it was included as one of the four main areas for consideration identified in the Declaration on the future of the Union attached to the Treaty of Nice. The Charter has been incorporated into the Draft Treaty establishing the Constitution, as Part II, and has binding legal force.

There have not been any major changes to the text of the Charter from Nice to the version in the Constitutional Treaty, except in incorporating the legally-binding nature of the Charter, so that it comes under the jurisdiction of the Court of Justice; this is defined in Article II-112.

In addition, the Praesidium has prepared updated explanations for the interpretation of the Charter, which includes a commentary on the scope of the Charter, stating that it will not extend the rights already included in national law and that the Charter will only apply to issues affected by Union law. The explanations are attached to the new Treaty in Declaration no. 12. The introduction to the explanations states that the explanations do not have the status of law, but that they are "a valuable tool of interpretation".

There are concerns over the structure of the Charter, in that it has some contradictions and uncertainties, in particular the potential conflict between individual rights and the common good, which would need to be decided by the national and European courts. For example, the right to strike is included in Article II-88 and this could lead to the Court of Justice overruling the UK's industrial legislation. The impact of the Charter will only be properly assessed when test cases are brought before the Court of Justice.

The Court of Justice has already begun to refer to the Charter in its judgements, in a supportive and non-contentious role, even though the Charter only has legal effect once the Constitutional Treaty enters into force. The Court has used the Charter in a wide range of issues, such as cartels, in *JFE Engineering v Commission* (T-67/00), disclosure of insider information, in *Grøngaard and Bang* (C-384-/02), persons unable to be tried twice, in *Tokai Carbon v Commission* (T-236/01) and the legality of Community measures, in *Commission v. Jégo-Quéré* (C-263/02P).

Taxation (Articles III-170 to III-171)

Under the existing treaties, the principal area of tax covered has been indirect taxes, such as VAT and all direct taxes have been excluded. The Court of Justice has ruled on corporation tax, under the provisions of non-discrimination in Article 43 TEC, now Article III-137.

Direct tax is one of the UK Government's 'red lines', where the veto on tax issues is retained. The veto is very narrowly drawn in that the issue is whether changes to tax in the Treaty are by unanimity or by qualified majority voting.

There were provisions that were proposed to be introduced into the Constitutional Treaty, which would have extended the Treaty to cover administrative co-operation and tax fraud and evasion in corporation tax, where the Council would act by qualified majority. In order to achieve an agreement on the Treaty, these articles were withdrawn by the IGC, at the behest of the UK Government.

Space Policy (Article III-254)

This is a new policy area and has been introduced as space is considered to be of vital importance to the economic and political security of the European Union. The area includes the guarantee of European independent access to space, covering defence policy needs, as well as weather forecasts, observation and satellite navigation services, as well as transport and agriculture.

Energy provisions (Article III-256 and Declaration no.22)

These provisions are new to the European treaties, although there are references to energy in the TEC, essentially in environmental matters, and these have been carried forward into the new Treaty in Article III-234(2)(c) and remain under unanimity. Other articles that have an impact on energy include the provisions on trans-European networks, which include pipelines (Articles III-246 to III-247), competition rules, state aid, approximation of laws and finally the flexibility clause which allows the Union to act where the objectives of the Constitution so require (Article I-18).

The new Article introduces energy as a shared competence and the Council may act by qualified majority. Since the terms of reference in the Article have been broadly drawn, the British have a number of serious concerns, including whether the United Kingdom has the ability to have competence over boundary issues, nuclear energy and treaty negotiations with countries outside the European Union.

A Declaration (Declaration no. 22) has been attached to the Treaty to indicate that the Member States could protect their energy supplies for the benefit of their internal security, as described in Article III-131. The Commission has stated that it considers these amendments would breach the terms of the internal market and in the final discussions leading up to the agreement of the Treaty, the article was withdrawn and then reinstated owing to these concerns.

There is a third paragraph added to this provision in the final discussions at the IGC in July 2004, with the Member States retaining control over fiscal policy as the Council will act by unanimity, and this will cover duties and taxation on energy.

European Public Prosecutor (Article III-274)

A European Prosecutor will be formed from Eurojust to investigate and prosecute people involved in crimes affecting the financial interests of the Union and it will be able to act as prosecutor in the national courts of the Member States. The UK government was opposed to this on the basis that it was unnecessary, however this was over-ruled and at the moment the remit is restricted to financial interests, however, there are concerns that this will be extended to cover other offences, and this is made possible by Article III-274(4), giving the European Council the ability to extend the powers to cover any crime of a cross-border dimension.

Creation of a new European Union (Article IV-438)

Under this Article, a new European Union will be established by the Constitution, which will be the successor to the Union established by the existing treaties. The existing Treaties will be repealed in their entirety, but all the existing legislation of the Union forming the *acquis* of the Union will continue to apply, including the case law of the Court of Justice (Declaration no. 1).

'Passerelle' or 'Escalator' Clauses

'Passerelle' means a footbridge or gangway and these provisions allow either the European Council or the Council, deciding by unanimity, to change the method of voting of the Council from unanimity to qualified majority voting in a particular area or case. This would mean that areas that have been negotiated in the Treaty revision procedure as being under unanimity could be changed without the matter passing through the normal Treaty ratification process.

There are eight passerelle clauses in the Treaty, of which six are new in the Constitution and the details are shown in the chapter on the provisions that have changed from unanimity to qualified majority voting.

The passerelle clause has also been termed the '*simplified revision procedure*' and this approach was first suggested during the debates leading up to the Treaty of Nice for some of the less essential provisions to introduce a certain amount of flexibility in revision in the Treaty. This concept has been developed in the Constitution and as well as the specific passerelle articles, there are two general Articles that concern the policies and action of the Union.

The principal passerelle article (Article IV-444) allows the European Council, acting by unanimity, to amend the provisions in Part III of the Treaty, so that the Council may act by qualified majority in that particular area. This will not apply to decisions concerning defence or military matters.

In a late amendment to the Treaty, an 'emergency brake' provision was added to the general passerelle procedure to include the national parliaments, so that a single national parliament can veto a European Council decision under the passerelle clause to change from unanimity to qualified majority voting, if the parliament notifies its opposition within six months of being notified of the proposed change; Article IV-444(3).

One passerelle clause in the existing Treaties has been superseded by the provisions of the Constitutional Treaty and so has been removed; this concerns asylum and immigration (Article 67 TEC). Under this Article, the Council could amend the provisions to be voted on by qualified majority voting five years after the Treaty of Amsterdam had come into force (i.e. May 2004).

Simplified revision procedure (Article IV-445)

The *passerelle* clause has also been included in the term the '*simplified revision procedure*'; this approach was first suggested during the debates leading up to the Treaty of Nice for some of the less essential provisions, to introduce a certain amount of flexibility in revision in the Treaty. This concept has been developed in the Constitution and as well as the specific *passerelle* articles, there are two general Articles that concern the policies and action of the Union.

The other general clause covers internal Union policies and action (Article IV-445) in Title III of Part III. This Title includes provisions on the internal market, EMU and freedom security and justice. The European Council, acting by unanimity, may adopt a European decision amending all or part of these provisions, but the Member States must pass the revisions by their respective constitutional procedures. This process avoids the need to have an Inter-Governmental Council meeting to agree the changes.

National Parliaments (Article I-II(3) and Protocols nos. 1 and 2)

National parliaments have been brought into the legislative process, in that they can review all prospective legislation, other than that which is under the exclusive competence of the Union (Article I-11(3)).

Two new protocols have been included in the Treaty, which has the intention of involving the national parliaments in the legislative procedure (Protocols no. 1 and no. 2). All legislative proposals will be sent to the national parliaments and the parliaments may send an opinion on whether the proposals comply with the principles of subsidiarity and proportionality. There is a six-week time limit for the parliaments to reply. More details are shown in the chapter on legislative procedures.

National parliaments are involved in the evaluation procedures on Eurojust and Europol, and the extent of implementation by Member States in the area of freedom, security and justice (Article I-42 and Articles III-260, III-273 and III-276).

The national parliaments are involved in the principal 'passerelle' clause, in that they have the availability of an 'emergency brake' provision in Article IV-444(3). Where the European Council intends to amend the voting procedure of provisions in Part III of the Treaty from unanimity to qualified majority voting, the national parliaments will be informed and if one national Parliament opposes the decision, that decision will not be adopted.

Weighting of Votes (Article I-25 and Protocol no. 34)

One of the main issues in the negotiations of the Constitutional Treaty was the change in the weighting of the votes in the Council to more accurately reflect the size of population of each Member State.

The Treaty of Nice introduced a new and more complicated system of voting in the Council, where the voting would be based on the number of votes and the proportion of the members. In addition, a member of the Council could request that the qualified majority must represent at least 62% of the population.

This system was introduced as part of the process of the enlargement of the Union and is intended to take effect for the 2004–2009 session. However, this new procedure did not satisfy many Member States, and there were disagreements over the different weighting of seats and populations.

There were certain anomalies in the allocation of the weightings introduced in the Treaty of Nice, such as between Portugal and the Czech Republic, where Portugal has a smaller population but more seats in the European Parliament. Spain had negotiated a higher number of votes relative to its population, to the disapproval of Germany.

The voting system has been changed in the Constitution, to take effect from 1 November 2009. This date was used because of the provisions of the Treaty of Nice will be in force until then, with the terms of office of the Commission and the European Parliament will run from 2004 to 2009. The change in the system in 2009 could cause some difficulties in the operation of the Union's institutions, owing to the consequences of enlargement.

The number of weighted votes in the Council have been changed in the Constitution in recognition of the disagreements which had arisen in Nice. However, the concerns of the smaller countries remain over the relative voting weights, since the six largest counties have 74.4% of the population, which in the new voting system from 2009 would potentially give them greater influence over the result of Council votes than the small countries could have.

Number of representatives in each institution after enlargement for 2004 to 2009

The Treaty of Nice laid down the size of the European Parliament and the weighting of votes in the Council, when the Council is acting by qualified majority vote for the period 2004 to 2009. These provisions would have applied to the Member States before enlargement. The numbers have been adjusted in the Constitutional Treaty to take into account enlargement and the disputes among the Member States over the size of the European Parliament.

After enlargement to 25 Member States, the number of weighted votes in the Council will be increased to 321 and the number of seats in the European Parliament will be increased to 732. The Constitutional Treaty stipulates that there will be a maximum of 750 members in the European Parliament, with a minimum of six members per Member State (Article I-20(2)). The changes in the voting and the number of seats in the European Parliament have been based on the size of the populations. The detailed numbers are shown in Protocol no. 34 and a table, prepared by the BMDF, is shown below.

The European Parliament will vote by a majority of its members (Article III-338) and the European Council and the Council of Ministers will vote under the following system:

1. On a proposal from the Commission, there have to be 232 votes (72.27%) in favour for the act to be passed, with a blocking minority being 90 votes.

2. In other cases, there must be 232 votes in favour, representing two-thirds of the members.

In addition, a member may request that the votes in favour represent at least 62% of the population of the Union.

With the populations of the three largest States representing 44.3% of the population of the enlarged European Union, they are in a position to block any proposal they object to.

Number of representatives in each institution after enlargement from 1 November 2009

In the earlier drafts of the Constitutional Treaty, the proportions of the Member States required to achieve a majority would be over 50% of the Member States, representing at least 60% of the Union population.

The voting system was the subject of lengthy debate and the final version is a compromise solution which will take effect from 1 November 2009 and will last until at least 2014, according to the terms of a European Decision, attached to the Treaty in Declaration no.5.

The European Parliament will continue to vote by a majority of its members (Article III-338). Under the terms of Article I-25, the European Council and the Council of Ministers will vote under the following system:

1. On a proposal from the Commission, or acting on the initiative of the Union Minister for Foreign Affairs, there has to be at least 55% of the Member States in favour for the act to be passed (i.e. 14 Member States), representing at least 65% of the population of the Union (i.e. 296.1 m.)

2. In other cases, there must be 72% of the Member States in favour, representing at least 65% of the population of the Union.

The request by a member that the votes in favour represent at least 62% of the population of the Union, introduced by the Treaty of Nice, no longer applies.

A **blocking minority** is defined as at least four Council members, if this number is not reached, a qualified majority is deemed to have been attained. This is intended to prevent the three largest Member States to block any proposal they object to, as they have 44.3% of the total EU population and the four largest Member States have 300.9 m. people or 56.9% of the population.

Complexities of the voting system from 1 November 2009

The intention of the review of the voting system agreed at Nice was to simplify the procedure from the double majority requirement to a more straightforward one. The compromise arrangements that were finally agreed will actually make the voting more complicated, particularly since in 2009, when these provisions take effect, it is likely that the Union will consist of 27 Member States, with the probable accession of Bulgaria and Romania.

The solution to the disagreements among the Member States during the final negotiations of the Constitutional Treaty led to a Decision being attached to the Treaty. This proposes a system based on the Ioannina Compromise, which had been arranged at a Council meeting on 29 March 1994 to recognise the concerns of the existing Member States over the changes in voting weights resulting from the accession of Austria, Finland and Sweden.

The compromise in the Constitution is that if Council members representing at least three-quarters of the population (i.e. 26.25%) or at least three-quarters of the number of Member States required to form a blocking minority (i.e. 3 Member States) state their opposition to a proposed act, the Council will continue discussions within a reasonable time-scale to reach a satisfactory solution, without affecting the time limits laid down by Union law. This compromise will operate until at least 2014. After that time the Council may repeal it.

Another complexity is that there is no adjustment for abstentions in the Treaty, hence if one Member State abstains, requirements for a blocking minority of four Member States remains, as does the requirement of the majority being 55% of the remaining Member States with 65% of the population.

Weighting of Votes in the Council and number of seats in the European Parliament (2004 to 2009)

Member States	Council Votes	European Parliament Seats	Population (million)	Population %
Germany	29	99	82.5	18.1
United Kingdom	29	78	59.5	13.1
France	29	78	59.5	13.1
Italy	29	78	57.5	12.6
Spain	27	54	41.9	9.2
Poland	27	54	38.2	8.3
Netherlands	13	27	16.2	3.6
Greece	12	24	11.0	2.4
Belgium	12	24	10.4	2.3
Portugal	12	24	10.4	2.3
Czech Republic	12	24	10.2	2.2
Hungary	12	24	10.1	2.2
Sweden	10	19	9.0	2.0
Austria	10	18	8.1	1.8
Slovakia	7	14	5.4	1.2
Denmark	7	14	5.4	1.2
Finland	7	14	5.2	1.1
Ireland	7	13	4.0	0.9
Lithuania	7	13	3.7	0.8
Latvia	4	9	2.7	0.6
Slovenia	4	7	1.5	0.3
Estonia	4	6	1.5	0.3
Cyprus	4	6	0.7	0.2
Luxembourg	4	6	0.5	0.1
Malta	3	5	0.4	0.1
Total:	321	732	455.5	100

Table by BMDF   Population Source: OECD

PERTINENT ARTICLES

The following articles, and extracts from articles, are intended to summarise the most important provisions in the Treaty. As a result, the majority are new rather than being modified versions of existing articles in the current Treaty on European Union and the Treaty establishing the European Community.

PART ONE

- **Article I-6**: *Union Law (new)*

  - The Constitution and law adopted by the institutions of the Union in exercising competences conferred on it **shall have primacy over the law of the Member States**.

- **Article I-7**: *Legal personality (new)*

  - The Union shall have legal personality.

- **Article I-8**: *The symbols of the Union (new)*

  - The flag of the Union shall be a circle of twelve golden stars on a blue background.
    The anthem of the Union shall be based on the "Ode to Joy" from the Ninth Symphony by Ludwig van Beethoven.
    The motto of the Union shall be: "United in diversity".
    The currency of the Union shall be the euro.
    Europe day shall be celebrated on 9 May throughout the Union.

- **Article I-9**: *Fundamental Rights (ex Article 6(2) TEU)*

  - The Union shall recognise the rights, freedoms and principles set out in the Charter of Fundamental Rights which constitutes **Part II**.

- **Article I-12**: *Categories of competence (new)*

  2. When the Constitution confers on the Union a **competence shared** with the Member States in a specific area, the Union and the Member States **may** legislate and adopt legally binding acts in that area. **The Member States shall exercise their competence *to the extent that the Union has not exercised, or has decided to cease exercising, its competence*.**

  3. The Member States shall co-ordinate their economic and employment policies within arrangements as determined by Part III, which **the Union shall have competence** to provide.

  4. The Union shall have competence to **define and implement a common foreign and security policy**, including the progressive framing of a common defence policy.

- **Article I-13**: *Areas of Exclusive competence (new)*

  1. The Union shall have **exclusive competence** in the following areas:
     (a) customs union,
     (b) **the establishing of the competition rules necessary for the functioning of the internal market**,
     (c) monetary policy, for the Member States whose currency is the euro,
     (d) the conservation of marine biological resources under the common fisheries policy,
     (e) common commercial policy.

2. The Union shall also have **exclusive competence for the conclusion of an international agreement** when its conclusion is provided for in a legislative act of the Union or is necessary to enable the Union to exercise its internal competence, or **insofar as its conclusion may affect common rules or alter their scope**

- **Article I-14:** *Areas of shared competence (new)*

    1. The Union shall share competence with the Members States where the Constitution confers on it a competence which does not relate to the areas referred to in Articles 1-13 and 1-17.

    2. **Shared competence** between the Union and the Member States applies in the following principal areas:
    (a) internal market,
    (b) social policy, for aspects defined in Part III,
    (c) economic, social and territorial cohesion,
    (d) agriculture and fisheries, excluding the conservation of marine biological resources,
    (e) environment,
    (f) consumer protection,
    (g) transport,
    (h) trans-European networks,
    (i) energy,
    (j) area of freedom, security and justice,
    (k) common safety concerns in public health matters, for aspects defined in Part III.

- **Article I-15:** *The co-ordination of economic and employment policies (new)*

    1. The Member States shall co-ordinate their economic policies within the Union. **To this end, the Council of Ministers shall adopt measures, in particular broad guidelines for these policies.**
    Specific provisions shall apply to those Member States **whose currency is** the euro.

    2. The Union shall take measures to ensure co-ordination of the employment policies of the Member States, in particular by defining guidelines for these policies.

    3. The Union may take initiatives to ensure co-ordination of Member States' social policies.

- **Article I-16:** *The common foreign and security policy (ex Articles 17 TEU and 11(2) TEU)*

    1. The Union's competence in matters of common foreign and security policy shall cover all areas of foreign policy and all questions relating to the Union's security, including the progressive framing of a common defence policy that might lead to a common defence.

    2. Member States shall actively and unreservedly support the Union's common foreign and security policy in a spirit of loyalty and mutual solidarity and shall comply with the Union's action in this area. They shall refrain from action contrary to the Union's interests or likely to impair its effectiveness.

- **Article I-17:** *Area of supporting, co-ordinating or complementary action (new)*

    1. The Union shall have competence to carry out supporting, co-ordinating or complementary action. Such action shall, at European level, be
        (a) protection and improvement of human health;
        (b) industry;
        (c) culture;
        (d) tourism; *(new)*
        (e) education, youth, sport and vocational training; *(sport - new)*
        (f) civil protection; *(new)*
        (g) administrative co-operation. *(new)*

- **Article I-22:** *The European Council President (new)*

  1. The European Council shall elect its President, by a qualified majority, for a term of two and a half years, renewable once. In the event of an impediment or serious misconduct, the European Council can end his or her term of office in accordance with the same procedure.

- **Article I-25:** *Qualified majority (new)*

  1. A qualified majority shall be defined as **at least 55%** of the members of the Council, comprising **at least fifteen** of them and representing Member States comprising **at least 65% of the population** of the Union.

      A **blocking minority** must include **at least four** Council members, failing which the qualified majority shall be deemed attained.

  2. By way of derogation from paragraph 1, when the Council is not acting on a proposal from the Commission or from the Union Minister for Foreign Affairs, the qualified majority shall be defined as **at least 72%** of the members of the Council, representing Member States comprising **at least 65% of the population** of the Union.

- **Article I-26:** *The European Commission (new)*

  1. The Commission shall promote the general interest of the Union and take appropriate initiatives to that end. It shall **ensure the application of the Constitution**, and measures adopted by the institutions pursuant to the Constitution. It shall **oversee the application of Union law** under the control of the Court of Justice of the European Union. It shall **execute the budget** and manage programmes. It shall **exercise co-ordinating, executive and management functions**, as laid down in the Constitution. With the exception of the common foreign and security policy, and other cases provided for in the Constitution, it shall **ensure the Union's external representation**. It shall initiate the Union's annual and multiannual programming with a view to achieving inter-institutional agreements.

  2. **Union legislative acts may be adopted only on the basis of a Commission proposal**, except where the Constitution provides otherwise. Other acts shall be adopted on the basis of a Commission proposal where the Constitution so provides.

  5. The **first Commission** appointed under the provisions of the Constitution shall consist of **one national of each Member State**, including its President and the Union Minister for Foreign Affairs who shall be one of its Vice-Presidents.

  6. As from the end of the term of office of the Commission referred to in paragraph 5, the Commission shall consist of a number of members, including its President and the Union Minister for Foreign Affairs, corresponding to **two thirds of the number of Member States**, unless the European Council, acting unanimously, decides to alter this number.

- **Article I-28:** *The Union Minister for Foreign Affairs (new)*

  1. The European Council, **acting by qualified majority**, with the agreement of the President of the Commission, shall appoint the **Union Minister for Foreign Affairs**. The European Council may end his or her tenure by the same procedure.

  3. The Union Minister for Foreign Affairs shall preside over the Foreign Affairs Council.

  4. The Union Minister for Foreign Affairs shall be one of the Vice-Presidents of the Commission. He or she shall **ensure the consistency of the Union's external action.** He or she shall be **responsible within the Commission** for responsibilities incumbent on it in **external relations** and for co-ordinating other aspects of **the Union's external action**.

- **Article I-33:** *The legal acts of the Union (ex Article 249 TEC)*

  1. **To exercise** the Union**'s competences the Institutions** shall use as legal instruments, in accordance with Part III, European laws, European framework laws, European regulations, European decisions, recommendations and opinions.

- **Article I-36:** *Delegated regulations (ex Article 202 TEC)*

  1. European laws and European framework laws may delegate to the Commission the power to adopt delegated regulations to supplement or amend certain non-essential elements of the law or framework law.

  [*BMDF note*: A *'sunset clause'*, which had been strongly recommended by the Better Regulation Task Force, was in the original draft as follows:

  "The provisions of the delegated regulation are to lapse after a period set by the law or framework law. They may be extended, on a proposal form the Commission, by decision of the European Parliament and of the Council."

  This clause was deleted by the Praesidium in one of the drafts of the Treaty after objections by some Convention members that it *'could be a source of uncertainty and problems for legal security'*.]

- **Article I-40:** *Specific provisions for implementing common foreign and security policy (new)*

  1. The European Union shall conduct a common foreign and security policy, based on the development of mutual political solidarity among Member States, the identification of questions of general interest and the achievement of **an ever-increasing degree of convergence of Member States' actions**.

  4. The common foreign and security policy shall be put into effect by the Union Minister for Foreign Affairs and by the Member States, **using national and Union resources.**

- **Article I-41:** *Specific provisions relating to the common security and defence policy (new)*

  1. The common security and defence policy shall be an integral part of the common foreign and security policy. It shall provide the Union with an operational capacity drawing on civil and military assets.

  2. The common security and defence policy shall include the progressive framing of a common Union defence policy. This will lead to a common defence, when the European Council, acting unanimously, so decides.

- **Article I-42:** *Specific provisions relating to the area of freedom, security and justice (ex Article 61 TEC)*

  1. The Union shall constitute an area of freedom, security and justice:
     (a) by adopting European laws and European framework laws intended, where necessary, to approximate national laws in the areas listed in Part III;
     (b) by promoting mutual confidence between the competent authorities of the Member States, in particular on the basis of mutual recognition of judicial and extrajudicial decisions.

- **Article I-43:** *Solidarity clause (new)*

  1. The Union and its Member States shall act jointly in a spirit of solidarity if a Member State is the object of a terrorist attack or the victim of a natural or man-made disaster. The Union shall mobilise all the instruments at its disposal, including the military resources made available by the Member States, to:
     (a) – prevent the terrorist threat in the territory of the Member States;
         – protect democratic institutions and the civilian population from any terrorist attack;
         – assist a Member State in its territory, at the request of its political authorities, in the event of a terrorist attack;
     (b) assist a Member State in its territory, at the request of its political authorities, in the event of a natural or man-made disaster.

- **Article I-44:** *Enhanced Co-operation (ex Article 11 TEC and Articles 43 – 45 TEU)*

  1.   Member States which wish to establish enhanced co-operation between themselves within the framework of the Union's non-exclusive competences may make use of its Institutions and exercise those competences by applying the relevant provisions of the Constitution. . .
  . .

  Enhanced co-operation shall aim to further the objectives of the Union, protect its interests and reinforce its integration process.

  4.   Acts adopted in the framework of enhanced co-operation shall bind only participating States. They shall not be regarded as an *acquis* which has to be accepted by candidates for accession to the Union.

- **Article I-48:** *The social partners and autonomous social dialogue (ex Article 138 TEC)*

  The Union recognises and promotes the role of the social partners at its level, taking into account the diversity of national systems; it shall facilitate dialogue between the social partners, respecting their autonomy.

- **Article I-54**: *The Union's own resources (ex Article 269 TEC)*

  1.   The Union shall provide itself with the means necessary to attain its objectives and carry through its policies.

  3.   A European law of the Council shall lay down the provisions relating to the system of own resources of the Union. In this context it may establish new categories of own resources or abolish an existing category. The Council shall act unanimously after consulting the European Parliament. **That law shall not enter into force until it is approved by the Member States in accordance with their respective constitutional requirements.**

  4.   A European law of the Council shall lay down implementing measures of the Union's own resources system insofar as this is provided for in the European law adopted on the basis of paragraph 3. The Council shall act after obtaining the consent of the European Parliament.

- **Article I-55:** *The multiannual financial framework (new)*

  1.   The multiannual financial framework shall ensure that Union expenditure develops in an orderly manner and within the limits of its own resources. It shall determine the amounts of the annual ceilings of appropriations for commitments by category of expenditure in accordance with Article III-402.

  4.   The European Council may, unanimously, adopt a European decision **authorising the Council to act by a qualified majority** when adopting the European law of the Council referred to in paragraph 2.

- **Article I- 60:** *Voluntary withdrawal from the Union (new)*

  1.   Any Member State may decide to withdraw from the European Union in accordance with its own constitutional requirements.

  2.   A Member State which decides to withdraw shall notify the European Council of its intention. … [T]he Union shall conclude an agreement with that State, setting out the arrangements for its withdrawal, taking account of the framework for its future relationship with the Union. That agreement shall be negotiated in accordance with Article III-325(3); it shall be concluded by the Council acting by a qualified majority on behalf of the Union, after obtaining the consent of the European Parliament.

PART TWO

- **Preamble** *to the Charter of Fundamental Rights*

  The peoples of Europe, in creating **an ever closer union** among them, are resolved to share a peaceful future based on common values.

  To this end, it is necessary to strengthen the protection of fundamental rights. . . . by making those rights more visible in a Charter.

  This charter reaffirms . . . . the rights as they result from . . . . the social charters adopted by the Union and the case law of the Court of Justice of the European Union and of the European Court of Human Rights. In this context the **Charter will be interpreted by the courts of the Union and the Member States with due regard to the explanations** prepared under the authority of the Praesidium of the Convention which drafted the Charter and updated under the responsibility of the Praesidium of the European Convention.

  The Union therefore recognises the rights, freedoms and principles set out hereafter.

PART THREE

- **Article III-115:** *General (new)*

  The Union shall ensure consistency between the different policies and activities referred to in this Part, taking all of the Union's objectives into account.

- **Article III-118** *Discrimination (new)*

  In defining and implementing the policies and activities referred to in this Part, the Union shall aim to combat discrimination based on sex, race or ethnic origin, religion or belief, disability, age or sexual orientation.

- **Article III-130**: *Establishment and functioning of the internal market* (*ex Articles 14 & 15 TEC*)

  1. The Union shall adopt measures with the aim of establishing **or ensuring the functioning of** the internal market, in accordance with **the relevant provisions of the Constitution.**

- **Article III-136**: *Social security* (*ex Article 42 TEC*)

  2. Where a member of the Council considers that a draft European law or framework law referred to in paragraph 1 would affect fundamental aspects of its social security system, including its scope, cost or financial structure, or would affect the financial balance of that system, it may request that the matter be referred to the European Council. In that case, the procedure referred to in Article III-396 shall be suspended. After discussion, the European Council shall, within four months of this suspension, either:
     (a) refer the draft back to the Council, which shall terminate the suspension of the procedure referred to in Article III-396, or
     (b) request the Commission to submit a new proposal; in that case, the act originally proposed shall be deemed not to have been adopted.

- **Article III-160:** *Capital and payments (new)*

  Where necessary to achieve the objectives set out in Article III-257, as regards preventing and combating terrorism and related activities, European laws **shall** define a framework for administrative measures with regard to capital movements and payments, such as the freezing of funds, financial assets or economic gains belonging to, or owned or held by, natural or legal persons, groups or non-state entities.

  The Council, on a proposal from the Commission, shall adopt European regulations or European decisions in order to implement the European laws referred to in the first paragraph.

- **Article III-176:** *Intellectual property rights (new)*

In the context of the establishment and functioning of the internal market, European laws or framework laws shall establish measures for the creation of European intellectual property rights to provide uniform intellectual property rights protection throughout the Union and for the setting up of centralised Union-wide authorisation, co-ordination and supervision arrangements.
A European law of the Council shall establish language arrangements for the European intellectual property rights. The Council shall act unanimously after consulting the European Parliament.

- **Article III-225:** *Common agriculture and fisheries policy (new)*

The Union shall define and implement a common agriculture and fisheries policy.

"Agricultural products" means the products of the soil, of stockfarming and of fisheries and products of first-stage processing directly related to these products. References to the common agricultural policy or to agriculture, and the use of the term "agricultural", shall be understood as also referring to fisheries, having regard to the specific characteristics of this sector.

- **Article III-254:** *Space policy (new)*

  1. To promote scientific and technical progress, industrial competitiveness and the implementation of its policies, the Union shall draw up a European space policy. To this end, it may promote joint initiatives, support research and technological development and co-ordinate the efforts needed for the exploration and exploitation of space.

  2. To contribute to attaining the objectives referred to in paragraph 1, European laws or framework laws shall establish the necessary measures, which may take the form of a European space programme.

- **Article III-256:** *Energy (new)*

  1. In the context of the establishment and functioning of the internal market and with regard for the need to preserve and improve the environment, Union policy on energy shall aim to:

     (a) ensure the functioning of the energy market;

     (b) ensure security of energy supply in the Union, and

     (c) promote energy efficiency and energy saving and the development of new and renewable forms of energy.

  2. Without prejudice to the application of other provisions of the Constitution, the objectives in paragraph 1 shall be achieved by measures enacted in European laws or framework laws. Such laws or framework laws shall be adopted after consultation of the Committee of the Regions and the Economic and Social Committee.

     Such European laws or framework laws shall not affect a Member State's **right to determine the conditions for exploiting its energy resources**, its choice between different energy sources and the general structure of its energy supply, without prejudice to Article III-234(2)(c).

  3. By way of derogation from paragraph 2, a European law or framework law of the Council shall establish the measures referred to therein when they are primarily of a fiscal nature. The Council shall act **unanimously** after consulting the European Parliament.

- **Article III-266:** *Policy on border checks, asylum and immigration (ex Article 63, points 1 and 2, and ex Article 64(2) TEC)*

  1. The Union shall develop a **common policy on asylum,** subsidiary protection and temporary protection with a view to offering appropriate status to any third-country national requiring international protection and ensuring compliance with the principle of *non-refoulement.*

- **Article III-267:** *Policy on border checks, asylum and immigration (ex Articles 29 and 31(1)(e) TEU and points 3 and 4 of ex Article 63 TEC)*

    1. The Union shall develop a **common immigration policy** aimed at ensuring, at all stages, the efficient management of migration flows, fair treatment of third-country nationals residing legally in Member States, and the prevention of, and enhanced measure to combat, illegal immigration and trafficking in human beings.

- **Article III-269:** *Judicial co-operation in civil matters (ex Article 65 TEC)*

    1. The Union shall develop **judicial co-operation in civil matters** having cross-border implications, based on the principle of mutual recognition of judgments and decisions in extra-judicial cases. Such co-operation shall include the adoption of measures for the approximation of the laws and regulations of the Member States.

    3. Notwithstanding paragraph 2, a European law or framework law of the Council shall establish measures concerning family law with cross-border implications. The Council shall act unanimously after consulting the European Parliament.
    The Council, on a proposal from the Commission, may adopt a European decision determining those aspects of **family law with cross-border implications** which may be the subject of **acts adopted by the ordinary legislative procedure**. The Council shall act unanimously after consulting the European Parliament.

- **Article III-270:** *Judicial co-operation in criminal matters (ex Article 31(1) TEU)*

    1. Judicial co-operation in criminal matters in the Union shall be based on the principle of mutual recognition of judgments and judicial decisions and shall include the approximation of the laws and regulations of the Member States in the areas referred to in paragraph 2 and in Article III-271.

    3. Where a member of the Council considers that a draft European framework law as referred to in paragraph 2 would affect fundamental aspects of its criminal justice system, it may request that the draft framework law be referred to the European Council. In that case, the procedure referred to in Article III-396 shall be suspended. After discussion, the European Council shall, within four months of this suspension, either:

        (a) refer the draft back to the Council, which shall terminate the suspension of the procedure referred to in Article III-396, or

        (b) request the Commission or the group of Member States from which the draft originates to submit a new draft; in that case, the act originally proposed shall be deemed not to have been adopted.

- **Article III-271:** *Serious crime with a cross-border dimension (new)*

    1. European framework laws may establish minimum rules concerning the definition of criminal offences and sanctions in the areas of particularly resulting from the nature or impact of such offences or from a special need to combat them on a common basis.

        These areas of crime are the following: terrorism, trafficking in human beings and sexual exploitation of women and children, illicit drug trafficking, illicit arms trafficking, money laundering, corruption, counterfeiting of means of payment, computer crime and organised crime.

    3. Where a member of the Council considers that a draft European framework law as referred to in paragraph 1 or 2 would affect fundamental aspects of its criminal justice system, it may request that the draft framework law be referred to the European Council. In that case, where the procedure referred to in Article III-396 is applicable, it shall be suspended. After discussion, the European Council shall, within four months of this suspension, either:

        (a) refer the draft back to the Council, which shall terminate the suspension of the procedure referred to in Article III-396 where it is applicable, or (b)　request the Commission or the group of Member States from which the draft originates to submit a new draft; in that case, the act originally proposed shall be deemed not to have been adopted.

- **Article III-274**: *European Public Prosecutor's Office* (*new*)

1. In order to combat crimes affecting the **financial** interests of the Union, a European law of the Council may establish a European Public Prosecutor's Office from Eurojust. The Council shall act unanimously after obtaining the consent of the European Parliament.

4. The European Council may, at the same time or subsequently, adopt a European decision amending paragraph 1 in order to extend the powers of the European Public Prosecutor's Office to include serious crime having a cross-border dimension.... The European Council shall act unanimously after obtaining the consent of the European Parliament and after consulting the Commission.

- **Article III-284**: *Civil protection (new)*

1. The Union shall encourage co-operation between Member States in order to improve the effectiveness of systems for preventing and protecting against natural or man-made disasters.

   Union action shall aim to:
   (a)　support and supplement Member States' action at national, regional and local level in risk prevention, in preparing their civil-protection personnel and in responding to natural or man-made disasters within the Union;
   (b)　promote swift, effective operational co-operation within the Union between national civil-protection services;
   (c)　promote consistency in international civil-protection work.

2. European laws or framework laws shall establish the measures necessary to help achieve the objectives referred to in paragraph 1, excluding any harmonisation of the laws and regulations of the Member States.

- **Article III-285**: *Administrative co-operation (new)*

1. Effective national implementation of Union law by the Member States, which is essential for the proper functioning of the Union, shall be regarded as a matter of common interest.

2. The Union may support the efforts of Member States to improve their administrative capacity to implement Union law. Such action may include facilitating the exchange of information and of civil servants as well as supporting training schemes. No Member State shall be obliged to avail itself of such support. European laws shall establish the necessary measures to this end, excluding any harmonisation of the laws and regulations of the Member States.

3. This Article shall be without prejudice to the obligations of the Member States to implement Union law or the prerogatives and duties of the Commission. It shall also be without prejudice to other provisions of the Constitution providing for administrative co-operation among the Member States and between them and the Union.

- **Article III-296**: *The Union Minister for Foreign Affairs* (*new*)

1. The Union Minister for Foreign Affairs, who shall chair the Foreign Affairs Council, shall contribute through his or her proposals towards the preparation of the common foreign and security policy and shall ensure implementation of the European decisions adopted by the European Council and the Council.

2. **The Minister for Foreign Affairs shall represent the Union** for matters relating to the common foreign and security policy. He or she shall conduct political dialogue with third parties on the Union's behalf and shall express the Union's position in international organisations and at international conferences.

3.   In fulfilling his or her mandate, the Union Minister for Foreign Affairs shall be assisted by a **European External Action Service**. This service shall work in co-operation with the diplomatic services of the Member States and shall **comprise officials from relevant departments of the General Secretariat of the Council and of the Commission as well as staff seconded from national diplomatic services of the Member States.** The organisation and functioning of the European External Action Service shall be established by a European decision of the Council. The Council shall act on a proposal from the Union Minister for Foreign Affairs after consulting the European Parliament and after obtaining the consent of the Commission.

- **Article III-305:** *International organisations and at international conferences* (*ex Article 19 TEU*)

  1.   Member States shall co-ordinate their action in international organisations and at international conferences. They shall uphold the Union's positions in such fora. The Union Minister for Foreign Affairs shall organise this co-ordination.

        In international organisations and at international conferences where not all the Member States participate, those which do take part shall uphold the Union's positions.

  2.   When the Union has defined a position on a subject which is on the United Nations Security Council agenda, those Member States which sit on the Security Council shall request that the Union Minister for Foreign Affairs be asked to present the Union's position.

- **Article III-312**: *Common Security and defence policy* (*new*)

  1.   Those Member States which wish to participate in the **permanent structured co-operation** referred to in Article I-41(6), which fulfil the criteria and have made the commitments on military capabilities set out in the Protocol on permanent structured co-operation shall notify their intention to the Council and to the Union Minister for Foreign Affairs.

  2.   Within three months following the notification referred to in paragraph 1 the Council shall adopt a European decision establishing permanent structured co-operation and determining the list of participating Member States. The Council shall act by a qualified majority after consulting the Union Minister for Foreign Affairs.

- **Article III-422**: *Enhanced co-operation 'passerelle' clause* (*new*)

  1.   Where a provision of the Constitution which may be applied in the context of enhanced co-operation stipulates that the Council shall act unanimously, the Council, acting unanimously in accordance with the arrangements laid down in Article I-44(3), may adopt a European decision stipulating that it will act by a qualified majority.

  2.   Where a provision of the Constitution which may be applied in the context of enhanced co-operation stipulates that the Council shall adopt European laws or framework laws under a special legislative procedure, the Council, acting unanimously in accordance with the arrangements laid down in Article I-44(3), may adopt a European decision stipulating that it will act under the ordinary legislative procedure. The Council shall act after consulting the European Parliament.

  3.   Paragraphs 1 and 2 shall not apply to decisions having military or defence implications.

PART FOUR

- **Article IV-437:** *Repeal of earlier Treaties (new)*

    1. This Treaty establishing a Constitution for Europe shall repeal the Treaty establishing the European Community, the Treaty on European Union and … the acts and treaties which have supplemented or amended them.

- **Article IV-438:** *Succession and legal continuity (new)*

    1. The European Union established by this Treaty **shall be the successor** to the European Union established by the Treaty on European Union and to the European Community.

    2. Until new provisions have been adopted in implementation of this Treaty or until the end of their term of office, the Institutions, bodies, offices and agencies existing on the date of the entry into force of this Treaty shall, subject to the provisions of Article IV-439, exercise their powers within the meaning of this Treaty in their composition on that date.

    3. The other components of the *acquis* of the Community and of the Union existing at the time of the entry into force of this Treaty … shall also be preserved until they have been deleted or amended.

    4. The case law of the Court of Justice … shall remain the source of interpretation of Union law and in particular of the comparable provisions of the Constitution.

    5. Continuity in administrative and legal procedures undertaken prior to the date of entry into force of this Treaty shall be ensured in compliance with the Constitution.

- **Article IV-443:** *Ordinary revision procedure (new)*

    4. If, two years after the signature of the treaty amending this Treaty, four fifths of the Member States have ratified it and one or more Member States have encountered difficulties in proceeding with ratification, the matter shall be referred to the European Council.

- **Article IV-444:** *Simplified revision procedure – general 'Passerelle' Clause (new)*

    1. Where Part III provides for the Council should act by unanimity in a given area or case, the **European Council may adopt a European decision authorising the Council to act by a qualified majority** in that area or in that case.
    This paragraph shall not apply to decisions with military implications or those in the area of defence.

    2. Where Part III provides for European laws and framework laws to be adopted by the Council according to a special legislative procedure, the European Council may adopt a European decision allowing for the adoption of such European laws or framework laws according to the ordinary legislative procedure.

    3. Any initiative taken by the European Council on the basis of paragraphs 1 or 2 shall be notified to the national Parliaments of the Member States. If a **national Parliament makes known its opposition within six months of the date of such notification, the European decision referred to in paragraphs 1 or 2 shall not be adopted**. In the absence of opposition, the European Council may adopt the decision.
    For the adoption of the European decisions referred to in paragraphs 1 and 2, the European Council shall act by unanimity after obtaining the consent of the European Parliament, which shall be given by a majority of its component members.

PROTOCOLS

Protocol no. 1 on the Role of National Parliaments in the European Union

- **Article 1**

Commission consultation documents (green and white papers and communications) shall be forwarded directly by the Commission to national Parliaments upon publication. The Commission shall also forward the annual legislative programme as well as any other instrument of legislative planning or policy to national Parliaments, at the same time as to the European Parliament and the Council.

- **Article 3**

National Parliaments may send to the Presidents of the European Parliament, the Council and the Commission a reasoned opinion on whether a draft European legislative act complies with the principle of subsidiarity, in accordance with the procedure laid down in the Protocol on the application of the principles of subsidiarity and proportionality.

- **Article 9**

The European Parliament and national Parliaments shall together determine the organisation and promotion of effective and regular inter-parliamentary co-operation within the Union.

Protocol no. 2 on the application of the principles of subsidiarity and proportionality

- **Article 2**

Before proposing European legislative acts, the Commission shall consult widely. Such consultations shall, where appropriate, take into account the regional and local dimension of the action envisaged. In cases of exceptional urgency, the Commission shall not conduct such consultations. It shall give reasons for the decision in its proposal.

- **Article 6**

The European Parliament, the Council of Ministers and the Commission, and, where appropriate, the group of Member States, the Court of Justice, the European Central Bank or the European Investment Bank if the draft legislative act comes from them, shall take account of the reasoned opinions issued by national Parliaments or by a chamber of a national Parliament.

- **Article 7**

The European Parliament, the Council and the Commission, and, where appropriate, the group of Member States, the Court of Justice, the European Central Bank or the European Investment Bank, if the draft legislative act originates from them, shall take account of the reasoned opinions issued by national Parliaments or by a chamber of a national Parliament.

Where reasoned opinions on a draft European legislative act's non-compliance with the principle of subsidiarity represent at **least one third** of all the votes allocated to the national Parliaments in accordance with the second paragraph, the draft must be reviewed. This threshold shall be **a quarter** in the case of a draft European legislative act submitted on the basis of Article III-264 of the Constitution on the area of freedom, security and justice.

After such review, the Commission or, where appropriate, the group of Member States, the European Parliament, the Court of Justice, the European Central Bank or the European Investment Bank, if the draft European legislative act originates from them, **may decide to maintain, amend or withdraw the draft**. Reasons must be given for this decision.

Protocol no. 12 on the Euro group

- **Article 1**

The Ministers of the Member States whose currency is the euro shall meet informally.

- **Article 2**

    The Ministers of the Member States whose currency is the euro shall elect a president for two and a half years, by a majority of those Member States.

Protocol no. 23 on permanent structured co-operation established by Article I-41(6) and Article III-312 of the constitution

- **Article 1**

    The permanent structured co-operation referred to in Article I-41(6) of the Constitution shall be open to any Member State which undertakes, from the date of entry into force of the Treaty establishing a Constitution for Europe, to:

    (a)   proceed more intensively to develop its defence capacities through the development of its national contributions and participation, where appropriate, in multinational forces, in the main European equipment programmes, and in the activity of the Agency in the field of defence capabilities development, research, acquisition and armaments (European Defence Agency), and

    (b)   have the capacity to supply by 2007 at the latest, either at national level or as a component of multinational force groups, targeted combat units for the missions planned, structured at a tactical level as a battle group, with support elements including transport and logistics, capable of carrying out the tasks referred to in Article III-309, within a period of 5 to 30 days, in particular in response to requests from the United Nations Organisation, and which can be sustained for an initial period of 30 days and be extended up to at least 120 days.

Protocol no. 34 on the transitional provisions relating to the institutions and bodies of the Union

- **Article 2**

    1.   The provisions of Article I-25(1), (2) and (3) of the Constitution on the definition of the qualified majority in the European Council and the Council shall take effect on 1 November 2009, after the 2009 European Parliament elections have taken place in accordance with Article I-20(2) of the Constitution.

DECLARATIONS

Declaration no. 1 on Article I-6

- The Conference notes that Article I-6 reflects existing case law of the Court of Justice of the European Communities and of the Court of First Instance.

Declaration no. 4 on Article I-24(7) concerning the European Council Decision on the exercise of the Presidency of the Council

- **Article 1**

    1.   The Presidency of the Council, with the exception of the Foreign Affairs configuration, shall be held by pre-established groups of three Member States for a period of 18 months. The groups shall be made up on a basis of equal rotation among the Member States, taking into account their diversity and geographical balance within the Union.

    2.   Each member of the group shall in turn chair for a six-month period all configurations of the Council, with the exception of the Foreign Affairs configuration. The other members of the group shall assist the Chair in all its responsibilities on the basis of a common programme. Members of the team may decide alternative arrangements among themselves.

Declaration no. 5 on Article I-25

- Whereas:
  (1) Provisions should be adopted allowing for a smooth transition from the system for decision-making in the Council by a qualified majority as defined in the Treaty of Nice and set out in Article 2(2) of the Protocol on the transitional provisions relating to the institutions and bodies of the Union annexed to the Constitution, which will continue to apply until 31 October 2009, to the voting system provided for in Article I-25 of the Constitution, which will apply with effect from 1 November 2009.

- **Article 1**

  If members of the Council, representing:
  (a)   at least three quarters of the population, or
  (b)   at least three quarters of the number of Member States
  necessary to constitute a blocking minority resulting from the application of Article I-25(1), first subparagraph, or Article I-25(2), indicate their opposition to the Council adopting an act by a qualified majority, the Council shall discuss the issue.

- **Article 4**

  This decision shall take effect on 1 November 2009. It shall remain in force at least until 2014. Thereafter the Council may adopt a European decision repealing it.

Declaration no. 22 on Article III-256

- The Conference believes that Article III-256 does not affect the right of the Member States to take the necessary measures to ensure their energy supply under the conditions provided for in Article III-131.

Declaration no. 12 concerning the explanations relating to the Charter of Fundamental Rights

- The Conference takes note of the explanations relating to the Charter of Fundamental Rights prepared under the authority of the Praesidium of the Convention which drafted the Charter and updated under the responsibility of the Praesidium of the European Convention, as set out below.

EXPLANATIONS RELATING TO THE CHARTER OF FUNDAMENTAL RIGHTS

These explanations were originally prepared under the authority of the Praesidium of the Convention which drafted the Charter of Fundamental Rights of the European Union. They have been updated under the responsibility of the Praesidium of the European Convention, in the light of the drafting adjustments made to the text of the Charter by that Convention (notably to Articles 51 and 52 [Articles II-111 and II-112 of the Constitution]) and of further developments of Union law. Although they do not as such have the status of law, they are a valuable tool of interpretation intended to clarify the provisions of the Charter.

BRITISH BUSINESS CONCERNS

Increased Regulatory Burden

Although the British Government has been able to obtain a number of modifications and qualifications to meet concerns, all sections of British industry still have serious reservations about the Constitution - particularly about its centralising approach with the likelihood of a further increase in detailed regulatory burden.

This is contrary to the spirit of the Laeken Declaration which required the division of power between Brussels and Member States to be clarified and reviewed to see, *inter alia,* whether significant powers could be repatriated to Member States under the subsidiarity principle.

In the event, although the importance of subsidiarity is underlined, there is no mechanism in the Constitution for reviewing the current 100,000 pages of the *'acquis communautaire'*[1] many of which are unduly prescriptive.

Some specific concerns are listed below.

Increase in Regulatory burden.

Rather than reducing the current burden of detailed regulations and directives emanating from Brussels this burden is likely to be significantly increased with the wider powers being granted to the EU Commission.

Concreting in the *'acquis communautaire'*.

There are now over 100,000 regulations encompassed in the *acquis communautaire* which the Treaty will concrete in[2].

It is not only the number of regulations that causes concern but the difficulty of amending such regulations if the circumstances change or if it can be seen they do not fit particular situations in some countries.

Deletion of the 'Sunset clause'.

The proposal by the Better Regulation Task Force to insert a *'sunset clause'* (so that regulations would lapse after a certain period of time and only be extended after reconsideration) was included in an earlier draft of the Constitutional Treaty in Article I-35.

It was removed subsequently by the Praesidium on the grounds that this clause *'could be a source of uncertainty and problems for legal security'*.

Subsidiarity

is a 'top down' concept making the principle difficult to apply in practice. Once the competence has been given to the Union the power firmly rests in the centre. To get a consensus for amendment with so many different countries with varying interests is normally not feasible.

There is much misunderstanding about this term. When John Major agreed to Maastricht he was confident that the new clauses on **subsidiarity** would enable perhaps 25% of the then current regulations to be repatriated to member states. In the event not one was able to be repatriated.

Competence acquired by the European Union is never returned to Member States. Disputes about subsidiarity only really arise in those areas of competence not yet acquired by the European Union.

---

[1] **The Convention Alternative Report** noted that the Draft Constitution failed to address this important point.

[2] In a late amendment to the **Preamble** to the Treaty (page 3) this 'concreting in' was underlined – *'Determined to continue the work accomplished within the framework of the Treaties establishing the European Communities and the Treaty on European Union, by **ensuring the continuity of the Community "acquis"**,'*

Gisela Stuart MP the British Government representative on the Praesidium (which was responsible for the draft Constitution) in her paper[3] underlined the fundamental point that the *acquis communautaire* is not reconcilable with the professed objective of subsidiarity (taking decisions at the lowest feasible level).

'Shared competencies'.

The addition of areas of '*shared competence*' (Articles I-11 and I-13) to those in which the Union has exclusive competence (Article I-12) further widens the powers of the Union (perhaps to over 70% of Government fields).

The term '*shared*' is misleading as the power has been shifted fully to the Union. Member states can only exercise their competence when and to the extent '*that the Union has not exercised or has decided to cease exercising the competence*'.

Increasing Impotence.

If this shift of power is coupled with the proposed considerable **extension of QMV** (see pages xxi-xxiii) it will be seen that the areas in which individual countries can take action in their own right on matters of particular concern or worry are being **progressively** eroded. With the increased areas which will come under **the jurisdiction of the European Court of Justice** there are grounds to be considerably worried about the tightening bureaucratic network on business.

Social partners.

The potential strengthening of the position of unions (see Article I-47 on the social partners) adds to the possibility of further problems to good management. These problems include the **right to strike** included in the Charter of Fundamental Rights, Article II-88. which could impact on the UK's industrial law.

Legal uncertainty.

In addition to much loose language, the Constitution leaves too much open to future interpretation. This problem is greatly enhanced by the inclusion of the **Charter of Fundamental Rights** to add to that of Human Rights. There are particularly serious and damaging implications for restrictive employment practices - and time wasting and expensive legal arguments.

---

[3] '*The Making of Europe's Constitution*' published by The Fabian Society (ISBN 0 7163 0609 3)

LEGISLATIVE PROCEDURES

Introduction

In the early stages of the Community, voting on any prospective legislation was done by the Council and the voting process did not directly involve the European Parliament, beyond its being informed of any prospective legislation and its opinion being sought. As the Community, and latterly the Union, has developed, the European Parliament's role in the legislative procedure has grown. Under the Constitution, the Parliament becomes the main legislature of the Union.

Co-Decision - Ordinary Legislative Procedure

The concept of the ordinary legislative procedure is to directly involve the three principal Union institutions, the Commission, the Council of Ministers and the European Parliament, in enacting legislation. This process has been termed the 'Community method'. This procedure covers European laws and European framework laws and they are jointly adopted by the two institutions that have legislative powers, the European Parliament and the Council.

One of the consequences of the Community method of voting is that the Member States have a reduced role in the process of legislation, since the proposed act is initiated by the Commission and the European Parliament is directly involved in the adoption of laws. The significance of the change of voting in the Council from qualified majority to the ordinary legislative procedure is that it indicates the progressive movement towards having the Community method operate in all proposed legislation. As a form of a check and balance to this, the national parliaments have an increased role in the prospective legislation, in that they can review the proposals for adherence to the principles of subsidiarity and proportionality.

Forms of Legislation

In the current Treaties, regulations and directives are the principal forms of instruments used; in addition, there are decisions, which are binding, and recommendations and opinions, which are for guidance. Overall, there are fifteen different types of legal instruments, including 'joint actions' and 'common positions'. The Convention decided that these should be simplified and that there should be a more clearly defined distinction between the various types of legislation. As a result, a number of changes have been introduced to the types of legislative instruments and these are described in Articles I-33 to I-39.

Two principal classes of legislative instruments have been introduced by the Constitution: legislative acts and non-legislative acts.

Legislative Acts consist of European laws and European framework laws. These two types of laws correspond to regulations and directives respectively in the current Treaties (Article 249 TEC) and are jointly adopted by the European Parliament and the Council.

Non-legislative Acts consist of European regulations and European decisions. The new type of regulation takes over the definition of the existing regulations and the existing directives; the term 'directive' will no longer be used. Non-legislative acts are adopted by the Commission and the Council.

Legislative Acts

These are the principal form of legislative instrument and European laws and European framework laws are defined in Article I-33 as follows:

- **European laws** shall be legislative acts of general application. They shall be binding in their entirety and directly applicable in all Member States.

- **European framework laws** shall be legislative acts binding, as to the result to be achieved, on the Member States to which they are addressed, but leaving the national authorities entirely free to choose the form and means of achieving those results.

Non-legislative Acts

These are used to implement the legislative acts and European regulations and European decisions are defined in Article I-33 as:

- **European regulations** shall be non-legislative acts of general application for the implementation of legislative acts and of certain specific provisions of the Constitution. They may either be binding in their entirety and directly applicable in all Member States, or be binding, as regards the result to be achieved, on all Member States to which they are addressed, but leaving the national authorities entirely free to choose the form and means of achieving that result.

- **European decisions** shall be non-legislative acts, binding in their entirety. Decisions that specify those to whom they are addressed shall be binding only on them.

Other Acts

In addition to the legislative and non-legislative acts, there are two other forms of legal instrument, defined in Articles I-36 and I-37:

- **delegated European regulations** are a new category of act and are intended to supplement or amend non-essential aspects of the legislative acts. These acts are used by the Commission and the Member States to enact the Legislative Acts.

- **implementing acts** will take the form of regulations or decisions and are intended to give the Commission authority to implement European laws in the national law of Member States.

The procedure for the adoption of the legal acts of the Union is laid down in Articles I-34 to I-39. Legislative acts will be adopted by the ordinary legislative procedure under the initiative of the Commission, unless specified in the text of the Treaty, where the process will be by a special legislative procedure.

Methods of voting

The two principal types of voting used by the Council are retained in the Constitutional Treaty. *Unanimity* is used in areas of sensitive national interests, such as tax, the common foreign and security policy and revision of the Treaties, but **qualified majority voting** is increasingly becoming the standard method. This has evolved as a way of avoiding the difficulties of passing Community legislation where there had been unanimity and a individual Member State could invoke the national veto and prevent a piece of legislation becoming law.

The procedure of qualified majority voting takes two forms. The first is where the Commission initiates and proposes legislative acts, and the Council, in conjunction with the European Parliament, adopts the legislation, which in the current treaties is termed the 'Community Method' or **co-decision**.

The other procedure is where the Council acts on its own and the involvement of the European Parliament is limited to giving its consent or its opinion. In certain cases, it will only be informed of the actions of the Council. In the current Treaties, the involvement of the European Parliament can be by consent and using the co-operation method, which is a modified version of co-decision.

The co-decision procedure was introduced in the Maastricht Treaty and has been progressively applied to more areas in the Treaties of Amsterdam and Nice; the intention is that the co-decision procedure will become the principal method of enacting legislation in the Union, with fewer areas subject to adoption by the Council acting on its own. As the Council consists of the Heads of Government or senior ministers representing their national interests, it acts in an intergovernmental manner. The move towards co-decision, with the increased involvement (and therefore importance) of the European Parliament, is intended to enable the Union to move away from a inter-governmental structure to one where the Union acts in its own right.

Ordinary legislative procedure

The Constitutional Treaty renames the co-decision method as the '**ordinary legislative procedure**' to indicate that this is intended to become the normal procedure to enact legislation in the Union. This is described in Article I-34. This method can either be under unanimity or qualified majority voting.

The detailed process for the adoption of legislation by the ordinary legislative procedure is laid out in Article III-396. The Commission will submit a proposal to both the Council and to the European Parliament. The European Parliament will vote on the proposal and pass its decision to the Council, which will make its own assessment. If the two bodies agree, the proposal is adopted as law. If there is no agreement, a conciliation committee is formed to attempt to reach an agreement. If there is no agreement within six weeks of the Committee being convened, the proposal will not be adopted. If there is agreement in the Committee within the six week period, the Council and the European Parliament will have a further six weeks to adopt the legislation.

Special legislative procedure

Where the Council acts in any manner other than by the ordinary legislative procedure, the method of enacting legislation is termed the '**special legislative procedure**' in the Constitutional Treaty. In this procedure, the European Parliament is not directly involved in the legislative process. It is intended to be the exception to the usual method of enacting legislation and is described in Article I-34(2). The Council may vote to change the method of voting from the special procedure to the ordinary procedure and this is described in Article IV-444(2).

The co-operation method in the current Treaties has been removed and the voting method used in the provisions that came under this system are now either adopted under the ordinary legislative procedure or with the consent of the European Parliament. This is described more fully below.

The Constitutional Treaty has changed the method of voting in the Council of Ministers in a number of areas from unanimity to qualified majority voting. The summary below shows the principal areas where the procedure of voting in the Council has been changed from unanimity, together with an indication of where the method of qualified majority voting has changed to the ordinary legislative procedure.

Primacy and application of legislation: direct application and direct effect

The concept of Community law having precedence, that is primacy, over the national law of Member States, was laid down by the Court of Justice in Costa v. ENEL [1964] ECR 585, so that Community law binds individuals and the Member States, and the national courts are obliged to apply Community law. In Article I-6, this principle of primacy is confirmed for Union law and also that the Constitution has primacy over the laws of the Member States.

The definition of European laws or European regulations in Article I-33 describes them as being of general application. This indicates the nature of their legislative character in that they are the principle mechanism to ensure the uniformity of Community Union law throughout the European Union.

Where the European laws and regulations are '**directly applicable**', they must be directly entered into the national law of the Member States, without any need for implementing measures by the national authorities. Once the legislation is in force, and provided that the provisions are clear and unconditional, it creates rights for individuals that can be claimed against the Member States in national and European courts, giving the legislation '**direct effect**'.

European framework laws and certain European regulations are binding as to the result to be achieved, but leave the individual Member States freedom in how they implement the legislation. If the legislation is not implemented correctly or by the time stated, then individuals affected by the legislation may acquire rights, and as a result, these types of legislation can have direct effect.

European decisions are binding and there is no discretion in the manner of implementation. As a result, individuals can acquire rights from the provisions of the decisions and therefore the legislation can have direct effect.

Vertical and horizontal provisions

Once direct effect is established, individuals can rely on the legislation in national and European courts in actions brought against other individuals (**horizontal** provisions) and against a state or the Union (**vertical** provisions).

Role of the European Parliament

In the legislative structure created by the original Treaty of Rome, signed in 1957, the Community acted on an inter-governmental basis and the principal role of adopting legislation was held by the Council. The involvement of the European Parliament was restricted to being a reviewing chamber with the ability to give opinions and consent to proposed legislation.

As the nature of the Community has changed, the legislative process has changed so that the Community institutions act independently from the Member States. An increasing number of areas of legislation have been progressively changed to be adopted by the Council acting in conjunction with the European Parliament using co-decision. As the Community has acquired new competences, these new areas have also been made subject to co-decision. The role of the European Parliament has become more important and the intention is that the Parliament should be the main legislature of the Union.

The Constitutional Treaty continues this process of moving the legislative process to co-decision and increases the number of areas where the Parliament acts in conjunction with the Council and as a consequence, the power of the Parliament has been substantially increased. The areas where the Parliament is involved are shown below.

Role of national parliaments

One of the issues raised in the Laeken Declaration was the importance of bringing the European Union closer to European citizens. As a consequence, national parliaments have been given an increased role in the legislative procedure by the Constitution and there are a number of instances in the main text of the Treaty, where the Union institutions are required to consult the national parliaments. The consultation procedure is part of the application of the principle of subsidiarity and therefore does not apply where the Union has exclusive competence.

The principal areas where the national parliaments are consulted are:

-   ensuring compliance by the Union institutions of the **principle of representative democracy** and the concept of subsidiarity (Articles I-11, I-18 and I-46);

-   accession of a European state to the Union (Article I-58(2));

-   review of activities in the **area of freedom, security and justice** (Articles I-42 and III-260), in particular in the monitoring of **Eurojust** (Article III-273) and **Europol** (Article III-276)

-   ordinary revision of the Treaty (Article IV-443);

-   revision procedure of Part III through the *passerelle* clause (Article IV-444).

In addition, two protocols (Protocols nos. 1 and 2) have been included in the Treaty setting out the extent of the involvement of the national parliaments. These protocols are on the role of national parliaments and the application of subsidiarity.

All legislative proposals will be sent to the national parliaments and they may send an opinion to the Presidents of the European Parliament, the Council and the Commission, on whether the proposals comply with the principles of subsidiarity and proportionality within a six-week time limit. Where the parliaments have two chambers, each chamber may send an opinion (Protocol no. 2, Articles 5 and 6).

Under the terms of the Protocol on subsidiarity (Article 7), a **voting system** is introduced for the national parliaments. Each national parliament is allocated two votes; for bicameral parliaments, each chamber has one vote.

If an opinion from the national parliaments or chambers of a parliament, representing one-third of all the votes allocated to the parliaments (i.e. 17 out of a possible 50), reflects the view that there has not been compliance with the principle of subsidiarity, the Commission is required to review its proposal. The threshold will be reduced to one quarter of the votes (i.e. 13 out of 50) where the proposed legislation originates from the Commission and if it proposal concerns the area of freedom, security and justice.

The Commission may decide to maintain, amend or withdraw its proposal. Although there is no obligation for the Commission to change its proposal, there is the possibility under the voting procedures in the Council that the proposal could be rejected at that stage, depending on which Member States disagree with the proposed legislation.

ORDINARY LEGISLATIVE PROCEDURE (Article III-396)

I.   CHANGES FROM UNANIMITY

Full details are given *'Changes from Unanimity to Qualified Majority'*. See page xli.

II.   CHANGES FROM QUALIFIED MAJORITY

Freedom of movement of establishment

-   Exclusion of certain activities in a Member State from the scope of the provisions on freedom of establishment; Article III-139, second paragraph. *(ex Article 45(2) TEC)*

Free movement of capital and payments

-   Adoption of measures on movement of capital to or from third countries, where constituting a step back in the liberalisation process under Community law. Council law adopted unanimously, after consulting the European Parliament; Article III-157. *(ex Article 57(2) TEC)*

-   Extension of the provisions on services to third-country nationals established within the Community; Article III-144, second paragraph. *(ex Article 49(2) TEC)*

-   Liberalisation of services; Article III-147. (*ex Article 52(1) TEC*)

-   Adoption of other measures on movement of capital to or from third countries; Article III-157(2) *(ex Article 57(2) TEC)*

Economic policy

-   Multilateral surveillance of Member States' economic policies by the Commission; Article III-179(6). *(ex Article 99(5) TEC).*
    This has changed from the co-operation procedure (see below).

Economic and social cohesion

-   Structural Funds and Cohesion Fund: tasks, priority objectives and organisation. The first provisions to take effect once the new Treaty comes into force to be adopted by unanimity and consent of the European Parliament, after this by QMV under the ordinary legislative procedure; Article III-223 *(ex Article 161 TEC) This has changed from QMV with assent of the European Parliament, under the provisions introduced by the Treaty of Nice, which would have come into effect on 1 January 2007.*

Monetary policy

-   Amendment of the Protocol on the Statute of the ESCB and of the ECB, on a recommendation from the ECB after consulting the Commission; Article III-187(5). *(ex Article 107(5) TEC)*

Agriculture and fisheries

-   Application of competition rules to the common agricultural policy; Article III-231(1). *(ex Article 37(2) TEC)*

-   Common agricultural policy legislation; Article III-231(2). *(ex Article 37(2) TEC)*

Common commercial policy

-   Commercial policy – implementing measures; Article III-315(2). *(ex Article 133 TEC)*

Court of Justice

- Penalties: provision for the Council to give the Court of Justice unlimited jurisdiction over the size and nature of penalties. Previously, regulations by the European Parliament and the Council, and the Council under the terms of the TEC; Article III-363 (*ex Article 229 TEC*)

Environment

- Cohesion Fund: financial support for transport infrastructure. The first provisions to take effect once the new Treaty comes into force to be adopted by unanimity and consent of the European Parliament, after this by QMV under the ordinary legislative procedure; Article III-223 *(ex Article 161 TEC) This has changed from QMV with assent of the European Parliament, under the provisions introduced by the Treaty of Nice, which would have come into effect on 1 January 2007.*

Trans-European Networks

- Cohesion Fund: financial support for transport infrastructure. The first provisions to take effect once the new Treaty comes into force to be adopted by unanimity and consent of the European Parliament, after this by QMV under the ordinary legislative procedure; Article III-223 *(ex Article 161 TEC) This has changed from QMV with assent of the European Parliament, under the provisions introduced by the Treaty of Nice, which would have come into effect on 1 January 2007.*

Economic, financial and technical co-operation with third countries

- Economic, financial and technical co-operation with third countries; Article III-319(2). *(ex Article 181a TEC)*

Financial provisions

- Adoption of financial rules, as from 2007; Article III-412. *(ex Article 279(1) TEC)*

- Enactment of Staff Regulations for officials of the European Community and Conditions of Employment of other servants of the Union; Article III-427. *(ex Article 283 TEC)*

III. CHANGES FROM QUALIFIED MAJORITY [CO-OPERATION PROCEDURE]

The co-operation procedure, introduced in the Maastricht Treaty, enabled the European Parliament to propose amendments to any intended legislation and was a modified version of the co-decision procedure. The Constitutional Treaty repeals the co-operation procedure and the areas covered by this procedure now come under the consultation procedure, except for the multilateral surveillance of Member States' economic policies by the Commission, which is now under the ordinary legislative procedure.

In the consultation procedure, the European Parliament is not directly involved in the legislative process, but the Council of Ministers will now obtain the consent of the European Parliament before voting on a particular proposal from the Commission.

Economic policy

- Application of the ban on privileged access; Article III-182 and Article 183(2). *(ex Article 102(2) TEC)*

- Application of the ban on assuming commitments or granting overdraft facilities; Article III-183(2). *(ex Article 103(2) TEC)*

Monetary policy

- Measures to harmonise the denominations and technical specifications of coins; Article III-186(2). *(ex Article 106(2) TEC)*

International Agreements

- Agreements between the Union and other states or international organisations, for the adoption of internal rules; Article III-303 and III-325(7). *(ex Article 300(3) TEC)*

SPECIAL LEGISLATIVE PROCEDURES

These procedures are a new description of any method of enacting legislation that does not involve the direct involvement of the European Parliament under the 'ordinary' procedure. 'Special' procedures cover the situations where the Council of Ministers votes on proposed legislation after either consulting the European Parliament or receiving its consent.

These procedures cover the legislative acts of European laws and European framework laws, together with non-legislative acts.

I. CHANGES FROM UNANIMITY

Full details are given *'Changes from Unanimity to Qualified Majority'.* See pages xxii to xxiii

II. CHANGES FROM QUALIFIED MAJORITY

European Parliament

- Arrangements for exercising the right of inquiry into mal-administration of Union law: European Parliament law, with the approval of the Council and an opinion from the Commission; Article III-333. *(ex Article 193 TEC)*

Financial provisions

- Annual budget; law adopted under a special procedure; Article III-404. *(ex Article 272(5) TEC)*

NEW PROVISIONS UNDER UNANIMITY

There are a number of provisions introduced by the Constitutional Treaty that are under voting by unanimity.

Energy

- Fiscal measures, relating to duties and taxation of energy policy, will be established by European laws or framework laws by unanimity; Article III-256(3). *New provision*.

Area of Freedom, Security and Justice

- Judicial co-operation in civil matters: European decision on family law having a cross-border implications. This is also subject to a passerelle clause; Article III-269(3). *New provision*

- Judicial co-operation in criminal matters: extension of the definition of criminal offences and sanctions concerning serious crimes to other areas of crime that meet the criteria; Article III-271(1). *New provision*.

- Public Prosecutor's Office to be established by a European law, with the Council acting *unanimously*. This will initially cover the general rules of operation, but may be extended to cover serious cross-border crime; Article III-274. *New provision*

Multi-annual financial framework

- Terms of the multi-annual financial framework. Council acting by unanimity, with the consent of the European Parliament.; Article I-55. *New provision*

PROVISIONS REMAINING UNDER UNANIMITY

These are provisions that were under unanimity in the Treaty on European Union and in the Treaty establishing the European Community and have not been altered by the Constitutional Treaty.

Common Foreign and Security Policy

- European Council decisions on common defence (Article III-300);
- Foreign policy and defence decisions (Article III-300).

General Provisions

- Changes to the Treaty (Article IV-443);
- Accession of new Member States to the Union (Article I-58).

Non-discrimination and citizenship

- Action against discrimination (other than incentive measures) (Article III-124);
- Provisions on passports, identity cards, residence permits, social security and social protection, (Article III-125);
- Arrangements for non-nationals to vote in European Parliament and municipal elections, (Article III-126);
- Additional rights of European Union citizenship (Article III-129).

Capital and Payments

- Derogation from liberalisation of capital movements (Article III-157).

Transport

- Approval for derogations from transport rules in favour of a Member State's own carriers, (Article III-237).

Aid granted by Member States

- Derogation for state aid rules in exceptional circumstance (Article III-168).

Taxation

- Harmonisation of indirect taxation (Article III-171).

Approximation of Laws

- Approximation (harmonisation) of laws affecting the internal market (Article III-173).

Economic and Monetary Policy

- Replacement of the Protocol on excessive deficits (Article III-184);

- Conferring of specific tasks on the European Central Bank (Article III-185.6);

- Decisions concerning the ERM (Article III-326);

- Institutional provisions relating to the ERM (Article III-198.3).

International Agreements

- Negotiation and conclusion of agreements in the field of cultural and audiovisual services and in the field of social, education and health services (Article III-315.4);

- Conclusion of international agreements where it concerns areas of Union law under unanimity and for association agreements (Article III-325.8).

Flexibility Clause

- Where the Treaty does not confer competence on the Union, it may adopt the appropriate measures to fulfil one of the objectives of the Treaty (Article I-18).

Social Policy

- Social provisions covering social security and social protection of workers, protection of workers on termination of employment, representation of workers and conditions of employment for third country nationals (Article III-210.3).

European Institutions

- Uniform electoral procedure for the European Parliament (Article III-330);

- Taxation provisions of the Statute for Members of the European Parliament (Article III-330);

- Decision not to fill a vacancy in the Commission College (Article III-348.2);

- Increase in number of Advocates-General in the Court of Justice (Article III-354);

- Appointment of Judges to the Court of Justice and to the High Court (Court of First Instance) and Advocates-General to the Court of Justice (Articles III-355 and III-356);

- Creation of judicial panels and appointment of members of the panels (Article III-359);

- Amendment of a proposal by the Commission, except for matters concerning the EU budget, which has been transferred to qualified majority voting (Article III-395 and III-396);

- The location of the seats of the European institutions (Article III-432).

Other Areas

- **Culture** (Article III-280);

- First set of rules concerning **structural and cohesion funds** after introduction of the Constitution, following the provisions in Article 161 TEC of unanimity until 2007 (Article III-223.2);

- Certain provisions in **environment** - fiscal nature, town and country planning, land use, (Article III-234.2);

- Rules and procedures for association of the overseas countries and territories with the Community, (Article III-290/291);

- Provisions concerning the Union resources - the Union's 'own resources' (Article I-54.3);

- The official languages of the Union (Article III-433);

- Derogations for trade in arms by Member States (Article III-436).

CHANGES FROM UNANIMITY TO QUALIFIED MAJORITY

The Constitutional Treaty has changed the method of voting in the European Council and the Council in a significant number of areas from unanimity to qualified majority voting. These tables show the principal areas where the procedure of voting in the Council has been changed from unanimity, with an indication of which are under the ordinary or special legislative procedures.

European Council

1. Election of the President of the European Council, by the members of the European Council;
   Article I-22(1). *New provision*.

2. Configurations of the European Council, other than the Foreign Affairs Council;
   Article I-24(4). *New provision*.

3. Conditions and rotation of presidencies of the European Council configurations;
   Article I-24(6) *(ex Article 203 TEC)*

4. Appointment of the Foreign Minister for Foreign Affairs; Article I-27(1).
   New provision.

5. Appointment of ECB President, Vice-President and executive board; Article III-382(2)
   (ex Article 112 and 113 TEC)

Council of Ministers

<u>Ordinary Legislative Procedure</u>

Exercise of Union competence: Implementing acts

- Arrangements for control of implementing powers (comitology); Article I-37(3) *(ex Article 202 TEC)*

Participation of EU Citizens in Union democracy

- Determination of the procedures and conditions for Citizens' initiative for legislation; Article I-47(4). *New provision*

Free movement of workers

- Internal market: **social security** measures, principally benefits, for Community migrant workers; Article III-136(1) *(ex Article 42 TEC)*.
  Where a Member State considers that a draft law would affect fundamental aspects of its social security system, it may request a referral to the European Council, which may refer back to the Council or request the Commission to submit a new proposal; Article III-136(2). *New Provision*.

Freedom of Establishment

- **Self-employed persons**: co-ordination of provisions laid down by law, regulation or administrative action in Member States concerning the taking-up and pursuit of activities as self-employed persons. Change from unanimity to QMV in the case of co-ordination of existing principles laid down by law governing the professions with respect to training and conditions of access for natural persons; Article III-141(1)(b) *(ex Article 47(2) TEC)*

Cont'd….

Areas where the Union may take co-ordinating, complementary or supporting action

- Culture, including education, conservation, cultural exchanges and artistic creation (except for recommendations); Article III-280 *(ex Article 151 TEC)*

- Tourism; Article III-281. *New provision*

- Sport - promotion of sporting issues, including sport's social and educational function; Article III-282(1). *New provision.*

- Civil protection against natural and man-made disasters; Article III-284. *New provision*

- Administrative co-ordination to help Member States administrative capacity to implement Union law; Article III-285. *New provision*

Policies in specific areas

- **Intellectual Property Rights**
  Measures to provide uniform intellectual property rights protection throughout the Union and setting up of the centralised Union-wide authorisation, co-ordination and supervision arrangements; Article III-176. *New provision.*

- **Space**
  Measures for drawing up a European space policy; Article III-254. *New provision*

- **Energy**
  Measures to ensure the functioning of the energy market, the security of supply of energy in the Union and energy efficiency and saving; Article III-256.
  New provision

- **Transport**
  Measures for drawing up a policy for transport across Member States, where there is serious effect on the standard of living and employment, and air and sea transport; Articles III-236 and III-245 *(ex Articles 71(2) TEC and 80(2) TEC).*

- **Common Security and Defence Policy**
  Measures for drawing up **permanent structured co-operation,** including selection of participating Member States, confirmation of fulfilment of criteria and suspension from this co-operation; Article III-312(2), (3)and (4). *New provision*

- **Common Commercial Policy**
  Measures for negotiation and conclusion of international agreements, including intellectual property and foreign direct investment (FDI is a new provision). Previously, the Union could act by unanimity on intellectual property matters and for internal rules or where there were no conferred powers; Article III-315.
  (ex Article 133 TEC)

- **Economic, financial and technical co-operation with third countries**
  Measures to implement association and accession agreements concerned with economic, financial and technical co-operation; Article III-319.
  (ex Article 181a TEC)

- **Humanitarian Aid**
  Measures for drawing up a framework for humanitarian aid operations, including the formation of European Voluntary Humanitarian Aid Corps; Article III-321(3).
  New provision.

- **European Union Administration**
  Measures for drawing up an open, efficient and independent European administration, or 'civil service' to support the EU institutions, including conditions of employment for the staff; Article III-398. *New provision.*

Cont'd....

Area of Freedom, Security and Justice

- Border controls, visa and short-term residence policy, freedom of travel of third country nationals, gradual integration of integrated external border management, absence of internal border controls; Article III-265 *(ex Articles 62, 64 and 67 TEC)*

- Asylum - uniform status of asylum and subsidiary status for nationals of third countries, common system of temporary protection, common procedures for granting and withdrawing uniform asylum or subsidiary protection status, standards for conditions for reception of applicants, co-operation with third countries to manage inflows of people; Article III-266 *(ex Articles 63, 64 and 67 TEC)*

- Immigration - conditions of entry and residence and standards on issue of long-term visas, definition of rights of third-country nationals living legally in the EU, illegal immigration and residence in the EU, combating trafficking in people, especially women and children; Article III-267(2) *(ex Articles 63, 64 and 67 TEC)*

- Integration of third country nationals - measures to provide incentives and support for Member States' actions; Article III-267(4) *(ex Articles 63, 64 and 67 TEC)*

- Judicial co-operation in civil matters - mutual recognition and enforcement of judgements and decisions and cross-border co-operation; Article III-269(2) *(ex Articles 65 and 67 TEC).*

Under the TEC, the Union could act by unanimity for the above areas until May 2004 (five-year transitional period after the entry into force of the Amsterdam Treaty). Through the use of a passerelle clause, the Union could vote by unanimity to act by QMV after May 2004.

The UK has an opt-out from these Articles, under Protocol no. 18, Article 1, and Protocol no. 19, Articles 1 and 2.

- Approximation of national laws and regulations in Part III; Article I-42(1)(a). *New provision.*

- Judicial co-operation in criminal matters - procedures, co-operation, training and minimum rules; an 'emergency brake' has been introduced; Article III-270 *(ex Article 31 TEU)*

- Minimum rules on establishing definitions of criminal offences and sanctions for serious crime with a cross-border dimension; also applies to areas subject to harmonisation measures; an 'emergency brake' has been introduced; Article III-271. *New provision.*

- Crime prevention - promotion and supporting measures; Article III-272. *New provision.*

- Eurojust - determination of structure, operation, field of action and tasks, together with arrangements for involvement of the European Parliament and national parliaments; Article III-273(1) *(ex Article 31(2) TEU)*

- Police co-operation - some aspects, including analysis and exchange of information and staff training; Article III-275(2) *(ex Article 30 TEU)*

- Europol - determination of structure, operation, field of action and tasks, together with arrangements for involvement of the European Parliament and national parliaments; Article III-276 *(ex Article 30(2) TEU)*

Economic and Monetary Policy

- Amendment of articles in the Protocol on the Statute of the ESCB and of the ECB on a proposal from the Commission. The articles concern collection of statistical information, and the functioning and operation of the ESCB and the ECB; Article III-187(3) *(ex Article 107(5) TEC)*

- Measures required for use of the euro; Article III-19. *New provision*

Cont'd....

Court of Justice

- Establishment of specialist courts [judicial panels] attached to General Court (previously, the Court of First Instance), rules on organisation and extent of jurisdiction; Article III-359
  (ex Article 225a TEC)

- Jurisdiction for the Court of Justice in intellectual property matters; Article III-364
  (ex Article 229a TEC)

- Amendment of the Statute of the Court of Justice (except for Title I); Article III-381
  (ex Article 245 TEC)

European Investment Bank

- Amendment of some articles of the Protocol on the Statute of the EIB;
  Article III-393, third paragraph. *(ex Article 266 TEC)*

Economic and social cohesion

- Structural Funds and Cohesion Fund: tasks, priority objectives and organisation. The first provisions to take effect once the new Treaty comes into force to be adopted by unanimity, after this by QMV; Article III-223 *(ex Article 161 TEC)*

Environment

- Cohesion Fund: financial support for transport infrastructure. The first provisions to take effect once the new Treaty comes into force to be adopted by unanimity and consent of the European Parliament, after this by QMV under the ordinary legislative procedure;
  Article III-223 *(ex Article 161 TEC)*

Trans-European networks

- Cohesion Fund: financial support for transport infrastructure. The first provisions to take effect once the new Treaty comes into force to be adopted by unanimity and consent of the European Parliament, after this by QMV under the ordinary legislative procedure;
  Article III-223 *(ex Article 161 TEC)*

Special Legislative Procedure

Voluntary withdrawal from the Union

- Agreement with the Member State wishing to leave the Union: Council acts by qualified majority; Article I-60(2). **New provision.**

The Union's finances and resources

- Own resources arrangements:
  Implementing measures on the system of own resources by European law adopted by the Council by a qualified majority, with the consent of the European Parliament **(the UK rebate is covered by unanimity under Article I-54(3))**; Article I-54(4) *(ex Article 269 TEC)*

Area of Freedom, Security and Justice

- Arrangements for how the Member States conduct evaluation of the implementation of Union policies in the area of freedom, security and justice (in particular, mutual recognition). The European Parliament and the national parliaments are to be informed of the results. The UK has an opt-out from this, under Protocol no. 19, Article 1; Article III-260. **New provision.**

Cont'd....

- Administrative co-operation by regulation; Article III-263
  (ex Articles 66 TEC and 30 and 31 TEU)

- Judicial co-operation in civil matters: European decision on family law having a cross-border implications; Article III-269(3). ***New provision***
  This is also subject to a passerelle clause, see below.

Culture

- Recommendations on cultural matters: majority in the Council; Article III-280(5)(b)
  (ex Article 151(5), second indent, TEC)

Common foreign and security policy

- The Council acts by a qualified majority under the CFSP when adopting a decision on the initiative of the Minister for Foreign Affairs, further to a request from the European Council; Article III-300(2)(b). ***New provision***

- European Defence Agency – statute, seat and operational rules; by qualified majority; Article III-311. ***New provision***

Economic, financial and technical co-operation with third countries

- Emergency aid: Urgent financial assistance for third countries: European decision by the Council; Article III-320. ***New provision.***

Economic and Monetary Union

- Establishment of common positions among the members of EMU on matters concerning the Euro in the international monetary system and to ensure unified representation. The Council will act after consulting the ECB; Article III-196(1) and (2). ***New provision.***

Financial provisions

- Establishment of the EU budget by the Council and the European Parliament, by the production of a European law; Article III-404 *(ex Article 272 TEC)*

- Arrangements for the budget funds provided from own resources being made available to the Commission: European regulation by the Council, qualified majority from 1 January 2007; Articles I-53(3) and (4) and III-412(2) *(ex Article 279(2) TEC)*

Services of General Economic Interest

- Establishment of the principles and conditions, especially economic and financial conditions, to provide, commission and to fund the services, to promote social and territorial cohesion. The Council acts after consultation with the European Parliament; Article III-122 *(ex Article 16 TEC)*.

Diplomatic and consular protection

- Protection of citizens in third countries, following the right defined in Article I-10(2). The Council will act after consulting the European Parliament; Article III-127 *(ex Article 20 TEC)*

Court of Justice

- Establishment of a panel to select judges and advocate-generals, including appointment of the panel and the panel's operating rules. The Council will act on the initiative of the President of the Court of Justice; Article III-357. ***New provision***.

Cont'd....

Solidarity clause

- Arrangements for the implementation of the solidarity clause, in the case of a Member State suffering a terrorist attack or a natural or man-made disaster. The Council will act on the initiative of the Commission and the Union Minister for Foreign Affairs, the European Parliament will be informed; Article III-329. *New provision.*

Passerelle Clauses

There are eight passerelle clauses in the Constitutional Treaty, of which two were also present in the Treaty establishing the European Community. The passerelle clauses allow the Council, or the European Council, to vote by unanimity to change the method of voting on a particular area from unanimity to qualified majority voting under the ordinary legislative procedure.

These areas are:

- **Common foreign and security policy**: European decisions on CFSP in Article III-300, other than military or defence matters; Article I-40(7). *New provision*;

- **Multi-annual financial framework** (described in Article III-402) where the European Council may decide to change the voting; Article I-55(4) *New provision*;

- **Social policy**, protection of workers' rights, where the Council may decide to change the method of voting; Article III-210(3) (*ex Article 137 TEC*);

- **Environmental protection**, where the Council may decide to change the method of voting; Article III-234(2) (*ex Article 175 TEC*);

- **Judicial co-operation in civil matters** – family law with cross-border implications, where the Council may decide to change the method of voting; Article III-269. *New provision*;

- **Common Foreign and Security** Policy: European decisions on CFSP, other than military or defence matters; Article III-300(3). *New provision*;

- **Enhanced co-operation**, excluding defence implications, where the Council may decide to change the method of voting; Article (III-422) *New provision*;

- **General passerelle clause**, where the European Council may decide by unanimity to change the method of voting in Part III of the Treaty, excluding defence or military matters; Article IV-444. *New provision.*

In a late amendment to the Treaty, an 'emergency brake' provision was added to the general passerelle procedure to include the national parliaments, so that a national parliament can veto a European Council decision under the passerelle clause to change from unanimity to qualified majority voting, if the parliament notifies its opposition within six months of being notified of the proposed change; Article IV-444(3). *New Provision.*

ADDITIONAL PAPERS

THE LAEKEN DECLARATION
THE FUTURE OF THE EUROPEAN UNION

Laeken, 15 December 2001

SN 273/01

I.   EUROPE AT A CROSSROADS

For centuries, peoples and states have taken up arms and waged war to win control of the European continent. The debilitating effects of two bloody wars and the weakening of Europe's position in the world brought a growing realisation that only peace and concerted action could make the dream of a strong, unified Europe come true. In order to banish once and for all the demons of the past, a start was made with a coal and steel community. Other economic activities, such as agriculture, were subsequently added in. A genuine single market was eventually established for goods, persons, services and capital, and a single currency was added in 1999. On 1 January 2002 the euro is to become a day-to-day reality for 300 million European citizens.

The European Union has thus gradually come into being. In the beginning, it was more of an economic and technical collaboration. Twenty years ago, with the first direct elections to the European Parliament, the Community's democratic legitimacy, which until then had lain with the Council alone, was considerably strengthened. Over the last ten years, construction of a political union has begun and co-operation been established on social policy, employment, asylum, immigration, police, justice, foreign policy and a common security and defence policy.

The European Union is a success story. For over half a century now, Europe has been at peace. Along with North America and Japan, the Union forms one of the three most prosperous parts of the world. As a result of mutual solidarity and fair distribution of the benefits of economic development, moreover, the standard of living in the Union's weaker regions has increased enormously and they have made good much of the disadvantage they were at.

Fifty years on, however, the Union stands at a crossroads, a defining moment in its existence. The unification of Europe is near. The Union is about to expand to bring in more than ten new Member States, predominantly Central and Eastern European, thereby finally closing one of the darkest chapters in European history: the Second World War and the ensuing artificial division of Europe. At long last, Europe is on its way to becoming one big family, without bloodshed, a real transformation clearly calling for a different approach from fifty years ago, when six countries first took the lead.

The democratic challenge facing Europe

At the same time, the Union faces twin challenges, one within and the other beyond its borders.

Within the Union, the European institutions must be brought closer to its citizens. Citizens undoubtedly support the Union's broad aims, but they do not always see a connection between those goals and the Union's everyday action. They want the European institutions to be less unwieldy and rigid and, above all, more efficient and open. Many also feel that the Union should involve itself more with their particular concerns, instead of intervening, in every detail, in matters by their nature better left to Member States' and regions' elected representatives. This is even perceived by some as a threat to their identity. More importantly, however, they feel that deals are all too often cut out of their sight and they want better democratic scrutiny.

Europe's new role in a globalised world

Beyond its borders, in turn, the European Union is confronted with a fast-changing, globalised world. Following the fall of the Berlin Wall, it looked briefly as though we would for a long while be living in a stable world order, free from conflict, founded upon human rights. Just a few years later, however, there is no such certainty. The eleventh of September has brought a rude awakening. The opposing forces have not gone away: religious fanaticism, ethnic nationalism, racism and terrorism are on the increase, and regional conflicts, poverty and underdevelopment still provide a constant seedbed for them.

What is Europe's role in this changed world? Does Europe not, now that is finally unified, have a leading role to play in a new world order, that of a power able both to play a stabilising role worldwide and to point the way ahead for many countries and peoples? Europe as the continent of humane values, the Magna Carta, the Bill of Rights, the French Revolution and the fall of the Berlin Wall; the continent of liberty, solidarity and above all diversity, meaning respect for others' languages, cultures and traditions. The European Union's one boundary is democracy and human rights. The Union is open only to countries which uphold basic values such as free elections, respect for minorities and respect for the rule of law.

Now that the Cold War is over and we are living in a globalised, yet also highly fragmented world, Europe needs to shoulder its responsibilities in the governance of globalisation. The role it has to play is that of a power resolutely doing battle against all violence, all terror and all fanaticism, but which also does not turn a blind eye to the world's heartrending injustices. In short, a power wanting to change the course of world affairs in such a way as to benefit not just the rich countries but also the poorest. A power seeking to set globalisation within a moral framework, in other words to anchor it in solidarity and sustainable development.

The expectations of Europe's citizens

The image of a democratic and globally engaged Europe admirably matches citizens' wishes. There have been frequent public calls for a greater EU role in justice and security, action against cross-border crime, control of migration flows and reception of asylum seekers and refugees from far-flung war zones. Citizens also want results in the fields of employment and combating poverty and social exclusion, as well as in the field of economic and social cohesion. They want a common approach on environmental pollution, climate change and food safety, in short, all trans-national issues which they instinctively sense can only be tackled by working together. Just as they also want to see Europe more involved in foreign affairs, security and defence, in other words, greater and better co-ordinated action to deal with trouble spots in and around Europe and in the rest of the world.

At the same time, citizens also feel that the Union is behaving too bureaucratically in numerous other areas. In co-ordinating the economic, financial and fiscal environment, the basic issue should continue to be proper operation of the internal market and the single currency, without this jeopardising Member States' individuality. National and regional differences frequently stem from history or tradition. They can be enriching. In other words, what citizens understand by "good governance" is opening up fresh opportunities, not imposing further red tape. What they expect is more results, better responses to practical issues and not a European superstate or European institutions inveigling their way into every nook and cranny of life.

In short, citizens are calling for a clear, open, effective, democratically controlled Community approach, developing a Europe which points the way ahead for the world. An approach that provides concrete results in terms of more jobs, better quality of life, less crime, decent education and better health care. There can be no doubt that this will require Europe to undergo renewal and reform.

II.   CHALLENGES AND REFORMS IN A RENEWED UNION

The Union needs to become more democratic, more transparent and more efficient. It also has to resolve three basic challenges: how to bring citizens, and primarily the young, closer to the European design and the European institutions, how to organise politics and the European political area in an enlarged Union and how to develop the Union into a stabilising factor and a model in the new, multi-polar world. In order to address them a number of specific questions need to be put.

A better division and definition of competence in the European Union

Citizens often hold expectations of the European Union that are not always fulfilled. And vice versa - they sometimes have the impression that the Union takes on too much in areas where its involvement is not always essential. Thus the important thing is to clarify, simplify and adjust the division of competence between the Union and the Member States in the light of the new challenges facing the Union. This can lead both to restoring tasks to the Member States and to assigning new missions to the Union, or to the extension of existing powers, while constantly bearing in mind the equality of the Member States and their mutual solidarity.

A first series of questions that needs to be put concerns how the division of competence can be made more transparent. Can we thus make a clearer distinction between three types of competence: the exclusive competence of the Union, the competence of the Member States and the shared competence of the Union and the Member States? At what level is competence exercised in the most efficient way? How is the principle of subsidiarity to be applied here? And should we not make it clear that any powers not assigned by the Treaties to the Union fall within the exclusive sphere of competence of the Member States? And what would be the consequences of this?

The next series of questions should aim, within this new framework and while respecting the "*acquis communautaire*", to determine whether there needs to be any reorganisation of competence. How can citizens' expectations be taken as a guide here? What missions would this produce for the Union? And, vice versa, what tasks could better be left to the Member States? What amendments should be made to the Treaty on the various policies? How, for example, should a more coherent common foreign policy and defence policy be developed? Should the Petersberg tasks be updated? Do we want to adopt a more integrated approach to police and criminal law co-operation? How can economic-policy co-ordination be stepped up? How can we intensify co-operation in the field of social inclusion, the environment, health and food safety? But then, should not the day-to-day administration and implementation of the Union's policy be left more emphatically to the Member States and, where their constitutions so provide, to the regions? Should they not be provided with guarantees that their spheres of competence will not be affected?

Lastly, there is the question of how to ensure that a redefined division of competence does not lead to a creeping expansion of the competence of the Union or to encroachment upon the exclusive areas of competence of the Member States and, where there is provision for this, regions. How are we to ensure at the same time that the European dynamic does not come to a halt? In the future as well the Union must continue to be able to react to fresh challenges and developments and must be able to explore new policy areas. Should Articles 95 and 308 of the Treaty be reviewed for this purpose in the light of the "*acquis jurisprudentiel*"?

Simplification of the Union's instruments

Who does what is not the only important question; the nature of the Union's action and what instruments it should use are equally important. Successive amendments to the Treaty have on each occasion resulted in a proliferation of instruments, and directives have gradually evolved towards more and more detailed legislation. The key question is therefore whether the Union's various instruments should not be better defined and whether their number should not be reduced.

In other words, should a distinction be introduced between legislative and executive measures? Should the number of legislative instruments be reduced: directly applicable rules, framework legislation and non-enforceable instruments (opinions, recommendations, open co-ordination)? Is it or is it not desirable to have more frequent recourse to framework legislation, which affords the Member States more room for manoeuvre in achieving policy objectives? For which areas of competence are open co-ordination and mutual recognition the most appropriate instruments? Is the principle of proportionality to remain the point of departure?

More democracy, transparency and efficiency in the European Union

The European Union derives its legitimacy from the democratic values it projects, the aims it pursues and the powers and instruments it possesses. However, the European project also derives its legitimacy from democratic, transparent and efficient institutions. The national parliaments also contribute towards the legitimacy of the European project. The declaration on the future of the Union, annexed to the Treaty of Nice, stressed the need to examine their role in European integration. More generally, the question arises as to what initiatives we can take to develop a European public area.

The first question is thus how we can increase the democratic legitimacy and transparency of the present institutions, a question which is valid for the three institutions.

How can the authority and efficiency of the European Commission be enhanced? How should the President of the Commission be appointed: by the European Council, by the European Parliament or should he be directly elected by the citizens? Should the role of the European Parliament be strengthened? Should we extend the right of co-decision or not? Should the way in which we elect the members of the European Parliament be reviewed? Should a European electoral constituency be created, or should constituencies continue to be determined nationally? Can the two systems be combined? Should the role of the Council be strengthened? Should the Council act in the same manner in its legislative and its executive capacities? With a view to greater transparency, should the meetings of the Council, at least in its legislative capacity, be public? Should citizens have more access to Council documents? How, finally, should the balance and reciprocal control between the institutions be ensured?

A second question, which also relates to democratic legitimacy, involves the role of national parliaments. Should they be represented in a new institution, alongside the Council and the European Parliament? Should they have a role in areas of European action in which the European Parliament has no competence? Should they focus on the division of competence between Union and Member States, for example through preliminary checking of compliance with the principle of subsidiarity?

The third question concerns how we can improve the efficiency of decision-making and the workings of the institutions in a Union of some thirty Member States. How could the Union set its objectives and priorities more effectively and ensure better implementation? Is there a need for more decisions by a qualified majority? How is the co-decision procedure between the Council and the European Parliament to be simplified and speeded up? What of the six-monthly rotation of the Presidency of the Union? What is the future role of the European Parliament? What of the future role and structure of the various Council formations? How should the coherence of European foreign policy be enhanced? How is synergy between the High Representative and the competent Commissioner to be reinforced? Should the external representation of the Union in international fora be extended further?

Towards a Constitution for European citizens

The European Union currently has four Treaties. The objectives, powers and policy instruments of the Union are currently spread across those Treaties. If we are to have greater transparency, simplification is essential.
Four sets of questions arise in this connection. The first concerns simplifying the existing Treaties without changing their content. Should the distinction between the Union and the Communities be reviewed? What of the division into three pillars?

Questions then arise as to the possible reorganisation of the Treaties. Should a distinction be made between a basic treaty and the other treaty provisions? Should this distinction involve separating the texts? Could this lead to a distinction between the amendment and ratification procedures for the basic treaty and for the other treaty provisions?

Thought would also have to be given to whether the Charter of Fundamental Rights should be included in the basic treaty and to whether the European Community should accede to the European Convention on Human Rights.

The question ultimately arises as to whether this simplification and reorganisation might not lead in the long run to the adoption of a constitutional text in the Union. What might the basic features of such a constitution be? The values which the Union cherishes, the fundamental rights and obligations of its citizens, the relationship between Member States in the Union?

III.   CONVENING OF A CONVENTION ON THE FUTURE OF EUROPE

In order to pave the way for the next Intergovernmental Conference as broadly and openly as possible, the European Council has decided to convene a Convention composed of the main parties involved in the debate on the future of the Union. In the light of the foregoing, it will be the task of that Convention to consider the key issues arising for the Union's future development and try to identify the various possible responses.
The European Council has appointed Mr V. Giscard d'Estaing as Chairman of the Convention and Mr G. Amato and Mr J.L. Dehaene as Vice-Chairmen.

Composition

In addition to its Chairman and Vice-Chairmen, the Convention will be composed of 15 representatives of the Heads of State or Government of the Member States (one from each Member State), 30 members of national parliaments (two from each Member State), 16 members of the European Parliament and two Commission representatives. The accession candidate countries will be fully involved in the Convention's proceedings. They will be represented in the same way as the current Member States (one government representative and two national parliament members) and will be able to take part in the proceedings without, however, being able to prevent any consensus which may emerge among the Member States.

The members of the Convention may only be replaced by alternate members if they are not present. The alternate members will be designated in the same way as full members.

The Praesidium of the Convention will be composed of the Convention Chairman and Vice-Chairmen and nine members drawn from the Convention (the representatives of all the governments holding the Council Presidency during the Convention, two national parliament representatives, two European Parliament representatives and two Commission representatives).

Three representatives of the Economic and Social Committee with three representatives of the European social partners; from the Committee of the Regions: six representatives (to be appointed by the Committee of the Regions from the regions, cities and regions with legislative powers), and the European Ombudsman will be invited to attend as observers. The Presidents of the Court of Justice and of the Court of Auditors may be invited by the Praesidium to address the Convention.

Length of proceedings

The Convention will hold its inaugural meeting on 1 March 2002, when it will appoint its Praesidium and adopt its rules of procedure. Proceedings will be completed after a year, that is to say in time for the Chairman of the Convention to present its outcome to the European Council.

Working methods

The Chairman will pave the way for the opening of the Convention's proceedings by drawing conclusions from the public debate. The Praesidium will serve to lend impetus and will provide the Convention with an initial working basis.

The Praesidium may consult Commission officials and experts of its choice on any technical aspect which it sees fit to look into. It may set up ad hoc working parties.

The Council will be kept informed of the progress of the Convention's proceedings. The Convention Chairman will give an oral progress report at each European Council meeting, thus enabling Heads of State or Government to give their views at the same time.

The Convention will meet in Brussels. The Convention's discussions and all official documents will be in the public domain. The Convention will work in the Union's eleven working languages.

Final document

The Convention will consider the various issues. It will draw up a final document which may comprise either different options, indicating the degree of support which they received, or recommendations if consensus is achieved.

Together with the outcome of national debates on the future of the Union, the final document will provide a starting point for discussions in the Intergovernmental Conference, which will take the ultimate decisions.

Forum

In order for the debate to be broadly based and involve all citizens, a Forum will be opened for organisations representing civil society (the social partners, the business world, non-governmental organisations, academia, etc.). It will take the form of a structured network of organisations receiving regular information on the Convention's proceedings. Their contributions will serve as input into the debate. Such organisations may be heard or consulted on specific topics in accordance with arrangements to be established by the Praesidium.

Secretariat

The Praesidium will be assisted by a Convention Secretariat, to be provided by the General Secretariat of the Council, which may incorporate Commission and European Parliament experts.

REPORT
FROM THE CONVENTION PRESIDENCY
TO THE PRESIDENT OF THE EUROPEAN COUNCIL

Brussels, 18 July 2003 CONV 851/03

1.   In response to the mandate from the European Council meeting in Laeken on 14 and 15 December 2001, the Convention on the Future of Europe has completed its task, and submits to the President of the European Council the outcome of its work: a draft Treaty establishing a Constitution for Europe.

2.   As envisaged in the Laeken Declaration, the President of the Convention gave progress reports to the European Council at its meetings in June 2002 (Seville), October 2002 (Brussels), December 2002 (Copenhagen), and April 2003 (Athens). He presented Parts I and II of the draft Treaty to the European Council in Thessaloniki on 20 June 2003: they have not been subsequently changed. Parts III and IV, interim texts of which were available at Thessaloniki, have since been finalised, and are now added.

3.   This concludes seventeen months of work by the Convention. The [members] met in plenary session on 26 occasions (52 days), hearing over 1,800 interventions. The Convention also established eleven Working Groups and three Discussion Circles, each with its own specific mandate, which met to address particular issues and make recommendations to the Convention as a whole. Convention members also provided 386 written contributions to the Convention as a whole, and 773 to Working Groups and Discussion circles.

4.   The Praesidium, met on 50 occasions, and submitted 52 papers to the Convention. Members of the Praesidium chaired the Working Groups and Discussion Circles, and presented their reports to the Convention.

5.   The Convention operated in a fully transparent manner: its meetings were open to the public, and all its official documents were available on its website, which received an average of 47,000 visitors per month, rising to 100,000 in June 2003. In addition it took a number of initiatives to ensure wider participation in its work. The Forum established in accordance with the Laeken Declaration received 1,264 contributions from NGOs, the business community, academia and others. Meetings were organised with a wide range of groups with an interest in the Convention. These included churches and religious organisations, Think tanks, representatives of local and regional organisations, and NGOs. In addition a special plenary session devoted to civil society took place in June 2002. A Youth Convention was organised in July 2002: its elected Chairman became an additional observer of the Convention's continuing work.

6.   A key element in the Convention's success was the full role played by its members from candidate countries. In accordance with the Laeken Declaration, they participated fully in the Convention's proceedings; the Convention decided to go further, and one of their representatives, elected by them, was invited to participate in all Praesidium discussions. Interpretation arrangements were also made to enable members from candidate countries to address the Convention in their own languages. The Decision by the European Council on enlargement in December 2002, and the subsequent ratification process in the candidate countries, underlines the significance of these practical decisions taken early on in the Convention's life.

7.   The task given to the Convention was founded on the four issues addressed in the "Nice Declaration on the future of the Union", and then developed further in the mandate set out by the European Council in Laeken. During its initial meetings, the Convention addressed issues such as the delimitation of competences and the simplification of the Union's instruments and procedures. These discussions in plenary, together with the outcome of the first wave of working groups, enabled the Convention to define, in October 2002, the most appropriate future treaty structure which would respond in particular to the requirements of clarity and simplification. The outcome of the Convention reflects this: a merge and reorganisation of the existing treaties in the form of a draft Constitution, and hence a single legal personality for the European Union. This approach secured support from a large number of Convention members, and enabled the Convention subsequently to reach broad consensus on the consolidated and complete text of a draft Treaty, in four Parts, which it presents to the European Council.

8.   The Convention agreed on a major enhancement of the democratic nature of the Union. The Constitution incorporates it, calling for a significant expansion of the role of the European Parliament, with a doubling of the scope of legislation taken by co-decision, which becomes the normal legislative process of the

Union, and a substantial simplification of corresponding procedures. In addition, new mechanisms to ensure improved information flow to national Parliaments, and their closer involvement in the Union's work, in particular on legislation, have been devised. The Union's competences have been clarified, categorised and stabilised, and its range of legal instruments reduced, in the interests of better public understanding, more effective action, and a clear distinction between the roles of the Union and of the Member States.

9.   To enable the Union's central Institutions to adapt to the new Enlargement dimension, means of strengthening all three, while retaining the balance between them, have been incorporated in the Constitution. The Convention is convinced that these reforms will substantially improve the Union's effectiveness.

10.   The Constitution incorporates, as its Part II, the Charter of Fundamental Rights proclaimed at the Nice European Council. The Convention noted that the "Explanations" drawn up at the instigation of the Praesidium of the Charter Convention, and updated under the authority of this Convention's Praesidium, are one important tool for the interpretation of the Charter.

11.   The Convention has prepared the texts of new Protocols on the Role of National Parliaments in the European Union and on the Application of the Principles of Subsidiarity and Proportionality, as well as on the Eurogroup and Euratom. It has not attempted to review existing Protocols to the current Treaties, nor therefore to prepare the texts of the Protocols mentioned in Articles IV-1 and IV-2 [*BMDF Note: now Article IV-437*]: it will fall to the Intergovernmental Conference to undertake the task. Similarly, it will be for the Intergovernmental Conference to conclude the lists, foreseen in Articles III-213 and III-214 [*BMDF Note: now Articles III-312, III-419 and III-420*], of those Member States participating in closer co-operation and on mutual defence; and to ensure a response to the call, set out in the relevant Convention Declaration, for the timely establishment of a European External Action Service.

12.   The attention of the European Council is drawn to two further specific issues which it may wish to follow up. Firstly, a large number of members of the Convention argued for a more ambitious approach to the issue of transparency, including specifically the automatic presumption of public right of access to all documents. The proposed Constitution imposes an obligation on the institutions to adopt rules on transparency. The level of ambition of these rules, and so the extent to which demands for access can be met, therefore needs to be addressed within the framework of subsequent legislation.

13.   Secondly, although some members wished to re-examine, and perhaps update, the provisions of the Euratom treaty, the Convention did not believe it had either the mandate or the time and competence to do so. The future of Euratom therefore remains an issue which the European Council may wish at some stage to address.

14.   Certain members of the Convention, though not seeking to block consensus, were unable to give their support to the draft Constitution. One group of 4 members considered that the Convention had not responded appropriately to the section of the Laeken mandate on increasing democratic legitimacy; their minority alternative report proposing a "Europe of democracies" is attached.

15.   Some other members of the Convention, whilst joining the broad consensus on the text of the draft Constitution, would have preferred an approach going rather further, particularly as regards the extension of Qualified Majority Voting and the procedures for future Amendment of the Constitution.

16.   It is thanks to the high degree of commitment and engagement of all its members that the Convention has been able successfully to complete its work, and to present what the Thessaloniki European Council considered to be a "good basis" for the forthcoming Intergovernmental Conference. It hopes that the momentum which has been generated, and the balance of the synthesis on which it found consensus after long and careful examination, will be maintained by the Intergovernmental Conference.

17.   Having fulfilled the mandate given to it by the Laeken European Council, the Convention has ended. In presenting the draft Treaty establishing a Constitution for Europe, and this report, its Presidency discharges its mission, and steps down.

18.   The archives of the Convention will be deposited at the Secretariat of the Council.

Valéry Giscard d'Estaing, President of the Convention;   **Jean-Luc Dehaene**, Vice-President;
Giuliano Amato, Vice-President;   **John Kerr**, Secretary-General.

Alternative Report: *'The Europe of Democracies'*

The European Convention

19 July 2003

This Report was presented as a minority report from the Convention to the European Council on 19 June 2003 by the following Convention Members:

William Abitbol (Alternate Member) European Parliament;

Jens-Peter Bonde (Member) European Parliament;

Per Dalgaard (Alternate Member) Denmark - Parliament;

John Gormley (Alternate Member) Ireland - Parliament;

David Heathcoat-Amory (Member) UK - Parliament;

Esko Seppanen (Alternate Member) European Parliament;

Peter Skaarup (Member) Denmark - Parliament;

Jan Zahradil (Member) Czech Republic - Parliament.

The Alternative Report was attached as Annex III to the Report from the Presidency of the Convention to the President of the European Council on 18 July 2003 [CONV 851/03].

LAEKEN'S LOST MISSIONS

As members of the Convention, we cannot endorse the draft European Constitution. It does not meet the requirements of the Laeken Declaration of December 2001.

LAEKEN:

Says "the Union must be brought closer to its citizens".
> The transfer of more decision making from Member States to the Union, concerning criminal justice matters and new areas of domestic policy, will make the Union more remote.

Adds that "the division of competences be made more transparent".
> But the new category of 'shared competences' gives no assurance about how power is to be shared, particularly as Member States will be forbidden to legislate in these areas if the Union decides to act. The European Union court in Luxembourg will decide on any doubt.

Describes the Union as "behaving too bureaucratically".
> The draft Constitution fails to address the 97,000 accumulated pages of the *acquis communautaire*, and proposes a new legal instrument, the 'Non-Legislative Act', whereby the non-elected Commission can pass binding laws.

Calls for the "European institutions to be less unwieldy and rigid".
> But the Constitution gives more power to all the existing European Union institutions and creates a Europe of Presidents, with more jobs for politicians and less influence for the people.

Highlights the importance of national parliaments, and the Nice Treaty "stressed the need to examine their role in European integration".
> National parliaments lose influence relative to the Commission, the European Parliament and the European Council. Their proposed new role in 'ensuring' compliance with the subsidiarity principle is in reality no more than a request which the Commission can ignore. Not one competence will be returned to Member States.

Calls for "more transparency and efficiency" in the Union.
>The Constitution concentrates more executive and budgetary power in the very European Union institutions which have been the subject of repeated and continuing scandals over mismanagement, waste and fraud.

Suggests the possibility of a constitution: "The question ultimately arises as to whether this simplification and reorganisation might not lead in the long run to the adoption of a constitutional text of the Union".
>The suggestion that the existing intergovernmental treaties be transformed into a new European Constitution was rapidly seized upon, but without any study of either the alternatives on offer or the long-term consequences of such an act.

Lastly, LAEKEN'S overriding aim was a Democratic Europe.
>The draft Constitution creates a new centralised European state, more powerful, more remote, with more politicians, more bureaucracy, and a wider gap between the rulers and the ruled.

THE EURATOM TREATY was brought into the Constitution in the last moment without any working group having the time to revise it.

THE DRAFT EUROPEAN UNION CONSTITUTION was never drafted through normal democratic methods:

- The applicant countries were treated as observers in the Praesidium and had no real say;

- Only three political families were represented in the powerful Praesidium which drafted the tunnel vision text;

- The members were refused the right to have their amendments translated, distributed, discussed and voted upon;

- The Convention had no members for that half of the population, which rejected the Maastricht Treaty in France or the Nice Treaty in Ireland.;

- Not one single Euro-sceptic or Euro-realist person was allowed to observe or participate in the work in the Praesidium, nor any of its assisting secretariats.

Giscard did not allow democracy and normal voting in the Convention. The draft Constitution runs counter to all democratic principles. We want a new draft from a much more representative convention, democratic in content and democratic in procedures.

We hereby submit the following 15 points to the consideration for our Prime Ministers and citizens:

1. *Europe of Democracies:*
The European Union shall not have a constitution. Instead, Europe should be organised on an inter-parliamentary basis by means of a Treaty on European Co-operation. If the European Union should have a new name, it should be 'Europe of Democracies'.

2. *A Slim-line Treaty:*
The present 97,000 pages of the *acquis communautaire* covering the European Union and European Economic Area must be radically simplified. Instead, focus shall be placed on cross-frontier issues where national parliaments cannot effectively act by themselves. Decisions on subsidiarity shall be resolved by the national parliaments.

3. *Open to all Democracies:*
Membership of the European Union shall be open to any democratic European state which is a signatory of, and respects fully, the European Convention on Human Rights.

4. *Simplified Decision-Making:*
The present 30 different ways of making decisions in the European Union shall be reduced to two: laws and recommendations. Where qualified majority voting applies, the proposal in question shall require 75% of the votes to be cast in favour, unless otherwise stated.

5. *A Veto on Vital Issues:*
Laws shall be valid only if they have been passed by national parliaments. A national parliament shall have a veto on an issue it deems important.

6. *The Common Core Issues:*
Laws shall deal with the rules for the Common Market and certain common minimum standards to protect employees, consumers, health, safety and the environment. In other areas the European Union shall have the power to issue recommendations for Member States, which are always free to adopt higher standards.

7. *Flexible Co-operation:*
The European Union may unanimously approve flexible co-operation for those nations that want to take part in closer co-operation. The European Union shall also recognise and support other pan-European organisations, such as the Council of Europe.

8. *Openness and Transparency:*
The decision-making process and relevant documents shall be open and accessible, unless a reasonable cause for exception is confirmed by qualified majority.

9. *Straightforward Council Voting:*
A simplified voting system shall operate in the Council, which may comprise each Member State possessing one vote in the European Union Council. A decision by qualified majority shall require the support of countries with more than half the total European Union population.

10. *National Parliaments Elect the Commission:*
Every national parliament should elect its own member of the Commission. The Commissioner shall attend the European Scrutiny Committees of the national parliament concerned. National parliaments shall have the power to dismiss their Commissioner. The President of the Commission shall be elected by the national parliaments. National parliaments shall decide on the annual legislative programme and the Commission shall correspondingly act as a secretariat for the Council and the national parliaments.

11. *No Legislation by the Court:*
Legal activism by the European Court in Luxembourg shall be curbed, and the Court shall respect the European Convention on Human Rights.

12. *Partnership Agreements:*
The Member States and the European Union may enter into partnership agreements of mutual interest with states or groups of states. The European Union shall respect the parliamentary democracy of its partners and may assist poorer ones with a financial aid, while fostering free trade agreements.

13. *Better Scrutiny:*
The European Ombudsman, the Court of Auditors and the Budget Control Committees of the European and national parliaments shall have access to all documents and all financial accounts.

14. *Equality of Languages:*
When legislating, all official European Union languages shall be treated equally.

15. *United Nations:*
The European Union shall not have its own army. Peacekeeping and peacemaking should be mandated by the United Nations and the Organisation for Security and Co-operation in Europe. Member States shall decide themselves whether they opt for a common defence through NATO, independent defence, or follow a neutrality policy.

the european convention
THE CHAIRMAN

ROME DECLARATION

V. GISCARD D'ESTAING

CHAIRMAN OF THE EUROPEAN CONVENTION

Rome, 18 July 2003

I.   On 18 July 2003 the Chairman of the Convention on the future of Europe, V. Giscard d'Estaing, accompanied by the two Vice-Chairmen, G. Amato and J.-L. Dehaene, on the Convention's behalf, officially handed over the full draft Treaty establishing a Constitution for Europe to the Italian Presidency of the European Council.

When meeting President Ciampi and Prime Minister Berlusconi, Mr Giscard d'Estaing paid tribute to the key contribution made by the Italian members of the Convention, G. Amato, as Vice-Chairman, G. Fini, representing the Italian Government, L. Dini, representing the Italian Senate, and M. Follini, representing the Italian Chamber of Deputies, and their alternates.

Mr Giscard d'Estaing called on the Italian Presidency to conduct the Intergovernmental Conference at the highest political level, so as to bring it to completion under the Italian Presidency, in December 2003.

After the Treaty of Rome, the Rome Constitution would thus come into being. Italy, as a founding member of the European Union, will have had a key hand in it.

The Constitution could then be signed in May 2004, just before the next European elections, which would set the seal of popular approval on it.

The ten new Member States will already be full members of the Union, by then, and the signing will come in time for the European elections in June 2004.

II.   **With this Constitution, Europe is taking a decisive step towards political union**[1]: a union of citizens and a union of Member States.

The Constitution:

➤   enshrines citizens' rights by incorporating the European Charter of Fundamental Rights;

➤   turns Europe towards its citizens by holding out new opportunities for them to participate;

---

[1]   **Bolding by BMDF**

> establishes a clear, transparent apportionment of powers between the Union and its Member States, enabling national parliaments to intervene. The Union's powers are extended in areas where that is what its citizens want:

> ⇨ implementation of an area of freedom, security and justice, with more effective action to combat major crime, and recognition by Member States of one another's different systems of civil law;

> ⇨ gradual development of a common foreign and defence policy, with a European Foreign Minister to act and speak for Europe in the world, and establishment of a European arms agency;

> ⇨ improvement of economic co-ordination between countries using the euro, so as to ensure the stability and success of our common currency;

> provides Europe with stable, democratic and effective institutions:

> ⇨ **the European Parliament** becomes the Union's main legislature. It will enact laws together with the Council. European legislation will be the product of agreement between citizens' elected representatives and States;

> ⇨ **the Council** will have a face and a measure of durability; its President will organise States' work and will be able to plan for the future and think ahead;

> ⇨ **the Commission**, organised so as to fulfil its European role, will act as a driving force and the main executive. It will embody the common European interest.

III. The draft Constitution is a success because it strikes the necessary balance between peoples, between States new and old, between institutions and between dream and reality.

The draft is a success because it is a finished product, with no loose ends to be tied up, no options left open.

It is in the general interest. With that in mind, the Chairman of the Convention, together with the two Vice-Chairmen, called on the Italian Presidency – and the President of the European Council, Silvio Berlusconi, in person – to have the text left as it stands. Reopening it, even in part, would cause it to unravel.

The Chairman of the Convention places his trust in the Italian Presidency, confident that it will live up to that responsibility and that on 9 May 2004 the European Union will be able to sign its Rome Constitution.

Silvio Berlusconi, Prime Minister of Italy

Speech at the signing of the European Constitution

Rome, 29 October 2004

Two dates: Rome, 25 March 1957. Rome, 29 October 2004. Nearly half a century has passed between those two dates. The room in which we will shortly be signing the Constitutional Treaty is the same one in which the six forerunner countries signed the Treaties of Rome.

Europe was split in two. Our peoples were still divided – in need of external aid, and engaged in a difficult process of economic and political reconstruction that was to go on for years. But there were some who were already beginning to think ahead with foresight and courage to the Europe of the future, and to lay the foundations for reunification.

The process of European integration that arose from this basis, amidst considerable scepticism and doubt, has proved to be the most fruitful and enduring vision of the period after the Second World War. It was seen, in the words of Erasmus of Rotterdam, as "far-sighted and visionary madness". But the seeming madness of our founding fathers had become a splendid reality, to which a new fundamental chapter is being added today.

Through these two dates – from 1957 to 2004 – there runs the thread of our identities, which at first were broken up, crushed and trampled upon in many countries by an evil totalitarianism, but which have now been finally rediscovered around a common ideal of liberty, democracy, justice and prosperity.

The Europe that strengthens its ties on the institutional level has arrived at this goal by successive steps forward taken with patience and tenacity, without ever having abandoned the consensus-building method: an economic area without internal barriers, the single currency, a policy of freedom and security, and an increasingly shared view in external relations and external policy.

Again in Rome, on 4 October 2003, we opened the Intergovernmental Conference. This was a time of great hope, but also great uncertainty. We were taking on heavy responsibilities towards our citizens. Failure was absolutely not an option. I said then that we were being called on to accomplish not simply an act of faith but an act of will, that the Conference should be a Conference of the European will.

Today, little more than a year after that momentous occasion, we have achieved our goal and honoured our commitment. Never in history have we seen an example of nations voluntarily deciding to exercise their sovereign powers jointly in the exclusive interest of their peoples, thus overcoming age-old impulses of rivalry and distrust. Never in history have the fundamental values of freedom and democracy had such an important role in securing the destiny of hundreds of millions of people.

Today's proceedings thus mark a historic date: Europe has at last acquired a Constitution based on the twofold and indivisible consensus of the citizens and the Member States.

In signing this Constitution we must keep firmly in mind that no constitution, no political institution, no legal institution is self-sustaining. The constitutional momentum of the united Europe will always depend on the continued affirmation of the desire of the peoples and nations of Europe to integrate still further at the political, social and economic level and to act together in a number of areas that are essential to their future. The Constitution that we are signing today will therefore need to be backed up by a continually renewed commitment on the part of both citizens and governments.

The united Europe is – and will increasingly be – a matter of daily consensus.

My friends, today sees the start of the process of ratification of the Constitutional Treaty by the Member States. We shall commit ourselves to ensuring that Italy ratifies the new Treaty without delay. The Europeanist sentiment is part of our history as Italians: it is unshaken, it is enthusiastic, and I hope it can also be infectious.

It is my firm belief, even more than it is my fervent hope, that all the peoples, parliaments and governments of the Member States will give their consent because they profoundly believe that their destiny of freedom, peace and prosperity is identical with that of the united Europe, that Europe which, here in this *urbs urbium,* this "city of cities", is today taking a historic step forward.

Romano Prodi, President of the European Commission
Speech at the signing of the European Constitution
Rome, 29 October 2004

In signing the European Constitution, the Heads of State and Government are showing political vision and looking beyond their own national interests. Over fifty years after Europe's founding fathers took the first steps that resulted in the signing of the Treaty of Rome in this very room, the *Sala degli Orazi e Curiazi*, the political vision shown here today will take the process of European integration to a new level.

On 25 March 1957 Europe's response to the horrors of modern warfare and the continuing Cold War was a ground-breaking endeavour to build a supranational democracy. Today, Europe is reaffirming the unique nature of its political organisation in response to the challenges of globalisation, to promote its values and play its rightful role on the international stage. The new Constitution does not simply consolidate the political and institutional system set up by the Treaty of Rome. It breaks new ground and makes the Union **more democratic, more effective and more transparent**.

- The Union will be more democratic because almost all European laws will be adopted jointly by the European Parliament and the Council of Ministers and, for the first time ever in a supranational organisation, Europeans will be able to call directly for European laws.

- The Union will be more effective because more decisions will be taken by majority vote, even if this change does not go as far as I had hoped. At the same time, the double majority system will facilitate the work of the Council and reflect the twofold legitimacy of the Union, which is a union of peoples and States.

- The Union will also be more transparent thanks to the new mechanisms introduced to encourage participatory democracy.

At the same time, the Union's legislative process has been simplified and given greater legitimacy.

- It is simpler because the Community method now extends to almost all legislative acts, while the number of procedures and legal instruments has been reduced. European laws will be European in both form and substance.

- It has greater legitimacy thanks to the clearer demarcation of legislative powers between the Union and the Member States and the fact that national parliaments will ensure that the principle of subsidiarity is upheld.

In the last few months there has been a lively debate on how far the European Constitution goes. While I respect the views of all political groups, I must stress that the new Constitution *goes beyond the existing Treaties*. The innovative content of the social rights, which are now recognised as primary legislation, and the new social clauses introduced in the Constitution are clear steps forward.

The signing of the European Constitution does not mean we have crossed the finishing line. In the months ahead the Governments of the Union's 25 Member States will need to use their best endeavours to persuade their Parliaments and citizens to ratify the new Constitutional Treaty. Those decisions we cannot take for granted. This Constitution originated in the European Convention, which adopted new, more transparent and democratic working methods. It is only natural that Europeans should now expect to play a greater role in the remaining stages of the process.

While the chief responsibility for ratifying the Constitution will lie with the signatory Governments, the European Institutions will play their part in providing the citizens of Europe with objective information concerning its content. Clearly, national political groups will need to voice their opinions on the Constitutional Treaty, but it will be up to the Governments to hold parliamentary debates and referendum campaigns on the Constitution and prevent them from becoming overshadowed by questions of national politics.

To draw on a famous passage in the Schuman Declaration of 9 May 1950, it must again be said that Europe has no need of empty words; it needs bold and constructive action. The Heads of State and Government who will sign the European Constitution have acted boldly and constructively. The consequences of their actions may be far-reaching. I am convinced they will be, because the new Europe, with its own Constitution, must become the driving force for the economic and social wellbeing of its peoples and for world peace.

THE

TREATY

ESTABLISHING A CONSTITUTION

FOR EUROPE

PREAMBLE

HIS MAJESTY THE KING OF THE BELGIANS,
THE PRESIDENT OF THE CZECH REPUBLIC,
HER MAJESTY THE QUEEN OF DENMARK,
THE PRESIDENT OF THE FEDERAL REPUBLIC OF GERMANY,
THE PRESIDENT OF THE REPUBLIC OF ESTONIA,
THE PRESIDENT OF THE HELLENIC REPUBLIC,
HIS MAJESTY THE KING OF SPAIN,
THE PRESIDENT OF THE FRENCH REPUBLIC,
THE PRESIDENT OF IRELAND,
THE PRESIDENT OF THE ITALIAN REPUBLIC,
THE PRESIDENT OF THE REPUBLIC OF CYPRUS,
THE PRESIDENT OF THE REPUBLIC OF LATVIA,
THE PRESIDENT OF THE REPUBLIC OF LITHUANIA,
HIS ROYAL HIGHNESS THE GRAND DUKE OF LUXEMBOURG,
THE PRESIDENT OF THE REPUBLIC OF HUNGARY,
THE PRESIDENT OF MALTA,
HER MAJESTY THE QUEEN OF THE NETHERLANDS,
THE FEDERAL PRESIDENT OF THE REPUBLIC OF AUSTRIA,
THE PRESIDENT OF THE REPUBLIC OF POLAND,
THE PRESIDENT OF THE PORTUGUESE REPUBLIC,
THE PRESIDENT OF THE REPUBLIC OF SLOVENIA,
THE PRESIDENT OF THE SLOVAK REPUBLIC,
THE PRESIDENT OF THE REPUBLIC OF FINLAND,
THE GOVERNMENT OF THE KINGDOM OF SWEDEN,
HER MAJESTY THE QUEEN OF THE UNITED KINGDOM OF GREAT BRITAIN AND NORTHERN IRELAND,

DRAWING INSPIRATION from the cultural, religious and humanist inheritance of Europe, from which have developed the universal values of the inviolable and inalienable rights of the human person, freedom, democracy, equality and the rule of law,

BELIEVING that Europe, reunited after bitter experiences, intends to continue along the path of civilisation, progress and prosperity, for the good of all its inhabitants, including the weakest and most deprived; that it wishes to remain a continent open to culture, learning and social progress; and that it wishes to deepen the democratic and transparent nature of its public life, and to strive for peace, justice and solidarity throughout the world,

CONVINCED that, while remaining proud of their own national identities and history, the peoples of Europe are determined to transcend their former divisions and, united ever more closely, to forge a common destiny,

CONVINCED that, thus "United in diversity", Europe offers them the best chance of pursuing, with due regard for the rights of each individual and in awareness of their responsibilities towards future generations and the Earth, the great venture which makes of it a special area of human hope,

DETERMINED to continue the work accomplished within the framework of the Treaties establishing the European Communities and the Treaty on European Union, by ensuring the continuity of the Community *acquis*,

GRATEFUL to the members of the European Convention for having prepared the draft of this Constitution on behalf of the citizens and States of Europe,

HAVE DESIGNATED AS THEIR PLENIPOTENTIARIES:

HIS MAJESTY THE KING OF THE BELGIANS,

Guy VERHOFSTADT
Prime Minister;

Karel DE GUCHT
Minister for Foreign Affairs;

THE PRESIDENT OF THE CZECH REPUBLIC,

Stanislav GROSS
Prime Minister

Cyril SVOBODA
Minister for Foreign Affairs

HER MAJESTY THE QUEEN OF DENMARK,

Anders Fogh RASMUSSEN
Prime Minister

Per Stig MØLLER
Minister for Foreign Affairs

THE PRESIDENT OF THE FEDERAL REPUBLIC OF GERMANY,

Gerhard SCHRÖDER
Federal Chancellor

Joschka FISCHER
Federal Minister for Foreign Affairs and Deputy Federal Chancellor

THE PRESIDENT OF THE REPUBLIC OF ESTONIA,

Juhan PARTS
Prime Minister

Kristiina OJULAND
Minister for Foreign Affairs

THE PRESIDENT OF THE HELLENIC REPUBLIC,

Kostas KARAMANLIS
Prime Minister

Petros G. MOLYVIATIS
Minister for Foreign Affairs

HIS MAJESTY THE KING OF SPAIN,

José Luis RODRÍGUEZ ZAPATERO
President of the Government

Miguel Angel MORATINOS CUYAUBÉ
Minister for External Affairs and Co-operation

THE PRESIDENT OF THE FRENCH REPUBLIC,

Jacques CHIRAC
President

Jean-Pierre RAFFARIN
Prime Minister

Michel BARNIER
Minister for Foreign Affairs

THE PRESIDENT OF IRELAND,

Bertie AHERN
Prime Minister

Dermot AHERN
Minister for Foreign Affairs

THE PRESIDENT OF THE ITALIAN REPUBLIC,

Silvio BERLUSCONI
Prime Minister

Franco FRATTINI
Minister for Foreign Affairs

THE PRESIDENT OF THE REPUBLIC OF CYPRUS,

Tassos PAPADOPOULOS
President

George IACOVOU
Minister for Foreign Affairs

THE PRESIDENT OF THE REPUBLIC OF LATVIA,

Vaira VĪĶE FREIBERGA
President

Indulis EMSIS
Prime Minister

Artis PABRIKS,
Minister for Foreign Affairs

THE PRESIDENT OF THE REPUBLIC OF LITHUANIA,

Valdas ADAMKUS
President

Algirdas Mykolas BRAZAUSKAS
Prime Minister

Antanas VALIONIS
Minister for Foreign Affairs

HIS ROYAL HIGHNESS THE GRAND DUKE OF LUXEMBOURG,

Jean-Claude JUNCKER
Prime Minister

Jean ASSELBORN,
Deputy Prime Minister, Minister for Foreign Affairs and Immigration

THE PRESIDENT OF THE REPUBLIC OF HUNGARY,

Ferenc GYURCSÁNY
Prime Minister

László KOVÁCS
Minister for Foreign Affairs

THE PRESIDENT OF MALTA,

The Hon Lawrence GONZI
Prime Minister

The Hon Michael FRENDO
Minister for Foreign Affairs

HER MAJESTY THE QUEEN OF THE NETHERLANDS,

Dr Jan Peter BALKENENDE
Prime Minister

Dr Bernard R. BOT
Minister for Foreign Affairs

THE FEDERAL PRESIDENT OF THE REPUBLIC OF AUSTRIA,

Dr Wolfgang SCHÜSSEL
Federal Chancellor

Ds Ursula PLASSNIK
Federal Minister for Foreign Affairs

THE PRESIDENT OF THE REPUBLIC OF POLAND,

Marek BELKA
Prime Minister

Włodzimierz CIMOSZEWICZ
Minister for Foreign Affairs

THE PRESIDENT OF THE PORTUGUESE REPUBLIC,

Pedro Santana LOPES
Prime Minister

António Victor MARTINS MONTEIRO
Minister for Foreign Affairs and the Portuguese Communities

THE PRESIDENT OF THE REPUBLIC OF SLOVENIA,

Anton ROP
President of the Government

Ivo VAJGL
Minister for Foreign Affairs

THE PRESIDENT OF THE SLOVAK REPUBLIC,

Mikuláš DZURINDA
Prime Minister

Eduard KUKAN
Minister for Foreign Affairs

THE PRESIDENT OF THE REPUBLIC OF FINLAND,

Matti VANHANEN
Prime Minister

Erkki TUOMIOJA
Minister for Foreign Affairs

THE GOVERNMENT OF THE KINGDOM OF SWEDEN,

Göran PERSSON
Prime Minister

Laila FREIVALDS
Minister for Foreign Affairs

HER MAJESTY THE QUEEN OF THE UNITED KINGDOM OF GREAT BRITAIN AND NORTHERN IRELAND,

The Rt. Hon Tony BLAIR
Prime Minister

The Rt. Hon Jack STRAW
Secretary of State for Foreign and Commonwealth Affairs

WHO, having exchanged their full powers, found in good and due form, have agreed as follows:

PART I

TITLE I

DEFINITION AND OBJECTIVES OF THE UNION

ARTICLE I-1 *Establishment of the Union (new)*
1.   Reflecting the will of the citizens and States of Europe to build a common future, this Constitution establishes the European Union, on which the Member States confer competences to attain objectives they have in common. The Union shall co-ordinate the policies by which the Member States aim to achieve these objectives, and shall exercise on a Community basis the competences they confer on it.

2.   The Union shall be open to all European States which respect its values and are committed to promoting them together.

ARTICLE I-2 *The Union's values (ex Article 6(1) TEU)*
The Union is founded on the values of respect for human dignity, freedom, democracy, equality, the rule of law and respect for human rights, including the rights of persons belonging to minorities. These values are common to the Member States in a society in which pluralism, non-discrimination, tolerance, justice, solidarity and equality between women and men prevail.

ARTICLE I-3 *The Union's objectives (ex Article 2 TEC and Article 2 TEU)*
1.   The Union's aim is to promote peace, its values and the well-being of its peoples.

2.   The Union shall offer its citizens an area of freedom, security and justice without internal frontiers, and an internal market where competition is free and undistorted.

3.   The Union shall work for the sustainable development of Europe based on balanced economic growth and price stability, a highly competitive social market economy, aiming at full employment and social progress, and a high level of protection and improvement of the quality of the environment. It shall promote scientific and technological advance.
It shall combat social exclusion and discrimination, and shall promote social justice and protection, equality between women and men, solidarity between generations and protection of the rights of the child.
It shall promote economic, social and territorial cohesion, and solidarity among Member States. It shall respect its rich cultural and linguistic diversity, and shall ensure that Europe's cultural heritage is safeguarded and enhanced.

4.   In its relations with the wider world, the Union shall uphold and promote its values and interests. It shall contribute to peace, security, the sustainable development of the Earth, solidarity and mutual respect among peoples, free and fair trade, eradication of poverty and the protection of human rights, in particular the rights of the child, as well as to the strict observance and the development of international law, including respect for the principles of the United Nations Charter.

5.   The Union shall pursue its objectives by appropriate means commensurate with the competences which are conferred upon it in the Constitution.

ARTICLE I-4 *Fundamental freedoms and non-discrimination (ex Article 3(1)(c) and Article 12 TEC)*
1.   The free movement of persons, services, goods and capital, and freedom of establishment shall be guaranteed within and by the Union, in accordance with the Constitution.

2.   Within the scope of the Constitution, and without prejudice to any of its specific provisions, any discrimination on grounds of nationality shall be prohibited.

ARTICLE I-5 *Relations between the Union and the Member States (ex Article 10 TEC and Article 6(3) TEU)*
1.   The Union shall respect the equality of Member States before the Constitution as well as their national identities, inherent in their fundamental structures, political and constitutional, inclusive of regional and local

self-government. It shall respect their essential State functions, including ensuring the territorial integrity of the State, maintaining law and order and safeguarding national security.

2.   Pursuant to the principle of sincere co-operation, the Union and the Member States shall, in full mutual respect, assist each other in carrying out tasks which flow from the Constitution.

The Member States shall take any appropriate measure, general or particular, to ensure fulfilment of the obligations arising out of the Constitution or resulting from the acts of the institutions of the Union.

The Member States shall facilitate the achievement of the Union's tasks and refrain from any measure which could jeopardise the attainment of the Union's objectives.

ARTICLE I-6 *Union law (new)*
The Constitution and law adopted by the institutions of the Union in exercising competences conferred on it shall have primacy over the law of the Member States.

ARTICLE I-7 *Legal personality (new)*
The Union shall have legal personality.

ARTICLE I-8 *The symbols of the Union (new)*
The flag of the Union shall be a circle of twelve golden stars on a blue background.

The anthem of the Union shall be based on the "Ode to Joy" from the Ninth Symphony by Ludwig van Beethoven.

The motto of the Union shall be: "United in diversity".

The currency of the Union shall be the euro.

Europe day shall be celebrated on 9 May throughout the Union.

TITLE II

FUNDAMENTAL RIGHTS AND CITIZENSHIP OF THE UNION

ARTICLE I-9 *Fundamental rights (ex Article 6(2) TEU)*
1.   The Union shall recognise the rights, freedoms and principles set out in the Charter of Fundamental Rights which constitutes Part II.

2.   The Union shall accede to the European Convention for the Protection of Human Rights and Fundamental Freedoms. Such accession shall not affect the Union's competences as defined in the Constitution.

3.   Fundamental rights, as guaranteed by the European Convention for the Protection of Human Rights and Fundamental Freedoms and as they result from the constitutional traditions common to the Member States, shall constitute general principles of the Union's law.

ARTICLE I-10 *Citizenship of the Union (ex Articles 17 to 21 TEC)*
1.   Every national of a Member State shall be a citizen of the Union. Citizenship of the Union shall be additional to national citizenship and shall not replace it.

2.   Citizens of the Union shall enjoy the rights and be subject to the duties provided for in the Constitution. They shall have:
(a)   the right to move and reside freely within the territory of the Member States;
(b)   the right to vote and to stand as candidates in elections to the European Parliament and in municipal elections in their Member State of residence, under the same conditions as nationals of that State;
(c)   the right to enjoy, in the territory of a third country in which the Member State of which they are nationals is not represented, the protection of the diplomatic and consular authorities of any Member State on the same conditions as the nationals of that State;
(d)   the right to petition the European Parliament, to apply to the European Ombudsman, and to address the institutions and advisory bodies of the Union in any of the Constitution's languages and to obtain a reply in the same language.

These rights shall be exercised in accordance with the conditions and limits defined by the Constitution and by the measures adopted thereunder.

TITLE III

UNION COMPETENCES

ARTICLE I-11 *Fundamental principles (Paragraphs 3 and 4 ex Article 5 TEC)*
1.   The limits of Union competences are governed by the principle of conferral. The use of Union competences is governed by the principles of subsidiarity and proportionality.

2.   Under the principle of conferral, the Union shall act within the limits of the competences conferred upon it by the Member States in the Constitution to attain the objectives set out in the Constitution. Competences not conferred upon the Union in the Constitution remain with the Member States.

3.   Under the principle of subsidiarity, in areas which do not fall within its exclusive competence, the Union shall act only if and insofar as the objectives of the proposed action cannot be sufficiently achieved by the Member States, either at central level or at regional and local level, but can rather, by reason of the scale or effects of the proposed action, be better achieved at Union level.
The institutions of the Union shall apply the principle of subsidiarity as laid down in the Protocol on the application of the principles of subsidiarity and proportionality. National Parliaments shall ensure compliance with that principle in accordance with the procedure set out in that Protocol.

4.   Under the principle of proportionality, the content and form of Union action shall not exceed what is necessary to achieve the objectives of the Constitution.
The institutions of the Union shall apply the principle of proportionality as laid down in the Protocol on the application of the principles of subsidiarity and proportionality.

ARTICLE I-12 *Categories of competence (new)*
1.   When the Constitution confers on the Union exclusive competence in a specific area, only the Union may legislate and adopt legally binding acts, the Member States being able to do so themselves only if so empowered by the Union or for the implementation of Union acts.

2.   When the Constitution confers on the Union a competence shared with the Member States in a specific area, the Union and the Member States may legislate and adopt legally binding acts in that area. The Member States shall exercise their competence to the extent that the Union has not exercised, or has decided to cease exercising, its competence.

3.   The Member States shall co-ordinate their economic and employment policies within arrangements as determined by Part III, which the Union shall have competence to provide.

4.   The Union shall have competence to define and implement a common foreign and security policy, including the progressive framing of a common defence policy.

5.   In certain areas and under the conditions laid down in the Constitution, the Union shall have competence to carry out actions to support, co-ordinate or supplement the actions of the Member States, without thereby superseding their competence in these areas.
Legally binding acts of the Union adopted on the basis of the provisions in Part III relating to these areas shall not entail harmonisation of Member States' laws or regulations.

6.   The scope of and arrangements for exercising the Union's competences shall be determined by the provisions relating to each area in Part III.

ARTICLE I-13 *Areas of exclusive competence (new)*
1.   The Union shall have exclusive competence in the following areas:
(a)   customs union;
(b)   the establishing of the competition rules necessary for the functioning of the internal market;
(c)   monetary policy for the Member States whose currency is the euro;
(d)   the conservation of marine biological resources under the common fisheries policy;
(e)   common commercial policy.

2.   The Union shall also have exclusive competence for the conclusion of an international agreement when its conclusion is provided for in a legislative act of the Union or is necessary to enable the Union to exercise its internal competence, or insofar as its conclusion may affect common rules or alter their scope.

ARTICLE I-14 *Areas of shared competence(new article, drawing on specified TEC articles)*
1.   The Union shall share competence with the Member States where the Constitution confers on it a competence which does not relate to the areas referred to in Articles I-13 and I-17.

2.   Shared competence between the Union and the Member States applies in the following principal areas:
(a)   internal market; *(ex Articles 14, 15 and 95 TEC)*
(b)   social policy, for the aspects defined in Part III; *(ex Article 137 TEC)*
(c)   economic, social and territorial cohesion; *(ex Article 159 TEC)*
(d)   agriculture and fisheries, excluding the conservation of marine biological resources; *(ex Article 37 TEC)*
(e)   environment; *(ex Article 174 TEC)*
(f)   consumer protection; *(ex Article 153 TEC)*
(g)   transport; *(ex Article 154 TEC)*
(h)   trans-European networks; *(ex Article 154 TEC)*
(i)   energy; *(new)*
(j)   area of freedom, security and justice; *(ex Articles 61 - 64 TEC)*
(k)   common safety concerns in public health matters, for the aspects defined in Part III. *(ex Article 152 TEC)*

3.   In the areas of research, technological development and space, the Union shall have competence to carry out activities, in particular to define and implement programmes; however, the exercise of that competence shall not result in Member States being prevented from exercising theirs.

4.   In the areas of development co-operation and humanitarian aid, the Union shall have competence to carry out activities and conduct a common policy; however, the exercise of that competence shall not result in Member States being prevented from exercising theirs.

ARTICLE I-15 *The co-ordination of economic and employment policies (new)*
1.   The Member States shall co-ordinate their economic policies within the Union. To this end, the Council of Ministers shall adopt measures, in particular broad guidelines for these policies.
Specific provisions shall apply to those Member States whose currency is the euro.

2.   The Union shall take measures to ensure co-ordination of the employment policies of the Member States, in particular by defining guidelines for these policies.

3.   The Union may take initiatives to ensure co-ordination of Member States' social policies.

ARTICLE I-16 *The common foreign and security policy (ex Articles 17 TEU and 11(2) TEU)*
1.   The Union's competence in matters of common foreign and security policy shall cover all areas of foreign policy and all questions relating to the Union's security, including the progressive framing of a common defence policy that might lead to a common defence.

2.   Member States shall actively and unreservedly support the Union's common foreign and security policy in a spirit of loyalty and mutual solidarity and shall comply with the Union's action in this area. They shall refrain from action contrary to the Union's interests or likely to impair its effectiveness.

ARTICLE I-17 *Areas of supporting, co-ordinating or complementary action (new article, drawing on specified TEC articles)*
The Union shall have competence to carry out supporting, co-ordinating or complementary action.
The areas of such action shall, at European level, be:
(a)   protection and improvement of human health; *(ex Article 152 TEC)*
(b)   industry; *(ex Article 157 TEC)*
(c)   culture; *(ex Article 151 TEC)*
(d)   tourism; *(new)*
(e)   education, youth, sport and vocational training; *(ex Article 149 TEC, sport - new)*
(f)   civil protection; *(new)*
(g)   administrative co-operation. *(new)*

ARTICLE I-18 *Flexibility clause (ex Article 308 TEC)*
1.   If action by the Union should prove necessary, within the framework of the policies defined in Part III, to attain one of the objectives set out in the Constitution, and the Constitution has not provided the necessary powers, the Council of Ministers, acting unanimously on a proposal from the European Commission and after obtaining the consent of the European Parliament, shall adopt the appropriate measures.

2.   Using the procedure for monitoring the subsidiarity principle referred to in Article I-11(3), the European Commission shall draw national Parliaments' attention to proposals based on this Article.

3.   Measures based on this Article shall not entail harmonisation of Member States' laws or regulations in cases where the Constitution excludes such harmonisation.

TITLE IV

THE UNION'S INSTITUTIONS AND BODIES

CHAPTER I

THE INSTITUTIONAL FRAMEWORK

ARTICLE I-19 *The Union's institutions (ex Article 7 TEC and Article 3 TEU)*
1.   The Union shall have an institutional framework which shall aim to:
–   promote its values,
–   advance its objectives,
–   serve its interests, those of its citizens and those of the Member States,
–   ensure the consistency, effectiveness and continuity of its policies and actions.
This institutional framework comprises:
–   The European Parliament,
–   The European Council,
–   The Council of Ministers (hereinafter referred to as the "Council"),
–   The European Commission (hereinafter referred to as the "Commission"),
–   The Court of Justice of the European Union.

2.   Each institution shall act within the limits of the powers conferred on it in the Constitution, and in conformity with the procedures and conditions set out in it. The institutions shall practise mutual sincere co-operation.

ARTICLE I-20 *The European Parliament (new)*
1.   The European Parliament shall, jointly with the Council, exercise legislative and budgetary functions. It shall exercise functions of political control and consultation as laid down in the Constitution. It shall elect the President of the Commission.

2.   The European Parliament shall be composed of representatives of the Union's citizens. They shall not exceed seven hundred and fifty in number. Representation of citizens shall be degressively proportional, with a minimum threshold of six members per Member State. No Member State shall be allocated more than ninety-six seats.
The European Council shall adopt by unanimity, on the initiative of the European Parliament and with its consent, a European decision establishing the composition of the European Parliament, respecting the principles referred to in the first subparagraph.

3.   The members of the European Parliament shall be elected for a term of five years by direct universal suffrage in a free and secret ballot.

4.   The European Parliament shall elect its President and its officers from among its members.

ARTICLE I-21 *The European Council (ex Article 4 TEU)*
1.   The European Council shall provide the Union with the necessary impetus for its development and shall define the general political directions and priorities thereof. It shall not exercise legislative functions.

2.   The European Council shall consist of the Heads of State or Government of the Member States, together with its President and the President of the Commission. The Union Minister for Foreign Affairs shall take part in its work.

3.   The European Council shall meet quarterly, convened by its President. When the agenda so requires, the members of the European Council may decide each to be assisted by a minister and, in the case of the President of the Commission, by a member of the Commission. When the situation so requires, the President shall convene a special meeting of the European Council.

4.   Except where the Constitution provides otherwise, decisions of the European Council shall be taken by consensus.

ARTICLE I-22 *The European Council President (new)*
1.   The European Council shall elect its President, by a qualified majority, for a term of two and a half years, renewable once. In the event of an impediment or serious misconduct, the European Council can end his or her term of office in accordance with the same procedure.

2.   The President of the European Council:
(a)   shall chair it and drive forward its work;
(b)   shall ensure the preparation and continuity of the work of the European Council in co-operation with the President of the Commission, and on the basis of the work of the General Affairs Council;
(c)   shall endeavour to facilitate cohesion and consensus within the European Council;
(d)   shall present a report to the European Parliament after each of the meetings of the European Council.
The President of the European Council shall, at his or her level and in that capacity, ensure the external representation of the Union on issues concerning its common foreign and security policy, without prejudice to the powers of the Union Minister for Foreign Affairs.

3.   The President of the European Council shall not hold a national office.

ARTICLE I-23 *The Council of Ministers (ex Articles 202, 203 and 205 TEC)*
1.   The Council shall, jointly with the European Parliament, exercise legislative and budgetary functions. It shall carry out policy-making and co-ordinating functions as laid down in the Constitution.

2.   The Council shall consist of a representative of each Member State at ministerial level, who may commit the government of the Member State in question and cast its vote.

3.   The Council shall act by a qualified majority except where the Constitution provides otherwise.

ARTICLE I-24 *Configurations of the Council of Ministers (new. Paragraph 7 ex Article 203 TEC)*
1.   The Council shall meet in different configurations.

2.   The General Affairs Council shall ensure consistency in the work of the different Council configurations.
It shall prepare and ensure the follow-up to meetings of the European Council, in liaison with the President of the European Council and the Commission.

3.   The Foreign Affairs Council shall elaborate the Union's external action on the basis of strategic guidelines laid down by the European Council and ensure that the Union's action is consistent.

4.   The European Council shall adopt by a qualified majority a European decision establishing the list of other Council configurations.

5.   A Committee of Permanent Representatives of the Governments of the Member States shall be responsible for preparing the work of the Council.

6.   The Council shall meet in public when it deliberates and votes on a draft legislative act. To this end, each Council meeting shall be divided into two parts, dealing respectively with deliberations on Union legislative acts and non-legislative activities.

7.   The Presidency of Council configurations, other than that of Foreign Affairs, shall be held by Member State representatives in the Council on the basis of equal rotation, in accordance with the conditions established by a European decision of the European Council. The European Council shall act by a qualified majority.

ARTICLE I-25 *Definition of qualified majority within the European Council and the Council (new)*
1.   A qualified majority shall be defined as at least 55% of the members of the Council, comprising at least fifteen of them and representing Member States comprising at least 65% of the population of the Union.

A blocking minority must include at least four Council members, failing which the qualified majority shall be deemed attained.

2.   By way of derogation from paragraph 1, when the Council does not act on a proposal from the Commission or from the Union Minister for Foreign Affairs, the qualified majority shall be defined as at least 72% of the members of the Council, representing Member States comprising at least 65% of the population of the Union.

3.   Paragraphs 1 and 2 shall apply to the European Council when it is acting by a qualified majority.

4.   Within the European Council, its President and the President of the Commission shall not take part in the vote.
[*BMDF Note: Paragraphs 1, 2 and 3 come into effect on 1 November 2009; Protocol no. 34, Article 2.*]

ARTICLE I-26 *The European Commission (new)*
1.   The Commission shall promote the general interest of the Union and take appropriate initiatives to that end. It shall ensure the application of the Constitution, and measures adopted by the institutions pursuant to the Constitution. It shall oversee the application of Union law under the control of the Court of Justice of the European Union. It shall execute the budget and manage programmes. It shall exercise co-ordinating, executive and management functions, as laid down in the Constitution. With the exception of the common foreign and security policy, and other cases provided for in the Constitution, it shall ensure the Union's external representation. It shall initiate the Union's annual and multiannual programming with a view to achieving inter-institutional agreements.

2.   Union legislative acts may be adopted only on the basis of a Commission proposal, except where the Constitution provides otherwise. Other acts shall be adopted on the basis of a Commission proposal where the Constitution so provides.

3.   The Commission's term of office shall be five years.

4.   The members of the Commission shall be chosen on the ground of their general competence and European commitment from persons whose independence is beyond doubt.

5.   The first Commission appointed under the provisions of the Constitution shall consist of one national of each Member State, including its President and the Union Minister for Foreign Affairs who shall be one of its Vice-Presidents. [*BMDF Note: This appointment will be on 1 November 2009.*]

6.   As from the end of the term of office of the Commission referred to in paragraph 5, the Commission shall consist of a number of members, including its President and the Union Minister for Foreign Affairs, corresponding to two thirds of the number of Member States, unless the European Council, acting unanimously, decides to alter this number.
The members of the Commission shall be selected from among the nationals of the Member States on the basis of a system of equal rotation between the Member States. This system shall be established by a European decision adopted unanimously by the European Council and on the basis of the following principles:
(a)   Member States shall be treated on a strictly equal footing as regards determination of the sequence of, and the time spent by, their nationals as members of the Commission; consequently, the difference between the total number of terms of office held by nationals of any given pair of Member States may never be more than one;
(b)   subject to point (a), each successive Commission shall be so composed as to reflect satisfactorily the demographic and geographical range of all the Member States.
[*BMDF Note: This paragraph will take effect on 1 November 2014.*]

7.   In carrying out its responsibilities, the Commission shall be completely independent. Without prejudice to Article I-28(2), the members of the Commission shall neither seek nor take instructions from any government or other institution, body, office or entity. They shall refrain from any action incompatible with their duties or the performance of their tasks.

8.   The Commission, as a body, shall be responsible to the European Parliament. In accordance with Article III-340, the European Parliament may vote on a censure motion on the Commission. If such a motion is carried, the members of the Commission shall resign as a body and the Union Minister for Foreign Affairs shall resign from the duties that he or she carries out in the Commission.

ARTICLE I-27 *The President of the European Commission (new)*
1.   Taking into account the elections to the European Parliament and after having held the appropriate consultations, the European Council, acting by a qualified majority, shall propose to the European Parliament a candidate for President of the Commission. This candidate shall be elected by the European Parliament by a majority of its component members. If he or she does not obtain the required majority, the European Council, acting by a qualified majority, shall within one month propose a new candidate who shall be elected by the European Parliament following the same procedure.

2.   The Council, by common accord with the President-elect, shall adopt the list of the other persons whom it proposes for appointment as members of the Commission. They shall be selected, on the basis of the suggestions made by Member States, in accordance with the criteria set out in Article I-26(4) and (6), second subparagraph.
The President, the Union Minister for Foreign Affairs and the other members of the Commission shall be subject as a body to a vote of consent by the European Parliament. On the basis of this consent the Commission shall be appointed by the European Council, acting by a qualified majority.

3.   The President of the Commission shall:
(a)   lay down guidelines within which the Commission is to work;
(b)   decide on the internal organisation of the Commission, ensuring that it acts consistently, efficiently and as a collegiate body;
(c)   appoint Vice-Presidents, other than the Union Minister for Foreign Affairs, from among the members of the Commission.
A member of the Commission shall resign if the President so requests. The Union Minister for Foreign Affairs shall resign, in accordance with the procedure set out in Article I-28(1), if the President so requests.

ARTICLE I-28 *The Union Minister for Foreign Affairs (new)*
1.   The European Council, acting by a qualified majority, with the agreement of the President of the Commission, shall appoint the Union Minister for Foreign Affairs. The European Council may end his or her term of office by the same procedure.

2.   The Union Minister for Foreign Affairs shall conduct the Union's common foreign and security policy. He or she shall contribute by his or her proposals to the development of that policy, which he or she shall carry out as mandated by the Council. The same shall apply to the common security and defence policy.

3.   The Union Minister for Foreign Affairs shall preside over the Foreign Affairs Council.

4.   The Union Minister for Foreign Affairs shall be one of the Vice-Presidents of the Commission. He or she shall ensure the consistency of the Union's external action. He or she shall be responsible within the Commission for responsibilities incumbent on it in external relations and for co-ordinating other aspects of the Union's external action. In exercising these responsibilities within the Commission, and only for these responsibilities, the Union Minister for Foreign Affairs shall be bound by Commission procedures to the extent that this is consistent with paragraphs 2 and 3.

ARTICLE I-29 *The Court of Justice of the European Union (ex Articles 220, 221, 222 and 234 TEC)*
1.   The Court of Justice of the European Union shall include the Court of Justice, the General Court and specialised courts. It shall ensure that in the interpretation and application of the Constitution the law is observed.
Member States shall provide remedies sufficient to ensure effective legal protection in the fields covered by Union law.

2.   The Court of Justice shall consist of one judge from each Member State. It shall be assisted by Advocates-General.
The General Court shall include at least one judge per Member State.
The judges and the Advocates-General of the Court of Justice and the judges of the General Court shall be chosen from persons whose independence is beyond doubt and who satisfy the conditions set out in Articles III-355 and III-356. They shall be appointed by common accord of the governments of the Member States for six years. Retiring judges and Advocates-General may be reappointed.

3.   The Court of Justice of the European Union shall in accordance with Part III:
(a)   rule on actions brought by a Member State, an institution or a natural or legal person;
(b)   give preliminary rulings, at the request of courts or tribunals of the Member States, on the interpretation of Union law or the validity of acts adopted by the institutions;
(c)   rule in other cases provided for in the Constitution.

CHAPTER II

THE OTHER UNION INSTITUTIONS AND ADVISORY BODIES

ARTICLE I-30 *The European Central Bank (ex Articles 8, 105 and 107 TEC)*
1.   The European Central Bank, together with the national central banks, shall constitute the European System of Central Banks. The European Central Bank, together with the national central banks of the Member States whose currency is the euro, which constitute the Eurosystem, shall conduct the monetary policy of the Union.

2.   The European System of Central Banks shall be governed by the decision-making bodies of the European Central Bank. The primary objective of the European System of Central Banks shall be to maintain price stability. Without prejudice to that objective, it shall support the general economic policies in the Union in order to contribute to the achievement of the latter's objectives. It shall conduct other Central Bank tasks in accordance with Part III and the Statute of the European System of Central Banks and of the European Central Bank.

3.   The European Central Bank is an institution. It shall have legal personality. It alone may authorise the issue of the euro. It shall be independent in the exercise of its powers and in the management of its finances. Union institutions, bodies, offices and agencies and the governments of the Member States shall respect that independence.

4.   The European Central Bank shall adopt such measures as are necessary to carry out its tasks in accordance with Articles III-185 to III-191 and Article III-196, and with the conditions laid down in the Statute of the European System of Central Banks and of the European Central Bank. In accordance with these same Articles, those Member States whose currency is not the euro, and their central banks, shall retain their powers in monetary matters.

5.   Within the areas falling within its responsibilities, the European Central Bank shall be consulted on all proposed Union acts, and all proposals for regulation at national level, and may give an opinion.

6.   The decision-making organs of the European Central Bank, their composition and operating methods are set out in Articles III-382 and III-383, as well as in the Statute of the European System of Central Banks and of the European Central Bank.

ARTICLE I-31 *The Court of Auditors (ex Articles 246 and 247 TEC)*
1.   The Court of Auditors is an institution. It shall carry out the Union's audit.

2.   It shall examine the accounts of all Union revenue and expenditure, and shall ensure good financial management.

3.   It shall consist of one national of each Member State. Its members shall be completely independent in the performance of their duties, in the Union's general interest.

ARTICLE I-32 *The Union's advisory bodies (ex Article 7 TEC and Articles 257 - 265 TEC)*
1.   The European Parliament, the Council and the Commission shall be assisted by a Committee of the Regions and an Economic and Social Committee, exercising advisory functions.

2.   The Committee of the Regions shall consist of representatives of regional and local bodies who either hold a regional or local authority electoral mandate or are politically accountable to an elected assembly.

3.   The Economic and Social Committee shall consist of representatives of organisations of employers, of the employed, and of other parties representative of civil society, notably in socio-economic, civic, professional and cultural areas.

4.   The members of the Committee of the Regions and the Economic and Social Committee shall not be bound by any mandatory instructions. They shall be completely independent in the performance of their duties, in the Union's general interest.

5.   Rules governing the composition of these Committees, the designation of their members, their powers and their operations are set out in Articles III-386 to III-392.

The rules referred to in paragraphs 2 and 3 governing the nature of their composition shall be reviewed at regular intervals by the Council to take account of economic, social and demographic developments within the Union. The Council, on a proposal from the Commission, shall adopt European decisions to that end.

TITLE V

EXERCISE OF UNION COMPETENCE

CHAPTER I

COMMON PROVISIONS

ARTICLE I-33 *The legal acts of the Union (ex Article 249 TEC)*
1.   To exercise the Union's competences the institutions shall use as legal instruments, in accordance with Part III, European laws, European framework laws, European regulations, European decisions, recommendations and opinions.
A European law shall be a legislative act of general application. It shall be binding in its entirety and directly applicable in all Member States.
A European framework law shall be a legislative act binding, as to the result to be achieved, upon each Member State to which it is addressed, but shall leave to the national authorities the choice of form and methods.
A European regulation shall be a non-legislative act of general application for the implementation of legislative acts and of certain provisions of the Constitution. It may either be binding in its entirety and directly applicable in all Member States, or be binding, as to the result to be achieved, upon each Member State to which it is addressed, but shall leave to the national authorities the choice of form and methods.
A European decision shall be a non-legislative act, binding in its entirety. A decision which specifies those to whom it is addressed shall be binding only on them.
Recommendations and opinions shall have no binding force.

2.   When considering draft legislative acts, the European Parliament and the Council shall refrain from adopting acts not provided for by the relevant legislative procedure in the area in question.

ARTICLE I-34 *Legislative acts (new)*
1.   European laws and framework laws shall be adopted, on the basis of proposals from the Commission, jointly by the European Parliament and the Council under the ordinary legislative procedure as set out in Article III-396. If the two institutions cannot reach agreement on an act, it shall not be adopted.

2.   In the specific cases provided for in the Constitution, European laws and framework laws shall be adopted by the European Parliament with the participation of the Council, or by the latter with the participation of the European Parliament, in accordance with special legislative procedures.

3.   In the specific cases provided for in the Constitution, European laws and framework laws may be adopted at the initiative of a group of Member States or of the European Parliament, on a recommendation from the European Central Bank or at the request of the Court of Justice or the European Investment Bank.

ARTICLE I-35 *Non-legislative acts (new)*
1.   The European Council shall adopt European decisions in the cases provided for in the Constitution.

2.   The Council and the Commission, in particular in the cases referred to in Articles I-36 and I-37, and the European Central Bank in the specific cases provided for in the Constitution, shall adopt European regulations and decisions.

3.   The Council shall adopt recommendations. It shall act on a proposal from the Commission in all cases where the Constitution provides that it shall adopt acts on a proposal from the Commission. It shall act unanimously in those areas in which unanimity is required for the adoption of a Union act. The Commission, and the European Central Bank in the specific cases provided for in the Constitution, shall adopt recommendations.

ARTICLE I-36 *Delegated European regulations (ex Article 202 TEC)*
1.   European laws and framework laws may delegate to the Commission the power to adopt delegated European regulations to supplement or amend certain non-essential elements of the law or framework law.
The objectives, content, scope and duration of the delegation of power shall be explicitly defined in the European laws and framework laws. The essential elements of an area shall be reserved for the European law or framework law and accordingly shall not be the subject of a delegation of power.

2.   European laws and framework laws shall explicitly lay down the conditions to which the delegation is subject; these conditions may be as follows:
(a)   the European Parliament or the Council may decide to revoke the delegation;
(b)   the delegated European regulation may enter into force only if no objection has been expressed by the European Parliament or the Council within a period set by the European law or framework law.
For the purposes of (a) and (b), the European Parliament shall act by a majority of its component members, and the Council by a qualified majority.

ARTICLE I-37 *Implementing acts (ex Article 202 TEC)*
1.   Member States shall adopt all measures of national law necessary to implement legally binding Union acts.

2.   Where uniform conditions for implementing legally binding Union acts are needed, those acts shall confer implementing powers on the Commission, or, in duly justified specific cases and in the cases provided for in Article I-40, on the Council.

3.   For the purposes of paragraph 2, European laws shall lay down in advance the rules and general principles concerning mechanisms for control by Member States of the Commission's exercise of implementing powers.

4.   Union implementing acts shall take the form of European implementing regulations or European implementing decisions.

ARTICLE I-38 *Principles common to the Union's legal acts (ex Article 253 TEC)*
1.   Where the Constitution does not specify the type of act to be adopted, the institutions shall select it on a case-by-case basis, in compliance with the applicable procedures and with the principle of proportionality referred to in Article I-11.

2.   Legal acts shall state the reasons on which they are based and shall refer to any proposals, initiatives, recommendations, requests or opinions required by the Constitution.

ARTICLE I-39 *Publication and entry into force (ex Article 254 TEC)*
1.   European laws and framework laws adopted under the ordinary legislative procedure shall be signed by the President of the European Parliament and by the President of the Council.
In other cases they shall be signed by the President of the institution which adopted them.
European laws and framework laws shall be published in the *Official Journal of the European Union* and shall enter into force on the date specified in them or, in the absence thereof, on the twentieth day following their publication.

2.   European regulations, and European decisions which do not specify to whom they are addressed, shall be signed by the President of the institution which adopted them.
European regulations, and European decisions when the latter do not specify to whom they are addressed, shall be published in the *Official Journal of the European Union* and shall enter into force on the date specified in them or, in the absence thereof, on the twentieth day following that of their publication.

3.   European decisions other than those referred to in paragraph 2 shall be notified to those to whom they are addressed and shall take effect upon such notification.

CHAPTER II

SPECIFIC PROVISIONS

ARTICLE I-40 *Specific provisions relating to the common foreign and security policy (new)*
1.   The European Union shall conduct a common foreign and security policy, based on the development of mutual political solidarity among Member States, the identification of questions of general interest and the achievement of an ever-increasing degree of convergence of Member States' actions.

2.   The European Council shall identify the Union's strategic interests and determine the objectives of its common foreign and security policy. The Council shall frame this policy within the framework of the strategic guidelines established by the European Council and in accordance with Part III.

3.   The European Council and the Council shall adopt the necessary European decisions.

4.   The common foreign and security policy shall be put into effect by the Union Minister for Foreign Affairs and by the Member States, using national and Union resources.

5.   Member States shall consult one another within the European Council and the Council on any foreign and security policy issue which is of general interest in order to determine a common approach. Before undertaking any action on the international scene or any commitment which could affect the Union's interests, each Member State shall consult the others within the European Council or the Council. Member States shall ensure, through the convergence of their actions, that the Union is able to assert its interests and values on the international scene. Member States shall show mutual solidarity.

6.   European decisions relating to the common foreign and security policy shall be adopted by the European Council and the Council unanimously, except in the cases referred to in Part III. The European Council and the Council shall act on an initiative from a Member State, on a proposal from the Union Minister for Foreign Affairs or on a proposal from that Minister with the Commission's support. European laws and framework laws shall be excluded.

7.   The European Council may, unanimously, adopt a European decision authorising the Council to act by a qualified majority in cases other than those referred to in Part III.

8.   The European Parliament shall be regularly consulted on the main aspects and basic choices of the common foreign and security policy. It shall be kept informed of how it evolves.

ARTICLE I-41 *Specific provisions relating to the common security and defence policy (new)*
1.   The common security and defence policy shall be an integral part of the common foreign and security policy. It shall provide the Union with an operational capacity drawing on civil and military assets. The Union may use them on missions outside the Union for peace-keeping, conflict prevention and strengthening international security in accordance with the principles of the United Nations Charter. The performance of these tasks shall be undertaken using capabilities provided by the Member States.

2.   The common security and defence policy shall include the progressive framing of a common Union defence policy. This will lead to a common defence, when the European Council, acting unanimously, so decides. It shall in that case recommend to the Member States the adoption of such a decision in accordance with their respective constitutional requirements.
The policy of the Union in accordance with this Article shall not prejudice the specific character of the security and defence policy of certain Member States, it shall respect the obligations of certain Member States, which see their common defence realised in the North Atlantic Treaty Organisation, under the North Atlantic Treaty, and be compatible with the common security and defence policy established within that framework.

3.   Member States shall make civilian and military capabilities available to the Union for the implementation of the common security and defence policy, to contribute to the objectives defined by the Council. Those Member States which together establish multinational forces may also make them available to the common security and defence policy.
Member States shall undertake progressively to improve their military capabilities. An Agency in the field of defence capabilities development, research, acquisition and armaments (European Defence Agency) shall be established to identify operational requirements, to promote measures to satisfy those requirements, to contribute to identifying and, where appropriate, implementing any measure needed to strengthen the

industrial and technological base of the defence sector, to participate in defining a European capabilities and armaments policy, and to assist the Council in evaluating the improvement of military capabilities.

4.　European decisions relating to the common security and defence policy, including those initiating a mission as referred to in this Article, shall be adopted by the Council acting unanimously on a proposal from the Union Minister for Foreign Affairs or an initiative from a Member State. The Union Minister for Foreign Affairs may propose the use of both national resources and Union instruments, together with the Commission where appropriate.

5.　The Council may entrust the execution of a task, within the Union framework, to a group of Member States in order to protect the Union's values and serve its interests. The execution of such a task shall be governed by Article III-310.

6.　Those Member States whose military capabilities fulfil higher criteria and which have made more binding commitments to one another in this area with a view to the most demanding missions shall establish permanent structured co-operation within the Union framework. Such co-operation shall be governed by Article III-312. It shall not affect the provisions of Article III-309.

7.　If a Member State is the victim of armed aggression on its territory, the other Member States shall have towards it an obligation of aid and assistance by all the means in their power, in accordance with Article 51 of the United Nations Charter. This shall not prejudice the specific character of the security and defence policy of certain Member States.
Commitments and co-operation in this area shall be consistent with commitments under the North Atlantic Treaty Organisation, which, for those States which are members of it, remains the foundation of their collective defence and the forum for its implementation.

8.　The European Parliament shall be regularly consulted on the main aspects and basic choices of the common security and defence policy. It shall be kept informed of how it evolves.

ARTICLE I-42 *Specific provisions relating to the area of freedom, security and justice (ex Article 61 TEC)*
1.　The Union shall constitute an area of freedom, security and justice:
(a)　by adopting European laws and framework laws intended, where necessary, to approximate laws and regulations of the Member States in the areas referred to in Part III;
(b)　by promoting mutual confidence between the competent authorities of the Member States, in particular on the basis of mutual recognition of judicial and extrajudicial decisions;
(c)　by operational co-operation between the competent authorities of the Member States, including the police, customs and other services specialising in the prevention and detection of criminal offences.

2.　National Parliaments may, within the framework of the area of freedom, security and justice, participate in the evaluation mechanisms provided for in Article III-260. They shall be involved in the political monitoring of Europol and the evaluation of Eurojust's activities in accordance with Articles III-276 and III-273.

3.　Member States shall have a right of initiative in the field of police and judicial co-operation in criminal matters, in accordance with Article III-264.

ARTICLE I-43 *Solidarity clause (new)*
1.　The Union and its Member States shall act jointly in a spirit of solidarity if a Member State is the object of a terrorist attack or the victim of a natural or man-made disaster. The Union shall mobilise all the instruments at its disposal, including the military resources made available by the Member States, to:
(a)　–　prevent the terrorist threat in the territory of the Member States;
　　　–　protect democratic institutions and the civilian population from any terrorist attack;
　　　–　assist a Member State in its territory, at the request of its political authorities, in the event of a terrorist attack;
(b)　assist a Member State in its territory, at the request of its political authorities, in the event of a natural or man-made disaster.

2.　The detailed arrangements for implementing this Article are set out in Article III-329.

CHAPTER III

ENHANCED CO-OPERATION

ARTICLE I-44 *Enhanced co-operation (ex Article 11 TEC and Articles 43 - 45 TEU)*
1.   Member States which wish to establish enhanced co-operation between themselves within the framework of the Union's non-exclusive competences may make use of its institutions and exercise those competences by applying the relevant provisions of the Constitution, subject to the limits and in accordance with the procedures laid down in this Article and in Articles III-416 to III-423.
Enhanced co-operation shall aim to further the objectives of the Union, protect its interests and reinforce its integration process. Such co-operation shall be open at any time to all Member States, in accordance with Article III-418.

2.   The European decision authorising enhanced co-operation shall be adopted by the Council as a last resort, when it has established that the objectives of such co-operation cannot be attained within a reasonable period by the Union as a whole, and provided that at least one third of the Member States participate in it. The Council shall act in accordance with the procedure laid down in Article III-419.

3.   All members of the Council may participate in its deliberations, but only members of the Council representing the Member States participating in enhanced co-operation shall take part in the vote.
Unanimity shall be constituted by the votes of the representatives of the participating Member States only.
A qualified majority shall be defined as at least 55% of the members of the Council representing the participating Member States, comprising at least 65% of the population of these States.
A blocking minority must include at least the minimum number of Council members representing more than 35% of the population of the participating Member States, plus one member, failing which the qualified majority shall be deemed attained.
By way of derogation from the third and fourth subparagraphs, where the Council does not act on a proposal from the Commission or from the Union Minister for Foreign Affairs, the required qualified majority shall be defined as at least 72% of the members of the Council representing the participating Member States, comprising at least 65% of the population of these States.
[BMDF Note: Sub-paragraphs 3, 4 and 5 come into effect on 1 November 2009; Protocol no. 34, Article 2(4).]

4.   Acts adopted in the framework of enhanced co-operation shall bind only participating Member States. They shall not be regarded as part of the *acquis* which has to be accepted by candidate States for accession to the Union.

TITLE VI

THE DEMOCRATIC LIFE OF THE UNION

ARTICLE I-45 *The principle of democratic equality (new)*
In all its activities, the Union shall observe the principle of the equality of its citizens, who shall receive equal attention from its institutions, bodies, offices and agencies.

ARTICLE I-46 *The principle of representative democracy (new)*
1.   The functioning of the Union shall be founded on representative democracy.

2.   Citizens are directly represented at Union level in the European Parliament.
Member States are represented in the European Council by their Heads of State or Government and in the Council by their governments, themselves democratically accountable either to their national Parliaments, or to their citizens.

3.   Every citizen shall have the right to participate in the democratic life of the Union. Decisions shall be taken as openly and as closely as possible to the citizen.

4.   Political parties at European level contribute to forming European political awareness and to expressing the will of citizens of the Union.

ARTICLE I-47 *The principle of participatory democracy (new)*
1.   The institutions shall, by appropriate means, give citizens and representative associations the opportunity to make known and publicly exchange their views in all areas of Union action.

2.   The institutions shall maintain an open, transparent and regular dialogue with representative associations and civil society.

3.   The Commission shall carry out broad consultations with parties concerned in order to ensure that the Union's actions are coherent and transparent.

4.   Not less than one million citizens who are nationals of a significant number of Member States may take the initiative of inviting the Commission, within the framework of its powers, to submit any appropriate proposal on matters where citizens consider that a legal act of the Union is required for the purpose of implementing the Constitution. European laws shall determine the provisions for the procedures and conditions required for such a citizens' initiative, including the minimum number of Member States from which such citizens must come.

ARTICLE I-48 *The social partners and autonomous social dialogue (ex Article 138 TEC)*
The Union recognises and promotes the role of the social partners at its level, taking into account the diversity of national systems. It shall facilitate dialogue between the social partners, respecting their autonomy.
The Tripartite Social Summit for Growth and Employment shall contribute to social dialogue.

ARTICLE I-49 *The European Ombudsman (ex Article 195 TEC)*
A European Ombudsman elected by the European Parliament shall receive, examine and report on complaints about maladministration in the activities of the Union institutions, bodies, offices or agencies, under the conditions laid down in the Constitution. The European Ombudsman shall be completely independent in the performance of his or her duties.

ARTICLE I-50 *Transparency of the proceedings of Union institutions, bodies, offices and agencies*
                    (ex Article 255 TEC)
1.   In order to promote good governance and ensure the participation of civil society, the Union institutions, bodies, offices and agencies shall conduct their work as openly as possible.

2.   The European Parliament shall meet in public, as shall the Council when considering and voting on a draft legislative act.

3.   Any citizen of the Union, and any natural or legal person residing or having its registered office in a Member State shall have, under the conditions laid down in Part III, a right of access to documents of the Union institutions, bodies, offices and agencies, whatever their medium.
European laws shall lay down the general principles and limits which, on grounds of public or private interest, govern the right of access to such documents.

4.   Each institution, body, office or agency shall determine in its own rules of procedure specific provisions regarding access to its documents, in accordance with the European laws referred to in paragraph 3.

ARTICLE I-51 *Protection of personal data (ex Article 286 TEC)*
1.   Everyone has the right to the protection of personal data concerning him or her.

2.   European laws or framework laws shall lay down the rules relating to the protection of individuals with regard to the processing of personal data by Union institutions, bodies, offices and agencies, and by the Member States when carrying out activities which fall within the scope of Union law, and the rules relating to the free movement of such data. Compliance with these rules shall be subject to the control of independent authorities.

ARTICLE I-52 *Status of churches and non-confessional organisations (new)*
1.   The Union respects and does not prejudice the status under national law of churches and religious associations or communities in the Member States.

2.   The Union equally respects the status under national law of philosophical and non-confessional organisations.

3.   Recognising their identity and their specific contribution, the Union shall maintain an open, transparent and regular dialogue with these churches and organisations.

TITLE VII

THE UNION'S FINANCES

ARTICLE I-53 *Budgetary and financial principles (ex Articles 268 to 280 TEC)*
1.   All items of Union revenue and expenditure shall be included in estimates drawn up for each financial year and shall be shown in the Union's budget, in accordance with Part III.

2.   The revenue and expenditure shown in the budget shall be in balance.

3.   The expenditure shown in the budget shall be authorised for the annual budgetary period in accordance with the European law referred to in Article III-412.

4.   The implementation of expenditure shown in the budget shall require the prior adoption of a legally binding Union act providing a legal basis for its action and for the implementation of the corresponding expenditure in accordance with the European law referred to in Article III-412, except in cases for which that law provides.

5.   With a view to maintaining budgetary discipline, the Union shall not adopt any act which is likely to have appreciable implications for the budget without providing an assurance that the expenditure arising from such an act is capable of being financed within the limit of the Union's own resources and in compliance with the multiannual financial framework referred to in Article I-55.

6.   The budget shall be implemented in accordance with the principle of sound financial management. Member States shall co-operate with the Union to ensure that the appropriations entered in the budget are used in accordance with this principle.

7.   The Union and the Member States, in accordance with Article III–415, shall counter fraud and any other illegal activities affecting the financial interests of the Union.

ARTICLE I-54 *The Union's own resources (ex Article 269 TEC)*
1.   The Union shall provide itself with the means necessary to attain its objectives and carry through its policies.

2.   Without prejudice to other revenue, the Union's budget shall be financed wholly from its own resources.

3.   A European law of the Council shall lay down the provisions relating to the system of own resources of the Union. In this context it may establish new categories of own resources or abolish an existing category. The Council shall act unanimously after consulting the European Parliament. That law shall not enter into force until it is approved by the Member States in accordance with their respective constitutional requirements.

4.   A European law of the Council shall lay down implementing measures of the Union's own resources system insofar as this is provided for in the European law adopted on the basis of paragraph 3. The Council shall act after obtaining the consent of the European Parliament.

ARTICLE I-55 *The multiannual financial framework (new)*
1.   The multiannual financial framework shall ensure that Union expenditure develops in an orderly manner and within the limits of its own resources. It shall determine the amounts of the annual ceilings of appropriations for commitments by category of expenditure in accordance with Article III-402.

2.   A European law of the Council shall lay down the multiannual financial framework. The Council shall act unanimously after obtaining the consent of the European Parliament, which shall be given by a majority of its component members.

3.   The annual budget of the Union shall comply with the multiannual financial framework.

4.   The European Council may, unanimously, adopt a European decision authorising the Council to act by a qualified majority when adopting the European law of the Council referred to in paragraph 2.

ARTICLE I-56 *The Union's budget (ex Article 272 TEC)*
A European law shall establish the Union's annual budget in accordance with Article III-404.

TITLE VIII

THE UNION AND ITS NEIGHBOURS

ARTICLE I-57 *The Union and its neighbours (ex Article 300 TEC)*
1.   The Union shall develop a special relationship with neighbouring countries, aiming to establish an area of prosperity and good neighbourliness, founded on the values of the Union and characterised by close and peaceful relations based on co-operation.

2.   For the purposes of paragraph 1, the Union may conclude specific agreements with the countries concerned. These agreements may contain reciprocal rights and obligations as well as the possibility of undertaking activities jointly. Their implementation shall be the subject of periodic consultation.

TITLE IX

UNION MEMBERSHIP

ARTICLE I-58 *Conditions of eligibility and procedure for accession to the Union (ex Article 49 TEU)*
1.   The Union shall be open to all European States which respect the values referred to in Article I–2, and are committed to promoting them together.

2.   Any European State which wishes to become a member of the Union shall address its application to the Council. The European Parliament and national Parliaments shall be notified of this application. The Council shall act unanimously after consulting the Commission and after obtaining the consent of the European Parliament, which shall act by a majority of its component members. The conditions and arrangements for admission shall be the subject of an agreement between the Member States and the candidate State. That agreement shall be subject to ratification by each contracting State, in accordance with its respective constitutional requirements.

ARTICLE I-59 *Suspension of certain rights resulting from Union membership (ex Article 7 TEU)*
1.   On the reasoned initiative of one third of the Member States or the reasoned initiative of the European Parliament or on a proposal from the Commission, the Council may adopt a European decision determining that there is a clear risk of a serious breach by a Member State of the values referred to in Article I-2. The Council shall act by a majority of four fifths of its members after obtaining the consent of the European Parliament.
Before making such a determination, the Council shall hear the Member State in question and, acting in accordance with the same procedure, may address recommendations to that State.
The Council shall regularly verify that the grounds on which such a determination was made continue to apply.

2.   The European Council, on the initiative of one third of the Member States or on a proposal from the Commission, may adopt a European decision determining the existence of a serious and persistent breach by a Member State of the values mentioned in Article I-2, after inviting the Member State in question to submit its observations. The European Council shall act unanimously after obtaining the consent of the European Parliament.

3.   Where a determination under paragraph 2 has been made, the Council, acting by a qualified majority, may adopt a European decision suspending certain of the rights deriving from the application of the Constitution to the Member State in question, including the voting rights of the member of the Council representing that State. The Council shall take into account the possible consequences of such a suspension for the rights and obligations of natural and legal persons.

In any case, that State shall continue to be bound by its obligations under the Constitution.

4.   The Council, acting by a qualified majority, may adopt a European decision varying or revoking measures adopted under paragraph 3 in response to changes in the situation which led to their being imposed.

5.   For the purposes of this Article, the member of the European Council or of the Council representing the Member State in question shall not take part in the vote and the Member State in question shall not be counted in the calculation of the one third or four fifths of Member States referred to in paragraphs 1 and 2. Abstentions by members present in person or represented shall not prevent the adoption of European decisions referred to in paragraph 2.

For the adoption of the European decisions referred to in paragraphs 3 and 4, a qualified majority shall be defined as at least 72% of the members of the Council, representing the participating Member States, comprising at least 65% of the population of these States.

Where, following a decision to suspend voting rights adopted pursuant to paragraph 3, the Council acts by a qualified majority on the basis of a provision of the Constitution, that qualified majority shall be defined as in the second subparagraph, or, where the Council acts on a proposal from the Commission or from the Union Minister for Foreign Affairs, as at least 55% of the members of the Council representing the participating Member States, comprising at least 65% of the population of these States. In the latter case, a blocking minority must include at least the minimum number of Council members representing more than 35% of the population of the participating Member States, plus one member, failing which the qualified majority shall be deemed attained.

[BMDF Note: Sub-paragraphs 2 and 3 come into effect on 1 November 2009; Protocol no. 34, Article 2(4).]

6.   For the purposes of this Article, the European Parliament shall act by a two-thirds majority of the votes cast, representing the majority of its component members.

ARTICLE I-60 *Voluntary withdrawal from the Union (new)*
1.   Any Member State may decide to withdraw from the Union in accordance with its own constitutional requirements.

2.   A Member State which decides to withdraw shall notify the European Council of its intention. In the light of the guidelines provided by the European Council, the Union shall negotiate and conclude an agreement with that State, setting out the arrangements for its withdrawal, taking account of the framework for its future relationship with the Union. That agreement shall be negotiated in accordance with Article III-325(3). It shall be concluded by the Council, acting by a qualified majority, after obtaining the consent of the European Parliament.

3.   The Constitution shall cease to apply to the State in question from the date of entry into force of the withdrawal agreement or, failing that, two years after the notification referred to in paragraph 2, unless the European Council, in agreement with the Member State concerned, unanimously decides to extend this period.

4.   For the purposes of paragraphs 2 and 3, the member of the European Council or of the Council representing the withdrawing Member State shall not participate in the discussions of the European Council or Council or in European decisions concerning it.

A qualified majority shall be defined as at least 72% of the members of the Council, representing the participating Member States, comprising at least 65% of the population of these States.

[BMDF Note: Sub-paragraph 2 comes into effect on 1 November 2009; Protocol no. 34, Article 2(4).]

5.   If a State which has withdrawn from the Union asks to rejoin, its request shall be subject to the procedure referred to in Article I-58.

PART II

THE CHARTER OF FUNDAMENTAL RIGHTS OF THE UNION

PREAMBLE

The peoples of Europe, in creating an ever closer union among them, are resolved to share a peaceful future based on common values.

Conscious of its spiritual and moral heritage, the Union is founded on the indivisible, universal values of human dignity, freedom, equality and solidarity; it is based on the principles of democracy and the rule of law. It places the individual at the heart of its activities, by establishing the citizenship of the Union and by creating an area of freedom, security and justice.

The Union contributes to the preservation and to the development of these common values while respecting the diversity of the cultures and traditions of the peoples of Europe as well as the national identities of the Member States and the organisation of their public authorities at national, regional and local levels; it seeks to promote balanced and sustainable development and ensures free movement of persons, services, goods and capital, and the freedom of establishment.

To this end, it is necessary to strengthen the protection of fundamental rights in the light of changes in society, social progress and scientific and technological developments by making those rights more visible in a Charter.

This Charter reaffirms, with due regard for the powers and tasks of the Union and the principle of subsidiarity, the rights as they result, in particular, from the constitutional traditions and international obligations common to the Member States, the European Convention for the Protection of Human Rights and Fundamental Freedoms, the Social Charters adopted by the Union and by the Council of Europe and the case law of the Court of Justice of the European Union and of the European Court of Human Rights. In this context the Charter will be interpreted by the courts of the Union and the Member States with due regard to the explanations prepared under the authority of the Praesidium of the Convention which drafted the Charter and updated under the responsibility of the Praesidium of the European Convention.

Enjoyment of these rights entails responsibilities and duties with regard to other persons, to the human community and to future generations.

The Union therefore recognises the rights, freedoms and principles set out hereafter.

TITLE I

DIGNITY

ARTICLE II-61 *Human dignity*
Human dignity is inviolable. It must be respected and protected.

ARTICLE II-62 *Right to life*
1.   Everyone has the right to life.

2.   No one shall be condemned to the death penalty, or executed.

ARTICLE II-63 *Right to the integrity of the person*
1.   Everyone has the right to respect for his or her physical and mental integrity.

2.   In the fields of medicine and biology, the following must be respected in particular:
(a)   the free and informed consent of the person concerned, according to the procedures laid down by law;
(b)   the prohibition of eugenic practices, in particular those aiming at the selection of persons;
(c)   the prohibition on making the human body and its parts as such a source of financial gain;
(d)   the prohibition of the reproductive cloning of human beings.

ARTICLE II-64 *Prohibition of torture and inhuman or degrading treatment or punishment*
No one shall be subjected to torture or to inhuman or degrading treatment or punishment.

ARTICLE II-65 *Prohibition of slavery and forced labour*
1.   No one shall be held in slavery or servitude.

2.   No one shall be required to perform forced or compulsory labour.

3.   Trafficking in human beings is prohibited.

TITLE II

FREEDOMS

ARTICLE II-66 *Right to liberty and security*
Everyone has the right to liberty and security of person.

ARTICLE II-67 *Respect for private and family life*
Everyone has the right to respect for his or her private and family life, home and communications.

ARTICLE II-68 *Protection of personal data*
1.   Everyone has the right to the protection of personal data concerning him or her.

2.   Such data must be processed fairly for specified purposes and on the basis of the consent of the person concerned or some other legitimate basis laid down by law. Everyone has the right of access to data which has been collected concerning him or her, and the right to have it rectified.

3.   Compliance with these rules shall be subject to control by an independent authority.

ARTICLE II-69 *Right to marry and right to found a family*
The right to marry and the right to found a family shall be guaranteed in accordance with the national laws governing the exercise of these rights.

ARTICLE II-70 *Freedom of thought, conscience and religion*
1.   Everyone has the right to freedom of thought, conscience and religion. This right includes freedom to change religion or belief and freedom, either alone or in community with others and in public or in private, to manifest religion or belief, in worship, teaching, practice and observance.

2.   The right to conscientious objection is recognised, in accordance with the national laws governing the exercise of this right.

ARTICLE II-71 *Freedom of expression and information*
1.   Everyone has the right to freedom of expression. This right shall include freedom to hold opinions and to receive and impart information and ideas without interference by public authority and regardless of frontiers.

2.   The freedom and pluralism of the media shall be respected.

ARTICLE II-72 *Freedom of assembly and of association*
1.   Everyone has the right to freedom of peaceful assembly and to freedom of association at all levels, in particular in political, trade union and civic matters, which implies the right of everyone to form and to join trade unions for the protection of his or her interests.

2.   Political parties at Union level contribute to expressing the political will of the citizens of the Union.

ARTICLE II-73 *Freedom of the arts and sciences*
The arts and scientific research shall be free of constraint. Academic freedom shall be respected.

ARTICLE II-74 *Right to education*
1.   Everyone has the right to education and to have access to vocational and continuing training.

2.   This right includes the possibility to receive free compulsory education.

3.   The freedom to found educational establishments with due respect for democratic principles and the right of parents to ensure the education and teaching of their children in conformity with their religious, philosophical and pedagogical convictions shall be respected, in accordance with the national laws governing the exercise of such freedom and right.

ARTICLE II-75 *Freedom to choose an occupation and right to engage in work*
1.   Everyone has the right to engage in work and to pursue a freely chosen or accepted occupation.

2.   Every citizen of the Union has the freedom to seek employment, to work, to exercise the right of establishment and to provide services in any Member State.

3.   Nationals of third countries who are authorised to work in the territories of the Member States are entitled to working conditions equivalent to those of citizens of the Union.

ARTICLE II-76 *Freedom to conduct a business*
The freedom to conduct a business in accordance with Union law and national laws and practices is recognised.

ARTICLE II-77 *Right to property*
1.   Everyone has the right to own, use, dispose of and bequeath his or her lawfully acquired possessions. No one may be deprived of his or her possessions, except in the public interest and in the cases and under the conditions provided for by law, subject to fair compensation being paid in good time for their loss. The use of property may be regulated by law insofar as is necessary for the general interest.

2.   Intellectual property shall be protected.

ARTICLE II-78 *Right to asylum*
The right to asylum shall be guaranteed with due respect for the rules of the Geneva Convention of 28 July 1951 and the Protocol of 31 January 1967 relating to the status of refugees and in accordance with the Constitution.

ARTICLE II-79 *Protection in the event of removal, expulsion or extradition*
1.   Collective expulsions are prohibited.

2.   No one may be removed, expelled or extradited to a State where there is a serious risk that he or she would be subjected to the death penalty, torture or other inhuman or degrading treatment or punishment.

TITLE III

EQUALITY

ARTICLE II-80 *Equality before the law*
Everyone is equal before the law.

ARTICLE II-81 *Non-discrimination*
1.   Any discrimination based on any ground such as sex, race, colour, ethnic or social origin, genetic features, language, religion or belief, political or any other opinion, membership of a national minority, property, birth, disability, age or sexual orientation shall be prohibited.

2.   Within the scope of application of the Constitution and without prejudice to any of its specific provisions, any discrimination on grounds of nationality shall be prohibited.

ARTICLE II-82 *Cultural, religious and linguistic diversity*
The Union shall respect cultural, religious and linguistic diversity.

ARTICLE II-83 *Equality between women and men*
Equality between women and men must be ensured in all areas, including employment, work and pay.
The principle of equality shall not prevent the maintenance or adoption of measures providing for specific advantages in favour of the under-represented sex.

ARTICLE II-84 *The rights of the child*
1.   Children shall have the right to such protection and care as is necessary for their well-being. They may express their views freely. Such views shall be taken into consideration on matters which concern them in accordance with their age and maturity.

2.   In all actions relating to children, whether taken by public authorities or private institutions, the child's best interests must be a primary consideration.

3.   Every child shall have the right to maintain on a regular basis a personal relationship and direct contact with both his or her parents, unless that is contrary to his or her interests.

ARTICLE II-85 *The rights of the elderly*
The Union recognises and respects the rights of the elderly to lead a life of dignity and independence and to participate in social and cultural life.

ARTICLE II-86 *Integration of persons with disabilities*
The Union recognises and respects the right of persons with disabilities to benefit from measures designed to ensure their independence, social and occupational integration and participation in the life of the community.

TITLE IV

SOLIDARITY

ARTICLE II-87 *Workers' right to information and consultation within the undertaking*
Workers or their representatives must, at the appropriate levels, be guaranteed information and consultation in good time in the cases and under the conditions provided for by Union law and national laws and practices.

ARTICLE II-88 *Right of collective bargaining and action*
Workers and employers, or their respective organisations, have, in accordance with Union law and national laws and practices, the right to negotiate and conclude collective agreements at the appropriate levels and, in cases of conflicts of interest, to take collective action to defend their interests, including strike action.

ARTICLE II-89 *Right of access to placement services*
Everyone has the right of access to a free placement service.

ARTICLE II-90 *Protection in the event of unjustified dismissal*
Every worker has the right to protection against unjustified dismissal, in accordance with Union law and national laws and practices.

ARTICLE II-91 *Fair and just working conditions*
1.   Every worker has the right to working conditions which respect his or her health, safety and dignity.

2.   Every worker has the right to limitation of maximum working hours, to daily and weekly rest periods and to an annual period of paid leave.

ARTICLE II-92 *Prohibition of child labour and protection of young people at work*
The employment of children is prohibited. The minimum age of admission to employment may not be lower than the minimum school-leaving age, without prejudice to such rules as may be more favourable to young people and except for limited derogations.
Young people admitted to work must have working conditions appropriate to their age and be protected against economic exploitation and any work likely to harm their safety, health or physical, mental, moral or social development or to interfere with their education.

ARTICLE II-93 *Family and professional life*
1.   The family shall enjoy legal, economic and social protection.

2.   To reconcile family and professional life, everyone shall have the right to protection from dismissal for a reason connected with maternity and the right to paid maternity leave and to parental leave following the birth or adoption of a child.

ARTICLE II-94 *Social security and social assistance*
1.   The Union recognises and respects the entitlement to social security benefits and social services providing protection in cases such as maternity, illness, industrial accidents, dependency or old age, and in the case of loss of employment, in accordance with the rules laid down by Union law and national laws and practices.

2.   Everyone residing and moving legally within the European Union is entitled to social security benefits and social advantages in accordance with Union law and national laws and practices.

3.   In order to combat social exclusion and poverty, the Union recognises and respects the right to social and housing assistance so as to ensure a decent existence for all those who lack sufficient resources, in accordance with the rules laid down by Union law and national laws and practices.

ARTICLE II-95 *Health care*
Everyone has the right of access to preventive health care and the right to benefit from medical treatment under the conditions established by national laws and practices. A high level of human health protection shall be ensured in the definition and implementation of all Union policies and activities.

ARTICLE II-96 *Access to services of general economic interest*
The Union recognises and respects access to services of general economic interest as provided for in national laws and practices, in accordance with the Constitution, in order to promote the social and territorial cohesion of the Union.

ARTICLE II-97 *Environmental protection*
A high level of environmental protection and the improvement of the quality of the environment must be integrated into the policies of the Union and ensured in accordance with the principle of sustainable development.

ARTICLE II-98 *Consumer protection*
Union policies shall ensure a high level of consumer protection.

TITLE V

CITIZENS' RIGHTS

ARTICLE II-99 *Right to vote and to stand as a candidate at elections to the European Parliament*
1.   Every citizen of the Union has the right to vote and to stand as a candidate at elections to the European Parliament in the Member State in which he or she resides, under the same conditions as nationals of that State.

2.   Members of the European Parliament shall be elected by direct universal suffrage in a free and secret ballot.

ARTICLE II-100 *Right to vote and to stand as a candidate at municipal elections*
Every citizen of the Union has the right to vote and to stand as a candidate at municipal elections in the Member State in which he or she resides under the same conditions as nationals of that State.

ARTICLE II-101 *Right to good administration*
1.   Every person has the right to have his or her affairs handled impartially, fairly and within a reasonable time by the institutions, bodies, offices and agencies of the Union.

2.   This right includes:
(a)   the right of every person to be heard, before any individual measure which would affect him or her adversely is taken;
(b)   the right of every person to have access to his or her file, while respecting the legitimate interests of confidentiality and of professional and business secrecy;
(c)   the obligation of the administration to give reasons for its decisions.

3.   Every person has the right to have the Union make good any damage caused by its institutions or by its servants in the performance of their duties, in accordance with the general principles common to the laws of the Member States.

4.   Every person may write to the institutions of the Union in one of the languages of the Constitution and must have an answer in the same language.

ARTICLE II-102 *Right of access to documents*
Any citizen of the Union, and any natural or legal person residing or having its registered office in a Member State, has a right of access to documents of the institutions, bodies, offices and agencies of the Union, whatever their medium.

ARTICLE II-103 *European Ombudsman*
Any citizen of the Union and any natural or legal person residing or having its registered office in a Member State has the right to refer to the European Ombudsman cases of maladministration in the activities of the institutions, bodies, offices or agencies of the Union, with the exception of the Court of Justice of the European Union acting in its judicial role.

ARTICLE II-104 *Right to petition*
Any citizen of the Union and any natural or legal person residing or having its registered office in a Member State has the right to petition the European Parliament.

ARTICLE II-105 *Freedom of movement and of residence*
1.   Every citizen of the Union has the right to move and reside freely within the territory of the Member States.

2.   Freedom of movement and residence may be granted, in accordance with the Constitution, to nationals of third countries legally resident in the territory of a Member State.

ARTICLE II-106 *Diplomatic and consular protection*
Every citizen of the Union shall, in the territory of a third country in which the Member State of which he or she is a national is not represented, be entitled to protection by the diplomatic or consular authorities of any Member State, on the same conditions as the nationals of that Member State.

TITLE VI

JUSTICE

ARTICLE II-107 *Right to an effective remedy and to a fair trial*

Everyone whose rights and freedoms guaranteed by the law of the Union are violated has the right to an effective remedy before a tribunal in compliance with the conditions laid down in this Article.

Everyone is entitled to a fair and public hearing within a reasonable time by an independent and impartial tribunal previously established by law. Everyone shall have the possibility of being advised, defended and represented.

Legal aid shall be made available to those who lack sufficient resources insofar as such aid is necessary to ensure effective access to justice.

ARTICLE II-108 *Presumption of innocence and right of defence*

1.   Everyone who has been charged shall be presumed innocent until proved guilty according to law.

2.   Respect for the rights of the defence of anyone who has been charged shall be guaranteed.

ARTICLE II-109 *Principles of legality and proportionality of criminal offences and penalties*

1.   No one shall be held guilty of any criminal offence on account of any act or omission which did not constitute a criminal offence under national law or international law at the time when it was committed. Nor shall a heavier penalty be imposed than that which was applicable at the time the criminal offence was committed. If, subsequent to the commission of a criminal offence, the law provides for a lighter penalty, that penalty shall be applicable.

2.   This Article shall not prejudice the trial and punishment of any person for any act or omission which, at the time when it was committed, was criminal according to the general principles recognised by the community of nations.

3.   The severity of penalties must not be disproportionate to the criminal offence.

ARTICLE II-110 *Right not to be tried or punished twice in criminal proceedings for the same criminal offence*

No one shall be liable to be tried or punished again in criminal proceedings for an offence for which he or she has already been finally acquitted or convicted within the Union in accordance with the law.

TITLE VII

GENERAL PROVISIONS GOVERNING THE INTERPRETATION AND APPLICATION OF THE CHARTER

ARTICLE II-111 *Field of application*

1.   The provisions of this Charter are addressed to the institutions, bodies, offices and agencies of the Union with due regard for the principle of subsidiarity and to the Member States only when they are implementing Union law. They shall therefore respect the rights, observe the principles and promote the application thereof in accordance with their respective powers and respecting the limits of the powers of the Union as conferred on it in the other Parts of the Constitution.

2.   This Charter does not extend the field of application of Union law beyond the powers of the Union or establish any new power or task for the Union, or modify powers and tasks defined in the other Parts of the Constitution.

ARTICLE II-112 *Scope and interpretation of rights and principles*

1.   Any limitation on the exercise of the rights and freedoms recognised by this Charter must be provided for by law and respect the essence of those rights and freedoms. Subject to the principle of proportionality, limitations may be made only if they are necessary and genuinely meet objectives of general interest recognised by the Union or the need to protect the rights and freedoms of others.

2.   Rights recognised by this Charter for which provision is made in other Parts of the Constitution shall be exercised under the conditions and within the limits defined by these relevant Parts.

3.   Insofar as this Charter contains rights which correspond to rights guaranteed by the Convention for the Protection of Human Rights and Fundamental Freedoms, the meaning and scope of those rights shall be the same as those laid down by the said Convention. This provision shall not prevent Union law providing more extensive protection.

4.   Insofar as this Charter recognises fundamental rights as they result from the constitutional traditions common to the Member States, those rights shall be interpreted in harmony with those traditions.

5.   The provisions of this Charter which contain principles may be implemented by legislative and executive acts taken by institutions, bodies, offices and agencies of the Union, and by acts of Member States when they are implementing Union law, in the exercise of their respective powers. They shall be judicially cognisable only in the interpretation of such acts and in the ruling on their legality.

6.   Full account shall be taken of national laws and practices as specified in this Charter.

7.   The explanations drawn up as a way of providing guidance in the interpretation of the Charter of Fundamental Rights shall be given due regard by the courts of the Union and of the Member States.

ARTICLE II-113 *Level of protection*

Nothing in this Charter shall be interpreted as restricting or adversely affecting human rights and fundamental freedoms as recognised, in their respective fields of application, by Union law and international law and by international agreements to which the Union or all the Member States are party, including the European Convention for the Protection of Human Rights and Fundamental Freedoms, and by the Member States' constitutions.

ARTICLE II-114 *Prohibition of abuse of rights*

Nothing in this Charter shall be interpreted as implying any right to engage in any activity or to perform any act aimed at the destruction of any of the rights and freedoms recognised in this Charter or at their limitation to a greater extent than is provided for herein.

PART III

THE POLICIES AND FUNCTIONING OF THE UNION

TITLE I

PROVISIONS OF GENERAL APPLICATION

ARTICLE III-115 (*new*)
The Union shall ensure consistency between the policies and activities referred to in this Part, taking all of its objectives into account and in accordance with the principle of conferral of powers.

ARTICLE III-116 (*ex Article 3(2)TEC*)
In all the activities referred to in this Part, the Union shall aim to eliminate inequalities, and to promote equality, between women and men.

ARTICLE III-117 (*new*)
In defining and implementing the policies and actions referred to in this Part, the Union shall take into account requirements linked to the promotion of a high level of employment, the guarantee of adequate social protection, the fight against social exclusion, and a high level of education, training and protection of human health.

ARTICLE III-118 (*new*)
In defining and implementing the policies and activities referred to in this Part, the Union shall aim to combat discrimination based on sex, racial or ethnic origin, religion or belief, disability, age or sexual orientation.

ARTICLE III-119 (*ex Article 6 TEC*)
Environmental protection requirements must be integrated into the definition and implementation of the policies and activities referred to in this Part, in particular with a view to promoting sustainable development.

ARTICLE III-120 (*ex Article 153(2) TEC*)
Consumer protection requirements shall be taken into account in defining and implementing other Union policies and activities.

ARTICLE III-121 (*new*)
In formulating and implementing the Union's agriculture, fisheries, transport, internal market, research and technological development and space policies, the Union and the Member States shall, since animals are sentient beings, pay full regard to the requirements of animal welfare, while respecting the legislative or administrative provisions and customs of Member States relating in particular to religious rites, cultural traditions and regional heritage.

ARTICLE III-122 (*ex Article 16 TEC*)
Without prejudice to Articles I-5, III-166, III-167 and III-238, and given the place occupied by services of general economic interest as services to which all in the Union attribute value as well as their role in promoting its social and territorial cohesion, the Union and the Member States, each within their respective competences and within the scope of application of the Constitution, shall take care that such services operate on the basis of principles and conditions, in particular economic and financial conditions, which enable them to fulfil their missions. European laws shall establish these principles and set these conditions without prejudice to the competence of Member States, in compliance with the Constitution, to provide, to commission and to fund such services.

TITLE II

NON-DISCRIMINATION AND CITIZENSHIP

ARTICLE III-123 (*ex Article 12 TEC*)
European laws or framework laws may lay down rules to prohibit discrimination on grounds of nationality as referred to in Article I-4(2).

ARTICLE III-124 (*ex Article 13 TEC*)
1.   Without prejudice to the other provisions of the Constitution and within the limits of the powers assigned by it to the Union, a European law or framework law of the Council may establish the measures needed to combat discrimination based on sex, racial or ethnic origin, religion or belief, disability, age or sexual orientation. The Council shall act unanimously after obtaining the consent of the European Parliament.

2.   By way of derogation from paragraph 1, European laws or framework laws may establish basic principles for Union incentive measures and define such measures, to support action taken by Member States in order to contribute to the achievement of the objectives referred to in paragraph 1, excluding any harmonisation of their laws and regulations.

ARTICLE III-125 (*ex Article 18 TEC*)
1.   If action by the Union should prove necessary to facilitate the exercise of the right, referred to in Article I-10(2)(a), of every citizen of the Union to move and reside freely and the Constitution has not provided the necessary powers, European laws or framework laws may establish measures for that purpose.

2.   For the same purposes as those referred to in paragraph 1 and if the Constitution has not provided the necessary powers, a European law or framework law of the Council may establish measures concerning passports, identity cards, residence permits or any other such document and measures concerning social security or social protection. The Council shall act unanimously after consulting the European Parliament.

ARTICLE III-126 (*ex Article 19 TEC*)
A European law or framework law of the Council shall determine the detailed arrangements for exercising the right, referred to in Article I-10(2)(b), for every citizen of the Union to vote and to stand as a candidate in municipal elections and elections to the European Parliament in his or her Member State of residence without being a national of that State. The Council shall act unanimously after consulting the European Parliament. These arrangements may provide for derogations where warranted by problems specific to a Member State.
The right to vote and to stand as a candidate in elections to the European Parliament shall be exercised without prejudice to Article III-330(1) and the measures adopted for its implementation.

ARTICLE III-127 (*ex Article 20 TEC*)
Member States shall adopt the necessary provisions to secure diplomatic and consular protection of citizens of the Union in third countries, as referred to in Article I-10(2)(c).
Member States shall commence the international negotiations required to secure this protection.
A European law of the Council may establish the measures necessary to facilitate such protection. The Council shall act after consulting the European Parliament.

ARTICLE III-128 (*ex Article 21 TEC*)
The languages in which every citizen of the Union has the right to address the institutions or bodies under Article I-10(2)(d), and to have an answer, are those listed in Article IV-448(1). The institutions and bodies referred to in Article I-10(2)(d) are those listed in Articles I-19(1), second subparagraph, I-30, I-31 and I-32 and also the European Ombudsman.

ARTICLE III-129 (*ex Article 22 TEC*)
The Commission shall report to the European Parliament, to the Council and to the Economic and Social Committee every three years on the application of Article I-10 and of this Title. This report shall take account of the development of the Union.
On the basis of this report, and without prejudice to the other provisions of the Constitution, a European law or framework law of the Council may add to the rights laid down in Article I-10. The Council shall act unanimously after obtaining the consent of the European Parliament. The law or framework law concerned shall not enter into force until it is approved by the Member States in accordance with their respective constitutional requirements.

TITLE III

INTERNAL POLICIES AND ACTION

CHAPTER I

INTERNAL MARKET

SECTION 1

ESTABLISHMENT AND FUNCTIONING OF THE INTERNAL MARKET

ARTICLE III-130 (*ex Articles 14 and 15 TEC*)
1.   The Union shall adopt measures with the aim of establishing or ensuring the functioning of the internal market, in accordance with the relevant provisions of the Constitution.

2.   The internal market shall comprise an area without internal frontiers in which the free movement of persons, services, goods and capital is ensured in accordance with the Constitution.

3.   The Council, on a proposal from the Commission, shall adopt European regulations and decisions determining the guidelines and conditions necessary to ensure balanced progress in all the sectors concerned.

4.   When drawing up its proposals for achieving the objectives set out in paragraphs 1 and 2, the Commission shall take into account the extent of the effort that certain economies showing differences in development will have to sustain for the establishment of the internal market and it may propose appropriate measures.
If these measures take the form of derogations, they must be of a temporary nature and must cause the least possible disturbance to the functioning of the internal market.   [*BMDF Note: The UK has an opt-out from the provisions of this Article in relation to border controls, under Protocol no. 18, Article 1.*]

ARTICLE III-131 (*ex Article 297 TEC*)
Member States shall consult each other with a view to taking together the steps needed to prevent the functioning of the internal market being affected by measures which a Member State may be called upon to take in the event of serious internal disturbances affecting the maintenance of law and order, in the event of war, serious international tension constituting a threat of war, or in order to carry out obligations it has accepted for the purpose of maintaining peace and international security.

ARTICLE III-132 (*ex Article 298 TEC*)
If measures taken in the circumstances referred to in Articles III-131 and III-436 have the effect of distorting the conditions of competition in the internal market, the Commission shall, together with the Member State concerned, examine how these measures can be adjusted to the rules laid down in the Constitution.
By way of derogation from the procedure laid down in Articles III-360 and III-361, the Commission or any Member State may bring the matter directly before the Court of Justice if the Commission or Member State considers that another Member State is making improper use of the powers provided for in Articles III-131 and III-436. The Court of Justice shall give its ruling in camera.

SECTION 2

FREE MOVEMENT OF PERSONS AND SERVICES

Subsection 1

Workers

ARTICLE III-133 (*ex Article 39 TEC*)
1.   Workers shall have the right to move freely within the Union.

2.   Any discrimination based on nationality between workers of the Member States as regards employment, remuneration and other conditions of work and employment shall be prohibited.

3.   Workers shall have the right, subject to limitations justified on grounds of public policy, public security or public health:

(a)   to accept offers of employment actually made;

(b)   to move freely within the territory of Member States for this purpose;

(c)   to stay in a Member State for the purpose of employment in accordance with the provisions governing the employment of nationals of that State laid down by law, regulation or administrative action;

(d)   to remain in the territory of a Member State after having been employed in that State, subject to conditions which shall be embodied in European regulations adopted by the Commission.

4.   This Article shall not apply to employment in the public service.

ARTICLE III-134 (*ex Article 40 TEC*)

European laws or framework laws shall establish the measures needed to bring about freedom of movement for workers, as defined in Article III-133. They shall be adopted after consultation of the Economic and Social Committee.

Such European laws or framework laws shall aim, in particular, to:

(a)   ensure close co-operation between national employment services;

(b)   abolish those administrative procedures and practices and those qualifying periods in respect of eligibility for available employment, whether resulting from national legislation or from agreements previously concluded between Member States, the maintenance of which would form an obstacle to liberalisation of the movement of workers;

(c)   abolish all such qualifying periods and other restrictions provided for either under national legislation or under agreements previously concluded between Member States as impose on workers of other Member States conditions regarding the free choice of employment other than those imposed on workers of the State concerned;

(d)   set up appropriate machinery to bring offers of employment into touch with applications for employment and to facilitate the achievement of a balance between supply and demand in the employment market in such a way as to avoid serious threats to the standard of living and level of employment in the various regions and industries.

ARTICLE III-135 (*ex Article 41 TEC*)

Member States shall, within the framework of a joint programme, encourage the exchange of young workers.

ARTICLE III-136 (*ex Article 42 TEC*)

1.   In the field of social security, European laws or framework laws shall establish such measures as are necessary to bring about freedom of movement for workers by making arrangements to secure for employed and self-employed migrant workers and their dependants:

(a)   aggregation, for the purpose of acquiring and retaining the right to benefit and of calculating the amount of benefit, of all periods taken into account under the laws of the different countries;

(b)   payment of benefits to persons resident in the territories of Member States.

2.   Where a member of the Council considers that a draft European law or framework law referred to in paragraph 1 would affect fundamental aspects of its social security system, including its scope, cost or financial structure, or would affect the financial balance of that system, it may request that the matter be referred to the European Council. In that case, the procedure referred to in Article III-396 shall be suspended. After discussion, the European Council shall, within four months of this suspension, either:

(a)   refer the draft back to the Council, which shall terminate the suspension of the procedure referred to in Article III-396, or

(b)   request the Commission to submit a new proposal; in that case, the act originally proposed shall be deemed not to have been adopted.

Subsection 2

Freedom of establishment

ARTICLE III-137 (*ex Article 43 TEC*)

Within the framework of this Subsection, restrictions on the freedom of establishment of nationals of a Member State in the territory of another Member State shall be prohibited. Such prohibition shall also apply to restrictions on the setting-up of agencies, branches or subsidiaries by nationals of any Member State established in the territory of any Member State.

Nationals of a Member State shall have the right, in the territory of another Member State, to take up and pursue activities as self-employed persons and to set up and manage undertakings, in particular companies or firms within the meaning of the second paragraph of Article III-142, under the conditions laid down for its own nationals by the law of the Member State where such establishment is effected, subject to Section 4 relating to capital and payments.

ARTICLE III-138 (*ex Article 44 TEC*)
1.   European framework laws shall establish measures to attain freedom of establishment as regards a particular activity. They shall be adopted after consultation of the Economic and Social Committee.

2.   The European Parliament, the Council and the Commission shall carry out the duties devolving upon them under paragraph 1, in particular:
(a)   by according, as a general rule, priority treatment to activities where freedom of establishment makes a particularly valuable contribution to the development of production and trade;
(b)   by ensuring close co-operation between the competent authorities in the Member States in order to ascertain the particular situation within the Union of the various activities concerned;
(c)   by abolishing those administrative procedures and practices, whether resulting from national legislation or from agreements previously concluded between Member States, the maintenance of which would form an obstacle to freedom of establishment;
(d)   by ensuring that workers from one Member State employed in the territory of another Member State may remain in that territory for the purpose of taking up activities therein as self-employed persons, where they satisfy the conditions which they would be required to satisfy if they were entering that State at the time when they intended to take up such activities;
(e)   by enabling a national of one Member State to acquire and use land and buildings situated in the territory of another Member State, insofar as this does not conflict with the principles laid down in Article III-227(2);
(f)   by effecting the progressive abolition of restrictions on freedom of establishment in every branch of activity under consideration, both as regards the conditions for setting up agencies, branches or subsidiaries in the territory of a Member State and as regards the conditions governing the entry of personnel belonging to the main establishment into managerial or supervisory posts in such agencies, branches or subsidiaries;
(g)   by co-ordinating to the necessary extent the safeguards which, for the protection of the interests of members and others, are required by Member States of companies or firms within the meaning of the second paragraph of Article III-142 with a view to making such safeguards equivalent throughout the Union;
(h)   by satisfying themselves that the conditions of establishment are not distorted by aids granted by Member States.

ARTICLE III-139 (*ex Article 45 TEC*)
This Subsection shall not apply, so far as any given Member State is concerned, to activities which in that State are connected, even occasionally, with the exercise of official authority.
European laws or framework laws may exclude certain activities from application of this Subsection.

ARTICLE III-140 (*ex Article 46 TEC*)
1.   This Subsection and measures adopted in pursuance thereof shall not prejudice the applicability of provisions laid down by law, regulation or administrative action in Member States providing for special treatment for foreign nationals on grounds of public policy, public security or public health.

2.   European framework laws shall co-ordinate the national provisions referred to in paragraph 1.

ARTICLE III-141 (*ex Article 47 TEC*)
1.   European framework laws shall make it easier for persons to take up and pursue activities as self-employed persons. They shall cover:
(a)   the mutual recognition of diplomas, certificates and other evidence of formal qualifications;
(b)   the co-ordination of the provisions laid down by law, regulation or administrative action in Member States concerning the taking-up and pursuit of activities as self-employed persons.

2.   In the case of the medical and allied and pharmaceutical professions, the progressive abolition of restrictions shall be dependent upon co-ordination of the conditions for the exercise of such professions in the various Member States.

ARTICLE III-142 (*ex Article 48 TEC*)
Companies or firms formed in accordance with the law of a Member State and having their registered office, central administration or principal place of business within the Union shall, for the purposes of this Subsection, be treated in the same way as natural persons who are nationals of Member States.

"Companies or firms" means companies or firms constituted under civil or commercial law, including co-operative societies, and other legal persons governed by public or private law, save for those which are non-profit-making.

ARTICLE III-143 (*ex Article 294 TEC*)
Member States shall accord nationals of the other Member States the same treatment as their own nationals as regards participation in the capital of companies or firms within the meaning of the second paragraph of Article III-142, without prejudice to the application of the other provisions of the Constitution.

Subsection 3

Freedom to provide services

ARTICLE III-144 (*ex Article 49 TEC*)
Within the framework of this Subsection, restrictions on freedom to provide services within the Union shall be prohibited in respect of nationals of Member States who are established in a Member State other than that of the person for whom the services are intended.
European laws or framework laws may extend this Subsection to service providers who are nationals of a third State and who are established within the Union.

ARTICLE III-145 (*ex Article 50 TEC*)
Services shall be considered to be "services" for the purposes of the Constitution where they are normally provided for remuneration, insofar as they are not governed by the provisions relating to freedom of movement for persons, goods and capital.
"Services" shall in particular include:
(a)   activities of an industrial character;
(b)   activities of a commercial character;
(c)   activities of craftsmen;
(d)   activities of the professions.
Without prejudice to Subsection 2 relating to freedom of establishment, the person providing a service may, in order to do so, temporarily pursue his or her activity in the Member State where the service is provided, under the same conditions as are imposed by that State on its own nationals.

ARTICLE III-146 (*ex Article 51 TEC*)
1.   Freedom to provide services in the field of transport shall be governed by Section 7 of Chapter III relating to transport.

2.   The liberalisation of banking and insurance services connected with movements of capital shall be effected in step with the liberalisation of movement of capital.

ARTICLE III-147 (*ex Article 52 TEC*)
1.   European framework laws shall establish measures to achieve the liberalisation of a specific service. They shall be adopted after consultation of the Economic and Social Committee.

2.   European framework laws referred to in paragraph 1 shall as a general rule give priority to those services which directly affect production costs or the liberalisation of which helps to promote trade in goods.

ARTICLE III-148 (*ex Article 53 TEC*)
The Member States shall endeavour to undertake liberalisation of services beyond the extent required by the European framework laws adopted pursuant to Article III-147(1), if their general economic situation and the situation of the economic sector concerned so permit.
To this end, the Commission shall make recommendations to the Member States concerned.

ARTICLE III-149 (*ex Article 54 TEC*)
As long as restrictions on freedom to provide services have not been abolished, the Member States shall apply such restrictions without distinction on grounds of nationality or of residence to all persons providing services within the meaning of the first paragraph of Article III-144.

ARTICLE III-150 (*ex Article 55 TEC*)
Articles III-139 to III-142 shall apply to the matters covered by this Subsection.

SECTION 3

FREE MOVEMENT OF GOODS

Subsection 1

Customs union

ARTICLE III-151 (*ex Articles 23/24/25/26/27 TEC*)

1.   The Union shall comprise a customs union which shall cover all trade in goods and which shall involve the prohibition between Member States of customs duties on imports and exports and of all charges having equivalent effect, and the adoption of a common customs tariff in their relations with third countries.

2.   Paragraph 4 and Subsection 3 on the prohibition of quantitative restrictions shall apply to products originating in Member States and to products coming from third countries which are in free circulation in Member States.

3.   Products coming from a third country shall be considered to be in free circulation in a Member State if the import formalities have been complied with and any customs duties or charges having equivalent effect which are payable have been levied in that Member State, and if they have not benefited from a total or partial drawback of such duties or charges.

4.   Customs duties on imports and exports and charges having equivalent effect shall be prohibited between Member States. This prohibition shall also apply to customs duties of a fiscal nature.

5.   The Council, on a proposal from the Commission, shall adopt the European regulations and decisions fixing Common Customs Tariff duties.

6.   In carrying out the tasks entrusted to it under this Article the Commission shall be guided by:
(a)   the need to promote trade between Member States and third countries;
(b)   developments in conditions of competition within the Union insofar as they lead to an improvement in the competitive capacity of undertakings;
(c)   the requirements of the Union as regards the supply of raw materials and semi-finished goods; in this connection the Commission shall take care to avoid distorting conditions of competition between Member States in respect of finished goods;
(d)   the need to avoid serious disturbances in the economies of Member States and to ensure rational development of production and an expansion of consumption within the Union.

Subsection 2

Customs co-operation

ARTICLE III-152 (*ex Article 135 TEC*)
Within the scope of application of the Constitution, European laws or framework laws shall establish measures in order to strengthen customs co-operation between Member States and between them and the Commission.

Subsection 3

Prohibition of quantitative restrictions

ARTICLE III-153 (*ex Articles 28 and 29 TEC*)
Quantitative restrictions on imports and exports and all measures having equivalent effect shall be prohibited between Member States.

ARTICLE III-154 (*ex Article 30 TEC*)
Article III-153 shall not preclude prohibitions or restrictions on imports, exports or goods in transit justified on grounds of public morality, public policy or public security; the protection of health and life of humans, animals or plants; the protection of national treasures possessing artistic, historic or archaeological value; or the protection of industrial and commercial property. Such prohibitions or restrictions shall not, however, constitute a means of arbitrary discrimination or a disguised restriction on trade between Member States.

ARTICLE III-155 (*ex Article 31 TEC*)
1.   Member States shall adjust any State monopolies of a commercial character so as to ensure that no discrimination regarding the conditions under which goods are procured and marketed exists between nationals of Member States.
This Article shall apply to any body through which a Member State, in law or in fact, either directly or indirectly supervises, determines or appreciably influences imports or exports between Member States. It shall likewise apply to monopolies delegated by the State to others.

2.   Member States shall refrain from introducing any new measure which is contrary to the principles laid down in paragraph 1 or which restricts the scope of the Articles dealing with the prohibition of customs duties and quantitative restrictions between Member States.

3.   If a State monopoly of a commercial character has rules which are designed to make it easier to dispose of agricultural products or obtain for them the best return, steps should be taken in applying this Article to ensure equivalent safeguards for the employment and standard of living of the producers concerned.

SECTION 4

CAPITAL AND PAYMENTS

ARTICLE III-156 (*ex Article 56 TEC*)
Within the framework of this Section, restrictions both on the movement of capital and on payments between Member States and between Member States and third countries shall be prohibited.

ARTICLE III-157 (*ex Article 57 TEC*)
1.   Article III-156 shall be without prejudice to the application to third countries of any restrictions which existed on 31 December 1993 under national or Union law adopted in respect of the movement of capital to or from third countries involving direct investment – including investment in real estate, establishment, the provision of financial services or the admission of securities to capital markets. With regard to restrictions which exist under national law in Estonia and Hungary, the date in question shall be 31 December 1999.

2.   European laws or framework laws shall enact measures on the movement of capital to or from third countries involving direct investment – including investment in real estate, establishment, the provision of financial services or the admission of securities to capital markets.
The European Parliament and the Council shall endeavour to achieve the objective of free movement of capital between Member States and third countries to the greatest extent possible and without prejudice to other provisions of the Constitution.

3.   Notwithstanding paragraph 2, only a European law or framework law of the Council may enact measures which constitute a step backwards in Union law as regards the liberalisation of the movement of capital to or from third countries. The Council shall act unanimously after consulting the European Parliament.

ARTICLE III-158 (*ex Article 58 TEC and new provision*)
1.   Article III-156 shall be without prejudice to the right of Member States:
(a)   to apply the relevant provisions of their tax law which distinguish between taxpayers who are not in the same situation with regard to their place of residence or with regard to the place where their capital is invested;
(b)   to take all requisite measures to prevent infringements of national provisions laid down by law or regulation, in particular in the field of taxation and the prudential supervision of financial institutions, or to lay down procedures for the declaration of capital movements for purposes of administrative or statistical information, or to take measures which are justified on grounds of public policy or public security.

2.   This Section shall be without prejudice to the applicability of restrictions on the right of establishment which are compatible with the Constitution.

3.   The measures and procedures referred to in paragraphs 1 and 2 shall not constitute a means of arbitrary discrimination or a disguised restriction on the free movement of capital and payments as defined in Article III-156.

4.	In the absence of a European law or framework law provided for in Article III-157(3), the Commission or, in the absence of a European decision of the Commission within three months from the request of the Member State concerned, the Council, may adopt a European decision stating that restrictive tax measures adopted by a Member State concerning one or more third countries are to be considered compatible with the Constitution insofar as they are justified by one of the objectives of the Union and compatible with the proper functioning of the internal market. The Council shall act unanimously on application by a Member State. (*new provision*)

ARTICLE III-159 (*ex Article 59 TEC*)

Where, in exceptional circumstances, movements of capital to or from third countries cause, or threaten to cause, serious difficulties for the functioning of economic and monetary union, the Council, on a proposal from the Commission, may adopt European regulations or decisions introducing safeguard measures with regard to third countries for a period not exceeding six months if such measures are strictly necessary. It shall act after consulting the European Central Bank.

ARTICLE III-160 (*new*)

Where necessary to achieve the objectives set out in Article III-257, as regards preventing and combating terrorism and related activities, European laws shall define a framework for administrative measures with regard to capital movements and payments, such as the freezing of funds, financial assets or economic gains belonging to, or owned or held by, natural or legal persons, groups or non-State entities.

The Council, on a proposal from the Commission, shall adopt European regulations or European decisions in order to implement the European laws referred to in the first paragraph.

The acts referred to in this Article shall include necessary provisions on legal safeguards.

SECTION 5

RULES ON COMPETITION

Subsection 1

Rules applying to undertakings

ARTICLE III-161 (*ex Article 81 TEC*)

1.	The following shall be prohibited as incompatible with the internal market: all agreements between undertakings, decisions by associations of undertakings and concerted practices which may affect trade between Member States and which have as their object or effect the prevention, restriction or distortion of competition within the internal market, and in particular those which:
(a)	directly or indirectly fix purchase or selling prices or any other trading conditions;
(b)	limit or control production, markets, technical development, or investment;
(c)	share markets or sources of supply;
(d)	apply dissimilar conditions to equivalent transactions with other trading parties, thereby placing them at a competitive disadvantage;
(e)	make the conclusion of contracts subject to acceptance by the other parties of supplementary obligations which, by their nature or according to commercial usage, have no connection with the subject of such contracts.

2.	Any agreements or decisions prohibited pursuant to this Article shall be automatically void.

3.	Paragraph 1 may, however, be declared inapplicable in the case of:
–	any agreement or category of agreements between undertakings,
–	any decision or category of decisions by associations of undertakings,
–	any concerted practice or category of concerted practices,
which contributes to improving the production or distribution of goods or to promoting technical or economic progress, while allowing consumers a fair share of the resulting benefit, and which does not:
(a)	impose on the undertakings concerned restrictions which are not indispensable to the attainment of these objectives;
(b)	afford such undertakings the possibility of eliminating competition in respect of a substantial part of the products in question.

ARTICLE III-162 (*ex Article 82 TEC*)

Any abuse by one or more undertakings of a dominant position within the internal market or in a substantial part of it shall be prohibited as incompatible with the internal market insofar as it may affect trade between Member States.

Such abuse may, in particular, consist in:

(a)   directly or indirectly imposing unfair purchase or selling prices or other unfair trading conditions;

(b)   limiting production, markets or technical development to the prejudice of consumers;

(c)   applying dissimilar conditions to equivalent transactions with other trading parties, thereby placing them at a competitive disadvantage;

(d)   making the conclusion of contracts subject to acceptance by the other parties of supplementary obligations which, by their nature or according to commercial usage, have no connection with the subject of such contracts.

ARTICLE III-163 (*ex Article 83 TEC*)

The Council, on a proposal from the Commission, shall adopt the European regulations to give effect to the principles set out in Articles III-161 and III-162. It shall act after consulting the European Parliament.

Such regulations shall be designed in particular:

(a)   to ensure compliance with the prohibitions laid down in Article III-161(1) and in Article III-162 by making provision for fines and periodic penalty payments;

(b)   to lay down detailed rules for the application of Article III-161(3), taking into account the need to ensure effective supervision on the one hand, and to simplify administration to the greatest possible extent on the other;

(c)   to define, if need be, in the various branches of the economy, the scope of Articles III-161 and III-162;

(d)   to define the respective functions of the Commission and of the Court of Justice of the European Union in applying the provisions laid down in this paragraph;

(e)   to determine the relationship between Member States' laws and this Subsection as well as the European regulations adopted pursuant to this Article.

ARTICLE III-164 (*ex Article 84 TEC*)

Until the entry into force of the European regulations adopted pursuant to Article III-163, the authorities in Member States shall rule on the admissibility of agreements, decisions and concerted practices and on abuse of a dominant position in the internal market in accordance with their national law and Article III-161, in particular paragraph 3, and Article III-162.

ARTICLE III-165 (*ex Article 85 TEC and new provision*)

1.   Without prejudice to Article III-164, the Commission shall ensure the application of the principles set out in Articles III-161 and III-162. On application by a Member State or on its own initiative, and in co-operation with the competent authorities in the Member States, which shall give it their assistance, the Commission shall investigate cases of suspected infringement of these principles. If it finds that there has been an infringement, it shall propose appropriate measures to bring it to an end.

2.   If the infringement referred to in paragraph 1 is not brought to an end, the Commission shall adopt a reasoned European decision recording the infringement of the principles. The Commission may publish its decision and authorise Member States to take the measures, the conditions and details of which it shall determine, needed to remedy the situation.

3.   The Commission may adopt European regulations relating to the categories of agreement in respect of which the Council has adopted a European regulation pursuant to Article III-163, second paragraph, (b).

ARTICLE III-166 (*ex Article 86 TEC*)

1.   In the case of public undertakings and undertakings to which Member States grant special or exclusive rights, Member States shall neither enact nor maintain in force any measure contrary to the Constitution, in particular Article I-4(2) and Articles III-161 to III-169.

2.   Undertakings entrusted with the operation of services of general economic interest or having the character of an income-producing monopoly shall be subject to the provisions of the Constitution, in particular to the rules on competition, insofar as the application of such provisions does not obstruct the performance, in law or in fact, of the particular tasks assigned to them. The development of trade must not be affected to such an extent as would be contrary to the Union's interests.

3.   The Commission shall ensure the application of this Article and shall, where necessary, adopt appropriate European regulations or decisions.

Subsection 2

Aids granted by Member States

ARTICLE III-167 (*ex Article 87 TEC*)
1.   Save as otherwise provided in the Constitution, any aid granted by a Member State or through State resources in any form whatsoever which distorts or threatens to distort competition by favouring certain undertakings or the production of certain goods shall, insofar as it affects trade between Member States, be incompatible with the internal market.

2.   The following shall be compatible with the internal market:
(a)   aid having a social character, granted to individual consumers, provided that such aid is granted without discrimination related to the origin of the products concerned;
(b)   aid to make good the damage caused by natural disasters or exceptional occurrences;
(c)   aid granted to the economy of certain areas of the Federal Republic of Germany affected by the division of Germany, insofar as such aid is required in order to compensate for the economic disadvantages caused by that division. Five years after the entry into force of the Treaty establishing a Constitution for Europe, the Council, acting on a proposal from the Commission, may adopt a European decision repealing this point.

3.   The following may be considered to be compatible with the internal market:
(a)   aid to promote the economic development of areas where the standard of living is abnormally low or where there is serious underemployment, and of the regions referred to in Article III-424, in view of their structural, economic and social situation;
(b)   aid to promote the execution of an important project of common European interest or to remedy a serious disturbance in the economy of a Member State;
(c)   aid to facilitate the development of certain economic activities or of certain economic areas, where such aid does not adversely affect trading conditions to an extent contrary to the common interest;
(d)   aid to promote culture and heritage conservation where such aid does not affect trading conditions and competition in the Union to an extent that is contrary to the common interest;
(e)   such other categories of aid as may be specified by European regulations or decisions adopted by the Council on a proposal from the Commission.

ARTICLE III-168 (*ex Article 88 TEC*)
1.   The Commission, in co-operation with Member States, shall keep under constant review all systems of aid existing in those States. It shall propose to the latter any appropriate measures required by the progressive development or by the functioning of the internal market.

2.   If, after giving notice to the parties concerned to submit their comments, the Commission finds that aid granted by a Member State or through State resources is not compatible with the internal market having regard to Article III-167, or that such aid is being misused, it shall adopt a European decision requiring the Member State concerned to abolish or alter such aid within a period of time to be determined by the Commission.
If the Member State concerned does not comply with this European decision within the prescribed time, the Commission or any other interested Member State may, in derogation from Articles III-360 and III-361, refer the matter to the Court of Justice of the European Union directly.
On application by a Member State, the Council may adopt unanimously a European decision that aid which that State is granting or intends to grant shall be considered to be compatible with the internal market, in derogation from Article III-167 or from European regulations provided for in Article III-169, if such a decision is justified by exceptional circumstances. If, as regards the aid in question, the Commission has already initiated the procedure provided for in the first subparagraph of this paragraph, the fact that the Member State concerned has made its application to the Council shall have the effect of suspending that procedure until the Council has made its attitude known.
If, however, the Council has not made its attitude known within three months of the said application being made, the Commission shall act.

3.   The Commission shall be informed by the Member States, in sufficient time to enable it to submit its comments, of any plans to grant or alter aid. If it considers that any such plan is not compatible with the internal market having regard to Article III-167, it shall without delay initiate the procedure provided for in paragraph 2 of this Article. The Member State concerned shall not put its proposed measures into effect until this procedure has resulted in a final decision.

4.   The Commission may adopt European regulations relating to the categories of State aid that the Council has, pursuant to Article III-169, determined may be exempted from the procedure provided for by paragraph 3 of this Article.

ARTICLE III-169 (*ex Article 89 TEC*)
The Council, on a proposal from the Commission, may adopt European regulations for the application of Articles III-167 and III-168 and for determining in particular the conditions in which Article III-168(3) shall apply and the categories of aid exempted from the procedure provided for in Article 168(3). It shall act after consulting the European Parliament.

SECTION 6

FISCAL PROVISIONS

ARTICLE III-170 (*ex Articles 90, 91 and 92 TEC*)
1.   No Member State shall impose, directly or indirectly, on the products of other Member States any internal taxation of any kind in excess of that imposed directly or indirectly on similar domestic products. Furthermore, no Member State shall impose on the products of other Member States any internal taxation of such a nature as to afford indirect protection to other products.

2.   Where products are exported by a Member State to the territory of another Member State, any repayment of internal taxation shall not exceed the internal taxation imposed on them whether directly or indirectly.

3.   In the case of charges other than turnover taxes, excise duties and other forms of indirect taxation, remissions and repayments in respect of exports to other Member States may not be granted and countervailing charges in respect of imports from Member States may not be imposed unless the provisions contemplated have been previously approved for a limited period by a European decision adopted by the Council on a proposal from the Commission.

ARTICLE III-171 (*ex Article 93 TEC*)
A European law or framework law of the Council shall establish measures for the harmonisation of legislation concerning turnover taxes, excise duties and other forms of indirect taxation provided that such harmonisation is necessary to ensure the establishment and the functioning of the internal market and to avoid distortion of competition. The Council shall act unanimously after consulting the European Parliament and the Economic and Social Committee.

SECTION 7

COMMON PROVISIONS

ARTICLE III-172 (*ex Article 95 TEC*)
1.   Save where otherwise provided in the Constitution, this Article shall apply for the achievement of the objectives set out in Article III-130. European laws or framework laws shall establish measures for the approximation of the provisions laid down by law, regulation or administrative action in Member States which have as their object the establishment and functioning of the internal market. Such laws shall be adopted after consultation of the Economic and Social Committee.

2.   Paragraph 1 shall not apply to fiscal provisions, to those relating to the free movement of persons or to those relating to the rights and interests of employed persons.

3.   The Commission, in its proposals submitted under paragraph 1 concerning health, safety, environmental protection and consumer protection, shall take as a base a high level of protection, taking account in particular of any new development based on scientific facts. Within their respective powers, the European Parliament and the Council shall also seek to achieve this objective.

4.   If, after the adoption of a harmonisation measure by means of a European law or framework law or by means of a European regulation of the Commission, a Member State deems it necessary to maintain national provisions on grounds of major needs referred to in Article III-154, or relating to the protection of the

environment or the working environment, it shall notify the Commission of these provisions as well as the grounds for maintaining them.

5.   Moreover, without prejudice to paragraph 4, if, after the adoption of a harmonisation measure by means of a European law or framework law or by means of a European regulation of the Commission, a Member State deems it necessary to introduce national provisions based on new scientific evidence relating to the protection of the environment or the working environment on grounds of a problem specific to that Member State arising after the adoption of the harmonisation measure, it shall notify the Commission of the envisaged provisions and the reasons for them.

6.   The Commission shall, within six months of the notifications referred to in paragraphs 4 and 5, adopt a European decision approving or rejecting the national provisions involved after having verified whether or not they are a means of arbitrary discrimination or a disguised restriction on trade between Member States and whether or not they constitute an obstacle to the functioning of the internal market.
In the absence of a decision by the Commission within this period the national provisions referred to in paragraphs 4 and 5 shall be deemed to have been approved.
When justified by the complexity of the matter and in the absence of danger to human health, the Commission may notify the Member State concerned that the period referred to in this paragraph will be extended for a further period of up to six months.

7.   When, pursuant to paragraph 6, a Member State is authorised to maintain or introduce national provisions derogating from a harmonisation measure, the Commission shall immediately examine whether to propose an adaptation to that measure.

8.   When a Member State raises a specific problem on public health in a field which has been the subject of prior harmonisation measures, it shall bring it to the attention of the Commission which shall immediately examine whether to propose appropriate measures.

9.   By way of derogation from the procedure laid down in Articles III-360 and III-361, the Commission and any Member State may bring the matter directly before the Court of Justice of the European Union if it considers that another Member State is making improper use of the powers provided for in this Article.

10.   The harmonisation measures referred to in this Article shall, in appropriate cases, include a safeguard clause authorising the Member States to take, for one or more of the non-economic reasons referred to in Article III-154, provisional measures subject to a Union control procedure.

ARTICLE III-173 (*ex Article 94 TEC*)
Without prejudice to Article III-172, a European framework law of the Council shall establish measures for the approximation of such laws, regulations or administrative provisions of the Member States as directly affect the establishment or functioning of the internal market. The Council shall act unanimously after consulting the European Parliament and the Economic and Social Committee.

ARTICLE III-174 (*ex Article 96 TEC*)
Where the Commission finds that a difference between the provisions laid down by law, regulation or administrative action in Member States is distorting the conditions of competition in the internal market and that the resultant distortion needs to be eliminated, it shall consult the Member States concerned.
If such consultation does not result in agreement, European framework laws shall establish the measures necessary to eliminate the distortion in question. Any other appropriate measures provided for in the Constitution may be adopted.

ARTICLE III-175 (*ex Article 97 TEC*)
1.   Where there is reason to fear that the adoption or amendment of a provision laid down by law, regulation or administrative action of a Member State may cause distortion within the meaning of Article III-174, a Member State desiring to proceed therewith shall consult the Commission. After consulting the Member States, the Commission shall address to the Member States concerned a recommendation on such measures as may be appropriate to avoid the distortion in question.

2.   If a Member State desiring to introduce or amend its own provisions does not comply with the recommendation addressed to it by the Commission, other Member States shall not be required, pursuant to Article III-174, to amend their own provisions in order to eliminate such distortion. If the Member State which has ignored the recommendation of the Commission causes distortion detrimental only to itself, Article III-174 shall not apply.

ARTICLE III-176 (*new*)
In the context of the establishment and functioning of the internal market, European laws or framework laws shall establish measures for the creation of European intellectual property rights to provide uniform intellectual property rights protection throughout the Union and for the setting up of centralised Union-wide authorisation, co-ordination and supervision arrangements.
A European law of the Council shall establish language arrangements for the European intellectual property rights. The Council shall act unanimously after consulting the European Parliament.

CHAPTER II

ECONOMIC AND MONETARY POLICY

ARTICLE III-177 (*ex Article 4 TEC*)
For the purposes set out in Article I-3, the activities of the Member States and the Union shall include, as provided in the Constitution, the adoption of an economic policy which is based on the close co-ordination of Member States' economic policies, on the internal market and on the definition of common objectives, and conducted in accordance with the principle of an open market economy with free competition.
Concurrently with the foregoing, and as provided in the Constitution and in accordance with the procedures set out therein, these activities shall include a single currency, the euro, and the definition and conduct of a single monetary policy and exchange-rate policy, the primary objective of both of which shall be to maintain price stability and, without prejudice to this objective, to support general economic policies in the Union, in accordance with the principle of an open market economy with free competition.
These activities of the Member States and the Union shall entail compliance with the following guiding principles: stable prices, sound public finances and monetary conditions and a stable balance of payments.

SECTION 1

ECONOMIC POLICY

ARTICLE III-178 (*ex Article 98 TEC*)
Member States shall conduct their economic policies in order to contribute to the achievement of the Union's objectives, as defined in Article I-3, and in the context of the broad guidelines referred to in Article III-179(2). The Member States and the Union shall act in accordance with the principle of an open market economy with free competition, favouring an efficient allocation of resources, and in compliance with the principles set out in Article III-177.

ARTICLE III-179 (*ex Article 99 TEC*)
1. Member States shall regard their economic policies as a matter of common concern and shall co-ordinate them within the Council, in accordance with Article III-178.

2. The Council, on a recommendation from the Commission, shall formulate a draft for the broad guidelines of the economic policies of the Member States and of the Union, and shall report its findings to the European Council.
The European Council, on the basis of the report from the Council, shall discuss a conclusion on the broad guidelines of the economic policies of the Member States and of the Union. On the basis of this conclusion, the Council shall adopt a recommendation setting out these broad guidelines. It shall inform the European Parliament of its recommendation. *[BMDF Note: This paragraph does not apply to the United Kingdom, due to its opt-out from the euro, Article III-197(2)]*

3. In order to ensure closer co-ordination of economic policies and sustained convergence of the economic performances of the Member States, the Council, on the basis of reports submitted by the Commission, shall monitor economic developments in each of the Member States and in the Union, as well as the consistency of economic policies with the broad guidelines referred to in paragraph 2, and shall regularly carry out an overall assessment.
For the purpose of this multilateral surveillance, Member States shall forward information to the Commission on important measures taken by them in the field of their economic policy and such other information as they deem necessary.

4.   Where it is established, under the procedure referred to in paragraph 3, that the economic policies of a Member State are not consistent with the broad guidelines referred to in paragraph 2 or that they risk jeopardising the proper functioning of economic and monetary union, the Commission may address a warning to the Member State concerned. The Council, on a recommendation from the Commission, may address the necessary recommendations to the Member State concerned. The Council, on a proposal from the Commission, may decide to make its recommendations public.

Within the scope of this paragraph, the Council shall act without taking into account the vote of the member of the Council representing the Member State concerned.

A qualified majority shall be defined as at least 55% of the other members of the Council, representing Member States comprising at least 65% of the population of the participating Member States.

A blocking minority must include at least the minimum number of these other Council members representing more than 35% of the population of the participating Member States, plus one member, failing which the qualified majority shall be deemed attained.

[BMDF Note: The voting rights of the United Kingdom are suspended concerning the provisions of this paragraph, due to the UK's opt-out from the euro, Article III-197(4). The final two sub-paragraphs come into force on 1 November 2009, under the terms of Protocol no. 34, Article 2.]

5.   The President of the Council and the Commission shall report to the European Parliament on the results of multilateral surveillance. The President of the Council may be invited to appear before the competent committee of the European Parliament if the Council has made its recommendations public.

6.   European laws may lay down detailed rules for the multilateral surveillance procedure referred to in paragraphs 3 and 4.

ARTICLE III-180 (*ex Article 100 TEC*)
1.   Without prejudice to any other procedures provided for in the Constitution, the Council, on a proposal from the Commission, may adopt a European decision laying down measures appropriate to the economic situation, in particular if severe difficulties arise in the supply of certain products.

2.   Where a Member State is in difficulties or is seriously threatened with severe difficulties caused by natural disasters or exceptional occurrences beyond its control, the Council, on a proposal from the Commission, may adopt a European decision granting, under certain conditions, Union financial assistance to the Member State concerned. The President of the Council shall inform the European Parliament of the decision adopted.

ARTICLE III-181 (*ex Article 101 TEC*)
1.   Overdraft facilities or any other type of credit facility with the European Central Bank or with the central banks of the Member States (hereinafter referred to as "national central banks") in favour of Union institutions, bodies, offices or agencies, central governments, regional, local or other public authorities, other bodies governed by public law, or public undertakings of Member States shall be prohibited, as shall the purchase directly from them by the European Central Bank or national central banks of debt instruments.

2.   Paragraph 1 shall not apply to publicly owned credit institutions which, in the context of the supply of reserves by central banks, shall be given the same treatment by national central banks and the European Central Bank as private credit institutions.

ARTICLE III-182 (*ex Article 102 TEC*)
Any measure or provision, not based on prudential considerations, establishing privileged access by Union institutions, bodies, offices or agencies, central governments, regional, local or other public authorities, other bodies governed by public law, or public undertakings of Member States to financial institutions shall be prohibited.

ARTICLE III-183 (*ex Article 103 TEC*)
1.   The Union shall not be liable for or assume the commitments of central governments, regional, local or other public authorities, other bodies governed by public law, or public undertakings of any Member State, without prejudice to mutual financial guarantees for the joint execution of a specific project. A Member State shall not be liable for or assume the commitments of central governments, regional, local or other public authorities, other bodies governed by public law, or public undertakings of another Member State, without prejudice to mutual financial guarantees for the joint execution of a specific project.

2.   The Council, on a proposal from the Commission, may adopt European regulations or decisions specifying definitions for the application of the prohibitions laid down in Articles III-181 and III-182 and in this Article. It shall act after consulting the European Parliament.

ARTICLE III-184 (*ex Article 104 TEC*)

1.   Member States shall avoid excessive government deficits.

2.   The Commission shall monitor the development of the budgetary situation and of the stock of government debt in the Member States in order to identify gross errors. In particular it shall examine compliance with budgetary discipline on the basis of the following two criteria:

(a)   whether the ratio of the planned or actual government deficit to gross domestic product exceeds a reference value, unless:

(i)   either the ratio has declined substantially and continuously and reached a level that comes close to the reference value, or

(ii)   alternatively, the excess over the reference value is only exceptional and temporary and the ratio remains close to the reference value;

(b)   whether the ratio of government debt to gross domestic product exceeds a reference value, unless the ratio is diminishing sufficiently and approaching the reference value at a satisfactory pace.

The reference values are specified in the Protocol on the excessive deficit procedure.

3.   If a Member State does not fulfil the requirements under one or both of these criteria, the Commission shall prepare a report. The Commission's report shall also take into account whether the government deficit exceeds government investment expenditure and take into account all other relevant factors, including the medium-term economic and budgetary position of the Member State.

The Commission may also prepare a report if, notwithstanding the fulfilment of the requirements under the criteria, it is of the opinion that there is a risk of an excessive deficit in a Member State.

4.   The Economic and Financial Committee set up under Article III-192 shall formulate an opinion on the Commission's report.

5.   If the Commission considers that an excessive deficit in a Member State exists or may occur, it shall address an opinion to the Member State concerned and shall inform the Council accordingly.

6.   The Council shall, on a proposal from the Commission, having considered any observations which the Member State concerned may wish to make and after an overall assessment, decide whether an excessive deficit exists. In that case it shall adopt, without undue delay, on a recommendation from the Commission, recommendations addressed to the Member State concerned with a view to bringing that situation to an end within a given period. Subject to paragraph 8, those recommendations shall not be made public.

Within the scope of this paragraph, the Council shall act without taking into account the vote of the member of the Council representing the Member State concerned.

A qualified majority shall be defined as at least 55% of the other members of the Council, representing Member States comprising at least 65% of the population of the participating Member States.

A blocking minority must include at least the minimum number of these other Council members representing more than 35% of the population of the participating Member States, plus one member, failing which the qualified majority shall be deemed attained.

[BMDF Note: The voting rights of the United Kingdom are suspended concerning the provisions of this paragraph, due to the UK's opt-out from the euro, Article III-197(4). The final two sub-paragraphs come into force on 1 November 2009, under the terms of Protocol no. 34, Article 2.]

7.   The Council, on a recommendation from the Commission, shall adopt the European decisions and recommendations referred to in paragraphs 8 to 11.

It shall act without taking into account the vote of the member of the Council representing the Member State concerned.

A qualified majority shall be defined as at least 55% of the other members of the Council, representing Member States comprising at least 65% of the population of the participating Member States.

A blocking minority must include at least the minimum number of these other Council members representing more than 35% of the population of the participating Member States, plus one member, failing which the qualified majority shall be deemed attained.

[BMDF Note: The voting rights of the United Kingdom are suspended concerning the provisions of this paragraph, due to the UK's opt-out from the euro, Article III-197(4). The final two sub-paragraphs come into force on 1 November 2009, under the terms of Protocol no. 34, Article 2.]

8.   Where it adopts a European decision establishing that there has been no effective action in response to its recommendations within the period laid down, the Council may make its recommendations public.

[BMDF Note: The voting rights of the United Kingdom are suspended concerning the provisions of this paragraph, due to the UK's opt-out from the euro, Article III-197(4).]

9.   If a Member State persists in failing to put the Council's recommendations into practice, the Council may adopt a European decision giving notice to the Member State to take, within a specified time-limit, measures for the deficit reduction which the Council judges necessary to remedy the situation.

In such a case, the Council may request the Member State concerned to submit reports in accordance with a specific timetable in order to examine the adjustment efforts of that Member State.

[BMDF Note: This paragraph does not apply to the United Kingdom, due to its opt-out from the euro, Article III-197(2)]

10.   As long as a Member State fails to comply with a European decision adopted in accordance with paragraph 9, the Council may decide to apply or, as the case may be, intensify one or more of the following measures:

(a)   require the Member State concerned to publish additional information, to be specified by the Council, before issuing bonds and securities;

(b)   invite the European Investment Bank to reconsider its lending policy towards the Member State concerned;

(c)   require the Member State concerned to make a non-interest-bearing deposit of an appropriate size with the Union until the Council considers that the excessive deficit has been corrected;

(d)   impose fines of an appropriate size.

The President of the Council shall inform the European Parliament of the measures adopted.

[BMDF Note: This paragraph does not apply to the United Kingdom, due to its opt-out from the euro, Article III-197(2)]

11.   The Council shall repeal some or all of the measures referred to in paragraph 6 and paragraphs 8, 9 and 10 if it considers the excessive deficit in the Member State concerned to have been corrected. If the Council has previously made public recommendations, it shall state publicly, as soon as the European decision referred to in paragraph 8 has been repealed, that there is no longer an excessive deficit in the Member State concerned.

[BMDF Note: The voting rights of the United Kingdom are suspended concerning the provisions of this paragraph, due to the UK's opt-out from the euro, Article III-197(4)]

12.   The rights to bring actions provided for in Articles III-360 and III-361 shall not be exercised within the framework of paragraphs 1 to 6 or paragraphs 8 and 9.

13.   Further provisions relating to the implementation of the procedure laid down in this Article are set out in the Protocol on the excessive deficit procedure.

A European law of the Council shall lay down the appropriate measures to replace the said Protocol. The Council shall act unanimously after consulting the European Parliament and the European Central Bank.

Subject to the other provisions of this paragraph, the Council, on a proposal from the Commission, shall adopt European regulations or decisions laying down detailed rules and definitions for the application of the said Protocol. It shall act after consulting the European Parliament.

SECTION 2

MONETARY POLICY

ARTICLE III-185 (*ex Article 105 TEC*)

1.   The primary objective of the European System of Central Banks shall be to maintain price stability. Without prejudice to this objective, the European System of Central Banks shall support the general economic policies in the Union in order to contribute to the achievement of its objectives as laid down in Article I-3. The European System of Central Banks shall act in accordance with the principle of an open market economy with free competition, favouring an efficient allocation of resources, and in compliance with the principles set out in Article III-177. *[BMDF Note: This paragraph does not apply to the United Kingdom, due to its opt-out from the euro, Article III-197(2)]*

2.   The basic tasks to be carried out through the European System of Central Banks shall be:

(a)   to define and implement the Union's monetary policy;

(b)   to conduct foreign-exchange operations consistent with Article III-326;

(c)   to hold and manage the official foreign reserves of the Member States;

(d)   to promote the smooth operation of payment systems.

[BMDF Note: This paragraph does not apply to the United Kingdom, due to its opt-out from the euro, Article III-197(2)]

3.   Paragraph 2(c) shall be without prejudice to the holding and management by the governments of Member States of foreign-exchange working balances. *[BMDF Note: This paragraph does not apply to the United Kingdom, due to its opt-out from the euro, Article III-197(2)]*

4.   The European Central Bank shall be consulted:
(a)   on any proposed Union act in areas within its powers;
(b)   by national authorities regarding any draft legislative provision in areas within its powers, but within the limits and under the conditions set out by the Council in accordance with the procedure laid down in Article III-187(4).
The European Central Bank may submit opinions to the Union institutions, bodies, offices or agencies or to national authorities on matters within its powers.

5.   The European System of Central Banks shall contribute to the smooth conduct of policies pursued by the competent authorities relating to the prudential supervision of credit institutions and the stability of the financial system. *[BMDF Note: This paragraph does not apply to the United Kingdom, due to its opt-out from the euro, Article III-197(2)]*

6.   A European law of the Council may confer specific tasks upon the European Central Bank concerning policies relating to the prudential supervision of credit institutions and other financial institutions with the exception of insurance undertakings. The Council shall act unanimously after consulting the European Parliament and the European Central Bank.

ARTICLE III-186 (*ex Article 106 TEC*)
1.   The European Central Bank shall have the exclusive right to authorise the issue of euro bank notes in the Union. The European Central Bank and the national central banks may issue such notes. Only the bank notes issued by the European Central Bank and the national central banks shall have the status of legal tender within the Union.

2.   Member States may issue euro coins subject to approval by the European Central Bank of the volume of the issue.
The Council, on a proposal from the Commission, may adopt European regulations laying down measures to harmonise the denominations and technical specifications of coins intended for circulation to the extent necessary to permit their smooth circulation within the Union. The Council shall act after consulting the European Parliament and the European Central Bank.
[BMDF Note: This Article does not apply to the United Kingdom, due to its opt-out from the euro, Article III-197(2)]

ARTICLE III-187 (*ex Article 107 TEC*)
1.   The European System of Central Banks shall be governed by the decision-making bodies of the European Central Bank, which shall be the Governing Council and the Executive Board.

2.   The Statute of the European System of Central Banks is laid down in the Protocol on the Statute of the European System of Central Banks and of the European Central Bank.

3.   Article 5(1), (2) and (3), Articles 17 and 18, Article 19(1), Articles 22, 23, 24 and 26, Article 32(2), (3), (4) and (6), Article 33(1)(a) and Article 36 of the Statute of the European System of Central Banks and of the European Central Bank may be amended by European laws:
(a)   either on a proposal from the Commission and after consultation of the European Central Bank;
(b)   or on a recommendation from the European Central Bank and after consultation of the Commission.

4.   The Council shall adopt the European regulations and decisions laying down the measures referred to in Article 4, Article 5(4), Article 19(2), Article 20, Article 28(1), Article 29(2), Article 30(4) and Article 34(3) of the Statute of the European System of Central Banks and of the European Central Bank. It shall act after consulting the European Parliament:
(a)   either on a proposal from the Commission and after consulting the European Central Bank;
(b)   or on a recommendation from the European Central Bank and after consulting the Commission.

ARTICLE III-188 (*ex Article 108 TEC*)
When exercising the powers and carrying out the tasks and duties conferred upon them by the Constitution and the Statute of the European System of Central Banks and of the European Central Bank, neither the European Central Bank, nor a national central bank, nor any member of their decision-making bodies shall seek or take instructions from Union institutions, bodies, offices or agencies, from any government of a Member State or from any other body. The Union institutions, bodies, offices or agencies and the

governments of the Member States undertake to respect this principle and not to seek to influence the members of the decision-making bodies of the European Central Bank or of the national central banks in the performance of their tasks.

ARTICLE III-189 (*ex Article 109 TEC*)
Each Member State shall ensure that its national legislation, including the statutes of its national central bank, is compatible with the Constitution and the Statute of the European System of Central Banks and of the European Central Bank.

ARTICLE III-190 (*ex Article 110 TEC*)
1.   In order to carry out the tasks entrusted to the European System of Central Banks, the European Central Bank shall, in accordance with the Constitution and under the conditions laid down in the Statute of the European System of Central Banks and of the European Central Bank, adopt:
(a)   European regulations to the extent necessary to implement the tasks defined in Article 3(1)(a), Article 19(1), Article 22 and Article 25(2) of the Statute of the European System of Central Banks and of the European Central Bank and in cases which shall be laid down in European regulations and decisions as referred to in Article III-187(4);
(b)   European decisions necessary for carrying out the tasks entrusted to the European System of Central Banks under the Constitution and the Statute of the European System of Central Banks and of the European Central Bank;
(c)   recommendations and opinions.

2.   The European Central Bank may decide to publish its European decisions, recommendations and opinions.

3.   The Council shall, under the procedure laid down in Article III-187(4), adopt the European regulations establishing the limits and conditions under which the European Central Bank shall be entitled to impose fines or periodic penalty payments on undertakings for failure to comply with obligations under its European regulations and decisions.
[BMDF Note: This Article does not apply to the United Kingdom, due to its opt-out from the euro, Article III-197(2)]

ARTICLE III-191 (*ex Article 123(4) TEC*)
Without prejudice to the powers of the European Central Bank, European laws or framework laws shall lay down the measures necessary for use of the euro as the single currency. Such laws or framework laws shall be adopted after consultation of the European Central Bank.
[BMDF Note: This Article does not apply to the United Kingdom, due to its opt-out from the euro, Article III-197(2)]

SECTION 3

INSTITUTIONAL PROVISIONS

ARTICLE III-192 (*ex Article 114(2) to (4) TEC*)
1.   In order to promote co-ordination of the policies of Member States to the full extent needed for the functioning of the internal market, an Economic and Financial Committee is hereby set up.

2.   The Committee shall have the following tasks:
(a)   to deliver opinions at the request of the Council or of the Commission, or on its own initiative, for submission to those institutions;
(b)   to keep under review the economic and financial situation of the Member States and of the Union and to report on it regularly to the Council and to the Commission, in particular with regard to financial relations with third countries and international institutions;
(c)   without prejudice to Article III-344, to contribute to the preparation of the work of the Council referred to in Article III-159, Article III-179(2), (3), (4) and (6), Articles III-180, III-183 and III-184, Article III-185(6), Article III-186(2), Article III-187(3) and (4), Articles III-191 and III-196, Article III-198(2) and (3), Article III-201, Article III-202(2) and (3) and Articles III-322 and III-326, and to carry out other advisory and preparatory tasks assigned to it by the Council;
(d)   to examine, at least once a year, the situation regarding the movement of capital and the freedom of payments, as they result from the application of the Constitution and of Union acts; the examination

shall cover all measures relating to capital movements and payments; the Committee shall report to the Commission and to the Council on the outcome of this examination.

The Member States, the Commission and the European Central Bank shall each appoint no more than two members of the Committee.

3.   The Council, on a proposal from the Commission, shall adopt a European decision laying down detailed provisions concerning the composition of the Economic and Financial Committee. It shall act after consulting the European Central Bank and the Committee. The President of the Council shall inform the European Parliament of that decision.

4.   In addition to the tasks referred to in paragraph 2, if and as long as there are Member States with a derogation as referred to in Article III-197, the Committee shall keep under review the monetary and financial situation and the general payments system of those Member States and report regularly to the Council and to the Commission on the matter.

ARTICLE III-193 (*ex Article 115 TEC*)

For matters within the scope of Article III-179(4), Article III-184 with the exception of paragraph 13, Articles III-191, III-196, Article III-198(3) and Article III-326, the Council or a Member State may request the Commission to make a recommendation or a proposal, as appropriate. The Commission shall examine this request and submit its conclusions to the Council without delay.

SECTION 4

PROVISIONS SPECIFIC TO MEMBER STATES WHOSE CURRENCY IS THE EURO

ARTICLE III-194 (*new*)

1.   In order to ensure the proper functioning of economic and monetary union, and in accordance with the relevant provisions of the Constitution, the Council shall, in accordance with the relevant procedure from among those referred to in Articles III-179 and III-184, with the exception of the procedure set out in Article III-184(13), adopt measures specific to those Member States whose currency is the euro:

(a)   to strengthen the co-ordination and surveillance of their budgetary discipline;

(b)   to set out economic policy guidelines for them, while ensuring that they are compatible with those adopted for the whole of the Union and are kept under surveillance.

2.   For those measures set out in paragraph 1, only members of the Council representing Member States whose currency is the euro shall take part in the vote.

A qualified majority shall be defined as at least 55% of these members of the Council, representing Member States comprising at least 65% of the population of the participating Member States.

A blocking minority must include at least the minimum number of these Council members representing more than 35% of the population of the participating Member States, plus one member, failing which the qualified majority shall be deemed attained.

[BMDF Note: The final two sub-paragraphs come into force on 1 November 2009, under the terms of Protocol no. 34, Article 2.]

ARTICLE III-195 (*new*)

Arrangements for meetings between ministers of those Member States whose currency is the euro are laid down by the Protocol on the Euro Group.

ARTICLE III-196 (*new*)

1.   In order to secure the euro's place in the international monetary system, the Council, on a proposal from the Commission, shall adopt a European decision establishing common positions on matters of particular interest for economic and monetary union within the competent international financial institutions and conferences. The Council shall act after consulting the European Central Bank. *[BMDF Note: This paragraph does not apply to the United Kingdom, due to the opt-out from the euro, Article III-197(2)]*

2.   The Council, on a proposal from the Commission, may adopt appropriate measures to ensure unified representation within the international financial institutions and conferences. The Council shall act after consulting the European Central Bank. *[BMDF Note: This paragraph does not apply to the United Kingdom, due to the opt-out from the euro, Article III-197(2)]*

3.   For the measures referred to in paragraphs 1 and 2, only members of the Council representing Member States whose currency is the euro shall take part in the vote.

A qualified majority shall be defined as at least 55% of these members of the Council, representing Member States comprising at least 65% of the population of the participating Member States.

A blocking minority must include at least the minimum number of these Council members representing more than 35% of the population of the participating Member States, plus one member, failing which the qualified majority shall be deemed attained.

[BMDF Note: The final two sub-paragraphs come into force on 1 November 2009, under the terms of Protocol no. 34, Article 2.]

SECTION 5

TRANSITIONAL PROVISIONS

ARTICLE III-197 (*ex Article 122(1) and (3) to (5) TEC*)

1.   Member States in respect of which the Council has not decided that they fulfil the necessary conditions for the adoption of the euro shall hereinafter be referred to as "Member States with a derogation".

2.   The following provisions of the Constitution shall not apply to Member States with a derogation:

(a)   adoption of the parts of the broad economic policy guidelines which concern the euro area generally (Article III-179(2));

(b)   coercive means of remedying excessive deficits (Article III-184(9) and (10));

(c)   the objectives and tasks of the European System of Central Banks (Article III-185(1), (2), (3) and (5));

(d)   issue of the euro (Article III-186);

(e)   acts of the European Central Bank (Article III-190);

(f)   measures governing the use of the euro (Article III-191);

(g)   monetary agreements and other measures relating to exchange-rate policy (Article III-326);

(h)   appointment of members of the Executive Board of the European Central Bank (Article III-382(2));

(i)   European decisions establishing common positions on issues of particular relevance for economic and monetary union within the competent international financial institutions and conferences (Article III-196(1));

(j)   measures to ensure unified representation within the international financial institutions and conferences (Article III-196(2)).

In the Articles referred to in points (a) to (j), "Member States" shall therefore mean Member States whose currency is the euro.

3.   Under Chapter IX of the Statute of the European System of Central Banks and of the European Central Bank, Member States with a derogation and their national central banks are excluded from rights and obligations within the European System of Central Banks.

4.   The voting rights of members of the Council representing Member States with a derogation shall be suspended for the adoption by the Council of the measures referred to in the Articles listed in paragraph 2, and in the following instances:

(a)   recommendations made to those Member States whose currency is the euro in the framework of multilateral surveillance, including on stability programmes and warnings (Article III-179(4));

(b)   measures relating to excessive deficits concerning those Member States whose currency is the euro (Article III-184(6), (7), (8) and (11)).

A qualified majority shall be defined as at least 55% of the other members of the Council, representing Member States comprising at least 65% of the population of the participating Member States.

A blocking minority must include at least the minimum number of these other Council members representing more than 35% of the population of the participating Member States, plus one member, failing which the qualified majority shall be deemed attained.

[BMDF Note: The final two sub-paragraphs come into force on 1 November 2009, under the terms of Protocol no. 34, Article 2.]

ARTICLE III-198 (*ex Articles 121, 122(2) and 123(5) TEC*)

1.   At least once every two years, or at the request of a Member State with a derogation, the Commission and the European Central Bank shall report to the Council on the progress made by the Member States with a derogation in fulfilling their obligations regarding the achievement of economic and monetary union. These reports shall include an examination of the compatibility between the national legislation of each of these Member States, including the statutes of its national central bank, and Articles III-188 and III-189 and the

Statute of the European System of Central Banks and of the European Central Bank. The reports shall also examine whether a high degree of sustainable convergence has been achieved, by analysing how far each of these Member States has fulfilled the following criteria:

(a) the achievement of a high degree of price stability; this is apparent from a rate of inflation which is close to that of, at most, the three best performing Member States in terms of price stability;

(b) the sustainability of the government financial position; this is apparent from having achieved a government budgetary position without a deficit that is excessive as determined in accordance with Article III-184(6);

(c) the observance of the normal fluctuation margins provided for by the exchange-rate mechanism of the European monetary system, for at least two years, without devaluing against the euro;

(d) the durability of convergence achieved by the Member State with a derogation and of its participation in the exchange-rate mechanism, being reflected in the long-term interest-rate levels.

The four criteria laid down in this paragraph and the relevant periods over which they are to be respected are developed further in the Protocol on the convergence criteria. The reports from the Commission and the European Central Bank shall also take account of the results of the integration of markets, the situation and development of the balances of payments on current account and an examination of the development of unit labour costs and other price indices.

2. After consulting the European Parliament and after discussion in the European Council, the Council, on a proposal from the Commission, shall adopt a European decision establishing which Member States with a derogation fulfil the necessary conditions on the basis of the criteria laid down in paragraph 1, and shall abrogate the derogations of the Member States concerned.

The Council shall act having received a recommendation of a qualified majority of those among its members representing Member States whose currency is the euro. These members shall act within six months of the Council receiving the Commission's proposal.

The qualified majority referred to in the second subparagraph shall be defined as at least 55% of these members of the Council, representing Member States comprising at least 65% of the population of the participating Member States. A blocking minority must include at least the minimum number of these Council members representing more than 35% of the population of the participating Member States, plus one member, failing which the qualified majority shall be deemed attained.

[BMDF Note: The final sub-paragraph comes into force on 1 November 2009; Protocol no. 34, Article 2.]

3. If it is decided, in accordance with the procedure set out in paragraph 2, to abrogate a derogation, the Council shall, on a proposal from the Commission, adopt the European regulations or decisions irrevocably fixing the rate at which the euro is to be substituted for the currency of the Member State concerned, and laying down the other measures necessary for the introduction of the euro as the single currency in that Member State. The Council shall act with the unanimous agreement of the members representing Member States whose currency is the euro and the Member State concerned, after consulting the European Central Bank.

ARTICLE III-199 (*ex Articles 123(3) and 117(2) TEC*)

1. If and as long as there are Member States with a derogation, and without prejudice to Article III-187(1), the General Council of the European Central Bank referred to in Article 45 of the Statute of the European System of Central Banks and of the European Central Bank shall be constituted as a third decision-making body of the European Central Bank.

2. If and as long as there are Member States with a derogation, the European Central Bank shall, as regards those Member States:

(a) strengthen co-operation between the national central banks;

(b) strengthen the co-ordination of the monetary policies of the Member States, with the aim of ensuring price stability;

(c) monitor the functioning of the exchange-rate mechanism;

(d) hold consultations concerning issues falling within the competence of the national central banks and affecting the stability of financial institutions and markets;

(e) carry out the former tasks of the European Monetary Co-operation Fund which had subsequently been taken over by the European Monetary Institute.

ARTICLE III-200 (*ex Article 124(1) TEC*)

Each Member State with a derogation shall treat its exchange-rate policy as a matter of common interest. In so doing, it shall take account of the experience acquired in co-operation within the framework of the exchange-rate mechanism.

ARTICLE III-201 (*ex Article 119 TEC*)

1. Where a Member State with a derogation is in difficulties or is seriously threatened with difficulties as regards its balance of payments either as a result of an overall disequilibrium in its balance of payments, or as a result of the type of currency at its disposal, and where such difficulties are liable in particular to jeopardise the functioning of the internal market or the implementation of the common commercial policy, the Commission shall immediately investigate the position of the State in question and the action which, making use of all the means at its disposal, that State has taken or may take in accordance with the Constitution. The Commission shall state what measures it recommends the Member State concerned to adopt.

If the action taken by a Member State with a derogation and the measures suggested by the Commission do not prove sufficient to overcome the difficulties which have arisen or which threaten, the Commission shall, after consulting the Economic and Financial Committee, recommend to the Council the granting of mutual assistance and appropriate methods.

The Commission shall keep the Council regularly informed of the situation and of how it evolves.

2. The Council shall adopt European regulations or decisions granting such mutual assistance and laying down the conditions and details of such assistance, which may take such forms as:

(a) a concerted approach to or within any other international organisations to which Member States with a derogation may have recourse;

(b) measures needed to avoid deflection of trade where the Member State with a derogation, which is in difficulties, maintains or reintroduces quantitative restrictions against third countries;

(c) the granting of limited credits by other Member States, subject to their agreement.

3. If the mutual assistance recommended by the Commission is not granted by the Council or if the mutual assistance granted and the measures taken are insufficient, the Commission shall authorise the Member State with a derogation, which is in difficulties, to take protective measures, the conditions and details of which the Commission shall determine.

Such authorisation may be revoked and such conditions and details may be changed by the Council.

ARTICLE III-202 (*ex Article 120 TEC*)

1. Where a sudden crisis in the balance of payments occurs and a European decision as referred to in Article III-201(2) is not immediately adopted, a Member State with a derogation may, as a precaution, take the necessary protective measures. Such measures must cause the least possible disturbance in the functioning of the internal market and must not be wider in scope than is strictly necessary to remedy the sudden difficulties which have arisen.

2. The Commission and the other Member States shall be informed of the protective measures referred to in paragraph 1 not later than when they enter into force. The Commission may recommend to the Council the granting of mutual assistance under Article III-201.

3. The Council, acting on a recommendation from the Commission and after consulting the Economic and Financial Committee may adopt a European decision stipulating that the Member State concerned shall amend, suspend or abolish the protective measures referred to in paragraph 1.

CHAPTER III

POLICIES IN OTHER AREAS

SECTION 1

EMPLOYMENT

ARTICLE III-203 (*ex Article 125 TEC*)

The Union and the Member States shall, in accordance with this Section, work towards developing a co-ordinated strategy for employment and particularly for promoting a skilled, trained and adaptable workforce and labour markets responsive to economic change with a view to achieving the objectives referred to in Article I-3.

ARTICLE III-204 (*ex Article 126 TEC*)

1. Member States, through their employment policies, shall contribute to the achievement of the objectives referred to in Article III-203 in a way consistent with the broad guidelines of the economic policies of the Member States and of the Union adopted pursuant to Article III-179(2).

2. Member States, having regard to national practices related to the responsibilities of management and labour, shall regard promoting employment as a matter of common concern and shall co-ordinate their action in this respect within the Council, in accordance with Article III-206.

ARTICLE III-205 (*ex Article 127 TEC*)

1. The Union shall contribute to a high level of employment by encouraging co-operation between Member States and by supporting and, if necessary, complementing their action. In doing so, the competences of the Member States shall be respected.

2. The objective of a high level of employment shall be taken into consideration in the formulation and implementation of Union policies and activities.

ARTICLE III-206 (*ex Article 128 TEC*)

1. The European Council shall each year consider the employment situation in the Union and adopt conclusions thereon, on the basis of a joint annual report by the Council and the Commission.

2. On the basis of the conclusions of the European Council, the Council, on a proposal from the Commission, shall each year adopt guidelines which the Member States shall take into account in their employment policies. It shall act after consulting the European Parliament, the Committee of the Regions, the Economic and Social Committee and the Employment Committee.
These guidelines shall be consistent with the broad guidelines adopted pursuant to Article III-179(2).

3. Each Member State shall provide the Council and the Commission with an annual report on the principal measures taken to implement its employment policy in the light of the guidelines for employment as referred to in paragraph 2.

4. The Council, on the basis of the reports referred to in paragraph 3 and having received the views of the Employment Committee, shall each year carry out an examination of the implementation of the employment policies of the Member States in the light of the guidelines for employment. The Council, on a recommendation from the Commission, may adopt recommendations which it shall address to Member States.

5. On the basis of the results of that examination, the Council and the Commission shall make a joint annual report to the European Council on the employment situation in the Union and on the implementation of the guidelines for employment.

ARTICLE III-207 (*ex Article 129 TEC*)

European laws or framework laws may establish incentive measures designed to encourage co-operation between Member States and to support their action in the field of employment through initiatives aimed at developing exchanges of information and best practices, providing comparative analysis and advice as well as promoting innovative approaches and evaluating experiences, in particular by recourse to pilot projects. They shall be adopted after consultation of the Committee of the Regions and the Economic and Social Committee.
Such European laws or framework laws shall not include harmonisation of the laws and regulations of the Member States.

ARTICLE III-208 (*ex Article 130 TEC*)

The Council shall, by a simple majority, adopt a European decision establishing an Employment Committee with advisory status to promote co-ordination between Member States on employment and labour market policies. It shall act after consulting the European Parliament.
The tasks of the Committee shall be:
(a) to monitor the employment situation and employment policies in the Union and the Member States;
(b) without prejudice to Article III-344, to formulate opinions at the request of either the Council or the Commission or on its own initiative, and to contribute to the preparation of the Council proceedings referred to in Article III-206.
In fulfilling its mandate, the Committee shall consult management and labour.
Each Member State and the Commission shall appoint two members of the Committee.

SECTION 2

SOCIAL POLICY

ARTICLE III-209 (*ex Article 136 TEC*)
The Union and the Member States, having in mind fundamental social rights such as those set out in the European Social Charter signed at Turin on 18 October 1961 and in the 1989 Community Charter of the Fundamental Social Rights of Workers, shall have as their objectives the promotion of employment, improved living and working conditions, so as to make possible their harmonisation while the improvement is being maintained, proper social protection, dialogue between management and labour, the development of human resources with a view to lasting high employment and the combating of exclusion.
To this end the Union and the Member States shall act taking account of the diverse forms of national practices, in particular in the field of contractual relations, and the need to maintain the competitiveness of the Union economy.
They believe that such a development will ensue not only from the functioning of the internal market, which will favour the harmonisation of social systems, but also from the procedures provided for in the Constitution and from the approximation of provisions laid down by law, regulation or administrative action of the Member States.

ARTICLE III-210 (*ex Article 137 TEC*)
1.   With a view to achieving the objectives of Article III-209, the Union shall support and complement the activities of the Member States in the following fields:
(a)   improvement in particular of the working environment to protect workers' health and safety;
(b)   working conditions;
(c)   social security and social protection of workers;
(d)   protection of workers where their employment contract is terminated;
(e)   the information and consultation of workers;
(f)   representation and collective defence of the interests of workers and employers, including co-determination, subject to paragraph 6;
(g)   conditions of employment for third-country nationals legally residing in Union territory;
(h)   the integration of persons excluded from the labour market, without prejudice to Article III-283;
(i)   equality between women and men with regard to labour market opportunities and treatment at work;
(j)   the combating of social exclusion;
(k)   the modernisation of social protection systems without prejudice to point (c).

2.   For the purposes of paragraph 1:
(a)   European laws or framework laws may establish measures designed to encourage co-operation between Member States through initiatives aimed at improving knowledge, developing exchanges of information and best practices, promoting innovative approaches and evaluating experiences, excluding any harmonisation of the laws and regulations of the Member States;
(b)   in the fields referred to in paragraph 1(a) to (i), European framework laws may establish minimum requirements for gradual implementation, having regard to the conditions and technical rules obtaining in each of the Member States. Such European framework laws shall avoid imposing administrative, financial and legal constraints in a way which would hold back the creation and development of small and medium-sized undertakings.
In all cases, such European laws or framework laws shall be adopted after consultation of the Committee of the Regions and the Economic and Social Committee.

3.   By way of derogation from paragraph 2, in the fields referred to in paragraph 1(c), (d), (f) and (g), European laws or framework laws shall be adopted by the Council acting unanimously after consulting the European Parliament, the Committee of the Regions and the Economic and Social Committee.
The Council may, on a proposal from the Commission, adopt a European decision making the ordinary legislative procedure applicable to paragraph 1(d), (f) and (g). It shall act unanimously after consulting the European Parliament.

4.   A Member State may entrust management and labour, at their joint request, with the implementation of European framework laws adopted pursuant to paragraphs 2 and 3 or, where appropriate, with the implementation of European regulations or decisions adopted in accordance with Article III-212.
In this case, it shall ensure that, no later than the date on which a European framework law must be transposed, or a European regulation or decision implemented, management and labour have introduced the necessary measures by agreement, the Member State concerned being required to take any necessary measure enabling it at any time to be in a position to guarantee the results imposed by that framework law, regulation or decision.

5.   The European laws and framework laws adopted pursuant to this Article:

(a)   shall not affect the right of Member States to define the fundamental principles of their social security systems and must not significantly affect the financial equilibrium of such systems;

(b)   shall not prevent any Member State from maintaining or introducing more stringent protective measures compatible with the Constitution.

6.   This Article shall not apply to pay, the right of association, the right to strike or the right to impose lock-outs.

ARTICLE III-211 (*ex Article 138 TEC*)

1.   The Commission shall promote the consultation of management and labour at Union level and shall adopt any relevant measure to facilitate their dialogue by ensuring balanced support for the parties.

2.   For the purposes of paragraph 1, before submitting proposals in the social policy field, the Commission shall consult management and labour on the possible direction of Union action.

3.   If, after the consultation referred to in paragraph 2, the Commission considers Union action desirable, it shall consult management and labour on the content of the envisaged proposal. Management and labour shall forward to the Commission an opinion or, where appropriate, a recommendation.

4.   On the occasion of the consultation referred to in paragraphs 2 and 3, management and labour may inform the Commission of their wish to initiate the process provided for in Article III-212(1). The duration of this process shall not exceed nine months, unless the management and labour concerned and the Commission decide jointly to extend it.

ARTICLE III-212 (*ex Article 139 TEC*)

1.   Should management and labour so desire, the dialogue between them at Union level may lead to contractual relations, including agreements.

2.   Agreements concluded at Union level shall be implemented either in accordance with the procedures and practices specific to management and labour and the Member States or, in matters covered by Article III-210, at the joint request of the signatory parties, by European regulations or decisions adopted by the Council on a proposal from the Commission. The European Parliament shall be informed.

Where the agreement in question contains one or more provisions relating to one of the areas for which unanimity is required pursuant to Article III-210(3), the Council shall act unanimously.

ARTICLE III-213 (*ex Article 140 TEC*)

With a view to achieving the objectives of Article III-209 and without prejudice to the other provisions of the Constitution, the Commission shall encourage co-operation between the Member States and facilitate the co-ordination of their action in all social policy fields under this Section, particularly in matters relating to:

(a)   employment;
(b)   labour law and working conditions;
(c)   basic and advanced vocational training;
(d)   social security;
(e)   prevention of occupational accidents and diseases;
(f)   occupational hygiene;
(g)   the right of association and collective bargaining between employers and workers.

To this end, the Commission shall act in close contact with Member States by making studies, delivering opinions and arranging consultations both on problems arising at national level and on those of concern to international organisations, in particular initiatives aiming at the establishment of guidelines and indicators, the organisation of exchange of best practice, and the preparation of the necessary elements for periodic monitoring and evaluation. The European Parliament shall be kept fully informed.

Before delivering the opinions provided for in this Article, the Commission shall consult the Economic and Social Committee.

ARTICLE III-214 (*ex Article 141 TEC*)

1.   Each Member State shall ensure that the principle of equal pay for female and male workers for equal work or work of equal value is applied.

2.   For the purpose of this Article, "pay" means the ordinary basic or minimum wage or salary and any other consideration, whether in cash or in kind, which the worker receives directly or indirectly, in respect of his employment, from his employer.

Equal pay without discrimination based on sex means:

(a)   that pay for the same work at piece rates shall be calculated on the basis of the same unit of measurement;

(b)   that pay for work at time rates shall be the same for the same job.

3.   European laws or framework laws shall establish measures to ensure the application of the principle of equal opportunities and equal treatment of women and men in matters of employment and occupation, including the principle of equal pay for equal work or work of equal value. They shall be adopted after consultation of the Economic and Social Committee.

4.   With a view to ensuring full equality in practice between women and men in working life, the principle of equal treatment shall not prevent any Member State from maintaining or adopting measures providing for specific advantages in order to make it easier for the under-represented sex to pursue a vocational activity, or to prevent or compensate for disadvantages in professional careers.

ARTICLE III-215 (*ex Article 142 TEC*)
Member States shall endeavour to maintain the existing equivalence between paid holiday schemes.

ARTICLE III-216 (*ex Article 143 TEC*)
The Commission shall draw up a report each year on progress in achieving the objectives of Article III-209, including the demographic situation within the Union. It shall forward the report to the European Parliament, the Council and the Economic and Social Committee.

ARTICLE III-217 (*ex Article 144 TEC*)
The Council shall, by a simple majority, adopt a European decision establishing a Social Protection Committee with advisory status to promote co-operation on social protection policies between Member States and with the Commission. The Council shall act after consulting the European Parliament.
The tasks of the Committee shall be:
(a)   to monitor the social situation and the development of social protection policies in the Member States and within the Union;
(b)   to promote exchanges of information, experience and good practice between Member States and with the Commission;
(c)   without prejudice to Article III-344, to prepare reports, formulate opinions or undertake other work within the scope of its powers, at the request of either the Council or the Commission or on its own initiative.
In fulfilling its mandate, the Committee shall establish appropriate contacts with management and labour.
Each Member State and the Commission shall appoint two members of the Committee.

ARTICLE III-218 (*ex Article 145 TEC*)
The Commission shall include a separate chapter on social developments within the Union in its annual report to the European Parliament.
The European Parliament may invite the Commission to draw up reports on any particular problems concerning social conditions.

ARTICLE III-219 (*ex Articles 146/147/148 TEC*)
1.   In order to improve employment opportunities for workers in the internal market and to contribute thereby to raising the standard of living, a European Social Fund is hereby established; it shall aim to render the employment of workers easier and to increase their geographical and occupational mobility within the Union, and to facilitate their adaptation to industrial changes and to changes in production systems, in particular through vocational training and retraining.

2.   The Commission shall administer the Fund. It shall be assisted in this task by a Committee presided over by a member of the Commission and composed of representatives of Member States, trade unions and employers' organisations.

3.   European laws shall establish implementing measures relating to the Fund. Such laws shall be adopted after consultation of the Committee of the Regions and the Economic and Social Committee.

SECTION 3

ECONOMIC, SOCIAL AND TERRITORIAL COHESION

ARTICLE III-220 (*ex Article 158 TEC*)

In order to promote its overall harmonious development, the Union shall develop and pursue its action leading to the strengthening of its economic, social and territorial cohesion.

In particular, the Union shall aim at reducing disparities between the levels of development of the various regions and the backwardness of the least favoured regions.

Among the regions concerned, particular attention shall be paid to rural areas, areas affected by industrial transition, and regions which suffer from severe and permanent natural or demographic handicaps such as the northernmost regions with very low population density and island, cross-border and mountain regions.

ARTICLE III-221 (*ex Article 159 TEC*)

Member States shall conduct their economic policies and shall co-ordinate them in such a way as, in addition, to attain the objectives set out in Article III-220. The formulation and implementation of the Union's policies and action and the implementation of the internal market shall take into account those objectives and shall contribute to their achievement. The Union shall also support the achievement of these objectives by the action it takes through the Structural Funds (European Agricultural Guidance and Guarantee Fund, Guidance Section; European Social Fund; European Regional Development Fund), the European Investment Bank and the other existing financial instruments.

The Commission shall submit a report to the European Parliament, the Council, the Committee of the Regions and the Economic and Social Committee every three years on the progress made towards achieving economic, social and territorial cohesion and on the manner in which the various means provided for in this Article have contributed to it. This report shall, if necessary, be accompanied by appropriate proposals.

European laws or framework laws may establish any specific measure outside the Funds, without prejudice to measures adopted within the framework of the Union's other policies. They shall be adopted after consultation of the Committee of the Regions and the Economic and Social Committee.

ARTICLE III-222 (*ex Article 160 TEC*)

The European Regional Development Fund is intended to help to redress the main regional imbalances in the Union through participation in the development and structural adjustment of regions whose development is lagging behind and in the conversion of declining industrial regions.

ARTICLE III-223 (*ex Article 161 TEC*)

1.   Without prejudice to Article III-224, European laws shall define the tasks, the priority objectives and the organisation of the Structural Funds, which may involve grouping the Funds, the general rules applicable to them and the provisions necessary to ensure their effectiveness and the co-ordination of the Funds with one another and with the other existing financial instruments.

A Cohesion Fund set up by a European law shall provide a financial contribution to projects in the fields of environment and trans-European networks in the area of transport infrastructure.

In all cases, such European laws shall be adopted after consultation of the Committee of the Regions and the Economic and Social Committee.

2.   The first provisions on the Structural Funds and the Cohesion Fund to be adopted following those in force on the date on which the Treaty establishing a Constitution for Europe is signed shall be established by a European law of the Council. The Council shall act unanimously after obtaining the consent of the European Parliament.

ARTICLE III-224 (*ex Article 162 TEC*)

European laws shall establish implementing measures relating to the European Regional Development Fund. Such laws shall be adopted after consultation of the Committee of the Regions and the Economic and Social Committee.

With regard to the European Agricultural Guidance and Guarantee Fund, Guidance Section, and the European Social Fund, Articles III-231 and III-219(3) respectively shall apply.

SECTION 4

AGRICULTURE AND FISHERIES

ARTICLE III-225 (*new*)
The Union shall define and implement a common agriculture and fisheries policy.
"Agricultural products" means the products of the soil, of stockfarming and of fisheries and products of first-stage processing directly related to these products. References to the common agricultural policy or to agriculture, and the use of the term "agricultural", shall be understood as also referring to fisheries, having regard to the specific characteristics of this sector.

ARTICLE III-226 (*ex Article 32(1), first sentence, and (2) to (4) TEC*)
1.   The internal market shall extend to agriculture and trade in agricultural products.

2.   Save as otherwise provided in Articles III-227 to III-232, the rules laid down for the establishment and functioning of the internal market shall apply to agricultural products.

3.   The products listed in Annex I shall be subject to Articles III-227 to III-232.

4.   The operation and development of the internal market for agricultural products must be accompanied by a common agricultural policy.

ARTICLE III-227 (*ex Article 33 TEC*)
1.   The objectives of the common agricultural policy shall be:
(a)   to increase agricultural productivity by promoting technical progress and by ensuring the rational development of agricultural production and the optimum utilisation of the factors of production, in particular labour;
(b)   thus to ensure a fair standard of living for the agricultural community, in particular by increasing the individual earnings of persons engaged in agriculture;
(c)   to stabilise markets;
(d)   to assure the availability of supplies;
(e)   to ensure that supplies reach consumers at reasonable prices.

2.   In working out the common agricultural policy and the special methods for its application, account shall be taken of:
(a)   the particular nature of agricultural activity, which results from the social structure of agriculture and from structural and natural disparities between the various agricultural regions;
(b)   the need to effect the appropriate adjustments by degrees;
(c)   the fact that in the Member States agriculture constitutes a sector closely linked with the economy as a whole.

ARTICLE III-228 (*ex Article 34 TEC*)
1.   In order to attain the objectives set out in Article III-227, a common organisation of agricultural markets shall be established.
This organisation shall take one of the following forms, depending on the product concerned:
(a)   common rules on competition;
(b)   compulsory co-ordination of the various national market organisations;
(c)   a European market organisation.

2.   The common organisation established in accordance with paragraph 1 may include all measures required to attain the objectives set out in Article III-227, in particular regulation of prices, aids for the production and marketing of the various products, storage and carryover arrangements and common machinery for stabilising imports or exports.
The common organisation shall be limited to pursuit of the objectives set out in Article III-227 and shall exclude any discrimination between producers or consumers within the Union.
Any common price policy shall be based on common criteria and uniform methods of calculation.

3.   In order to enable the common organisation referred to in paragraph 1 to attain its objectives, one or more agricultural guidance and guarantee funds may be set up.

ARTICLE III-229 (*ex Article 35 TEC*)
To enable the objectives set out in Article III-227 to be attained, provision may be made within the framework of the common agricultural policy for measures such as:

(a) an effective co-ordination of efforts in the spheres of vocational training, of research and of the dissemination of agricultural knowledge; this may include joint financing of projects or institutions;

(b) joint measures to promote consumption of certain products.

ARTICLE III-230 (*ex Article 36 TEC*)

1. The Section relating to rules on competition shall apply to production of and trade in agricultural products only to the extent determined by European laws or framework laws in accordance with Article III-231(2), having regard to the objectives set out in Article III-227.

2. The Council, on a proposal from the Commission, may adopt a European regulation or decision authorising the granting of aid:

(a) for the protection of enterprises handicapped by structural or natural conditions;

(b) within the framework of economic development programmes.

ARTICLE III-231 (*ex Article 37 TEC*)

1. The Commission shall submit proposals for working out and implementing the common agricultural policy, including the replacement of the national organisations by one of the forms of common organisation provided for in Article III-228(1), and for implementing the measures referred to in this Section.

These proposals shall take account of the interdependence of the agricultural matters referred to in this Section.

2. European laws or framework laws shall establish the common organisation of the market provided for in Article III-228(1) and the other provisions necessary for the pursuit of the objectives of the common agricultural policy and the common fisheries policy. They shall be adopted after consultation of the Economic and Social Committee.

3. The Council, on a proposal from the Commission, shall adopt the European regulations or decisions on fixing prices, levies, aid and quantitative limitations and on the fixing and allocation of fishing opportunities.

4. In accordance with paragraph 2, the national market organisations may be replaced by the common organisation provided for in Article III-228(1) if:

(a) the common organisation offers Member States which are opposed to this measure and which have an organisation of their own for the production in question equivalent safeguards for the employment and standard of living of the producers concerned, account being taken of the adjustments that will be possible and the specialisation that will be needed with the passage of time, and

(b) such an organisation ensures conditions for trade within the Union similar to those existing in a national market.

5. If a common organisation for certain raw materials is established before a common organisation exists for the corresponding processed products, such raw materials as are used for processed products intended for export to third countries may be imported from outside the Union.

ARTICLE III-232 (*ex Article 38 TEC*)

Where in a Member State a product is subject to a national market organisation or to internal rules having equivalent effect which affect the competitive position of similar production in another Member State, a countervailing charge shall be applied by Member States to imports of this product coming from the Member State where such organisation or rules exist, unless that State applies a countervailing charge on export.

The Commission shall adopt European regulations or decisions fixing the amount of these charges at the level required to redress the balance. It may also authorise other measures, the conditions and details of which it shall determine.

SECTION 5

ENVIRONMENT

ARTICLE III-233 (*ex Article 174 TEC*)

1. Union policy on the environment shall contribute to the pursuit of the following objectives:

(a) preserving, protecting and improving the quality of the environment;

(b) protecting human health;

(c) prudent and rational utilisation of natural resources;

(d)   promoting measures at international level to deal with regional or worldwide environmental problems.

2.   Union policy on the environment shall aim at a high level of protection taking into account the diversity of situations in the various regions of the Union. It shall be based on the precautionary principle and on the principles that preventive action should be taken, that environmental damage should as a priority be rectified at source and that the polluter should pay.

In this context, harmonisation measures answering environmental protection requirements shall include, where appropriate, a safeguard clause allowing Member States to take provisional steps, for non-economic environmental reasons, subject to a procedure of inspection by the Union.

3.   In preparing its policy on the environment, the Union shall take account of:
(a)   available scientific and technical data;
(b)   environmental conditions in the various regions of the Union;
(c)   the potential benefits and costs of action or lack of action;
(d)   the economic and social development of the Union as a whole and the balanced development of its regions.

4.   Within their respective spheres of competence, the Union and the Member States shall co-operate with third countries and with the competent international organisations. The arrangements for the Union's co-operation may be the subject of agreements between the Union and the third parties concerned.

The first subparagraph shall be without prejudice to Member States' competence to negotiate in international bodies and to conclude international agreements.

ARTICLE III-234 (*ex Article 175/176 TEC*)
1.   European laws or framework laws shall establish what action is to be taken in order to achieve the objectives referred to in Article III-233. They shall be adopted after consultation of the Committee of the Regions and the Economic and Social Committee.

2.   By way of derogation from paragraph 1 and without prejudice to Article III-172, the Council shall unanimously adopt European laws or framework laws establishing:
(a)   provisions primarily of a fiscal nature;
(b)   measures affecting:
        (i)   town and country planning;
        (ii)   quantitative management of water resources or affecting, directly or indirectly, the availability of those resources;
        (iii)   land use, with the exception of waste management;
(c)   measures significantly affecting a Member State's choice between different energy sources and the general structure of its energy supply.

The Council, on a proposal from the Commission, may unanimously adopt a European decision making the ordinary legislative procedure applicable to the matters referred to in the first subparagraph.

In all cases, the Council shall act after consulting the European Parliament, the Committee of the Regions and the Economic and Social Committee.

3.   European laws shall establish general action programmes which set out priority objectives to be attained. Such laws shall be adopted after consultation of the Committee of the Regions and the Economic and Social Committee.

The measures necessary for the implementation of these programmes shall be adopted under the terms of paragraph 1 or 2, as the case may be.

4.   Without prejudice to certain measures adopted by the Union, the Member States shall finance and implement the environment policy.

5.   Without prejudice to the principle that the polluter should pay, if a measure based on paragraph 1 involves costs deemed disproportionate for the public authorities of a Member State, such measure shall provide in appropriate form for:
(a)   temporary derogations, and/or
(b)   financial support from the Cohesion Fund.

6.   The protective measures adopted pursuant to this Article shall not prevent any Member State from maintaining or introducing more stringent protective measures. Such measures must be compatible with the Constitution. They shall be notified to the Commission.

SECTION 6

CONSUMER PROTECTION

ARTICLE III-235 (*ex Article 153 TEC*)
1.   In order to promote the interests of consumers and to ensure a high level of consumer protection, the Union shall contribute to protecting the health, safety and economic interests of consumers, as well as to promoting their right to information, education and to organise themselves in order to safeguard their interests.

2.   The Union shall contribute to the attainment of the objectives referred to in paragraph 1 through:
(a)   measures adopted pursuant to Article III-172 in the context of the establishment and functioning of the internal market;
(b)   measures which support, supplement and monitor the policy pursued by the Member States.

3.   European laws or framework laws shall establish the measures referred to in paragraph 2(b). Such laws shall be adopted after consultation of the Economic and Social Committee.

4.   Acts adopted pursuant to paragraph 3 shall not prevent any Member State from maintaining or introducing more stringent protective provisions. Such provisions must be compatible with the Constitution. They shall be notified to the Commission.

SECTION 7

TRANSPORT

ARTICLE III-236 (*ex Articles 70 and 71 TEC*)
1.   The objectives of the Constitution shall, in matters governed by this Section, be pursued within the framework of a common transport policy.

2.   European laws or framework laws shall implement paragraph 1, taking into account the distinctive features of transport. They shall be adopted after consultation of the Committee of the Regions and the Economic and Social Committee.
Such European laws or framework laws shall establish:
(a)   common rules applicable to international transport to or from the territory of a Member State or passing across the territory of one or more Member States;
(b)   the conditions under which non-resident carriers may operate transport services within a Member State;
(c)   measures to improve transport safety;
(d)   any other appropriate measure.

3.   When the European laws or framework laws referred to in paragraph 2 are adopted, account shall be taken of cases where their application might seriously affect the standard of living and level of employment in certain regions, and the operation of transport facilities.

ARTICLE III-237 (*ex Article 72 TEC*)
Until the European laws or framework laws referred to in Article III-236(2) have been adopted, no Member State may, unless the Council has unanimously adopted a European decision granting a derogation, make the various provisions governing the subject on 1 January 1958 or, for acceding States, the date of their accession less favourable in their direct or indirect effect on carriers of other Member States as compared with carriers who are nationals of that State.

ARTICLE III-238 (*ex Article 73 TEC*)
Aids shall be compatible with the Constitution if they meet the needs of co-ordination of transport or if they represent reimbursement for the discharge of certain obligations inherent in the concept of a public service.

ARTICLE III-239 (*ex Article 74 TEC*)
Any measures adopted within the framework of the Constitution in respect of transport rates and conditions shall take account of the economic circumstances of carriers.

ARTICLE III-240 (*ex Article 75 TEC*)

1.   In the case of transport within the Union, discrimination which takes the form of carriers charging different rates and imposing different conditions for the carriage of the same goods over the same transport links on grounds of the Member State of origin or of destination of the goods in question shall be prohibited.

2.   Paragraph 1 shall not prevent the adoption of other European laws or framework laws pursuant to Article III-236(2).

3.   The Council, on a proposal from the Commission, shall adopt European regulations or decisions for implementing paragraph 1. It shall act after consulting the European Parliament and the Economic and Social Committee.
The Council may in particular adopt the European regulations and decisions needed to enable the institutions to secure compliance with the rule laid down in paragraph 1 and to ensure that users benefit from it to the full.

4.   The Commission, acting on its own initiative or on application by a Member State, shall investigate any cases of discrimination falling within paragraph 1 and, after consulting any Member State concerned, adopt the necessary European decisions within the framework of the European regulations and decisions referred to in paragraph 3.

ARTICLE III-241 (*ex Article 76 TEC*)

1.   The imposition by a Member State, in respect of transport operations carried out within the Union, of rates and conditions involving any element of support or protection in the interest of one or more particular undertakings or industries shall be prohibited, unless authorised by a European decision of the Commission.

2.   The Commission, acting on its own initiative or on application by a Member State, shall examine the rates and conditions referred to in paragraph 1, taking account in particular of the requirements of an appropriate regional economic policy, the needs of underdeveloped areas and the problems of areas seriously affected by political circumstances on the one hand, and of the effects of such rates and conditions on competition between the different modes of transport on the other.
After consulting each Member State concerned, the Commission shall adopt the necessary European decisions.

3.   The prohibition provided for in paragraph 1 shall not apply to tariffs fixed to meet competition.

ARTICLE III-242 (*ex Article 77 TEC*)

Charges or dues in respect of the crossing of frontiers which are charged by a carrier in addition to the transport rates shall not exceed a reasonable level after taking the costs actually incurred thereby into account. Member States shall endeavour to reduce these costs.
The Commission may make recommendations to Member States for the application of this Article.

ARTICLE III-243 (*ex Article 78 TEC*)

The provisions of this Section shall not form an obstacle to the application of measures taken in the Federal Republic of Germany to the extent that such measures are required in order to compensate for the economic disadvantages caused by the division of Germany to the economy of certain areas of the Federal Republic affected by that division. Five years after the entry into force of the Treaty establishing a Constitution for Europe, the Council, acting on a proposal from the Commission, may adopt a European decision repealing this Article.

ARTICLE III-244 (*ex Article 79 TEC*)

An Advisory Committee consisting of experts designated by the governments of the Member States shall be attached to the Commission. The Commission, whenever it considers it desirable, shall consult the Committee on transport matters.

ARTICLE III-245 (*ex Article 80 TEC*)

1.   This Section shall apply to transport by rail, road and inland waterway.

2.   European laws or framework laws may lay down appropriate measures for sea and air transport. They shall be adopted after consultation of the Committee of the Regions and the Economic and Social Committee.

SECTION 8

TRANS-EUROPEAN NETWORKS

ARTICLE III-246 (*ex Article 154 TEC*)
1.   To help achieve the objectives referred to in Articles III-130 and III-220 and to enable citizens of the Union, economic operators and regional and local communities to derive full benefit from the setting-up of an area without internal frontiers, the Union shall contribute to the establishment and development of trans-European networks in the areas of transport, telecommunications and energy infrastructures.

2.   Within the framework of a system of open and competitive markets, action by the Union shall aim at promoting the interconnection and interoperability of national networks as well as access to such networks. It shall take account in particular of the need to link island, landlocked and peripheral regions with the central regions of the Union.

ARTICLE III-247 (*ex Articles 155 TEC and 156 TEC*)
1.   In order to achieve the objectives referred to in Article III-246, the Union:
(a)   shall establish a series of guidelines covering the objectives, priorities and broad lines of measures envisaged in the sphere of trans-European networks; these guidelines shall identify projects of common interest;
(b)   shall implement any measures that may prove necessary to ensure the interoperability of the networks, in particular in the field of technical standardisation;
(c)   may support projects of common interest supported by Member States, which are identified in the framework of the guidelines referred to in point (a), particularly through feasibility studies, loan guarantees or interest-rate subsidies; the Union may also contribute, through the Cohesion Fund, to the financing of specific projects in Member States in the area of transport infrastructure.
The Union's activities shall take into account the potential economic viability of the projects.

2.   European laws or framework laws shall establish the guidelines and other measures referred to in paragraph 1. Such laws shall be adopted after consultation of the Committee of the Regions and the Economic and Social Committee.
Guidelines and projects of common interest which relate to the territory of a Member State shall require the agreement of that Member State.

3.   Member States shall, in liaison with the Commission, co-ordinate among themselves the policies pursued at national level which may have a significant impact on the achievement of the objectives referred to in Article III-246. The Commission may, in close co-operation with the Member States, take any useful initiative to promote such co-ordination.

4.   The Union may co-operate with third countries to promote projects of mutual interest and to ensure the interoperability of networks.

SECTION 9

RESEARCH AND TECHNOLOGICAL DEVELOPMENT AND SPACE

ARTICLE III-248 (*ex Article 163 TEC*)
1.   The Union shall aim to strengthen its scientific and technological bases by achieving a European research area in which researchers, scientific knowledge and technology circulate freely, and encourage it to become more competitive, including in its industry, while promoting all the research activities deemed necessary by virtue of other Chapters of the Constitution.

2.   For the purposes referred to in paragraph 1 the Union shall, throughout the Union, encourage undertakings, including small and medium-sized undertakings, research centres and universities in their research and technological development activities of high quality. It shall support their efforts to co-operate with one another, aiming, notably, at permitting researchers to co-operate freely across borders and at enabling undertakings to exploit the internal market potential, in particular through the opening-up of national public contracts, the definition of common standards and the removal of legal and fiscal obstacles to that co-operation.

3.   All the Union's activities in the area of research and technological development, including demonstration projects, shall be decided on and implemented in accordance with this Section.

ARTICLE III-249 (*ex Article 164 TEC*)
In pursuing the objectives referred to in Article III-248, the Union shall carry out the following activities, complementing the activities carried out in the Member States:
(a)   implementation of research, technological development and demonstration programmes, by promoting co-operation with and between undertakings, research centres and universities;
(b)   promotion of co-operation in the field of the Union's research, technological development and demonstration with third countries and international organisations;
(c)   dissemination and optimisation of the results of activities in the Union's research, technological development and demonstration;
(d)   stimulation of the training and mobility of researchers in the Union.

ARTICLE III-250 (*ex Article 165 TEC*)
1.   The Union and the Member States shall co-ordinate their research and technological development activities so as to ensure that national policies and the Union's policy are mutually consistent.

2.   In close co-operation with the Member States, the Commission may take any useful initiative to promote the co-ordination referred to in paragraph 1, in particular initiatives aiming at the establishment of guidelines and indicators, the organisation of exchange of best practice, and the preparation of the necessary elements for periodic monitoring and evaluation. The European Parliament shall be kept fully informed.

ARTICLE III-251 (*ex Article 166 TEC*)
1.   European laws shall establish a multiannual framework programme, setting out all the activities financed by the Union. Such laws shall be adopted after consultation of the Economic and Social Committee. The framework programme shall:
(a)   establish the scientific and technological objectives to be achieved by the activities provided for in Article III-249 and lay down the relevant priorities;
(b)   indicate the broad lines of such activities;
(c)   lay down the maximum overall amount and the detailed rules for the Union's financial participation in the framework programme and the respective shares in each of the activities provided for.

2.   The multiannual framework programme shall be adapted or supplemented as the situation changes.

3.   A European law of the Council shall establish specific programmes to implement the multiannual framework programme within each activity. Each specific programme shall define the detailed rules for implementing it, fix its duration and provide for the means deemed necessary. The sum of the amounts deemed necessary, fixed in the specific programmes, shall not exceed the overall maximum amount fixed for the framework programme and each activity. Such a law shall be adopted after consulting the European Parliament and the Economic and Social Committee.

4.   As a complement to the activities planned in the multiannual framework programme, European laws shall establish the measures necessary for the implementation of the European research area. Such laws shall be adopted after consulting the Economic and Social Committee.

ARTICLE III-252 (*ex Articles 167, 168, 169, 170 and second paragraph of ex Article 172 TEC*)
1.   For the implementation of the multiannual framework programme, European laws or framework laws shall establish:
(a)   the rules for the participation of undertakings, research centres and universities;
(b)   the rules governing the dissemination of research results.
Such European laws or framework laws shall be adopted after consultation of the Economic and Social Committee.

2.   In implementing the multiannual framework programme, European laws may establish supplementary programmes involving the participation of certain Member States only, which shall finance them subject to possible participation by the Union.
Such European laws shall determine the rules applicable to supplementary programmes, particularly as regards the dissemination of knowledge as well as access by other Member States. They shall be adopted after consultation of the Economic and Social Committee and with the agreement of the Member States concerned.

3.   In implementing the multiannual framework programme, European laws may make provision, in agreement with the Member States concerned, for participation in research and development programmes

undertaken by several Member States, including participation in the structures created for the execution of those programmes.

Such European laws shall be adopted after consultation of the Economic and Social Committee.

4.   In implementing the multiannual framework programme the Union may make provision for co-operation in the Union's research, technological development and demonstration with third countries or international organisations.

The detailed arrangements for such co-operation may be the subject of agreements between the Union and the third parties concerned.

ARTICLE III-253 (*ex Article 171 and first paragraph of ex Article 172 TEC*)

The Council, on a proposal from the Commission, may adopt European regulations or decisions to set up joint undertakings or any other structure necessary for the efficient execution of the Union's research, technological development and demonstration programmes. It shall act after consulting the European Parliament and the Economic and Social Committee.

ARTICLE III-254 (*new*)

1.   To promote scientific and technical progress, industrial competitiveness and the implementation of its policies, the Union shall draw up a European space policy. To this end, it may promote joint initiatives, support research and technological development and co-ordinate the efforts needed for the exploration and exploitation of space.

2.   To contribute to attaining the objectives referred to in paragraph 1, European laws or framework laws shall establish the necessary measures, which may take the form of a European space programme.

3.   The Union shall establish any appropriate relations with the European Space Agency.

ARTICLE III-255 (*ex Article 173 TEC*)

At the beginning of each year the Commission shall send a report to the European Parliament and the Council. The report shall include information on activities relating to research, technological development and the dissemination of results during the previous year, and the work programme for the current year.

SECTION 10

ENERGY

ARTICLE III-256 (*new*)

1.   In the context of the establishment and functioning of the internal market and with regard for the need to preserve and improve the environment, Union policy on energy shall aim to:
(a)   ensure the functioning of the energy market;
(b)   ensure security of energy supply in the Union, and
(c)   promote energy efficiency and energy saving and the development of new and renewable forms of energy.

2.   Without prejudice to the application of other provisions of the Constitution, the objectives in paragraph 1 shall be achieved by measures enacted in European laws or framework laws. Such laws or framework laws shall be adopted after consultation of the Committee of the Regions and the Economic and Social Committee.

Such European laws or framework laws shall not affect a Member State's right to determine the conditions for exploiting its energy resources, its choice between different energy sources and the general structure of its energy supply, without prejudice to Article III-234(2)(c).

3.   By way of derogation from paragraph 2, a European law or framework law of the Council shall establish the measures referred to therein when they are primarily of a fiscal nature. The Council shall act unanimously after consulting the European Parliament.

CHAPTER IV

AREA OF FREEDOM, SECURITY AND JUSTICE

SECTION 1

GENERAL PROVISIONS

ARTICLE III-257 (*ex Articles 29 TEU and 61 TEC*)
1.   The Union shall constitute an area of freedom, security and justice with respect for fundamental rights and the different legal systems and traditions of the Member States.

2.   It shall ensure the absence of internal border controls for persons and shall frame a common policy on asylum, immigration and external border control, based on solidarity between Member States, which is fair towards third-country nationals. For the purpose of this Chapter, stateless persons shall be treated as third-country nationals.

3.   The Union shall endeavour to ensure a high level of security through measures to prevent and combat crime, racism and xenophobia, and through measures for co-ordination and co-operation between police and judicial authorities and other competent authorities, as well as through the mutual recognition of judgments in criminal matters and, if necessary, through the approximation of criminal laws.

4.   The Union shall facilitate access to justice, in particular through the principle of mutual recognition of judicial and extrajudicial decisions in civil matters.

ARTICLE III-258 (*new*)
The European Council shall define the strategic guidelines for legislative and operational planning within the area of freedom, security and justice.

ARTICLE III-259 (*new*)
National Parliaments shall ensure that the proposals and legislative initiatives submitted under Sections 4 and 5 of this Chapter comply with the principle of subsidiarity, in accordance with the arrangements laid down by the Protocol on the application of the principles of subsidiarity and proportionality.

ARTICLE III-260 (*new*)
Without prejudice to Articles III-360 to III-362, the Council may, on a proposal from the Commission, adopt European regulations or decisions laying down the arrangements whereby Member States, in collaboration with the Commission, conduct objective and impartial evaluation of the implementation of the Union policies referred to in this Chapter by Member States' authorities, in particular in order to facilitate full application of the principle of mutual recognition. The European Parliament and national Parliaments shall be informed of the content and results of the evaluation.

ARTICLE III-261 (*ex Article 36 TEU*)
A standing committee shall be set up within the Council in order to ensure that operational co-operation on internal security is promoted and strengthened within the Union. Without prejudice to Article III-344, it shall facilitate co-ordination of the action of Member States' competent authorities. Representatives of the Union bodies, offices and agencies concerned may be involved in the proceedings of this committee. The European Parliament and national Parliaments shall be kept informed of the proceedings.

ARTICLE III-262 (*ex Article 33 TEU and ex Article 64(1) TEC*)
This Chapter shall not affect the exercise of the responsibilities incumbent upon Member States with regard to the maintenance of law and order and the safeguarding of internal security.

ARTICLE III-263 (*ex Article 66 TEC*)
The Council shall adopt European regulations to ensure administrative co-operation between the relevant departments of the Member States in the areas covered by this Chapter, as well as between those departments and the Commission. It shall act on a Commission proposal, subject to Article III-264, and after consulting the European Parliament.

ARTICLE III-264 (*new*)
The acts referred to in Sections 4 and 5, together with the European regulations referred to in Article III-263 which ensure administrative co-operation in the areas covered by these Sections, shall be adopted:

(a)   on a proposal from the Commission, or

(b)   on the initiative of a quarter of the Member States.

SECTION 2

POLICIES ON BORDER CHECKS, ASYLUM AND IMMIGRATION

ARTICLE III-265 (*ex Articles 62 TEC and 64(1) TEC*)

1.   The Union shall develop a policy with a view to:

(a)   ensuring the absence of any controls on persons, whatever their nationality, when crossing internal borders;

(b)   carrying out checks on persons and efficient monitoring of the crossing of external borders;

(c)   the gradual introduction of an integrated management system for external borders.

2.   For the purposes of paragraph 1, European laws or framework laws shall establish measures concerning:

(a)   the common policy on visas and other short-stay residence permits;

(b)   the checks to which persons crossing external borders are subject;

(c)   the conditions under which nationals of third countries shall have the freedom to travel within the Union for a short period;

(d)   any measure necessary for the gradual establishment of an integrated management system for external borders;

(e)   the absence of any controls on persons, whatever their nationality, when crossing internal borders.

3.   This Article shall not affect the competence of the Member States concerning the geographical demarcation of their borders, in accordance with international law. [*BMDF Note: The UK has an opt-out from this Article, under Protocol no. 18, Article 1.*]

ARTICLE III-266 (*ex Article 63, points 1 and 2, and ex Article 64(2) TEC*)

1.   The Union shall develop a common policy on asylum, subsidiary protection and temporary protection with a view to offering appropriate status to any third-country national requiring international protection and ensuring compliance with the principle of *non-refoulement*. This policy must be in accordance with the Geneva Convention of 28 July 1951 and the Protocol of 31 January 1967 relating to the status of refugees, and other relevant treaties.

2.   For the purposes of paragraph 1, European laws or framework laws shall lay down measures for a common European asylum system comprising:

(a)   a uniform status of asylum for nationals of third countries, valid throughout the Union;

(b)   a uniform status of subsidiary protection for nationals of third countries who, without obtaining European asylum, are in need of international protection;

(c)   a common system of temporary protection for displaced persons in the event of a massive inflow;

(d)   common procedures for the granting and withdrawing of uniform asylum or subsidiary protection status;

(e)   criteria and mechanisms for determining which Member State is responsible for considering an application for asylum or subsidiary protection;

(f)   standards concerning the conditions for the reception of applicants for asylum or subsidiary protection;

(g)   partnership and co-operation with third countries for the purpose of managing inflows of people applying for asylum or subsidiary or temporary protection.

3.   In the event of one or more Member States being confronted by an emergency situation characterised by a sudden inflow of nationals of third countries, the Council, on a proposal from the Commission, may adopt European regulations or decisions comprising provisional measures for the benefit of the Member State(s) concerned. It shall act after consulting the European Parliament.

ARTICLE III-267 (*ex Articles 29 and 31(1)(e) TEU, ex Article 63 TEC (points 3 and 4) and new provisions*)

1.   The Union shall develop a common immigration policy aimed at ensuring, at all stages, the efficient management of migration flows, fair treatment of third-country nationals residing legally in Member States, and the prevention of, and enhanced measures to combat, illegal immigration and trafficking in human beings.

2.   For the purposes of paragraph 1, European laws or framework laws shall establish measures in the following areas:
(a)   the conditions of entry and residence, and standards on the issue by Member States of long-term visas and residence permits, including those for the purpose of family reunion;
(b)   the definition of the rights of third-country nationals residing legally in a Member State, including the conditions governing freedom of movement and of residence in other Member States;
(c)   illegal immigration and unauthorised residence, including removal and repatriation of persons residing without authorisation;
(d)   combating trafficking in persons, in particular women and children.

3.   The Union may conclude agreements with third countries for the readmission to their countries of origin or provenance of third-country nationals who do not or who no longer fulfil the conditions for entry, presence or residence in the territory of one of the Member States.

4.   European laws or framework laws may establish measures to provide incentives and support for the action of Member States with a view to promoting the integration of third-country nationals residing legally in their territories, excluding any harmonisation of the laws and regulations of the Member States.

5.   This Article shall not affect the right of Member States to determine volumes of admission of third-country nationals coming from third countries to their territory in order to seek work, whether employed or self-employed.

ARTICLE III-268 (*new*)
The policies of the Union set out in this Section and their implementation shall be governed by the principle of solidarity and fair sharing of responsibility, including its financial implications, between the Member States. Whenever necessary, the Union acts adopted pursuant to this Section shall contain appropriate measures to give effect to this principle.
[*BMDF Note: The UK has an opt-out from the provisions of this Section, under Protocol no.19, Article 1.*]

SECTION 3

JUDICIAL CO-OPERATION IN CIVIL MATTERS

ARTICLE III-269 (*ex Article 65 TEC*)
1.   The Union shall develop judicial co-operation in civil matters having cross-border implications, based on the principle of mutual recognition of judgments and decisions in extra-judicial cases. Such co-operation may include the adoption of measures for the approximation of the laws and regulations of the Member States.

2.   For the purposes of paragraph 1, European laws or framework laws shall establish measures, particularly when necessary for the proper functioning of the internal market, aimed at ensuring:
(a)   the mutual recognition and enforcement between Member States of judgments and decisions in extra-judicial cases;
(b)   the cross-border service of judicial and extra-judicial documents;
(c)   the compatibility of the rules applicable in the Member States concerning conflict of laws and of jurisdiction;
(d)   co-operation in the taking of evidence;
(e)   effective access to justice;
(f)   the elimination of obstacles to the proper functioning of civil proceedings, if necessary by promoting the compatibility of the rules on civil procedure applicable in the Member States;
(g)   the development of alternative methods of dispute settlement;
(h)   support for the training of the judiciary and judicial staff.

3.   Notwithstanding paragraph 2, a European law or framework law of the Council shall establish measures concerning family law with cross-border implications. The Council shall act unanimously after consulting the European Parliament.
The Council, on a proposal from the Commission, may adopt a European decision determining those aspects of family law with cross-border implications which may be the subject of acts adopted by the ordinary legislative procedure. The Council shall act unanimously after consulting the European Parliament.
[*BMDF Note: The UK has an opt-out from the provisions of this Section, under Protocol no.19, Article 1.*]

SECTION 4

JUDICIAL CO-OPERATION IN CRIMINAL MATTERS

ARTICLE III-270 (*ex Article 31(1) TEU*)

1.   Judicial co-operation in criminal matters in the Union shall be based on the principle of mutual recognition of judgments and judicial decisions and shall include the approximation of the laws and regulations of the Member States in the areas referred to in paragraph 2 and in Article III-271.

European laws or framework laws shall establish measures to:

(a)   lay down rules and procedures for ensuring recognition throughout the Union of all forms of judgments and judicial decisions;

(b)   prevent and settle conflicts of jurisdiction between Member States;

(c)   support the training of the judiciary and judicial staff;

(d)   facilitate co-operation between judicial or equivalent authorities of the Member States in relation to proceedings in criminal matters and the enforcement of decisions.

2.   To the extent necessary to facilitate mutual recognition of judgments and judicial decisions and police and judicial co-operation in criminal matters having a cross-border dimension, European framework laws may establish minimum rules. Such rules shall take into account the differences between the legal traditions and systems of the Member States.

They shall concern:

(a)   mutual admissibility of evidence between Member States;

(b)   the rights of individuals in criminal procedure;

(c)   the rights of victims of crime;

(d)   any other specific aspects of criminal procedure which the Council has identified in advance by a European decision; for the adoption of such a decision, the Council shall act unanimously after obtaining the consent of the European Parliament.

Adoption of the minimum rules referred to in this paragraph shall not prevent Member States from maintaining or introducing a higher level of protection for individuals.

3.   Where a member of the Council considers that a draft European framework law as referred to in paragraph 2 would affect fundamental aspects of its criminal justice system, it may request that the draft framework law be referred to the European Council. In that case, the procedure referred to in Article III-396 shall be suspended. After discussion, the European Council shall, within four months of this suspension, either:

(a)   refer the draft back to the Council, which shall terminate the suspension of the procedure referred to in Article III-396, or

(b)   request the Commission or the group of Member States from which the draft originates to submit a new draft; in that case, the act originally proposed shall be deemed not to have been adopted.

4.   If, by the end of the period referred to in paragraph 3, either no action has been taken by the European Council or if, within 12 months from the submission of a new draft under paragraph 3(b), the European framework law has not been adopted, and at least one third of the Member States wish to establish enhanced co-operation on the basis of the draft framework law concerned, they shall notify the European Parliament, the Council and the Commission accordingly.

In such a case, the authorisation to proceed with enhanced co-operation referred to in Articles I-44(2) and III-419(1) shall be deemed to be granted and the provisions on enhanced co-operation shall apply.

ARTICLE III-271 (*new*)

1.   European framework laws may establish minimum rules concerning the definition of criminal offences and sanctions in the areas of particularly serious crime with a cross-border dimension resulting from the nature or impact of such offences or from a special need to combat them on a common basis.

These areas of crime are the following: terrorism, trafficking in human beings and sexual exploitation of women and children, illicit drug trafficking, illicit arms trafficking, money laundering, corruption, counterfeiting of means of payment, computer crime and organised crime.

On the basis of developments in crime, the Council may adopt a European decision identifying other areas of crime that meet the criteria specified in this paragraph. It shall act unanimously after obtaining the consent of the European Parliament.

2.   If the approximation of criminal laws and regulations of the Member States proves essential to ensure the effective implementation of a Union policy in an area which has been subject to harmonisation measures, European framework laws may establish minimum rules with regard to the definition of criminal offences and

sanctions in the area concerned. Such framework laws shall be adopted by the same procedure as was followed for the adoption of the harmonisation measures in question, without prejudice to Article III-264.

3.   Where a member of the Council considers that a draft European framework law as referred to in paragraph 1 or 2 would affect fundamental aspects of its criminal justice system, it may request that the draft framework law be referred to the European Council. In that case, where the procedure referred to in Article III-396 is applicable, it shall be suspended. After discussion, the European Council shall, within four months of this suspension, either:
(a)   refer the draft back to the Council, which shall terminate the suspension of the procedure referred to in Article III-396 where it is applicable, or
(b)   request the Commission or the group of Member States from which the draft originates to submit a new draft; in that case, the act originally proposed shall be deemed not to have been adopted.

4.   If, by the end of the period referred to in paragraph 3, either no action has been taken by the European Council or if, within 12 months from the submission of a new draft under paragraph 3(b), the European framework law has not been adopted, and at least one third of the Member States wish to establish enhanced co-operation on the basis of the draft framework law concerned, they shall notify the European Parliament, the Council and the Commission accordingly.
In such a case, the authorisation to proceed with enhanced co-operation referred to in Articles I-44(2) and III-419(1) shall be deemed to be granted and the provisions on enhanced co-operation shall apply.

ARTICLE III-272 (*new*)
European laws or framework laws may establish measures to promote and support the action of Member States in the field of crime prevention, excluding any harmonisation of the laws and regulations of the Member States.

ARTICLE III-273 (*ex Article 31(2) TEU*)
1.   Eurojust's mission shall be to support and strengthen co-ordination and co-operation between national investigating and prosecuting authorities in relation to serious crime affecting two or more Member States or requiring a prosecution on common bases, on the basis of operations conducted and information supplied by the Member States' authorities and by Europol.
In this context, European laws shall determine Eurojust's structure, operation, field of action and tasks. Those tasks may include:
(a)   the initiation of criminal investigations, as well as proposing the initiation of prosecutions, conducted by competent national authorities, particularly those relating to offences against the financial interests of the Union;
(b)   the co-ordination of investigations and prosecutions referred to in point (a);
(c)   the strengthening of judicial co-operation, including by resolution of conflicts of jurisdiction and by close co-operation with the European Judicial Network.
European laws shall also determine arrangements for involving the European Parliament and national Parliaments in the evaluation of Eurojust's activities.

2.   In the prosecutions referred to in paragraph 1, and without prejudice to Article III-274, formal acts of judicial procedure shall be carried out by the competent national officials.

ARTICLE III-274 (*new*)
1.   In order to combat crimes affecting the financial interests of the Union, a European law of the Council may establish a European Public Prosecutor's Office from Eurojust. The Council shall act unanimously after obtaining the consent of the European Parliament.

2.   The European Public Prosecutor's Office shall be responsible for investigating, prosecuting and bringing to judgment, where appropriate in liaison with Europol, the perpetrators of, and accomplices in, offences against the Union's financial interests, as determined by the European law provided for in paragraph 1. It shall exercise the functions of prosecutor in the competent courts of the Member States in relation to such offences.

3.   The European law referred to in paragraph 1 shall determine the general rules applicable to the European Public Prosecutor's Office, the conditions governing the performance of its functions, the rules of procedure applicable to its activities, as well as those governing the admissibility of evidence, and the rules applicable to the judicial review of procedural measures taken by it in the performance of its functions.

4.   The European Council may, at the same time or subsequently, adopt a European decision amending paragraph 1 in order to extend the powers of the European Public Prosecutor's Office to include serious crime

having a cross-border dimension and amending accordingly paragraph 2 as regards the perpetrators of, and accomplices in, serious crimes affecting more than one Member State. The European Council shall act unanimously after obtaining the consent of the European Parliament and after consulting the Commission.

SECTION 5

POLICE CO-OPERATION

ARTICLE III-275 (*ex Article 30(1) TEU*)

1.   The Union shall establish police co-operation involving all the Member States' competent authorities, including police, customs and other specialised law enforcement services in relation to the prevention, detection and investigation of criminal offences.

2.   For the purposes of paragraph 1, European laws or framework laws may establish measures concerning:
(a)   the collection, storage, processing, analysis and exchange of relevant information;
(b)   support for the training of staff, and co-operation on the exchange of staff, on equipment and on research into crime-detection;
(c)   common investigative techniques in relation to the detection of serious forms of organised crime.

3.   A European law or framework law of the Council may establish measures concerning operational co-operation between the authorities referred to in this Article. The Council shall act unanimously after consulting the European Parliament.

ARTICLE III-276 (*ex Article 30(2) TEU*)

1.   Europol's mission shall be to support and strengthen action by the Member States' police authorities and other law enforcement services and their mutual co-operation in preventing and combating serious crime affecting two or more Member States, terrorism and forms of crime which affect a common interest covered by a Union policy.

2.   European laws shall determine Europol's structure, operation, field of action and tasks. These tasks may include:
(a)   the collection, storage, processing, analysis and exchange of information forwarded particularly by the authorities of the Member States or third countries or bodies;
(b)   the co-ordination, organisation and implementation of investigative and operational action carried out jointly with the Member States' competent authorities or in the context of joint investigative teams, where appropriate in liaison with Eurojust.
European laws shall also lay down the procedures for scrutiny of Europol's activities by the European Parliament, together with national Parliaments.

3.   Any operational action by Europol must be carried out in liaison and in agreement with the authorities of the Member State or States whose territory is concerned. The application of coercive measures shall be the exclusive responsibility of the competent national authorities.

ARTICLE III-277 (*ex-Article 32 TEU*)

A European law or framework law of the Council shall lay down the conditions and limitations under which the competent authorities of the Member States referred to in Articles III-270 and III-275 may operate in the territory of another Member State in liaison and in agreement with the authorities of that State. The Council shall act unanimously after consulting the European Parliament.

CHAPTER V

AREAS WHERE THE UNION MAY TAKE CO-ORDINATING, COMPLEMENTARY OR SUPPORTING ACTION

SECTION 1

PUBLIC HEALTH

ARTICLE III-278 (*ex Article 152 TEC*)
1.   A high level of human health protection shall be ensured in the definition and implementation of all the Union's policies and activities.
Action by the Union, which shall complement national policies, shall be directed towards improving public health, preventing human illness and diseases, and obviating sources of danger to physical and mental health. Such action shall cover:
(a)   the fight against the major health scourges, by promoting research into their causes, their transmission and their prevention, as well as health information and education;
(b)   monitoring, early warning of and combating serious cross-border threats to health.
The Union shall complement the Member States' action in reducing drug-related health damage, including information and prevention.

2.   The Union shall encourage co-operation between the Member States in the areas referred to in this Article and, if necessary, lend support to their action. It shall in particular encourage co-operation between the Member States to improve the complementarity of their health services in cross-border areas.
Member States shall, in liaison with the Commission, co-ordinate among themselves their policies and programmes in the areas referred to in paragraph 1. The Commission may, in close contact with the Member States, take any useful initiative to promote such co-ordination, in particular initiatives aiming at the establishment of guidelines and indicators, the organisation of exchange of best practice, and the preparation of the necessary elements for periodic monitoring and evaluation. The European Parliament shall be kept fully informed.

3.   The Union and the Member States shall foster co-operation with third countries and the competent international organisations in the sphere of public health.

4.   By way of derogation from Article I-12(5) and Article I-17(a) and in accordance with Article I-14(2)(k), European laws or framework laws shall contribute to the achievement of the objectives referred to in this Article by establishing the following measures in order to meet common safety concerns:
(a)   measures setting high standards of quality and safety of organs and substances of human origin, blood and blood derivatives; these measures shall not prevent any Member State from maintaining or introducing more stringent protective measures;
(b)   measures in the veterinary and phytosanitary fields which have as their direct objective the protection of public health;
(c)   measures setting high standards of quality and safety for medicinal products and devices for medical use;
(d)   measures concerning monitoring, early warning of and combating serious cross-border threats to health.
Such European laws or framework laws shall be adopted after consultation of the Committee of the Regions and the Economic and Social Committee.

5.   European laws or framework laws may also establish incentive measures designed to protect and improve human health and in particular to combat the major cross-border health scourges, as well as measures which have as their direct objective the protection of public health regarding tobacco and the abuse of alcohol, excluding any harmonisation of the laws and regulations of the Member States. They shall be adopted after consultation of the Committee of the Regions and the Economic and Social Committee.

6.   For the purposes of this Article, the Council, on a proposal from the Commission, may also adopt recommendations.

7.   Union action shall respect the responsibilities of the Member States for the definition of their health policy and for the organisation and delivery of health services and medical care. The responsibilities of the Member States shall include the management of health services and medical care and the allocation of the

resources assigned to them. The measures referred to in paragraph 4(a) shall not affect national provisions on the donation or medical use of organs and blood.

SECTION 2

INDUSTRY

ARTICLE III-279 (*ex Article 157 TEC*)

1.   The Union and the Member States shall ensure that the conditions necessary for the competitiveness of the Union's industry exist.

For that purpose, in accordance with a system of open and competitive markets, their action shall be aimed at:

(a)   speeding up the adjustment of industry to structural changes;

(b)   encouraging an environment favourable to initiative and to the development of undertakings throughout the Union, particularly small and medium-sized undertakings;

(c)   encouraging an environment favourable to co-operation between undertakings;

(d)   fostering better exploitation of the industrial potential of policies of innovation, research and technological development.

2.   The Member States shall consult each other in liaison with the Commission and, where necessary, shall co-ordinate their action. The Commission may take any useful initiative to promote such co-ordination, in particular initiatives aiming at the establishment of guidelines and indicators, the organisation of exchange of best practice, and the preparation of the necessary elements for periodic monitoring and evaluation. The European Parliament shall be kept fully informed.

3.   The Union shall contribute to the achievement of the objectives set out in paragraph 1 through the policies and activities it pursues under other provisions of the Constitution. European laws or framework laws may establish specific measures in support of action taken in the Member States to achieve the objectives set out in paragraph 1, excluding any harmonisation of the laws and regulations of the Member States. They shall be adopted after consultation of the Economic and Social Committee.

This Section shall not provide a basis for the introduction by the Union of any measure which could lead to distortion of competition or contains tax provisions or provisions relating to the rights and interests of employed persons.

SECTION 3

CULTURE

ARTICLE III-280 (*ex Article 151 TEC*)

1.   The Union shall contribute to the flowering of the cultures of the Member States, while respecting their national and regional diversity and at the same time bringing the common cultural heritage to the fore.

2.   Action by the Union shall be aimed at encouraging co-operation between Member States and, if necessary, supporting and complementing their action in the following areas:

(a)   improvement of the knowledge and dissemination of the culture and history of the European peoples;

(b)   conservation and safeguarding of cultural heritage of European significance;

(c)   non-commercial cultural exchanges;

(d)   artistic and literary creation, including in the audiovisual sector.

3.   The Union and the Member States shall foster co-operation with third countries and the competent international organisations in the sphere of culture, in particular the Council of Europe.

4.   The Union shall take cultural aspects into account in its action under other provisions of the Constitution, in particular in order to respect and to promote the diversity of its cultures.

5.   In order to contribute to the achievement of the objectives referred to in this Article:

(a)   European laws or framework laws shall establish incentive measures, excluding any harmonisation of the laws and regulations of the Member States. They shall be adopted after consultation of the Committee of the Regions;

(b)   the Council, on a proposal from the Commission, shall adopt recommendations.

SECTION 4

TOURISM

ARTICLE III-281 (*new*)
1.   The Union shall complement the action of the Member States in the tourism sector, in particular by promoting the competitiveness of Union undertakings in that sector.
To that end, Union action shall be aimed at:
(a)   encouraging the creation of a favourable environment for the development of undertakings in this sector;
(b)   promoting co-operation between the Member States, particularly by the exchange of good practice;

2.   European laws or framework laws shall establish specific measures to complement actions within the Member States to achieve the objectives referred to in this Article, excluding any harmonisation of the laws and regulations of the Member States.

SECTION 5

EDUCATION, YOUTH, SPORT AND VOCATIONAL TRAINING

ARTICLE III-282 (*ex Article 149 TEC*)
1.   The Union shall contribute to the development of quality education by encouraging co-operation between Member States and, if necessary, by supporting and complementing their action. It shall fully respect the responsibility of the Member States for the content of teaching and the organisation of education systems and their cultural and linguistic diversity.
The Union shall contribute to the promotion of European sporting issues, while taking account of the specific nature of sport, its structures based on voluntary activity and its social and educational function.
Union action shall be aimed at:
(a)   developing the European dimension in education, particularly through the teaching and dissemination of the languages of the Member States;
(b)   encouraging mobility of students and teachers, inter alia by encouraging the academic recognition of diplomas and periods of study;
(c)   promoting co-operation between educational establishments;
(d)   developing exchanges of information and experience on issues common to the education systems of the Member States;
(e)   encouraging the development of youth exchanges and of exchanges of socio-educational instructors and encouraging the participation of young people in democratic life in Europe;
(f)   encouraging the development of distance education;
(g)   developing the European dimension in sport, by promoting fairness and openness in sporting competitions and co-operation between bodies responsible for sports, and by protecting the physical and moral integrity of sportsmen and sportswomen, especially young sportsmen and sportswomen.

2.   The Union and the Member States shall foster co-operation with third countries and the competent international organisations in the field of education and sport, in particular the Council of Europe.

3.   In order to contribute to the achievement of the objectives referred to in this Article:
(a)   European laws or framework laws shall establish incentive measures, excluding any harmonisation of the laws and regulations of the Member States. They shall be adopted after consultation of the Committee of the Regions and the Economic and Social Committee;
(b)   the Council, on a proposal from the Commission, shall adopt recommendations.

ARTICLE III-283 (*ex Article 150 TEC*)
1.   The Union shall implement a vocational training policy which shall support and complement the action of the Member States, while fully respecting the responsibility of the Member States for the content and organisation of vocational training.
Union action shall aim to:
(a)   facilitate adaptation to industrial change, in particular through vocational training and retraining;
(b)   improve initial and continuing vocational training in order to facilitate vocational integration and reintegration into the labour market;
(c)   facilitate access to vocational training and encourage mobility of instructors and trainees and particularly young people;

(d)   stimulate co-operation on training between educational or training establishments and firms;

(e)   develop exchanges of information and experience on issues common to the training systems of the Member States.

2.   The Union and the Member States shall foster co-operation with third countries and the competent international organisations in the sphere of vocational training.

3.   In order to contribute to the achievement of the objectives referred to in this Article:

(a)   European laws or framework laws shall establish the necessary measures, excluding any harmonisation of the laws and regulations of the Member States. They shall be adopted after consultation of the Committee of the Regions and the Economic and Social Committee;

(b)   the Council, on a proposal from the Commission, shall adopt recommendations.

SECTION 6

CIVIL PROTECTION

ARTICLE III-284 (*new*)

1.   The Union shall encourage co-operation between Member States in order to improve the effectiveness of systems for preventing and protecting against natural or man-made disasters.

Union action shall aim to:

(a)   support and complement Member States' action at national, regional and local level in risk prevention, in preparing their civil-protection personnel and in responding to natural or man-made disasters within the Union;

(b)   promote swift, effective operational co-operation within the Union between national civil-protection services;

(c)   promote consistency in international civil-protection work.

2.   European laws or framework laws shall establish the measures necessary to help achieve the objectives referred to in paragraph 1, excluding any harmonisation of the laws and regulations of the Member States.

SECTION 7

ADMINISTRATIVE CO-OPERATION

ARTICLE III-285 (*new*)

1.   Effective implementation of Union law by the Member States, which is essential for the proper functioning of the Union, shall be regarded as a matter of common interest.

2.   The Union may support the efforts of Member States to improve their administrative capacity to implement Union law. Such action may include facilitating the exchange of information and of civil servants as well as supporting training schemes. No Member State shall be obliged to avail itself of such support. European laws shall establish the necessary measures to this end, excluding any harmonisation of the laws and regulations of the Member States.

3.   This Article shall be without prejudice to the obligations of the Member States to implement Union law or to the prerogatives and duties of the Commission. It shall also be without prejudice to other provisions of the Constitution providing for administrative co-operation among the Member States and between them and the Union.

TITLE IV

ASSOCIATION OF THE OVERSEAS COUNTRIES AND TERRITORIES

ARTICLE III-286 (*ex Article 182 TEC*)

1.   The non-European countries and territories which have special relations with Denmark, France, the Netherlands and the United Kingdom shall be associated with the Union. These countries and territories, hereinafter called the "countries and territories", are listed in Annex II.

This title shall apply to Greenland, subject to the specific provisions of the Protocol on special arrangements for Greenland.

2.   The purpose of association shall be to promote the economic and social development of the countries and territories and to establish close economic relations between them and the Union.

Association shall serve primarily to further the interests and prosperity of the inhabitants of these countries and territories in order to lead them to the economic, social and cultural development to which they aspire.

ARTICLE III-287 (*ex Article 183 TEC*)

Association shall have the following objectives:

(a)   Member States shall apply to their trade with the countries and territories the same treatment as they accord each other pursuant to the Constitution;

(b)   each country or territory shall apply to its trade with Member States and with the other countries and territories the same treatment as that which it applies to the European State with which it has special relations;

(c)   Member States shall contribute to the investments required for the progressive development of these countries and territories;

(d)   for investments financed by the Union, participation in tenders and supplies shall be open on equal terms to all natural and legal persons who are nationals of a Member State or of one of the countries and territories;

(e)   in relations between Member States and the countries and territories, the right of establishment of nationals and companies or firms shall be regulated in accordance with the provisions of Subsection 2 of Section 2 of Chapter I of Title III relating to the freedom of establishment and under the procedures laid down in that Subsection, and on a non-discriminatory basis, subject to any acts adopted pursuant to Article III-291.

ARTICLE III-288 (*ex Article 184 TEC*)

1.   Customs duties on imports into the Member States of goods originating in the countries and territories shall be prohibited in conformity with the prohibition of customs duties between Member States provided for in the Constitution.

2.   Customs duties on imports into each country or territory from Member States or from the other countries or territories shall be prohibited in accordance with Article III-151(4).

3.   The countries and territories may, however, levy customs duties which meet the needs of their development and industrialisation or produce revenue for their budgets.

The duties referred to in the first subparagraph shall not exceed the level of those imposed on imports of products from the Member State with which each country or territory has special relations.

4.   Paragraph 2 shall not apply to countries and territories which, by reason of the particular international obligations by which they are bound, already apply a non-discriminatory customs tariff.

5.   The introduction of or any change in customs duties imposed on goods imported into the countries and territories shall not, either in law or in fact, give rise to any direct or indirect discrimination between imports from the various Member States.

ARTICLE III-289 (*ex Article 185 TEC*)

If the level of the duties applicable to goods from a third country on entry into a country or territory is liable, when Article III-288(1) has been applied, to cause deflections of trade to the detriment of any Member State, the latter may request the Commission to propose to the other Member States that they take the necessary measures to remedy the situation.

ARTICLE III-290 (*ex Article 186 TEC*)
Subject to the provisions relating to public health, public security or public policy, freedom of movement within Member States for workers from the countries and territories, and within the countries and territories for workers from Member States, shall be regulated by acts adopted in accordance with Article III-291.

ARTICLE III-291 (*ex Article 187 TEC*)
The Council, on a proposal from the Commission, shall adopt unanimously, on the basis of the experience acquired under the association of the countries and territories with the Union, European laws, framework laws, regulations and decisions as regards the detailed rules and the procedure for the association of the countries and territories with the Union. These laws and framework laws shall be adopted after consultation of the European Parliament.

TITLE V

THE UNION'S EXTERNAL ACTION

CHAPTER I

PROVISIONS HAVING GENERAL APPLICATION

ARTICLE III-292 (*Article 3, second paragraph, TEU and ex Article 11 TEU*)
1.   The Union's action on the international scene shall be guided by the principles which have inspired its own creation, development and enlargement, and which it seeks to advance in the wider world: democracy, the rule of law, the universality and indivisibility of human rights and fundamental freedoms, respect for human dignity, the principles of equality and solidarity, and respect for the principles of the United Nations Charter and international law.
The Union shall seek to develop relations and build partnerships with third countries, and international, regional or global organisations which share the principles referred to in the first subparagraph. It shall promote multilateral solutions to common problems, in particular in the framework of the United Nations.

2.   The Union shall define and pursue common policies and actions, and shall work for a high degree of co-operation in all fields of international relations, in order to:
(a)   safeguard its values, fundamental interests, security, independence and integrity;
(b)   consolidate and support democracy, the rule of law, human rights and the principles of international law;
(c)   preserve peace, prevent conflicts and strengthen international security, in accordance with the purposes and principles of the United Nations Charter, with the principles of the Helsinki Final Act and with the aims of the Charter of Paris, including those relating to external borders;
(d)   foster the sustainable economic, social and environmental development of developing countries, with the primary aim of eradicating poverty;
(e)   encourage the integration of all countries into the world economy, including through the progressive abolition of restrictions on international trade;
(f)   help develop international measures to preserve and improve the quality of the environment and the sustainable management of global natural resources, in order to ensure sustainable development;
(g)   assist populations, countries and regions confronting natural or man-made disasters;
(h)   promote an international system based on stronger multilateral co-operation and good global governance.

3.   The Union shall respect the principles and pursue the objectives set out in paragraphs 1 and 2 in the development and implementation of the different areas of the Union's external action covered by this Title and the external aspects of its other policies.
The Union shall ensure consistency between the different areas of its external action and between these and its other policies. The Council and the Commission, assisted by the Union Minister for Foreign Affairs, shall ensure that consistency and shall co-operate to that effect.

ARTICLE III-293 (*new*)
1.   On the basis of the principles and objectives set out in Article III-292, the European Council shall identify the strategic interests and objectives of the Union.

European decisions of the European Council on the strategic interests and objectives of the Union shall relate to the common foreign and security policy and to other areas of the external action of the Union. Such decisions may concern the relations of the Union with a specific country or region or may be thematic in approach. They shall define their duration, and the means to be made available by the Union and the Member States.

The European Council shall act unanimously on a recommendation from the Council, adopted by the latter under the arrangements laid down for each area. European decisions of the European Council shall be implemented in accordance with the procedures provided for in the Constitution.

2.   The Union Minister for Foreign Affairs, for the area of common foreign and security policy, and the Commission, for other areas of external action, may submit joint proposals to the Council.

CHAPTER II

COMMON FOREIGN AND SECURITY POLICY

SECTION 1

COMMON PROVISIONS

ARTICLE III-294 (*ex Articles 11 and 12 TEU*)
1.   In the context of the principles and objectives of its external action, the Union shall define and implement a common foreign and security policy covering all areas of foreign and security policy.

2.   The Member States shall support the common foreign and security policy actively and unreservedly in a spirit of loyalty and mutual solidarity.
The Member States shall work together to enhance and develop their mutual political solidarity. They shall refrain from any action which is contrary to the interests of the Union or likely to impair its effectiveness as a cohesive force in international relations.
The Council and the Union Minister for Foreign Affairs shall ensure that these principles are complied with.

3.   The Union shall conduct the common foreign and security policy by:
(a)   defining the general guidelines;
(b)   adopting European decisions defining:
    (i)   actions to be undertaken by the Union;
    (ii)   positions to be taken by the Union;
    (iii)   arrangements for the implementation of the European decisions referred to in points (i) and (ii);
(c)   strengthening systematic co-operation between Member States in the conduct of policy.

ARTICLE III-295 (*ex Article 13 TEU*)
1.   The European Council shall define the general guidelines for the common foreign and security policy, including for matters with defence implications.
If international developments so require, the President of the European Council shall convene an extraordinary meeting of the European Council in order to define the strategic lines of the Union's policy in the face of such developments.

2.   The Council shall adopt the European decisions necessary for defining and implementing the common foreign and security policy on the basis of the general guidelines and strategic lines defined by the European Council.

ARTICLE III-296 (*new*)
1.   The Union Minister for Foreign Affairs, who shall chair the Foreign Affairs Council, shall contribute through his or her proposals towards the preparation of the common foreign and security policy and shall ensure implementation of the European decisions adopted by the European Council and the Council.

2.   The Minister for Foreign Affairs shall represent the Union for matters relating to the common foreign and security policy. He or she shall conduct political dialogue with third parties on the Union's behalf and shall express the Union's position in international organisations and at international conferences.

3. In fulfilling his or her mandate, the Union Minister for Foreign Affairs shall be assisted by a European External Action Service. This service shall work in co-operation with the diplomatic services of the Member States and shall comprise officials from relevant departments of the General Secretariat of the Council and of the Commission as well as staff seconded from national diplomatic services of the Member States. The organisation and functioning of the European External Action Service shall be established by a European decision of the Council. The Council shall act on a proposal from the Union Minister for Foreign Affairs after consulting the European Parliament and after obtaining the consent of the Commission.

ARTICLE III-297 (*ex Article 14 TEU*)

1. Where the international situation requires operational action by the Union, the Council shall adopt the necessary European decisions. Such decisions shall lay down the objectives, the scope, the means to be made available to the Union, if necessary the duration, and the conditions for implementation of the action.

If there is a change in circumstances having a substantial effect on a question subject to such a European decision, the Council shall review the principles and objectives of that decision and adopt the necessary European decisions.

2. The European decisions referred to in paragraph 1 shall commit the Member States in the positions they adopt and in the conduct of their activity.

3. Whenever there is any plan to adopt a national position or take national action pursuant to a European decision as referred to in paragraph 1, information shall be provided by the Member State concerned in time to allow, if necessary, for prior consultations within the Council. The obligation to provide prior information shall not apply to measures which are merely a national transposition of such a decision.

4. In cases of imperative need arising from changes in the situation and failing a review of the European decision pursuant to the second subparagraph of paragraph 1, Member States may take the necessary measures as a matter of urgency, having regard to the general objectives of that decision. The Member State concerned shall inform the Council immediately of any such measures.

5. Should there be any major difficulties in implementing a European decision as referred to in this Article, a Member State shall refer them to the Council which shall discuss them and seek appropriate solutions. Such solutions shall not run counter to the objectives of the action or impair its effectiveness.

ARTICLE III-298 (*ex Article 15 TEU*)

The Council shall adopt European decisions which shall define the approach of the Union to a particular matter of a geographical or thematic nature. Member States shall ensure that their national policies conform to the positions of the Union.

ARTICLE III-299 (*ex Article 22 TEU*)

1. Any Member State, the Union Minister for Foreign Affairs, or that Minister with the Commission's support, may refer any question relating to the common foreign and security policy to the Council and may submit to it initiatives or proposals as appropriate.

2. In cases requiring a rapid decision, the Union Minister for Foreign Affairs, of the Minister's own motion or at the request of a Member State, shall convene an extraordinary meeting of the Council within forty-eight hours or, in an emergency, within a shorter period.

ARTICLE III-300 (*ex Article 23 TEU*)

1. The European decisions referred to in this Chapter shall be adopted by the Council acting unanimously.

When abstaining in a vote, any member of the Council may qualify its abstention by making a formal declaration. In that case, it shall not be obliged to apply the European decision, but shall accept that the latter commits the Union. In a spirit of mutual solidarity, the Member State concerned shall refrain from any action likely to conflict with or impede Union action based on that decision and the other Member States shall respect its position. If the members of the Council qualifying their abstention in this way represent at least one third of the Member States comprising at least one third of the population of the Union, the decision shall not be adopted.

2. By way of derogation from paragraph 1, the Council shall act by a qualified majority:

(a) when adopting European decisions defining a Union action or position on the basis of a European decision of the European Council relating to the Union's strategic interests and objectives, as referred to in Article III-293(1);

(b)   when adopting a European decision defining a Union action or position, on a proposal which the Union Minister for Foreign Affairs has presented following a specific request to him or her from the European Council, made on its own initiative or that of the Minister;

(c)   when adopting a European decision implementing a European decision defining a Union action or position;

(d)   when adopting a European decision concerning the appointment of a special representative in accordance with Article III-302.

If a member of the Council declares that, for vital and stated reasons of national policy, it intends to oppose the adoption of a European decision to be adopted by a qualified majority, a vote shall not be taken. The Union Minister for Foreign Affairs will, in close consultation with the Member State involved, search for a solution acceptable to it. If he or she does not succeed, the Council may, acting by a qualified majority, request that the matter be referred to the European Council for a European decision by unanimity.

3.   In accordance with Article I-40(7) the European Council may unanimously adopt a European decision stipulating that the Council shall act by a qualified majority in cases other than those referred to in paragraph 2 of this Article.

4.   Paragraphs 2 and 3 shall not apply to decisions having military or defence implications.

ARTICLE III-301 (*new*)

1.   When the European Council or the Council has defined a common approach of the Union within the meaning of Article I-40(5), the Union Minister for Foreign Affairs and the Ministers for Foreign Affairs of the Member States shall co-ordinate their activities within the Council.

2.   The diplomatic missions of the Member States and the Union delegations in third countries and at international organisations shall co-operate and shall contribute to formulating and implementing the common approach referred to in paragraph 1.

ARTICLE III-302 (*ex Article 18(5) TEU*)

The Council may appoint, on a proposal from the Union Minister for Foreign Affairs, a special representative with a mandate in relation to particular policy issues. The special representative shall carry out his or her mandate under the Minister's authority.

ARTICLE III-303 (*ex Article 24 TEU and Article 300 TEC*)

The Union may conclude agreements with one or more States or international organisations in areas covered by this Chapter.

ARTICLE III-304 (*ex Article 21 TEU*)

1.   The Union Minister for Foreign Affairs shall consult and inform the European Parliament in accordance with Article I-40(8) and Article I-41(8). He or she shall ensure that the views of the European Parliament are duly taken into consideration. Special representatives may be involved in briefing the European Parliament.

2.   The European Parliament may ask questions of the Council and of the Union Minister for Foreign Affairs or make recommendations to them. Twice a year it shall hold a debate on progress in implementing the common foreign and security policy, including the common security and defence policy.

ARTICLE III-305 (*ex Article 19 TEU*)

1.   Member States shall co-ordinate their action in international organisations and at international conferences. They shall uphold the Union's positions in such fora. The Union Minister for Foreign Affairs shall organise this co-ordination.

In international organisations and at international conferences where not all the Member States participate, those which do take part shall uphold the Union's positions.

2.   In accordance with Article I-16(2), Member States represented in international organisations or international conferences where not all the Member States participate shall keep the latter, as well as the Union Minister for Foreign Affairs, informed of any matter of common interest.

Member States which are also members of the United Nations Security Council shall concert and keep the other Member States and the Union Minister for Foreign Affairs fully informed. Member States which are members of the Security Council will, in the execution of their functions, defend the positions and the interests of the Union, without prejudice to their responsibilities under the United Nations Charter.

When the Union has defined a position on a subject which is on the United Nations Security Council agenda, those Member States which sit on the Security Council shall request that the Union Minister for Foreign Affairs be asked to present the Union's position.

ARTICLE III-306 (*ex Article 20 TEU*)

The diplomatic and consular missions of the Member States and the Union delegations in third countries and international conferences, and their representations to international organisations, shall co-operate in ensuring that the European decisions defining Union positions and actions adopted pursuant to this Chapter are complied with and implemented. They shall step up co-operation by exchanging information and carrying out joint assessments.

They shall contribute to the implementation of the right of European citizens to protection in the territory of third countries as referred to in Article I-10(2)(c) and the measures adopted pursuant to Article III-127.

ARTICLE III-307 (*ex Article 25 TEU*)

1.   Without prejudice to Article III-344, a Political and Security Committee shall monitor the international situation in the areas covered by the common foreign and security policy and contribute to the definition of policies by delivering opinions to the Council at the request of the latter, or of the Union Minister for Foreign Affairs, or on its own initiative. It shall also monitor the implementation of agreed policies, without prejudice to the powers of the Union Minister for Foreign Affairs.

2.   Within the scope of this Chapter, the Political and Security Committee shall exercise, under the responsibility of the Council and of the Union Minister for Foreign Affairs, the political control and strategic direction of the crisis management operations referred to in Article III-309.

The Council may authorise the Committee, for the purpose and for the duration of a crisis management operation, as determined by the Council, to take the relevant measures concerning the political control and strategic direction of the operation.

ARTICLE III-308 (*ex Articles 46(f) and 47 TEU*)

The implementation of the common foreign and security policy shall not affect the application of the procedures and the extent of the powers of the institutions laid down by the Constitution for the exercise of the Union competences referred to in Articles I-13 to I-15 and I-17.

Similarly, the implementation of the policies listed in those Articles shall not affect the application of the procedures and the extent of the powers of the institutions laid down by the Constitution for the exercise of the Union competences under this Chapter.

SECTION 2

THE COMMON SECURITY AND DEFENCE POLICY

ARTICLE III-309 (*ex Article 17(2) TEU*)

1.   The tasks referred to in Article I-41(1), in the course of which the Union may use civilian and military means, shall include joint disarmament operations, humanitarian and rescue tasks, military advice and assistance tasks, conflict prevention and peace-keeping tasks, tasks of combat forces in crisis management, including peace-making and post-conflict stabilisation. All these tasks may contribute to the fight against terrorism, including by supporting third countries in combating terrorism in their territories.

2.   The Council shall adopt European decisions relating to the tasks referred to in paragraph 1, defining their objectives and scope and the general conditions for their implementation. The Union Minister for Foreign Affairs, acting under the authority of the Council and in close and constant contact with the Political and Security Committee, shall ensure co-ordination of the civilian and military aspects of such tasks.

ARTICLE III-310 (*new*)

1.   Within the framework of the European decisions adopted in accordance with Article III-309, the Council may entrust the implementation of a task to a group of Member States which are willing and have the necessary capability for such a task. Those Member States, in association with the Union Minister for Foreign Affairs, shall agree among themselves on the management of the task.

2.   Member States participating in the task shall keep the Council regularly informed of its progress on their own initiative or at the request of another Member State. Those States shall inform the Council immediately should the completion of the task entail major consequences or require amendment of the

objective, scope and conditions determined for the task in the European decisions referred to in paragraph 1. In such cases, the Council shall adopt the necessary European decisions.

ARTICLE III-311 (*new*)

1. The Agency in the field of defence capabilities development, research, acquisition and armaments (European Defence Agency), established by Article I-41(3) and subject to the authority of the Council, shall have as its task to:

(a)   contribute to identifying the Member States' military capability objectives and evaluating observance of the capability commitments given by the Member States;

(b)   promote harmonisation of operational needs and adoption of effective, compatible procurement methods;

(c)   propose multilateral projects to fulfil the objectives in terms of military capabilities, ensure co-ordination of the programmes implemented by the Member States and management of specific co-operation programmes;

(d)   support defence technology research, and co-ordinate and plan joint research activities and the study of technical solutions meeting future operational needs;

(e)   contribute to identifying and, if necessary, implementing any useful measure for strengthening the industrial and technological base of the defence sector and for improving the effectiveness of military expenditure.

2. The European Defence Agency shall be open to all Member States wishing to be part of it. The Council, acting by a qualified majority, shall adopt a European decision defining the Agency's statute, seat and operational rules. That decision should take account of the level of effective participation in the Agency's activities. Specific groups shall be set up within the Agency bringing together Member States engaged in joint projects. The Agency shall carry out its tasks in liaison with the Commission where necessary.

ARTICLE III-312 (*new*)

1. Those Member States which wish to participate in the permanent structured co-operation referred to in Article I-41(6), which fulfil the criteria and have made the commitments on military capabilities set out in the Protocol on permanent structured co-operation shall notify their intention to the Council and to the Union Minister for Foreign Affairs.

2. Within three months following the notification referred to in paragraph 1 the Council shall adopt a European decision establishing permanent structured co-operation and determining the list of participating Member States. The Council shall act by a qualified majority after consulting the Union Minister for Foreign Affairs.

3. Any Member State which, at a later stage, wishes to participate in the permanent structured co-operation shall notify its intention to the Council and to the Union Minister for Foreign Affairs.

The Council shall adopt a European decision confirming the participation of the Member State concerned which fulfils the criteria and makes the commitments referred to in Articles 1 and 2 of the Protocol on permanent structured co-operation. The Council shall act by a qualified majority after consulting the Union Minister for Foreign Affairs. Only members of the Council representing the participating Member States shall take part in the vote.

A qualified majority shall be defined as at least 55% of the members of the Council representing the participating Member States, comprising at least 65% of the population of these States.

A blocking minority must include at least the minimum number of Council members representing more than 35% of the population of the participating Member States, plus one member, failing which the qualified majority shall be deemed attained. *[BMDF Note: The final two sub-paragraphs come into force on 1 November 2009, under the terms of Protocol no. 34, Article 2.]*

4. If a participating Member State no longer fulfils the criteria or is no longer able to meet the commitments referred to in Articles 1 and 2 of the Protocol on permanent structured co-operation, the Council may adopt a European decision suspending the participation of the Member State concerned.

The Council shall act by a qualified majority. Only members of the Council representing the participating Member States, with the exception of the Member State in question, shall take part in the vote.

A qualified majority shall be defined as at least 55% of the members of the Council representing the participating Member States, comprising at least 65% of the population of these States.

A blocking minority must include at least the minimum number of Council members representing more than 35% of the population of the participating Member States, plus one member, failing which the qualified majority shall be deemed attained. *[BMDF Note: The final two sub-paragraphs come into force on 1 November 2009, under the terms of Protocol no. 34, Article 2.]*

5.   Any participating Member State which wishes to withdraw from permanent structured co-operation shall notify its intention to the Council, which shall take note that the Member State in question has ceased to participate.

6.   The European decisions and recommendations of the Council within the framework of permanent structured co-operation, other than those provided for in paragraphs 2 to 5, shall be adopted by unanimity. For the purposes of this paragraph, unanimity shall be constituted by the votes of the representatives of the participating Member States only.

SECTION 3

FINANCIAL PROVISIONS

ARTICLE III-313 (*ex Article 28 TEU*)

1.   Administrative expenditure which the implementation of this Chapter entails for the institutions shall be charged to the Union budget.

2.   Operating expenditure to which the implementation of this Chapter gives rise shall also be charged to the Union budget, except for such expenditure arising from operations having military or defence implications and cases where the Council decides otherwise.

In cases where expenditure is not charged to the Union budget it shall be charged to the Member States in accordance with the gross national product scale, unless the Council decides otherwise. As for expenditure arising from operations having military or defence implications, Member States whose representatives in the Council have made a formal declaration under Article III-300(1), second subparagraph, shall not be obliged to contribute to the financing thereof.

3.   The Council shall adopt a European decision establishing the specific procedures for guaranteeing rapid access to appropriations in the Union budget for urgent financing of initiatives in the framework of the common foreign and security policy, and in particular for preparatory activities for the tasks referred to in Article I-41(1) and Article III-309. It shall act after consulting the European Parliament.

Preparatory activities for the tasks referred to in Article I-41(1) and Article III-309 which are not charged to the Union budget shall be financed by a start-up fund made up of Member States' contributions.

The Council shall adopt by a qualified majority, on a proposal from the Union Minister for Foreign Affairs, European decisions establishing:

(a)   the procedures for setting up and financing the start-up fund, in particular the amounts allocated to the fund;

(b)   the procedures for administering the start-up fund;

(c)   the financial control procedures.

When the task planned in accordance with Article I-41(1) and Article III-309 cannot be charged to the Union budget, the Council shall authorise the Union Minister for Foreign Affairs to use the fund. The Union Minister for Foreign Affairs shall report to the Council on the implementation of this remit.

CHAPTER III

COMMON COMMERCIAL POLICY

ARTICLE III-314 (*ex Article 131 TEC*)

By establishing a customs union in accordance with Article III-151, the Union shall contribute, in the common interest, to the harmonious development of world trade, the progressive abolition of restrictions on international trade and on foreign direct investment, and the lowering of customs and other barriers.

ARTICLE III-315 (*ex Article 133 TEC*)

1.   The common commercial policy shall be based on uniform principles, particularly with regard to changes in tariff rates, the conclusion of tariff and trade agreements relating to trade in goods and services, and the commercial aspects of intellectual property, foreign direct investment, the achievement of uniformity in measures of liberalisation, export policy and measures to protect trade such as those to be taken in the event of dumping or subsidies. The common commercial policy shall be conducted in the context of the principles and objectives of the Union's external action.

2.   European laws shall establish the measures defining the framework for implementing the common commercial policy.

3.   Where agreements with one or more third countries or international organisations need to be negotiated and concluded, Article III-325 shall apply, subject to the special provisions of this Article.

The Commission shall make recommendations to the Council, which shall authorise it to open the necessary negotiations. The Council and the Commission shall be responsible for ensuring that the agreements negotiated are compatible with internal Union policies and rules.

The Commission shall conduct these negotiations in consultation with a special committee appointed by the Council to assist the Commission in this task and within the framework of such directives as the Council may issue to it. The Commission shall report regularly to the special committee and to the European Parliament on the progress of negotiations.

4.   For the negotiation and conclusion of the agreements referred to in paragraph 3, the Council shall act by a qualified majority.

For the negotiation and conclusion of agreements in the fields of trade in services and the commercial aspects of intellectual property, as well as foreign direct investment, the Council shall act unanimously where such agreements include provisions for which unanimity is required for the adoption of internal rules.

The Council shall also act unanimously for the negotiation and conclusion of agreements:

(a)   in the field of trade in cultural and audiovisual services, where these agreements risk prejudicing the Union's cultural and linguistic diversity;

(b)   in the field of trade in social, education and health services, where these agreements risk seriously disturbing the national organisation of such services and prejudicing the responsibility of Member States to deliver them.

5.   The negotiation and conclusion of international agreements in the field of transport shall be subject to Section 7 of Chapter III of Title III and to Article III-325.

6.   The exercise of the competences conferred by this Article in the field of the common commercial policy shall not affect the delimitation of competences between the Union and the Member States, and shall not lead to harmonisation of legislative or regulatory provisions of the Member States insofar as the Constitution excludes such harmonisation.

CHAPTER IV

CO-OPERATION WITH THIRD COUNTRIES AND HUMANITARIAN AID

SECTION 1

DEVELOPMENT CO-OPERATION

ARTICLE III-316 (ex Article 177 TEC)

1.   Union policy in the field of development co-operation shall be conducted within the framework of the principles and objectives of the Union's external action. The Union's development co-operation policy and that of the Member States shall complement and reinforce each other.

Union development co-operation policy shall have as its primary objective the reduction and, in the long term, the eradication of poverty. The Union shall take account of the objectives of development co-operation in the policies that it implements which are likely to affect developing countries.

2.   The Union and the Member States shall comply with the commitments and take account of the objectives they have approved in the context of the United Nations and other competent international organisations.

ARTICLE III-317 (ex Articles 179 and 181 TEC)

1.   European laws or framework laws shall establish the measures necessary for the implementation of development co-operation policy, which may relate to multiannual co-operation programmes with developing countries or programmes with a thematic approach.

2.   The Union may conclude with third countries and competent international organisations any agreement helping to achieve the objectives referred to in Articles III-292 and III-316.

The first subparagraph shall be without prejudice to Member States' competence to negotiate in international bodies and to conclude agreements.

3. The European Investment Bank shall contribute, under the terms laid down in its Statute, to the implementation of the measures referred to in paragraph 1.

ARTICLE III-318 (*ex Articles 180 and 181 TEC*)
1. In order to promote the complementarity and efficiency of their action, the Union and the Member States shall co-ordinate their policies on development co-operation and shall consult each other on their aid programmes, including in international organisations and during international conferences. They may undertake joint action. Member States shall contribute if necessary to the implementation of Union aid programmes.

2. The Commission may take any useful initiative to promote the co-ordination referred to in paragraph 1.

3. Within their respective spheres of competence, the Union and the Member States shall co-operate with third countries and the competent international organisations.

SECTION 2

ECONOMIC, FINANCIAL AND TECHNICAL CO-OPERATION WITH THIRD COUNTRIES

ARTICLE III-319 (*ex Article 181a TEC*)
1. Without prejudice to the other provisions of the Constitution, and in particular Articles III-316 to III-318, the Union shall carry out economic, financial and technical co-operation measures, including assistance, in particular financial assistance, with third countries other than developing countries. Such measures shall be consistent with the development policy of the Union and shall be carried out within the framework of the principles and objectives of its external action. The Union's measures and those of the Member States shall complement and reinforce each other.

2. European laws or framework laws shall establish the measures necessary for the implementation of paragraph 1.

3. Within their respective spheres of competence, the Union and the Member States shall co-operate with third countries and the competent international organisations. The arrangements for Union co-operation may be the subject of agreements between the Union and the third parties concerned.
The first subparagraph shall be without prejudice to Member States' competence to negotiate in international bodies and to conclude agreements.

ARTICLE III-320 *(new)*
When the situation in a third country requires urgent financial assistance from the Union, the Council shall adopt the necessary European decisions on a proposal from the Commission.

SECTION 3

HUMANITARIAN AID

ARTICLE III-321 *(new)*
1. The Union's operations in the field of humanitarian aid shall be conducted within the framework of the principles and objectives of the external action of the Union. Such operations shall be intended to provide ad hoc assistance and relief and protection for people in third countries who are victims of natural or man-made disasters, in order to meet the humanitarian needs resulting from these different situations. The Union's operations and those of the Member States shall complement and reinforce each other.

2. Humanitarian aid operations shall be conducted in compliance with the principles of international law and with the principles of impartiality, neutrality and non-discrimination.

3.   European laws or framework laws shall establish the measures defining the framework within which the Union's humanitarian aid operations shall be implemented.

4.   The Union may conclude with third countries and competent international organisations any agreement helping to achieve the objectives referred to in paragraph 1 and in Article III-292.
The first subparagraph shall be without prejudice to Member States' competence to negotiate in international bodies and to conclude agreements.

5.   In order to establish a framework for joint contributions from young Europeans to the humanitarian aid operations of the Union, a European Voluntary Humanitarian Aid Corps shall be set up. European laws shall determine the rules and procedures for the operation of the Corps.

6.   The Commission may take any useful initiative to promote co-ordination between actions of the Union and those of the Member States, in order to enhance the efficiency and complementarity of Union and national humanitarian aid measures.

7.   The Union shall ensure that its humanitarian aid operations are co-ordinated and consistent with those of international organisations and bodies, in particular those forming part of the United Nations system.

CHAPTER V

RESTRICTIVE MEASURES

ARTICLE III-322 (*ex Article 301 TEC*)
1.   Where a European decision, adopted in accordance with Chapter II, provides for the interruption or reduction, in part or completely, of economic and financial relations with one or more third countries, the Council, acting by a qualified majority on a joint proposal from the Union Minister for Foreign Affairs and the Commission, shall adopt the necessary European regulations or decisions. It shall inform the European Parliament thereof.

2.   Where a European decision adopted in accordance with Chapter II so provides, the Council may adopt restrictive measures under the procedure referred to in paragraph 1 against natural or legal persons and groups or non-State entities.

3.   The acts referred to in this Article shall include necessary provisions on legal safeguards.

CHAPTER VI

INTERNATIONAL AGREEMENTS

ARTICLE III-323 (*ex Article 24 TEU and Article 300(7) TEC*)
1.   The Union may conclude an agreement with one or more third countries or international organisations where the Constitution so provides or where the conclusion of an agreement is necessary in order to achieve, within the framework of the Union's policies, one of the objectives referred to in the Constitution, or is provided for in a legally binding Union act or is likely to affect common rules or alter their scope.

2.   Agreements concluded by the Union are binding on the institutions of the Union and on its Member States.

ARTICLE III-324 (*ex Article 310 TEC*)
The Union may conclude an association agreement with one or more third countries or international organisations in order to establish an association involving reciprocal rights and obligations, common actions and special procedures.

ARTICLE III-325 (*ex Article 300 TEC*)
1.   Without prejudice to the specific provisions laid down in Article III-315, agreements between the Union and third countries or international organisations shall be negotiated and concluded in accordance with the following procedure.

2.   The Council shall authorise the opening of negotiations, adopt negotiating directives, authorise the signing of agreements and conclude them.

3.   The Commission, or the Union Minister for Foreign Affairs where the agreement envisaged relates exclusively or principally to the common foreign and security policy, shall submit recommendations to the Council, which shall adopt a European decision authorising the opening of negotiations and, depending on the subject of the agreement envisaged, nominating the Union negotiator or head of the Union's negotiating team.

4.   The Council may address directives to the negotiator and designate a special committee in consultation with which the negotiations must be conducted.

5.   The Council, on a proposal by the negotiator, shall adopt a European decision authorising the signing of the agreement and, if necessary, its provisional application before entry into force.

6.   The Council, on a proposal by the negotiator, shall adopt a European decision concluding the agreement.
Except where agreements relate exclusively to the common foreign and security policy, the Council shall adopt the European decision concluding the agreement:
(a)   after obtaining the consent of the European Parliament in the following cases:
        (i)   association agreements;
        (ii)   Union accession to the European Convention for the Protection of Human Rights and Fundamental Freedoms;
        (iii)   agreements establishing a specific institutional framework by organising co-operation procedures;
        (iv)   agreements with important budgetary implications for the Union;
        (v)   agreements covering fields to which either the ordinary legislative procedure applies, or the special legislative procedure where consent by the European Parliament is required.
        The European Parliament and the Council may, in an urgent situation, agree upon a time-limit for consent.
(b)   after consulting the European Parliament in other cases. The European Parliament shall deliver its opinion within a time-limit which the Council may set depending on the urgency of the matter. In the absence of an opinion within that time-limit, the Council may act.

7.   When concluding an agreement, the Council may, by way of derogation from paragraphs 5, 6 and 9, authorise the negotiator to approve on the Union's behalf modifications to the agreement where it provides for them to be adopted by a simplified procedure or by a body set up by the agreement. The Council may attach specific conditions to such authorisation.

8.   The Council shall act by a qualified majority throughout the procedure.
However, it shall act unanimously when the agreement covers a field for which unanimity is required for the adoption of a Union act as well as for association agreements and the agreements referred to in Article III-319 with the States which are candidates for accession.

9.   The Council, on a proposal from the Commission or the Union Minister for Foreign Affairs, shall adopt a European decision suspending application of an agreement and establishing the positions to be adopted on the Union's behalf in a body set up by an agreement, when that body is called upon to adopt acts having legal effects, with the exception of acts supplementing or amending the institutional framework of the agreement.

10.   The European Parliament shall be immediately and fully informed at all stages of the procedure.

11.   A Member State, the European Parliament, the Council or the Commission may obtain the opinion of the Court of Justice as to whether an agreement envisaged is compatible with the Constitution. Where the opinion of the Court of Justice is adverse, the agreement envisaged may not enter into force unless it is amended or the Constitution is revised.

ARTICLE III-326 (ex Article 111 TEC)
1.   By way of derogation from Article III-325, the Council, either on a recommendation from the European Central Bank or on a recommendation from the Commission and after consulting the European Central Bank, in an endeavour to reach a consensus consistent with the objective of price stability, may conclude formal agreements on an exchange-rate system for the euro in relation to the currencies of third States. The Council shall act unanimously after consulting the European Parliament and in accordance with the procedure provided for in paragraph 3.

The Council, either on a recommendation from the European Central Bank or on a recommendation from the Commission and after consulting the European Central Bank, in an endeavour to reach a consensus consistent with the objective of price stability, may adopt, adjust or abandon the central rates of the euro within the exchange-rate system. The President of the Council shall inform the European Parliament of the adoption, adjustment or abandonment of the central rates of the euro.

2. In the absence of an exchange-rate system in relation to one or more currencies of third States as referred to in paragraph 1, the Council, acting either on a recommendation from the European Central Bank or on a recommendation from the Commission and after consulting the European Central Bank, may formulate general orientations for exchange-rate policy in relation to these currencies. These general orientations shall be without prejudice to the primary objective of the European System of Central Banks, to maintain price stability.

3. By way of derogation from Article III-325, where agreements on matters relating to the monetary or exchange-rate system are to be the subject of negotiations between the Union and one or more third States or international organisations, the Council, acting on a recommendation from the Commission and after consulting the European Central Bank, shall decide the arrangements for the negotiation and for the conclusion of such agreements. These arrangements shall ensure that the Union expresses a single position. The Commission shall be fully associated with the negotiations.

4. Without prejudice to Union competence and Union agreements as regards economic and monetary union, Member States may negotiate in international bodies and conclude agreements.
[BMDF Note: This article does not apply to the United Kingdom, due to its opt-out from the euro, Article III-197(2)]

CHAPTER VII

THE UNION'S RELATIONS WITH INTERNATIONAL ORGANISATIONS AND THIRD COUNTRIES AND UNION DELEGATIONS

ARTICLE III-327 (*ex Articles 302, 303 and 304 TEC*)
1. The Union shall establish all appropriate forms of co-operation with the organs of the United Nations and its specialised agencies, the Council of Europe, the Organisation for Security and Co-operation in Europe and the Organisation for Economic Co-operation and Development.
The Union shall also maintain such relations as are appropriate with other international organisations.

2. The Union Minister for Foreign Affairs and the Commission shall be instructed to implement this Article.

ARTICLE III-328 (*new*)
1. Union delegations in third countries and at international organisations shall represent the Union.

2. Union delegations shall be placed under the authority of the Union Minister for Foreign Affairs. They shall act in close co-operation with Member States' diplomatic and consular missions.

CHAPTER VIII

IMPLEMENTATION OF THE SOLIDARITY CLAUSE

ARTICLE III-329 (*new*)
1. Should a Member State be the object of a terrorist attack or the victim of a natural or man-made disaster, the other Member States shall assist it at the request of its political authorities. To that end, the Member States shall co-ordinate between themselves in the Council.

2. The arrangements for the implementation by the Union of the solidarity clause referred to in Article I-43 shall be defined by a European decision adopted by the Council acting on a joint proposal by the Commission and the Union Minister for Foreign Affairs. The Council shall act in accordance with Article III-300(1) where this decision has defence implications. The European Parliament shall be informed.

For the purposes of this paragraph and without prejudice to Article III-344, the Council shall be assisted by the Political and Security Committee with the support of the structures developed in the context of the common security and defence policy and by the Committee referred to in Article III-261; the two committees shall, if necessary, submit joint opinions.

3.   The European Council shall regularly assess the threats facing the Union in order to enable the Union and its Member States to take effective action.

TITLE VI

THE FUNCTIONING OF THE UNION

CHAPTER I

PROVISIONS GOVERNING THE INSTITUTIONS

SECTION 1

THE INSTITUTIONS

Subsection 1

The European Parliament

ARTICLE III-330 (*ex Article 190 TEC*)
1.   A European law or framework law of the Council shall establish the necessary measures for the election of the Members of the European Parliament by direct universal suffrage in accordance with a uniform procedure in all Member States or in accordance with principles common to all Member States.
The Council shall act unanimously on initiative from, and after obtaining the consent of, the European Parliament, which shall act by a majority of its component members. This law or framework law shall enter into force after it has been approved by the Member States in accordance with their respective constitutional requirements.

2.   A European law of the European Parliament shall lay down the regulations and general conditions governing the performance of the duties of its Members. The European Parliament shall act on its own initiative after seeking an opinion from the Commission and after obtaining the consent of the Council. The Council shall act unanimously on all rules or conditions relating to the taxation of Members or former Members.

ARTICLE III-331 (*ex Article 191 TEC*)
European laws shall lay down the regulations governing the political parties at European level referred to in Article I-46(4), and in particular the rules regarding their funding.

ARTICLE III-332 (*ex Article 192 TEC*)
The European Parliament may, by a majority of its component Members, request the Commission to submit any appropriate proposal on matters on which it considers that a Union act is required for the purpose of implementing the Constitution. If the Commission does not submit a proposal, it shall inform the European Parliament of the reasons.

ARTICLE III-333 (*ex Article 193 TEC*)
In the course of its duties, the European Parliament may, at the request of a quarter of its component Members, set up a temporary Committee of Inquiry to investigate, without prejudice to the powers conferred by the Constitution on other institutions or bodies, alleged contraventions or maladministration in the implementation of Union law, except where the alleged facts are being examined before a court and while the case is still subject to legal proceedings.
The temporary Committee of Inquiry shall cease to exist on submission of its report.

A European law of the European Parliament shall lay down the detailed provisions governing the exercise of the right of inquiry. The European Parliament shall act on its own initiative after obtaining the consent of the Council and of the Commission.

ARTICLE III-334 (*ex Article 194 TEC*)
In accordance with Article I-10(2)(d), any citizen of the Union, and any natural or legal person residing or having its registered office in a Member State, shall have the right to address, individually or in association with other persons, a petition to the European Parliament on a matter which comes within the Union's fields of activity and which affects him, her or it directly.

ARTICLE III-335 (*ex Article 195 TEC*)
1.   The European Parliament shall elect a European Ombudsman. In accordance with Articles I-10(2)(d) and I-49, he or she shall be empowered to receive complaints from any citizen of the Union or any natural or legal person residing or having its registered office in a Member State concerning instances of maladministration in the activities of the Union's institutions, bodies, offices or agencies, with the exception of the Court of Justice of the European Union acting in its judicial role.
In accordance with his or her duties, the Ombudsman shall conduct inquiries for which he or she finds grounds, either on his or her own initiative or on the basis of complaints submitted to him or her direct or through a member of the European Parliament, except where the alleged facts are or have been the subject of legal proceedings. Where the Ombudsman establishes an instance of maladministration, he or she shall refer the matter to the institution, body, office or agency concerned, which shall have a period of three months in which to inform him or her of its views. The European Ombudsman shall then forward a report to the European Parliament and the institution, body, office or agency concerned. The person lodging the complaint shall be informed of the outcome of such inquiries.
The Ombudsman shall submit an annual report to the European Parliament on the outcome of his or her inquiries.

2.   The Ombudsman shall be elected after each election of the European Parliament for the duration of its term of office. The Ombudsman shall be eligible for reappointment.
The Ombudsman may be dismissed by the Court of Justice at the request of the European Parliament if he or she no longer fulfils the conditions required for the performance of his or her duties or if he or she is guilty of serious misconduct.

3.   The Ombudsman shall be completely independent in the performance of his or her duties. In the performance of those duties he or she shall neither seek nor take instructions from any institution, body, office or agency. The Ombudsman shall not, during his or her term of office, engage in any other occupation, whether gainful or not.

4.   A European law of the European Parliament shall lay down the regulations and general conditions governing the performance of the Ombudsman's duties. The European Parliament shall act on its own initiative after seeking an opinion from the Commission and after obtaining the consent of the Council.

ARTICLE III-336 (*ex Article 196 TEC*)
The European Parliament shall hold an annual session. It shall meet, without requiring to be convened, on the second Tuesday in March.
The European Parliament may meet in extraordinary part-session at the request of a majority of its component members or at the request of the Council or of the Commission.

ARTICLE III-337 (*ex Articles 197 and 200 TEC*)
1.   The European Council and the Council shall be heard by the European Parliament in accordance with the conditions laid down in the Rules of Procedure of the European Council and those of the Council.

2.   The Commission may attend all the meetings of the European Parliament and shall, at its request, be heard. It shall reply orally or in writing to questions put to it by the European Parliament or by its members.

3.   The European Parliament shall discuss in open session the annual general report submitted to it by the Commission.

ARTICLE III-338 (*ex Article 198 TEC*)
Save as otherwise provided in the Constitution, the European Parliament shall act by a majority of the votes cast. Its Rules of Procedure shall determine the quorum.

ARTICLE III-339 (*ex Article 199 TEC*)

The European Parliament shall adopt its Rules of Procedure, by a majority of its component members.

The proceedings of the European Parliament shall be published in the manner laid down in the Constitution and the Rules of Procedure of the European Parliament.

ARTICLE III-340 (*ex Article 201 TEC*)

If a motion of censure on the activities of the Commission is tabled before it, the European Parliament shall not vote thereon until at least three days after the motion has been tabled and shall do so only by open vote.

If the motion of censure is carried by a two-thirds majority of the votes cast, representing a majority of the component members of the European Parliament, the members of the Commission shall resign as a body and the Union Minister for Foreign Affairs shall resign from duties that he or she carries out in the Commission. They shall remain in office and continue to deal with current business until they are replaced in accordance with Articles I-26 and I-27. In this case, the term of office of the members of the Commission appointed to replace them shall expire on the date on which the term of office of the members of the Commission obliged to resign as a body would have expired.

Subsection 2

The European Council

ARTICLE III-341 (*new*)

1.   Where a vote is taken, any member of the European Council may also act on behalf of not more than one other member.

Abstentions by members present in person or represented shall not prevent the adoption by the European Council of acts which require unanimity.

2.   The President of the European Parliament may be invited to be heard by the European Council.

3.   The European Council shall act by a simple majority for procedural questions and for the adoption of its Rules of Procedure.

4.   The European Council shall be assisted by the General Secretariat of the Council.

Subsection 3

The Council of Ministers

ARTICLE III-342 (*ex Articles 203 and 204 TEC*)

The Council shall meet when convened by its President on his or her own initiative, or at the request of one of its members or of the Commission.

ARTICLE III-343 (*ex Articles 205 and 206 TEC*)

1.   Where a vote is taken, any member of the Council may act on behalf of not more than one other member.

2.   Where it is required to act by a simple majority, the Council shall act by a majority of its component members.

3.   Abstentions by members present in person or represented shall not prevent the adoption by the Council of acts which require unanimity.

ARTICLE III-344 (*ex Article 207 TEC*)

1.   A committee consisting of the Permanent Representatives of the Governments of the Member States shall be responsible for preparing the work of the Council and for carrying out the tasks assigned to it by the latter. The Committee may adopt procedural decisions in cases provided for in the Council's Rules of Procedure.

2.   The Council shall be assisted by a General Secretariat, under the responsibility of a Secretary-General appointed by the Council.

The Council shall decide on the organisation of the General Secretariat by a simple majority.

3.   The Council shall act by a simple majority regarding procedural matters and for the adoption of its Rules of Procedure.

ARTICLE III-345 (*ex Article 208 TEC*)
The Council, by a simple majority, may request the Commission to undertake any studies the Council considers desirable for the attainment of the common objectives, and to submit any appropriate proposals to it. If the Commission does not submit a proposal, it shall inform the Council of the reasons.

ARTICLE III-346 (*ex Article 209 TEC*)
The Council shall adopt European decisions laying down the rules governing the committees provided for in the Constitution. It shall act by a simple majority after consulting the Commission.

Subsection 4

The European Commission

ARTICLE III-347 (*ex Article 213(2) TEC*)
The members of the Commission shall refrain from any action incompatible with their duties. Member States shall respect their independence and shall not seek to influence them in the performance of their tasks.
The members of the Commission shall not, during their term of office, engage in any other occupation, whether gainful or not. When entering upon their duties they shall give a solemn undertaking that, both during and after their term of office, they will respect the obligations arising therefrom and in particular their duty to behave with integrity and discretion as regards the acceptance, after they have ceased to hold office, of certain appointments or benefits. In the event of any breach of these obligations, the Court of Justice may, on application by the Council, acting by a simple majority, or the Commission, rule that the person concerned be, according to the circumstances, either compulsorily retired in accordance with Article III-349 or deprived of his or her right to a pension or other benefits in its stead.

ARTICLE III-348 (*ex Article 215 TEC*)
1.   Apart from normal replacement, or death, the duties of a member of the Commission shall end when he or she resigns or is compulsorily retired.

2.   A vacancy caused by resignation, compulsory retirement or death shall be filled for the remainder of the member's term of office by a new member of the same nationality appointed by the Council, by common accord with the President of the Commission, after consulting the European Parliament and in accordance with the criteria set out in Article I-26(4).
The Council may, acting unanimously on a proposal from the President of the Commission, decide that such a vacancy need not be filled, in particular when the remainder of the member's term of office is short.

3.   In the event of resignation, compulsory retirement or death, the President shall be replaced for the remainder of his or her term of office in accordance with Article I-27(1).

4.   In the event of resignation, compulsory retirement or death, the Union Minister for Foreign Affairs shall be replaced, for the remainder of his or her term of office, in accordance with Article I-28(1).

5.   In the case of the resignation of all the members of the Commission, they shall remain in office and continue to deal with current business until they have been replaced, for the remainder of their term of office, in accordance with Articles I-26 and I-27.

ARTICLE III-349 (*ex Article 216 TEC*)
If any member of the Commission no longer fulfils the conditions required for the performance of his or her duties or if he or she has been guilty of serious misconduct, the Court of Justice may, on application by the Council, acting by a simple majority, or by the Commission, compulsorily retire him or her.

ARTICLE III-350 (*ex Article 217 TEC*)
Without prejudice to Article I-28(4), the responsibilities incumbent upon the Commission shall be structured and allocated among its members by its President, in accordance with Article I-27(3). The President may reshuffle the allocation of those responsibilities during the Commission's term of office. The members of the Commission shall carry out the duties devolved upon them by the President under his or her authority.

ARTICLE III-351 (*ex Article 219 TEC*)
The Commission shall act by a majority of its members. Its Rules of Procedure shall determine the quorum.

ARTICLE III-352 (*ex Articles 218 and 212 TEC*)
1.   The Commission shall adopt its Rules of Procedure so as to ensure both its own operation and that of its departments. It shall ensure that these rules are published.

2.   The Commission shall publish annually, not later than one month before the opening of the session of the European Parliament, a general report on the activities of the Union.

Subsection 5

The Court of Justice of the European Union

ARTICLE III-353 (*ex Article 221 TEC*)
The Court of Justice shall sit in chambers, as a Grand Chamber or as a full Court, in accordance with the Statute of the Court of Justice of the European Union.

ARTICLE III-354 (*ex Article 222 TEC*)
The Court of Justice shall be assisted by eight Advocates-General. Should the Court of Justice so request, the Council may, acting unanimously, adopt a European decision to increase the number of Advocates-General.
It shall be the duty of the Advocate-General, acting with complete impartiality and independence, to make, in open court, reasoned submissions on cases which, in accordance with the Statute of the Court of Justice of the European Union, require his or her involvement.

ARTICLE III-355 (*ex Article 223 TEC*)
The Judges and Advocates-General of the Court of Justice shall be chosen from persons whose independence is beyond doubt and who possess the qualifications required for appointment to the highest judicial offices in their respective countries or who are jurisconsults of recognised competence; they shall be appointed by common accord of the governments of the Member States after consultation of the panel provided for in Article III-357.
Every three years there shall be a partial replacement of the Judges and Advocates-General, in accordance with the conditions laid down in the Statute of the Court of Justice of the European Union.
The Judges shall elect the President of the Court of Justice from among their number for a term of three years. He or she may be re-elected.
The Court of Justice shall adopt its Rules of Procedure. Those Rules shall require the consent of the Council.

ARTICLE III-356 (*ex Article 224 TEC*)
The number of Judges of the General Court shall be determined by the Statute of the Court of Justice of the European Union. The Statute may provide for the General Court to be assisted by Advocates-General.
The members of the General Court shall be chosen from persons whose independence is beyond doubt and who possess the ability required for appointment to high judicial office. They shall be appointed by common accord of the governments of the Member States after consultation of the panel provided for in Article III-357.
The membership of the General Court shall be partially renewed every three years.
The Judges shall elect the President of the General Court from among their number for a term of three years. He or she may be re-elected.
The General Court shall establish its Rules of Procedure in agreement with the Court of Justice.
The Rules shall be subject to the consent of the Council.
Unless the Statute provides otherwise, the provisions of the Constitution relating to the Court of Justice shall apply to the General Court.

ARTICLE III-357 (*new*)
A panel shall be set up in order to give an opinion on candidates' suitability to perform the duties of Judge and Advocate-General of the Court of Justice and the General Court before the governments of the Member States make the appointments referred to in Articles III-355 and III-356.
The panel shall comprise seven persons chosen from among former members of the Court of Justice and the General Court, members of national supreme courts and lawyers of recognised competence, one of whom shall be proposed by the European Parliament. The Council shall adopt a European decision establishing the panel's operating rules and a European decision appointing its members. It shall act on the initiative of the President of the Court of Justice.

ARTICLE III-358 (*ex Article 225 TEC*)
1.   The General Court shall have jurisdiction to hear and determine at first instance actions or proceedings referred to in Articles III-365, III-367, III-370, III-372 and III-374, with the exception of those assigned to a

specialised court set up under Article III-359 and those reserved in the Statute of the Court of Justice of the European Union for the Court of Justice. The Statute may provide for the General Court to have jurisdiction for other classes of action or proceeding.

Decisions given by the General Court under this paragraph may be subject to a right of appeal to the Court of Justice on points of law only, under the conditions and within the limits laid down by the Statute.

2.   The General Court shall have jurisdiction to hear and determine actions or proceedings brought against decisions of the specialised courts.

Decisions given by the General Court under this paragraph may exceptionally be subject to review by the Court of Justice, under the conditions and within the limits laid down by the Statute of the Court of Justice of the European Union, where there is a serious risk of the unity or consistency of Union law being affected.

3.   The General Court shall have jurisdiction to hear and determine questions referred for a preliminary ruling under Article III-369, in specific areas laid down by the Statute of the Court of Justice of the European Union.

Where the General Court considers that the case requires a decision of principle likely to affect the unity or consistency of Union law, it may refer the case to the Court of Justice for a ruling.

Decisions given by the General Court on questions referred for a preliminary ruling may exceptionally be subject to review by the Court of Justice, under the conditions and within the limits laid down by the Statute, where there is a serious risk of the unity or consistency of Union law being affected.

ARTICLE III-359 (*ex Article 225a TEC*)
1.   European laws may establish specialised courts attached to the General Court to hear and determine at first instance certain classes of action or proceeding brought in specific areas. They shall be adopted either on a proposal from the Commission after consultation of the Court of Justice or at the request of the Court of Justice after consultation of the Commission.

2.   The European law establishing a specialised court shall lay down the rules on the organisation of the court and the extent of the jurisdiction conferred upon it.

3.   Decisions given by specialised courts may be subject to a right of appeal on points of law only or, when provided for in the European law establishing the specialised court, a right of appeal also on matters of fact, before the General Court.

4.   The members of the specialised courts shall be chosen from persons whose independence is beyond doubt and who possess the ability required for appointment to judicial office. They shall be appointed by the Council, acting unanimously.

5.   The specialised courts shall establish their Rules of Procedure in agreement with the Court of Justice. Those Rules shall require the consent of the Council.

6.   Unless the European law establishing the specialised court provides otherwise, the provisions of the Constitution relating to the Court of Justice of the European Union and the provisions of the Statute of the Court of Justice of the European Union shall apply to the specialised courts. Title I of the Statute and Article 64 thereof shall in any case apply to the specialised courts.

ARTICLE III-360 (*ex Article 226 TEC*)
If the Commission considers that a Member State has failed to fulfil an obligation under the Constitution, it shall deliver a reasoned opinion on the matter after giving the State concerned the opportunity to submit its observations.

If the State concerned does not comply with the opinion within the period laid down by the Commission, the latter may bring the matter before the Court of Justice of the European Union.

ARTICLE III-361 (*ex Article 227 TEC*)
A Member State which considers that another Member State has failed to fulfil an obligation under the Constitution may bring the matter before the Court of Justice of the European Union.

Before a Member State brings an action against another Member State for an alleged infringement of an obligation under the Constitution, it shall bring the matter before the Commission.

The Commission shall deliver a reasoned opinion after each of the States concerned has been given the opportunity to submit its own case and its observations on the other party's case both orally and in writing.

If the Commission has not delivered an opinion within three months of the date on which the matter was brought before it, the absence of such opinion shall not prevent the matter from being brought before the Court.

ARTICLE III-362 (*ex Article 228 TEC*)

1.   If the Court of Justice of the European Union finds that a Member State has failed to fulfil an obligation under the Constitution, that State shall be required to take the necessary measures to comply with the judgment of the Court.

2.   If the Commission considers that the Member State concerned has not taken the necessary measures to comply with the judgment referred to in paragraph 1, it may bring the case before the Court of Justice of the European Union after giving that State the opportunity to submit its observations. It shall specify the amount of the lump sum or penalty payment to be paid by the Member State concerned which it considers appropriate in the circumstances.
If the Court finds that the Member State concerned has not complied with its judgment it may impose a lump sum or penalty payment on it.
This procedure shall be without prejudice to Article III-361.

3.   When the Commission brings a case before the Court of Justice of the European Union pursuant to Article III-360 on the grounds that the Member State concerned has failed to fulfil its obligation to notify measures transposing a European framework law, it may, when it deems appropriate, specify the amount of the lump sum or penalty payment to be paid by the Member State concerned which it considers appropriate in the circumstances.
If the Court finds that there is an infringement it may impose a lump sum or penalty payment on the Member State concerned not exceeding the amount specified by the Commission. The payment obligation shall take effect on the date set by the Court in its judgment.

ARTICLE III-363 (*ex Article 229 TEC*)

European laws and regulations of the Council may give the Court of Justice of the European Union unlimited jurisdiction with regard to the penalties provided for in them.

ARTICLE III-364 (*ex Article 229a TEC*)

Without prejudice to the other provisions of the Constitution, a European law may confer on the Court of Justice of the European Union, to the extent that it shall determine, jurisdiction in disputes relating to the application of acts adopted on the basis of the Constitution which create European intellectual property rights.

ARTICLE III-365 (*ex Article 230 TEC*)

1.   The Court of Justice of the European Union shall review the legality of European laws and framework laws, of acts of the Council, of the Commission and of the European Central Bank, other than recommendations and opinions, and of acts of the European Parliament and of the European Council intended to produce legal effects vis-à-vis third parties. It shall also review the legality of acts of bodies, offices or agencies of the Union intended to produce legal effects vis-à-vis third parties.

2.   For the purposes of paragraph 1, the Court of Justice of the European Union shall have jurisdiction in actions brought by a Member State, the European Parliament, the Council or the Commission on grounds of lack of competence, infringement of an essential procedural requirement, infringement of the Constitution or of any rule of law relating to its application, or misuse of powers.

3.   The Court of Justice of the European Union shall have jurisdiction under the conditions laid down in paragraphs 1 and 2 in actions brought by the Court of Auditors, by the European Central Bank and by the Committee of the Regions for the purpose of protecting their prerogatives.

4.   Any natural or legal person may, under the conditions laid down in paragraphs 1 and 2, institute proceedings against an act addressed to that person or which is of direct and individual concern to him or her, and against a regulatory act which is of direct concern to him or her and does not entail implementing measures.

5.   Acts setting up bodies, offices and agencies of the Union may lay down specific conditions and arrangements concerning actions brought by natural or legal persons against acts of these bodies, offices or agencies intended to produce legal effects in relation to them.

6.   The proceedings provided for in this Article shall be instituted within two months of the publication of the act, or of its notification to the plaintiff, or, in the absence thereof, of the day on which it came to the plaintiff's knowledge, as the case may be.

ARTICLE III-366 (*ex Article 231 TEC*)
If the action is well founded, the Court of Justice of the European Union shall declare the act concerned to be void.
However, the Court shall, if it considers this necessary, state which of the effects of the act which it has declared void shall be considered as definitive.

ARTICLE III-367 (*ex Article 232 TEC*)
Should the European Parliament, the European Council, the Council, the Commission or the European Central Bank, in infringement of the Constitution, fail to act, the Member States and the other institutions of the Union may bring an action before the Court of Justice of the European Union to have the infringement established. This Article shall apply, under the same conditions, to bodies, offices and agencies of the Union which fail to act.
The action shall be admissible only if the institution, body, office or agency concerned has first been called upon to act. If, within two months of being so called upon, the institution, body, office or agency concerned has not defined its position, the action may be brought within a further period of two months.
Any natural or legal person may, under the conditions laid down in the first and second paragraphs, complain to the Court that an institution, body, office or agency of the Union has failed to address to that person any act other than a recommendation or an opinion.

ARTICLE III-368 (*ex Article 233 TEC*)
The institution, body, office or agency whose act has been declared void, or whose failure to act has been declared contrary to the Constitution, shall be required to take the necessary measures to comply with the judgment of the Court of Justice of the European Union.
This obligation shall not affect any obligation which may result from the application of the second paragraph of Article III-431.

ARTICLE III-369 (*ex Article 234 TEC*)
The Court of Justice of the European Union shall have jurisdiction to give preliminary rulings concerning:
(a)   the interpretation of the Constitution;
(b)   the validity and interpretation of acts of the institutions, bodies, offices and agencies of the Union.
Where such a question is raised before any court or tribunal of a Member State, that court or tribunal may, if it considers that a decision on the question is necessary to enable it to give judgment, request the Court to give a ruling thereon.
Where any such question is raised in a case pending before a court or tribunal of a Member State against whose decisions there is no judicial remedy under national law, that court or tribunal shall bring the matter before the Court.
If such a question is raised in a case pending before a court or tribunal of a Member State with regard to a person in custody, the Court shall act with the minimum of delay.

ARTICLE III-370 (*ex Article 235 TEC*)
The Court of Justice of the European Union shall have jurisdiction in disputes relating to compensation for damage provided for in the second and third paragraphs of Article III-431.

ARTICLE III-371 (*ex Article 46 (e) TEU*)
The Court of Justice shall have jurisdiction to decide on the legality of an act adopted by the European Council or by the Council pursuant to Article I-59 solely at the request of the Member State concerned by a determination of the European Council or of the Council and in respect solely of the procedural stipulations contained in that Article.
Such a request must be made within one month from the date of such determination. The Court shall rule within one month from the date of the request.

ARTICLE III-372 (*ex Article 236 TEC*)
The Court of Justice of the European Union shall have jurisdiction in any dispute between the Union and its servants within the limits and under the conditions laid down in the Staff Regulations of Officials and the Conditions of Employment of other servants of the Union.

ARTICLE III-373 (*ex Article 237 TEC*)
The Court of Justice of the European Union shall, within the limits hereinafter laid down, have jurisdiction in disputes concerning:
(a)   the fulfilment by Member States of obligations under the Statute of the European Investment Bank. In this connection, the Board of Directors of the Bank shall enjoy the powers conferred upon the Commission by Article III-360;

(b)   measures adopted by the Board of Governors of the European Investment Bank. In this connection, any Member State, the Commission or the Board of Directors of the Bank may institute proceedings under the conditions laid down in Article III-365;

(c)   measures adopted by the Board of Directors of the European Investment Bank. Proceedings against such measures may be instituted only by Member States or by the Commission, under the conditions laid down in Article III-365, and solely on the grounds of non-compliance with the procedure provided for in Article 19(2), (5), (6) and (7) of the Statute of the Bank;

(d)   the fulfilment by national central banks of obligations under the Constitution and the Statute of the European System of Central Banks and of the European Central Bank. In this connection, the powers of the Governing Council of the European Central Bank in respect of national central banks shall be the same as those conferred upon the Commission in respect of Member States by Article III-360. If the Court of Justice of the European Union finds that a national central bank has failed to fulfil an obligation under the Constitution, that bank shall be required to take the necessary measures to comply with the judgment of the Court.

ARTICLE III-374 (*ex Articles 238 TEC*)

The Court of Justice of the European Union shall have jurisdiction to give judgment pursuant to any arbitration clause contained in a contract concluded by or on behalf of the Union, whether that contract be governed by public or private law.

ARTICLE III-375 (*ex Articles 240, 292 and 239 TEC*)

1.   Save where jurisdiction is conferred on the Court of Justice of the European Union by the Constitution, disputes to which the Union is a party shall not on that ground be excluded from the jurisdiction of the courts or tribunals of the Member States.

2.   Member States undertake not to submit a dispute concerning the interpretation or application of the Constitution to any method of settlement other than those provided for therein.

3.   The Court of Justice shall have jurisdiction in any dispute between Member States which relates to the subject-matter of the Constitution if the dispute is submitted to it under a special agreement between the parties.

ARTICLE III-376 (*new*)

The Court of Justice of the European Union shall not have jurisdiction with respect to Articles I-40 and I-41 and the provisions of Chapter II of Title V concerning the common foreign and security policy and Article III-293 insofar as it concerns the common foreign and security policy.

However, the Court shall have jurisdiction to monitor compliance with Article III-308 and to rule on proceedings, brought in accordance with the conditions laid down in Article III-365(4), reviewing the legality of European decisions providing for restrictive measures against natural or legal persons adopted by the Council on the basis of Chapter II of Title V.

ARTICLE III-377 (*ex Article 35(5) TEU*)

In exercising its powers regarding the provisions of Sections 4 and 5 of Chapter IV of Title III relating to the area of freedom, security and justice, the Court of Justice of the European Union shall have no jurisdiction to review the validity or proportionality of operations carried out by the police or other law-enforcement services of a Member State or the exercise of the responsibilities incumbent upon Member States with regard to the maintenance of law and order and the safeguarding of internal security.

ARTICLE III-378 (*ex Article 241 TEC*)

Notwithstanding the expiry of the period laid down in Article III-365(6), any party may, in proceedings in which an act of general application adopted by an institution, body, office or agency of the Union is at issue, plead the grounds specified in Article III-365(2) in order to invoke before the Court of Justice of the European Union the inapplicability of that act.

ARTICLE III-379 (*ex Article 242 and 243 TEC*)

1.   Actions brought before the Court of Justice of the European Union shall not have suspensory effect. The Court may, however, if it considers that circumstances so require, order that application of the contested act be suspended.

2.   The Court of Justice of the European Union may in any cases before it prescribe any necessary interim measures.

ARTICLE III-380 (*ex Article 244 TEC*)
The judgments of the Court of Justice of the European Union shall be enforceable under the conditions laid down in Article III-401.

ARTICLE III-381 (*ex Article 245 TEC*)
The Statute of the Court of Justice of the European Union shall be laid down in a Protocol.
A European law may amend the provisions of the Statute, with the exception of Title I and Article 64. It shall be adopted either at the request of the Court of Justice and after consultation of the Commission, or on a proposal from the Commission and after consultation of the Court of Justice.

Subsection 6

The European Central Bank

ARTICLE III-382 (*ex Article 112 TEC*)
1.   The Governing Council of the European Central Bank shall comprise the members of the Executive Board of the European Central Bank and the Governors of the national central banks of the Member States without a derogation as referred to in Article III-197.

2.   The Executive Board shall comprise the President, the Vice-President and four other members.
The President, the Vice-President and the other members of the Executive Board shall be appointed by the European Council, acting by a qualified majority, from among persons of recognised standing and professional experience in monetary or banking matters, on a recommendation from the Council and after consulting the European Parliament and the Governing Council of the European Central Bank.
Their term of office shall be eight years and shall not be renewable.
Only nationals of Member States may be members of the Executive Board.
[BMDF Note: This provision does not apply to the United Kingdom, due to its opt-out from the euro, Article III-197(2)]

ARTICLE III-383 (*ex Article 113 TEC*)
1.   The President of the Council and a member of the Commission may participate, without having the right to vote, in meetings of the Governing Council of the European Central Bank.
The President of the Council may submit a motion for deliberation to the Governing Council of the European Central Bank.

2.   The President of the European Central Bank shall be invited to participate in meetings of the Council when it is discussing matters relating to the objectives and tasks of the European System of Central Banks.

3.   The European Central Bank shall address an annual report on the activities of the European System of Central Banks and on the monetary policy of both the previous and the current year to the European Parliament, the European Council, the Council and the Commission. The President of the European Central Bank shall present this report to the European Parliament, which may hold a general debate on that basis, and to the Council.
The President of the European Central Bank and the other members of the Executive Board may, at the request of the European Parliament or on their own initiative, be heard by the competent bodies of the European Parliament.

Subsection 7

The Court of Auditors

ARTICLE III-384 (*ex Article 248 TEC*)
1.   The Court of Auditors shall examine the accounts of all revenue and expenditure of the Union. It shall also examine the accounts of all revenue and expenditure of any body, office or agency set up by the Union insofar as the instrument establishing that body, office or agency does not preclude such examination.
The Court of Auditors shall provide the European Parliament and the Council with a statement of assurance as to the reliability of the accounts and the legality and regularity of the underlying transactions which shall be published in the *Official Journal of the European Union*. This statement may be supplemented by specific assessments for each major area of Union activity.

2.   The Court of Auditors shall examine whether all revenue has been received and all expenditure incurred in a lawful and regular manner and whether the financial management has been sound. In doing so, it shall report in particular on any cases of irregularity.

The audit of revenue shall be carried out on the basis of the amounts established as due and the amounts actually paid to the Union.

The audit of expenditure shall be carried out on the basis both of commitments undertaken and payments made.

These audits may be carried out before the closure of accounts for the financial year in question.

3.   The audit shall be based on records and, if necessary, performed on the spot in the other institutions, or on the premises of any body, office or agency which manages revenue or expenditure on behalf of the Union and in the Member States, including on the premises of any natural or legal person in receipt of payments from the budget. In the Member States the audit shall be carried out in liaison with national audit bodies or, if these do not have the necessary powers, with the competent national departments. The Court of Auditors and the national audit bodies of the Member States shall co-operate in a spirit of trust while maintaining their independence. These bodies or departments shall inform the Court of Auditors whether they intend to take part in the audit.

The other institutions, any bodies, offices or agencies managing revenue or expenditure on behalf of the Union, any natural or legal person in receipt of payments from the budget, and the national audit bodies or, if these do not have the necessary powers, the competent national departments, shall forward to the Court of Auditors, at its request, any document or information necessary to carry out its task.

In respect of the European Investment Bank's activity in managing Union revenue and expenditure, rights of access by the Court of Auditors to information held by the Bank shall be governed by an agreement between the Court of Auditors, the Bank and the Commission. In the absence of an agreement, the Court of Auditors shall nevertheless have access to information necessary for the audit of Union expenditure and revenue managed by the Bank.

4.   The Court of Auditors shall draw up an annual report after the close of each financial year. It shall be forwarded to the other institutions and shall be published, together with the replies of these institutions to the observations of the Court of Auditors, in the *Official Journal of the European Union*.

The Court of Auditors may also, at any time, submit observations, particularly in the form of special reports, on specific questions and deliver opinions at the request of one of the other institutions.

It shall adopt its annual reports, special reports or opinions by a majority of its component members. However, it may establish internal chambers in order to adopt certain categories of reports or opinions under the conditions laid down by its Rules of Procedure.

It shall assist the European Parliament and the Council in exercising their powers of control over the implementation of the budget.

It shall adopt its Rules of Procedure. Those rules shall require the consent of the Council .

ARTICLE III-385 (*ex Article 247 TEC*)
1.   The members of the Court of Auditors shall be chosen from among persons who belong or have belonged in their respective States to external audit bodies or who are especially qualified for this office. Their independence must be beyond doubt.

2.   The members of the Court of Auditors shall be appointed for a term of six years. Their term of office shall be renewable. The Council shall adopt a European decision establishing the list of members drawn up in accordance with the proposals made by each Member State. It shall act after consulting the European Parliament.

The members of the Court of Auditors shall elect their President from among their number for a term of three years. He or she may be re-elected.

3.   In the performance of their duties, members of the Court of Auditors shall neither seek nor take instructions from any government or from any other body. They shall refrain from any action incompatible with their duties.

4.   Members of the Court of Auditors shall not, during their term of office, engage in any other occupation, whether gainful or not. When entering upon their duties they shall give a solemn undertaking that, both during and after their term of office, they will respect the obligations arising therefrom and in particular their duty to behave with integrity and discretion as regards the acceptance, after they have ceased to hold office, of certain appointments or benefits.

5.   Apart from normal replacement, or death, the duties of a member of the Court of Auditors shall end when he or she resigns, or is compulsorily retired by a ruling of the Court of Justice pursuant to paragraph 6.

The vacancy thus caused shall be filled for the remainder of the member's term of office.

Save in the case of compulsory retirement, members of the Court of Auditors shall remain in office until they have been replaced.

6. A member of the Court of Auditors may be deprived of his or her office or of his or her right to a pension or other benefits in its stead only if the Court of Justice, at the request of the Court of Auditors, finds that he or she no longer fulfils the requisite conditions or meets the obligations arising from his or her office.

SECTION 2

THE UNION'S ADVISORY BODIES

Subsection 1

The Committee of the Regions

ARTICLE III-386 (*ex Article 263 TEC*)

The number of members of the Committee of the Regions shall not exceed 350. The Council, acting unanimously on a proposal from the Commission, shall adopt a European decision determining the Committee's composition.

The members of the Committee and an equal number of alternate members shall be appointed for five years. Their term of office shall be renewable. No member of the Committee shall at the same time be a member of the European Parliament.

The Council shall adopt the European decision establishing the list of members and alternate members drawn up in accordance with the proposals made by each Member State.

When the mandate referred to in Article I-32(2) on the basis of which they were proposed comes to an end, the term of office of members of the Committee shall terminate automatically and they shall then be replaced for the remainder of the said term of office in accordance with the same procedure.

ARTICLE III-387 (*ex Article 264 TEC*)

The Committee of the Regions shall elect its chairman and officers from among its members for a term of two and a half years.

It shall be convened by its chairman at the request of the European Parliament, of the Council or of the Commission. It may also meet on its own initiative.

It shall adopt its Rules of Procedure.

ARTICLE III-388 (*ex Article 265 TEC*)

The Committee of the Regions shall be consulted by the European Parliament, by the Council or by the Commission where the Constitution so provides and in all other cases in which one of these institutions considers it appropriate, in particular those which concern cross-border co-operation.

The European Parliament, the Council or the Commission shall, if it considers it necessary, set the Committee, for the submission of its opinion, a time-limit which shall not be less than one month from the date on which the chairman receives notification to this effect. Upon expiry of the time-limit, the absence of an opinion shall not prevent further action.

Where the Economic and Social Committee is consulted, the Committee of the Regions shall be informed by the European Parliament, the Council or the Commission of the request for an opinion. Where it considers that specific regional interests are involved, the Committee of the Regions may issue an opinion on the matter. It may also issue an opinion on its own initiative.

The opinion of the Committee, together with a record of its proceedings, shall be forwarded to the European Parliament, to the Council and to the Commission.

Subsection 2

The Economic and Social Committee

ARTICLE III-389 (*ex Article 258 TEC*)

The number of members of the Economic and Social Committee shall not exceed 350.

The Council, acting unanimously on a proposal from the Commission, shall adopt a European decision determining the Committee's composition.

ARTICLE III-390 (*ex Article 259 TEC*)
The members of the Economic and Social Committee shall be appointed for five years. Their term of office shall be renewable.
The Council shall adopt the European decision establishing the list of members drawn up in accordance with the proposals made by each Member State.
The Council shall act after consulting the Commission. It may obtain the opinion of European bodies which are representative of the various economic and social sectors and of civil society to which the Union's activities are of concern.

ARTICLE III-391 (*ex Article 260 TEC*)
The Economic and Social Committee shall elect its chairman and officers from among its members for a term of two and a half years.
It shall be convened by its chairman at the request of the European Parliament, of the Council or of the Commission. It may also meet on its own initiative.
It shall adopt its Rules of Procedure.

ARTICLE III-392 (*ex Article 262 TEC*)
The Economic and Social Committee shall be consulted by the European Parliament, by the Council or by the Commission where the Constitution so provides. It may be consulted by these institutions in all cases in which they consider it appropriate. It may also issue an opinion on its own initiative.
The European Parliament, the Council or the Commission shall, if it considers it necessary, set the Committee, for the submission of its opinion, a time-limit which shall not be less than one month from the date on which the chairman receives notification to this effect. Upon expiry of the time-limit, the absence of an opinion shall not prevent further action.
The opinion of the Committee, together with a record of its proceedings, shall be forwarded to the European Parliament, to the Council and to the Commission.

SECTION 3

THE EUROPEAN INVESTMENT BANK

ARTICLE III-393 (*ex Article 266 TEC*)
The European Investment Bank shall have legal personality.
Its members shall be the Member States.
The Statute of the European Investment Bank is laid down in a Protocol.
A European law of the Council may amend the Statute of the European Investment Bank. The Council shall act unanimously, either at the request of the European Investment Bank and after consulting the European Parliament and the Commission, or on a proposal from the Commission and after consulting the European Parliament and the European Investment Bank.

ARTICLE III-394 (*ex Article 267 TEC*)
The task of the European Investment Bank shall be to contribute, by having recourse to the capital markets and utilising its own resources, to the balanced and steady development of the internal market in the Union's interest. For this purpose the European Investment Bank shall, operating on a non-profit-making basis, in particular grant loans and give guarantees which facilitate the financing of the following projects in all sectors of the economy:
(a)   projects for developing less-developed regions;
(b)   projects for modernising or converting undertakings or for developing fresh activities called for by the establishment or functioning of the internal market, where these projects are of such a size or nature that they cannot be entirely financed by the various means available in the individual Member States;
(c)   projects of common interest to several Member States which are of such a size or nature that they cannot be entirely financed by the various means available in the individual Member States.
In carrying out its task, the European Investment Bank shall facilitate the financing of investment programmes in conjunction with assistance from the Structural Funds and other Union financial instruments.

SECTION 4

PROVISIONS COMMON TO UNION INSTITUTIONS, BODIES, OFFICES AND AGENCIES

ARTICLE III-395 (*ex Article 250 TEC*)

1.   Where, pursuant to the Constitution, the Council acts on a proposal from the Commission, it may amend that proposal only by acting unanimously, except in the cases referred to in Articles I-55, I-56, III-396(10) and (13), III-404 and III-405(2).

2.   As long as the Council has not acted, the Commission may alter its proposal at any time during the procedures leading to the adoption of a Union act.

ARTICLE III-396 (*ex Article 251 TEC*)

1.   Where, pursuant to the Constitution, European laws or framework laws are adopted under the ordinary legislative procedure, the following provisions shall apply.

2.   The Commission shall submit a proposal to the European Parliament and the Council.

First reading

3.   The European Parliament shall adopt its position at first reading and communicate it to the Council.

4.   If the Council approves the European Parliament's position, the act concerned shall be adopted in the wording which corresponds to the position of the European Parliament.

5.   If the Council does not approve the European Parliament's position, it shall adopt its position at first reading and communicate it to the European Parliament.

6.   The Council shall inform the European Parliament fully of the reasons which led it to adopt its position at first reading. The Commission shall inform the European Parliament fully of its position.

Second reading

7.   If, within three months of such communication, the European Parliament:
(a)   approves the Council's position at first reading or has not taken a decision, the act concerned shall be deemed to have been adopted in the wording which corresponds to the position of the Council;
(b)   rejects, by a majority of its component members, the Council's position at first reading, the proposed act shall be deemed not to have been adopted;
(c)   proposes, by a majority of its component members, amendments to the Council's position at first reading, the text thus amended shall be forwarded to the Council and to the Commission, which shall deliver an opinion on those amendments.

8.   If, within three months of receiving the European Parliament's amendments, the Council, acting by a qualified majority:
(a)   approves all those amendments, the act in question shall be deemed to have been adopted;
(b)   does not approve all the amendments, the President of the Council, in agreement with the President of the European Parliament, shall within six weeks convene a meeting of the Conciliation Committee.

9.   The Council shall act unanimously on the amendments on which the Commission has delivered a negative opinion.

Conciliation

10.   The Conciliation Committee, which shall be composed of the members of the Council or their representatives and an equal number of members representing the European Parliament, shall have the task of reaching agreement on a joint text, by a qualified majority of the members of the Council or their representatives and by a majority of the members representing the European Parliament within six weeks of its being convened, on the basis of the positions of the European Parliament and the Council at second reading.

11.   The Commission shall take part in the Conciliation Committee's proceedings and shall take all necessary initiatives with a view to reconciling the positions of the European Parliament and the Council.

12.   If, within six weeks of its being convened, the Conciliation Committee does not approve the joint text, the proposed act shall be deemed not to have been adopted.

Third reading

13.   If, within that period, the Conciliation Committee approves a joint text, the European Parliament, acting by a majority of the votes cast, and the Council, acting by a qualified majority, shall each have a period of six weeks from that approval in which to adopt the act in question in accordance with the joint text. If they fail to do so, the proposed act shall be deemed not to have been adopted.

14.   The periods of three months and six weeks referred to in this Article shall be extended by a maximum of one month and two weeks respectively at the initiative of the European Parliament or the Council.

Special provisions

15.   Where, in the cases provided for in the Constitution, a law or framework law is submitted to the ordinary legislative procedure on the initiative of a group of Member States, on a recommendation by the European Central Bank, or at the request of the Court of Justice, paragraph 2, the second sentence of paragraph 6, and paragraph 9 shall not apply.
In such cases, the European Parliament and the Council shall communicate the proposed act to the Commission with their positions at first and second readings. The European Parliament or the Council may request the opinion of the Commission throughout the procedure, which the Commission may also deliver on its own initiative. It may also, if it deems it necessary, take part in the Conciliation Committee in accordance with paragraph 11.

ARTICLE III-397 (*ex Article 218(1) TEC and new provision*)
The European Parliament, the Council and the Commission shall consult each other and by common agreement make arrangements for their co-operation. To that end, they may, in compliance with the Constitution, conclude inter-institutional agreements which may be of a binding nature.

ARTICLE III-398 (*new*)
1.   In carrying out their missions, the institutions, bodies, offices and agencies of the Union shall have the support of an open, efficient and independent European administration.

2.   In compliance with the Staff Regulations and the Conditions of Employment adopted on the basis of Article III-427, European laws shall establish provisions to that end.

ARTICLE III-399 (*ex Article 255 TEC*)
1.   The institutions, bodies, offices and agencies of the Union shall ensure transparency in their work and shall, pursuant to Article I-50, determine in their rules of procedure specific provisions for public access to their documents. The Court of Justice of the European Union, the European Central Bank and the European Investment Bank shall be subject to the provisions of Article I-50(3) and to this Article only when exercising their administrative tasks.

2.   The European Parliament and the Council shall ensure publication of the documents relating to the legislative procedures under the terms laid down by the European law referred to in Article I-50(3).

ARTICLE III-400 (*ex Articles 210 and 247(8) TEC*)
1.   The Council shall adopt European regulations and decisions determining:
(a)   the salaries, allowances and pensions of the President of the European Council, the President of the Commission, the Union Minister for Foreign Affairs, the members of the Commission, the Presidents, members and Registrars of the Court of Justice of the European Union, and the Secretary-General of the Council;
(b)   the conditions of employment, in particular the salaries, allowances and pensions, of the President and members of the Court of Auditors;
(c)   any payment to be made instead of remuneration to the persons referred to in points (a) and (b).

2.   The Council shall adopt European regulations and decisions determining the allowances of the members of the Economic and Social Committee.

ARTICLE III-401 (*ex Article 256 TEC*)
Acts of the Council, of the Commission or of the European Central Bank which impose a pecuniary obligation on persons other than Member States shall be enforceable.

Enforcement shall be governed by the rules of civil procedure in force in the Member State in the territory of which it is carried out. The order for its enforcement shall be appended to the decision, without other formality than verification of the authenticity of the decision, by the national authority which the government of each Member State shall designate for this purpose and shall make known to the Commission and the Court of Justice of the European Union.

When these formalities have been completed on application by the party concerned, the latter may proceed to enforcement by bringing the matter directly before the competent authority, in accordance with the national law.

Enforcement may be suspended only by a decision of the Court of Justice of the European Union. However, the courts of the country concerned shall have jurisdiction over complaints that enforcement is being carried out in an irregular manner.

CHAPTER II

FINANCIAL PROVISIONS

SECTION 1

THE MULTIANNUAL FINANCIAL FRAMEWORK

ARTICLE III-402 (*new*)
1.   The multiannual financial framework shall be established for a period of at least five years in accordance with Article I-55.

2.   The financial framework shall determine the amounts of the annual ceilings on commitment appropriations by category of expenditure and of the annual ceiling on payment appropriations. The categories of expenditure, limited in number, shall correspond to the Union's major sectors of activity.

3.   The financial framework shall lay down any other provisions required for the annual budgetary procedure to run smoothly.

4.   Where no European law of the Council determining a new financial framework has been adopted by the end of the previous financial framework, the ceilings and other provisions corresponding to the last year of that framework shall be extended until such time as that law is adopted.

5.   Throughout the procedure leading to the adoption of the financial framework, the European Parliament, the Council and the Commission shall take any measure necessary to facilitate the successful completion of the procedure.

SECTION 2

THE UNION'S ANNUAL BUDGET

ARTICLE III-403 (*ex Article 272(1) TEC*)
The financial year shall run from 1 January to 31 December.

ARTICLE III-404 (*ex Article 272(2) to (10) TEC*)
European laws shall establish the Union's annual budget in accordance with the following provisions:
1.   Each institution shall, before 1 July, draw up estimates of its expenditure for the following financial year. The Commission shall consolidate these estimates in a draft budget which may contain different estimates.
The draft budget shall contain an estimate of revenue and an estimate of expenditure.

2.   The Commission shall submit a proposal containing the draft budget to the European Parliament and to the Council not later than 1 September of the year preceding that in which the budget is to be implemented. The Commission may amend the draft budget during the procedure until such time as the Conciliation Committee, referred to in paragraph 5, is convened.

3.   The Council shall adopt its position on the draft budget and forward it to the European Parliament not later than 1 October of the year preceding that in which the budget is to be implemented. The Council shall inform the European Parliament in full of the reasons which led it to adopt its position.

4.   If, within forty-two days of such communication, the European Parliament:
(a)   approves the position of the Council, the European law establishing the budget shall be adopted;
(b)   has not taken a decision, the European law establishing the budget shall be deemed to have been adopted;
(c)   adopts amendments by a majority of its component members, the amended draft shall be forwarded to the Council and to the Commission. The President of the European Parliament, in agreement with the President of the Council, shall immediately convene a meeting of the Conciliation Committee. However, if within ten days of the draft being forwarded the Council informs the European Parliament that it has approved all its amendments, the Conciliation Committee shall not meet.

5.   The Conciliation Committee, which shall be composed of the members of the Council or their representatives and an equal number of members representing the European Parliament, shall have the task of reaching agreement on a joint text, by a qualified majority of the members of the Council or their representatives and by a majority of the representatives of the European Parliament within twenty-one days of its being convened, on the basis of the positions of the European Parliament and the Council.
The Commission shall take part in the Conciliation Committee's proceedings and shall take all the necessary initiatives with a view to reconciling the positions of the European Parliament and the Council.

6.   If, within the twenty-one days referred to in paragraph 5, the Conciliation Committee agrees on a joint text, the European Parliament and the Council shall each have a period of fourteen days from the date of that agreement in which to approve the joint text.

7.   If, within the period of fourteen days referred to in paragraph 6:
(a)   the European Parliament and the Council both approve the joint text or fail to take a decision, or if one of these institutions approves the joint text while the other one fails to take a decision, the European law establishing the budget shall be deemed to be definitively adopted in accordance with the joint text, or
(b)   the European Parliament, acting by a majority of its component members, and the Council both reject the joint text, or if one of these institutions rejects the joint text while the other one fails to take a decision, a new draft budget shall be submitted by the Commission, or
(c)   the European Parliament, acting by a majority of its component members, rejects the joint text while the Council approves it, a new draft budget shall be submitted by the Commission, or
(d)   the European Parliament approves the joint text whilst the Council rejects it, the European Parliament may, within fourteen days from the date of the rejection by the Council and acting by a majority of its component members and three-fifths of the votes cast, decide to confirm all or some of the amendments referred to in paragraph 4(c). Where a European Parliament amendment is not confirmed, the position agreed in the Conciliation committee on the budget heading which is the subject of the amendment shall be retained. The European law establishing the budget shall be deemed to be definitively adopted on this basis.

8.   If, within the twenty-one days referred to in paragraph 5, the Conciliation Committee does not agree on a joint text, a new draft budget shall be submitted by the Commission.

9.   When the procedure provided for in this Article has been completed, the President of the European Parliament shall declare that the European law establishing the budget has been definitively adopted.

10.   Each institution shall exercise the powers conferred upon it under this Article in compliance with the Constitution and the acts adopted thereunder, with particular regard to the Union's own resources and the balance between revenue and expenditure.

ARTICLE III-405 (*ex Article 273 TEC*)
1.   If at the beginning of a financial year no European law establishing the budget has been definitively adopted, a sum equivalent to not more than one twelfth of the budget appropriations entered in the chapter in question of the budget for the preceding financial year may be spent each month in respect of any chapter in accordance with the European law referred to in Article III-412; that sum shall not, however, exceed one twelfth of the appropriations provided for in the same chapter of the draft budget.

2.   The Council, on a proposal by the Commission and in compliance with the other conditions laid down in paragraph 1, may adopt a European decision authorising expenditure in excess of one twelfth, in

accordance with the European law referred to in Article III-412. The Council shall forward the decision immediately to the European Parliament.

The European decision shall lay down the necessary measures relating to resources to ensure application of this Article, in accordance with the European laws referred to in Article I-54(3) and (4).

It shall enter into force thirty days following its adoption if the European Parliament, acting by a majority of its component members, has not decided to reduce this expenditure within that time-limit.

ARTICLE III-406 (*ex Article 271 TEC*)

In accordance with the conditions laid down by the European law referred to in Article III-412, any appropriations, other than those relating to staff expenditure, that are unexpended at the end of the financial year may be carried forward to the next financial year only.

Appropriations shall be classified under different chapters grouping items of expenditure according to their nature or purpose and subdivided in accordance with the European law referred to in Article III-412.

The expenditure of
–   the European Parliament,
–   the European Council and the Council,
–   the Commission, and
–   the Court of Justice of the European Union

shall be set out in separate sections of the budget, without prejudice to special arrangements for certain common items of expenditure.

SECTION 3

IMPLEMENTATION OF THE BUDGET AND DISCHARGE

ARTICLE III-407 (*ex Article 274 TEC*)

The Commission shall implement the budget in co-operation with the Member States, in accordance with the European law referred to in Article III-412, on its own responsibility and within the limits of the appropriations allocated, having regard to the principles of sound financial management. Member States shall co-operate with the Commission to ensure that the appropriations are used in accordance with those principles.

The European law referred to in Article III-412 shall establish the control and audit obligations of the Member States in the implementation of the budget and the resulting responsibilities. It shall establish the responsibilities and detailed rules for each institution concerning its part in effecting its own expenditure.

Within the budget the Commission may, subject to the limits and conditions laid down by the European law referred to in Article III-412, transfer appropriations from one chapter to another or from one subdivision to another.

ARTICLE III-408 (*ex Article 275 TEC*)

The Commission shall submit annually to the European Parliament and to the Council the accounts of the preceding financial year relating to the implementation of the budget. The Commission shall also forward to them a financial statement of the Union's assets and liabilities.

The Commission shall also submit to the European Parliament and to the Council an evaluation report on the Union's finances based on the results achieved, in particular in relation to the indications given by the European Parliament and the Council pursuant to Article III-409.

ARTICLE III-409 (*ex Article 276 TEC*)

1.   The European Parliament, on a recommendation from the Council, shall give a discharge to the Commission in respect of the implementation of the budget. To this end, the Council and the European Parliament in turn shall examine the accounts, the financial statement and the evaluation report referred to in Article III-408, the annual report by the Court of Auditors together with the replies of the institutions under audit to the observations of the Court of Auditors, the statement of assurance referred to in the second subparagraph of Article III-384(1) and any relevant special reports by the Court of Auditors.

2.   Before giving a discharge to the Commission, or for any other purpose in connection with the exercise of its powers over the implementation of the budget, the European Parliament may ask to hear the Commission give evidence with regard to the execution of expenditure or the operation of financial control systems. The Commission shall submit any necessary information to the European Parliament at the latter's request.

3.   The Commission shall take all appropriate steps to act on the observations in the decisions giving discharge and on other observations by the European Parliament relating to the execution of expenditure, as well as on comments accompanying the recommendations on discharge adopted by the Council.

4.   At the request of the European Parliament or the Council, the Commission shall report on the measures taken in the light of these observations and comments and in particular on the instructions given to the departments which are responsible for the implementation of the budget. These reports shall also be forwarded to the Court of Auditors.

SECTION 4

COMMON PROVISIONS

ARTICLE III-410 (*ex Article 277 TEC*)
The multiannual financial framework and the annual budget shall be drawn up in euro.

ARTICLE III-411 (*ex Article 278 TEC*)
The Commission may, provided it notifies the competent authorities of the Member States concerned, transfer into the currency of one of the Member States its holdings in the currency of another Member State, to the extent necessary to enable them to be used for purposes which come within the scope of the Constitution. The Commission shall as far as possible avoid making such transfers if it possesses cash or liquid assets in the currencies which it needs.
The Commission shall deal with each Member State concerned through the authority designated by that State. In carrying out financial operations the Commission shall employ the services of the bank of issue of the Member State concerned or of any other financial institution approved by that State.

ARTICLE III-412 (*ex Article 279 TEC*)
1.   European laws shall establish:
(a)   the financial rules which determine in particular the procedure to be adopted for establishing and implementing the budget and for presenting and auditing accounts;
(b)   rules providing for checks on the responsibility of financial actors, in particular authorising officers and accounting officers.
Such European laws shall be adopted after consultation of the Court of Auditors.

2.   The Council shall, on a proposal from the Commission, adopt a European regulation laying down the methods and procedure whereby the budget revenue provided under the arrangements relating to the Union's own resources shall be made available to the Commission, and the measures to be applied, if need be, to meet cash requirements. The Council shall act after consulting the European Parliament and the Court of Auditors.

3.   The Council shall act unanimously until 31 December 2006 in all the cases referred to by this Article.

ARTICLE III-413 (*new*)
The European Parliament, the Council and the Commission shall ensure that the financial means are made available to allow the Union to fulfil its legal obligations in respect of third parties.

ARTICLE III-414 (*new*)
Regular meetings between the Presidents of the European Parliament, the Council and the Commission shall be convened, on the initiative of the Commission, under the budgetary procedures referred to in this Chapter. The Presidents shall take all the necessary steps to promote consultation and the reconciliation of the positions of the institutions over which they preside in order to facilitate the implementation of this Chapter.

SECTION 5

COMBATING FRAUD

ARTICLE III-415 (*ex Article 280 TEC*)
1.   The Union and the Member States shall counter fraud and any other illegal activities affecting the Union's financial interests through measures taken in accordance with this Article. These measures shall act

as a deterrent and be such as to afford effective protection in the Member States and in all the Union's institutions, bodies, offices and agencies.

2.   Member States shall take the same measures to counter fraud affecting the Union's financial interests as they take to counter fraud affecting their own financial interests.

3.   Without prejudice to other provisions of the Constitution, the Member States shall co-ordinate their action aimed at protecting the Union's financial interests against fraud. To this end they shall organise, together with the Commission, close and regular co-operation between the competent authorities.

4.   European laws or framework laws shall lay down the necessary measures in the fields of the prevention of and fight against fraud affecting the Union's financial interests with a view to affording effective and equivalent protection in the Member States and in all the Union's institutions, bodies, offices and agencies. They shall be adopted after consultation of the Court of Auditors.

5.   The Commission, in co-operation with Member States, shall each year submit to the European Parliament and to the Council a report on the measures taken for the implementation of this Article.

CHAPTER III

ENHANCED CO-OPERATION

ARTICLE III-416 (*ex Article 43(e) TEU*)
Any enhanced co-operation shall comply with the Constitution and the law of the Union.
Such co-operation shall not undermine the internal market or economic, social and territorial cohesion. It shall not constitute a barrier to or discrimination in trade between Member States, nor shall it distort competition between them.

ARTICLE III-417 (*ex Articles 43(h) and 44(2) TEU*)
Any enhanced co-operation shall respect the competences, rights and obligations of those Member States which do not participate in it. Those Member States shall not impede its implementation by the participating Member States.

ARTICLE III-418 (*ex Article 43b TEU and new provisions*)
1.   When enhanced co-operation is being established, it shall be open to all Member States, subject to compliance with any conditions of participation laid down by the European authorising decision. It shall also be open to them at any other time, subject to compliance with the acts already adopted within that framework, in addition to any such conditions.
The Commission and the Member States participating in enhanced co-operation shall ensure that they promote participation by as many Member States as possible.

2.   The Commission and, where appropriate, the Union Minister for Foreign Affairs shall keep the European Parliament and the Council regularly informed regarding developments in enhanced co-operation.

ARTICLE III-419 (*ex Article 27c TEU*)
1.   Member States which wish to establish enhanced co-operation between themselves in one of the areas covered by the Constitution, with the exception of fields of exclusive competence and the common foreign and security policy, shall address a request to the Commission, specifying the scope and objectives of the enhanced co-operation proposed. The Commission may submit a proposal to the Council to that effect. In the event of the Commission not submitting a proposal, it shall inform the Member States concerned of the reasons for not doing so.
Authorisation to proceed with enhanced co-operation shall be granted by a European decision of the Council, which shall act on a proposal from the Commission and after obtaining the consent of the European Parliament.

2.   The request of the Member States which wish to establish enhanced co-operation between themselves within the framework of the common foreign and security policy shall be addressed to the Council. It shall be forwarded to the Union Minister for Foreign Affairs, who shall give an opinion on whether the enhanced co-operation proposed is consistent with the Union's common foreign and security policy, and to the Commission, which shall give its opinion in particular on whether the enhanced co-operation proposed is consistent with other Union policies. It shall also be forwarded to the European Parliament for information.

Authorisation to proceed with enhanced co-operation shall be granted by a European decision of the Council acting unanimously.

ARTICLE III-420 (*ex Article 11a TEC and Article 27e TEU*)
1.   Any Member State which wishes to participate in enhanced co-operation in progress in one of the areas referred to in Article III-419(1) shall notify its intention to the Council and the Commission.
The Commission shall, within four months of the date of receipt of the notification, confirm the participation of the Member State concerned. It shall note where necessary that the conditions of participation have been fulfilled and shall adopt any transitional measures necessary with regard to the application of the acts already adopted within the framework of enhanced co-operation.
However, if the Commission considers that the conditions of participation have not been fulfilled, it shall indicate the arrangements to be adopted to fulfil those conditions and shall set a deadline for re-examining the request. On the expiry of that deadline, it shall re-examine the request, in accordance with the procedure set out in the second subparagraph. If the Commission considers that the conditions of participation have still not been met, the Member State concerned may refer the matter to the Council, which shall decide on the request. The Council shall act in accordance with Article I-44(3). It may also adopt the transitional measures referred to in the second subparagraph on a proposal from the Commission.

2.   Any Member State which wishes to participate in enhanced co-operation in progress in the framework of the common foreign and security policy shall notify its intention to the Council, the Union Minister for Foreign Affairs and the Commission.
The Council shall confirm the participation of the Member State concerned, after consulting the Union Minister for Foreign Affairs and after noting, where necessary, that the conditions of participation have been fulfilled. The Council, on a proposal from the Union Minister for Foreign Affairs, may also adopt any transitional measures necessary with regard to the application of the acts already adopted within the framework of enhanced co-operation. However, if the Council considers that the conditions of participation have not been fulfilled, it shall indicate the arrangements to be adopted to fulfil those conditions and shall set a deadline for re-examining the request for participation.
For the purposes of this paragraph, the Council shall act unanimously and in accordance with Article I-44(3).

ARTICLE III-421 (*ex Article 44a TEU*)
Expenditure resulting from implementation of enhanced co-operation, other than administrative costs entailed for the institutions, shall be borne by the participating Member States, unless all members of the Council, acting unanimously after consulting the European Parliament, decide otherwise.

ARTICLE III-422 (*new*)
1.   Where a provision of the Constitution which may be applied in the context of enhanced co-operation stipulates that the Council shall act unanimously, the Council, acting unanimously in accordance with the arrangements laid down in Article I-44(3), may adopt a European decision stipulating that it will act by a qualified majority.

2.   Where a provision of the Constitution which may be applied in the context of enhanced co-operation stipulates that the Council shall adopt European laws or framework laws under a special legislative procedure, the Council, acting unanimously in accordance with the arrangements laid down in Article I-44(3), may adopt a European decision stipulating that it will act under the ordinary legislative procedure. The Council shall act after consulting the European Parliament.

3.   Paragraphs 1 and 2 shall not apply to decisions having military or defence implications.

ARTICLE III-423 (*ex Article 45 TEU*)
The Council and the Commission shall ensure the consistency of activities undertaken in the context of enhanced co-operation and the consistency of such activities with the policies of the Union, and shall co-operate to that end.

TITLE VII

COMMON PROVISIONS

ARTICLE III-424 (*ex Article 299 TEC*)

Taking account of the structural economic and social situation of Guadeloupe, French Guiana, Martinique, Réunion, the Azores, Madeira and the Canary Islands, which is compounded by their remoteness, insularity, small size, difficult topography and climate, economic dependence on a few products, the permanence and combination of which severely restrain their development, the Council, on a proposal from the Commission, shall adopt European laws, framework laws, regulations and decisions aimed, in particular, at laying down the conditions of application of the Constitution to those regions, including common policies. It shall act after consulting the European Parliament.

The acts referred to in the first paragraph concern in particular areas such as customs and trade policies, fiscal policy, free zones, agriculture and fisheries policies, conditions for supply of raw materials and essential consumer goods, State aids and conditions of access to structural funds and to horizontal Union programmes.

The Council shall adopt the acts referred to in the first paragraph taking into account the special characteristics and constraints of the outermost regions without undermining the integrity and the coherence of the Union legal order, including the internal market and common policies.

ARTICLE III-425 (*ex Article 295 TEC*)

The Constitution shall in no way prejudice the rules in Member States governing the system of property ownership.

ARTICLE III-426 (*ex Article 282 TEC*)

In each of the Member States, the Union shall enjoy the most extensive legal capacity accorded to legal persons under their laws; it may, in particular, acquire or dispose of movable and immovable property and may be a party to legal proceedings. To this end, the Union shall be represented by the Commission. However, the Union shall be represented by each of the institutions, by virtue of their administrative autonomy, in matters relating to their respective operation.

ARTICLE III-427 (*ex Article 283 TEC*)

The Staff Regulations of officials and the Conditions of Employment of other servants of the Union shall be laid down by a European law. It shall be adopted after consultation of the institutions concerned.

ARTICLE III-428 (*ex Article 284 TEC*)

The Commission may, within the limits and under conditions laid down by a European regulation or decision adopted by a simple majority by the Council, collect any information and carry out any checks required for the performance of the tasks entrusted to it.

ARTICLE III-429 (*ex Article 285 TEC*)

1.   Without prejudice to Article 5 of the Protocol on the Statute of the European System of Central Banks and of the European Central Bank, measures for the production of statistics shall be laid down by a European law or framework law where necessary for the performance of the Union's activities.

2.   The production of statistics shall conform to impartiality, reliability, objectivity, scientific independence, cost-effectiveness and statistical confidentiality. It shall not entail excessive burdens on economic operators.

ARTICLE III-430 (*ex Article 287 TEC*)

The members of the Union's institutions, the members of committees, and the officials and other servants of the Union shall be required, even after their duties have ceased, not to disclose information of the kind covered by the obligation of professional secrecy, in particular information about undertakings, their business relations or their cost components.

ARTICLE III-431 (*ex Article 288 TEC*)

The Union's contractual liability shall be governed by the law applicable to the contract in question.

In the case of non-contractual liability, the Union shall, in accordance with the general principles common to the laws of the Member States, make good any damage caused by its institutions or by its servants in the performance of their duties.

Notwithstanding the second paragraph, the European Central Bank shall, in accordance with the general principles common to the laws of the Member States, make good any damage caused by it or by its servants in the performance of their duties.

The personal liability of its servants towards the Union shall be governed by the provisions laid down in their Staff Regulations or in the Conditions of Employment applicable to them.

ARTICLE III-432 (*ex Article 289 TEC*)

The seat of the Union's institutions shall be determined by common accord of the governments of the Member States.

ARTICLE III-433 (*ex Article 290 TEC*)

The Council shall adopt unanimously a European regulation laying down the rules governing the languages of the Union's institutions, without prejudice to the Statute of the Court of Justice of the European Union.

ARTICLE III-434 (*ex Article 291 TEC*)

The Union shall enjoy in the territories of the Member States such privileges and immunities as are necessary for the performance of its tasks, under the conditions laid down in the Protocol on the privileges and immunities of the European Union.

ARTICLE III-435 (*ex Article 307 TEC*)

The rights and obligations arising from agreements concluded before 1 January 1958 or, for acceding States, before the date of their accession, between one or more Member States on the one hand, and one or more third countries on the other, shall not be affected by the Constitution.

To the extent that such agreements are not compatible with the Constitution, the Member State or States concerned shall take all appropriate steps to eliminate the incompatibilities established. Member States shall, where necessary, assist each other to this end and shall, where appropriate, adopt a common attitude.

In applying the agreements referred to in the first paragraph, Member States shall take into account the fact that the advantages accorded under the Constitution by each Member State form an integral part of the Union and are thereby inseparably linked with the creation of institutions on which powers have been conferred by the Constitution and the granting of identical advantages by all the other Member States.

ARTICLE III-436 (*ex Article 296 TEC*)

1.   The Constitution shall not preclude the application of the following rules:
(a)   no Member State shall be obliged to supply information the disclosure of which it considers contrary to the essential interests of its security;
(b)   any Member State may take such measures as it considers necessary for the protection of the essential interests of its security which are connected with the production of or trade in arms, munitions and war material; such measures shall not adversely affect the conditions of competition in the internal market regarding products which are not intended for specifically military purposes.

2.   The Council, on a proposal from the Commission, may unanimously adopt a European decision making changes to the list of 15 April 1958 of the products to which the provisions of paragraph 1(b) apply.

PART IV

GENERAL AND FINAL PROVISIONS

ARTICLE IV-437 *Repeal of earlier Treaties* (*new*)
1.   This Treaty establishing a Constitution for Europe shall repeal the Treaty establishing the European Community, the Treaty on European Union and, under the conditions laid down in the Protocol on the acts and treaties having supplemented or amended the Treaty establishing the European Community and the Treaty on European Union, the acts and treaties which have supplemented or amended them, subject to paragraph 2 of this Article.

2.   The Treaties on the Accession:
(a)   of the Kingdom of Denmark, Ireland and the United Kingdom of Great Britain and Northern Ireland;
(b)   of the Hellenic Republic;
(c)   of the Kingdom of Spain and the Portuguese Republic;
(d)   of the Republic of Austria, the Republic of Finland and the Kingdom of Sweden, and
(e)   of the Czech Republic, the Republic of Estonia, the Republic of Cyprus, the Republic of Latvia, the Republic of Lithuania, the Republic of Hungary, the Republic of Malta, the Republic of Poland, the Republic of Slovenia and the Slovak Republic, shall be repealed.
Nevertheless:
–   the provisions of the Treaties referred to in points (a) to (d) and set out or referred to in the Protocol on the Treaties and Acts of Accession of the Kingdom of Denmark, Ireland and the United Kingdom of Great Britain and Northern Ireland, of the Hellenic Republic, of the Kingdom of Spain and the Portuguese Republic, and of the Republic of Austria, the Republic of Finland and the Kingdom of Sweden shall remain in force and their legal effects shall be preserved in accordance with that Protocol,
–   the provisions of the Treaty referred to in point (e) and which are set out or referred to in the Protocol on the Treaty and Act of Accession of the Czech Republic, the Republic of Estonia, the Republic of Cyprus, the Republic of Latvia, the Republic of Lithuania, the Republic of Hungary, the Republic of Malta, the Republic of Poland, the Republic of Slovenia and the Slovak Republic shall remain in force and their legal effects shall be preserved in accordance with that Protocol.

ARTICLE IV-438 *Succession and legal continuity* (*new*)
1.   The European Union established by this Treaty shall be the successor to the European Union established by the Treaty on European Union and to the European Community.

2.   Until new provisions have been adopted in implementation of this Treaty or until the end of their term of office, the institutions, bodies, offices and agencies existing on the date of the entry into force of this Treaty shall, subject to Article IV-439, exercise their powers within the meaning of this Treaty in their composition on that date.

3.   The acts of the institutions, bodies, offices and agencies adopted on the basis of the treaties and acts repealed by Article IV-437 shall remain in force. Their legal effects shall be preserved until those acts are repealed, annulled or amended in implementation of this Treaty. The same shall apply to agreements concluded between Member States on the basis of the treaties and acts repealed by Article IV-437.
The other components of the *acquis* of the Community and of the Union existing at the time of the entry into force of this Treaty, in particular the inter-institutional agreements, decisions and agreements arrived at by the Representatives of the Governments of the Member States, meeting within the Council, the agreements concluded by the Member States on the functioning of the Union or of the Community or linked to action by the Union or by the Community, the declarations, including those made in the context of intergovernmental conferences, as well as the resolutions or other positions adopted by the European Council or the Council and those relating to the Union or to the Community adopted by common accord by the Member States, shall also be preserved until they have been deleted or amended.

4.   The case law of the Court of Justice of the European Communities and of the Court of First Instance on the interpretation and application of the treaties and acts repealed by Article IV-437, as well as of the acts

and conventions adopted for their application, shall remain, *mutatis mutandis*, the source of interpretation of Union law and in particular of the comparable provisions of the Constitution.

5.   Continuity in administrative and legal procedures commenced prior to the date of entry into force of this Treaty shall be ensured in compliance with the Constitution. The institutions, bodies, offices and agencies responsible for those procedures shall take all appropriate measures to that effect.

ARTICLE IV-439 *Transitional provisions relating to certain institutions (new)*
The transitional provisions relating to the composition of the European Parliament, to the definition of a qualified majority in the European Council and in the Council, including those cases where not all members of the European Council or Council vote, and to the composition of the Commission, including the Union Minister for Foreign Affairs, shall be laid down in the Protocol on the transitional provisions relating to the institutions and bodies of the Union.

ARTICLE IV-440 *Scope (ex Article 299 TEC)*
1.   This Treaty shall apply to the Kingdom of Belgium, the Czech Republic, the Kingdom of Denmark, the Federal Republic of Germany, the Republic of Estonia, the Hellenic Republic, the Kingdom of Spain, the French Republic, Ireland, the Italian Republic, the Republic of Cyprus, the Republic of Latvia, the Republic of Lithuania, the Grand Duchy of Luxembourg, the Republic of Hungary, the Republic of Malta, the Kingdom of the Netherlands, the Republic of Austria, the Republic of Poland, the Portuguese Republic, the Republic of Slovenia, the Slovak Republic, the Republic of Finland, the Kingdom of Sweden and the United Kingdom of Great Britain and Northern Ireland.

2.   This Treaty shall apply to Guadeloupe, French Guiana, Martinique, Réunion, the Azores, Madeira and the Canary Islands in accordance with Article III-424.

3.   The special arrangements for association set out in Title IV of Part III shall apply to the overseas countries and territories listed in Annex II.
This Treaty shall not apply to overseas countries and territories having special relations with the United Kingdom of Great Britain and Northern Ireland which are not included in that list.

4.   This Treaty shall apply to the European territories for whose external relations a Member State is responsible.

5.   This Treaty shall apply to the Åland Islands with the derogations which originally appeared in the Treaty referred to in Article IV-437(2)(d) and which have been incorporated in Section 5 of Title V of the Protocol on the Treaties and Acts of Accession of the Kingdom of Denmark, Ireland and the United Kingdom of Great Britain and Northern Ireland, of the Hellenic Republic, of the Kingdom of Spain and the Portuguese Republic, and of the Republic of Austria, the Republic of Finland and the Kingdom of Sweden.

6.   Notwithstanding paragraphs 1 to 5:
(a)   this Treaty shall not apply to the Faeroe Islands;
(b)   this Treaty shall apply to Akrotiri and Dhekelia, the sovereign base areas of the United Kingdom of Great Britain and Northern Ireland in Cyprus, only to the extent necessary to ensure the implementation of the arrangements originally provided for in the Protocol on the Sovereign Base Areas of the United Kingdom of Great Britain and Northern Ireland in Cyprus, annexed to the Act of Accession which is an integral part of the Treaty referred to in Article IV-437(2)(e), and which have been incorporated in Title III of Part II of the Protocol on the Treaty and Act of Accession of the Czech Republic, the Republic of Estonia, the Republic of Cyprus, the Republic of Latvia, the Republic of Lithuania, the Republic of Hungary, the Republic of Malta, the Republic of Poland, the Republic of Slovenia and the Slovak Republic;
(c)   this Treaty shall apply to the Channel Islands and the Isle of Man only to the extent necessary to ensure the implementation of the arrangements for those islands originally set out in the Treaty referred to in Article IV-437(2)(a), and which have been incorporated in Section 3 of Title II of the Protocol on the Treaties and Acts of Accession of the Kingdom of Denmark, Ireland and the United Kingdom of Great Britain and Northern Ireland, of the Hellenic Republic, of the Kingdom of Spain and the Portuguese Republic, and of the Republic of Austria, the Republic of Finland and the Kingdom of Sweden.

7. The European Council may, on the initiative of the Member State concerned, adopt a European decision amending the status, with regard to the Union, of a Danish, French or Netherlands country or territory referred to in paragraphs 2 and 3. The European Council shall act unanimously after consulting the Commission.

ARTICLE IV-441 *Regional unions* (*ex Article 306 TEC*)
This Treaty shall not preclude the existence or completion of regional unions between Belgium and Luxembourg, or between Belgium, Luxembourg and the Netherlands, to the extent that the objectives of these regional unions are not attained by application of the said Treaty.

ARTICLE IV-442 *Protocols and Annexes* (*ex Article 311 TEC*)
The Protocols and Annexes to this Treaty shall form an integral part thereof.

ARTICLE IV-443 *Ordinary revision procedure* (*ex Article 48 TEU*)
1.   The government of any Member State, the European Parliament or the Commission may submit to the Council proposals for the amendment of this Treaty. These proposals shall be submitted to the European Council by the Council and the national Parliaments shall be notified.

2.   If the European Council, after consulting the European Parliament and the Commission, adopts by a simple majority a decision in favour of examining the proposed amendments, the President of the European Council shall convene a Convention composed of representatives of the national Parliaments, of the Heads of State or Government of the Member States, of the European Parliament and of the Commission. The European Central Bank shall also be consulted in the case of institutional changes in the monetary area. The Convention shall examine the proposals for amendments and shall adopt by consensus a recommendation to a conference of representatives of the governments of the Member States as provided for in paragraph 3.
The European Council may decide by a simple majority, after obtaining the consent of the European Parliament, not to convene a Convention should this not be justified by the extent of the proposed amendments. In the latter case, the European Council shall define the terms of reference for a conference of representatives of the governments of the Member States.

3.   A conference of representatives of the governments of the Member States shall be convened by the President of the Council for the purpose of determining by common accord the amendments to be made to this Treaty.
The amendments shall enter into force after being ratified by all the Member States in accordance with their respective constitutional requirements.

4.   If, two years after the signature of the treaty amending this Treaty, four fifths of the Member States have ratified it and one or more Member States have encountered difficulties in proceeding with ratification, the matter shall be referred to the European Council.

ARTICLE IV-444 *Simplified revision procedure* (*new*)
1.   Where Part III provides for the Council to act by unanimity in a given area or case, the European Council may adopt a European decision authorising the Council to act by a qualified majority in that area or in that case.
This paragraph shall not apply to decisions with military implications or those in the area of defence.

2.   Where Part III provides for European laws and framework laws to be adopted by the Council in accordance with a special legislative procedure, the European Council may adopt a European decision allowing for the adoption of such European laws or framework laws in accordance with the ordinary legislative procedure.

3.   Any initiative taken by the European Council on the basis of paragraphs 1 or 2 shall be notified to the national Parliaments. If a national Parliament makes known its opposition within six months of the date of such notification, the European decision referred to in paragraphs 1 or 2 shall not be adopted. In the absence of opposition, the European Council may adopt the decision.
For the adoption of the European decisions referred to in paragraphs 1 and 2, the European Council shall act by unanimity after obtaining the consent of the European Parliament, which shall be given by a majority of its component members.

ARTICLE IV-445 *Simplified revision procedure concerning internal Union policies and action* (*new*)
1.   The Government of any Member State, the European Parliament or the Commission may submit to the European Council proposals for revising all or part of the provisions of Title III of Part III on the internal policies and action of the Union.

2.   The European Council may adopt a European decision amending all or part of the provisions of Title III of Part III. The European Council shall act by unanimity after consulting the European Parliament and the Commission, and the European Central Bank in the case of institutional changes in the monetary area.

Such a European decision shall not come into force until it has been approved by the Member States in accordance with their respective constitutional requirements.

3.　　The European decision referred to in paragraph 2 shall not increase the competences conferred on the Union in this Treaty.

ARTICLE IV-446 *Duration* (*ex Articles 51 TEU and 312 TEC*)
This Treaty is concluded for an unlimited period.

ARTICLE IV-447 *Ratification and entry into force* (*ex Articles 52 TEU and 313 TEC*)
1.　　This Treaty shall be ratified by the High Contracting Parties in accordance with their respective constitutional requirements. The instruments of ratification shall be deposited with the Government of the Italian Republic.

2.　　This Treaty shall enter into force on 1 November 2006, provided that all the instruments of ratification have been deposited, or, failing that, on the first day of the second month following the deposit of the instrument of ratification by the last signatory State to take this step.

ARTICLE IV-448 *Authentic texts and translations* (*ex Articles 53 TEU and 314 TEC*)
1.　　This Treaty, drawn up in a single original in the Czech, Danish, Dutch, English, Estonian, Finnish, French, German, Greek, Hungarian, Irish, Italian, Latvian, Lithuanian, Maltese, Polish, Portuguese, Slovak, Slovenian, Spanish and Swedish languages, the texts in each of these languages being equally authentic, shall be deposited in the archives of the Government of the Italian Republic, which will transmit a certified copy to each of the governments of the other signatory States.

2.　　This Treaty may also be translated into any other languages as determined by Member States among those which, in accordance with their constitutional order, enjoy official status in all or part of their territory. A certified copy of such translations shall be provided by the Member States concerned to be deposited in the archives of the Council.

IN WITNESS WHEREOF, the undersigned plenipotentiaries have signed this Treaty.

Done at … this …

[*BMDF Note: For each Member State, the names of the Heads of State, the names of the Plenipotentiaries and the signatures of the Plenipotentiaries follow here.*]

ANNEX I

LIST
referred to in Article III-226 of the Constitution

- 1 -	- 2 -
Number in the Brussels nomenclature	Description of products
CHAPTER 1	Live animals
CHAPTER 2	Meat and edible meat offal
CHAPTER 3	Fish, crustaceans and molluscs
CHAPTER 4	Dairy produce; birds' eggs; natural honey
CHAPTER 5	
05.04	Guts, bladders and stomachs of animals (other than fish), whole and pieces thereof
05.15	Animal products not elsewhere specified or included; dead animals of Chapter 1 or Chapter 3, unfit for human consumption
CHAPTER 6	Live trees and other plants; bulbs, roots and the like; cut flowers and ornamental foliage
CHAPTER 7	Edible vegetables and certain roots and tubers
CHAPTER 8	Edible fruit and nuts; peel of melons or citrus fruit
CHAPTER 9	Coffee, tea and spices, excluding maté (heading No 09.03)
CHAPTER 10	Cereals
CHAPTER 11	Products of the milling industry; malt and starches; gluten; inulin
CHAPTER 12	Oil seeds and oleaginous fruit; miscellaneous grains, seeds and fruit; industrial and medical plants; straw and fodder
CHAPTER 13	
ex 13.03	Pectin
CHAPTER 15	
15.01	Lard and other rendered pig fat; rendered poultry fat
15.02	Unrendered fats of bovine cattle, sheep or goats; tallow (including "premier jus") produced from those fats
15.03	Lard stearin, oleostearin and tallow stearin; lard oil, oleo-oil and tallow oil, not emulsified or mixed or prepared in any way
15.04	Fats and oil, of fish and marine mammals, whether or not refined
15.07	Fixed vegetable oils, fluid or solid, crude, refined or purified
15.12	Animal or vegetable fats and oils, hydrogenated, whether or not refined, but not further prepared
15.13	Margarine, imitation lard and other prepared edible fats
15.17	Residues resulting from the treatment of fatty substances or animal or vegetable waxes
CHAPTER 16	Preparations of meat, of fish, of crustaceans or molluscs

- 1 -	- 2 -
Number in the Brussels nomenclature	Description of products

CHAPTER 17	
17.01	Beet sugar and cane sugar, solid
17.02	Other sugars; sugar syrups; artificial honey (whether or not mixed with natural honey); caramel
17.03	Molasses, whether or not decolourised
17.05 (*)	Flavoured or coloured sugars, syrups and molasses, but not including fruit juices containing added sugar in any proportion
CHAPTER 18	
18.01	Cocoa beans, whole or broken, raw or roasted
18.02	Cocoa shells, husks, skins and waste
CHAPTER 20	Preparations of vegetables, fruit or other parts of plants
CHAPTER 22	
22.04	Grape must, in fermentation or with fermentation arrested otherwise than by the addition of alcohol
22.05	Wine of fresh grapes; grape must with fermentation arrested by the addition of alcohol
22.07	Other fermented beverages (for example, cider, perry and mead)
ex 22.08 (*) ex 22.09 (*)	Ethyl alcohol or neutral spirits, whether or not denatured, of any strength, obtained from agricultural products listed in this Annex, excluding liqueurs and other spirituous beverages and compound alcoholic preparations (known as "concentrated extracts") for the manufacture of beverages
ex 22.10 (*)	Vinegar and substitutes for vinegar
CHAPTER 23	Residues and waste from the food industries; prepared animal fodder
CHAPTER 24	
24.01	Unmanufactured tobacco, tobacco refuse
CHAPTER 45	
45.01	Natural cork, unworked, crushed, granulated or ground; waste cork
CHAPTER 54	
54.01	Flax, raw or processed but not spun; flax tow and waste (including pulled or garnetted rags)
CHAPTER 57	
57.01	True hemp (*Cannabis sativa*), raw or processed but not spun; tow and waste of true hemp (including pulled or garnetted rags or ropes)

(*)   Heading added by Article 1 of Regulation No 7a of the Council of the European Economic Community of 18 December 1959 (OJ No 7, 30.1.1961, p. 71. Special edition (English edition) 1959-1962, p. 68).

ANNEX II

OVERSEAS COUNTRIES AND TERRITORIES

to which
Title IV in Part III of the Constitution apply

–   Greenland,

–   New Caledonia and Dependencies,

–   French Polynesia,

–   French Southern and Antarctic Territories,

–   Wallis and Futuna Islands,

–   Mayotte,

–   Saint Pierre and Miquelon,

–   Aruba,

–   Netherlands Antilles:

    –   Bonaire,

    –   Curaçao,

    –   Saba,

    –   Sint Eustatius,

    –   Sint Maarten.

–   Anguilla,

–   Cayman Islands,

–   Falkland Islands,

–   South Georgia and the South Sandwich Islands,

–   Montserrat,

–   Pitcairn,

–   Saint Helena and Dependencies,

–   British Antarctic Territory,

–   British Indian Ocean Territory,

–   Turks and Caicos Islands,

–   British Virgin Islands,

–   Bermuda.

FINAL ACT

THE CONFERENCE OF THE REPRESENTATIVES OF THE GOVERNMENTS OF THE MEMBER STATES, convened in Brussels on 30 September 2003 to adopt by common accord the Treaty establishing a Constitution for Europe, has adopted the following texts:

I. Treaty establishing a Constitution for Europe

II. Protocols annexed to the Treaty establishing a Constitution for Europe

1. Protocol on the role of national Parliaments in the European Union

2. Protocol on the application of the principles of subsidiarity and proportionality

3. Protocol on the Statute of the Court of Justice of the European Union

4. Protocol on the Statute of the European System of Central Banks and of the European Central Bank

5. Protocol on the Statute of the European Investment Bank

6. Protocol on the location of the seats of the institutions and of certain bodies, offices, agencies and departments of the European Union

7. Protocol on the privileges and immunities of the European Union

8. Protocol on the Treaties and Acts of Accession of the Kingdom of Denmark, Ireland and the United Kingdom of Great Britain and Northern Ireland, of the Hellenic Republic, of the Kingdom of Spain and the Portuguese Republic, and of the Republic of Austria, the Republic of Finland and the Kingdom of Sweden

9. Protocol on the Treaty and the Act of Accession of the Czech Republic, the Republic of Estonia, the Republic of Cyprus, the Republic of Latvia, the Republic of Lithuania, the Republic of Hungary, the Republic of Malta, the Republic of Poland, the Republic of Slovenia and the Slovak Republic

10. Protocol on the excessive deficit procedure

11. Protocol on the convergence criteria

12. Protocol on the Euro Group

13. Protocol on certain provisions relating to the United Kingdom of Great Britain and Northern Ireland as regards economic and monetary union

14. Protocol on certain provisions relating to Denmark as regards economic and monetary union

15. Protocol on certain tasks of the National Bank of Denmark

16. Protocol on the Pacific Financial Community franc system

17. Protocol on the Schengen *acquis* integrated into the framework of the European Union

18. Protocol on the application of certain aspects of Article III-130 of the Constitution to the United Kingdom and to Ireland

19. Protocol on the position of the United Kingdom and Ireland on policies in respect of border controls, asylum and immigration, judicial co-operation in civil matters and on police co-operation

20. Protocol on the position of Denmark

21. Protocol on external relations of the Member States with regard to the crossing of external borders

22. Protocol on asylum for nationals of Member States

The Conference has adopted the following declarations annexed to this Final Act.

Furthermore, the Conference has noted the declarations listed hereafter and annexed to this Final Act:

42. Declaration by the Kingdom of the Netherlands on Article I-55

43. Declaration by the Kingdom of the Netherlands on Article IV-440

44. Declaration by the Federal Republic of Germany, Ireland, the Republic of Hungary, the Republic of Austria and the Kingdom of Sweden

45. Declaration by the Kingdom of Spain and the United Kingdom of Great Britain and Northern Ireland

46. Declaration by the United Kingdom of Great Britain and Northern Ireland on the definition of the term "nationals"

47. Declaration by the Kingdom of Spain on the definition of the term "nationals"

48. Declaration by the United Kingdom of Great Britain and Northern Ireland on the franchise for elections to the European Parliament

49. Declaration by the Kingdom of Belgium on national parliaments

50. Declaration by the Republic of Latvia and the Republic of Hungary on the spelling of the name of the single currency in the Treaty establishing a Constitution for Europe

Done at Rome this twenty-ninth day of October in the year two thousand and four.
....
(all languages)

For ....
....

[*BMDF Note: For each Member State, the names of the Heads of State, the names of the Plenipotentiaries and the signatures of the Plenipotentiaries follow here.*]

The following have also signed this Final Act, in their capacity as candidate States for accession to the European Union, having been observers to the Conference:

For Bulgaria, ...

For Romania, ...

For Turkey, ...

PROTOCOLS
ANNEXED TO THE TREATY ESTABLISHING
A CONSTITUTION FOR EUROPE

BMDF notes are shown in brackets and in italics after certain of the protocol titles, to give an indication of the subject matter.

* * * * *

PROTOCOLS

ANNEXED TO THE TREATY ESTABLISHING A CONSTITUTION FOR EUROPE

1. PROTOCOL ON THE ROLE OF NATIONAL PARLIAMENTS IN THE EUROPEAN UNION

THE HIGH CONTRACTING PARTIES,

RECALLING that the way in which national Parliaments scrutinise their governments in relation to the activities of the Union is a matter for the particular constitutional organisation and practice of each Member State;

DESIRING to encourage greater involvement of national Parliaments in the activities of the European Union and to enhance their ability to express their views on draft European legislative acts as well as on other matters which may be of particular interest to them,

HAVE AGREED UPON the following provisions, which shall be annexed to the Treaty establishing a Constitution for Europe and to the Treaty establishing the European Atomic Energy Community:

TITLE I

INFORMATION FOR NATIONAL PARLIAMENTS

ARTICLE 1
Commission consultation documents (green and white papers and communications) shall be forwarded directly by the Commission to national Parliaments upon publication. The Commission shall also forward the annual legislative programme as well as any other instrument of legislative planning or policy to national Parliaments, at the same time as to the European Parliament and the Council.

ARTICLE 2
Draft European legislative acts sent to the European Parliament and to the Council shall be forwarded to national Parliaments.
For the purposes of this Protocol, "draft European legislative acts" shall mean proposals from the Commission, initiatives from a group of Member States, initiatives from the European Parliament, requests from the Court of Justice, recommendations from the European Central Bank and requests from the European Investment Bank for the adoption of a European legislative act.
Draft European legislative acts originating from the Commission shall be forwarded to national Parliaments directly by the Commission, at the same time as to the European Parliament and the Council.
Draft European legislative acts originating from the European Parliament shall be forwarded to national Parliaments directly by the European Parliament.
Draft European legislative acts originating from a group of Member States, the Court of Justice, the European Central Bank or the European Investment Bank shall be forwarded to national Parliaments by the Council.

ARTICLE 3
National Parliaments may send to the Presidents of the European Parliament, the Council and the Commission a reasoned opinion on whether a draft European legislative act complies with the principle of subsidiarity, in accordance with the procedure laid down in the Protocol on the application of the principles of subsidiarity and proportionality.
If the draft European legislative act originates from a group of Member States, the President of the Council shall forward the reasoned opinion or opinions to the governments of those Member States.
If the draft European legislative act originates from the Court of Justice, the European Central Bank or the European Investment Bank, the President of the Council shall forward the reasoned opinion or opinions to the institution or body concerned.

ARTICLE 4

A six-week period shall elapse between a draft European legislative act being made available to national Parliaments in the official languages of the Union and the date when it is placed on a provisional agenda for the Council for its adoption or for adoption of a position under a legislative procedure. Exceptions shall be possible in cases of urgency, the reasons for which shall be stated in the act or position of the Council. Save in urgent cases for which due reasons have been given, no agreement may be reached on a draft European legislative act during those six weeks. Save in urgent cases for which due reasons have been given, a ten-day period shall elapse between the placing of a draft European legislative act on the provisional agenda for the Council and the adoption of a position.

ARTICLE 5

The agendas for and the outcome of meetings of the Council, including the minutes of meetings where the Council is deliberating on draft European legislative acts, shall be forwarded directly to national Parliaments, at the same time as to Member States' governments.

ARTICLE 6

When the European Council intends to make use of Article IV-444(1) or (2) of the Constitution, national Parliaments shall be informed of the initiative of the European Council at least six months before any European decision is adopted.

ARTICLE 7

The Court of Auditors shall forward its annual report to national Parliaments, for information, at the same time as to the European Parliament and to the Council.

ARTICLE 8

Where the national Parliamentary system is not unicameral, Articles 1 to 7 shall apply to the component chambers.

TITLE II

INTER-PARLIAMENTARY CO-OPERATION

ARTICLE 9

The European Parliament and national Parliaments shall together determine the organisation and promotion of effective and regular inter-parliamentary co-operation within the Union.

ARTICLE 10

A conference of Parliamentary Committees for Union Affairs may submit any contribution it deems appropriate for the attention of the European Parliament, the Council and the Commission. That conference shall in addition promote the exchange of information and best practice between national Parliaments and the European Parliament, including their special committees. It may also organise inter-parliamentary conferences on specific topics, in particular to debate matters of common foreign and security policy, including common security and defence policy. Contributions from the conference shall not bind national Parliaments and shall not prejudge their positions.

2. PROTOCOL ON THE APPLICATION OF THE PRINCIPLES OF SUBSIDIARITY AND PROPORTIONALITY

THE HIGH CONTRACTING PARTIES,

WISHING to ensure that decisions are taken as closely as possible to the citizens of the Union;

RESOLVED to establish the conditions for the application of the principles of subsidiarity and proportionality, as laid down in Article I-11 of the Constitution, and to establish a system for monitoring the application of those principles,

HAVE AGREED UPON the following provisions, which shall be annexed to the Treaty establishing a Constitution for Europe:

ARTICLE 1

Each institution shall ensure constant respect for the principles of subsidiarity and proportionality, as laid down in Article I-11 of the Constitution.

ARTICLE 2

Before proposing European legislative acts, the Commission shall consult widely. Such consultations shall, where appropriate, take into account the regional and local dimension of the action envisaged. In cases of exceptional urgency, the Commission shall not conduct such consultations. It shall give reasons for its decision in its proposal.

ARTICLE 3

For the purposes of this Protocol, "draft European legislative acts" shall mean proposals from the Commission, initiatives from a group of Member States, initiatives from the European Parliament, requests from the Court of Justice, recommendations from the European Central Bank and requests from the European Investment Bank for the adoption of a European legislative act.

ARTICLE 4

The Commission shall forward its draft European legislative acts and its amended drafts to national Parliaments at the same time as to the Union legislator.

The European Parliament shall forward its draft European legislative acts and its amended drafts to national Parliaments.

The Council shall forward draft European legislative acts originating from a group of Member States, the Court of Justice, the European Central Bank or the European Investment Bank and amended drafts to national Parliaments.

Upon adoption, legislative resolutions of the European Parliament and positions of the Council shall be forwarded by them to national Parliaments.

ARTICLE 5

Draft European legislative acts shall be justified with regard to the principles of subsidiarity and proportionality. Any draft European legislative act should contain a detailed statement making it possible to appraise compliance with the principles of subsidiarity and proportionality. This statement should contain some assessment of the proposal's financial impact and, in the case of a European framework law, of its implications for the rules to be put in place by Member States, including, where necessary, the regional legislation. The reasons for concluding that a Union objective can be better achieved at Union level shall be substantiated by qualitative and, wherever possible, quantitative indicators. Draft European legislative acts shall take account of the need for any burden, whether financial or administrative, falling upon the Union, national governments, regional or local authorities, economic operators and citizens, to be minimised and commensurate with the objective to be achieved.

ARTICLE 6

Any national Parliament or any chamber of a national Parliament may, within six weeks from the date of transmission of a draft European legislative act, send to the Presidents of the European Parliament, the Council and the Commission a reasoned opinion stating why it considers that the draft in question does not comply with the principle of subsidiarity. It will be for each national Parliament or each chamber of a national Parliament to consult, where appropriate, regional parliaments with legislative powers.

If the draft European legislative act originates from a group of Member States, the President of the Council shall forward the opinion to the governments of those Member States.

If the draft European legislative act originates from the Court of Justice, the European Central Bank or the European Investment Bank, the President of the Council shall forward the opinion to the institution or body concerned.

ARTICLE 7

The European Parliament, the Council and the Commission, and, where appropriate, the group of Member States, the Court of Justice, the European Central Bank or the European Investment Bank, if the draft legislative act originates from them, shall take account of the reasoned opinions issued by national Parliaments or by a chamber of a national Parliament.

Each national Parliament shall have two votes, shared out on the basis of the national Parliamentary system. In the case of a bicameral Parliamentary system, each of the two chambers shall have one vote.

Where reasoned opinions on a draft European legislative act's non-compliance with the principle of subsidiarity represent at least one third of all the votes allocated to the national Parliaments in accordance with the second paragraph, the draft must be reviewed. This threshold shall be a quarter in the case of a draft European legislative act submitted on the basis of Article III-264 of the Constitution on the area of freedom, security and justice.

After such review, the Commission or, where appropriate, the group of Member States, the European Parliament, the Court of Justice, the European Central Bank or the European Investment Bank, if the draft European legislative act originates from them, may decide to maintain, amend or withdraw the draft. Reasons must be given for this decision.

ARTICLE 8

The Court of Justice of the European Union shall have jurisdiction in actions on grounds of infringement of the principle of subsidiarity by a European legislative act, brought in accordance with the rules laid down in Article III-365 of the Constitution by Member States, or notified by them in accordance with their legal order on behalf of their national Parliament or a chamber of it.

In accordance with the rules laid down in the said Article, the Committee of the Regions may also bring such actions against European legislative acts for the adoption of which the Constitution provides that it be consulted.

ARTICLE 9

The Commission shall submit each year to the European Council, the European Parliament, the Council and national Parliaments a report on the application of Article I-11 of the Constitution. This annual report shall also be forwarded to the Committee of the Regions and to the Economic and Social Committee.

3. PROTOCOL ON THE STATUTE OF THE COURT OF JUSTICE OF THE EUROPEAN UNION

THE HIGH CONTRACTING PARTIES

DESIRING to lay down the Statute of the Court of Justice of the European Union provided for in Article III-381 of the Constitution,

HAVE AGREED upon the following provisions, which shall be annexed to the Treaty establishing a Constitution for Europe and the Treaty establishing the European Atomic Energy Community:

ARTICLE 1

The Court of Justice of the European Union shall be constituted and shall function in accordance with the Constitution, with the Treaty establishing the European Atomic Energy Community (EAEC Treaty) and with this Statute.

TITLE I

JUDGES AND ADVOCATES-GENERAL

ARTICLE 2

Before taking up his duties each Judge shall, before the Court of Justice sitting in open court, take an oath to perform his duties impartially and conscientiously and to preserve the secrecy of the deliberations of the Court.

ARTICLE 3

The Judges shall be immune from legal proceedings. After they have ceased to hold office, they shall continue to enjoy immunity in respect of acts performed by them in their official capacity, including words spoken or written.

The Court of Justice, sitting as a full Court, may waive the immunity. If the decision concerns a member of the General Court or of a specialised court, the Court shall decide after consulting the court concerned.

Where immunity has been waived and criminal proceedings are instituted against a Judge, he shall be tried, in any of the Member States, only by the court competent to judge the members of the highest national judiciary.

Articles 11 to 14 and Article 17 of the Protocol on the privileges and immunities of the Union shall apply to the Judges, Advocates-General, Registrars and Assistant Rapporteurs of the Court of Justice of the European Union, without prejudice to the provisions relating to immunity from legal proceedings of Judges which are set out in the first, second and third paragraphs of this Article.

ARTICLE 4

The Judges may not hold any political or administrative office.

They may not engage in any occupation, whether gainful or not, unless exemption is exceptionally granted by a European decision of the Council, acting by a simple majority.

When taking up their duties, they shall give a solemn undertaking that, both during and after their term of office, they will respect the obligations arising therefrom, in particular the duty to behave with integrity and discretion as regards the acceptance, after they have ceased to hold office, of certain appointments or benefits. Any doubt on this point shall be settled by decision of the Court of Justice. If the decision concerns a member of the General Court or of a specialised court, the Court shall decide after consulting the court concerned.

ARTICLE 5

Apart from normal replacement, or death, the duties of a Judge shall end when he resigns.

Where a Judge resigns, his letter of resignation shall be addressed to the President of the Court of Justice for transmission to the President of the Council. Upon this notification a vacancy shall arise on the bench.

Save where Article 6 applies, a Judge shall continue to hold office until his successor takes up his duties.

ARTICLE 6

A Judge may be deprived of his office or of his right to a pension or other benefits in its stead only if, in the unanimous opinion of the Judges and Advocates-General of the Court of Justice, he no longer fulfils the requisite conditions or meets the obligations arising from his office. The Judge concerned shall not take part in any such deliberations. If the person concerned is a member of the General Court or of a specialised court, the Court shall decide after consulting the court concerned.

The Registrar of the Court of Justice shall communicate the decision of the Court of Justice to the President of the European Parliament and to the President of the Commission and shall notify it to the President of the Council.

In the case of a decision depriving a Judge of his office, a vacancy shall arise on the bench upon this latter notification.

ARTICLE 7

A Judge who is to replace a member of the Court of Justice whose term of office has not expired shall be appointed for the remainder of his predecessor's term.

ARTICLE 8

The provisions of Articles 2 to 7 shall apply to the Advocates-General.

TITLE II

ORGANISATION OF THE COURT OF JUSTICE

ARTICLE 9

When, every three years, the Judges are partially replaced, thirteen and twelve Judges shall be replaced alternately.

When, every three years, the Advocates-General are partially replaced, four Advocates-General shall be replaced on each occasion.

ARTICLE 10

The Registrar shall take an oath before the Court of Justice to perform his duties impartially and conscientiously and to preserve the secrecy of the deliberations of the Court of Justice.

ARTICLE 11

The Court of Justice shall arrange for replacement of the Registrar on occasions when he is prevented from attending the Court of Justice.

ARTICLE 12

Officials and other servants shall be attached to the Court of Justice to enable it to function. They shall be responsible to the Registrar under the authority of the President.

ARTICLE 13

A European law may provide for the appointment of Assistant Rapporteurs and lay down the rules governing their service. It shall be adopted at the request of the Court of Justice. The Assistant Rapporteurs may be required, under conditions laid down in the Rules of Procedure, to participate in preparatory inquiries in cases pending before the Court of Justice and to co-operate with the Judge who acts as Rapporteur.

The Assistant Rapporteurs shall be chosen from persons whose independence is beyond doubt and who possess the necessary legal qualifications; they shall be appointed by a European decision of the Council, acting by a simple majority. They shall take an oath before the Court of Justice to perform their duties impartially and conscientiously and to preserve the secrecy of the deliberations of the Court of Justice.

ARTICLE 14

The Judges, the Advocates-General and the Registrar shall be required to reside at the place where the Court of Justice has its seat.

ARTICLE 15

The Court of Justice shall remain permanently in session. The duration of the judicial vacations shall be determined by the Court of Justice with due regard to the needs of its business.

ARTICLE 16

The Court of Justice shall form chambers consisting of three and five Judges. The Judges shall elect the Presidents of the chambers from among their number. The Presidents of the chambers of five Judges shall be elected for three years. They may be re-elected once.

The Grand Chamber shall consist of thirteen Judges. It shall be presided over by the President of the Court of Justice. The Presidents of the chambers of five Judges and other Judges appointed in accordance with the conditions laid down in the Rules of Procedure shall also form part of the Grand Chamber.

The Court of Justice shall sit in a Grand Chamber when a Member State or an institution of the Union that is party to the proceedings so requests.

The Court of Justice shall sit as a full Court where cases are brought before it pursuant to Article III-335(2), the second paragraph of Article III-347, Article III-349 or Article III-385(6) of the Constitution.

Moreover, where it considers that a case before it is of exceptional importance, the Court of Justice may decide, after hearing the Advocate-General, to refer the case to the full Court.

ARTICLE 17

Decisions of the Court of Justice shall be valid only when an uneven number of its members is sitting in the deliberations.

Decisions of the chambers consisting of either three or five Judges shall be valid only if they are taken by three Judges.

Decisions of the Grand Chamber shall be valid only if nine Judges are sitting.

Decisions of the full Court shall be valid only if fifteen Judges are sitting.

In the event of one of the Judges of a chamber being prevented from attending, a Judge of another chamber may be called upon to sit in accordance with conditions laid down in the Rules of Procedure.

ARTICLE 18

No Judge or Advocate-General may take part in the disposal of any case in which he has previously taken part as agent or adviser or has acted for one of the parties, or in which he has been called upon to pronounce as a member of a court or tribunal, of a commission of inquiry or in any other capacity.

If, for some special reason, any Judge or Advocate-General considers that he should not take part in the judgment or examination of a particular case, he shall so inform the President. If, for some special reason, the President considers that any Judge or Advocate-General should not sit or make submissions in a particular case, he shall notify him accordingly.

Any difficulty arising as to the application of this Article shall be settled by decision of the Court of Justice.

A party may not apply for a change in the composition of the Court of Justice or of one of its chambers on the grounds of either the nationality of a Judge or the absence from the Court or from the chamber of a Judge of the nationality of that party.

TITLE III

PROCEDURE BEFORE THE COURT OF JUSTICE

ARTICLE 19

The Member States and the institutions of the Union shall be represented before the Court of Justice by an agent appointed for each case. The agent may be assisted by an adviser or by a lawyer.

The States, other than the Member States, which are parties to the Agreement on the European Economic Area and also the European Free Trade Association (EFTA) Surveillance Authority referred to in that Agreement shall be represented in same manner.

Other parties must be represented by a lawyer.

Only a lawyer authorised to practise before a court of a Member State or of another State which is a party to the Agreement on the European Economic Area may represent or assist a party before the Court of Justice.

Such agents, advisers and lawyers shall, when they appear before the Court of Justice, enjoy the rights and immunities necessary to the independent exercise of their duties, under conditions laid down in the Rules of Procedure.

As regards such advisers and lawyers who appear before it, the Court of Justice shall have the powers normally accorded to courts of law, under conditions laid down in the Rules of Procedure.

University teachers being nationals of a Member State whose law accords them a right of audience shall have the same rights before the Court of Justice as are accorded by this Article to lawyers.

ARTICLE 20

The procedure before the Court of Justice shall consist of two parts: written and oral.

The written procedure shall consist of the communication to the parties and to the institutions, bodies, offices or agencies of the Union whose acts are in dispute, of applications, statements of case, defences and observations, and of replies, if any, as well as of all papers and documents in support or of certified copies of them.

Communications shall be made by the Registrar in the order and within the time laid down in the Rules of Procedure.

The oral procedure shall consist of the reading of the report presented by a Judge acting as Rapporteur, the hearing by the Court of Justice of agents, advisers and lawyers and of the submissions of the Advocate-General, as well as the hearing, if any, of witnesses and experts.

Where it considers that the case raises no new point of law, the Court of Justice may decide, after hearing the Advocate-General, that the case shall be determined without a submission from the Advocate-General.

ARTICLE 21

A case shall be brought before the Court of Justice by a written application addressed to the Registrar. The application shall contain the applicant's name and permanent address and the description of the signatory, the name of the party or names of the parties against whom the application is made, the subject-matter of the dispute, the form of order sought and a brief statement of the pleas in law on which the application is based.

The application shall be accompanied, where appropriate, by the measure the annulment of which is sought or, in the circumstances referred to in Article III-367 of the Constitution, by documentary evidence of the date on which an institution was, in accordance with that Article, requested to act. If the documents are not submitted with the application, the Registrar shall ask the party concerned to produce them within a reasonable period, but in that event the rights of the party shall not lapse even if such documents are produced after the time-limit for bringing proceedings.

ARTICLE 22

A case governed by Article 18 of the EAEC Treaty shall be brought before the Court of Justice by an appeal addressed to the Registrar. The appeal shall contain the name and permanent address of the applicant and the description of the signatory, a reference to the decision against which the appeal is brought, the names of the respondents, the subject-matter of the dispute, the submissions and a brief statement of the grounds on which the appeal is based.

The appeal shall be accompanied by a certified copy of the decision of the Arbitration Committee which is contested.

If the Court rejects the appeal, the decision of the Arbitration Committee shall become final.

If the Court annuls the decision of the Arbitration Committee, the matter may be re-opened, where appropriate, on the initiative of one of the parties in the case, before the Arbitration Committee. The latter shall conform to any decisions on points of law given by the Court.

ARTICLE 23

In the cases governed by Article III-369 of the Constitution, the decision of the court or tribunal of a Member State which suspends its proceedings and refers a case to the Court of Justice shall be notified to the Court of Justice by the court or tribunal concerned. The decision shall then be notified by the Registrar of the Court of Justice to the parties, to the Member States and to the Commission, and to the institution, body, office or agency which adopted the act the validity or interpretation of which is in dispute.

Within two months of this notification, the parties, the Member States, the Commission and, where appropriate, the institution, body, office or agency which adopted the act the validity or interpretation of which is in dispute, shall be entitled to submit statements of case or written observations to the Court of Justice.

The decision of the national court or tribunal shall, moreover, be notified by the Registrar of the Court of Justice to the States, other than the Member States, which are parties to the Agreement on the European Economic Area and also to the EFTA Surveillance Authority referred to in that Agreement which may, within two months of notification, where one of the fields of application of that Agreement is concerned, submit statements of case or written observations to the Court of Justice. This paragraph shall not apply to questions falling within the scope of the EAEC Treaty.

Where an agreement relating to a specific subject matter, concluded by the Council and one or more non-member countries, provides that those countries are to be entitled to submit statements of case or written observations where a court or tribunal of a Member State refers to the Court of Justice for a preliminary ruling on a question falling within the scope of the agreement, the decision of the national court or tribunal containing that question shall also be notified to the non-member countries concerned. Within two months from such notification, those countries may lodge at the Court of Justice statements of case or written observations.

ARTICLE 24

The Court of Justice may require the parties to produce all documents and to supply all information which the Court of Justice considers desirable. Formal note shall be taken of any refusal.

The Court of Justice may also require the Member States and institutions, bodies, offices and agencies of the Union not being parties to the case to supply all information which the Court of Justice considers necessary for the proceedings.

ARTICLE 25

The Court of Justice may at any time entrust any individual, body, authority, committee or other organisation it chooses with the task of giving an expert opinion.

ARTICLE 26

Witnesses may be heard under conditions laid down in the Rules of Procedure.

ARTICLE 27

With respect to defaulting witnesses the Court of Justice shall have the powers generally granted to courts and tribunals and may impose pecuniary penalties under conditions laid down in the Rules of Procedure.

ARTICLE 28

Witnesses and experts may be heard on oath taken in the form laid down in the Rules of Procedure or in the manner laid down by the law of the country of the witness or expert.

ARTICLE 29

The Court of Justice may order that a witness or expert be heard by the judicial authority of his place of permanent residence.

The order shall be sent for implementation to the competent judicial authority under conditions laid down in the Rules of Procedure. The documents drawn up in compliance with the letters rogatory shall be returned to the Court of Justice under the same conditions.

The Court of Justice shall defray the expenses, without prejudice to the right to charge them, where appropriate, to the parties.

ARTICLE 30

A Member State shall treat any violation of an oath by a witness or expert in the same manner as if the offence had been committed before one of its courts with jurisdiction in civil proceedings. At the instance of the Court of Justice, the Member State concerned shall prosecute the offender before its competent court.

ARTICLE 31

The hearing in court shall be public, unless the Court of Justice, of its own motion or on application by the parties, decides otherwise for serious reasons.

ARTICLE 32

During the hearings the Court of Justice may examine the experts, the witnesses and the parties themselves. The latter, however, may address the Court of Justice only through their representatives.

ARTICLE 33

Minutes shall be made of each hearing and signed by the President and the Registrar.

ARTICLE 34

The case list shall be established by the President.

ARTICLE 35

The deliberations of the Court of Justice shall be and shall remain secret.

ARTICLE 36
Judgments shall state the reasons on which they are based. They shall contain the names of the Judges who took part in the deliberations.

ARTICLE 37
Judgments shall be signed by the President and the Registrar. They shall be read in open court.

ARTICLE 38
The Court of Justice shall adjudicate upon costs.

ARTICLE 39
The President of the Court of Justice may, by way of summary procedure, which may, insofar as necessary, differ from some of the rules contained in this Statute and which shall be laid down in the Rules of Procedure, adjudicate upon applications to suspend execution, as provided for in Article III-379(1) of the Constitution and Article 157 of the EAEC Treaty, or to prescribe interim measures in pursuance of Article III-379(2) of the Constitution, or to suspend enforcement in accordance with the fourth paragraph of Article III-401 of the Constitution or the third paragraph of Article 164 of the EAEC Treaty.
Should the President be prevented from attending, his place shall be taken by another Judge under conditions laid down in the Rules of Procedure.
The ruling of the President or of the Judge replacing him shall be provisional and shall in no way prejudice the decision of the Court of Justice on the substance of the case.

ARTICLE 40
Member States and institutions of the Union may intervene in cases before the Court of Justice.
The same right shall be open to the bodies, offices and agencies of the Union and to any other person which can establish an interest in the result of a case submitted to the Court of Justice. Natural or legal persons shall not intervene in cases between Member States, between institutions of the Union or between Member States and institutions of the Union.
Without prejudice to the second paragraph, the States, other than the Member States, which are parties to the Agreement on the European Economic Area, and also the EFTA Surveillance Authority referred to in that Agreement, may intervene in cases before the Court of Justice where one of the fields of application of that Agreement is concerned.
An application to intervene shall be limited to supporting the form of order sought by one of the parties.

ARTICLE 41
Where the defending party, after having been duly summoned, fails to file written submissions in defence, judgment shall be given against that party by default. An objection may be lodged against the judgment within one month of it being notified. The objection shall not have the effect of staying enforcement of the judgment by default unless the Court of Justice decides otherwise.

ARTICLE 42
Member States, institutions, bodies, offices and agencies of the Union and any other natural or legal persons may, in cases and under conditions laid down in the Rules of Procedure, institute third-party proceedings to contest a judgment rendered without their being heard, where the judgment is prejudicial to their rights.

ARTICLE 43
If the meaning or scope of a judgment is in doubt, the Court of Justice shall construe it on application by any party or any institution of the Union establishing an interest therein.

ARTICLE 44
An application for revision of a judgment may be made to the Court of Justice only on discovery of a fact which is of such a nature as to be a decisive factor, and which, when the judgment was given, was unknown to the Court and to the party claiming the revision.
The revision shall be opened by a judgment of the Court expressly recording the existence of a new fact, recognising that it is of such a character as to lay the case open to revision and declaring the application admissible on this ground.
No application for revision may be made after the lapse of ten years from the date of the judgment.

ARTICLE 45
Periods of grace based on considerations of distance shall be laid down in the Rules of Procedure.
No right shall be prejudiced in consequence of the expiry of a time-limit if the party concerned proves the existence of unforeseeable circumstances or of *force majeure*.

ARTICLE 46

Proceedings against the Union in matters arising from non-contractual liability shall be barred after a period of five years from the occurrence of the event giving rise thereto. The period of limitation shall be interrupted if proceedings are instituted before the Court of Justice or if prior to such proceedings an application is made by the aggrieved party to the relevant institution of the Union. In the latter event the proceedings must be instituted within the period of two months provided for in Article III-365 of the Constitution. The second paragraph of Article III-367 of the Constitution shall apply.

This Article shall also apply to proceedings against the European Central Bank regarding non-contractual liability.

TITLE IV

THE GENERAL COURT

ARTICLE 47

The first paragraph of Article 9, Articles 14 and 15, the first, second, fourth and fifth paragraphs of Article 17 and Article 18 shall apply to the General Court and its members.

Articles 10, 11 and 14 shall apply to the Registrar of the General Court *mutatis mutandis*.

ARTICLE 48

The General Court shall consist of twenty-five Judges.

ARTICLE 49

The members of the General Court may be called upon to perform the task of an Advocate-General.

It shall be the duty of the Advocate-General, acting with complete impartiality and independence, to

make, in open court, reasoned submissions on certain cases brought before the General Court in order to assist that Court in the performance of its task.

The criteria for selecting such cases, as well as the procedures for designating the Advocates-General, shall be laid down in the Rules of Procedure of the General Court.

A member called upon to perform the task of Advocate-General in a case may not take part in the judgment of the case.

ARTICLE 50

The General Court shall sit in chambers of three or five Judges. The Judges shall elect the Presidents of the chambers from among their number. The Presidents of the chambers of five Judges shall be elected for three years. They may be re-elected once.

The composition of the chambers and the assignment of cases to them shall be governed by the Rules of Procedure. In certain cases governed by the Rules of Procedure, the General Court may sit as a full court or be constituted by a single Judge.

The Rules of Procedure may also provide that the General Court may sit in a Grand Chamber in cases and under the conditions specified therein.

ARTICLE 51

By way of derogation from the rule laid down in Article III-358(1) of the Constitution, jurisdiction shall be reserved to the Court of Justice in the actions referred to in Articles III-365 and III-367 of the Constitution when they are brought by a Member State against:

(a)   an act of or failure to act by the European Parliament or the Council, or both those institutions acting jointly, except for:
- European decisions adopted by the Council under the third subparagraph of Article III-168(2) of the Constitution;
- acts of the Council adopted pursuant to a Council act concerning measures to protect trade within the meaning of Article III-315 of the Constitution;
- acts of the Council by which the Council exercises implementing powers in accordance with Article I-37(2) of the Constitution;

(b)   against an act of or failure to act by the Commission under Article III-420(1) of the Constitution.

Jurisdiction shall also be reserved to the Court of Justice in the actions referred to in the same Articles when they are brought by an institution of the Union against an act of or failure to act by the European Parliament or the Council or both of those institutions acting jointly or the Commission, or brought by an institution against an act of or failure to act by the European Central Bank.

ARTICLE 52

The President of the Court of Justice and the President of the General Court shall determine, by common accord, the conditions under which officials and other servants attached to the Court of Justice shall render their services to the General Court to enable it to function. Certain officials or other servants shall be responsible to the Registrar of the General Court under the authority of the President of the General Court.

ARTICLE 53

The procedure before the General Court shall be governed by Title III.

Such further and more detailed provisions as may be necessary shall be laid down in its Rules of Procedure. The Rules of Procedure may derogate from the fourth paragraph of Article 40 and from Article 41 in order to take account of the specific features of litigation in the field of intellectual property.

Notwithstanding the fourth paragraph of Article 20, the Advocate-General may make his reasoned submissions in writing.

ARTICLE 54

Where an application or other procedural document addressed to the General Court is lodged by mistake with the Registrar of the Court of Justice, it shall be transmitted immediately by that Registrar to the Registrar of the General Court. Likewise, where an application or other procedural document addressed to the Court of Justice is lodged by mistake with the Registrar of the General Court, it shall be transmitted immediately by that Registrar to the Registrar of the Court of Justice.

Where the General Court finds that it does not have jurisdiction to hear and determine an action in respect of which the Court of Justice has jurisdiction, it shall refer that action to the Court of Justice. Likewise, where the Court of Justice finds that an action falls within the jurisdiction of the General Court, it shall refer that action to the General Court, whereupon that Court may not decline jurisdiction.

Where the Court of Justice and the General Court are seised of cases in which the same relief is sought, the same issue of interpretation is raised or the validity of the same act is called in question, the General Court may, after hearing the parties, stay the proceedings before it until such time as the Court of Justice has delivered judgment, or, where the action is one brought pursuant to Article III-365 of the Constitution or pursuant to Article 146 of the EAEC Treaty, may decline jurisdiction so as to allow the Court of Justice to rule on such actions. In the same circumstances, the Court of Justice may also decide to stay the proceedings before it. In that event, the proceedings before the General Court shall continue.

Where a Member State and an institution are challenging the same act, the General Court shall decline jurisdiction so that the Court of Justice may rule on those applications.

ARTICLE 55

Final decisions of the General Court, decisions disposing of the substantive issues in part only or disposing of a procedural issue concerning a plea of lack of competence or inadmissibility, shall be notified by the Registrar of the General Court to all parties as well as all Member States and the institutions of the Union even if they did not intervene in the case before the General Court.

ARTICLE 56

An appeal may be brought before the Court of Justice, within two months of the notification of the decision appealed against, against final decisions of the General Court and decisions of that Court disposing of the substantive issues in part only or disposing of a procedural issue concerning a plea of lack of competence or inadmissibility.

Such an appeal may be brought by any party which has been unsuccessful, in whole or in part, in its submissions. However, interveners other than the Member States and the institutions of the Union may bring such an appeal only where the decision of the General Court directly affects them.

With the exception of cases relating to disputes between the Union and its servants, an appeal may also be brought by Member States and institutions of the Union which did not intervene in the proceedings before the General Court. Such Member States and institutions shall be in the same position as Member States or institutions which intervened at first instance.

ARTICLE 57

Any person whose application to intervene has been dismissed by the General Court may appeal to the Court of Justice within two weeks from the notification of the decision dismissing the application.

The parties to the proceedings may appeal to the Court of Justice against any decision of the General Court made pursuant to Article III-379(1) or (2) or the fourth paragraph of Article III-401 of the Constitution, or Article 157 or the third paragraph of Article 164 of the EAEC Treaty, within two months from their notification.

The appeal referred to in the first two paragraphs shall be heard and determined under the procedure referred to in Article 39.

ARTICLE 58

An appeal to the Court of Justice shall be limited to points of law. It shall lie on the grounds of lack of competence of the General Court, a breach of procedure before it which adversely affects the interests of the appellant as well as the infringement of Union law by the General Court.

No appeal shall lie regarding only the amount of the costs or the party ordered to pay them.

ARTICLE 59

Where an appeal is brought against a decision of the General Court, the procedure before the Court of Justice shall consist of a written part and an oral part. In accordance with conditions laid down in the Rules of Procedure, the Court of Justice, having heard the Advocate-General and the parties, may dispense with the oral procedure.

ARTICLE 60

Without prejudice to Article III-379(1) and (2) of the Constitution or Article 157 of the EAEC Treaty, an appeal shall not have suspensory effect.

By way of derogation from Article III-380 of the Constitution, decisions of the General Court declaring a European law or European regulation binding in its entirety and directly applicable in all Member States to be void shall take effect only as from the date of expiry of the period referred to in the first paragraph of Article 56 of this Statute or, if an appeal shall have been brought within that period, as from the date of dismissal of the appeal, without prejudice, however, to the right of a party to apply to the Court of Justice, pursuant to Article III-379(1) and (2) of the Constitution, and Article 157 of the EAEC Treaty for the suspension of the effects of the European law or European regulation which has been declared void or for the prescription of any other interim measure.

ARTICLE 61

If the appeal is well founded, the Court of Justice shall quash the decision of the General Court. It may itself give final judgment in the matter, where the state of the proceedings so permits, or refer the case back to the General Court for judgment.

Where a case is referred back to the General Court, that Court shall be bound by the decision of the Court of Justice on points of law.

When an appeal brought by a Member State or an institution of the Union, which did not intervene in the proceedings before the General Court, is well founded, the Court of Justice may, if it considers this necessary, state which of the effects of the decision of the General Court which has been quashed shall be considered as definitive in respect of the parties to the litigation.

ARTICLE 62

In the cases provided for in Article III-358(2) and (3) of the Constitution, where the First Advocate-General considers that there is a serious risk of the unity or consistency of Union law being affected, he may propose that the Court of Justice review the decision of the General Court.

The proposal must be made within one month of delivery of the decision by the General Court. Within one month of receiving the proposal made by the First Advocate-General, the Court of Justice shall decide whether or not the decision should be reviewed.

TITLE V

FINAL PROVISIONS

ARTICLE 63

The Rules of Procedure of the Court of Justice and of the General Court shall contain any provisions necessary for applying and, where required, supplementing this Statute.

ARTICLE 64

The rules governing the language arrangements applicable at the Court of Justice of the European Union shall be laid down by a European regulation of the Council acting unanimously. This regulation shall be adopted either at the request of the Court of Justice and after consultation of the Commission and the European Parliament, or on a proposal from the Commission and after consultation of the Court of Justice and of the European Parliament.

Until those rules have been adopted, the provisions of the Rules of Procedure of the Court of Justice and of the Rules of Procedure of the General Court governing language arrangements shall apply. By way of derogation from Articles III-355 and III-356 of the Constitution, those provisions may only be amended or repealed with the unanimous consent of the Council.

ARTICLE 65
1.   By way of derogation from Article IV-437 of the Constitution, any amendment to the Protocol on the Statute of the Court of Justice, annexed to the Treaty on European Union, to the Treaty establishing the European Community and to the EAEC Treaty, which is adopted between the signing and the entry into force of the Treaty establishing a Constitution for Europe, shall remain in force.

2.   In order to incorporate them into the enacting terms of this Statute, the amendments referred to in paragraph 1 shall be subject to official codification by a European law of the Council, adopted at the request of the Court of Justice. When such codifying European law enters into force, this Article shall be repealed.

4.   PROTOCOL ON THE STATUTE OF THE EUROPEAN SYSTEM OF CENTRAL BANKS AND OF THE EUROPEAN CENTRAL BANK

THE HIGH CONTRACTING PARTIES,

DESIRING to lay down the Statute of the European System of Central Banks and of the European Central Bank provided for in Articles I-30 and III-187(2) of the Constitution,

HAVE AGREED upon the following provisions, which shall be annexed to the Treaty establishing a Constitution for Europe:

CHAPTER I

THE EUROPEAN SYSTEM OF CENTRAL BANKS

ARTICLE 1 *The European System of Central Banks*
1.   In accordance with Article I-30(1) of the Constitution, the European Central Bank and the national central banks shall constitute the European System of Central Banks. The European Central Bank and the national central banks of those Member States whose currency is the euro shall constitute the Eurosystem.

2.   The European System of Central Banks and the European Central Bank shall perform their tasks and carry on their activities in accordance with the Constitution and this Statute.

CHAPTER II

OBJECTIVES AND TASKS OF THE EUROPEAN SYSTEM OF CENTRAL BANKS

ARTICLE 2 *Objectives*
In accordance with Articles I-30(2) and III-185(1) of the Constitution, the primary objective of the European System of Central Banks shall be to maintain price stability. Without prejudice to that objective, it shall support the general economic policies in the Union in order to contribute to the achievement of the latter's objectives as laid down in Article I-3 of the Constitution. The European System of Central Banks shall act in accordance with the principle of an open market economy with free competition, favouring an efficient allocation of resources, and in compliance with the principles set out in Article III-177 of the Constitution.

ARTICLE 3 *Tasks*
1.   In accordance with Article III-185(2) of the Constitution, the basic tasks to be carried out through the European System of Central Banks shall be:
(a)   to define and implement the Union's monetary policy;
(b)   to conduct foreign-exchange operations consistent with Article III-326 of the Constitution;
(c)   to hold and manage the official foreign reserves of the Member States;
(d)   to promote the smooth operation of payment systems.

2.   In accordance with Article III-185(3) of the Constitution, paragraph 1(c) of this Article shall be without prejudice to the holding and management by the governments of Member States of foreign-exchange working balances.

3.   In accordance with Article III-185(5) of the Constitution, the European System of Central Banks shall contribute to the smooth conduct of policies pursued by the competent authorities relating to the prudential supervision of credit institutions and the stability of the financial system.

ARTICLE 4 *Advisory functions*
In accordance with Article III-185(4) of the Constitution, the European Central Bank shall be consulted:
(a)   on any proposed Union act in areas within its powers;
(b)   by national authorities regarding any draft legislative provision in its fields of competence, but within the limits and under the conditions set out by the Council in accordance with the procedure laid down in Article 41;
The European Central Bank may submit opinions to the Union institutions, bodies, offices or agencies or to national authorities on matters within its powers.

ARTICLE 5 *Collection of statistical information*
1.   In order to undertake the tasks of the European System of Central Banks, the European Central Bank, assisted by the national central banks, shall collect the necessary statistical information either from the competent national authorities or directly from economic agents. For these purposes it shall co-operate with Union institutions, bodies, offices or agencies and with the competent authorities of the Member States or third countries and with international organisations.

2.   The national central banks shall carry out, to the extent possible, the tasks referred to in paragraph 1.

3.   The European Central Bank shall contribute to the harmonisation, where necessary, of the rules and practices governing the collection, compilation and distribution of statistics in the areas within its powers.

4.   The Council, in accordance with the procedure laid down in Article 41, shall define the natural and legal persons subject to reporting requirements, the confidentiality regime and the appropriate provisions for enforcement.

ARTICLE 6 *International co-operation*
1.   In the field of international co-operation involving the tasks entrusted to the European System of Central Banks, the European Central Bank shall decide how the European System of Central Banks shall be represented.

2.   The European Central Bank and, subject to its approval, the national central banks may participate in international monetary institutions.

3.   Paragraphs 1 and 2 shall be without prejudice to Article III-196 of the Constitution.

CHAPTER III

ORGANISATION OF THE EUROPEAN SYSTEM OF CENTRAL BANKS

ARTICLE 7 *Independence*
In accordance with Article III-188 of the Constitution, when exercising the powers and carrying out the tasks and duties conferred upon them by the Constitution and this Statute, neither the European Central Bank, nor a national central bank, nor any member of their decision-making bodies shall seek or take instructions from Union institutions, bodies, offices or agencies, from any government of a Member State or from any other body. The Union institutions, bodies, offices and agencies and the governments of the Member States undertake to respect this principle and not to seek to influence the members of the decision-making bodies of the European Central Bank or of the national central banks in the performance of their tasks.

ARTICLE 8 *General principle*
The European System of Central Banks shall be governed by the decision-making bodies of the European Central Bank.

ARTICLE 9 *The European Central Bank*
1.   The European Central Bank, which, in accordance with Article I-30(3) of the Constitution, has legal personality, shall enjoy in each of the Member States the most extensive legal capacity accorded to legal persons under its law. It may, in particular, acquire or dispose of movable and immovable property and may be a party to legal proceedings.

2.   The European Central Bank shall ensure that the tasks conferred upon the European System of Central Banks under Article III-185(2), (3) and (5) of the Constitution are implemented either by itself pursuant to this Statute or through the national central banks pursuant to Article 12(1) and Article 14.

3.   In accordance with Article III-187(1) of the Constitution, the decision-making bodies of the European Central Bank shall be the Governing Council and the Executive Board.

ARTICLE 10 *The Governing Council*
1.   In accordance with Article III-382(1) of the Constitution, the Governing Council shall comprise the members of the Executive Board of the European Central Bank and the Governors of the national central banks of the Member States without a derogation as referred to in Article III-197 of the Constitution.

2.   Each member of the Governing Council shall have one vote. As from the date on which the number of members of the Governing Council exceeds 21, each member of the Executive Board shall have one vote and the number of governors with a voting right shall be 15. The latter voting rights shall be assigned and shall rotate as follows:
(a)   as from the date on which the number of governors exceeds 15 and until it reaches 22, the governors shall be allocated to two groups, according to a ranking of the size of the share of their national central bank's Member State in the aggregate gross domestic product at market prices and in the total aggregated balance sheet of the monetary financial institutions of the Member States whose currency is the euro. The shares in the aggregate gross domestic product at market prices and in the total aggregated balance sheet of the monetary financial institutions shall be assigned weights of 5/6 and 1/6, respectively. The first group shall be composed of five governors and the second group of the remaining governors. The frequency of voting rights of the governors allocated to the first group shall not be lower than the frequency of voting rights of those of the second group. Subject to the previous sentence, the first group shall be assigned four voting rights and the second group eleven voting rights;
(b)   as from the date on which the number of governors reaches 22, the governors shall be allocated to three groups according to a ranking based on the criteria laid down in (a). The first group shall be composed of five governors and shall be assigned four voting rights. The second group shall be composed of half of the total number of governors, with any fraction rounded up to the nearest integer, and shall be assigned eight voting rights. The third group shall be composed of the remaining governors and shall be assigned three voting rights;
(c)   within each group, the governors shall have their voting rights for equal amounts of time;
(d)   for the calculation of the shares in the aggregate gross domestic product at market prices Article 29(2) shall apply. The total aggregated balance sheet of the monetary financial institutions shall be calculated in accordance with the statistical framework applying in the Union at the time of the calculation;
(e)   whenever the aggregate gross domestic product at market prices is adjusted in accordance with Article 29(3), or whenever the number of governors increases, the size and/or composition of the groups shall be adjusted in accordance with the principles laid down in this subparagraph;
(f)   the Governing Council, acting by a two-thirds majority of all its members, with and without a voting right, shall take all measures necessary for the implementation of the principles laid down in this subparagraph and may decide to postpone the start of the rotation system until the date on which the number of governors exceeds 18.
The right to vote shall be exercised in person. By way of derogation from this rule, the Rules of Procedure referred to in Article 12(3) may lay down that members of the Governing Council may cast their vote by means of teleconferencing. These Rules shall also provide that a member of the Governing Council who is prevented from attending meetings of the Governing Council for a prolonged period may appoint an alternate as a member of the Governing Council.
The first and second subparagraphs are without prejudice to the voting rights of all members of the Governing Council, with and without a voting right, under paragraph 3 and Article 40(2) and (3). Save as otherwise provided for in this Statute, the Governing Council shall act by a simple majority of the members having a voting right. In the event of a tie, the President shall have the casting vote.
In order for the Governing Council to vote, there shall be a quorum of two thirds of the members having a voting right. If the quorum is not met, the President may convene an extraordinary meeting at which decisions may be taken without regard to the quorum.

3.   For any decisions to be taken under Articles 28, 29, 30, 32, 33 and 49, the votes in the Governing Council shall be weighted according to the national central banks' shares in the subscribed capital of the European Central Bank. The weighting of the votes of the members of the Executive Board shall be zero. A decision requiring a qualified majority shall be adopted if the votes cast in favour represent at least two thirds of the subscribed capital of the European Central Bank and represent at least half of the shareholders. If a Governor is unable to be present, he may nominate an alternate to cast his weighted vote.

4.   The proceedings of the meetings shall be confidential. The Governing Council may decide to make the outcome of its deliberations public.

5.   The Governing Council shall meet at least ten times a year.

ARTICLE 11 *The Executive Board*
1.   In accordance with the first subparagraph of Article III-382(2) of the Constitution, the Executive Board shall comprise the President, the Vice-President and four other members.
The members shall perform their duties on a full-time basis. No member shall engage in any occupation, whether gainful or not, unless exemption is exceptionally granted by the Governing Council.

2.   In accordance with Article III-382(2) of the Constitution, the President, the Vice-President and the other members of the Executive Board shall be appointed by the European Council, acting by a qualified majority, from among persons of recognised standing and professional experience in monetary or banking matters, on a recommendation from the Council and after consulting the European Parliament and the Governing Council.
Their term of office shall be eight years and shall not be renewable.
Only nationals of Member States may be members of the Executive Board.

3.   The terms and conditions of employment of the members of the Executive Board, in particular their salaries, pensions and other social security benefits shall be the subject of contracts with the European Central Bank and shall be fixed by the Governing Council on a proposal from a Committee comprising three members appointed by the Governing Council and three members appointed by the Council. The members of the Executive Board shall not have the right to vote on matters referred to in this paragraph.

4.   If a member of the Executive Board no longer fulfils the conditions required for the performance of his duties or if he has been guilty of serious misconduct, the Court of Justice may, on application by the Governing Council or the Executive Board, compulsorily retire him.

5.   Each member of the Executive Board present in person shall have the right to vote and shall have, for that purpose, one vote. Save as otherwise provided, the Executive Board shall act by a simple majority of the votes cast. In the event of a tie, the President shall have the casting vote. The voting arrangements shall be specified in the Rules of Procedure referred to in Article 12(3).

6.   The Executive Board shall be responsible for the current business of the European Central Bank.

7.   Any vacancy on the Executive Board shall be filled by the appointment of a new member in accordance with paragraph 2.

ARTICLE 12 *Responsibilities of the decision-making bodies*
1.   The Governing Council shall adopt the guidelines and take the decisions necessary to ensure the performance of the tasks entrusted to the European System of Central Banks under the Constitution and this Statute. The Governing Council shall formulate the monetary policy of the Union including, as appropriate, decisions relating to intermediate monetary objectives, key interest rates and the supply of reserves in the European System of Central Banks, and shall establish the necessary guidelines for their implementation.
The Executive Board shall implement monetary policy in accordance with the guidelines and decisions laid down by the Governing Council. In doing so the Executive Board shall give the necessary instructions to national central banks. In addition the Executive Board may have certain powers delegated to it where the Governing Council so decides.
To the extent deemed possible and appropriate and without prejudice to the provisions of this Article, the European Central Bank shall have recourse to the national central banks to carry out operations which form part of the tasks of the European System of Central Banks.

2.   The Executive Board shall have responsibility for the preparation of meetings of the Governing Council.

3.   The Governing Council shall adopt Rules of Procedure which determine the internal organisation of the European Central Bank and its decision-making bodies.

4.   The Governing Council shall exercise the advisory functions referred to in Article 4.

5.   The Governing Council shall take the decisions referred to in Article 6.

ARTICLE 13 *The President*

1.   The President or, in his absence, the Vice-President shall chair the Governing Council and the Executive Board of the European Central Bank.

2.   Without prejudice to Article 38, the President or his nominee shall represent the European Central Bank externally.

ARTICLE 14 *National central banks*

1.   In accordance with Article III-189 of the Constitution, each Member State shall ensure that its national legislation, including the statutes of its national central bank, is compatible with the Constitution and this Statute.

2.   The statutes of the national central banks shall, in particular, provide that the term of office of a Governor of a national central bank shall be no less than five years.

A Governor may be relieved from office only if he no longer fulfils the conditions required for the performance of his duties or if he has been guilty of serious misconduct. A decision to this effect may be referred to the Court of Justice by the Governor concerned or the Governing Council on grounds of infringement of the Constitution or of any rule of law relating to its application. Such proceedings shall be instituted within two months of the publication of the decision or of its notification to the plaintiff or, in the absence thereof, of the day on which it came to the knowledge of the latter, as the case may be.

3.   The national central banks are an integral part of the European System of Central Banks and shall act in accordance with the guidelines and instructions of the European Central Bank. The Governing Council shall take the necessary steps to ensure compliance with the guidelines and instructions of the European Central Bank, and shall require that any necessary information be given to it.

4.   National central banks may perform functions other than those specified in this Statute unless the Governing Council finds, by a majority of two thirds of the votes cast, that these interfere with the objectives and tasks of the European System of Central Banks. Such functions shall be performed on the responsibility and liability of national central banks and shall not be regarded as being part of the functions of the European System of Central Banks.

ARTICLE 15 *Reporting commitments*

1.   The European Central Bank shall draw up and publish reports on the activities of the European System of Central Banks at least quarterly.

2.   A consolidated financial statement of the European System of Central Banks shall be published each week.

3.   In accordance with Article III-383(3) of the Constitution, the European Central Bank shall address an annual report on the activities of the European System of Central Banks and on the monetary policy of both the previous and the current year to the European Parliament, the European Council, the Council and the Commission.

4.   The reports and statements referred to in this Article shall be made available to interested parties free of charge.

ARTICLE 16 *Banknotes*

In accordance with Article III-186(1) of the Constitution, the Governing Council shall have the exclusive right to authorise the issue of euro banknotes within the Union. The European Central Bank and the national central banks may issue such notes. The banknotes issued by the European Central Bank and the national central banks shall be the only such notes to have the status of legal tender within the Union.

The European Central Bank shall respect as far as possible existing practices regarding the issue and design of banknotes.

CHAPTER IV

MONETARY FUNCTIONS AND OPERATIONS OF THE EUROPEAN SYSTEM OF CENTRAL BANKS

ARTICLE 17 *Accounts with the European Central Bank and the national central banks*
In order to conduct their operations, the European Central Bank and the national central banks may open accounts for credit institutions, public entities and other market participants, and accept assets, including book entry securities, as collateral.

ARTICLE 18 *Open market and credit operations*
1.   In order to achieve the objectives of the European System of Central Banks and to carry out its tasks, the European Central Bank and the national central banks may:
(a)   operate in the financial markets by buying and selling outright (spot and forward) or under repurchase agreement and by lending or borrowing claims and marketable instruments, whether in euro or other currencies, as well as precious metals;
(b)   conduct credit operations with credit institutions and other market participants, with lending being based on adequate collateral.

2.   The European Central Bank shall establish general principles for open market and credit operations carried out by itself or the national central banks, including for the announcement of conditions under which they stand ready to enter into such transactions.

ARTICLE 19 *Minimum reserves*
1.   Subject to Article 2, the European Central Bank may require credit institutions established in Member States to hold minimum reserves on accounts with the European Central Bank and national central banks in pursuance of monetary policy objectives. Detailed rules concerning the calculation and determination of the required minimum reserves may be established by the Governing Council. In cases of non-compliance the European Central Bank shall be entitled to levy penalty interest and to impose other sanctions with comparable effect.

2.   For the application of this Article, the Council shall, in accordance with the procedure laid down in Article 41, define the basis for minimum reserves and the maximum permissible ratios between those reserves and their basis, as well as the appropriate sanctions in cases of non-compliance.

ARTICLE 20 *Other instruments of monetary control*
The Governing Council may, by a majority of two thirds of the votes cast, decide upon the use of such other operational methods of monetary control as it sees fit, respecting Article 2.
The Council shall, in accordance with the procedure laid down in Article 41, define the scope of such methods if they impose obligations on third parties.

ARTICLE 21 *Operations with public entities*
1.   In accordance with Article III-181 of the Constitution, overdrafts or any other type of credit facility with the European Central Bank or with the national central banks in favour of Union institutions, bodies, offices or agencies, central governments, regional, local or other public authorities, other bodies governed by public law, or public undertakings of Member States shall be prohibited, as shall the purchase directly from them by the European Central Bank or national central banks of debt instruments.

2.   The European Central Bank and national central banks may act as fiscal agents for the entities referred to in paragraph 1.

3.   The provisions of this Article shall not apply to publicly owned credit institutions which, in the context of the supply of reserves by central banks, shall be given the same treatment by national central banks and the European Central Bank as private credit institutions.

ARTICLE 22 *Clearing and payment systems*
The European Central Bank and national central banks may provide facilities, and the European Central Bank may make regulations, to ensure efficient and sound clearing and payment systems within the Union and with other countries.

ARTICLE 23 *External operations*
The European Central Bank and national central banks may:
(a)   establish relations with central banks and financial institutions in other countries and, where appropriate, with international organisations;

(b)   acquire and sell spot and forward all types of foreign exchange assets and precious metals; the term "foreign exchange asset" shall include securities and all other assets in the currency of any country or units of account and in whatever form held;

(c)   hold and manage the assets referred to in this Article;

(d)   conduct all types of banking transactions in relations with third countries and international organisations, including borrowing and lending operations.

ARTICLE 24 *Other operations*

In addition to operations arising from their tasks, the European Central Bank and national central banks may enter into operations for their administrative purposes or for their staff.

CHAPTER V

PRUDENTIAL SUPERVISION

ARTICLE 25 *Prudential supervision*

1.   The European Central Bank may offer advice to and be consulted by the Council, the Commission and the competent authorities of the Member States on the scope and implementation of legally binding acts of the Union relating to the prudential supervision of credit institutions and to the stability of the financial system.

2.   In accordance with any European law adopted under Article III-185(6) of the Constitution, the European Central Bank may perform specific tasks concerning policies relating to the prudential supervision of credit institutions and other financial institutions with the exception of insurance undertakings.

CHAPTER VI

FINANCIAL PROVISIONS OF THE EUROPEAN SYSTEM OF CENTRAL BANKS

ARTICLE 26 *Financial accounts*

1.   The financial year of the European Central Bank and national central banks shall begin on the first day of January and end on the last day of December.

2.   The annual accounts of the European Central Bank shall be drawn up by the Executive Board, in accordance with the principles established by the Governing Council. The accounts shall be approved by the Governing Council and shall thereafter be published.

3.   For analytical and operational purposes, the Executive Board shall draw up a consolidated balance sheet of the European System of Central Banks, comprising those assets and liabilities of the national central banks that fall within the European System of Central Banks.

4.   For the application of this Article, the Governing Council shall establish the necessary rules for standardising the accounting and reporting of operations undertaken by the national central banks.

ARTICLE 27 *Auditing*

1.   The accounts of the European Central Bank and national central banks shall be audited by independent external auditors recommended by the Governing Council and approved by the Council. The auditors shall have full power to examine all books and accounts of the European Central Bank and national central banks and obtain full information about their transactions.

2.   Article III-384 of the Constitution shall only apply to an examination of the operational efficiency of the management of the European Central Bank.

ARTICLE 28 *Capital of the European Central Bank*

1.   The capital of the European Central Bank, shall be 5,000 million euro. The capital may be increased by such amounts as stipulated by a European decision by the Governing Council acting by the qualified majority provided for in Article 10(3), within the limits and under the conditions set by the Council under the procedure laid down in Article 41.

2.   The national central banks shall be the sole subscribers to and holders of the capital of the European Central Bank. The subscription of capital shall be according to the key established in accordance with Article 29.

3.   The Governing Council, acting by the qualified majority provided for in Article 10(3), shall determine the extent to which and the form in which the capital shall be paid up.

4.   Subject to paragraph 5, the shares of the national central banks in the subscribed capital of the European Central Bank may not be transferred, pledged or attached.

5.   If the key referred to in Article 29 is adjusted, the national central banks shall transfer among themselves capital shares to the extent necessary to ensure that the distribution of capital shares corresponds to the adjusted key. The Governing Council shall determine the terms and conditions of such transfers.

ARTICLE 29 *Key for capital subscription*
1.   The key for subscription of the European Central Bank's capital, fixed for the first time in 1998 when the European System of Central Banks was established, shall be determined by assigning to each national central bank a weighting in this key equal to the sum of:
–   50% of the share of its respective Member State in the population of the Union in the penultimate year preceding the establishment of the European System of Central Banks;
–   50% of the share of its respective Member State in the Union's gross domestic product at market prices as recorded in the last five years preceding the penultimate year before the establishment of the European System of Central Banks.
The percentages shall be rounded up or down to the nearest multiple of 0.0001 percentage points.

2.   The statistical data to be used for the application of this Article shall be provided by the Commission in accordance with the rules laid down by the Council under the procedure provided for in Article 41.

3.   The weightings assigned to the national central banks shall be adjusted every five years after the establishment of the European System of Central Banks by analogy with paragraph 1. The adjusted key shall apply with effect from the first day of the following year.

4.   The Governing Council shall take all other measures necessary for the application of this Article.

ARTICLE 30 *Transfer of foreign reserve assets to the European Central Bank*
1.   Without prejudice to Article 28, the European Central Bank shall be provided by the national central banks with foreign reserve assets, other than Member States' currencies, euro, International Monetary Fund reserve positions and special drawing rights, up to an amount equivalent to 50,000 million euro. The Governing Council shall decide upon the proportion to be called up by the European Central Bank. The European Central Bank shall have the full right to hold and manage the foreign reserves that are transferred to it and to use them for the purposes set out in this Statute.

2.   The contributions of each national central bank shall be fixed in proportion to its share in the subscribed capital of the European Central Bank.

3.   Each national central bank shall be credited by the European Central Bank with a claim equivalent to its contribution. The Governing Council shall determine the denomination and remuneration of such claims.

4.   Further calls of foreign reserve assets beyond the limit set in paragraph 1 may be effected by the European Central Bank, in accordance with paragraph 2, within the limits and under the conditions laid down by the Council in accordance with the procedure laid down in Article 41.

5.   The European Central Bank may hold and manage International Monetary Fund reserve positions and special drawing rights and provide for the pooling of such assets.

6.   The Governing Council shall take all other measures necessary for the application of this Article.

ARTICLE 31 *Foreign reserve assets held by national central banks*
1.   The national central banks shall be allowed to perform transactions in fulfilment of their obligations towards international organisations in accordance with Article 23.

2.   All other operations in foreign reserve assets remaining with the national central banks after the transfers referred to in Article 30, and Member States' transactions with their foreign exchange working balances shall, above a certain limit to be established within the framework of paragraph 3, be subject to approval by the European Central Bank in order to ensure consistency with the exchange rate and monetary policies of the Union.

3.   The Governing Council shall issue guidelines with a view to facilitating such operations.

ARTICLE 32 *Allocation of monetary income of national central banks*
1.   The income accruing to the national central banks in the performance of the monetary policy function of the European System of Central Banks (hereinafter referred to as "monetary income") shall be allocated at the end of each financial year in accordance with the provisions of this Article.

2.   The amount of each national central bank's monetary income shall be equal to its annual income derived from its assets held against notes in circulation and deposit liabilities to credit institutions. These assets shall be earmarked by national central banks in accordance with guidelines to be established by the Governing Council.

3.   If, after the start of the third stage, the balance sheet structures of the national central banks do not, in the judgment of the Governing Council, permit the application of paragraph 2, the Governing Council, acting by a qualified majority, may decide that, by way of derogation from paragraph 2, monetary income shall be measured according to an alternative method for a period of not more than five years.

4.   The amount of each national central bank's monetary income shall be reduced by an amount equivalent to any interest paid by that central bank on its deposit liabilities to credit institutions in accordance with Article 19.
The Governing Council may decide that national central banks shall be indemnified against costs incurred in connection with the issue of banknotes or in exceptional circumstances for specific losses arising from monetary policy operations undertaken for the European System of Central Banks. Indemnification shall be in a form deemed appropriate in the judgment of the Governing Council. These amounts may be offset against the national central banks' monetary income.

5.   The sum of the national central banks' monetary income shall be allocated to the national central banks in proportion to their paid–up shares in the capital of the European Central Bank, subject to any decision taken by the Governing Council pursuant to Article 33(2).

6.   The clearing and settlement of the balances arising from the allocation of monetary income shall be carried out by the European Central Bank in accordance with guidelines established by the Governing Council.

7.   The Governing Council shall take all other measures necessary for the application of this Article.

ARTICLE 33 *Allocation of net profits and losses of the European Central Bank*
1.   The net profit of the European Central Bank shall be transferred in the following order:
(a)   an amount to be determined by the Governing Council, which may not exceed 20% of the net profit, shall be transferred to the general reserve fund subject to a limit equal to 100% of the capital;
(b)   the remaining net profit shall be distributed to the shareholders of the European Central Bank in proportion to their paid-up shares.

2.   In the event of a loss incurred by the European Central Bank, the shortfall may be offset against the general reserve fund of the European Central Bank and, if necessary, following a decision by the Governing Council, against the monetary income of the relevant financial year in proportion and up to the amounts allocated to the national central banks in accordance with Article 32(5).

CHAPTER VII

GENERAL PROVISIONS

ARTICLE 34 *Legal acts*
1.   In accordance with Article III-190 of the Constitution, the European Central Bank shall adopt:
(a)   European regulations to the extent necessary to implement the tasks defined in Article 3(1), (a), Article 19(1), Article 22 or Article 25(2) of this Statute and in cases which shall be laid down in the European regulations and decisions referred to in Article 41;
(b)   the European decisions necessary for carrying out the tasks entrusted to the European System of Central Banks under the Constitution and this Statute;
(c)   recommendations and deliver opinions.

2.   The European Central Bank may decide to publish its European decisions, recommendations and opinions.

3.   Within the limits and under the conditions adopted by the Council under the procedure laid down in Article 41, the European Central Bank shall be entitled to impose fines or periodic penalty payments on undertakings for failure to comply with obligations under its European regulations and decisions.

ARTICLE 35 *Judicial control and related matters*
1.   The acts or omissions of the European Central Bank shall be open to review or interpretation by the Court of Justice of the European Union in the cases and under the conditions laid down in the Constitution. The European Central Bank may institute proceedings in the cases and under the conditions laid down in the Constitution.

2.   Disputes between the European Central Bank, on the one hand, and its creditors, debtors or any other person, on the other, shall be decided by the competent national courts, save where jurisdiction has been conferred upon the Court of Justice of the European Union.

3.   The European Central Bank shall be subject to the liability regime provided for in Article III-431 of the Constitution. The national central banks shall be liable according to their respective national laws.

4.   The Court of Justice of the European Union shall have jurisdiction to give judgment pursuant to any arbitration clause contained in a contract concluded by or on behalf of the European Central Bank, whether that contract be governed by public or private law.

5.   A decision of the European Central Bank to bring an action before the Court of Justice of the European Union shall be taken by the Governing Council.

6.   The Court of Justice of the European Union shall have jurisdiction in disputes concerning the fulfilment by a national central bank of obligations under the Constitution and this Statute. If the European Central Bank considers that a national central bank has failed to fulfil an obligation under the Constitution and this Statute, it shall deliver a reasoned opinion on the matter after giving the national central bank concerned the opportunity to submit its observations. If the national central bank concerned does not comply with the opinion within the period laid down by the European Central Bank, the latter may bring the matter before the Court of Justice of the European Union.

ARTICLE 36 *Staff*
1.   The Governing Council, on a proposal from the Executive Board, shall lay down the conditions of employment of the staff of the European Central Bank.

2.   The Court of Justice of the European Union shall have jurisdiction in any dispute between the European Central Bank and its servants within the limits and under the conditions laid down in the conditions of employment.

ARTICLE 37 *Professional secrecy*
1.   Members of the governing bodies and the staff of the European Central Bank and the national central banks shall be required, even after their duties have ceased, not to disclose information of the kind covered by the obligation of professional secrecy.

2.   Persons having access to data covered by a legally binding Union act imposing an obligation of secrecy shall be subject to that obligation.

ARTICLE 38 *Signatories*
The European Central Bank shall be legally committed to third parties by the President or by two members of the Executive Board or by the signatures of two members of the staff of the European Central Bank who have been duly authorised by the President to sign on behalf of the European Central Bank.

ARTICLE 39 *Privileges and immunities*
The European Central Bank shall enjoy in the territories of the Member States such privileges and immunities as are necessary for the performance of its tasks, under the conditions laid down in the Protocol on the privileges and immunities of the European Union.

CHAPTER VIII

AMENDMENT OF THE STATUTE AND COMPLEMENTARY RULES

ARTICLE 40 *Simplified amendment procedures*
1.   In accordance with Article III-187(3) of the Constitution, Articles 5(1), (2) and (3), 17, 18, 19(1), 22, 23, 24, 26, 32(2), (3), (4) and (6), 33(1)(a) and 36 of this Statute may be amended by European laws:
(a)   on a proposal from the Commission and after consulting the European Central Bank, or
(b)   on a recommendation from the European Central Bank and after consulting the Commission.

2.   Article 10(2) may be amended by a European decision of the European Council, acting unanimously, either on a recommendation from the European Central Bank and after consulting the European Parliament and the Commission, or on a recommendation from the Commission and after consulting the European Parliament and the European Central Bank. These amendments shall not enter into force until they are approved by the Member States in accordance with their respective constitutional requirements.

3.   A recommendation made by the European Central Bank under this Article shall require a unanimous decision by the Governing Council.

ARTICLE 41 *Complementary rules*
In accordance with Article III-187(4) of the Constitution, the Council shall adopt European regulations and decisions establishing the measures referred to in Articles 4, 5(4), 19(2), 20, 28(1), 29(2), 30(4) and 34(3) of this Statute. It shall act after consulting the European Parliament either:
(a)   on a proposal from the Commission and after consulting the European Central Bank or
(b)   on a recommendation from the European Central Bank and after consulting the Commission.

CHAPTER IX

TRANSITIONAL AND OTHER PROVISIONS FOR THE EUROPEAN SYSTEM OF CENTRAL BANKS

ARTICLE 42 *General provisions*
1.   A derogation as referred to in Article III-197(1) of the Constitution shall entail that the following Articles of this Statute shall not confer any rights or impose any obligations on the Member State concerned: 3, 6, 9(2), 12(1), 14(3), 16, 18, 19, 20, 22, 23, 26(2), 27, 30, 31, 32, 33, 34 and 50.

2.   The central banks of Member States with a derogation as specified in Article III-197(1) of the Constitution shall retain their powers in the field of monetary policy according to national law.

3.   In accordance with the second subparagraph of Article III-197(2) of the Constitution, in Articles 3, 11(2) and 19 of this Statute "Member States" shall mean Member States whose currency is the euro.

4.   In Articles 9(2), 10(2) and (3), 12(1), 16, 17, 18, 22, 23, 27, 30, 31, 32, 33(2) and 50 of this Statute, "national central banks" shall mean central banks of Member States whose currency is the euro.

5.   In Articles 10(3) and 33(1), "shareholders" shall mean national central banks of Member States whose currency is the euro.

6.   In Articles 10(3) and 30(2), "subscribed capital" shall mean capital of the European Central Bank subscribed by the national central banks of Member States whose currency is the euro.

ARTICLE 43 *Transitional tasks of the European Central Bank*
The European Central Bank shall take over the former functions of the European Monetary Institute referred to in Article III-199(2) of the Constitution which, because of the derogations of one or more Member States, still have to be performed after the introduction of the euro.
The European Central Bank shall give advice in the preparations for the abrogation of the derogations referred to in Article III-198 of the Constitution.

ARTICLE 44 *The General Council of the European Central Bank*
1.   Without prejudice to Article III-187(1) of the Constitution, the General Council shall be constituted as a third decision-making body of the European Central Bank.

2.   The General Council shall comprise the President and Vice-President of the European Central Bank and the Governors of the national central banks. The other members of the Executive Board may participate, without having the right to vote, in meetings of the General Council.

3.   The responsibilities of the General Council are listed in full in Article 46.

ARTICLE 45 *Functioning of the General Council*
1.   The President or, in his absence, the Vice-President of the European Central Bank shall chair the General Council of the European Central Bank.

2.   The President of the Council and a Member of the Commission may participate, without having the right to vote, in meetings of the General Council.

3.   The President shall prepare the meetings of the General Council.

4.   By way of derogation from Article 12(3), the General Council shall adopt its Rules of Procedure.

5.   The Secretariat of the General Council shall be provided by the European Central Bank.

ARTICLE 46 *Responsibilities of the General Council*
1.   The General Council shall:
(a)   perform the tasks referred to in Article 43;
(b)   contribute to the advisory functions referred to in Articles 4 and 25(1).

2.   The General Council shall contribute to:
(a)   the collection of statistical information as referred to in Article 5;
(b)   the reporting activities of the European Central Bank as referred to in Article 15;
(c)   the establishment of the necessary rules for the application of Article 26 as referred to in Article 26(4);
(d)   the taking of all other measures necessary for the application of Article 29 as referred to in Article 29(4);
(e)   the laying down of the conditions of employment of the staff of the European Central Bank as referred to in Article 36.

3.   The General Council shall contribute to the necessary preparations for irrevocably fixing the exchange rates of the currencies of Member States with a derogation against the euro as referred to in Article III-198(3) of the Constitution.

4.   The General Council shall be informed by the President of the European Central Bank of decisions of the Governing Council.

ARTICLE 47 *Transitional provisions for the capital of the European Central Bank*
In accordance with Article 29, each national central bank shall be assigned a weighting in the key for subscription of the European Central Bank's capital. By way of derogation from Article 28(3), central banks of Member States with a derogation shall not pay up their subscribed capital unless the General Council, acting by a majority representing at least two thirds of the subscribed capital of the European Central Bank and at least half of the shareholders, decides that a minimal percentage has to be paid up as a contribution to the operational costs of the European Central Bank.

ARTICLE 48 *Deferred payment of capital, reserves and provisions of the European Central Bank*
1.   The central bank of a Member State whose derogation has been abrogated shall pay up its subscribed share of the capital of the European Central Bank to the same extent as the central banks of other Member States whose currency is the euro, and shall transfer to the European Central Bank foreign reserve assets in accordance with Article 30(1). The sum to be transferred shall be determined by multiplying the euro value at current exchange rates of the foreign reserve assets which have already been transferred to the European Central Bank in accordance with Article 30(1), by the ratio between the number of shares subscribed by the national central bank concerned and the number of shares already paid up by the other national central banks.

2.   In addition to the payment to be made in accordance with paragraph 1, the national central bank concerned shall contribute to the reserves of the European Central Bank, to those provisions equivalent to reserves, and to the amount still to be appropriated to the reserves and provisions corresponding to the balance of the profit and loss account as at 31 December of the year prior to the abrogation of the derogation. The sum to be contributed shall be determined by multiplying the amount of the reserves, as defined above and as

stated in the approved balance sheet of the European Central Bank, by the ratio between the number of shares subscribed by the central bank concerned and the number of shares already paid up by the other central banks.

3.   Upon one or more countries becoming Member States and their respective national central banks becoming part of the European System of Central Banks, the subscribed capital of the European Central Bank and the limit on the amount of foreign reserve assets that may be transferred to the European Central Bank shall be automatically increased. The increase shall be determined by multiplying the respective amounts then prevailing by the ratio, within the expanded capital key, between the weighting of the entering national central banks concerned and the weighting of the national central banks already members of the European System of Central Banks. Each national central bank's weighting in the capital key shall be calculated by analogy with Article 29(1) and in compliance with Article 29(2). The reference periods to be used for the statistical data shall be identical to those applied for the latest quinquennial adjustment of the weightings under Article 29(3).

ARTICLE 49 *Derogation from Article 32*
1.   If, after the start of the third stage, the Governing Council decides that the application of Article 32 results in significant changes in national central banks' relative income positions, the amount of income to be allocated pursuant to Article 32 shall be reduced by a uniform percentage which shall not exceed 60% in the first financial year after the start of the third stage and which shall decrease by at least 12 percentage points in each subsequent financial year.

2.   Paragraph 1 shall be applicable for not more than five financial years after the start of the third stage.

ARTICLE 50 *Exchange of banknotes in Member States' currencies*
Following the irrevocable fixing of exchange rates in accordance with Article III-198(3) of the Constitution, the Governing Council shall take the necessary measures to ensure that banknotes denominated in the currencies of Member States with irrevocably fixed exchange rates are exchanged by the national central banks at their respective par values.

ARTICLE 51 *Applicability of the transitional provisions*
If and as long as there are Member States with a derogation Articles 42 to 47 shall be applicable.

5.   PROTOCOL ON THE STATUTE OF THE EUROPEAN INVESTMENT BANK

THE HIGH CONTRACTING PARTIES,

DESIRING to lay down the Statute of the European Investment Bank provided for in
Article III-393 of the Constitution,

HAVE AGREED upon the following provisions, which shall be annexed to the Treaty establishing a Constitution for Europe:

ARTICLE 1
The European Investment Bank referred to in Article III-393 of the Constitution (hereinafter called the "Bank") is hereby constituted; it shall perform its functions and carry on its activities in accordance with the provisions of the Constitution and of this Statute.

ARTICLE 2
The task of the Bank shall be that defined in Article III-394 of the Constitution.

ARTICLE 3
In accordance with Article III-393 of the Constitution, the Bank's members shall be the Member States.

ARTICLE 4

1.   The capital of the Bank shall be 163,653,737,000 euro, subscribed by the Member States as follows:

Germany	26,649,532,500
France	26,649,532,500
Italy	26,649,532,500
United Kingdom	26,649,532,500
Spain	15,989,719,500
Belgium	7,387,065,000
Netherlands	7,387,065,000
Sweden	4,900,585,500
Denmark	3,740,283,000
Austria	3,666,973,500
Poland	3,411,263,500
Finland	2,106,816,000
Greece	2,003,725,500
Portugal	1,291,287,000
Czech Republic	1,258,785,500
Hungary	1,190,868,500
Ireland	935,070,000
Slovakia	428,490,500
Slovenia	397,815,000
Lithuania	249,617,500
Luxembourg	187,015,500
Cyprus	183,382,000
Latvia	152,335,000
Estonia	117,640,000
Malta	69,804,000

The Member States shall be liable only up to the amount of their share of the capital subscribed and not paid up.

2.   The admission of a new member shall entail an increase in the subscribed capital corresponding to the capital brought in by the new member.

3.   The Board of Governors may, acting unanimously, decide to increase the subscribed capital.

4.   The share of a member in the subscribed capital may not be transferred, pledged or attached.

ARTICLE 5

1.   The subscribed capital shall be paid in by Member States to the extent of 5% on average of the amounts laid down in Article 4(1).

2.   In the event of an increase in the subscribed capital, the Board of Governors, acting unanimously, shall fix the percentage to be paid up and the arrangements for payment. Cash payments shall be made exclusively in euro.

3.   The Board of Directors may require payment of the balance of the subscribed capital, to such extent as may be required for the Bank to meet its obligations.
Each Member State shall make this payment in proportion to its share of the subscribed capital.

ARTICLE 6

The Bank shall be directed and managed by a Board of Governors, a Board of Directors and a Management Committee.

ARTICLE 7

1.   The Board of Governors shall consist of the ministers designated by the Member States.

2.   The Board of Governors shall lay down general directives for the credit policy of the Bank, in accordance with the Union's objectives.
The Board of Governors shall ensure that these directives are implemented.

3.   The Board of Governors shall in addition:
(a)   decide whether to increase the subscribed capital in accordance with Article 4(3) and Article 5(2);
(b)   for the purposes of Article 9(1), determine the principles applicable to financing operations undertaken within the framework of the Bank's task;
(c)   exercise the powers provided in Articles 9 and 11 in respect of the appointment and the compulsory retirement of the members of the Board of Directors and of the Management Committee, and those powers provided for in the second subparagraph of Article 11(1);
(d)   take decisions in respect of the granting of finance for investment operations to be carried out, in whole or in part, outside the territories of the Member States in accordance with Article 16(1);
(e)   approve the annual report of the Board of Directors;
(f)   approve the annual balance sheet and profit and loss account;
(g)   approve the Rules of Procedure of the Bank;
(h)   exercise the other powers conferred by this Statute.

4.   Within the framework of the Constitution and this Statute, the Board of Governors, acting unanimously, may take any decisions concerning the suspension of the operations of the Bank and, should the event arise, its liquidation.

ARTICLE 8
1.   Save as otherwise provided in this Statute, decisions of the Board of Governors shall be taken by a majority of its members. This majority must represent at least 50% of the subscribed capital.
A qualified majority shall require eighteen votes in favour and 68% of the subscribed capital.

2.   Abstentions by members present in person or represented shall not prevent the adoption of decisions requiring unanimity.

ARTICLE 9
1.   The Board of Directors shall take decisions in respect of granting finance, in particular in the form of loans and guarantees, and raising loans; it shall fix the interest rates on loans granted and the commission and other charges. It may, on the basis of a decision taken by a qualified majority, delegate some of its functions to the Management Committee. It shall determine the terms and conditions for such delegation and shall supervise its execution.
The Board of Directors shall see that the Bank is properly run; it shall ensure that the Bank is managed in accordance with the Constitution and this Statute and with the general directives laid down by the Board of Governors.
At the end of the financial year the Board of Directors shall submit a report to the Board of Governors and shall publish it when approved.

2.   The Board of Directors shall consist of twenty-six directors and sixteen alternate directors.
The directors shall be appointed by the Board of Governors for five years, one nominated by each Member State. One shall also be nominated by the Commission.
The alternate directors shall be appointed by the Board of Governors for five years as shown below:
–   two alternates nominated by the Federal Republic of Germany,
–   two alternates nominated by the French Republic,
–   two alternates nominated by the Italian Republic,
–   two alternates nominated by the United Kingdom of Great Britain and Northern Ireland,
–   one alternate nominated by common accord between the Kingdom of Spain and the Portuguese Republic,
–   one alternate nominated by common accord between the Kingdom of Belgium, the Grand Duchy of Luxembourg and the Kingdom of the Netherlands,
–   one alternate nominated by common accord between the Kingdom of Denmark, the Hellenic Republic and Ireland,
–   one alternate nominated by common accord between the Republic of Austria, the Republic of Finland and the Kingdom of Sweden,
–   three alternates nominated by common accord between the Czech Republic, the Republic of Estonia, the Republic of Cyprus, the Republic of Latvia, the Republic of Lithuania, the Republic of Hungary, the Republic of Malta, the Republic of Poland, the Republic of Slovenia and the Slovak Republic,
–   one alternate director nominated by the Commission.
The Board of Directors shall co-opt six non-voting experts: three as members and three as alternates.
The appointments of the directors and the alternates shall be renewable.
The Rules of Procedure shall lay down the arrangements for participating in the meetings of the Board of Directors and the provisions applicable to alternates and co-opted experts.

The President of the Management Committee or, in his absence, one of the Vice-Presidents, shall preside over meetings of the Board of Directors but shall not vote.

Members of the Board of Directors shall be chosen from persons whose independence and competence are beyond doubt. They shall be responsible only to the Bank.

3. A director may be compulsorily retired by the Board of Governors only if he no longer fulfils the conditions required for the performance of his duties; the Board must act by a qualified majority.

If the annual report is not approved, the Board of Directors shall resign.

4. Any vacancy arising as a result of death, voluntary resignation, compulsory retirement or collective resignation shall be filled in accordance with paragraph 2. A member shall be replaced for the remainder of his term of office, save where the entire Board of Directors is being replaced.

5. The Board of Governors shall determine the remuneration of members of the Board of Directors. The Board of Governors shall lay down what activities are incompatible with the duties of a director or an alternate.

ARTICLE 10

1. Each director shall have one vote on the Board of Directors. He may delegate his vote in all cases, according to procedures to be laid down in the Rules of Procedure of the Bank.

2. Save as otherwise provided in this Statute, decisions of the Board of Directors shall be taken by at least one third of the members entitled to vote, representing at least 50% of the subscribed capital. A qualified majority shall require eighteen votes and 68% of the subscribed capital in favour. The Rules of Procedure of the Bank shall lay down how many members of the Board of Directors constitute the quorum needed for the adoption of decisions.

ARTICLE 11

1. The Management Committee shall consist of a President and eight Vice-Presidents appointed for a period of six years by the Board of Governors on a proposal from the Board of Directors. Their appointments shall be renewable.

The Board of Governors, acting unanimously, may vary the number of members on the Management Committee.

2. On a proposal from the Board of Directors adopted by a qualified majority, the Board of Governors may, acting by a qualified majority, compulsorily retire a member of the Management Committee.

3. The Management Committee shall be responsible for the current business of the Bank, under the authority of the President and the supervision of the Board of Directors.

It shall prepare the decisions of the Board of Directors, including decisions on the raising of loans and the granting of finance, in particular in the form of loans and guarantees. It shall ensure that these decisions are implemented.

4. The Management Committee, acting by a majority, shall adopt opinions on proposals for raising loans or granting finance, in particular in the form of loans and guarantees.

5. The Board of Governors shall determine the remuneration of members of the Management Committee and shall lay down what activities are incompatible with their duties.

6. The President or, if he is prevented, a Vice-President shall represent the Bank in judicial and other matters.

7. The staff of the Bank shall be under the authority of the President. They shall be engaged and discharged by him. In the selection of staff, account shall be taken not only of personal ability and qualifications but also of an equitable representation of nationals of Member States. The Rules of Procedure shall determine which organ is competent to adopt the provisions applicable to staff.

8. The Management Committee and the staff of the Bank shall be responsible only to the Bank and shall be completely independent in the performance of their duties.

ARTICLE 12
1.   A Committee consisting of six members, appointed on the grounds of their competence by the Board of Governors, shall verify that the activities of the Bank conform to best banking practice and shall be responsible for the auditing of its accounts.

2.   The Committee referred to in paragraph 1 shall annually ascertain that the operations of the Bank have been conducted and its books kept in a proper manner. To this end, it shall verify that the Bank's operations have been carried out in compliance with the formalities and procedures laid down by this Statute and the Rules of Procedure.

3.   The Committee referred to in paragraph 1 shall confirm that the financial statements, as well as any other financial information contained in the annual accounts drawn up by the Board of Directors, give a true and fair view of the financial position of the Bank in respect of its assets and liabilities, and of the results of its operations and its cash flows for the financial year under review.

4.   The Rules of Procedure shall specify the qualifications required of the members of the Committee and lay down the terms and conditions for the Committee's activity.

ARTICLE 13
The Bank shall deal with each Member State through the authority designated by that State. In the conduct of financial operations the Bank shall have recourse to the national central bank of the Member State concerned or to other financial institutions approved by that State.

ARTICLE 14
1.   The Bank shall co-operate with all international organisations active in fields similar to its own.

2.   The Bank shall seek to establish all appropriate contacts in the interests of co-operation with banking and financial institutions in the countries to which its operations extend.

ARTICLE 15
At the request of a Member State or of the Commission, or on its own initiative, the Board of Governors shall, in accordance with the same provisions as governed their adoption, interpret or supplement the directives laid down by it under Article 7.

ARTICLE 16
1.   Within the framework of the task set out in Article III-394 of the Constitution, the Bank shall grant finance, in particular in the form of loans and guarantees to its members or to private or public undertakings for investments to be carried out in the territories of Member States, to the extent that funds are not available from other sources on reasonable terms.
However, by decision of the Board of Governors, acting by a qualified majority on a proposal from the Board of Directors, the Bank may grant financing for investment to be carried out, in whole or in part, outside the territories of Member States.

2.   As far as possible, loans shall be granted only on condition that other sources of finance are also used.

3.   When granting a loan to an undertaking or to a body other than a Member State, the Bank shall make the loan conditional either on a guarantee from the Member State in whose territory the investment will be carried out, on adequate guarantees, or on the financial strength of the debtor.
Furthermore, in accordance with the principles established by the Board of Governors pursuant to Article 7(3)(b), and where the implementation of projects provided for in Article III-394 of the Constitution so requires, the Board of Directors shall, acting by a qualified majority, lay down the terms and conditions of any financing operation presenting a specific risk profile and thus considered to be a special activity.

4.   The Bank may guarantee loans contracted by public or private undertakings or other bodies for the purpose of carrying out projects provided for in Article III-394 of the Constitution.

5.   The aggregate amount outstanding at any time of loans and guarantees granted by the Bank shall not exceed 250% of its subscribed capital, reserves, non-allocated provisions and profit and loss account surplus. The latter aggregate amount shall be reduced by an amount equal to the amount subscribed (whether or not paid in) for any equity participation of the Bank.
The amount of the Bank's disbursed equity participations shall not exceed at any time an amount corresponding to the total of its paid-in subscribed capital, reserves, non-allocated provisions and profit and loss account surplus.

By way of exception, the special activities of the Bank, as decided by the Board of Governors and the Board of Directors in accordance with paragraph 3, will have a specific allocation of reserve.

This paragraph shall also apply to the consolidated accounts of the Bank.

6. The Bank shall protect itself against exchange risks by including in contracts for loans and guarantees such clauses as it considers appropriate.

ARTICLE 17

1. Interest rates on loans to be granted by the Bank and commission and other charges shall be adjusted to conditions prevailing on the capital market and shall be calculated in such a way that the income therefrom shall enable the Bank to meet its obligations, to cover its expenses and risks and to build up a reserve fund as provided for in Article 22.

2. The Bank shall not grant any reduction in interest rates. Where a reduction in the interest rate appears desirable in view of the nature of the investment to be financed, the Member State concerned or some other agency may grant aid towards the payment of interest to the extent that this is compatible with Article III-167 of the Constitution.

ARTICLE 18

In its financing operations, the Bank shall observe the following principles:

1. It shall ensure that its funds are employed in the most rational way in the interests of the Union.

It may grant loans or guarantees only:

(a)   where, in the case of investments by undertakings in the production sector, interest and amortisation payments are covered out of operating profits or, in the case of other investments, either by a commitment entered into by the State in which the investment is made or by some other means; and,

(b)   where the execution of the investment contributes to an increase in economic productivity in general and promotes the establishment or functioning of the internal market.

2. It shall neither acquire any interest in an undertaking nor assume any responsibility in its management unless this is required to safeguard the rights of the Bank in ensuring recovery of funds lent.

However, in accordance with the principles determined by the Board of Governors pursuant to Article 7(3)(b), and where the implementation of operations provided for in Article III-394 of the Constitution so requires, the Board of Directors shall, acting by a qualified majority, lay down the terms and conditions for taking an equity participation in a commercial undertaking, normally as a complement to a loan or a guarantee, insofar as this is required to finance an investment or programme.

3. It may dispose of its claims on the capital market and may, to this end, require its debtors to issue bonds or other securities.

4. Neither the Bank nor the Member States shall impose conditions requiring funds lent by the Bank to be spent within a specified Member State.

5. The Bank may make its loans conditional on international invitations to tender being arranged.

6. The Bank shall not finance, in whole or in part, any investment opposed by the Member State in whose territory it is to be carried out.

7. As a complement to its lending activity, the Bank may provide technical assistance services in accordance with the terms and conditions laid down by the Board of Governors, acting by a qualified majority, and in compliance with this Statute.

ARTICLE 19

1. Any undertaking or public or private entity may apply directly to the Bank for financing.

Applications to the Bank may also be made either through the Commission or through the Member State on whose territory the investment will be carried out.

2. Applications made through the Commission shall be submitted for an opinion to the Member State in whose territory the investment will be carried out. Applications made through a Member State shall be submitted to the Commission for an opinion. Applications made direct by an undertaking shall be submitted to the Member State concerned and to the Commission.

The Member State concerned and the Commission shall deliver their opinions within two months. If no reply is received within this period, the Bank may assume that there is no objection to the investment in question.

3.   The Board of Directors shall rule on financing operations submitted to it by the Management Committee.

4.   The Management Committee shall examine whether financing operations submitted to it comply with the provisions of this Statute, in particular with Articles 16 and 18. Where the Management Committee is in favour of the financing operation, it shall submit the corresponding proposal to the Board of Directors. The Committee may make its favourable opinion subject to such conditions as it considers essential. Where the Management Committee is against granting the finance, it shall submit the relevant documents together with its opinion to the Board of Directors.

5.   Where the Management Committee delivers an unfavourable opinion, the Board of Directors may not grant the finance concerned unless its decision is unanimous.

6.   Where the Commission delivers an unfavourable opinion, the Board of Directors may not grant the finance concerned unless its decision is unanimous, the director nominated by the Commission abstaining.

7.   Where both the Management Committee and the Commission deliver an unfavourable opinion, the Board of Directors may not grant the finance.

8.   In the event that a financing operation relating to an approved investment has to be restructured in order to safeguard the Bank's rights and interests, the Management Committee shall take without delay the emergency measures which it deems necessary, subject to immediate reporting thereon to the Board of Directors.

ARTICLE 20
1.   The Bank shall borrow on the capital markets the funds necessary for the performance of its tasks.

2.   The Bank may borrow on the capital markets of the Member States in accordance with the legal provisions applying to those markets.
The competent authorities of a Member State with a derogation within the meaning of Article III-197(1) of the Constitution may oppose this only if there is reason to fear serious disturbances on the capital market of that State.

ARTICLE 21
1.   The Bank may employ any available funds which it does not immediately require to meet its obligations in the following ways:
(a)   it may invest on the money markets;
(b)   it may, subject to the provisions of Article 18(2), buy and sell securities;
(c)   it may carry out any other financial operation linked with its objectives.

2.   Without prejudice to the provisions of Article 23, the Bank shall not, in managing its investments, engage in any currency arbitrage not directly required to carry out its lending operations or fulfil commitments arising out of loans raised or guarantees granted by it.

3.   The Bank shall, in the fields covered by this Article, act in agreement with the competent authorities or with the national central bank of the Member State concerned.

ARTICLE 22
1.   A reserve fund of up to 10% of the subscribed capital shall be built up progressively. If the state of the liabilities of the Bank should so justify, the Board of Directors may decide to set aside additional reserves. Until such time as the reserve fund has been fully built up, it shall be fed by:
(a)   interest received on loans granted by the Bank out of sums to be paid up by the Member States pursuant to Article 5;
(b)   interest received on loans granted by the Bank out of funds derived from repayment of the loans referred to in (a);
to the extent that this income is not required to meet the obligations of the Bank or to cover its expenses.

2.   The resources of the reserve fund shall be so invested as to be available at any time to meet the purpose of the fund.

ARTICLE 23
1.   The Bank shall at all times be entitled to transfer its assets into the currency of a Member State whose currency is not the euro in order to carry out financial operations corresponding to the task set out in Article

III-394 of the Constitution, taking into account the provisions of Article 21 of this Statute. The Bank shall, as far as possible, avoid making such transfers if it has cash or liquid assets in the currency required.

2. The Bank may not convert its assets in the currency of a Member State whose currency is not the euro into the currency of a third country without the agreement of the Member State concerned.

3. The Bank may freely dispose of that part of its capital which is paid up and of any currency borrowed on markets outside the Union.

4. The Member States undertake to make available to the debtors of the Bank the currency needed to repay the capital and pay the interest on loans or commission on guarantees granted by the Bank for investment to be carried out in their territory.

ARTICLE 24

If a Member State fails to meet the obligations of membership arising from this Statute, in particular the obligation to pay its share of the subscribed capital or to service its borrowings, the granting of loans or guarantees to that Member State or its nationals may be suspended by a decision of the Board of Governors, acting by a qualified majority.
Such decision shall not release either the Member State or its nationals from their obligations towards the Bank.

ARTICLE 25

1. If the Board of Governors decides to suspend the operations of the Bank, all its activities shall cease forthwith, except those required to ensure the due realisation, protection and preservation of its assets and the settlement of its liabilities.

2. In the event of liquidation, the Board of Governors shall appoint the liquidators and give them instructions for carrying out the liquidation. It shall ensure that the rights of the members of staff are safeguarded.

ARTICLE 26

1. In each of the Member States, the Bank shall enjoy the most extensive legal capacity accorded to legal persons under their laws. It may, in particular, acquire or dispose of movable or immovable property and may be a party to legal proceedings.

2. The property of the Bank shall be exempt from all forms of requisition or expropriation.

ARTICLE 27

1. Disputes between the Bank on the one hand, and its creditors, debtors or any other person on the other, shall be decided by the competent national courts, save where jurisdiction has been conferred on the Court of Justice of the European Union. The Bank may provide for arbitration in any contract.

2. The Bank shall have an address for service in each Member State. It may, however, in any contract, specify a particular address for service.

3. The property and assets of the Bank shall not be liable to attachment or to seizure by way of execution except by decision of a court.

ARTICLE 28

1. The Board of Governors may, acting unanimously, decide to establish subsidiaries or other entities, which shall have legal personality and financial autonomy.

2. The Board of Governors, acting unanimously, shall establish the Statutes of the bodies referred to in paragraph 1, defining, in particular, their objectives, structure, capital, membership, the location of their seat, their financial resources, means of intervention and auditing arrangements, as well as their relationship with the organs of the Bank.

3. The Bank may participate in the management of these bodies and contribute to their subscribed capital up to the amount determined by the Board of Governors, acting unanimously.

4. The Protocol on the privileges and immunities of the European Union shall apply to the bodies referred to in paragraph 1 insofar as they are incorporated under Union law, to the members of their organs in

the performance of their duties as such and to their staff, under the same terms and conditions as those applicable to the Bank.

Those dividends, capital gains or other forms of revenue stemming from such bodies to which the members, other than the European Union and the Bank, are entitled, shall however remain subject to the fiscal provisions of the applicable legislation.

5.   The Court of Justice of the European Union shall, within the limits hereinafter laid down, hear disputes concerning measures adopted by organs of a body incorporated under Union law.

Proceedings against such measures may be instituted by any member of such a body in its capacity as such or by Member States under the conditions laid down in Article III-365 of the Constitution.

6.   The Board of Governors may, acting unanimously, decide to admit the staff of bodies incorporated under Union law to joint schemes with the Bank, in compliance with the respective internal procedures.

6.   PROTOCOL ON THE LOCATION OF THE SEATS OF THE INSTITUTIONS AND OF CERTAIN BODIES, OFFICES, AGENCIES AND DEPARTMENTS OF THE EUROPEAN UNION

THE HIGH CONTRACTING PARTIES,

HAVING REGARD to Article III-432 of the Constitution,

RECALLING AND CONFIRMING the Decision of 8 April 1965, and without prejudice to the decisions concerning the seat of future institutions, bodies, offices, agencies and departments,

HAVE AGREED UPON the following provisions, which shall be annexed to the Treaty establishing a Constitution for Europe and to the Treaty establishing the European Atomic Energy Community:

SOLE ARTICLE

1.   The European Parliament shall have its seat in Strasbourg, where the 12 periods of monthly plenary sessions, including the budget session, shall be held. The periods of additional plenary sessions shall be held in Brussels. The committees of the European Parliament shall meet in Brussels. The General Secretariat of the European Parliament and its departments shall remain in Luxembourg.

2.   The Council shall have its seat in Brussels. During the months of April, June and October, the Council shall hold its meetings in Luxembourg.

3.   The Commission shall have its seat in Brussels. The departments listed in Articles 7, 8 and 9 of the Decision of 8 April 1965 shall be established in Luxembourg.

4.   The Court of Justice of the European Union shall have its seat in Luxembourg.

5.   The European Central Bank shall have its seat in Frankfurt.

6.   The Court of Auditors shall have its seat in Luxembourg.

7.   The Committee of the Regions shall have its seat in Brussels.

8.   The Economic and Social Committee shall have its seat in Brussels.

9.   The European Investment Bank shall have its seat in Luxembourg.

10.   Europol shall have its seat in The Hague.

7. PROTOCOL ON THE PRIVILEGES AND IMMUNITIES OF THE EUROPEAN UNION

THE HIGH CONTRACTING PARTIES,

CONSIDERING that, in accordance with Article III-434 of the Constitution, the Union shall enjoy in the territories of the Member States such privileges and immunities as are necessary for the performance of its tasks,

HAVE AGREED upon the following provisions, which shall be annexed to the Treaty establishing a Constitution for Europe and to the Treaty establishing the European Atomic Energy Community:

CHAPTER I

PROPERTY, FUNDS, ASSETS AND OPERATIONS OF THE UNION

ARTICLE 1
The premises and buildings of the Union shall be inviolable. They shall be exempt from search, requisition, confiscation or expropriation. The property and assets of the Union shall not be the subject of any administrative or legal measure of constraint without the authorisation of the Court of Justice.

ARTICLE 2
The archives of the Union shall be inviolable.

ARTICLE 3
The Union, its assets, revenues and other property shall be exempt from all direct taxes.
The governments of the Member States shall, wherever possible, take the appropriate measures to remit or refund the amount of indirect taxes or sales taxes included in the price of movable or immovable property, where the Union makes, for its official use, substantial purchases the price of which includes taxes of this kind. These provisions shall not be applied, however, so as to have the effect of distorting competition within the Union.
No exemption shall be granted in respect of taxes and dues which amount merely to charges for public utility services.

ARTICLE 4
The Union shall be exempt from all customs duties, prohibitions and restrictions on imports and exports in respect of articles intended for its official use. Articles so imported shall not be disposed of, whether or not in return for payment, in the territory of the State into which they have been imported, except under conditions approved by the government of that State.
The Union shall also be exempt from any customs duties and any prohibitions and restrictions on import and exports in respect of its publications.

CHAPTER II

COMMUNICATIONS AND *LAISSEZ-PASSER*

ARTICLE 5
For their official communications and the transmission of all their documents, the institutions of the Union shall enjoy in the territory of each Member State the treatment accorded by that State to diplomatic missions. Official correspondence and other official communications of the institutions of the Union shall not be subject to censorship.

ARTICLE 6
1.   *Laissez-passer* in a form to be prescribed by a European regulation of the Council acting by a simple majority, which shall be recognised as valid travel documents by the authorities of the Member States, may be issued to members and servants of the institutions of the Union by the Presidents of these institutions. These *laissez-passer* shall be issued to officials and other servants under conditions laid down in the Staff Regulations of officials and the Conditions of Employment of other servants of the Union.
The Commission may conclude agreements for these *laissez-passer* to be recognised as valid travel documents within the territory of third States.

CHAPTER III

MEMBERS OF THE EUROPEAN PARLIAMENT

ARTICLE 7

No administrative or other restriction shall be imposed on the free movement of members of the European Parliament travelling to or from the place of meeting of the European Parliament.

Members of the European Parliament shall, in respect of customs and exchange control, be accorded:

(a)   by their own governments, the same facilities as those accorded to senior officials travelling abroad on temporary official missions;

(b)   by the governments of other Member States, the same facilities as those accorded to representatives of foreign governments on temporary official missions.

ARTICLE 8

Members of the European Parliament shall not be subject to any form of inquiry, detention or legal proceedings in respect of opinions expressed or votes cast by them in the performance of their duties.

ARTICLE 9

During the sessions of the European Parliament, its members shall enjoy:

(a)   in the territory of their own State, the immunities accorded to members of their Parliament;

(b)   in the territory of any other Member State, immunity from any measure of detention and from legal proceedings.

Immunity shall likewise apply to members while they are travelling to and from the place of meeting of the European Parliament.

Immunity cannot be claimed when a member is found in the act of committing an offence and shall not prevent the European Parliament from exercising its right to waive the immunity of one of its members.

CHAPTER IV

REPRESENTATIVES OF MEMBER STATES TAKING PART IN THE WORK OF THE INSTITUTIONS OF THE UNION

ARTICLE 10

Representatives of Member States taking part in the work of the institutions of the Union, their advisers and technical experts shall, in the performance of their duties and during their travel to and from the place of meeting, enjoy the customary privileges, immunities and facilities.

This Article shall also apply to members of the advisory bodies of the Union.

CHAPTER V

OFFICIALS AND OTHER SERVANTS OF THE UNION

ARTICLE 11

In the territory of each Member State and whatever their nationality, officials and other servants of the Union shall:

(a)   subject to the provisions of the Constitution relating, on the one hand, to the rules on the liability of officials and other servants towards the Union and, on the other hand, to the jurisdiction of the Court of Justice of the European Union in disputes between the Union and its officials and other servants, be immune from legal proceedings in respect of acts performed by them in their official capacity, including their words spoken or written. They shall continue to enjoy this immunity after they have ceased to hold office;

(b)   together with their spouses and dependent members of their families, not be subject to immigration restrictions or to formalities for the registration of aliens;

(c)   in respect of currency or exchange regulations, be accorded the same facilities as are customarily accorded to officials of international organisations;

(d)   enjoy the right to import free of duty their furniture and effects at the time of first taking up their post in the State concerned, and the right to re-export free of duty their furniture and effects, on termination of their duties in that State, subject in either case to the conditions considered to be necessary by the government of the State in which this right is exercised;

(e)   have the right to import free of duty a motor car for their personal use, acquired either in the State of their last residence or in the State of which they are nationals on the terms ruling in the home market in that State, and to re-export it free of duty, subject in either case to the conditions considered to be necessary by the government of the State concerned.

ARTICLE 12

Officials and other servants of the Union shall be liable to a tax, for the benefit of the Union, on salaries, wages and emoluments paid to them by the Union, in accordance with the conditions and procedure laid down by a European law. That law shall be adopted after consultation of the institutions concerned.

Officials and other servants of the Union shall be exempt from national taxes on salaries, wages and emoluments paid by the Union.

ARTICLE 13

In the application of income tax, wealth tax and death duties and in the application of conventions on the avoidance of double taxation concluded between Member States of the Union, officials and other servants of the Union who, solely by reason of the performance of their duties in the service of the Union, establish their residence in the territory of a Member State other than their State of domicile for tax purposes at the time of entering the service of the Union, shall be considered, both in the State of their actual residence and in the State of domicile for tax purposes, as having maintained their domicile in the latter State provided that it is a member of the Union. This provision shall also apply to a spouse, to the extent that the latter is not separately engaged in a gainful occupation, and to children dependent on and in the care of the persons referred to in this Article.

Movable property belonging to persons referred to in the first paragraph and situated in the territory of the State where they are staying shall be exempt from death duties in that State. Such property shall, for the assessment of such duty, be considered as being in the State of domicile for tax purposes, subject to the rights of third States and to the possible application of provisions of international conventions on double taxation.

Any domicile acquired solely by reason of the performance of duties in the service of other international organisations shall not be taken into consideration in applying the provisions of this Article.

ARTICLE 14

The scheme of social security benefits for officials and other servants of the Union shall be laid down by a European law. That law shall be adopted after consultation of the institutions concerned.

ARTICLE 15

The categories of officials and other servants of the Union to whom Article 11, the second paragraph of Article 12, and Article 13 shall apply, in whole or in part, shall be determined by a European law. That law shall be adopted after consultation of the institutions concerned.

The names, grades and addresses of officials and other servants included in such categories shall be communicated periodically to the governments of the Member States.

CHAPTER VI

PRIVILEGES AND IMMUNITIES OF MISSIONS OF THIRD STATES ACCREDITED TO THE UNION

ARTICLE 16

The Member State in whose territory the Union has its seat shall accord the customary diplomatic privileges and immunities to missions of third States accredited to the Union.

CHAPTER VII

GENERAL PROVISIONS

ARTICLE 17

Privileges, immunities and facilities shall be accorded to officials and other servants of the Union solely in the interests of the Union.

Each institution of the Union shall be required to waive the immunity accorded to an official or other servant wherever that institution considers that the waiver of such immunity is not contrary to the interests of the Union.

ARTICLE 18

The institutions of the Union shall, for the purpose of applying this Protocol, co-operate with the responsible authorities of the Member States concerned.

ARTICLE 19
Articles 11 to 14 and Article 17 shall apply to members of the Commission.

ARTICLE 20
Articles 11 to 14 and Article 17 shall apply to the Judges, the Advocates-General, the Registrars and the Assistant Rapporteurs of the Court of Justice of the European Union, without prejudice to the provisions of Article 3 of the Protocol on the Statute of the Court of Justice of the European Union concerning immunity from legal proceedings of Judges and Advocates-General.
Articles 11 to 14 and Article 17 shall also apply to the members of the Court of Auditors.

ARTICLE 21
This Protocol shall also apply to the European Central Bank, to the members of its organs and to its staff, without prejudice to the Protocol on the Statute of the European System of Central Banks and of the European Central Bank.
The European Central Bank shall, in addition, be exempt from any form of taxation or imposition of a like nature on the occasion of any increase in its capital and from the various formalities which may be connected therewith in the State where the Bank has its seat. The activities of the Bank and of its organs carried on in accordance with the Statute of the European System of Central Banks and of the European Central Bank shall not be subject to any turnover tax.

ARTICLE 22
This Protocol shall also apply to the European Investment Bank, to the members of its organs, to its staff and to the representatives of the Member States taking part in its activities, without prejudice to the Protocol on the Statute of the Bank.
The European Investment Bank shall in addition be exempt from any form of taxation or imposition of a like nature on the occasion of any increase in its capital and from the various formalities which may be connected therewith in the State where the Bank has its seat. Similarly, its dissolution or liquidation shall not give rise to any imposition. Finally, the activities of the Bank and of its organs carried on in accordance with its Statute shall not be subject to any turnover tax.

8. **PROTOCOL ON THE TREATIES AND ACTS OF ACCESSION OF THE KINGDOM OF DENMARK, IRELAND AND THE UNITED KINGDOM OF GREAT BRITAIN AND NORTHERN IRELAND, OF THE HELLENIC REPUBLIC, OF THE KINGDOM OF SPAIN AND THE PORTUGUESE REPUBLIC, AND OF THE REPUBLIC OF AUSTRIA, THE REPUBLIC OF FINLAND AND THE KINGDOM OF SWEDEN**

THE HIGH CONTRACTING PARTIES,

RECALLING that the Kingdom of Denmark, Ireland and the United Kingdom of Great Britain and Northern Ireland acceded to the European Communities on 1 January 1973; that the Hellenic Republic acceded to the European Communities on 1 January 1981; that the Kingdom of Spain and the Portuguese Republic acceded to the European Communities on 1 January 1986; that the Republic of Austria, the Republic of Finland and the Kingdom of Sweden acceded to the European Communities and to the European Union established by the Treaty on European Union on 1 January 1995;

CONSIDERING THAT Article IV-437(2) of the Constitution provides that the Treaties concerning the accessions referred to above shall be repealed;

CONSIDERING THAT certain provisions appearing in those Accession Treaties and in the Acts annexed thereto remain relevant; and that Article IV-437(2) of the Constitution provides that such provisions must be set out or referred to in a Protocol, so that they remain in force and that their legal effects are preserved;

WHEREAS the provisions in question require the technical adjustments necessary to bring them into line with the Constitution without altering their legal effect,

HAVE AGREED upon the following provisions, which shall be annexed to the Treaty establishing a Constitution for Europe and the Treaty establishing the European Atomic Energy Community:

TITLE I

COMMON PROVISIONS

ARTICLE 1 (*new*)
The rights and obligations resulting from the Accession Treaties referred to in Article IV-437(2)(a) to (d) of the Constitution took effect, under the conditions laid down in those Treaties, on the following dates:
(a) 1 January 1973, for the Treaty concerning the accession of the Kingdom of Denmark, Ireland and the United Kingdom of Great Britain and Northern Ireland;
(b) 1 January 1981, for the Treaty concerning the accession of the Hellenic Republic;
(c) 1 January 1986, for the Treaty concerning the accession of the Kingdom of Spain and the Portuguese Republic;
(d) 1 January 1995, for the Treaty concerning the accession of the Republic of Austria, the Republic of Finland and the Kingdom of Sweden.

ARTICLE 2 (*new*)
1.   The acceding States referred to in Article 1 shall be required to accede to the following agreements or conventions concluded before their respective accessions, insofar as such agreements or conventions are still in force:
(a) agreements or conventions concluded between the other Member States which are based on the Treaty establishing the European Community, the Treaty establishing the European Atomic Energy Community or the Treaty on European Union, or which are inseparable from the attainment of the objectives of those Treaties, or which relate to the functioning of the Communities or of the Union or which are connected with the activities thereof;
(b) agreements or conventions concluded by the other Member States, acting jointly with the European Communities, with one or more third States or with an international organisation, and the agreements which are related to those agreements or conventions. The Union and the other Member States shall assist the acceding States referred to in Article 1 in this respect.

2.   The acceding States referred to in Article 1 shall take appropriate measures, where necessary, to adjust their position in relation to international organisations, and in relation to those international agreements to which the Union or the European Atomic Energy Community or other Member States are also parties, to the rights and obligations arising from their accession.

ARTICLE 3 (*new*)
Provisions of the Acts of Accession, as interpreted by the Court of Justice of the European Communities and the Court of First Instance, the purpose or effect of which is to repeal or amend, otherwise than as a transitional measure, acts adopted by the institutions, bodies, offices or agencies of the European Communities or of the European Union established by the Treaty on European Union shall remain in force subject to the second paragraph.
The provisions referred to in the first paragraph shall have the same status in law as the acts which they repeal or amend and shall be subject to the same rules as those acts.

ARTICLE 4 (*new*)
The texts of the acts of the institutions, bodies, offices and agencies of the European Communities or of the European Union established by the Treaty on European Union which were adopted before the accessions referred to in Article 1 and which were subsequently drawn up successively in the English and Danish languages, in the Greek language, in the Spanish and Portuguese languages, and in the Finnish and Swedish languages, shall be authentic from the date of the respective accessions referred to in Article 1, under the same conditions as the texts drawn up and authentic in the other languages.

ARTICLE 5 (*new*)
A European law of the Council may repeal the transitional provisions set out in this Protocol, when they are no longer applicable. The Council shall act unanimously after consulting the European Parliament.

TITLE II

PROVISIONS TAKEN FROM THE ACT CONCERNING THE CONDITIONS OF ACCESSION OF THE KINGDOM OF DENMARK, IRELAND AND THE UNITED KINGDOM OF GREAT BRITAIN AND NORTHERN IRELAND

SECTION 1

PROVISIONS ON GIBRALTAR

ARTICLE 6 (*ex Article 28 AA 1972*)
1.   Acts of the institutions relating to the products in Annex I to the Constitution and the products subject, on importation into the Union, to specific rules as a result of the implementation of the common agricultural policy, as well as the acts on the harmonisation of legislation of Member States concerning turnover taxes, shall not apply to Gibraltar unless the Council adopts a European decision which provides otherwise. The Council shall act unanimously on a proposal from the Commission.

2.   The situation of Gibraltar defined in point VI of Annex II [OJ L 73, 27.3.1972, p. 47] to the Act concerning the conditions of accession of the Kingdom of Denmark, Ireland and the United Kingdom of Great Britain and Northern Ireland shall be maintained.

SECTION 2

PROVISIONS ON THE FAROE ISLANDS

ARTICLE 7 (*ex Protocol No 2 AA 1972*)
Danish nationals resident in the Faroe Islands shall be considered to be nationals of a Member State within the meaning of the Constitution only from the date on which the Constitution becomes applicable to those islands.

SECTION 3

PROVISIONS ON THE CHANNEL ISLANDS AND THE ISLE OF MAN

ARTICLE 8 (*ex Article 1 of Protocol No 3 AA 1972*)
1.   The Union rules on customs matters and quantitative restrictions, in particular customs duties, charges having equivalent effect and the Common Customs Tariff, shall apply to the Channel Islands and the Isle of Man under the same conditions as they apply to the United Kingdom.

2.   In respect of agricultural products and products processed therefrom which are the subject of a special trade regime, the levies and other import measures laid down in Union rules and applicable by the United Kingdom shall be applied to third countries.
Such provisions of Union rules as are necessary to allow free movement and observance of normal conditions of competition in trade in these products shall also be applicable.
The Council, on a proposal from the Commission, shall adopt the European regulations or decisions establishing the conditions under which the provisions referred to in the first and second subparagraphs shall be applicable to these territories.

ARTICLE 9 (*ex Article 2 of Protocol No 3 AA 1972*)
The rights enjoyed by Channel Islanders or Manxmen in the United Kingdom shall not be affected by Union law. However, such persons shall not benefit from provisions of Union law relating to the free movement of persons and services.

ARTICLE 10 (*ex Article 3 of Protocol No 3 AA 1972*)
The provisions of the Treaty establishing the European Atomic Energy Community applicable to persons or undertakings within the meaning of Article 196 of that Treaty shall apply to those persons or undertakings when they are established in the territories referred to in Article 8 of this Protocol.

ARTICLE 11 (*ex Article 4 of Protocol No 3 AA 1972*)
The authorities of the territories referred to in Article 8 shall apply the same treatment to all natural and legal persons of the Union.

ARTICLE 12 (*ex Article 5 of Protocol No 3 AA 1972*)

If, during the application of the arrangements defined in this Section, difficulties appear on either side in relations between the Union and the territories referred to in Article 8, the Commission shall without delay propose to the Council such safeguard measures as it believes necessary, specifying their terms and conditions of application.

The Council shall adopt the appropriate European regulations or decisions within one month.

ARTICLE 13 (*ex Article 6 of Protocol No 3 AA 1972*)

In this Section, Channel Islander or Manxman shall mean any British citizen who holds that citizenship by virtue of the fact that he, a parent or grandparent was born, adopted, naturalised or registered in the island in question; but such a person shall not for this purpose be regarded as a Channel Islander or Manxman if he, a parent or a grandparent was born, adopted, naturalised or registered in the United Kingdom. Nor shall he be so regarded if he has at any time been ordinarily resident in the United Kingdom for five years.

The administrative arrangements necessary to identify these persons will be notified to the Commission.

SECTION 4

PROVISIONS ON THE IMPLEMENTATION OF THE POLICY OF INDUSTRIALISATION AND ECONOMIC DEVELOPMENT IN IRELAND

ARTICLE 14 (*ex Protocol No 30 AA 1972*)

The Member States take note of the fact that the Government of Ireland has embarked upon the implementation of a policy of industrialisation and economic development designed to align the standards of living in Ireland with those of the other Member States and to eliminate under-employment while progressively evening out regional differences in levels of development.

They recognise it to be in their common interest that the objectives of this policy be so attained and agree to recommend to this end that the institutions implement all the means and procedures laid down by the Constitution, particularly by making adequate use of the Union resources intended for the realisation of its objectives.

The Member States recognise in particular that, in the application of Articles III-167 and III-168 of the Constitution, it will be necessary to take into account the objectives of economic expansion and the raising of the standard of living of the population.

SECTION 5

PROVISIONS ON THE EXCHANGE OF INFORMATION WITH DENMARK IN THE FIELD OF NUCLEAR ENERGY

ARTICLE 15 (*ex Article 1 of Protocol No 25 AA 1972*)

1.   From 1 January 1973, such information as has been communicated to Member States, persons and undertakings, in accordance with Article 13 of the Treaty establishing the European Atomic Energy Community, shall be placed at the disposal of Denmark, which shall give it limited distribution within its territory under the conditions laid down in that Article.

2.   From 1 January 1973, Denmark shall place at the disposal of the European Atomic Energy Community an equivalent volume of information in the sectors specified in paragraph 3. This information shall be set forth in detail in a document transmitted to the Commission. The Commission shall communicate this information to Community undertakings under the conditions laid down in Article 13 of the Treaty establishing the European Atomic Energy Community.

3.   The sectors in which Denmark shall make information available to the European Atomic Energy Community are as follows:

(a)   DOR heavy water moderated organic cooled reactor;
(b)   DT-350, DK-400 heavy water pressure vessel reactors;
(c)   high temperature gas loop;
(d)   instrumentation systems and special electronic equipment;
(e)   reliability;
(f)   reactor physics, reactor dynamics and heat exchange;
(g)   in-pile testing of materials and equipment.

4.   Denmark shall undertake to supply the European Atomic Energy Community with any information complementary to the reports which it shall communicate, in particular during visits by European Atomic Energy Community personnel or personnel from the Member States to the Risö Centre, under conditions to be determined by mutual agreement in each case.

ARTICLE 16 (*ex Article 2 of Protocol No 25 AA 1972*)
1.   In those sectors in which Denmark places information at the disposal of the European Atomic Energy Community, the competent authorities shall grant upon request licences on commercial terms to Member States, persons and undertakings of the Community where they possess exclusive rights to patents filed in Member States and insofar as they have no obligation or commitment in respect of third parties to grant or offer to grant an exclusive or partially exclusive licence to the rights in these patents.

2.   Where an exclusive or partially exclusive licence has been granted, Denmark shall encourage and facilitate the granting of sublicences on commercial terms to Member States, persons and undertakings of the Community by the holders of such licences.
Such exclusive or partially exclusive licences shall be granted on a normal commercial basis.

SECTION 6

PROVISIONS ON THE EXCHANGE OF INFORMATION WITH IRELAND IN THE FIELD OF
NUCLEAR ENERGY

ARTICLE 17 (*ex Article 1 of Protocol No 26 AA 1972*)
1.   From 1 January 1973, such information as has been communicated to Member States, persons and undertakings, in accordance with Article 13 of the Treaty establishing the European Atomic Energy Community, shall be placed at the disposal of Ireland, which shall give it limited distribution within its territory under the conditions laid down in that Article.

2.   From 1 January 1973, Ireland shall place at the disposal of the European Atomic Energy Community information obtained in the nuclear field in Ireland, which is given limited distribution, insofar as strictly commercial applications are not involved. The Commission shall communicate this information to Community undertakings under the conditions laid down in Article 13 of the Treaty establishing the European Atomic Energy Community.

3.   The information referred to in paragraphs 1 and 2 shall mainly concern studies for the development of a power reactor and work on radioisotopes and their application in medicine, including the problems of radiation protection.

ARTICLE 18 (*ex Article 2 of Protocol No 26 AA 1972*)
1.   In those sectors in which Ireland places information at the disposal of the European Atomic Energy Community, the competent authorities shall grant upon request licences on commercial terms to Member States, persons and undertakings of the Community where they possess exclusive rights to patents filed in Member States and insofar as they have no obligation or commitment in respect of third parties to grant or offer to grant an exclusive or partially exclusive licence to the rights in these patents.

2.   Where an exclusive or partially exclusive licence has been granted, Ireland shall encourage and facilitate the granting of sublicences on commercial terms to Member States, persons and undertakings of the Community by the holders of such licences.
Such exclusive or partially exclusive licences shall be granted on a normal commercial basis.

SECTION 7

PROVISIONS ON THE EXCHANGE OF INFORMATION WITH THE UNITED KINGDOM IN THE
FIELD OF NUCLEAR ENERGY

ARTICLE 19 (*ex Article 1 of Protocol No 28 AA 1972*)
1.   From 1 January 1973, such information as has been communicated to Member States, persons and undertakings, in accordance with Article 13 of the Treaty establishing the European Atomic Energy Community, shall be placed at the disposal of the United Kingdom, which shall give it limited distribution within its territory under the conditions laid down in that Article.

2.   From 1 January 1973, the United Kingdom shall place at the disposal of the European Atomic Energy Community an equivalent volume of information in the sectors set out in the list contained in the Annex [OJ L 73, 27.3.1972, p. 84] to Protocol No 28 to the Act concerning the conditions of accession of the Kingdom of Denmark, Ireland and the United Kingdom of Great Britain and Northern Ireland. This information shall be set forth in detail in a document transmitted to the Commission. The Commission shall communicate this information to Community undertakings under the conditions laid down in Article 13 of the Treaty establishing the European Atomic Energy Community.

3.   In view of the European Atomic Energy Community's greater interest in certain sectors, the United Kingdom shall lay special emphasis on the transmission of information in the following sectors:
(a)   fast reactor research and development (including safety);
(b)   fundamental research (applicable to reactor types);
(c)   reactor safety (other than fast reactors);
(d)   metallurgy, steel, zirconium alloys and concrete;
(e)   compatibility of structural materials;
(f)   experimental fuel fabrication;
(g)   thermohydrodynamics;
(h)   instrumentation.

ARTICLE 20 (*ex Article 2 of Protocol No 28 AA 1972*)
1.   In those fields in which the United Kingdom places information at the disposal of the European Atomic Energy Community, the competent authorities shall grant upon request licences on commercial terms to Member States, persons and undertakings of the Community where they possess exclusive rights to patents filed in the Member States of the Community and insofar as they have no obligation or commitment in respect of third parties to grant or offer to grant an exclusive or partially exclusive licence to the rights in these patents.

2.   Where an exclusive or partially exclusive licence has been granted, the United Kingdom shall encourage and facilitate the granting of sublicences on commercial terms to the Member States, persons and undertakings of the Community by the holders of such licences.
Such exclusive or partially exclusive licences shall be granted on a normal commercial basis.

TITLE III

PROVISIONS TAKEN FROM THE ACT CONCERNING THE CONDITIONS OF ACCESSION OF THE HELLENIC REPUBLIC

SECTION 1

PROVISIONS ON THE GRANTING BY GREECE OF EXEMPTION FROM CUSTOMS DUTIES ON THE IMPORT OF CERTAIN GOODS

ARTICLE 21 (*ex Protocol No 3 AA 1979*)
Article III-151 of the Constitution shall not prevent the Hellenic Republic from maintaining measures of exemption granted before 1 January 1979 pursuant to:
(a)   Law No 4171/61 (General measures to aid development of the country's economy),
(b)   Decree Law No 2687/53 (Investment and protection of foreign capital),
(c)   Law No 289/76 (Incentives with a view to promoting the development of frontier regions and governing all pertinent questions),
until the expiry of the agreements concluded by the Hellenic Government with those persons benefiting from these measures.

SECTION 2

PROVISIONS ON TAXATION

ARTICLE 22 (*ex Article 128 AA 1979*)
The acts listed in point II. [OJ L 291, 19.11.1979, p. 163] of Annex VIII 1 to the Act concerning the conditions of accession of the Hellenic Republic shall apply in respect of the Hellenic Republic under the conditions laid down in that Annex, with the exception of the references to points 9 and 18(b) thereof.

SECTION 3

PROVISIONS ON COTTON

ARTICLE 23 (*ex Protocol No 4 AA 1979, amended by Protocol No 14 AA 1985*)

1.   This Section concerns cotton, not carded or combed, falling within subheading No 520 100 of the Combined Nomenclature.

2.   A system shall be introduced in the Union particularly to:

(a)   support the production of cotton in regions of the Union where it is important for the agricultural economy,

(b)   permit the producers concerned to earn a fair income,

(c)   stabilise the market by structural improvements at the level of supply and marketing.

3.   The system referred to in paragraph 2 shall include the grant of an aid to production.

4.   In order to allow cotton producers to concentrate supply and to adapt production to market requirements, a system shall be introduced to encourage the formation of producer groups and federations of such groups.

This system shall provide for the grant of aids with a view to providing incentives for the formation and facilitating the functioning of producer groups.

The only groups that may benefit from this system must:

(a)   be formed on the initiative of the producers themselves,

(b)   offer a sufficient guarantee for the duration and effectiveness of their action,

(c)   be recognised by the Member State concerned.

5.   The Union trading system with third countries shall not be affected. In this respect, in particular, no measure restricting imports may be laid down.

6.   A European law of the Council shall establish the adjustments necessary to the system introduced pursuant to this Section.

The Council, on a proposal from the Commission, shall adopt the European regulations and decisions establishing the general rules necessary for implementing the provisions of this Section.

The Council shall act after consulting the European Parliament.

SECTION 4

PROVISIONS ON THE ECONOMIC AND INDUSTRIAL DEVELOPMENT OF GREECE

ARTICLE 24 (*ex Protocol No 7 AA 1979*)

The Member States take note of the fact that the Hellenic Government has embarked upon the implementation of a policy of industrialisation and economic development designed to align the standards of living in Greece with those of the other Member States and to eliminate underemployment while progressively evening out regional differences in levels of development.

They recognise it to be in their common interest that the objectives of this policy be so attained. To this end, the institutions shall implement all the means and procedures laid down by the Constitution, particularly by making adequate use of the Union resources intended for the realisation of its objectives.

In particular, in the application of Articles III-167 and III-168 of the Constitution, it will be necessary to take into account the objectives of economic expansion and the raising of the standard of living of the population.

SECTION 5

PROVISIONS ON THE EXCHANGE OF INFORMATION WITH GREECE IN THE FIELD OF NUCLEAR ENERGY

ARTICLE 25 (*ex Article 1 of Protocol No 6 AA 1979*)

1.   From 1 January 1981, such information as has been communicated to Member States, persons and undertakings, in accordance with Article 13 of the Treaty establishing the European Atomic Energy Community, shall be placed at the disposal of the Hellenic Republic, which shall give it limited distribution within its territory under the conditions laid down in that Article.

2.   From 1 January 1981, the Hellenic Republic shall place at the disposal of the European Atomic Energy Community information obtained in the nuclear field in Greece which is given limited distribution, insofar as strictly commercial applications are not involved. The Commission shall communicate this information to Community undertakings under the conditions laid down in Article 13 of the Treaty establishing the European Atomic Energy Community.

3.   The information referred to in paragraphs 1 and 2 shall mainly concern:
(a)   studies on the application of radioisotopes in the following fields: medicine, agriculture, entomology and environmental protection,
(b)   the application of nuclear technology to archeometry,
(c)   the development of electronic medical apparatus,
(d)   the development of methods of radioactive ore prospecting.

ARTICLE 26 (*ex Article 2 of Protocol No 6 AA 1979*)
1.   In those sectors in which the Hellenic Republic places information at the disposal of the European Atomic Energy Community, the competent authorities shall grant upon request licences on commercial terms to Member States, persons and undertakings of the Community where they possess exclusive rights to patents filed in Member States of the Community and insofar as they have no obligation or commitment in respect of third parties to grant or offer to grant an exclusive or partially exclusive licence to the rights in these patents.

2.   Where an exclusive or partially exclusive licence has been granted, the Hellenic Republic shall encourage and facilitate the granting of sublicences on commercial terms to Member States, persons and undertakings of the European Atomic Energy Community by the holders of such licences.
Such exclusive or partially exclusive licences shall be granted on a normal commercial basis.

TITLE IV

PROVISIONS TAKEN FROM THE ACT CONCERNING THE CONDITIONS OF ACCESSION OF THE KINGDOM OF SPAIN AND THE PORTUGUESE REPUBLIC

SECTION 1

FINANCIAL PROVISIONS

ARTICLE 27 (*ex Article 187 AA 1985*)
The own resources accruing from value added tax shall be calculated and checked as if the Canary Islands and Ceuta and Melilla were included in the territorial field of application of Sixth Council Directive 77/388/EEC of 17 May 1977 on the harmonisation of the laws of the Member States relating to turnover taxes – Common system of value added tax: uniform basis of assessment.

SECTION 2

PROVISIONS ON PATENTS

ARTICLE 28 (*ex Protocol No 8 AA 1985*)
The provisions of Spanish national law relating to the burden of proof, which were adopted under paragraph 2 of Protocol No 8 to the Act concerning the conditions of accession of the Kingdom of Spain and the Portuguese Republic, shall not apply if the infringement proceedings are brought against the holder of another process patent for the manufacture of a product identical to that obtained as the result of the patented process of the plaintiff, if that other patent was issued before 1 January 1986.
In cases where shifting the burden of proof does not apply, the Kingdom of Spain shall continue to require the patent holder to adduce proof of infringement. In all these cases the Kingdom of Spain shall apply a judicial procedure known as "distraint-description".
"Distraint-description" means a procedure forming part of the system referred to in the first and second paragraphs by which any person entitled to bring an action for infringement may, after obtaining a court order, granted on his application, cause a detailed description to be made, at the premises of the alleged infringer, by a bailiff assisted by experts, of the processes in question, in particular by photocopying technical documents, with or without actual distraint. This court order may order the payment of a security, intended to grant damages to the alleged infringer in case of injury caused by the "distraint-description".

ARTICLE 29 (*ex Protocol No 19 AA 1985*)

The provisions of Portuguese national law relating to the burden of proof, which were adopted under paragraph 2 of Protocol No 19 to the Act concerning the conditions of accession of the Kingdom of Spain and the Portuguese Republic, shall not apply if the infringement proceedings are brought against the holder of another process patent for the manufacture of a product identical to that obtained as the result of the patented process of the plaintiff, if that other patent was issued before 1 January 1986.

In cases where shifting the burden of proof does not apply, the Portuguese Republic shall continue to require the patent holder to adduce proof of infringement. In all these cases, the Portuguese Republic shall apply a judicial procedure known as "distraint-description".

"Distraint-description" means a procedure forming part of the system referred to in the first and second paragraphs by which any person entitled to bring an action for infringement may, after obtaining a court order, granted on his application, cause a detailed description to be made, at the premises of the alleged infringer, by a bailiff assisted by experts, of the processes in question, in particular by photocopying technical documents, with or without actual distraint. This court order may order the payment of a security, intended to grant damages to the alleged infringer in case of injury caused by the "distraint-description".

SECTION 3

PROVISIONS ON THE MECHANISM FOR ADDITIONAL RESPONSIBILITIES WITHIN THE FRAMEWORK OF FISHERIES AGREEMENTS CONCLUDED BY THE UNION WITH THIRD COUNTRIES

ARTICLE 30 (*ex Protocol No 4 AA 1985*)

1.   A specific system is hereby established for the execution of operations carried out as a complement to fishing activities undertaken by vessels flying the flag of a Member State in waters falling under the sovereignty or within the jurisdiction of a third country within the framework of responsibilities created under fisheries agreements concluded by the Union with the third countries in question.

2.   Operations considered likely to occur by way of addition to fishing activities subject to the conditions and within the limits referred to in paragraphs 3 and 4 relate to:

(a)   the processing, in the territory of the third country concerned, of fishery products caught by vessels flying the flag of a Member State in the waters of that third country in the course of fishing activities carried out by virtue of a fisheries agreement, with a view to those products being put on the Union market under tariff headings falling within Chapter 3 of the Common Customs Tariff,

(b)   the loading or transhipment aboard a vessel flying the flag of a Member State occurring within the framework of activities provided for under such a fisheries agreement, of fishery products falling within Chapter 3 of the Common Customs Tariff with a view to their transport and any processing for the purpose of being put on the Union market.

3.   The import into the Union of products having been the subject of the operations referred to in paragraph 2 shall be carried out subject to suspension, in part or in whole, of the Common Customs Tariff duties or subject to a special system of charges, under the conditions and within the limits of additionality fixed annually in relation to the volume of fishing possibilities deriving from the agreements in question and from their accompanying detailed rules.

4.   European laws or framework laws shall lay down the general rules of application of this system and in particular the criteria for fixing and apportioning the quantities concerned. The detailed implementing rules of this system and the quantities concerned shall be adopted in accordance with the procedure laid down in Article 37 of Regulation (EC) No 104/2000.

SECTION 4

PROVISIONS ON CEUTA AND MELILLA

Subsection 1

General provisions

ARTICLE 31 (*ex Article 25 AA 1985*)

1.   The Constitution and the acts of the institutions shall apply to Ceuta and to Melilla, subject to the derogations referred to in paragraphs 2 and 3 and to the other provisions of this Section.

2.   The conditions under which the provisions of the Constitution concerning the free movement of goods, and the acts of the institutions concerning customs legislation and commercial policy, shall apply to Ceuta and to Melilla are set out in Subsection 3 of this Section.

3.   Without prejudice to the specific provisions of Article 32, the acts of the institutions concerning the common agricultural policy and the common fisheries policy shall not apply to Ceuta or to Melilla.

4.   At the request of the Kingdom of Spain, a European law or framework law of the Council may:
(a)   include Ceuta and Melilla in the customs territory of the Union;
(b)   define the appropriate measures aimed at extending to Ceuta and to Melilla the provisions of Union law in force.
On a proposal from the Commission acting on its own initiative or at the request of a Member State, the Council may adopt a European law or framework law adjusting the arrangements applicable to Ceuta and to Melilla if necessary.
The Council shall act unanimously after consulting the European Parliament.

Subsection 2

Provisions relating to the Common Fisheries Policy

ARTICLE 32 (*ex Article 155 AA 1985*)
1.   Subject to paragraph 2 and without prejudice to Subsection 3, the common fisheries policy shall not apply to Ceuta or to Melilla.

2.   The Council, on a proposal from the Commission, shall adopt the European laws, framework laws, regulations or decisions which:
(a)   determine the structural measures which may be adopted in favour of Ceuta and Melilla;
(b)   determine the procedures appropriate to take into consideration all or part of the interests of Ceuta and Melilla when it adopts acts, case by case, with a view to the negotiations by the Union aimed at the resumption or conclusion of fisheries agreements with third countries and to the specific interests of Ceuta and Melilla within international conventions concerning fisheries, to which the Union is a contracting party.

3.   The Council, on a proposal from the Commission, shall adopt the European laws, framework laws, regulations or decisions which determine, where appropriate, the possibilities and conditions of mutual access to respective fishing zones and to the resources thereof. It shall act unanimously.

4.   The European laws and framework laws referred to in paragraphs 2 and 3 shall be adopted after consultation of the European Parliament.

Subsection 3

Provisions on free movement of goods, customs legislation and commercial policy

ARTICLE 33 (*ex Article 1 of Protocol No 2 AA 1985*)
1.   Products originating in Ceuta or in Melilla and products coming from third countries imported into Ceuta or into Melilla under the arrangements which are applicable there to them shall not be deemed, when released for free circulation in the customs territory of the Union, to be goods fulfilling the conditions of paragraphs 1 to 3 of Article III-151 of the Constitution.

2.   The customs territory of the Union shall not include Ceuta and Melilla.

3.   Except where otherwise provided for in this Subsection, the acts of the institutions regarding customs legislation for foreign trade shall apply under the same conditions to trade between the customs territory of the Union, on the one hand, and Ceuta and Melilla, on the other.

4.   Except where otherwise provided for in this Subsection, the acts of the institutions regarding the common commercial policy, be they autonomous or enacted by agreement, directly linked to the import or export of goods, shall not be applicable to Ceuta or to Melilla.

5.	Except where otherwise provided for in this Title, the Union shall apply in its trade with Ceuta and Melilla, for products falling within Annex I to the Constitution, the general arrangements which it applies in its foreign trade.

ARTICLE 34 (*ex Article 2 of Protocol No 2 AA 1985*)
1.	Subject to Article 35, customs duties on the import into the customs territory of the Union of products originating in Ceuta or in Melilla shall be abolished.

ARTICLE 35 (*ex Article 3 of Protocol No 2 AA 1985*)
1.	Fishery products falling within heading Nos 03.01, 03.02, 03.03, 16.04, 16.05 and subheadings 05.11.91 and 23.01.20 of the Common Customs Tariff and originating in Ceuta or in Melilla, shall, within the limit of tariff quotas calculated by product and on the average quantities actually disposed of during 1982, 1983 and 1984, qualify for exemption from customs duties throughout the customs territory of the Union.
The release for free circulation of products imported into the customs territory of the Union, under these tariff quotas, shall be subject to compliance with the rules laid down by the common organisation of markets and in particular with respect to reference prices.

2.	The Council, on a proposal from the Commission, shall each year adopt European regulations or decisions opening and allocating tariff quotas in accordance with the detailed rules laid down in paragraph 1.

ARTICLE 36 (*ex Article 5 of Protocol No 2 AA 1985*)
1.	Where application of Article 34 could lead to a substantial increase in the import of certain products originating in Ceuta or in Melilla such as might prejudice Union producers, the Council, on a proposal from the Commission, may adopt European regulations or decisions to subject the access of these products to the customs territory of the Union to special conditions.

2.	Where, because the common commercial policy and the Common Customs Tariff are not applied to the import of raw materials or intermediate products into Ceuta or into Melilla, imports of a product originating in Ceuta or in Melilla cause, or may cause, serious injury to a producer activity exercised in one or more Member States, the Commission, at the request of a Member State or on its own initiative, may take the appropriate measures.

ARTICLE 37 (*ex Article 6 of Protocol No 2 AA 1985*)
The customs duties on import into Ceuta and into Melilla of products originating in the customs territory of the Union, and charges having equivalent effect, shall be abolished.

ARTICLE 38 (*ex Article 7 of Protocol No 2 AA 1985*)
The customs duties and charges having an effect equivalent to such duties and the trade arrangements applied on the import into Ceuta and into Melilla of goods coming from a third country may not be less favourable than those applicable by the Union in accordance with its international commitments or its preferential arrangements with regard to such third country, providing that the same third country grants, to imports from Ceuta and from Melilla, the same treatment as that which it grants to the Union. However, the arrangements applied to imports into Ceuta and into Melilla with regard to goods coming from such third country may not be more favourable than those applied with regard to the imports of products originating in the customs territory of the Union.

ARTICLE 39 (*ex Article 9 of Protocol No 2 AA 1985*)
The Council, on a proposal from the Commission, shall adopt European regulations or decisions laying down the rules for the application of this Subsection and in particular the rules of origin applicable to trade, as referred to in Articles 34, 35 and 37, including the provisions concerning the identification of originating products and the control of origin.
The rules will include, in particular, provisions on marking and/or labelling of products, on the conditions of registration of vessels, on the application of the rule on mixed origin for fishery products, and also provisions enabling the origin of products to be determined.

SECTION 5

PROVISIONS ON THE REGIONAL DEVELOPMENT OF SPAIN

ARTICLE 40 (*ex Protocol No 12 AA 1985*)

The Member States take note of the fact that the Spanish Government has embarked upon the implementation of a policy of regional development designed in particular to stimulate economic growth in the less-developed regions and areas of Spain.

They recognise it to be in their common interest that the objectives of this policy be attained.

They agree, in order to help the Spanish Government to accomplish this task, to recommend that the institutions use all the means and procedures laid down by the Constitution, particularly by making adequate use of the Union resources intended for the realisation of its objectives.

The Member States recognise in particular that, in the application of Articles III-167 and III-168 of the Constitution, it will be necessary to take into account the objectives of economic expansion and the raising of the standard of living of the population of the less-developed regions and areas of Spain.

SECTION 6

PROVISIONS ON THE ECONOMIC AND INDUSTRIAL DEVELOPMENT OF PORTUGAL

ARTICLE 41 (*ex Protocol No 21 AA 1985*)

The Member States take note of the fact that the Portuguese Government has embarked upon the implementation of a policy of industrialisation and economic development designed to align the standard of living in Portugal with that of the other Member States and to eliminate underemployment while progressively evening out regional differences in levels of development.

They recognise it to be in their common interest that the objectives of this policy be attained.

They agree to recommend to this end that the institutions use all the means and procedures laid down by the Constitution, particularly by making adequate use of the Union resources intended for the realisation of its objectives.

The Member States recognise in particular that, in the application of Articles III-167 and III-168 of the Constitution, it will be necessary to take into account the objectives of economic expansion and the raising of the standard of living of the population.

SECTION 7

PROVISIONS ON THE EXCHANGE OF INFORMATION WITH THE KINGDOM OF SPAIN IN THE FIELD OF NUCLEAR ENERGY

ARTICLE 42 (*ex Article 1 of Protocol No 13 AA 1985*)

1.   From 1 January 1986, such information as has been communicated to Member States, persons and undertakings, in accordance with Article 13 of the Treaty establishing the European Atomic Energy Community, shall be placed at the disposal of the Kingdom of Spain, which shall give it limited distribution within its territory under the conditions laid down in that Article.

2.   From 1 January 1986, the Kingdom of Spain shall place at the disposal of the European Atomic Energy Community information obtained in the nuclear field in Spain which is given limited distribution, insofar as strictly commercial applications are not involved. The Commission shall communicate this information to Community undertakings under the conditions laid down in Article 13 of the Treaty establishing the European Atomic Energy Community.

3.   The information referred to in paragraphs 1 and 2 shall mainly concern:
(a)   nuclear physics (low and high-energy);
(b)   radiation protection;
(c)   isotope applications, in particular those of stable isotopes;
(d)   research reactors and relevant fuels;
(e)   research into the field of the fuel cycle (more especially the mining and processing of low-grade uranium ore; optimisation of fuel elements for power reactors).

ARTICLE 43 (*ex Article 2 of Protocol No 13 AA 1985*)

1.   In those sectors in which the Kingdom of Spain places information at the disposal of the European Atomic Energy Community, the competent authorities shall grant upon request licences on commercial terms

to Member States, persons and undertakings of the Community where they possess exclusive rights to patents filed in Member States and insofar as they have no obligation or commitment in respect of third parties to grant or offer to grant an exclusive or partially exclusive licence to the rights in these patents.

2.   Where an exclusive or partially exclusive licence has been granted, the Kingdom of Spain shall encourage and facilitate the granting of sublicences on commercial terms to Member States, persons and undertakings of the Community by the holders of such licences.
Such exclusive or partially exclusive licences shall be granted on a normal commercial basis.

SECTION 8

PROVISIONS ON THE EXCHANGE OF INFORMATION WITH THE PORTUGUESE REPUBLIC IN THE FIELD OF NUCLEAR ENERGY

ARTICLE 44 (*ex Article 1 of Protocol No 22 AA 1985*)
1.   From 1 January 1986, such information as has been communicated to Member States, persons and undertakings, in accordance with Article 13 of the Treaty establishing the European Atomic Energy Community, shall be placed at the disposal of the Portuguese Republic, which shall give it limited distribution within its territory under the conditions laid down in that Article.

2.   From 1 January 1986, the Portuguese Republic shall place at the disposal of the European Atomic Energy Community information obtained in the nuclear field in Portugal which is given limited distribution, insofar as strictly commercial applications are not involved. The Commission shall communicate this information to Community undertakings under the conditions laid down in Article 13 of the Treaty establishing the European Atomic Energy Community.

3.   The information referred to in paragraphs 1 and 2 shall mainly concern:
(a)   reactor dynamics;
(b)   radiation protection;
(c)   application of nuclear measuring techniques (in the industrial, agricultural, archaeological and geological fields);
(d)   atomic physics (effective measuring of cross sections, pipeline techniques);
(e)   extractive metallurgy of uranium.

ARTICLE 45 (*ex Article 2 of Protocol No 22 AA 1985*)
1.   In those sectors in which the Portuguese Republic places information at the disposal of the European Atomic Energy Community, the competent authorities shall grant upon request licences on commercial terms to Member States, persons and undertakings of the Community where they possess exclusive rights to patents filed in Member States and insofar as they have no obligation or commitment in respect of third parties to grant or offer to grant an exclusive or partially exclusive licence to the rights in these patents.

2.   Where an exclusive or partially exclusive licence has been granted, the Portuguese Republic shall encourage and facilitate the granting of sublicences on commercial terms to Member States, persons and undertakings of the Community by the holders of such licences.
Such exclusive or partially exclusive licences shall be granted on a normal commercial basis.

TITLE V

PROVISIONS TAKEN FROM THE ACT CONCERNING THE CONDITIONS OF ACCESSION OF THE REPUBLIC OF AUSTRIA, THE REPUBLIC OF FINLAND AND THE KINGDOM OF SWEDEN

SECTION 1

FINANCIAL PROVISIONS

ARTICLE 46 (*ex Article 108 AA 1994*)
Own resources accruing from value added tax shall be calculated and checked as though the Åland Islands were included in the territorial scope of Sixth Council Directive 77/388/EEC of 17 May 1977 on the harmonisation of the laws of the Member States relating to turnover taxes – Common system of value added tax: uniform basis of assessment.

SECTION 2

PROVISIONS ON AGRICULTURE

ARTICLE 47 (*ex Article 141 AA 1994*)

Where there are serious difficulties resulting from accession which remain after full utilisation of Article 48 and of the other measures resulting from the rules existing in the Union, the Commission may adopt a European decision authorising Finland to grant national aids to producers so as to facilitate their full integration into the common agricultural policy.

ARTICLE 48 (*ex Article 142 AA 1994*)

1.   The Commission shall adopt European decisions authorising Finland and Sweden to grant long-term national aids with a view to ensuring that agricultural activity is maintained in specific regions. These regions should cover the agricultural areas situated to the north of the 62nd Parallel and some adjacent areas south of that parallel affected by comparable climatic conditions rendering agricultural activity particularly difficult.

2.   The regions referred to in paragraph 1 shall be determined by the Commission, taking into consideration in particular:
(a)   the low population density;
(b)   the portion of agricultural land in the overall surface area;
(c)   the portion of agricultural land devoted to arable crops intended for human consumption, in the agricultural surface area used.

3.   The national aids provided for in paragraph 1 may be related to physical factors of production, such as hectares of agricultural land or heads of animal taking account of the relevant limits laid down in the common organisations of the market, as well as the historical production patterns of each farm, but must not:
(a)   be linked to future production;
(b)   or lead to an increase in production or in the level of overall support recorded during a reference period preceding 1 January 1995, to be determined by the Commission.
These aids may be differentiated by region.
These aids must be granted in particular in order to:
(a)   maintain traditional primary production and processing naturally suited to the climatic conditions of the regions concerned;
(b)   improve the structures for the production, marketing and processing of agricultural products;
(c)   facilitate the disposal of the said products;
(d)   ensure that the environment is protected and the countryside preserved.

ARTICLE 49 (*ex Article 143 AA 1994*)

1.   The aids provided for in Articles 47 and 48 and any other national aid subject to Commission authorisation under this Title shall be notified to the Commission. They may not be applied until such authorisation has been given.

2.   As regards the aids provided for in Article 48, the Commission shall submit to the Council every five years as from 1 January 1996 a report on:
(a)   the authorisations granted;
(b)   the results of the aid granted under such authorisations.
In preparation for drawing up such reports, Member States in receipt of such authorisations shall supply the Commission in good time with information on the effects of the aids granted, illustrating the development noted in the agricultural economy of the regions in question.

ARTICLE 50 (*ex Article 144 AA 1994*)

In the field of the aids provided for in Articles III-167 and III-168 of the Constitution:
(a)   among the aids applied in Austria, Finland and Sweden prior to 1 January 1995, only those notified to the Commission by 30 April 1995 will be deemed to be existing aids within the meaning of Article III-168(1) of the Constitution;
(b)   existing aids and plans intended to grant or alter aids which were notified to the Commission prior to 1 January 1995 shall be deemed to have been notified on that date.

ARTICLE 51 (*ex Article 148 AA 1994*)

1.   Unless otherwise stipulated in specific cases, the Council, on a proposal from the Commission, shall adopt the necessary European regulations or decisions to implement this Section.

2.   A European law of the Council may make the adaptations to the provisions appearing in this Section which may prove necessary as a result of a modification in Union law. The Council shall act unanimously after consulting the European Parliament.

ARTICLE 52 (*ex Article 149 AA 1994*)
1.   If transitional measures are necessary to facilitate the transition from the existing regime in Austria, Finland and Sweden to that resulting from application of the common organisation of the markets under the conditions set out in the Act concerning the conditions of accession of the Republic of Austria, the Republic of Finland and the Kingdom of Sweden, such measures shall be adopted in accordance with the procedure laid down in Article 38 of Regulation No 136/66/EEC or, as appropriate, in the corresponding Articles of the other Regulations on the common organisation of agricultural markets. These measures may be taken during a period expiring on 31 December 1997 and their application shall be limited to that date.

2.   A European law of the Council may extend the period referred to in paragraph 1. The Council shall act unanimously after consulting the European Parliament.

ARTICLE 53 (*ex Articles 88(2) and 115(2) AA 1994*)
Articles 51 and 52 shall be applicable to fishery products.

SECTION 3

PROVISIONS ON TRANSITIONAL MEASURES

ARTICLE 54 (*ex Article 151 AA 1994*)
The Acts listed in points VII.B.I, VII.D.1, VII.D.2.c, IX.2.b, c, f, g, h, i, j, l, m, n, x, y, z and aa, and X.a, b and c of Annex XV [OJ C 241, 29.8.1994, p. 322] to the Act concerning the conditions of accession of the Republic of Austria, the Republic of Finland and the Kingdom of Sweden shall apply in respect of Austria, Finland and Sweden under the conditions laid down in that Annex.
With regard to point IX.2.x of Annex XV referred to in the first paragraph, the reference to the provisions of the Treaty establishing the European Community, in particular to Articles 90 and 91 thereof, must be understood as referring to the provisions of the Constitution, in particular to Article III-170(1) and (2) thereof.

SECTION 4

PROVISIONS ON THE APPLICABILITY OF CERTAIN ACTS

ARTICLE 55 (*ex Article 172(4), (5) and (7) AA 1994*)
1.   Any individual exemption decisions taken and negative clearance decisions taken before 1 January 1995 under Article 53 of the Agreement on the European Economic Area (EEA) or Article 1 of Protocol 25 to that Agreement, whether by the Surveillance Authority of the European Free Trade Association (EFTA) or the Commission, and which concern cases which fall under Article 81 of the Treaty establishing the European Community as a result of accession shall remain valid for the purposes of Article III-161 of the Constitution until the time limit specified therein expires or until the Commission adopts a duly motivated European decision to the contrary, in accordance with Union law.

2.   All decisions taken by the EFTA Surveillance Authority before 1 January 1995 pursuant to Article 61 of the EEA Agreement and which fall under Article 87 of the Treaty establishing the European Community as a result of accession shall remain valid with respect to Article III-167 of the Constitution unless the Commission adopts a European decision to the contrary pursuant to Article III-168 of the Constitution. This paragraph shall not apply to decisions subject to the proceedings provided for in Article 64 of the EEA Agreement.

3.   Without prejudice to paragraphs 1 and 2, the decisions taken by the EFTA Surveillance Authority remain valid after 1 January 1995 unless the Commission takes a duly motivated decision to the contrary in accordance with Union law.

SECTION 5

PROVISIONS ON THE ÅLAND ISLANDS

ARTICLE 56 (*ex Article 1 of Protocol No 2 AA 1994*)

The provisions of the Constitution shall not preclude the application of the existing provisions in force on 1 January 1994 on the Åland islands on:

(a) restrictions, on a non-discriminatory basis, on the right of natural persons who do not enjoy hembygdsrätt/kotiseutuoikeus (regional citizenship) in Åland, and for legal persons, to acquire and hold real property on the Åland islands without permission by the competent authorities of the Åland islands;

(b) restrictions, on a non-discriminatory basis, on the right of establishment and the right to provide services by natural persons who do not enjoy hembygdsrätt/kotiseutuoikeus (regional citizenship) in Åland, or by legal persons without permission by the competent authorities of the Åland islands.

ARTICLE 57 (*ex Article 2 of Protocol No 2 AA 1994*)

1.   The territory of the Åland Islands – being considered as a third territory, as defined in the third indent of Article 3(1) of Council Directive 77/388/EEC, and as a national territory falling outside the field of application of the excise harmonisation directives as defined in Article 2 of Council Directive 92/12/EEC – shall be excluded from the territorial application of Union law in the fields of harmonisation of the laws of the Member States on turnover taxes and on excise duties and other forms of indirect taxation. This paragraph shall not apply to the provisions of Council Directive 69/335/EEC relating to capital duty.

2.   The derogation provided for in paragraph 1 is aimed at maintaining a viable local economy in the islands and shall not have any negative effects on the interests of the Union nor on its common policies. If the Commission considers that the provisions in paragraph 1 are no longer justified, particularly in terms of fair competition or own resources, it shall submit appropriate proposals to the Council, which shall adopt the necessary acts in accordance with the pertinent articles of the Constitution.

ARTICLE 58 (*ex Article 3 of Protocol No 2 AA 1994*)

The Republic of Finland shall ensure that the same treatment applies to all natural and legal persons of the Member States in the Åland islands.

ARTICLE 59 (*new*)

The provisions of this Section shall apply in the light of the Declaration on the Åland Islands, which incorporates, without altering its legal effect, the wording of the preamble to Protocol No 2 to the Act concerning the conditions of accession of the Republic of Austria, the Republic of Finland and the Kingdom of Sweden.

SECTION 6

PROVISIONS ON THE SAMI PEOPLE

ARTICLE 60 (*ex Article 1 of Protocol No 3 AA 1994*)

Notwithstanding the provisions of the Constitution, exclusive rights to reindeer husbandry within traditional Sami areas may be granted to the Sami people.

ARTICLE 61 (*ex Article 2 of Protocol No 3 AA 1994*)

This Section may be extended to take account of any further development of exclusive Sami rights linked to their traditional means of livelihood. A European law of the Council may make the necessary amendments to this Section. The Council shall act unanimously after consulting the European Parliament and the Committee of the Regions.

ARTICLE 62 (*new*)

The provisions of this Section shall apply in the light of the Declaration on the Sami people, which incorporates, without altering its legal effect, the wording of the preamble to Protocol No 3 to the Act concerning the conditions of accession of the Republic of Austria, the Republic of Finland and the Kingdom of Sweden.

SECTION 7

SPECIAL PROVISIONS IN THE FRAMEWORK OF THE STRUCTURAL FUNDS IN FINLAND AND SWEDEN

ARTICLE 63 (*ex Article 2 of Protocol No 6 AA 1994*)
Areas covered by the objective of promoting the development and structural adjustment of regions with an extremely low population density shall in principle represent or belong to regions at NUTS level II with a population density of 8 persons per km^2 or less. Union assistance may, subject to the requirement of concentration, also extend to adjacent and contiguous smaller areas fulfilling the same population density criterion. The regions and areas referred to in this Article, are listed in Annex 1 [OJ C 241, 29.8.1994, p. 355] to Protocol No 6 to the Act concerning the conditions of accession of the Republic of Austria, the Republic of Finland and the Kingdom of Sweden.

SECTION 8

PROVISIONS ON RAIL AND COMBINED TRANSPORT IN AUSTRIA

ARTICLE 64 (*ex Article 1 of Protocol No 9 AA 1994*)
1.   For the purposes of this Section, the following definitions shall apply:
(a)   "heavy goods vehicle" shall mean any motor vehicle with a maximum authorised weight of over 7,5 tonnes registered in a Member State designed to carry goods or haul trailers, including semi-trailer tractor units, and trailers with a maximum authorised weight of over 7,5 tonnes and hauled by a motor vehicle registered in a Member State with a maximum authorised weight of 7,5 tonnes or less;
(b)   "combined transport" shall mean the carriage of goods by heavy goods vehicles or loading units which complete part of their journey by rail and either begin or end the journey by road, whereby transit traffic may under no circumstances cross Austrian territory on its way to or from a rail terminal by road alone.

2.   Articles 65 to 71 shall apply to measures relating to the provision of rail and combined transport crossing the territory of Austria.

ARTICLE 65 (*ex Article 3 of Protocol No 9 AA 1994*)
The Union and the Member States concerned shall, within the framework of their respective competences, adopt and closely co-ordinate measures for the development and promotion of rail and combined transport for the trans-Alpine carriage of goods.

ARTICLE 66 (*ex Article 4 of Protocol No 9 AA 1994*)
When establishing the guidelines provided for in Article III-247 of the Constitution, the Union shall ensure that the axes defined in Annex 1 [OJ C 241, 29.8.1994, p. 364] to Protocol No 9 to the Act concerning the conditions of accession of the Republic of Austria, the Republic of Finland and the Kingdom of Sweden form part of the trans-European networks for rail and combined transport and are furthermore identified as projects of common interest.

ARTICLE 67 (*ex Article 5 of Protocol No 9 AA 1994*)
The Union and the Member States concerned shall, within the framework of their respective competences, implement the measures listed in Annex 2 [OJ C 241, 29.8.1994, p. 365] to Protocol No 9 to the Act concerning the conditions of accession of the Republic of Austria, the Republic of Finland and the Kingdom of Sweden.

ARTICLE 68 (*ex Article 6 of Protocol No 9 AA 1994*)
The Union and the Member States concerned shall use their best endeavours to develop and utilise the additional railway capacity referred to in Annex 3 [OJ C 241, 29.8.1994, p. 367] to Protocol No 9 to the Act concerning the conditions of accession of the Republic of Austria, the Republic of Finland and the Kingdom of Sweden.

ARTICLE 69 (*ex Article 7 of Protocol No 9 AA 1994*)
The Union and the Member States concerned shall take measures to enhance the provision of rail and combined transport. Where appropriate, and subject to the provisions of the Constitution, such measures shall be established in close consultation with railway companies and other railway service providers. Priority should be given to those measures set out in the provisions of Union law on railways and combined transport. In implementing any measures, particular attention shall be attached to the competitiveness, effectiveness and

cost transparency of rail and combined transport. In particular, the Member States concerned shall endeavour to take such measures so as to ensure that prices for combined transport are competitive with those for other modes of transport. Any aid granted to these ends shall comply with Union law.

ARTICLE 70 (*ex Article 8 of Protocol No 9 AA 1994*)
The Union and the Member States concerned shall, in the event of a serious disturbance in rail transit, such as a natural disaster, take all possible concerted action to maintain the flow of traffic. Priority shall be given to sensitive loads, such as perishable foods.

ARTICLE 71 (*ex Article 9 of Protocol No 9 AA 1994*)
The Commission, acting in accordance with the procedure laid down in Article 73(2), shall review the operation of this Section.

ARTICLE 72 (*new*)
1.   This Article shall apply to the carriage of goods by road on journeys carried out within the territory of the Community.

2.   For journeys which involve transit of goods by road through Austria, the regime established for journeys on own account and for journeys for hire or reward under the First Council Directive of 23 July 1962 and Council Regulation (EEC) No 881/92 shall apply subject to the provisions of this Article.

3.   Until 1 January 1998, the following provisions shall apply:
(a)   The total of NOx emissions from heavy goods vehicles crossing Austria in transit shall be reduced by 60% in the period between 1 January 1992 and 31 December 2003, according to the table in Annex 4.
(b)   The reductions in total NOx emissions from heavy goods vehicles shall be administered according to an ecopoints system. Under that system any heavy goods vehicle crossing Austria in transit shall require a number of ecopoints equivalent to its NOx emissions (authorised under the Conformity of Production (COP) value or type-approval value). The method of calculation and administration of such points is described in Annex 5.
(c)   If the number of transit journeys in any year exceeds the reference figure established for 1991 by more than 8%, the Commission, acting in accordance with the procedure laid down in Article 16, shall adopt appropriate measures in accordance with paragraph 3 of Annex 5.
(d)   Austria shall issue and make available in good time the ecopoints cards required for the administration of the ecopoints system, pursuant to Annex 5, for heavy goods vehicles crossing Austria in transit.
(e)   The ecopoints shall be distributed by the Commission among Member States in accordance with provisions to be established in accordance with paragraph 7.

4.   Before 1 January 1998, the Council, on the basis of a report by the Commission, shall review the operation of provisions concerning transit of goods by road through Austria. The review shall take place in conformity with basic principles of Community law, such as the proper functioning of the internal market, in particular the free movement of goods and freedom to provide services, protection of the environment in the interest of the Community as a whole, and traffic safety. Unless the Council, acting unanimously on a proposal from the Commission and after consulting the European Parliament, decides otherwise, the transitional period shall be extended to 1 January 2001, during which the provisions of paragraph 3 shall apply.

5.   Before 1 January 2001, the Commission, in co-operation with the European Environment Agency, shall make a scientific study of the degree to which the objective concerning reduction of pollution set out in paragraph 3(a) has been achieved. If the Commission concludes that this objective has been achieved on a sustainable basis, the provisions of paragraph 3 shall cease to apply on 1 January 2001. If the Commission concludes that this objective has not been achieved on a sustainable basis, the Council, acting in accordance with Article 75 of the EC Treaty, may adopt measures, within a Community framework, which ensure equivalent protection of the environment, in particular a 60% reduction of pollution. If the Council does not adopt such measures, the transitional period shall be automatically extended for a final period of three years, during which the provisions of paragraph 3 shall apply.

6.   At the end of the transitional period, the Community *acquis* in its entirety shall be applied.

7.   The Commission, acting in accordance with the procedure laid down in Article 16, shall adopt detailed measures concerning the procedures relating to the ecopoints system, the distribution of ecopoints and technical questions concerning the application of this Article, which shall enter into force on the date of accession of Austria.

The measures referred to in the first subparagraph shall ensure that the factual situation for the present Member States resulting from the application of Council Regulation (EEC) No 3637/92 and of the Administrative Arrangement, signed on 23 December 1992, setting the date of entry into force and the procedures for the introduction of the ecopoints system referred to in the Transit Agreement, is maintained. All necessary efforts shall be made to ensure that the share of ecopoints allocated to Greece takes sufficient account of Greek needs in this context.

ARTICLE 73 (*ex Article 16 of Protocol No 9 AA 1994*)
1.   The Commission shall be assisted by a Committee.

2.   In cases where reference is made to this paragraph, Articles 3 and 7 of Decision 1999/468/EC shall apply.

3.   The Committee shall adopt its Rules of Procedure.

SECTION 9

PROVISIONS ON THE USE OF SPECIFIC AUSTRIAN TERMS OF THE GERMAN LANGUAGE IN THE FRAMEWORK OF THE EUROPEAN UNION

ARTICLE 74 (*ex Sole Article of Protocol No 10 AA 1994*)
1.   The specific Austrian terms of the German language contained in the Austrian legal order and listed in the Annex [OJ C 241, 29.8.1994, p. 370] to Protocol No 10 to the Act concerning the conditions of accession of the Republic of Austria, the Republic of Finland and the Kingdom of Sweden shall have the same status and may be used with the same legal effect as the corresponding terms used in Germany listed in that Annex.

2.   In the German language version of new legal acts the specific Austrian terms referred to in the Annex to Protocol No 10 to the Act concerning the conditions of accession of the Republic of Austria, the Republic of Finland and the Kingdom of Sweden shall be added in appropriate form to the corresponding terms used in Germany.

9.   **PROTOCOL ON THE TREATY AND THE ACT OF ACCESSION OF THE CZECH REPUBLIC, THE REPUBLIC OF ESTONIA, THE REPUBLIC OF CYPRUS, THE REPUBLIC OF LATVIA, THE REPUBLIC OF LITHUANIA, THE REPUBLIC OF HUNGARY, THE REPUBLIC OF MALTA, THE REPUBLIC OF POLAND, THE REPUBLIC OF SLOVENIA AND THE SLOVAK REPUBLIC**

THE HIGH CONTRACTING PARTIES,

RECALLING that the Czech Republic, the Republic of Estonia, the Republic of Cyprus, the Republic of Latvia, the Republic of Lithuania, the Republic of Hungary, the Republic of Malta, the Republic of Poland, the Republic of Slovenia and the Slovak Republic acceded to the European Communities and to the European Union established by the Treaty on European Union on 1 May 2004;

CONSIDERING that Article IV-437(2)(e) of the Constitution provides that the Treaty of 16 April 2003 concerning the accessions referred to above shall be repealed;

CONSIDERING that many of the provisions of the Act annexed to that Treaty of Accession remain relevant; that Article IV-437(2) of the Constitution provides that those provisions must be set out or referred to in a Protocol, so that they remain in force and their legal effects are preserved;

CONSIDERING that some of those provisions require the technical adjustments necessary to bring them into line with the Constitution without altering their legal effect,

HAVE AGREED UPON the following provisions, which shall be annexed to the Treaty establishing a Constitution for Europe and to the Treaty establishing the European Atomic Energy Community:

PART ONE

PROVISIONS RELATING TO THE ACT OF ACCESSION OF 16 APRIL 2003

TITLE I

PRINCIPLES

ARTICLE 1 (*ex Article 1 AA 2003*)
For the purposes of this Protocol:
(a)   the expression "Act of Accession of 16 April 2003" means the Act concerning the conditions of accession of the Czech Republic, the Republic of Estonia, the Republic of Cyprus, the Republic of Latvia, the Republic of Lithuania, the Republic of Hungary, the Republic of Malta, the Republic of Poland, the Republic of Slovenia and the Slovak Republic and the adjustments to the Treaties on which the European Union is founded;
(b)   the expressions "Treaty establishing the European Community" ("EC Treaty") and "Treaty establishing the European Atomic Energy Community" ("EAEC Treaty") mean those Treaties as supplemented or amended by treaties or other acts which entered into force before 1 May 2004;
(c)   the expression "Treaty on European Union" ("EU Treaty") means that Treaty as supplemented or amended by treaties or other acts which entered into force before 1 May 2004;
(d)   the expression "the Community" means one or both of the Communities referred to in (b) as the case may be;
(e)   the expression "present Member States" means the following Member States: the Kingdom of Belgium, the Kingdom of Denmark, the Federal Republic of Germany, the Hellenic Republic, the Kingdom of Spain, the French Republic, Ireland, the Italian Republic, the Grand Duchy of Luxembourg, the Kingdom of the Netherlands, the Republic of Austria, the Portuguese Republic, the Republic of Finland, the Kingdom of Sweden and the United Kingdom of Great Britain and Northern Ireland;
(f)   the expression "new Member States" means the following Member States: the Czech Republic, the Republic of Estonia, the Republic of Cyprus, the Republic of Latvia, the Republic of Lithuania, the Republic of Hungary, the Republic of Malta, the Republic of Poland, the Republic of Slovenia and the Slovak Republic.

ARTICLE 2 (*ex Article 2 AA 2003*)
The rights and obligations resulting from the Treaty on the Accession of the Czech Republic, the Republic of Estonia, the Republic of Cyprus, the Republic of Latvia, the Republic of Lithuania, the Republic of Hungary, the Republic of Malta, the Republic of Poland, the Republic of Slovenia and the Slovak Republic, referred to in Article IV-437(2)(e) of the Constitution, took effect, under the conditions laid down in that Treaty, as from 1 May 2004.

ARTICLE 3 (*ex Article 3 AA 2003*)
1.   The provisions of the Schengen *acquis* integrated into the framework of the Union by the Protocol annexed to the Treaty establishing a Constitution for Europe (hereinafter referred to as the "Schengen Protocol") and the acts building upon it or otherwise related to it, listed in Annex I to the Act of Accession of 16 April 2003, as well as any further such acts adopted before 1 May 2004, shall be binding on and applicable in the new Member States from 1 May 2004.

2.   Those provisions of the Schengen *acquis* as integrated into the framework of the Union and the acts building upon it or otherwise related to it not referred to in paragraph 1, while binding on the new Member States from 1 May 2004, shall apply in a new Member State only pursuant to a European decision of the Council to that effect after verification in accordance with the applicable Schengen evaluation procedures that the necessary conditions for the application of all parts of the *acquis* concerned have been met in that new Member State.
The Council shall take its decision, after consulting the European Parliament, acting with the unanimity of its members representing the Governments of the Member States in respect of which the provisions referred to in the present paragraph have already been put into effect and of the representative of the Government of the Member State in respect of which those provisions are to be put into effect. The members of the Council representing the Governments of Ireland and of the United Kingdom of Great Britain and Northern Ireland shall take part in such a decision insofar as it relates to the provisions of the Schengen *acquis* and the acts building upon it or otherwise related to it in which these Member States participate.

3.   The Agreements concluded by the Council under Article 6 of the Schengen Protocol shall be binding on the new Member States from 1 May 2004.

4.   The new Member States shall be required in respect of those conventions or instruments in the field of justice and home affairs which are inseparable from the attainment of the objectives of the EU Treaty:

(a)   to accede to those which, by 1 May 2004, have been opened for signature by the present Member States, and to those which have been drawn up by the Council in accordance with Title VI of the EU Treaty and recommended to the Member States for adoption;

(b)   to introduce administrative and other arrangements, such as those adopted by 1 May 2004 by the present Member States or by the Council, to facilitate practical co-operation between the Member States' institutions and organisations working in the field of justice and home affairs.

ARTICLE 4 (*ex Article 4 AA 2003*)

Each of the new Member States shall participate in Economic and Monetary Union from 1 May 2004 as a Member State with a derogation within the meaning of Article III-197 of the Constitution.

ARTICLE 5 (*ex Article 5 AA 2003*)

1.   The new Member States, which have acceded by the Act of Accession of 16 April 2003 to the decisions and agreements adopted by the Representatives of the Governments of the Member States, meeting within the Council, shall be required to accede to all other agreements concluded by the present Member States relating to the functioning of the Union or connected with the activities thereof.

2.   The new Member States shall be required to accede to the conventions provided for in Article 293 of the EC Treaty and to those that are inseparable from the attainment of the objectives of the EC Treaty, insofar as they are still in force, and also to the protocols on the interpretation of those conventions by the Court of Justice of the European Communities, signed by the present Member States, and to this end they shall be required to enter into negotiations with the present Member States in order to make the necessary adjustments thereto.

ARTICLE 6 (*ex Article 6 AA 2003*)

1.   The new Member States shall be required to accede, under the conditions laid down in this Protocol, to the agreements or conventions concluded or provisionally applied by the present Member States and the Union or the European Atomic Energy Community, acting jointly, and to the agreements concluded by those States which are related to those agreements or conventions.

The accession of the new Member States to the agreements or conventions mentioned in paragraph 4, as well as the agreements with Belarus, China, Chile, Mercosur and Switzerland which have been concluded or signed by the Community and its present Member States jointly shall be agreed by the conclusion of a protocol to such agreements or conventions between the Council, acting unanimously on behalf of the Member States, and the third country or countries or international organisation concerned. This procedure is without prejudice to the Union's and the European Atomic Energy Community's own competences and does not affect the allocation of powers between the Union and the European Atomic Energy Community and the Member States as regards the conclusion of such agreements in the future or any other amendments not related to accession. The Commission shall negotiate these protocols on behalf of the Member States on the basis of negotiating directives approved by the Council, acting by unanimity, and in consultation with a committee comprised of the representatives of the Member States. It shall submit a draft of the protocols for conclusion to the Council.

2.   Upon acceding to the agreements and conventions referred to in paragraph 1 the new Member States shall acquire the same rights and obligations under those agreements and conventions as the present Member States.

3.   The new Member States shall be required to accede, under the conditions laid down in this Protocol, to the Agreement on the European Economic Area [OJ L 1, 3.1.1994, p. 3], in accordance with Article 128 of that Agreement.

4.   As from 1 May 2004, and, where appropriate, pending the conclusion of the necessary protocols referred to in paragraph 1, the new Member States shall apply the provisions of the Agreements concluded by the present Member States and, jointly, the Community, with Algeria, Armenia, Azerbaijan, Bulgaria, Croatia, Egypt, the former Yugoslav Republic of Macedonia, Georgia, Israel, Jordan, Kazakhstan, Kyrgyzstan, Lebanon, Mexico, Moldova, Morocco, Romania, the Russian Federation, San Marino, South Africa, South Korea, Syria, Tunisia, Turkey, Turkmenistan, Ukraine and Uzbekistan as well as the provisions of other agreements concluded jointly by the present Member States and the Community before 1 May 2004.

Any adjustments to these Agreements shall be the subject of protocols concluded with the co-contracting countries in conformity with the provisions of the second subparagraph of paragraph 1. Should the protocols not have been concluded by 1 May 2004, the Union, the European Atomic Energy Community and the

Member States shall take, in the framework of their respective competences, the necessary measures to deal with that situation.

5.   As from 1 May 2004, the new Member States shall apply the bilateral textile agreements and arrangements concluded by the Community with third countries.
The quantitative restrictions applied by the Union on imports of textile and clothing products shall be adjusted to take account of the accession of the new Member States.
Should the amendments to the bilateral textile agreements and arrangements not have entered into force by 1 May 2004, the Union shall make the necessary adjustments to its rules for the import of textile and clothing products from third countries to take into account the accession of the new Member States.

6.   The quantitative restrictions applied by the Union on imports of steel and steel products shall be adjusted on the basis of imports by new Member States during the years immediately preceding the signing of the Accession Treaty of steel products originating in the supplier countries concerned.

7.   Fisheries agreements concluded before 1 May 2004 by the new Member States with third countries shall be managed by the Union.
The rights and obligations resulting for the new Member States from those agreements shall not be affected during the period in which the provisions of those agreements are provisionally maintained.
As soon as possible, and in any event before the expiry of the agreements referred to in the first subparagraph, appropriate European decisions for the continuation of fishing activities resulting from those agreements shall be adopted in each case by the Council on a proposal from the Commission, including the possibility of extending certain agreements for periods not exceeding one year.

8.   With effect from 1 May 2004, the new Member States shall withdraw from any free trade agreements with third countries, including the Central European Free Trade Agreement.
To the extent that agreements between one or more of the new Member States on the one hand, and one or more third countries on the other, are not compatible with the obligations arising from the Constitution and in particular from this Protocol, the new Member States shall take all appropriate steps to eliminate the incompatibilities established. If a new Member State encounters difficulties in adjusting an agreement concluded with one or more third countries before accession, it shall, according to the terms of the agreement, withdraw from that agreement.

9.   The new Member States shall take appropriate measures, where necessary, to adjust their position in relation to international organisations, and in relation to those international agreements to which the Union or the European Atomic Energy Community or other Member States are also parties, to the rights and obligations arising from their accession to the Union.
They shall in particular withdraw at 1 May 2004 or the earliest possible date thereafter from international fisheries agreements and organisations to which the Union is also a party, unless their membership relates to matters other than fisheries.

ARTICLE 7 (*ex Article 8 AA 2003*)
Acts adopted by the institutions to which the transitional provisions laid down in this Protocol relate shall retain their status in law; in particular, the procedures for amending those acts shall continue to apply.

ARTICLE 8 (*ex Article 9 AA 2003*)
Provisions of the Act of Accession of 16 April 2003, as interpreted by the Court of Justice of the European Communities and the Court of First Instance, the purpose or effect of which is to repeal or amend, otherwise than as a transitional measure, acts adopted by the institutions, bodies, offices or agencies of the Community or of the European Union established by the Treaty on European Union shall remain in force subject to the application of the second paragraph.
These provisions shall have the same status in law as the acts which they repeal or amend and shall be subject to the same rules as those acts.

ARTICLE 9 (*ex Article 58 AA 2003*)
The texts of the acts of the institutions, bodies, offices and agencies of the Community or of the European Union established by the Treaty on European Union and the texts of acts of the European Central Bank which were adopted before 1 May 2004 and which were drawn up in the Czech, Estonian, Latvian, Lithuanian, Hungarian, Maltese, Polish, Slovenian and Slovak languages shall be authentic from that date, under the same conditions as the texts drawn up and authentic in the other languages.

ARTICLE 10 (*new*)

A European law of the Council may repeal the transitional provisions set out in this Protocol, when they are no longer applicable. The Council shall act unanimously after consulting the European Parliament.

ARTICLE 11 (*ex Article 10 AA 2003*)

The application of the Constitution and acts adopted by the institutions shall, as a transitional measure, be subject to the derogations provided for in this Protocol.

TITLE II

PERMANENT PROVISIONS

ARTICLE 12 (*ex Article 21 AA 2003*)

The adaptations to the acts listed in Annex III to the Act of Accession of 16 April 2003 made necessary by accession shall be drawn up in conformity with the guidelines set out in that Annex and in accordance with the procedure and under the conditions laid down in Article 36.

ARTICLE 13 (*ex Article 22 AA 2003*)

The measures listed in Annex IV to the Act of Accession of 16 April 2003 shall be applied under the conditions laid down in that Annex.

ARTICLE 14 (*ex Article 23 AA 2003*)

A European law of the Council may make the adaptations to the provisions of this Protocol relating to the common agricultural policy which may prove necessary as a result of a modification of Union law. The Council shall act unanimously after consulting the European Parliament.

TITLE III

TEMPORARY PROVISIONS

ARTICLE 15 (*ex Article 24 AA 2003*)

The measures listed in Annexes V, VI, VII, VIII, IX, X, XI, XII, XIII and XIV to the Act of Accession of 16 April 2003 shall apply in respect of the new Member States under the conditions laid down in those Annexes.

ARTICLE 16 (*ex Article 27 AA 2003*)

1. The revenue designated as "Common Customs Tariff duties and other duties" referred to in Article 2(1)(b) of Council Decision 2000/597/EC, Euratom of 29 September 2000 on the system of the European Communities' own resources [OJ L 253, 7.10.2000, p. 42], or the corresponding provision in any Decision replacing it, shall include the customs duties calculated on the basis of the rates resulting from the Common Customs Tariff and any tariff concession relating thereto applied by the Union in the new Member States' trade with third countries.

2. For the year 2004, the harmonised VAT assessment base and the GNI (gross national income) base of each new Member State, referred to in Article 2(1)(c) and (d) of Council Decision 2000/597/EC, Euratom shall be equal to two thirds of the annual base. The GNI base of each new Member State to be taken into account for the calculation of the financing of the correction in respect of budgetary imbalances granted to the United Kingdom, referred to in Article 5(1) of Council Decision 2000/597/EC, Euratom shall likewise be equal to two thirds of the annual base.

3. For the purposes of determining the frozen rate for 2004 according to Article 2(4)(b) of Council Decision 2000/597/EC, Euratom the capped VAT bases of the new Member States shall be calculated on the basis of two thirds of their uncapped VAT base and two thirds of their GNI.

ARTICLE 17 (*ex Article 28 AA 2003*)

1. The budget of the Union for the financial year 2004 shall be adapted to take into account the accession of the new Member States through an amending budget taking effect on 1 May 2004.

2. The twelve monthly twelfths of VAT and GNI-based resources to be paid by the new Member States under the amending budget referred to in paragraph 1, as well as the retroactive adjustment of the monthly twelfths for the period January-April 2004 that only apply to the present Member States, shall be converted into eighths to be called during the period May-December 2004. The retroactive adjustments that result from

any subsequent amending budget adopted in 2004 shall likewise be converted into equal parts to be called during the remainder of the year.

ARTICLE 18 (*ex Article 29 AA 2003*)
On the first working day of each month the Union shall pay the Czech Republic, Cyprus, Malta and Slovenia, as an item of expenditure under the Union budget, one eighth in 2004, as of 1 May 2004, and one twelfth in 2005 and 2006 of the following amounts of temporary budgetary compensation:

	2004	2005	2006
		(€ million, 1999 prices)	
Czech Republic	125.4	178.0	85.1
Cyprus	68.9	119.2	112.3
Malta	37.8	65.6	62.9
Slovenia	29.5	66.4	35.5

ARTICLE 19 (*ex Article 30 AA 2003*)
On the first working day of each month the Union shall pay the Czech Republic, Estonia, Cyprus, Latvia, Lithuania, Hungary, Malta, Poland, Slovenia and Slovakia, as an item of expenditure under the Union budget, one eighth in 2004, as of 1 May 2004, and one twelfth in 2005 and 2006 of the following amounts of a special lump-sum cash-flow facility:

	2004	2005	2006
	(€ million, 1999 prices)		
Czech Republic	174.70	91.55	91.55
Estonia	15.80	2.90	2.90
Cyprus	27.70	5.05	5.05
Latvia	19.50	3.40	3.40
Lithuania	34.80	6.30	6.30
Hungary	155.30	27.95	27.95
Malta	12.20	27.15	27.15
Poland	442.80	550.00	450.00
Slovenia	65.40	17.85	17.85
Slovakia	63.20	11.35	11.35

€1 thousand million for Poland and €100 million for the Czech Republic included in the special lump-sum cash-flow facility shall be taken into account for any calculations on the distribution of Structural Funds for the years 2004, 2005 and 2006.

ARTICLE 20 (*ex Article 31 AA 2003*)
1.   The new Member States listed below shall pay the following amounts to the Research Fund for Coal and Steel referred to in Decision 2002/234/ECSC of the Representatives of the Governments of the Member States, meeting within the Council, of 27 February 2002 on the financial consequences of the expiry of the ECSC Treaty and on the Research Fund for Coal and Steel [OJ L 79, 22.3.2002, p. 42]:

	(€ million, current prices)
Czech Republic	39.88
Estonia	2.50
Latvia	2.69
Hungary	9.93
Poland	92.46
Slovenia	2.36
Slovakia	20.11

2.   The contributions to the Research Fund for Coal and Steel shall be made in four instalments starting in 2006 and paid as follows, in each case on the first working day of the first month of each year:

2006:	15%
2007:	20%
2008:	30%
2009:	35%.

ARTICLE 21 (*ex Article 32 AA 2003*)

1.   Save as otherwise provided for in this Protocol, no financial commitments shall be made under the Phare programme [Regulation (EEC) No 3906/89 (OJ L 375, 23.12.1989, p. 11)], the Phare Cross-Border Co-operation programme [Regulation (EC) No 2760/98 (OJ L 345, 19.12.1998, p. 49)], pre-accession funds for Cyprus and Malta [Regulation (EC) No 555/2000 (OJ L 68, 16.3.2000, p. 3)], the ISPA programme [Regulation (EC) No 1267/1999 (OJ L 161, 26.6.1999, p. 73)] and the SAPARD programme [Regulation (EC) No 1268/1999 (OJ L 161, 26.6.1999, p. 87)] in favour of the new Member States after 31 December 2003. The new Member States shall receive the same treatment as the present Member States as regards expenditure under the first three Headings of the Financial Perspective, as defined in the Inter-institutional Agreement of 6 May 1999 [Inter-institutional Agreement of 6 May 1999 between the European Parliament, the Council and the Commission on budgetary discipline and improvement of the budgetary procedure (OJ C 172, 18.6.1999, p. 1)], as from 1 January 2004, subject to the individual specifications and exceptions below or as otherwise provided for in this Protocol. The maximum additional appropriations for headings 1, 2, 3 and 5 of the Financial Perspective related to enlargement are set out in Annex XV to the Act of Accession of 16 April 2003. However, no financial commitment under the 2004 budget for any programme or agency concerned may be made before the accession of the relevant new Member State has taken place.

2.   Paragraph 1 shall not apply to expenditure under the European Agricultural Guidance and Guarantee Fund, Guarantee Section, according to Articles 2(1), 2(2), and 3(3) of Council Regulation (EC) No 1258/1999 of 17 May 1999 on the financing of the common agricultural policy [OJ L 160, 26.6.1999, p. 103], which will become eligible for Community funding only from 1 May 2004, in accordance with Article 2 of this Protocol. However, paragraph 1 of this Article shall apply to expenditure for rural development under the European Agricultural Guidance and Guarantee Fund, Guarantee Section, according to Article 47a of Council Regulation (EC) No 1257/1999 of 17 May 1999 on support for rural development from the European Agricultural Guidance and Guarantee Fund (EAGGF) and amending and repealing certain regulations [OJ L 160, 26.6.1999, p. 80], subject to the conditions set out in the amendment of that Regulation in Annex II to the Act of Accession of 16 April 2003.

3.   Subject to the last sentence of paragraph 1, as of 1 January 2004, the new Member States shall participate in Union programmes and agencies according to the same terms and conditions as the present Member States with funding from the general budget of the Union.

4.   If any measures are necessary to facilitate the transition from the pre-accession regime to that resulting from the application of this Article, the Commission shall adopt the required measures.

ARTICLE 22 (*ex Article 33 AA 2003*)

1.   Tendering, contracting, implementation and payments for pre-accession assistance under the Phare programme, the Phare Cross-Border Co-operation programme and pre-accession funds for Cyprus and Malta shall be managed by implementing agencies in the new Member States as from 1 May 2004.

The Commission shall adopt European decisions to waive the ex-ante control by the Commission over tendering and contracting following a positively assessed Extended Decentralised Implementation System (EDIS) in accordance with the criteria and conditions laid down in the Annex to Council Regulation (EC) No 1266/1999 of 21 June 1999 on co-ordinating aid to the applicant countries in the framework of the pre-accession strategy and amending Regulation (EEC) No 3906/89 [OJ L 232, 2.9.1999, p. 34].

If these decisions to waive ex-ante control have not been adopted before 1 May 2004, any contracts signed between 1 May 2004 and the date on which the Commission decisions are taken shall not be eligible for pre-accession assistance.

However, exceptionally, if the Commission decisions to waive ex-ante control are delayed beyond 1 May 2004 for reasons not attributable to the authorities of a new Member State, the Commission may accept, in duly justified cases, eligibility for pre-accession assistance of contracts signed between 1 May 2004 and the date of these decisions, and the continued implementation of pre-accession assistance for a limited period, subject to ex-ante control by the Commission over tendering and contracting.

2.   Global budget commitments made before 1 May 2004 under the pre-accession financial instruments referred to in paragraph 1, including the conclusion and registration of subsequent individual legal commitments and payments made after 1 May 2004, shall continue to be governed by the rules and regulations of the pre-accession financing instruments and be charged to the corresponding budget chapters until closure of the programmes and projects concerned. Notwithstanding this, public procurement procedures initiated after 1 May 2004 shall be carried out in accordance with the relevant Union acts.

3.   The last programming exercise for the pre-accession assistance referred to in paragraph 1 shall take place in the last full calendar year preceding 1 May 2004. Actions under these programmes will have to be contracted within the following two years and disbursements made as provided for in the Financing

Memorandum [As set out in the Phare Guidelines (SEC (1999) 1596, updated on 6.9.2002 by C 3303/2)], usually by the end of the third year after the commitment. No extensions shall be granted for the contracting period. Exceptionally and in duly justified cases, limited extensions in terms of duration may be granted for disbursement.

4.   In order to ensure the necessary phasing out of the pre-accession financial instruments referred to in paragraph 1 as well as the ISPA programme, and a smooth transition from the rules applicable before and after 1 May 2004, the Commission may take all appropriate measures to ensure that the necessary statutory staff is maintained in the new Member States for a maximum of fifteen months following that date. During this period, officials assigned to posts in the new Member States before accession and who are required to remain in service in those States after 1 May 2004 shall benefit, as an exception, from the same financial and material conditions as were applied by the Commission before 1 May 2004 in accordance with Annex X to the Staff Regulations of officials and the conditions of employment of other servants of the European Communities laid down in Regulation (EEC, Euratom, ECSC) No 259/68 [OJ L 56, 4.3.1968, p. 1]. The administrative expenditure, including salaries for other staff, necessary for the management of the pre-accession assistance shall be covered, for all of 2004 and until the end of July 2005, under the heading "support expenditure for operations" (former part B of the budget) or equivalent headings for the financial instruments referred to in paragraph 1 as well as the ISPA programme, of the relevant pre-accession budgets.

5.   Where projects approved under Regulation (EC) No 1258/1999 can no longer be funded under that instrument, they may be integrated into rural development programming and financed under the European Agricultural Guidance and Guarantee Fund. Should specific transitional measures be necessary in this regard, these shall be adopted by the Commission in accordance with the procedures laid down in Article 50(2) of Council Regulation (EC) No 1260/1999 of 21 June 1999 laying down general provisions on the Structural Funds [OJ L 161, 26.6.1999, p. 1].

ARTICLE 23 (*ex Article 34 AA 2003*)
1.   Between 1 May 2004 and the end of 2006, the Union shall provide temporary financial assistance, hereinafter referred to as the "Transition Facility", to the new Member States to develop and strengthen their administrative capacity to implement and enforce Union and European Atomic Energy Community law and to foster exchange of best practice among peers.

2.   Assistance shall address the continued need for strengthening institutional capacity in certain areas through action which cannot be financed by the Structural Funds, in particular in the following areas:
(a)   justice and home affairs (strengthening of the judicial system, external border controls, anti-corruption strategy, strengthening of law enforcement capacities);
(b)   financial control;
(c)   protection of the financial interests of the Union and of the European Atomic Energy Community and the fight against fraud;
(d)   internal market, including customs union;
(e)   environment;
(f)   veterinary services and administrative capacity-building relating to food safety;
(g)   administrative and control structures for agriculture and rural development, including the Integrated Administration and Control System (IACS);
(h)   nuclear safety (strengthening the effectiveness and competence of nuclear safety authorities and their technical support organisations as well as public radioactive waste management agencies);
(i)   statistics;
(j)   strengthening public administration according to needs identified in the Commission's comprehensive monitoring report which are not covered by the Structural Funds.

3.   Assistance under the Transition Facility shall be decided in accordance with the procedure laid down in Article 8 of Council Regulation (EEC) No 3906/89 of 18 December 1989 on economic aid to certain countries of Central and Eastern Europe [OJ L 375, 23.12.1989, p. 11].

4.   The programme shall be implemented in accordance with Article 53(1)(a) and (b) of the Financial Regulation applicable to the general budget of the European Communities [Regulation (EC, Euratom) No 1605/2002 (OJ L 248, 16.9.2002, p. 1)] or the European law replacing it. For twinning projects between public administrations for the purpose of institution-building, the procedure for call for proposals through the network of contact points in the Member States shall continue to apply, as established in the Framework Agreements with the present Member States for the purpose of pre-accession assistance.
The commitment appropriations for the Transition Facility, at 1999 prices, shall be €200 million in 2004, €120 million in 2005 and €60 million in 2006. The annual appropriations shall be authorised by the budgetary

authority within the limits of the Financial Perspective as defined by the Inter-institutional Agreement of 6 May 1999.

ARTICLE 24 (*ex Article 35 AA 2003*)

1.   A Schengen Facility is hereby created as a temporary instrument to help beneficiary Member States between 1 May 2004 and the end of 2006 to finance actions at the new external borders of the Union for the implementation of the Schengen *acquis* and external border control.

In order to address the shortcomings identified in the preparation for participation in Schengen, the following types of action shall be eligible for financing under the Schengen Facility:

(a)   investment in construction, renovation or upgrading of border-crossing infrastructure and related buildings;

(b)   investments in any kind of operating equipment (e.g. laboratory equipment, detection tools, Schengen Information System – SIS II hardware and software, means of transport);

(c)   training of border guards;

(d)   support to costs for logistics and operations.

2.   The following amounts shall be made available under the Schengen Facility in the form of lump-sum grant payments as of 1 May 2004 to the beneficiary Member States listed below:

	2004	2005	2006
		(€ million, 1999 prices)	
Estonia	22.90	22.90	22.90
Latvia	23.70	23.70	23.70
Lithuania	44.78	61.07	29.85
Hungary	49.30	49.30	49.30
Poland	93.34	93.33	93.33
Slovenia	35.64	35.63	35.63
Slovakia	15.94	15.93	15.93

3.   The beneficiary Member States shall be responsible for selecting and implementing individual operations in compliance with this Article. They shall also be responsible for co-ordinating use of the Schengen Facility with assistance from other Union instruments, ensuring compatibility with Union policies and measures and compliance with the Financial Regulation applicable to the general budget of the European Communities or with the European law replacing it.

The lump-sum grant payments shall be used within three years from the first payment and any unused or unjustifiably spent funds shall be recovered by the Commission. The beneficiary Member States shall submit, no later than six months after expiry of the three-year deadline, a comprehensive report on the financial execution of the lump-sum grant payments with a statement justifying the expenditure.

The beneficiary State shall exercise this responsibility without prejudice to the Commission's responsibility for the implementation of the Union's budget and in accordance with the provisions applicable to decentralised management in the said Financial Regulation or in the European law replacing it.

4.   The Commission retains the right of verification, through the Anti-Fraud Office (OLAF). The Commission and the Court of Auditors may also carry out on-the-spot checks in accordance with the appropriate procedures.

5.   The Commission may adopt any technical provisions necessary for the operation of the Schengen Facility.

ARTICLE 25 (*ex Article 36 AA 2003*)

The amounts referred to in Articles 18, 19, 23 and 24 shall be adjusted each year, as part of the technical adjustment provided for in paragraph 15 of the Interinstitutional Agreement of 6 May 1999.

ARTICLE 26 (*ex Article 37 AA 2003*)

1.   If, until the end of a period of up to three years after 1 May 2004, difficulties arise which are serious and liable to persist in any sector of the economy or which could bring about serious deterioration in the economic situation of a given area, a new Member State may apply for authorisation to take protective measures in order to rectify the situation and adjust the sector concerned to the economy of the internal market.

In the same circumstances, any present Member State may apply for authorisation to take protective measures with regard to one or more of the new Member States.

2.   Upon request by the State concerned, the Commission shall, by emergency procedure, adopt the European regulations or decisions establishing the protective measures which it considers necessary, specifying the conditions and modalities under which they are to be put into effect.

In the event of serious economic difficulties and at the express request of the Member State concerned, the Commission shall act within five working days of the receipt of the request accompanied by the relevant background information. The measures thus decided on shall be applicable forthwith, shall take account of the interests of all parties concerned and shall not entail frontier controls.

3.   The measures authorised under paragraph 2 may involve derogations from the rules of the Constitution, and in particular from this Protocol, to such an extent and for such periods as are strictly necessary in order to attain the objectives referred to in paragraph 1. Priority shall be given to such measures as will least disturb the functioning of the internal market.

ARTICLE 27 (*ex Article 38 AA 2003*)

If a new Member State has failed to implement commitments undertaken in the context of the accession negotiations, causing a serious breach of the functioning of the internal market, including any commitments in all sectoral policies which concern economic activities with cross-border effect, or an imminent risk of such breach, the Commission may, until the end of a period of up to three years after 1 May 2004, upon the motivated request of a Member State or on its own initiative, adopt European regulations or decisions establishing appropriate measures.

Measures shall be proportional and priority shall be given to measures which least disturb the functioning of the internal market and, where appropriate, to the application of the existing sectoral safeguard mechanisms. Such safeguard measures shall not be invoked as a means of arbitrary discrimination or a disguised restriction on trade between Member States. The measures shall be maintained no longer than strictly necessary, and, in any case, will be lifted when the relevant commitment is implemented. They may however be applied beyond the period specified in the first paragraph as long as the relevant commitments have not been fulfilled. In response to progress made by the new Member State concerned in fulfilling its commitments, the Commission may adapt the measures as appropriate. The Commission shall inform the Council in good time before revoking the European regulations or decisions establishing the safeguard measures, and it shall take duly into account any observations of the Council in this respect.

ARTICLE 28 (*ex Article 39 AA 2003*)

If there are serious shortcomings or any imminent risks of such shortcomings in a new Member State in the transposition, state of implementation or the application of the framework decisions or any other relevant commitments, instruments of co-operation and decisions relating to mutual recognition in the area of criminal law under Title VI of the EU Treaty, Directives and Regulations relating to mutual recognition in civil matters under Title IV of the EC Treaty, and European laws and framework laws adopted on the basis of Sections 3 and 4 of Chapter IV of Title III of Part III of the Constitution, the Commission may, until the end of a period of up to three years after 1 May 2004, upon the motivated request of a Member State or on its own initiative and after consulting the Member States, adopt European regulations or decisions establishing appropriate measures and specify the conditions and modalities under which these measures are put into effect.

These measures may take the form of temporary suspension of the application of relevant provisions and decisions in the relations between a new Member State and any other Member State or Member States, without prejudice to the continuation of close judicial co-operation. The measures shall be maintained no longer than strictly necessary, and, in any case, will be lifted when the shortcomings are remedied. They may however be applied beyond the period specified in the first paragraph as long as these shortcomings persist. In response to progress made by the new Member State concerned in rectifying the identified shortcomings, the Commission may adapt the adopted measures as appropriate after consulting the Member States. The Commission shall inform the Council in good time before revoking safeguard measures, and it shall take duly into account any observations of the Council in this respect.

ARTICLE 29 (*ex Article 40 AA 2003*)

In order not to hamper the proper functioning of the internal market, the enforcement of the new Member States' national rules during the transitional periods referred to in Annexes V to XIV to the Act of Accession of 16 April 2003 shall not lead to border controls between Member States.

ARTICLE 30 (*ex Article 41 AA 2003*)

If transitional measures are necessary to facilitate the transition from the existing regime in the new Member States to that resulting from the application of the common agricultural policy under the conditions set out in this Protocol, such measures shall be adopted by the Commission in accordance with the procedure referred to in Article 42(2) of Council Regulation (EC) No 1260/2001 of 19 June 2001 on the common organisation of the markets in the sugar sector [OJ L 178, 30.6.2001, p. 1], or as appropriate, in the corresponding Articles of the other Regulations on the common organisation of agricultural markets or of the European laws replacing them or the relevant procedure as determined in the applicable legislation. The transitional measures referred to in this Article may be adopted during a period of three years after 1 May 2004 and their application shall be limited to that period. A European law of the Council may extend this period. The Council shall act unanimously after consulting the European Parliament.

ARTICLE 31 (*ex Article 42 AA 2003*)

If transitional measures are necessary to facilitate the transition from the existing regime in the new Member States to that resulting from the application of the Union veterinary and phytosanitary rules, such measures shall be adopted by the Commission in accordance with the relevant procedure as determined in the applicable legislation. These measures shall be taken during a period of three years after 1 May 2004 and their application shall be limited to that period.

ARTICLE 32 (*ex Article 52 AA 2003*)

1.   The terms of office of the new members of the Committees, groups and other bodies listed in Annex XVI to the Act of Accession of 16 April 2003 shall expire at the same time as those of the members in office on 1 May 2004.

2.   The terms of office of the new members of the Committees and groups set up by the Commission which are listed in Annex XVII to the Act of Accession of 16 April 2003 shall expire at the same time as those of the members in office on 1 May 2004.

TITLE IV

APPLICABILITY OF THE ACTS OF THE INSTITUTIONS

ARTICLE 33 (*ex Article 53 AA 2003*)

As from 1 May 2004, the new Member States shall be considered as being addressees of directives and decisions within the meaning of Article 249 of the EC Treaty and of Article 161 of the EAEC Treaty, provided that those directives and decisions have been addressed to all the present Member States. Except with regard to directives and decisions which enter into force pursuant to Article 254(1) and (2) of the EC Treaty, the new Member States shall be considered as having received notification of such directives and decisions upon 1 May 2004.

ARTICLE 34 (*ex Article 54 AA 2003*)

The new Member States shall put into effect the measures necessary for them to comply, from 1 May 2004, with the provisions of directives and decisions within the meaning of Article 249 of the EC Treaty and of Article 161 of the EAEC Treaty, unless another time-limit is provided for in the Annexes referred to in Article 15 or in any other provisions of this Protocol.

ARTICLE 35 (*ex Article 56 AA 2003*)

Unless otherwise stipulated, the Council, on a proposal from the Commission, shall adopt the necessary European regulations and decisions to implement the provisions contained in Annexes III and IV to the Act of Accession of 16 April 2003 referred to in Articles 12 and 13 of this Protocol.

ARTICLE 36 (*ex Article 57 AA 2003*)

1.   Where acts of the institutions prior to 1 May 2004 require adaptation by reason of accession, and the necessary adaptations have not been provided for in this Protocol, those adaptations shall be made in accordance with the procedure laid down by paragraph 2. Those adaptations shall enter into force as from 1 May 2004.

2.   The Council, on a proposal from the Commission, or the Commission, according to which of these two institutions adopted the original acts, shall to this end adopt the necessary acts.

ARTICLE 37 (*ex Article 59 AA 2003*)

Provisions laid down by law, regulation or administrative action designed to ensure the protection of the health of workers and the general public in the territory of the new Member States against the dangers arising from ionising radiations shall, in accordance with Article 33 of the EAEC Treaty, be communicated by those States to the Commission within three months from 1 May 2004.

PART TWO

PROVISIONS ON THE PROTOCOLS ANNEXED TO THE ACT OF ACCESSION OF 16 APRIL 2003

TITLE I

TRANSITIONAL PROVISIONS ON THE EUROPEAN INVESTMENT BANK

ARTICLE 38 (*ex Article 2 of Protocol No 1 AA 2003*)
The Kingdom of Spain shall pay the amount of €309,686,775 as its share of the capital paid in for the subscribed capital increase. This contribution shall be paid in eight equal instalments falling due on 30 September 2004, 30 September 2005, 30 September 2006, 31 March 2007, 30 September 2007, 31 March 2008, 30 September 2008 and 31 March 2009.
The Kingdom of Spain shall contribute, in eight equal instalments falling due on those dates, to the reserves and provisions equivalent to reserves, as well as to the amount still to be appropriated to the reserves and provisions, comprising the balance of the profit and loss account, established at the end of the month of April 2004, as entered on the balance sheet of the Bank, in amounts corresponding to 4.1292% of the reserves and provisions.

ARTICLE 39 (*ex Article 3 of Protocol No 1 AA 2003*)
From 1 May 2004, the new Member States shall pay the following amounts corresponding to their share of the capital paid in for the subscribed capital as defined in Article 4 of the Statute of the European Investment Bank.

Poland	€ 170,563,175
Czech Republic	€ 62,939,275
Hungary	€ 59,543,425
Slovakia	€ 21,424,525
Slovenia	€ 19,890,750
Lithuania	€ 12,480,875
Cyprus	€ 9,169,100
Latvia	€ 7,616,750
Estonia	€ 5,882,000
Malta	€ 3,490,200

These contributions shall be paid in eight equal instalments falling due on 30 September 2004, 30 September 2005, 30 September 2006, 31 March 2007, 30 September 2007, 31 March 2008, 30 September 2008 and 31 March 2009.

ARTICLE 40 (*ex Article 4 of Protocol No 1 AA 2003*)
The new Member States shall contribute, in eight equal instalments falling due on the dates referred to in Article 39, to the reserves and provisions equivalent to reserves, as well as to the amount still to be appropriated to the reserves and provisions, comprising the balance of the profit and loss account, established at the end of the month of April 2004, as entered on the balance sheet of the European Investment Bank, in amounts corresponding to the following percentages of the reserves and provisions:

Poland	2.2742%
Czech Republic	0.8392%
Hungary	0.7939%
Slovakia	0.2857%
Slovenia	0.2652%
Lithuania	0.1664%
Cyprus	0.1223%
Latvia	0.1016%
Estonia	0.0784%
Malta	0.0465%

ARTICLE 41 (*ex Article 5 of Protocol No 1 AA 2003*)
The capital and payments provided for in Articles 38, 39 and 40 shall be paid in by the Kingdom of Spain and the new Member States in cash in euro, save by way of derogation decided unanimously by the Board of Governors.

TITLE II

PROVISIONS ON THE RESTRUCTURING OF THE CZECH STEEL INDUSTRY

ARTICLE 42 (*ex Protocol No 2 AA 2003*)

1.   Notwithstanding Articles III-167 and III-168 of the Constitution, State aid granted by the Czech Republic for restructuring purposes to specified parts of the Czech steel industry from 1997 to 2003 shall be deemed to be compatible with the internal market provided that:

(a)   the period provided for in Article 8(4) of Protocol 2 on ECSC products to the Europe Agreement establishing an association between the European Communities and their Member States, of the one part, and the Czech Republic, of the other part [OJ L 360, 31.12.1994, p. 2], has been extended until 1 May 2004;

(b)   the terms set out in the restructuring plan on the basis of which the abovementioned Protocol was extended are adhered to throughout the period 2002-2006;

(c)   the conditions set out in this Title are met, and

(d)   no State aid for restructuring is to be paid to the Czech steel industry after 1 May 2004.

2.   Restructuring of the Czech steel sector, as described in the individual business plans of the companies listed in Annex 1 to Protocol No 2 to the Act of Accession of 16 April 2003 (hereinafter referred to as "benefiting companies"), and in line with the conditions set out in this Title, shall be completed no later than 31 December 2006 (hereinafter referred to as "the end of the restructuring period").

3.   Only benefiting companies shall be eligible for State aid in the framework of the Czech steel restructuring programme.

4.   A benefiting company may not:

(a)   in the case of a merger with a company not included in Annex 1 to Protocol No 2 to the Act of Accession of 16 April 2003, pass on the benefit of the aid granted to the benefiting company;

(b)   take over the assets of any company not included in Annex 1 to Protocol No 2 to the Act of Accession of 16 April 2003 which is declared bankrupt in the period up to 31 December 2006.

5.   Any subsequent privatisation of any of the benefiting companies shall respect the conditions and principles regarding viability, State aids and capacity reduction defined in this Title.

6.   The total restructuring aid to be granted to the benefiting companies shall be determined by the justifications set out in the approved Czech steel restructuring plan and individual business plans as approved by the Council. But in any case, the aid paid out in the period 1997-2003 is limited to a maximum amount of CZK 14,147,425,201. Of this total figure, Nová Huť receives a maximum of CZK 5,700,075,201, Vítkovice Steel receives a maximum of CZK 8,155,350,000 and Válcovny Plechu Frýdek Místek receives a maximum of CZK 292,000,000 depending on the requirements as set out in the approved restructuring plan. The aid shall only be granted once. No further State aid shall be granted by the Czech Republic for restructuring purposes to the Czech steel industry.

7.   The net capacity reduction to be achieved by the Czech Republic for finished products during the period 1997-2006 shall be 590,000 tonnes.
Capacity reduction shall be measured only on the basis of permanent closure of production facilities by physical destruction such that the facilities cannot be restored to service. A declaration of bankruptcy of a steel company shall not qualify as capacity reduction.
The above level of net capacity reduction, together with any other capacity reductions identified as necessary in the restructuring programmes, shall be completed in line with the timetable in Annex 2 to Protocol No 2 to the Act of Accession of 16 April 2003.

8.   The Czech Republic shall remove trade barriers in the coal market in accordance with the *acquis* by accession, enabling Czech steel companies to obtain access to coal at international market prices.

9.   The business plan for the benefiting company Nová Huť shall be implemented. In particular:

(a)   the Vysoké Pece Ostrava (VPO) plant shall be brought into the organisational framework of Nová Huť by acquisition of full ownership. A target date shall be set for this merger, including assignation of responsibility for its implementation;

(b)   restructuring efforts shall concentrate on the following:

        (i)   evolving Nová Huť from being production-oriented to being marketing-oriented and improving the efficiency and effectiveness of its business management, including greater transparency on costs;

    (ii)   Nová Huť reviewing its product mix and entry into higher added-value markets;

    (iii)   Nová Huť making the necessary investments in order to achieve a higher quality of finished products in the short term;

(c)   employment restructuring shall be implemented; levels of productivity comparable to those obtained by the Union's steel industry product groups shall be reached as at 31 December 2006, on the basis of the consolidated figures of the benefiting companies concerned;

(d)   compliance with the relevant Community *acquis* in the field of environmental protection shall be achieved by 1 May 2004 including the necessary investments addressed in the business plan. In accordance with the business plan the necessary future IPPC-related investment shall also be made, in order to ensure compliance with Council Directive 96/61/EC of 24 September 1996 concerning integrated pollution prevention and control [OJ L 257, 10.10.1996, p. 26] by 1 November 2007.

10.   The business plan for the benefiting company Vítkovice Steel shall be implemented. In particular:

(a)   the Duo Mill shall be permanently closed no later than 31 December 2006. In the event of purchase of the company by a strategic investor, the purchase contract shall be made conditional on this closure by this date;

(b)   restructuring efforts shall concentrate on the following:

    (i)   an increase in direct sales and a greater focus on cost reduction, this being essential for more efficient business management,

    (ii)   adapting to market demand and shifting towards higher value-added products,

    (iii) bringing forward the proposed investment in the secondary steel-making process from 2004 to 2003, in order to allow the company to compete on quality rather than on price;

(c)   compliance with the relevant Community *acquis* in the field of environmental protection shall be achieved by 1 May 2004 including the necessary investments addressed in the business plan, which include the need for future IPPC-related investment.

11.   The business plan for the benefiting company Válcovny Plechu Frýdek Místek (VPFM) shall be implemented. In particular:

(a)   Hot Rolling Mills Nos 1 and 2 shall be permanently closed at the end of 2004;

(b)   restructuring efforts shall concentrate on the following:

    (i)   making the necessary investment in order to reach a higher quality of finished product in the short term after the signing of the Treaty of Accession,

    (ii)   giving priority to the implementation of key identified profit improvement opportunities (including employment restructuring, cost reductions, yield improvements and distribution reorientation).

12.   Any subsequent changes in the overall restructuring plan and the individual plans must be agreed by the Commission and, where appropriate, by the Council.

13.   The implementation of the restructuring shall take place under conditions of full transparency and on the basis of sound market economy principles.

14.   The Commission and the Council shall closely monitor the implementation of the restructuring and the fulfilment of the conditions set out in this Title concerning viability, State aid and capacity reductions before and after 1 May 2004 until the end of the restructuring period, in accordance with paragraphs 15 to 18. For this purpose the Commission shall report to the Council.

15.   The Commission and the Council shall monitor the restructuring benchmarks set out in Annex 3 to Protocol No 2 to the Act of Accession of 16 April 2003. The references in that Annex to paragraph 16 of the said Protocol shall be construed as being made to paragraph 16 of this Article.

16.   Monitoring shall include an independent evaluation to be carried out in 2003, 2004, 2005 and 2006. The Commission's viability test shall be an important element in ensuring that viability is achieved.

17.   The Czech Republic shall co-operate fully with all the arrangements for monitoring. In particular:

(a)   the Czech Republic shall supply the Commission with six-monthly reports concerning the restructuring of the benefiting companies, no later than 15 March and 15 September of each year, until the end of the restructuring period,

(b)   the first report shall reach the Commission by 15 March 2003 and the last report by 15 March 2007, unless the Commission decides otherwise,

(c)   the reports shall contain all the information necessary to monitor the restructuring process and the reduction and use of capacity and shall provide sufficient financial data to allow an assessment to be made of whether the conditions and requirements contained in this Title have been fulfilled. The reports shall at the least contain the information set out in Annex 4 to Protocol No 2 to the Act of Accession of 16 April 2003, which the Commission reserves the right to modify in line with its experiences during the monitoring process. In addition to the individual business reports of the benefiting companies, there shall also be a report on the overall situation of the Czech steel sector, including recent macroeconomic developments,

(d)   the Czech Republic shall oblige the benefiting companies to disclose all relevant data which might, under other circumstances, be considered as confidential. In its reporting to the Council, the Commission shall ensure that company-specific confidential information is not disclosed.

18.   The Commission may at any time decide to mandate an independent consultant to evaluate the monitoring results, undertake any research necessary and report to the Commission and the Council.

19.   If the Commission establishes, on the basis of the reports referred to in paragraph 17, that substantial deviations from the financial data on which the viability assessment has been made have occurred, it may require the Czech Republic to take appropriate measures to reinforce the restructuring measures of the benefiting companies concerned.

20.   Should the monitoring show that:
(a)   the conditions for the transitional arrangements contained in this Title have not been fulfilled, or that
(b)   the commitments made in the framework of the extension of the period during which the Czech Republic may exceptionally grant State support for the restructuring of its steel industry under the Europe Agreement establishing an association between the European Communities and their Member States, of the one part, and the Czech Republic, of the other part [OJ L 360, 31.12.1994, p. 2] have not been fulfilled, or that
(c)   the Czech Republic in the course of the restructuring period has granted additional incompatible State aid to the steel industry and to the benefiting companies in particular,
the transitional arrangements contained in this Title shall not have effect.
The Commission shall take appropriate steps requiring any company concerned to reimburse any aid granted in breach of the conditions laid down in this Title.

TITLE III

PROVISIONS ON THE SOVEREIGN BASE AREAS OF THE UNITED KINGDOM OF GREAT BRITAIN AND NORTHERN IRELAND IN CYPRUS

ARTICLE 43 (*ex Article 2 of Protocol No 3 AA 2003*)
1.   The Sovereign Base Areas shall be included within the customs territory of the Union and, for this purpose, the customs and common commercial policy acts of the Union listed in Part One of the Annex to Protocol No 3 to the Act of Accession of 16 April 2003 shall apply to the Sovereign Base Areas with the amendments set out in that Annex. In that Annex, reference to "this Protocol" shall be construed as being to this Title.

2.   The Union acts on turnover taxes, excise duties and other forms of indirect taxation listed in Part Two of the Annex to Protocol No 3 to the Act of Accession of 16 April 2003 shall apply to the Sovereign Base Areas with the amendments set out in that Annex as well as the relevant provisions applying to Cyprus as set out in this Protocol.

3.   The Union acts listed in Part Three of the Annex to Protocol No 3 to the Act of Accession of 16 April 2003 shall be amended as set out in that Annex to enable the United Kingdom to maintain the reliefs and exemptions from duties and taxes on supplies to its forces and associated personnel which are granted by the Treaty concerning the Establishment of the Republic of Cyprus (hereinafter referred to as the "Treaty of Establishment").

ARTICLE 44 (*ex Article 3 of Protocol No 3 AA 2003*)
Articles III-225 to III-232 of the Constitution, together with the provisions adopted on that basis, and the provisions adopted in accordance with Article III-278(4)(b)of the Constitution shall apply to the Sovereign Base Areas.

ARTICLE 45 (*ex Article 4 of Protocol No 3 AA 2003*)
Persons resident or employed in the territory of the Sovereign Base Areas who, under arrangements made pursuant to the Treaty of Establishment and the associated Exchange of Notes dated 16 August 1960, are

subject to the social security legislation of the Republic of Cyprus shall be treated for the purposes of Council Regulation (EEC) No 1408/71 of 14 June 1971 on the application of social security schemes to employed persons, to self-employed persons and to members of their families moving within the Community [OJ L 149, 5.7.1971, p. 2] as if they were resident or employed in the territory of the Republic of Cyprus.

ARTICLE 46 (*ex Article 5 of Protocol No 3 AA 2003*)

1. The Republic of Cyprus shall not be required to carry out checks on persons crossing its land and sea boundaries with the Sovereign Base Areas and any Union restrictions on the crossing of external borders shall not apply in relation to such persons.

2. The United Kingdom shall exercise controls on persons crossing the external borders of the Sovereign Base Areas in accordance with the undertakings set out in Part Four of the Annex to Protocol No 3 to the Act of Accession of 16 April 2003.

ARTICLE 47 (*ex Article 6 of Protocol No 3 AA 2003*)

The Council, on a proposal from the Commission, may, in order to ensure effective implementation of the objectives of this Title, adopt a European decision amending Articles 43 to 46, including the Annex to Protocol No 3 to the Act of Accession of 16 April 2003, or applying other provisions of the Constitution and Union acts to the Sovereign Base Areas on such terms and subject to such conditions as it may specify. The Council shall act unanimously. The Commission shall consult the United Kingdom and the Republic of Cyprus before bringing forward a proposal.

ARTICLE 48 (*ex Article 7 of Protocol No 3 AA 2003*)

1. Subject to paragraph 2, the United Kingdom shall be responsible for the implementation of this Title in the Sovereign Base Areas. In particular:
(a) the United Kingdom shall be responsible for the application of the Union measures specified in this Title in the fields of customs, indirect taxation and the common commercial policy in relation to goods entering or leaving the island of Cyprus through a port or airport within the Sovereign Base Areas;
(b) customs controls on goods imported into or exported from the island of Cyprus by the forces of the United Kingdom through a port or airport in the Republic of Cyprus may be carried out within the Sovereign Base Areas;
(c) the United Kingdom shall be responsible for issuing any licences, authorisations or certificates which may be required under any applicable Union measure in respect of goods imported into or exported from the island of Cyprus by the forces of the United Kingdom.

2. The Republic of Cyprus shall be responsible for the administration and payment of any Union funds to which persons in the Sovereign Base Areas may be entitled pursuant to the application of the common agricultural policy in the Sovereign Base Areas under Article 44, and the Republic of Cyprus shall be accountable to the Commission for such expenditure.

3. Without prejudice to paragraphs 1 and 2, the United Kingdom may delegate to the competent authorities of the Republic of Cyprus, in accordance with arrangements made pursuant to the Treaty of Establishment, the performance of any functions imposed on a Member State by or under any provision referred to in Articles 43 to 46.

4. The United Kingdom and the Republic of Cyprus shall co-operate to ensure the effective implementation of this Title in the Sovereign Base Areas and, where appropriate, shall conclude further arrangements concerning the delegation of the implementation of any of the provisions referred to in Articles 43 to 46. A copy of any such arrangements shall be submitted to the Commission.

ARTICLE 49 (*ex Article 8 of Protocol No 3 AA 2003*)

The arrangements provided for in this Title shall have the sole purpose of regulating the particular situation of the Sovereign Base Areas of the United Kingdom in Cyprus and shall not apply to any other territory of the Union, nor serve as a precedent, in whole or in part, for any other special arrangements which either already exist or which might be set up in another European territory provided for in Article IV-440 of the Constitution.

ARTICLE 50 (*ex Article 9 of Protocol No 3 AA 2003*)

The Commission shall report to the European Parliament and the Council every five years as from 1 May 2004 on the implementation of the provisions of this Title.

ARTICLE 51 (*new*)

The provisions of this Title shall apply in the light of the Declaration on the Sovereign Base Areas of the United Kingdom of Great Britain and Northern Ireland in Cyprus, which incorporates, without altering its legal effect, the wording of the preamble to Protocol No 3 to the Act of Accession of 16 April 2003.

TITLE IV

PROVISIONS ON THE IGNALINA NUCLEAR POWER PLANT IN LITHUANIA

ARTICLE 52 (*ex Article 1 of Protocol No 4 AA 2003*)

Acknowledging the readiness of the Union to provide adequate additional assistance to the efforts by Lithuania to decommission the Ignalina Nuclear Power Plant and highlighting this expression of solidarity, Lithuania has undertaken to close Unit 1 of the Ignalina Nuclear Power Plant before 2005 and Unit 2 of this plant by 31 December 2009 at the latest and subsequently decommission these units.

ARTICLE 53 (*ex Article 2 of Protocol No 4 AA 2003*)

1.   During the period 2004-2006, the Union shall provide Lithuania with additional financial assistance in support of its efforts to decommission, and to address the consequences of the closure and decommissioning of, the Ignalina Nuclear Power Plant (hereinafter "the Ignalina Programme").

2.   Measures under the Ignalina Programme shall be decided and implemented in accordance with the provisions laid down in Council Regulation (EEC) No 3906/89 of 18 December 1989 on economic aid to certain countries of Central and Eastern Europe [OJ L 375, 23.12.1989, p. 11].

3.   The Ignalina Programme shall, inter alia, cover: measures in support of the decommissioning of the Ignalina Nuclear Power Plant; measures for the environmental upgrading in line with the *acquis* and modernisation measures of conventional production capacity to replace the production capacity of the two Ignalina Nuclear Power Plant reactors; and other measures which are consequential to the decision to close and decommission this plant and which contribute to the necessary restructuring, environmental upgrading and modernisation of the energy production, transmission and distribution sectors in Lithuania as well as to enhancing the security of energy supply and improving energy efficiency in Lithuania.

4.   The Ignalina Programme shall include measures to support plant personnel in maintaining a high level of operational safety at the Ignalina Nuclear Power Plant in the periods prior to the closure and during the decommissioning of the said reactor units.

5.   For the period 2004-2006 the Ignalina Programme shall amount to €285 million in commitment appropriations, to be committed in equal annual tranches.

6.   The contribution under the Ignalina Programme may, for certain measures, amount to up to 100% of the total expenditure. Every effort should be made to continue the co-financing practice established under the pre-accession assistance for Lithuania's decommissioning effort as well as to attract co-financing from other sources, as appropriate.

7.   The assistance under the Ignalina Programme, or parts thereof, may be made available as a Union contribution to the Ignalina International Decommissioning Support Fund, managed by the European Bank for Reconstruction and Development.

8.   Public aid from national, Union and international sources:

(a)   for the environmental upgrading in line with the *acquis* and modernisation measures of the Lithuanian Thermal Power Plant in Elektrenai as the key replacement for the production capacity of the two Ignalina Nuclear Power Plant reactors; and

(b)   for the decommissioning of the Ignalina Nuclear Power Plant

shall be compatible with the internal market as defined in the Constitution.

9.   Public aid from national, Union and international sources in support of Lithuania's efforts to address the consequences of the closure and of the decommissioning of the Ignalina Nuclear Power Plant may, on a case by case basis, be considered to be compatible – under the Constitution – with the internal market, in particular public aid provided for enhancing the security of energy supply.

ARTICLE 54 (*ex Article 3 of Protocol No 4 AA 2003*)

1.　　Recognising that the decommissioning of the Ignalina Nuclear Power Plant is of a long-term nature and represents for Lithuania an exceptional financial burden not commensurate with its size and economic strength, the Union shall, in solidarity with Lithuania, provide adequate additional assistance to the decommissioning effort beyond 2006.

2.　　The Ignalina Programme shall be, for this purpose, seamlessly continued and extended beyond 2006.Implementing provisions for the extended Ignalina Programme shall be adopted in accordance with the procedure laid down in Article 35 of this Protocol and enter into force, at the latest, by the date of expiry of the Financial Perspective as defined in the Interinstitutional Agreement of 6 May 1999.

3.　　The Ignalina Programme, as extended in accordance with the provisions of paragraph 2, shall be based on the same elements and principles as described in Article 53.

4.　　For the period of the subsequent Financial Perspective, the overall average appropriations under the extended Ignalina Programme shall be appropriate. Programming of these resources will be based on actual payment needs and absorption capacity.

ARTICLE 55 (*ex Article 4 of Protocol No 4 AA 2003*)

Without prejudice to the provisions of Article 52, the general safeguard clause referred to in Article 26 shall apply until 31 December 2012 if energy supply is disrupted in Lithuania.

ARTICLE 56 (*new*)

This Title shall apply in the light of the Declaration on the Ignalina Nuclear Power Plant in Lithuania which incorporates, without altering its legal effect, the wording of the preamble to Protocol No 4 to the Act of Accession of 16 April 2003.

TITLE V

PROVISIONS ON THE TRANSIT OF PERSONS BY LAND BETWEEN THE REGION OF KALININGRAD AND OTHER PARTS OF THE RUSSIAN FEDERATION

ARTICLE 57 (*ex Article 1 of Protocol No 5 AA 2003*)

The Union rules and arrangements on transit of persons by land between the region of Kaliningrad and other parts of the Russian Federation, and in particular the Council Regulation (EC) No 693/2003 of 14 April 2003 establishing a specific Facilitated Transit Document (FTD), a Facilitated Rail Transit Document (FRTD) and amending the Common Consular Instructions and the Common Manual [OJ L 99, 17.4.2003, p. 8], shall not in themselves delay or prevent the full participation of Lithuania in the Schengen *acquis*, including the removal of internal border controls.

ARTICLE 58 (*ex Article 2 of Protocol No 5 AA 2003*)

The Union shall assist Lithuania in implementing the rules and arrangements for the transit of persons between the region of Kaliningrad and the other parts of the Russian Federation with a view to Lithuania's full participation in the Schengen area as soon as possible.
The Union shall assist Lithuania in managing the transit of persons between the region of Kaliningrad and the other parts of the Russian Federation and shall, notably, bear any additional costs incurred by implementing the specific provisions of the *acquis* provided for such transit.

ARTICLE 59 (*ex Article 2 of Protocol No 5 AA 2003*)

Without prejudice to the sovereign rights of Lithuania, any further act concerning the transit of persons between the region of Kaliningrad and other parts of the Russian Federation shall be adopted by the Council on a proposal from the Commission. The Council shall act unanimously.

ARTICLE 60 (*new*)

This Title shall apply in the light of the Declaration on the transit of persons by land between the region of Kaliningrad and other parts of the Russian Federation, which incorporates, without altering its legal affect, the wording of the preamble to Protocol No 5 to the Act of Accession of 16 April 2003.

TITLE VI

PROVISIONS ON THE ACQUISITION OF SECONDARY RESIDENCES IN MALTA

ARTICLE 61 (*ex Protocol No 6 AA 2003*)

Bearing in mind the very limited number of residences in Malta and the very limited land available for construction purposes, which can only cover the basic needs created by the demographic development of the present residents, Malta may on a non-discriminatory basis maintain in force the rules on the acquisition and holding of immovable property for secondary residence purposes by nationals of the Member States who have not legally resided in Malta for at least five years laid down in the Immovable Property (Acquisition by Non-Residents) Act (Chapter 246).

Malta shall apply authorisation procedures for the acquisition of immovable property for secondary residence purposes in Malta, which shall be based on published, objective, stable and transparent criteria. These criteria shall be applied in a non-discriminatory manner and shall not differentiate between nationals of Malta and of other Member States. Malta shall ensure that in no instance shall a national of a Member State be treated in a more restrictive way than a national of a third country.

In the event that the value of one such property bought by a national of a Member State exceeds the thresholds provided for in Malta's legislation, namely 30,000 Maltese lira for apartments and 50,000 Maltese lira for any type of property other than apartments and property of historical importance, authorisation shall be granted. Malta may revise the thresholds established by such legislation to reflect changes in prices in the property market in Malta.

TITLE VII

PROVISIONS ON ABORTION IN MALTA

ARTICLE 62 (*ex Protocol No 7 AA 2003*)

Nothing in the Treaty establishing a Constitution for Europe or in the Treaties and Acts modifying or supplementing it shall affect the application in the territory of Malta of national legislation relating to abortion.

TITLE VIII

PROVISIONS ON THE RESTRUCTURING OF THE POLISH STEEL INDUSTRY

ARTICLE 63 (*ex Protocol No 8 AA 2003*)

1.   Notwithstanding Articles III-167 and III-168 of the Constitution, State aid granted by Poland for restructuring purposes to specified parts of the Polish steel industry shall be deemed to be compatible with the internal market provided that:

(a)   the period provided for in Article 8(4) of Protocol 2 on ECSC products to the Europe Agreement establishing an association between the European Communities and their Member States, of the one part, and Poland, of the other part [OJ L 348, 31.12.1993, p. 2], has been extended until 1 May 2004,

(b)   the terms set out in the restructuring plan, on the basis of which the abovementioned Protocol was extended are adhered to throughout the period 2002-2006,

(c)   the conditions set out in this Title are met, and

(d)   no State aid for restructuring is to be paid to the Polish steel industry after 1 May 2004.

2.   Restructuring of the Polish steel sector, as described in the individual business plans of the companies listed in Annex 1 to Protocol No 8 to the Act of Accession of 16 April 2003 (hereinafter referred to as "benefiting companies"), and in line with the conditions set out in this Title, shall be completed no later than 31 December 2006 (hereinafter referred to as "the end of the restructuring period").

3.   Only benefiting companies shall be eligible for State aid in the framework of the Polish steel restructuring programme.

4.   A benefiting company may not:

(a)   in the case of a merger with a company not included in Annex 1 to Protocol No 8 to the Act of Accession of 16 April 2003, pass on the benefit of the aid granted to the benefiting company;

(b)   take over the assets of any company not included in Annex 1 to Protocol No 8 to the Act of Accession of 16 April 2003 which is declared bankrupt in the period up to 31 December 2006.

5.   Any subsequent privatisation of any of the benefiting companies shall take place on a basis that respects the need for transparency and shall respect the conditions and principles regarding viability, State aids and capacity reduction defined in this Title. No further State aid shall be granted as part of the sale of any company or individual assets.

6.   The restructuring aid granted to the benefiting companies shall be determined by the justifications set out in the approved Polish steel restructuring plan and individual business plans as approved by the Council. But, in any case, the aid paid out in the period of 1997-2003 in its total amount shall not exceed PLN 3,387,070,000.
Of this total figure:

(a)   as regards Polskie Huty Stali (hereinafter referred to as "PHS"), the restructuring aid already granted or to be granted from 1997 until the end of 2003 shall not exceed PLN 3,140,360,000. PHS has already received PLN 62,360,000 of restructuring aid in the period 1997-2001; it shall receive further restructuring aid of no more than PLN 3,078,000,000 in 2002 and 2003 depending on the requirements set out in the approved restructuring plan (to be entirely paid out in 2002 if the extension of the grace period under Protocol 2 of the Europe Agreement establishing an association between the European Communities and their Member States, of the one part, and Poland, of the other part, is granted by the end of 2002, or otherwise in 2003);

(b)   as regards Huta Andrzej S.A., Huta Bankowa Sp. z o.o., Huta Batory S.A., Huta Buczek S.A., Huta L.W. Sp. z o.o., Huta Łabędy S.A., and Huta Pokój S.A. (hereinafter referred to as "other benefiting companies"), the steel restructuring aid already granted or to be granted from 1997 until the end of 2003 shall not exceed PLN 246,710,000. These firms have already received PLN 37,160,000 of restructuring aid in the period 1997-2001; they shall receive further restructuring aid of no more than PLN 210,210,000 depending on the requirements set out in the approved restructuring plan (of which PLN 182,170,000 in 2002 and PLN 27,380,000 in 2003 if the extension of the grace period under Protocol 2 of the Europe Agreement establishing an association between the European Communities and their Member States, of the one part, and Poland, of the other part, is granted by the end of 2002, or otherwise PLN 210,210,000 in 2003).
No further State aid shall be granted by Poland for restructuring purposes to the Polish steel industry.

7.   The net capacity reduction to be achieved by Poland for finished products during the period 1997-2006 shall be a minimum of 1,231,000 tonnes. This overall amount includes net capacity reductions of at least 715,000 tpy in hot-rolled products and 716,000 tpy in cold-rolled products, as well as an increase of at most 200,000 tpy of other finished products.
Capacity reduction shall be measured only on the basis of permanent closure of production facilities by physical destruction such that the facilities cannot be restored to service. A declaration of bankruptcy of a steel company shall not qualify as capacity reduction.
The net capacity reductions shown in Annex 2 to Protocol No 8 to the Act of Accession of 16 April 2003 are minima and actual net capacity reductions to be achieved and the time frame for doing so shall be established on the basis of Poland's final restructuring programme and individual business plans under the Europe Agreement establishing an association between the European Communities and their Member States, of the one part, and Poland, of the other part, taking into account the objective to ensure the viability of benefiting companies as at 31 December 2006.

8.   The business plan for the benefiting company PHS shall be implemented. In particular:
(a)   restructuring efforts shall concentrate on the following:
      (i)   reorganising PHS production facilities on a product basis and ensuring horizontal organisation by function (purchasing, production, sales),
      (ii)   establishing in PHS a unified management structure enabling full realisation of synergies in the consolidation,
      (iii)   evolving the strategic focus of PHS from being production-oriented to being marketing-oriented,
      (iv)   improving the efficiency and effectiveness of PHS business management and also ensuring better control of direct sales,
      (v)   PHS reviewing, on the basis of sound economic considerations, the strategy of spin-off companies and, where appropriate, reintegrating services into the parent company,
      (vi)   PHS reviewing its product mix, reducing over-capacity on long semi-finished products and generally moving further into the higher value-added product market,
      (vii)   PHS investing in order to achieve a higher quality of finished products; special attention shall be given to attaining by the date set in the timetable for the implementation of the PHS restructuring programme and at the latest by the end of 2006 3-Sigma production quality level at the PHS site in Kraków;

(b)   cost savings shall be maximised in PHS during the restructuring period through energy efficiency gains, improved purchasing and ensuring productivity yields comparable to Union levels;

(c)   employment restructuring shall be implemented; levels of productivity comparable to those obtained by Union steel industry product groups shall be reached as at 31 December 2006, based on consolidated figures including indirect employment in the wholly owned service companies;

(d)   any privatisation shall be on a basis that respects the need for transparency and fully respects the commercial value of PHS. No further State aid shall be granted as part of the sale.

9.   The business plan for the other benefiting companies shall be implemented. In particular:

(a)   for all of the other benefiting companies, restructuring efforts shall concentrate on the following:

    (i)   evolving the strategic focus from being production-oriented to being marketing-oriented,

    (ii)   improving the efficiency and effectiveness of the companies' business management and also ensuring better control of direct sales,

    (iii)   reviewing, on the basis of sound economic considerations, the strategy of spin-off companies and, where appropriate, reintegrating services into the parent companies;

(b)   for Huta Bankowa, implementing the cost savings programme;

(c)   for Huta Buczek, obtaining the necessary financial support from creditors and local financial institutions and implementing the cost savings programme, including reducing the investment cost by adapting existing production facilities;

(d)   for Huta Łabędy, implementing the cost savings programme and reducing reliance on the mining industry;

(e)   for Huta Pokój, achieving international productivity standards in the subsidiaries, implementing energy consumption savings and cancelling the proposed investment in the processing and construction department;

(f)   for Huta Batory, reaching agreement with creditors and financial institutions on debt rescheduling and investment loans. The company shall also ensure substantial additional cost savings associated with employment restructuring and improved yields;

(g)   for Huta Andrzej, securing a stable financial base for its development by negotiating an agreement between the company's current lenders, long-term creditors, trade creditors and financial institutions. Additional investments in the hot tube mill as well as the implementation of the staff reduction programme must take place;

(h)   for Huta L.W., carrying out investments in relation to the company's hot-rolling mills project, lifting equipment, and environmental standing. This company shall also achieve higher productivity levels, through staff restructuring and reducing the costs of external services.

10.   Any subsequent changes in the overall restructuring plan and the individual plans must be agreed by the Commission and, where appropriate, by the Council.

11.   The implementation of the restructuring shall take place under conditions of full transparency and on the basis of sound market economy principles.

12.   The Commission and the Council shall closely monitor the implementation of the restructuring and the fulfilment of the conditions set out in this Title concerning viability, State aid and capacity reductions before and after 1 May 2004, until the end of the restructuring period, in accordance with paragraphs 13 to 18. For this purpose the Commission shall report to the Council.

13.   In addition to the monitoring of State aid, the Commission and the Council shall monitor the restructuring benchmarks set out in Annex 3 to Protocol No 8 to the Act of Accession of 16 April 2003. References made in that Annex to paragraph 14 of the Protocol shall be construed as being made to paragraph 14 of this Article.

14.   Monitoring shall include an independent evaluation to be carried out in 2003, 2004, 2005 and 2006. The Commission's viability test shall be applied and productivity shall be measured as part of the evaluation.

15.   Poland shall co-operate fully with all the arrangements for monitoring. In particular:

(a)   Poland shall supply the Commission with six-monthly reports concerning the restructuring of the benefiting companies, no later than 15 March and 15 September of each year, until the end of the restructuring period;

(b)   the first report shall reach the Commission by 15 March 2003 and the last report by 15 March 2007, unless the Commission decides otherwise;

(c)   the reports shall contain all the information necessary to monitor the restructuring process, the State aid and the reduction and use of capacity and shall provide sufficient financial data to allow an assessment to be made of whether the conditions and requirements contained in this Title have been fulfilled. The reports shall at the least contain the information set out in Annex 4 to Protocol No 8 to the Act of Accession of 16 April 2003, which the Commission reserves the right to modify in line with its experiences during the monitoring process. In Annex 4 to Protocol No 8 to the Act of Accession of 16 April 2003, the reference to paragraph 14 of the Protocol shall be construed as being to paragraph 14 of this Article. In addition to the individual business reports of the benefiting companies there shall also be a report on the overall situation of the Polish steel sector, including recent macroeconomic developments;

(d)   all additional information necessary for the independent evaluation provided for in paragraph 14 must, furthermore, be provided by Poland;

(e)   Poland shall oblige the benefiting companies to disclose all relevant data which might, under other circumstances, be considered as confidential. In its reporting to the Council, the Commission shall ensure that company-specific confidential information is not disclosed.

16.   The Commission may at any time decide to mandate an independent consultant to evaluate the monitoring results, undertake any research necessary and report to the Commission and the Council.

17.   If the Commission establishes, on the basis of the monitoring, that substantial deviations from the financial data on which the viability assessment has been made have occurred, it may require Poland to take appropriate measures to reinforce or modify the restructuring measures of the benefiting companies concerned.

18.   Should the monitoring show that:

(a)   the conditions for the transitional arrangements contained in this Title have not been fulfilled, or that

(b)   the commitments made in the framework of the extension of the period during which Poland may exceptionally grant State support for the restructuring of its steel industry under the Europe Agreement establishing an association between the European Communities and their Member States, of the one part, and Poland, of the other part, have not been fulfilled, or that

(c)   Poland in the course of the restructuring period has granted additional incompatible State aid to the steel industry and to the benefiting companies in particular,

the transitional arrangements contained in this Title shall not have effect.

The Commission shall take appropriate steps requiring any company concerned to reimburse any aid granted in breach of the conditions laid down in this Title.

TITLE IX

PROVISIONS ON UNIT 1 AND UNIT 2 OF THE BOHUNICE V1 NUCLEAR POWER PLANT IN SLOVAKIA

ARTICLE 64 (*ex Article 1 of Protocol No 9 AA 2003*)
Slovakia has undertaken to close Unit 1 of the Bohunice V1 Nuclear Power Plant by 31 December 2006 at the latest and Unit 2 of this plant by 31 December 2008 at the latest and subsequently decommission these units.

ARTICLE 65 (*ex Article 2 of Protocol No 9 AA 2003*)
1.   During the period 2004-2006, the Union shall provide Slovakia with financial assistance in support of its efforts to decommission, and to address the consequences of the closure and decommissioning of, Unit 1 and Unit 2 of the Bohunice V1 Nuclear Power Plant (hereinafter referred to as "the Assistance").

2.   The Assistance shall be decided and implemented in accordance with the provisions laid down in Council Regulation (EEC) No 3906/89 of 18 December 1989 on economic aid to certain countries of Central and Eastern Europe [OJ L 375, 23.12.1989, p. 11].

3.   For the period 2004-2006 the Assistance shall amount to €90 million in commitment appropriations, to be committed in equal annual tranches.

4.   The Assistance or parts thereof may be made available as a Union contribution to the Bohunice International Decommissioning Support Fund, managed by the European Bank for Reconstruction and Development.

ARTICLE 66 (*ex Article 3 of Protocol No 9 AA 2003*)
The Union acknowledges that the decommissioning of the Bohunice V1 Nuclear Power plant must continue beyond the Financial Perspective as defined in the Interinstitutional Agreement of 6 May 1999, and that this

effort represents for Slovakia a significant financial burden. Decisions on the continuation of Union assistance in this field after 2006 will take the situation into account.

ARTICLE 67 (*new*)

The provisions of this Title shall apply in the light of the Declaration on Unit 1 and Unit 2 of the Bohunice V1 Nuclear Power Plant in Slovakia which incorporates, without altering its legal effect, the wording of the preamble to Protocol No 9 to the Act of Accession of 16 April 2003.

TITLE X

PROVISIONS ON CYPRUS

ARTICLE 68 (*ex Article 1 of Protocol No 10 AA 2003*)

1.   The application of the Community and Union *acquis* shall be suspended in those areas of the Republic of Cyprus in which the Government of the Republic of Cyprus does not exercise effective control.

2.   The Council, on the basis of a proposal from the Commission, shall decide on the withdrawal of the suspension referred to in paragraph 1. It shall act unanimously.

ARTICLE 69 (*ex Article 2 of Protocol No 10 AA 2003*)

1.   The Council, on the basis of a proposal from the Commission, shall define the terms under which the provisions of Union law shall apply to the line between those areas referred to in Article 68 and the areas in which the Government of the Republic of Cyprus exercises effective control. The Council shall act unanimously.

2.   The boundary between the Eastern Sovereign Base Area and those areas referred to in Article 68 shall be treated as part of the external borders of the Sovereign Base Areas for the purpose of Part Four of the Annex to Protocol No 3 to the Act of Accession of 16 April 2003 on the Sovereign Base Areas of the United Kingdom of Great Britain and Northern Ireland in Cyprus for the duration of the suspension of the application of the Community and Union *acquis* according to Article 68.

ARTICLE 70 (*ex Article 3 of Protocol No 10 AA 2003*)

1.   Nothing in this Title shall preclude measures with a view to promoting the economic development of the areas referred to in Article 68.

2.   Such measures shall not affect the application of the Community and Union *acquis* under the conditions set out in this Protocol in any other part of the Republic of Cyprus.

ARTICLE 71 (*ex Article 4 of Protocol No 10 AA 2003*)

In the event of settlement of the Cyprus problem, the Council, on the basis of a proposal from the Commission, shall decide on the adaptations to the terms concerning the accession of Cyprus to the Union with regard to the Turkish Cypriot Community. The Council shall act unanimously.

ARTICLE 72 (*new*)

This Title shall apply in the light of the declaration on Cyprus which incorporates, without altering its legal effect, the wording of the preamble to Protocol No 10 to the Act of Accession of 16 April 2003.

PART THREE

PROVISIONS ON THE ANNEXES TO THE ACT OF ACCESSION OF 16 APRIL 2003

ARTICLE 73 (*new*)

Annex I and Annexes III to XVII to the Act of Accession of 16 April 2003, their appendices, and the Annexes to Protocols 2, 3 and 8 to the Act of Accession of 16 April 2003 [OJ L 236, 23.9.2003, p. 33] form an integral part of this Protocol.

ARTICLE 74 (*new*)

1.   The references made to the "Treaty of Accession" in the Annexes referred to in Article 73 of this Protocol shall be construed as being made to the Treaty referred to in Article IV-437(2)(e) of the Constitution, those made to the date or time of signing of that Treaty shall be construed as being made to 16 April 2003 and those made to the date of accession shall be construed as being made to 1 May 2004.

2.   Without prejudice to the second subparagraph, the references made to "this Act" in the Annexes referred to in Article 73 of this Protocol shall be construed as being made to the Act of Accession of 16 April 2003.

The references made to the provisions of the Act of Accession of 16 April 2003 in the Annexes referred to in Article 73 of this Protocol shall be construed as being made to this Protocol, in accordance with the following table of equivalence.

Act of Accession of 16 April 2003	*Protocol*
Article 21	Article 12
Article 22	Article 13
Article 24	Article 15
Article 32	Article 21
Article 37	Article 26
Article 52	Article 32

3.   The expressions, which appear in the Annexes referred to in Article 73, shall be construed as having the meaning assigned to them in the following table of equivalence, unless they refer exclusively to legal situations preceding the entry into force of the Treaty establishing a Constitution for Europe.

Expressions used in the Annexes	*Meaning*
Treaty establishing the European Community	Constitution
Treaty on European Union	Constitution
Treaties on which the European Union is founded	Constitution
(European) Community	Union
Enlarged Community	Union
Community	Union
EU	Union
Enlarged Union or enlarged EU	Union

By way of derogation from the first subparagraph, the meaning of the expression "Community" where it is used to qualify the terms "preference" and "fisheries" shall remain unchanged.

4.   The references made to parts or to provisions of the Treaty establishing the European Community in the Annexes referred to in Article 73 of this Protocol shall be construed as being made to parts or to provisions of the Constitution, in accordance with the following table of equivalence.

EC Treaty	*Constitution*
(Part Three) Title I	Part III, Title III, Chapter I, Section 3
Part Three, Title I, Chapter 1	Part III, Title III, Chapter I, Section 3 Sub-Section 1
Part Three, Title II	Part III, Title III, Chapter III, Section 4
Agriculture	Agriculture and Fisheries
(Part Three) Title III	Part III, Title III, Chapter I
(Part Three) Title VI, Chapter 1	Part III, Title III, Chapter I, Section 5
Article 31	Article III-44
Article 39	Article III-18
Article 49	Article III-29
Article 58	Article III-47
Article 87	Article III-56
Article 88	Article III-57
Article 226	Article III-265
Annex I	Annex I

5.   Where the Annexes referred to in Article 73 of this Protocol provide that the Council or the Commission shall adopt legal acts, those acts shall take the form of European regulations or decisions.

10. PROTOCOL ON THE EXCESSIVE DEFICIT PROCEDURE

THE HIGH CONTRACTING PARTIES,

DESIRING to lay down the details of the excessive deficit procedure referred to in Article III-184 of the Constitution,

HAVE AGREED upon the following provisions, which shall be annexed to the Treaty establishing a Constitution for Europe:

ARTICLE 1
The reference values referred to in Article III-184(2) of the Constitution are:
(a)   3% for the ratio of the planned or actual government deficit to gross domestic product at market prices;
(b)   60% for the ratio of government debt to gross domestic product at market prices.

ARTICLE 2
For the purposes of Article III-184 of the Constitution and of this Protocol:
(a)   "government" means general government, that is central government, regional or local government and social security funds, to the exclusion of commercial operations, as defined in the European System of Integrated Economic Accounts;
(b)   "deficit" means net borrowing as defined in the European System of Integrated Economic Accounts;
(c)   "investment" means gross fixed capital formation as defined in the European System of Integrated Economic Accounts;
(d)   "debt" means total gross debt at nominal value outstanding at the end of the year and consolidated between and within the sectors of general government as defined in point (a).

ARTICLE 3
In order to ensure the effectiveness of the excessive deficit procedure, the governments of the Member States shall be responsible under this procedure for the deficits of general government as defined in Article 2(a). The Member States shall ensure that national procedures in the budgetary area enable them to meet their obligations in this area deriving from the Constitution. The Member States shall report their planned and actual deficits and the levels of their debt promptly and regularly to the Commission.

ARTICLE 4
The statistical data to be used for the application of this Protocol shall be provided by the Commission.

11. PROTOCOL ON THE CONVERGENCE CRITERIA

THE HIGH CONTRACTING PARTIES,

DESIRING to lay down the details of the convergence criteria which shall guide the Union in taking decisions referred to in Article III-198 of the Constitution to end the derogations of those Member States with a derogation,

HAVE AGREED upon the following provisions, which shall be annexed to the Treaty establishing a Constitution for Europe:

ARTICLE 1
The criterion on price stability referred to in Article III-198(1)(a) of the Constitution shall mean that the Member State concerned has a price performance that is sustainable and an average rate of inflation, observed over a period of one year before the examination, that does not exceed by more than 1,5 percentage points that of, at most, the three best performing Member States in terms of price stability. Inflation shall be measured by means of the consumer price index on a comparable basis, taking into account differences in national definitions.

ARTICLE 2

The criterion on the government budgetary position referred to in Article III-198(1)(b) of the Constitution shall mean that at the time of the examination the Member State concerned is not the subject of a European decision of the Council under Article III-184(6) of the Constitution that an excessive deficit exists.

ARTICLE 3

The criterion on participation in the exchange-rate mechanism of the European Monetary System referred to in Article III-198(1)(c) of the Constitution shall mean that the Member State concerned has respected the normal fluctuation margins provided for by the exchange-rate mechanism of the European Monetary System without severe tensions for at least the last two years before the examination. In particular, the Member State shall not have devalued its currency's bilateral central rate against the euro on its own initiative for the same period.

ARTICLE 4

The criterion on the convergence of interest rates referred to in Article III-198(1)(d) of the Constitution shall mean that, observed over a period of one year before the examination, the Member State concerned has had an average nominal long-term interest rate that does not exceed by more than 2 percentage points that of, at most, the three best performing Member States in terms of price stability. Interest rates shall be measured on the basis of long-term government bonds or comparable securities, taking into account differences in national definitions.

ARTICLE 5

The statistical data to be used for the application of this Protocol shall be provided by the Commission.

ARTICLE 6

The Council shall, acting unanimously on a proposal from the Commission and after consulting the European Parliament, the European Central Bank, and the Economic and Financial Committee referred to in Article III-192 of the Constitution, adopt appropriate provisions to lay down the details of the convergence criteria referred to in Article III-198 of the Constitution, which shall then replace this Protocol.

12.   PROTOCOL ON THE EURO GROUP

THE HIGH CONTRACTING PARTIES,

DESIRING to promote conditions for stronger economic growth in the European Union and, to that end, to develop ever-closer co-ordination of economic policies within the euro area,

CONSCIOUS of the need to lay down special provisions for enhanced dialogue between the Member States whose currency is the euro, pending the euro becoming the currency of all Member States of the Union,

HAVE AGREED upon the following provisions, which are annexed to the Treaty establishing a Constitution for Europe:

ARTICLE 1

The Ministers of the Member States whose currency is the euro shall meet informally. Such meetings shall take place, when necessary, to discuss questions related to the specific responsibilities they share with regard to the single currency. The Commission shall take part in the meetings. The European Central Bank shall be invited to take part in such meetings, which shall be prepared by the representatives of the Ministers with responsibility for finance of the Member States whose currency is the euro and of the Commission.

ARTICLE 2

The Ministers of the Member States whose currency is the euro shall elect a president for two and a half years, by a majority of those Member States.

13. PROTOCOL ON CERTAIN PROVISIONS RELATING TO THE UNITED KINGDOM OF GREAT BRITAIN AND NORTHERN IRELAND AS REGARDS ECONOMIC AND MONETARY UNION

THE HIGH CONTRACTING PARTIES,

RECOGNISING that the United Kingdom shall not be obliged or committed to adopt the euro without a separate decision to do so by its government and Parliament;

GIVEN that on 16 October 1996 and 30 October 1997 the United Kingdom government notified the Council of its intention not to participate in the third stage of economic and monetary union, under the terms of paragraph 1 of the Protocol on certain provisions relating to the United Kingdom of Great Britain and Northern Ireland, annexed to the Treaty establishing the European Community;

NOTING the practice of the government of the United Kingdom to fund its borrowing requirement by the sale of debt to the private sector,

HAVE AGREED upon the following provisions, which shall be annexed to the Treaty establishing a Constitution for Europe:

ARTICLE 1
Unless the United Kingdom notifies the Council that it intends to adopt the euro, it shall be under no obligation to do so.

ARTICLE 2
In view of the notice given to the Council by the United Kingdom government on 16 October 1996 and 30 October 1997, Articles 3 to 8 and 10 shall apply to the United Kingdom.

ARTICLE 3
The United Kingdom shall retain its powers in the field of monetary policy according to national law.

ARTICLE 4
Articles I-30(2), with the exception of the first and last sentences thereof, I-30(5), III-177, second paragraph, III-184(1), (9) and (10), III-185(1) to (5), III-186, III-188, III-189, III-190, III-191, III-196, III-198(3), III-326 and III-382 of the Constitution shall not apply to the United Kingdom. The same applies to Article III-179(2) of the Constitution as regards the adoption of the parts of the broad economic policy guidelines which concern the euro area generally.
In the provisions referred to in the first paragraph, references to the Union or the Member States shall not include the United Kingdom and references to national central banks shall not include the Bank of England.

ARTICLE 5
The United Kingdom shall endeavour to avoid an excessive government deficit.
Articles III-192(4) and III-200 of the Constitution shall apply to the United Kingdom as if it had a derogation. Articles III-201 and III-202 of the Constitution shall continue to apply to the United Kingdom.

ARTICLE 6
The voting rights of the United Kingdom shall be suspended for the adoption by the Council of the measures referred to in the Articles listed in Article 4 and in the instances referred to in the first subparagraph of Article III-197(4) of the Constitution. For this purpose the second and third subparagraphs of Article III-197(4) of the Constitution shall apply.
The United Kingdom shall also have no right to participate in the appointment of the President, the Vice-President and the other members of the Executive Board of the European Central Bank under the second, third and fourth subparagraphs of Article III-382(2) of the Constitution.

ARTICLE 7
Articles 3, 4, 6, 7, 9(2), 10(1), (2) and (3), 11(2), 12(1), 14, 16, 18, 19, 20, 22, 23, 26, 27, 30, 31, 32, 33, 34 and 50 of the Protocol on the Statute of the European System of Central Banks and of the European Central Bank ("the Statute") shall not apply to the United Kingdom.
In those Articles, references to the Union or the Member States shall not include the United Kingdom and references to national central banks or shareholders shall not include the Bank of England.
References in Articles 10(3) and 30(2) of the Statute to "subscribed capital of the European Central Bank" shall not include capital subscribed by the Bank of England.

ARTICLE 8

Article III-199 of the Constitution and Articles 43 to 47 of the Statute shall have effect, whether or not there is any Member State with a derogation, subject to the following amendments:

(a)   References in Article 43 of the Statute to the tasks of the European Central Bank and the European Monetary Institute shall include those tasks that still need to be performed after the introduction of the euro owing to the decision of the United Kingdom not to adopt the euro.

(b)   In addition to the tasks referred to in Article 46 of the Statute, the European Central Bank shall also give advice in relation to and contribute to the preparation of any European regulation or any European decision of the Council with regard to the United Kingdom taken in accordance with Article 9(a) and (c) of this Protocol.

(c)   The Bank of England shall pay up its subscription to the capital of the European Central Bank as a contribution to its operational costs on the same basis as national central banks of Member States with a derogation.

ARTICLE 9

The United Kingdom may notify the Council at any time of its intention to adopt the euro. In that event:

(a)   The United Kingdom shall have the right to adopt the euro provided only that it satisfies the necessary conditions. The Council, acting at the request of the United Kingdom and under the conditions and in accordance with the procedure laid down in Article III-198(1) and (2) of the Constitution, shall decide whether it fulfils the necessary conditions.

(b)   The Bank of England shall pay up its subscribed capital, transfer to the European Central Bank foreign reserve assets and contribute to its reserves on the same basis as the national central bank of a Member State whose derogation has been abrogated.

(c)   The Council, acting under the conditions and in accordance with the procedure laid down in Article III-198(3) of the Constitution, shall take all other necessary decisions to enable the United Kingdom to adopt the euro.

If the United Kingdom adopts the euro pursuant to the provisions of this Article, Articles 3 to 8 shall cease to have effect.

ARTICLE 10

Notwithstanding Article III-181 of the Constitution and Article 21(1) of the Statute, the Government of the United Kingdom may maintain its "ways and means" facility with the Bank of England if and so long as the United Kingdom does not adopt the euro.

14.   PROTOCOL ON CERTAIN PROVISIONS RELATING TO DENMARK AS REGARDS ECONOMIC AND MONETARY UNION

THE HIGH CONTRACTING PARTIES,

TAKING INTO ACCOUNT that the Danish Constitution contains provisions which may imply a referendum in Denmark prior to Denmark renouncing its exemption;

GIVEN THAT, on 3 November 1993, the Danish Government notified the Council of its intention not to participate in the third stage of economic and monetary union, under the terms of paragraph 1 of the Protocol on certain provisions relating to Denmark, annexed to the Treaty establishing the European Community,

HAVE AGREED upon the following provisions, which shall be annexed to the Treaty establishing a Constitution for Europe:

ARTICLE 1

In view of the notice given to the Council by the Danish Government on 3 November 1993, Denmark shall have an exemption. The effect of the exemption shall be that all provisions of the Constitution and the Statute of the European System of Central Banks and the European Central Bank referring to a derogation shall be applicable to Denmark.

ARTICLE 2

As for the abrogation of the exemption, the procedure referred to in Article III-198 of the Constitution shall only be initiated at the request of Denmark.

ARTICLE 3
In the event of abrogation of the exemption status, the provisions of this Protocol shall cease to apply.

15. PROTOCOL ON CERTAIN TASKS OF THE NATIONAL BANK OF DENMARK

THE HIGH CONTRACTING PARTIES,

DESIRING to settle certain particular problems relating to Denmark;

HAVE AGREED upon the following provisions, which shall be annexed to the Treaty establishing a Constitution for Europe:

SOLE ARTICLE
Article 14 of the Protocol on the Statute of the European System of Central Banks and of the European Central Bank shall not affect the right of the National Bank of Denmark to carry out its existing tasks concerning those parts of Denmark which are not part of the Union.

16. PROTOCOL ON THE PACIFIC FINANCIAL COMMUNITY FRANC SYSTEM

THE HIGH CONTRACTING PARTIES,

DESIRING to take into account a particular point relating to France,

HAVE AGREED upon the following provisions, which shall be annexed to the Treaty establishing a Constitution for Europe:

SOLE ARTICLE
France may keep the privilege of monetary emission in New Caledonia, French Polynesia and Wallis and Futuna under the terms established by its national laws and shall be solely entitled to determine the parity of the Pacific Financial Community franc.

17. PROTOCOL ON THE SCHENGEN *ACQUIS* INTEGRATED INTO THE FRAMEWORK OF THE EUROPEAN UNION

THE HIGH CONTRACTING PARTIES,

RECALLING that the provisions of the Schengen *acquis* consisting of the Agreements on the gradual abolition of checks at common borders, signed by some Member States of the European Union in Schengen on 14 June 1985 and on 19 June 1990, as well as related agreements and rules adopted on the basis of these agreements, have been integrated into the framework of the European Union by a Protocol annexed to the Treaty on European Union and to the Treaty establishing the European Community;

DESIRING to preserve the Schengen *acquis*, as developed since the entry into force of the abovementioned Protocol, within the framework of the Constitution, and to develop this *acquis* in order to contribute towards achieving the objective of offering citizens of the Union an area of freedom, security and justice without internal borders;

TAKING INTO ACCOUNT the special position of Denmark;

TAKING INTO ACCOUNT the fact that Ireland and the United Kingdom of Great Britain and Northern Ireland do not participate in all the provisions of the Schengen *acquis*; provision should, however, be made to allow those Member States to accept other provisions of this *acquis* in full or in part;

RECOGNISING that, as a consequence, it is necessary to make use of the provisions of the Constitution concerning closer co-operation between some Member States;

TAKING INTO ACCOUNT the need to maintain a special relationship with the Republic of Iceland and the Kingdom of Norway, both States being bound by the provisions of the Nordic passport union, together with the Nordic States which are members of the European Union;

HAVE AGREED UPON the following provisions, which shall be annexed to the Treaty establishing a Constitution for Europe,

ARTICLE 1

The Kingdom of Belgium, the Czech Republic, the Kingdom of Denmark, the Federal Republic of Germany, the Republic of Estonia, the Hellenic Republic, the Kingdom of Spain, the French Republic, the Italian Republic, the Republic of Cyprus, the Republic of Latvia, the Republic of Lithuania, the Grand Duchy of Luxembourg, the Republic of Hungary, the Republic of Malta, the Kingdom of the Netherlands, the Republic of Austria, the Republic of Poland, the Portuguese Republic, the Republic of Slovenia, the Slovak Republic, the Republic of Finland and the Kingdom of Sweden shall be authorised to implement closer co-operation among themselves in areas covered by provisions defined by the Council which constitute the Schengen *acquis*. This co-operation shall be conducted within the institutional and legal framework of the Union and with respect for the relevant provisions of the Constitution.

ARTICLE 2

The Schengen *acquis* shall apply to the Member States referred to in Article 1, without prejudice to Article 3 of the Protocol on the Treaty and the Act of Accession of the Czech Republic, the Republic of Estonia, the Republic of Cyprus, the Republic of Latvia, the Republic of Lithuania, the Republic of Hungary, the Republic of Malta, the Republic of Poland, the Republic of Slovenia and the Slovak Republic. The Council will substitute itself for the Executive Committee established by the Schengen agreements.

ARTICLE 3

The participation of Denmark in the adoption of measures constituting a development of the Schengen *acquis*, as well as the implementation of these measures and their application to Denmark, shall be governed by the relevant provisions of the Protocol on the position of Denmark.

ARTICLE 4

Ireland and the United Kingdom of Great Britain and Northern Ireland, may at any time request to take part in some or all of the provisions of the Schengen *acquis*.

The Council shall adopt a European decision on this request. It shall act by a unanimous decision of the members referred to in Article 1 and of the member representing the government of the Member State concerned.

ARTICLE 5

Proposals and initiatives to build upon the Schengen *acquis* shall be subject to the relevant provisions of the Constitution.

In this context, where either Ireland or the United Kingdom or both have not notified the President of the Council in writing within a reasonable period that they wish to take part, the authorisation referred to in Article III-419(1) of the Constitution shall be deemed to have been granted to the Member States referred to in Article 1 and to Ireland or the United Kingdom where either of them wishes to take part in the areas of co-operation in question.

ARTICLE 6

The Republic of Iceland and the Kingdom of Norway shall be associated with the implementation of the Schengen *acquis* and its further development. Appropriate procedures shall be agreed to that effect in an Agreement to be concluded with those States by the Council, acting by the unanimity of its members mentioned in Article 1. That Agreement shall include provisions on the contribution of Iceland and Norway to any financial consequences resulting from the implementation of this Protocol.

A separate Agreement shall be concluded by the Council, acting unanimously, with Iceland and Norway for the establishment of rights and obligations between Ireland and the United Kingdom of Great Britain and

Northern Ireland on the one hand, and Iceland and Norway on the other, in domains of the Schengen *acquis* which apply to these States.

ARTICLE 7

For the purposes of the negotiations for the admission of new Member States into the European Union, the Schengen *acquis* and further measures adopted by the institutions within its scope shall be regarded as an *acquis* which must be accepted in full by all States candidates for admission.

18. PROTOCOL ON THE APPLICATION OF CERTAIN ASPECTS OF ARTICLE III-130 OF THE CONSTITUTION TO THE UNITED KINGDOM AND TO IRELAND

THE HIGH CONTRACTING PARTIES,

DESIRING to settle certain questions relating to the United Kingdom and Ireland;

HAVING REGARD to the existence for many years of special travel arrangements between the United Kingdom and Ireland,

HAVE AGREED UPON the following provisions, which shall be annexed to the Treaty establishing a Constitution for Europe:

ARTICLE 1

The United Kingdom shall be entitled, notwithstanding Articles III-130 and III-265 of the Constitution, any other provision of the Constitution, any measure adopted under the Constitution, or any international agreement concluded by the Union or by the Union and its Member States with one or more third States, to exercise at its frontiers with other Member States such controls on persons seeking to enter the United Kingdom as it may consider necessary for the purpose:
(a) of verifying the right to enter the United Kingdom of citizens of Member States and of their dependants exercising rights conferred by Union law, as well as citizens of other States on whom such rights have been conferred by an agreement by which the United Kingdom is bound; and
(b) of determining whether or not to grant other persons permission to enter the United Kingdom.
Nothing in Articles III-130 and III-265 of the Constitution or in any other provision of the Constitution or in any measure adopted under it shall prejudice the right of the United Kingdom to adopt or exercise any such controls. References to the United Kingdom in this Article shall include territories for whose external relations the United Kingdom is responsible.

ARTICLE 2

The United Kingdom and Ireland may continue to make arrangements between themselves relating to the movement of persons between their territories ("the Common Travel Area"), while fully respecting the rights of persons referred to in Article 1, first paragraph, point (a), of this Protocol. Accordingly, as long as they maintain such arrangements, the provisions of Article 1 of this Protocol shall apply to Ireland under the same terms and conditions as for the United Kingdom. Nothing in Articles III-130 and III-265 of the Constitution, in any other provision of the Constitution or in any measure adopted under it shall affect any such arrangements.

ARTICLE 3

The other Member States shall be entitled to exercise at their frontiers or at any point of entry into their territory such controls on persons seeking to enter their territory from the United Kingdom or any territories whose external relations are under its responsibility for the same purposes stated in Article 1 of this Protocol, or from Ireland as long as the provisions of Article 1 of this Protocol apply to Ireland.
Nothing in Articles III-130 and III-265 of the Constitution or in any other provision of the Constitution or in any measure adopted under it shall prejudice the right of the other Member States to adopt or exercise any such controls.

ARTICLE 4

This Protocol shall also apply to acts which remain in force by virtue of Article IV-438 of the Constitution.

19. PROTOCOL ON THE POSITION OF THE UNITED KINGDOM AND IRELAND ON POLICIES IN RESPECT OF BORDER CONTROLS, ASYLUM AND IMMIGRATION, JUDICIAL CO-OPERATION IN CIVIL MATTERS AND ON POLICE CO-OPERATION

THE HIGH CONTRACTING PARTIES,

DESIRING to settle certain questions relating to the United Kingdom and Ireland;

HAVING REGARD to the Protocol on the application of certain aspects of Article III-130 of the Constitution to the United Kingdom and Ireland,

HAVE AGREED UPON the following provisions which shall be annexed to the Treaty establishing a Constitution for Europe:

ARTICLE 1

Subject to Article 3, the United Kingdom and Ireland shall not take part in the adoption by the Council of proposed measures pursuant to Section 2 or Section 3 of Chapter IV of Title III of Part III of the Constitution or to Article III-260 thereof, insofar as that Article relates to the areas covered by those Sections, to Article III-263 or to Article III-275(2)(a) of the Constitution. The unanimity of the members of the Council, with the exception of the representatives of the governments of the United Kingdom and Ireland, shall be necessary for acts of the Council which must be adopted unanimously.

For the purposes of this Article, a qualified majority shall be defined as at least 55% of the members of the Council representing the participating Member States, comprising at least 65% of the population of these States.

A blocking minority must include at least the minimum number of Council members representing more than 35% of the population of the participating Member States, plus one member, failing which the qualified majority shall be deemed attained.

By way of derogation from the second and third paragraphs, where the Council does not act on a proposal from the Commission or from the Union Minister for Foreign Affairs, the required qualified majority shall be defined as at least 72% of the members of the Council representing the participating Member States, comprising at least 65% of the population of these States.

ARTICLE 2

In consequence of Article 1 and subject to Articles 3, 4 and 6, none of the provisions of Section 2 or Section 3 of Chapter IV of Title III of Part III of the Constitution or of Article III-260 of the Constitution, insofar as that Article relates to the areas covered by those Sections, or of Article III-263 or Article III-275(2)(a) of the Constitution, no measure adopted pursuant to those Sections or Articles, no provision of any international agreement concluded by the Union pursuant to those Sections or Articles, and no decision of the Court of Justice of the European Union interpreting any such provision or measure shall be binding upon or applicable in the United Kingdom or Ireland; and no such provision, measure or decision shall in any way affect the competences, rights and obligations of those States; and no such provision, measure or decision shall in any way affect the Community or Union *acquis* nor form part of Union law as they apply to the United Kingdom or Ireland.

ARTICLE 3

1.   The United Kingdom or Ireland may notify the Council in writing, within three months after a proposal has been presented to the Council pursuant to Section 2 or Section 3 of Chapter IV of Title III of Part III of the Constitution or after a proposal or initiative has been presented to the Council pursuant to Article III-263 or to Article III-275(2)(a) of the Constitution, that it wishes to take part in the adoption and application of any such proposed measure, whereupon that State shall be entitled to do so. The unanimity of the members of the Council, with the exception of a member which has not made such a notification, shall be necessary for acts of the Council which must be adopted unanimously. A measure adopted under this paragraph shall be binding upon all Member States which took part in its adoption. The European regulations or decisions adopted pursuant to Article III-260 of the Constitution shall lay down the conditions for the participation of the United Kingdom and Ireland in the evaluations concerning the areas covered by Section 2 or Section 3 of Chapter IV of Title III of Part III of the Constitution.

For the purposes of this Article, a qualified majority shall be defined as at least 55% of the members of the Council representing the participating Member States, comprising at least 65% of the population of these States.

A blocking minority must include at least the minimum number of Council members representing more than 35% of the population of the participating Member States, plus one member, failing which the qualified majority shall be deemed attained.

By way of derogation from the second and third subparagraphs, where the Council does not act on a proposal from the Commission or from the Union Minister for Foreign Affairs, the required qualified majority shall be defined as at least 72% of the members of the Council representing the participating Member States, comprising at least 65% of the population of these States.

2.　　If after a reasonable period of time a measure referred to in paragraph 1 cannot be adopted with the United Kingdom or Ireland taking part, the Council may adopt such measure in accordance with Article 1 without the participation of the United Kingdom or Ireland. In that case Article 2 applies.

ARTICLE 4
The United Kingdom or Ireland may, at any time after the adoption of a measure pursuant to Section 2 or Section 3 of Chapter IV of Title III of Part III of the Constitution or to Article III-263 or to Article III-275(2)(a) of the Constitution, notify its intention to the Council and to the Commission that it wishes to accept that measure. In that case, the procedure provided for in Article III-420(1) of the Constitution shall apply *mutatis mutandis*.

ARTICLE 5
A Member State which is not bound by a measure adopted pursuant to Section 2 or Section 3 of Chapter IV of Title III of Part III of the Constitution, to Article III-263 or to Article III-275(2)(a) of the Constitution, shall bear no financial consequences of that measure other than administrative costs entailed for the institutions, unless all members of the Council, acting unanimously after consulting the European Parliament, decide otherwise.

ARTICLE 6
Where, in cases referred to in this Protocol, the United Kingdom or Ireland is bound by a measure adopted pursuant to Section 2 or Section 3 of Chapter IV of Title III of Part III of the Constitution, to Article III-260 of the Constitution, insofar as that Article relates to the areas covered by those Sections, to Article III-263 or to Article III-275(2)(a) of the Constitution, the relevant provisions of the Constitution shall apply to that State in relation to that measure.

ARTICLE 7
Articles 3 and 4 shall be without prejudice to the Protocol on the Schengen *acquis* integrated into the framework of the European Union.

ARTICLE 8
Ireland may notify the Council in writing that it no longer wishes to be covered by the terms of this Protocol. In that case, this Protocol shall no longer apply to Ireland.

20.　PROTOCOL ON THE POSITION OF DENMARK

THE HIGH CONTRACTING PARTIES,

RECALLING the decision of the Heads of State or Government, meeting within the European Council at Edinburgh on 12 December 1992, concerning certain problems raised by Denmark on the Treaty on European Union;

HAVING NOTED the position of Denmark with regard to citizenship, economic and monetary union, defence policy, and justice and home affairs as laid down in the Edinburgh decision;

CONSCIOUS of the fact that a continuation under the Constitution of the legal regime originating in the Edinburgh decision will significantly limit Denmark's participation in important areas of co-operation of the Union, and that it would be in the best interest of the Union to ensure the integrity of the *acquis* in the area of freedom, security and justice;

WISHING therefore to establish a legal framework that will provide an option for Denmark to participate in the adoption of measures proposed on the basis of Chapter IV of Title III of Part III of the Constitution and welcoming the intention of Denmark to avail itself of this option when possible in accordance with its constitutional requirements;

NOTING that Denmark will not prevent the other Member States from further developing their co-operation with respect to measures not binding on Denmark;

BEARING IN MIND the Protocol on the Schengen *acquis* integrated into the framework of the European Union,

HAVE AGREED UPON the following provisions, which shall be annexed to the Constitution:

PART I

ARTICLE 1

Denmark shall not take part in the adoption by the Council of proposed measures pursuant to Chapter IV of Title III of Part III of the Constitution. The unanimity of the members of the Council, with the exception of the representative of the government of Denmark, shall be necessary for the acts of the Council which must be adopted unanimously.

For the purposes of this Article, a qualified majority shall be defined as at least 55% of the members of the Council representing the participating Member States, comprising at least 65% of the population of these States.

A blocking minority must include at least the minimum number of Council members representing more than 35% of the population of the participating Member States, plus one member, failing which the qualified majority shall be deemed attained.

By way of derogation from the second and third paragraphs, where the Council does not act on a proposal from the Commission or from the Union Minister for Foreign Affairs, the required qualified majority shall be defined as at least 72% of the members of the Council representing the participating Member States, comprising at least 65% of the population of these States.

ARTICLE 2

None of the provisions of Chapter IV of Title III of Part III of the Constitution, no measure adopted pursuant to that Chapter, no provision of any international agreement concluded by the Union pursuant to that Chapter, and no decision of the Court of Justice of the European Union interpreting any such provision or measure shall be binding upon or applicable in Denmark; and no such provision, measure or decision shall in any way affect the competences, rights and obligations of Denmark; and no such provision, measure or decision shall in any way affect the Community or Union *acquis* nor form part of Union law as they apply to Denmark.

ARTICLE 3

Denmark shall bear no financial consequences of measures referred to in Article 1, other than administrative costs entailed for the institutions.

ARTICLE 4

1.   Denmark shall decide within a period of six months after the adoption of a measure to build upon the Schengen *acquis* covered by Part I whether it will implement this measure in its national law. If it decides to do so, this measure will create an obligation under international law between Denmark and the other Member States bound by the measure.

If Denmark decides not to implement such a measure, the Member States bound by that measure and Denmark will consider appropriate measures to be taken.

2.   Denmark shall maintain the rights and obligations existing before the entry into force of the Treaty establishing a Constitution for Europe with regard to the Schengen *acquis*.

PART II

ARTICLE 5

With regard to measures adopted by the Council pursuant to Article I-41, Article III-295(1) and Articles III-309 to III-313 of the Constitution, Denmark does not participate in the elaboration and the implementation of decisions and actions of the Union which have defence implications. Therefore Denmark shall not participate in their adoption. Denmark will not prevent the other Member States from further developing their co-operation in this area. Denmark shall not be obliged to contribute to the financing of operational expenditure arising from such measures, nor to make military capabilities available to the Union.

The unanimity of the members of the Council, with the exception of the representative of the government of Denmark, shall be necessary for the acts of the Council which must be adopted unanimously.

For the purposes of this Article, a qualified majority shall be defined as at least 55% of the members of the Council representing the participating Member States, comprising at least 65% of the population of these States.

A blocking minority must include at least the minimum number of Council members representing more than 35% of the population of the participating Member States, plus one member, failing which the qualified majority shall be deemed attained.

By way of derogation from the third and fourth paragraphs, where the Council does not act on a proposal from the Commission or from the Union Minister for Foreign Affairs, the required qualified majority shall be defined as at least 72% of the members of the Council representing the participating Member States, comprising at least 65% of the population of these States.

PART III

ARTICLE 6

This Protocol shall also apply to measures remaining in force by virtue of Article IV-438 of the Constitution, which were covered, prior to the entry into force of the Treaty establishing a Constitution for Europe, by the Protocol on the position of Denmark annexed to the Treaty on European Union and to the Treaty establishing the European Community.

ARTICLE 7

Articles 1, 2 and 3 shall not apply to measures determining the third countries whose nationals must be in possession of a visa when crossing the external borders of the Member States, or measures relating to a uniform format for visas.

PART IV

ARTICLE 8

At any time Denmark may, in accordance with its constitutional requirements, inform the other Member States that it no longer wishes to avail itself of all or part of this Protocol. In that event, Denmark will apply in full all relevant measures then in force taken within the framework of the Union.

ARTICLE 9

1.   At any time and without prejudice to Article 8, Denmark may, in accordance with its constitutional requirements, notify the other Member States that, with effect from the first day of the month following the notification, Part I shall consist of the provisions in the Annex. In that case Articles 5 to 9 shall be renumbered in consequence.

2.   Six months after the date on which the notification referred to in paragraph 1 takes effect all Schengen *acquis* and measures adopted to build upon this *acquis*, which until then have been binding on Denmark as obligations under international law, shall be binding upon Denmark as Union law.

ANNEX

ARTICLE 1

Subject to Article 3, Denmark shall not take part in the adoption by the Council of measures proposed pursuant to Chapter IV of Title III of Part III of the Constitution. The unanimity of the members of the Council, with the exception of the representative of the government of Denmark, shall be necessary for the acts of the Council which must be adopted unanimously.

For the purposes of this Article, a qualified majority shall be defined as at least 55% of the members of the Council representing the participating Member States, comprising at least 65% of the population of these States.

A blocking minority must include at least the minimum number of Council members representing more than 35% of the population of the participating Member States, plus one member, failing which the qualified majority shall be deemed attained.

By way of derogation from the second and third paragraphs, where the Council does not act on a proposal from the Commission or from the Union Minister for Foreign Affairs, the required qualified majority shall be defined as at least 72% of the members of the Council representing the participating Member States, comprising at least 65% of the population of these States.

ARTICLE 2

Pursuant to Article 1 and subject to Articles 3, 4 and 6, none of the provisions in Chapter IV of Title III of Part III of the Constitution, no measure adopted pursuant to that Chapter, no provision of any international agreements concluded by the Union pursuant to that Chapter, no decision of the Court of Justice of the European Union interpreting any such provision or measure shall be binding upon or applicable in Denmark; and no such provision, measure or decision shall in any way affect the competences, rights and obligations of Denmark; and no such provision, measure or decision shall in any way affect the Community or Union *acquis* nor form part of Union law as they apply to Denmark.

ARTICLE 3

1.   Denmark may notify the President of the Council in writing, within three months after a proposal or initiative has been presented to the Council pursuant to Chapter IV of Title III of Part III of the Constitution, that it wishes to take part in the adoption and application of any such proposed measure, whereupon Denmark shall be entitled to do so.

2.   If after a reasonable period of time a measure referred to in paragraph 1 cannot be adopted with Denmark taking part, the Council may adopt that measure referred to in paragraph 1 in accordance with Article 1 without the participation of Denmark. In that case Article 2 applies.

ARTICLE 4

Denmark may at any time after the adoption of a measure pursuant to Chapter IV of Title III of Part III of the Constitution notify its intention to the Council and the Commission that it wishes to accept that measure. In that case, the procedure provided for in Article III-420(1) of the Constitution shall apply *mutatis mutandis*.

ARTICLE 5

1.   Notification pursuant to Article 4 shall be submitted no later than six months after the final adoption of a measure if this measure builds upon the Schengen *acquis*.

If Denmark does not submit a notification in accordance with Articles 3 or 4 regarding a measure building upon the Schengen *acquis*, the Member States bound by that measure and Denmark will consider appropriate measures to be taken.

2.   A notification pursuant to Article 3 with respect to a measure building upon the Schengen *acquis* shall be deemed irrevocably to be a notification pursuant to Article 3 with respect to any further proposal or initiative aiming to build upon that measure to the extent that such proposal or initiative builds upon the Schengen *acquis*.

ARTICLE 6

Where, in cases referred to in this Part, Denmark is bound by a measure adopted by the Council pursuant to Chapter IV of Title III of Part III of the Constitution, the relevant provisions of the Constitution shall apply to Denmark in relation to that measure.

ARTICLE 7

Where Denmark is not bound by a measure adopted pursuant to Chapter IV of Title III of Part III of the Constitution, it shall bear no financial consequences of that measure other than administrative costs entailed for the institutions unless the Council, acting unanimously after consulting the European Parliament, decides otherwise.

21. PROTOCOL ON EXTERNAL RELATIONS OF THE MEMBER STATES WITH REGARD TO THE CROSSING OF EXTERNAL BORDERS

THE HIGH CONTRACTING PARTIES,

TAKING INTO ACCOUNT the need of the Member States to ensure effective controls at their external borders, in co-operation with third countries where appropriate,

HAVE AGREED UPON the following provision, which shall be annexed to the Treaty establishing a Constitution for Europe:

SOLE ARTICLE

The provisions on the measures on the crossing of external borders included in Article III-265(2)(b) of the Constitution shall be without prejudice to the competence of Member States to negotiate or conclude agreements with third countries as long as they respect Union law and other relevant international agreements.

22. PROTOCOL ON ASYLUM FOR NATIONALS OF MEMBER STATES

THE HIGH CONTRACTING PARTIES,

WHEREAS, in accordance with Article I-9(1) of the Constitution, the Union recognises the rights, freedoms and principles set out in the Charter of Fundamental Rights;

WHEREAS pursuant to Article I-9(3) of the Constitution, fundamental rights, as guaranteed by the European Convention for the Protection of Human Rights and Fundamental Freedoms, constitute part of the Union's law as general principles;

WHEREAS the Court of Justice of the European Union has jurisdiction to ensure that in the interpretation and application of Article I-9(1) and (3) of the Constitution the law is observed by the Union;

WHEREAS pursuant to Article I-58 of the Constitution, any European State, when applying to become a member of the Union, must respect the values set out in Article I-2 of the Constitution;

BEARING IN MIND that Article I-59 of the Constitution establishes a mechanism for the suspension of certain rights in the event of a serious and persistent breach by a Member State of those values;

RECALLING that each national of a Member State, as a citizen of the Union, enjoys a special status and protection which shall be guaranteed by the Member States in accordance with the provisions of Title II of Part I and Title II of Part III of the Constitution;

BEARING IN MIND that the Constitution establishes an area without internal frontiers and grants every citizen of the Union the right to move and reside freely within the territory of the Member States;

WISHING to prevent the institution of asylum being resorted to for purposes alien to those for which it is intended;

WHEREAS this Protocol respects the finality and the objectives of the Geneva Convention of 28 July 1951 relating to the status of refugees,

HAVE AGREED UPON the following provisions which shall be annexed to the Treaty establishing a Constitution for Europe:

SOLE ARTICLE

Given the level of protection of fundamental rights and freedoms by the Member States of the European Union, Member States shall be regarded as constituting safe countries of origin in respect of each other for all legal and practical purposes in relation to asylum matters. Accordingly, any application for asylum made by a national of a Member State may be taken into consideration or declared admissible for processing by another Member State only in the following cases:

(a)   if the Member State of which the applicant is a national proceeds, availing itself of the provisions of Article 15 of the European Convention for the Protection of Human Rights and Fundamental Freedoms, to take measures derogating in its territory from its obligations under that Convention;

(b)   if the procedure referred to in Article I-59(1) or (2) of the Constitution has been initiated and until the Council, or, where appropriate, the European Council, adopts a European decision in respect thereof with regard to the Member State of which the applicant is a national;

(c)   if the Council has adopted a European decision in accordance with Article I-59(1) of the Constitution in respect of the Member State of which the applicant is a national or if the European Council has adopted a European decision in accordance with Article I-59(2) of the Constitution in respect of the Member State of which the applicant is a national;

(d)   if a Member State should so decide unilaterally in respect of the application of a national of another Member State; in that case the Council shall be immediately informed; the application shall be dealt with on the basis of the presumption that it is manifestly unfounded without affecting in any way, whatever the case may be, the decision-making power of the Member State.

23. PROTOCOL ON PERMANENT STRUCTURED CO-OPERATION ESTABLISHED BY ARTICLE I-41(6) AND ARTICLE III-312 OF THE CONSTITUTION

THE HIGH CONTRACTING PARTIES,

HAVING REGARD TO Article I-41(6) and Article III-312 of the Constitution,

RECALLING that the Union is pursuing a common foreign and security policy based on the achievement of growing convergence of action by Member States;

RECALLING that the common security and defence policy is an integral part of the common foreign and security policy; that it provides the Union with operational capacity drawing on civil and military assets; that the Union may use such assets in the tasks referred to in Article III-309 of the Constitution outside the Union for peace-keeping, conflict prevention and strengthening international security in accordance with the principles of the United Nations Charter; that the performance of these tasks is to be undertaken using capabilities provided by the Member States in accordance with the principle of a single set of forces;

RECALLING that the common security and defence policy of the Union does not prejudice the specific character of the security and defence policy of certain Member States;

RECALLING that the common security and defence policy of the Union respects the obligations under the North Atlantic Treaty of those Member States, which see their common defence realised in the North Atlantic Treaty Organisation, which remains the foundation of the collective defence of its members, and is compatible with the common security and defence policy established within that framework;

CONVINCED that a more assertive Union role in security and defence matters will contribute to the vitality of a renewed Atlantic Alliance, in accordance with the Berlin Plus arrangements;

DETERMINED to ensure that the Union is capable of fully assuming its responsibilities within the international community;

RECOGNISING that the United Nations Organisation may request the Union's assistance for the urgent implementation of missions undertaken under Chapters VI and VII of the United Nations Charter;

RECOGNISING that the strengthening of the security and defence policy will require efforts by Member States in the area of capabilities;

CONSCIOUS that embarking on a new stage in the development of the European security and defence policy involves a determined effort by the Member States concerned;

RECALLING the importance of the Minister for Foreign Affairs being fully involved in proceedings relating to permanent structured co-operation,

HAVE AGREED UPON the following provisions, which shall be annexed to the Constitution:

ARTICLE 1
The permanent structured co-operation referred to in Article I-41(6) of the Constitution shall be open to any Member State which undertakes, from the date of entry into force of the Treaty establishing a Constitution for Europe, to:
(a) proceed more intensively to develop its defence capacities through the development of its national contributions and participation, where appropriate, in multinational forces, in the main European equipment programmes, and in the activity of the Agency in the field of defence capabilities development, research, acquisition and armaments (European Defence Agency), and
(b) have the capacity to supply by 2007 at the latest, either at national level or as a component of multinational force groups, targeted combat units for the missions planned, structured at a tactical level as a battle group, with support elements including transport and logistics, capable of carrying out the tasks referred to in Article III-309, within a period of 5 to 30 days, in particular in response to requests from the United Nations Organisation, and which can be sustained for an initial period of 30 days and be extended up to at least 120 days.

ARTICLE 2
To achieve the objectives laid down in Article 1, Member States participating in permanent structured co-operation shall undertake to:
(a) co-operate, as from the entry into force of the Treaty establishing a Constitution for Europe, with a view to achieving approved objectives concerning the level of investment expenditure on defence equipment, and regularly review these objectives, in the light of the security environment and of the Union's international responsibilities;
(b) bring their defence apparatus into line with each other as far as possible, particularly by harmonising the identification of their military needs, by pooling and, where appropriate, specialising their defence means and capabilities, and by encouraging co-operation in the fields of training and logistics;
(c) take concrete measures to enhance the availability, interoperability, flexibility and deployability of their forces, in particular by identifying common objectives regarding the commitment of forces, including possibly reviewing their national decision-making procedures;
(d) work together to ensure that they take the necessary measures to make good, including through multinational approaches, and without prejudice to undertakings in this regard within the North Atlantic Treaty Organisation, the shortfalls perceived in the framework of the "Capability Development Mechanism";
(e) take part, where appropriate, in the development of major joint or European equipment programmes in the framework of the European Defence Agency.

ARTICLE 3
The European Defence Agency shall contribute to the regular assessment of participating Member States' contributions with regard to capabilities, in particular contributions made in accordance with the criteria to be established inter alia on the basis of Article 2, and shall report thereon at least once a year. The assessment may serve as a basis for Council recommendations and European decisions adopted in accordance with Article III-312 of the Constitution.

24. PROTOCOL ON ARTICLE I-41(2) OF THE CONSTITUTION

THE HIGH CONTRACTING PARTIES,

BEARING IN MIND the need to implement fully the provisions of Article I-41(2) of the Constitution;

BEARING IN MIND that the policy of the Union in accordance with Article I-41(2) of the Constitution shall not prejudice the specific character of the security and defence policy of certain Member States and shall respect the obligations of certain Member States, which see their common defence realised in the North Atlantic Treaty Organisation, under the North Atlantic Treaty and be compatible with the common security and defence policy established within that framework,

HAVE AGREED UPON the following provision, which is annexed to the Treaty establishing a Constitution for Europe:

SOLE ARTICLE
The Union shall draw up, together with the Western European Union, arrangements for enhanced co-operation between them.

25. PROTOCOL CONCERNING IMPORTS INTO THE EUROPEAN UNION OF PETROLEUM PRODUCTS REFINED IN THE NETHERLANDS ANTILLES

THE HIGH CONTRACTING PARTIES,

BEING DESIROUS of giving fuller details about the system of trade applicable to imports into the Union of petroleum products refined in the Netherlands Antilles,

HAVE AGREED on the following provisions, which shall be annexed to the Treaty establishing a Constitution for Europe:

ARTICLE 1
This Protocol is applicable to petroleum products coming under the Combined Nomenclature numbers 27.10, 27.11, 27.12 (paraffin wax and petroleum wax), ex 27.13 (paraffin residues) and 27.14 (shale wax), imported for use in the Member States.

ARTICLE 2
Member States shall undertake to grant to petroleum products refined in the Netherlands Antilles the tariff preferences resulting from the Association of the latter with the Union, under the conditions provided for by this Protocol. These provisions shall hold good whatever may be the rules of origin applied by the Member States.

ARTICLE 3
1.   When the Commission, at the request of a Member State or on its own initiative, establishes that imports into the Union of petroleum products refined in the Netherlands Antilles under the system provided for in Article 2 are giving rise to real difficulties on the market of one or more Member States, it shall adopt a European decision establishing that customs duties on the said imports shall be introduced, increased or re-introduced by the Member States in question, to such an extent and for such a period as may be necessary to meet that situation. The rates of the customs duties thus introduced, increased or re-introduced may not exceed the customs duties applicable to third countries for these same products.

2.   The provisions of paragraph 1 can in any case be applied when imports into the Union of petroleum products refined in the Netherlands Antilles reach two million tonnes a year.

3.   The Council shall be informed of European decisions adopted by the Commission in pursuance of paragraphs 1 and 2, including those directed at rejecting the request of a Member State. The Council shall, at the request of any Member State, assume responsibility for the matter and may at any time adopt a European decision to amend or revoke such decisions.

ARTICLE 4
1.   If a Member State considers that imports of petroleum products refined in the Netherlands Antilles, made either directly or through another Member State under the system provided for in Article 2, are giving rise to real difficulties on its market and that immediate action is necessary to meet them, it may on its own initiative decide to apply customs duties to such imports, the rate of which may not exceed those of the customs duties applicable to third countries in respect of the same products. It shall notify its decision to the Commission, which shall within one month adopt a European decision establishing whether the measures taken by the State should be maintained or must be amended or cancelled. Article 3(3) shall be applicable to such decision of the Commission.

2.   When the quantities of petroleum products refined in the Netherlands Antilles imported either directly or through another Member State, under the system provided for in Article 2, into a Member State or States exceed during a calendar year the tonnage shown in the Annex to this Protocol, the measures taken in pursuance of paragraph 1 by that or those Member States for the current year shall be considered to be justified. The Commission shall, after assuring itself that the tonnage fixed has been reached, formally record the measures taken. In such a case the other Member States shall abstain from formally placing the matter before the Council.

ARTICLE 5
If the Union decides to apply quantitative restrictions to petroleum products, no matter whence they are imported, these restrictions may also be applied to imports of such products from the Netherlands Antilles. In this case preferential treatment shall be granted to the Netherlands Antilles as compared with third countries.

ARTICLE 6
1.   Articles 2 to 5 may be reviewed by the Council, by unanimous decision, after consulting the European Parliament and the Commission, when a common definition of origin for petroleum products from third countries and associated countries is adopted, or when decisions are taken within the framework of a common commercial policy for the products in question or when a common energy policy is established.

2.   When such revision is made, however, equivalent preferences shall in any case be maintained in favour of the Netherlands Antilles in a suitable form and for a minimum quantity of 2½ million tonnes of petroleum products.

3.   The Union's commitments in regard to equivalent preferences as referred to in paragraph 2 may, if necessary, be broken down State by State taking into account the tonnage indicated in the Annex to this Protocol.

ARTICLE 7
For the implementation of this Protocol, the Commission is responsible for following the pattern of imports into the Member States of petroleum products refined in the Netherlands Antilles. Member States shall communicate to the Commission, which shall see that it is circulated, all useful information to that end in accordance with the administrative conditions recommended by it.

ANNEX

For the implementation of Article 4(2), the High Contracting Parties have decided that the quantity of 2 million metric tons of petroleum products from the Antilles shall be allocated among the Member States as follows:

Germany	625,000 metric tons
Belgo/Luxembourg Economic Union	200,000 metric tons
France	75,000 metric tons
Italy	100,000 metric tons
Netherlands	1,000,000 metric tons

26. PROTOCOL ON THE ACQUISITION OF PROPERTY IN DENMARK

THE HIGH CONTRACTING PARTIES,

DESIRING to settle certain particular problems relating to Denmark,

HAVE AGREED upon the following provision, which shall be annexed to the Treaty establishing a Constitution for Europe:

SOLE ARTICLE
Notwithstanding the provisions of the Constitution, Denmark may maintain the existing legislation on the acquisition of second homes.

27. PROTOCOL ON THE SYSTEM OF PUBLIC BROADCASTING IN THE MEMBER STATES

THE HIGH CONTRACTING PARTIES,

CONSIDERING that the system of public broadcasting in the Member States is directly related to the democratic, social and cultural needs of each society and to the need to preserve media pluralism,

HAVE AGREED UPON the following interpretative provisions, which shall be annexed to the Treaty establishing a Constitution for Europe:

SOLE ARTICLE
The provisions of the Constitution shall be without prejudice to the competence of Member States to provide for the funding of public service broadcasting insofar as such funding is granted to broadcasting organisations for the fulfilment of the public service remit as conferred, defined and organised by each Member State, and insofar as such funding does not affect trading conditions and competition in the Union to an extent which would be contrary to the common interest, while the realisation of the remit of that public service shall be taken into account.

28. PROTOCOL CONCERNING ARTICLE III-214 OF THE CONSTITUTION

THE HIGH CONTRACTING PARTIES,

HAVE AGREED upon the following provision, which shall be annexed to the Treaty establishing a Constitution for Europe:

SOLE ARTICLE
For the purposes of Article III-214 of the Constitution, benefits under occupational social security schemes shall not be considered as remuneration if and insofar as they are attributable to periods of employment prior to 17 May 1990, except in the case of workers or those claiming under them who have before that date initiated legal proceedings or introduced an equivalent claim under the applicable national law.

29. PROTOCOL ON ECONOMIC, SOCIAL AND TERRITORIAL COHESION

THE HIGH CONTRACTING PARTIES,

RECALLING that Article I-3 of the Constitution includes the objective of promoting economic, social and territorial cohesion and solidarity between Member States and that the said cohesion figures among the areas of shared competence of the Union listed in Article I-14(2)(c) of the Constitution;

RECALLING that the provisions of Section 3 of Chapter III of Title III of Part III of the Constitution, on economic, social and territorial cohesion as a whole provide the legal basis for consolidating and further developing the Union's action in this field, including the creation of a fund;

RECALLING that Article III-223 of the Constitution envisages setting up a Cohesion Fund;

NOTING that the European Investment Bank is lending large and increasing amounts for the benefit of the poorer regions;

NOTING the desire for greater flexibility in the arrangements for allocations from the Structural Funds;

NOTING the desire for modulation of the levels of Union participation in programmes and projects in certain Member States;

NOTING the proposal to take greater account of the relative prosperity of Member States in the system of own resources,

HAVE AGREED upon the following provisions, which shall be annexed to the Treaty establishing a Constitution for Europe:

SOLE ARTICLE
1.   The Member States reaffirm that the promotion of economic, social and territorial cohesion is vital to the full development and enduring success of the Union.

2.   The Member States reaffirm their conviction that the Structural Funds should continue to play a considerable part in the achievement of Union objectives in the field of cohesion.

3.   The Member States reaffirm their conviction that the European Investment Bank should continue to devote the majority of its resources to the promotion of economic, social and territorial cohesion, and declare their willingness to review the capital needs of the European Investment Bank as soon as this is necessary for that purpose.

4.   The Member States agree that the Cohesion Fund shall provide Union financial contributions to projects in the fields of environment and trans-European networks in Member States with a per capita GNP of less than 90% of the Union average which have a programme leading to the fulfilment of the conditions of economic convergence as set out in Article III-184 of the Constitution.

5.   The Member States declare their intention of allowing a greater margin of flexibility in allocating financing from the Structural Funds to specific needs not covered under the present Structural Funds regulations.

6.   The Member States declare their willingness to modulate the levels of Union participation in the context of programmes and projects of the Structural Funds, with a view to avoiding excessive increases in budgetary expenditure in the less prosperous Member States.

7.   The Member States recognise the need to monitor regularly the progress made towards achieving economic, social and territorial cohesion, and state their willingness to study all necessary measures in this respect.

8.   The Member States declare their intention of taking greater account of the contributive capacity of individual Member States in the system of own resources, and of examining means of correcting, for the less prosperous Member States, regressive elements existing in the present own resources system.

30.   PROTOCOL ON SPECIAL ARRANGEMENTS FOR GREENLAND

THE HIGH CONTRACTING PARTIES,

HAVE AGREED upon the following provisions, which shall be annexed to the Treaty establishing a Constitution for Europe:

SOLE ARTICLE
1.   The treatment on import into the Union of products subject to the common organisation of the market in fishery products and originating in Greenland shall, while complying with the mechanisms of the common market organisation, involve exemption from customs duties and charges having equivalent effect and the absence of quantitative restrictions or measures having equivalent effect if the possibilities for access to Greenland fishing zones granted to the Union pursuant to an agreement between the Union and the authority responsible for Greenland are satisfactory to the Union.

2.   The measures relating to the import arrangements for the products referred to in paragraph 1 shall be adopted in accordance with the procedures laid down in Article III-231 of the Constitution.

31. PROTOCOL ON ARTICLE 40.3.3 OF THE CONSTITUTION OF IRELAND

THE HIGH CONTRACTING PARTIES

HAVE AGREED upon the following provision, which shall be annexed to the Treaty establishing a Constitution for Europe and to the Treaty establishing the European Atomic Energy Community:

SOLE ARTICLE

Nothing in the Treaty establishing a Constitution for Europe or in the Treaties or Acts modifying or supplementing it shall affect the application in Ireland of Article 40.3.3 of the Constitution of Ireland.

32. PROTOCOL RELATING TO ARTICLE I-9(2) OF THE CONSTITUTION ON THE ACCESSION OF THE UNION TO THE EUROPEAN CONVENTION ON THE PROTECTION OF HUMAN RIGHTS AND FUNDAMENTAL FREEDOMS

THE HIGH CONTRACTING PARTIES

HAVE AGREED on the following provisions, which shall be annexed to the Treaty establishing a Constitution for Europe:

ARTICLE 1

The agreement relating to the accession of the Union to the European Convention on the Protection of Human Rights and Fundamental Freedoms (hereinafter referred to as the "European Convention") provided for in Article I-9(2) of the Constitution shall make provision for preserving the specific characteristics of the Union and Union law, in particular with regard to:

(a)   the specific arrangements for the Union's possible participation in the control bodies of the European Convention;

(b)   the mechanisms necessary to ensure that proceedings by non-Member States and individual applications are correctly addressed to Member States and/or the Union as appropriate.

ARTICLE 2

The agreement referred to in Article 1 shall ensure that accession of the Union shall not affect the competences of the Union or the powers of its institutions. It shall ensure that nothing therein affects the situation of Member States in relation to the European Convention, in particular in relation to the Protocols thereto, measures taken by Member States derogating from the European Convention in accordance with Article 15 thereof and reservations to the European Convention made by Member States in accordance with Article 57 thereof.

ARTICLE 3

Nothing in the agreement referred to in Article 1 shall affect Article III-375(2) of the Constitution.

33. PROTOCOL ON THE ACTS AND TREATIES WHICH HAVE SUPPLEMENTED OR AMENDED THE TREATY ESTABLISHING THE EUROPEAN COMMUNITY AND THE TREATY ON EUROPEAN UNION

THE HIGH CONTRACTING PARTIES,

WHEREAS Article IV-437(1) of the Constitution repeals the Treaty establishing the European Community and the Treaty on European Union and the Acts and Treaties which have supplemented or amended them;

WHEREAS a list should be drawn up of the acts and treaties referred to in Article IV-437(1);

WHEREAS the substance of Article 9(7) of the Treaty of Amsterdam should be incorporated;

RECALLING that the Act of 20 September 1976 concerning the election of representatives of the European Parliament by direct universal suffrage is to remain in force,

HAVE AGREED upon the following provisions, which are annexed to the Treaty establishing a Constitution for Europe and to the Treaty establishing the European Atomic Energy Community:

ARTICLE 1

1.   The following Acts and Treaties which have supplemented or amended the Treaty establishing the European Community are hereby repealed:

(a)   the Protocol of 8 April 1965 on the privileges and immunities of the European Communities annexed to the Treaty establishing a single Council and a single Commission (OJ 152, 13.7.1967, p. 13);

(b)   the Treaty of 22 April 1970 amending certain budgetary provisions of the Treaties establishing the European Communities and of the Treaty establishing a single Council and a single Commission of the European Communities (OJ L 2, 2.1.1971, p. 1);

(c)   the Treaty of 22 July 1975 amending certain financial provisions of the Treaties establishing the European Communities and of the Treaty establishing a single Council and a single Commission of the European Communities (OJ L 359, 31.12.1977, p. 4);

(d)   the Treaty of 10 July 1975 amending certain provisions of the Protocol on the Statute of the European Investment Bank (OJ L 91, 6.4.1978, p. 1);

(e)   the Treaty of 13 March 1984 amending, with regard to Greenland, the Treaties establishing the European Communities (OJ L 29, 1.2.1985, p. 1);

(f)   the Single European Act of 17 February 1986 and 28 February 1986 (OJ L 169, 29.6.1987, p. 1);

(g)   the Act of 25 March 1993 amending the Protocol on the Statute of the European Investment Bank, empowering the Board of Governors to establish a European Investment Fund (OJ L 173, 7.7.1994, p. 14);

(h)   Decision 2003/223/EC of the Council, meeting in the composition of the Heads of State or Government, of 21 March 2003 on an amendment to Article 10.2 of the Statute of the European System of Central Banks and of the European Central Bank (OJ L 83, 1.4.2003, p. 66).

2.   The Treaty of Amsterdam of 2 October 1997 amending the Treaty on European Union, the Treaties establishing the European Communities and certain related acts is hereby repealed (OJ C 340, 10.11.1997, p. 1).

3.   The Treaty of Nice of 26 February 2001 amending the Treaty on European Union, the Treaties establishing the European Communities and certain related acts is hereby repealed (OJ C 80, 10.3.2001, p. 1).

ARTICLE 2

1.   Without prejudice to the application of Article III-432 of the Constitution and Article 189 of the Treaty establishing the European Atomic Energy Community, the representatives of the Governments of the Member States shall adopt by common accord the necessary provisions for the purpose of dealing with certain problems particular to the Grand Duchy of Luxembourg which arise from the creation of a Single Council and a Single Commission of the European Communities.

2.   The Act concerning the election of representatives of the European Parliament by direct universal suffrage, annexed to Council Decision 76/787/ECSC, EEC, Euratom (OJ L 278, 8.10.1976, p. 1), as it stands at the time of entry into force of the Treaty establishing a Constitution for Europe remains in force. In order to bring it into line with the Constitution, this Act is hereby amended as follows:

(a)   Article 1(3) shall be deleted.

(b)   This amendment does not concern the English text.

(c)   In Article 6(2), the words "of 8 April 1965" shall be deleted; and the term "European Communities" shall be replaced by "European Union".

(d)   In the second indent of Article 7(1), the term "Commission of the European Communities" shall be replaced by "European Commission".

(e)   In the third indent of Article 7(1), the phrase "Court of Justice of the European Communities or of the Court of First Instance" shall be replaced by "Court of Justice of the European Union".

(f)   In the fifth indent of Article 7(1), the term "Court of Auditors of the European Communities" shall be replaced by "Court of Auditors".

(g)   In the sixth indent of Article 7(1), the term "Ombudsman of the European Communities" shall be replaced by "European Ombudsman".

(h)   In the seventh indent of Article 7(1), the phrase "of the European Economic Community and of the European Atomic Energy Community" shall be replaced by "of the European Union".

(i)   In the ninth indent of Article 7(1), the phrase "pursuant to the Treaties establishing the European Economic Community and the European Atomic Energy Community" shall be replaced by "pursuant to the Treaty establishing a Constitution for Europe and the Treaty establishing the European Atomic Energy Community"; and the term "Communities'" shall be replaced by "Union's".

(j)   In the eleventh indent of Article 7(1), the phrase "institutions of the European Communities or of the specialised bodies attached to them or of the European Central Bank" shall be replaced by "institutions, bodies, offices or agencies of the European Union".

(k)   The indents of Article 7(1) shall become points (a) to (k) respectively.

(l)   The indents of the second subparagraph of Article 7(2) shall become points (a) and (b) respectively.

(m)   In the second subparagraph of Article 11(2), the term "Community" shall be replaced by "Union"; the word "determine" shall be replaced by "adopt a European decision which shall determine"; and the words "preceding subparagraph" shall be replaced by "first subparagraph".

(n)   In Article 11(3), the phrase "without prejudice to Article 139 of the Treaty establishing the European Community" shall be replaced by "without prejudice to Article III-336 of the Constitution".

(o)   In Article 14, the term "a proposal" shall be replaced by "an initiative"; and the phrase "adopt such measures" shall be replaced by "adopt the necessary European regulations or decisions".

34.   PROTOCOL ON THE TRANSITIONAL PROVISIONS RELATING TO THE INSTITUTIONS AND BODIES OF THE UNION

THE HIGH CONTRACTING PARTIES,

WHEREAS, in order to organise the transition from the European Union established by the Treaty on European Union and the European Community to the European Union established by the Treaty establishing a Constitution for Europe which is their successor, it is necessary to lay down transitional provisions which will apply before all the provisions of the Constitution and the instruments necessary for their implementation take full effect,

HAVE AGREED UPON the following provisions, which shall be annexed to the Treaty establishing a Constitution for Europe and to the Treaty establishing the European Atomic Energy Community:

TITLE I

PROVISIONS CONCERNING THE EUROPEAN PARLIAMENT

ARTICLE 1

1.   In accordance with the second subparagraph of Article I-20(2) of the Constitution, the European Council shall adopt a European decision determining the composition of the European Parliament sufficiently in advance of the 2009 European Parliament elections.

2.   During the 2004-2009 parliamentary term, the composition and the number of representatives elected to the European Parliament in each Member State shall remain the same as on the date of the entry into force of the Treaty establishing a Constitution for Europe, the number of representatives being as follows:

Belgium	24	Luxembourg	6
Czech Republic	24	Hungary	24
Denmark	14	Malta	5
Germany	99	Netherlands	27
Estonia	6	Austria	18
Greece	24	Poland	54
Spain	54	Portugal	24
France	78	Slovenia	7
Ireland	13	Slovakia	14
Italy	78	Finland	14
Cyprus	6	Sweden	19
Latvia	9	United Kingdom	78
Lithuania	13		

TITLE II

PROVISIONS CONCERNING THE EUROPEAN COUNCIL AND THE COUNCIL

ARTICLE 2

1.   The provisions of Article I-25(1), (2) and (3) of the Constitution on the definition of the qualified majority in the European Council and the Council shall take effect on 1 November 2009, after the 2009 European Parliament elections have taken place in accordance with Article I-20(2) of the Constitution.

2.   The following provisions shall remain in force until 31 October 2009, without prejudice to Article I-25(4) of the Constitution.

For acts of the European Council and of the Council requiring a qualified majority, members' votes shall be weighted as follows:

Belgium	12	Luxembourg	4
Czech Republic	12	Hungary	12
Denmark	7	Malta	3
Germany	29	Netherlands	13
Estonia	4	Austria	10
Greece	12	Poland	27
Spain	27	Portugal	12
France	29	Slovenia	4
Ireland	7	Slovakia	7
Italy	29	Finland	7
Cyprus	4	Sweden	10
Latvia	4	United Kingdom	29
Lithuania	7		

Acts shall be adopted if there are at least 232 votes in favour representing a majority of the members where, under the Constitution, they must be adopted on a proposal from the Commission. In other cases decisions shall be adopted if there are at least 232 votes in favour representing at least two thirds of the members.

A member of the European Council or the Council may request that, where an act is adopted by the European Council or the Council by a qualified majority, a check is made to ensure that the Member States comprising the qualified majority represent at least 62% of the total population of the Union. If that proves not to be the case, the act shall not be adopted.

3.   For subsequent accessions, the threshold referred to in paragraph 2 shall be calculated to ensure that the qualified majority threshold expressed in votes does not exceed that resulting from the table in the Declaration on the enlargement of the European Union in the Final Act of the Conference which adopted the Treaty of Nice.

4.   The provisions of the following Articles shall take effect on 1 November 2009:
-       Article I-44(3), third, fourth and fifth subparagraphs, of the Constitution,
-       Article I-59(5), second and third subparagraphs, of the Constitution,
-       Article I-60(4), second subparagraph, of the Constitution,
-       Article III-179(4), third and fourth subparagraphs, of the Constitution,
-       Article III-184(6), third and fourth subparagraphs, of the Constitution,
-       Article III-184(7), third and fourth subparagraphs, of the Constitution,
-       Article III-194(2), second and third subparagraphs, of the Constitution,
-       Article III-196(3), second and third subparagraphs, of the Constitution,
-       Article III-197(4), second and third subparagraphs, of the Constitution,
-       Article III-198(2), third subparagraph, of the Constitution,
-       Article III-312(3), third and fourth subparagraphs, of the Constitution,
-       Article III-312(4), third and fourth subparagraphs, of the Constitution,
-       Article 1, second, third and fourth paragraphs, and Article 3(1), second, third and fourth subparagraphs, of the Protocol on the position of the United Kingdom and Ireland on policies in respect of border controls, asylum and immigration, judicial co-operation in civil matters and on police co-operation,
-       Article 1, second, third and fourth paragraphs and Article 5, third, fourth and fifth paragraphs, of the Protocol on the position of Denmark.

Until 31 October 2009, the qualified majority shall, in cases where not all the members of the Council participate in voting, namely in the cases referred to in the articles mentioned in the first subparagraph, be defined as the same proportion of the weighted votes and the same proportion of the number of the Council members and, if appropriate, the same percentage of the population of the Member States concerned as laid down in paragraph 2.

ARTICLE 3
Until the entry into force of the European decision referred to in Article I-24(4) of the Constitution, the Council may meet in the configurations laid down in Article I-24(2) and (3) and in the other configurations on the list established by a European decision of the General Affairs Council, acting by a simple majority.

TITLE III

PROVISIONS CONCERNING THE COMMISSION, INCLUDING THE UNION MINISTER FOR FOREIGN AFFAIRS

ARTICLE 4
The members of the Commission in office on the date of entry into force of the Treaty establishing a Constitution for Europe shall remain in office until the end of their term of office. However, on the day of the appointment of the Union Minister for Foreign Affairs, the term of office of the member having the same nationality as the Union Minister for Foreign Affairs shall end.

TITLE IV

PROVISIONS CONCERNING THE SECRETARY-GENERAL OF THE COUNCIL, HIGH REPRESENTATIVE FOR THE COMMON FOREIGN AND SECURITY POLICY, AND THE DEPUTY SECRETARY-GENERAL OF THE COUNCIL

ARTICLE 5
The terms of office of the Secretary-General of the Council, High Representative for the common foreign and security policy, and the Deputy Secretary-General of the Council shall end on the date of entry into force of the Treaty establishing a Constitution for Europe. The Council shall appoint a Secretary-General in conformity with Article III-344(2) of the Constitution.

TITLE V

PROVISIONS CONCERNING ADVISORY BODIES

ARTICLE 6
Until entry into force of the European decision referred to in Article III-386 of the Constitution, the allocation of members of the Committee of the Regions shall be as follows:

Belgium	12	Luxembourg	6
Czech Republic	12	Hungary	12
Denmark	9	Malta	5
Germany	24	Netherlands	12
Estonia	7	Austria	12
Greece	12	Poland	21
Spain	21	Portugal	12
France	24	Slovenia	7
Ireland	9	Slovakia	9
Italy	24	Finland	9
Cyprus	6	Sweden	12
Latvia	7	United Kingdom	24
Lithuania	9		

ARTICLE 7
Until entry into force of the European decision referred to in Article III-389 of the Constitution, the allocation of members of the Economic and Social Committee shall be as follows:

Belgium	12	Luxembourg	6
Czech Republic	12	Hungary	12
Denmark	9	Malta	5
Germany	24	Netherlands	12
Estonia	7	Austria	12
Greece	12	Poland	21
Spain	21	Portugal	12
France	24	Slovenia	7
Ireland	9	Slovakia	9
Italy	24	Finland	9
Cyprus	6	Sweden	12
Latvia	7	United Kingdom	24
Lithuania	9		

35. PROTOCOL ON THE FINANCIAL CONSEQUENCES OF THE EXPIRY OF THE TREATY ESTABLISHING THE EUROPEAN COAL AND STEEL COMMUNITY AND ON THE RESEARCH FUND FOR COAL AND STEEL

THE HIGH CONTRACTING PARTIES,

RECALLING that all assets and liabilities of the European Coal and Steel Community, as they existed on 23 July 2002, were transferred to the European Community on 24 July 2002;

TAKING ACCOUNT of the desire to use these funds for research in sectors related to the coal and steel industry and therefore the necessity to provide for certain special rules in this regard,

HAVE AGREED UPON the following provisions, which shall be annexed to the Treaty establishing a Constitution for Europe:

ARTICLE 1
1.	The net worth of the assets and liabilities of the European Coal and Steel Community, as they appear in the balance sheet of the European Coal and Steel Community of 23 July 2002, subject to any increase or

decrease which may occur as a result of the liquidation operations, shall be considered as Union assets intended for research in sectors related to the coal and steel industry, referred to as the "European Coal and Steel Community in liquidation". On completion of the liquidation they shall be referred to as the "Assets of the Research Fund for Coal and Steel".

2.   The revenue from these assets, referred to as the "Research Fund for Coal and Steel", shall be used exclusively for research, outside the research framework programme, in sectors related to the coal and steel industry in accordance with this Protocol and with acts adopted under it.

ARTICLE 2
1.   A European law of the Council shall lay down all the necessary provisions for the implementation of this Protocol, including essential principles. The Council shall act after obtaining the consent of the European Parliament.

2.   The Council shall adopt, on a proposal from the Commission, the European regulations or decisions establishing multiannual financial guidelines for managing the assets of the Research Fund for Coal and Steel and technical guidelines for the research programme of the Research Fund for Coal and Steel. It shall act after consulting the European Parliament.

ARTICLE 3
Except as otherwise provided in this Protocol and in the acts adopted under it, the provisions of the Constitution shall apply.

36. PROTOCOL AMENDING THE TREATY ESTABLISHING THE EUROPEAN ATOMIC ENERGY COMMUNITY

THE HIGH CONTRACTING PARTIES,

RECALLING the necessity that the provisions of the Treaty establishing the European Atomic Energy Community should continue to have full legal effect;

DESIRING to adapt that Treaty to the new rules laid down by the Treaty establishing a Constitution for Europe, in particular in the institutional and financial fields,

HAVE AGREED UPON the following provisions, which shall be annexed to the Treaty establishing a Constitution for Europe and which amend the Treaty establishing the European Atomic Energy Community as follows:

ARTICLE 1
This Protocol shall amend the Treaty establishing the European Atomic Energy Community (hereinafter referred to as the "EAEC Treaty") in its version in force at the time of entry into force of the Treaty establishing a Constitution for Europe.
Notwithstanding the provisions of Article IV-437 of the Treaty establishing a Constitution for Europe and without prejudice to the other provisions of this Protocol, the legal effects of the amendments made to the EAEC Treaty by the Treaties and Acts repealed pursuant to Article IV-437 of the Treaty establishing a Constitution for Europe and the legal effects of the acts in force adopted on the basis of the EAEC Treaty shall not be affected.

ARTICLE 2
The heading of Title III of the EAEC Treaty "Institutional provisions" shall be replaced by the heading: "Institutional and financial provisions".

ARTICLE 3
The following chapter shall be inserted at the beginning of Title III of the EAEC Treaty:

"CHAPTER I

APPLICATION OF CERTAIN PROVISIONS OF THE TREATY ESTABLISHING A CONSTITUTION FOR EUROPE

ARTICLE 106a
1.   Articles I-19 to I-29, Articles I-31 to I-39, Articles I-49 and I-50, Articles I-53 to I-56, Articles I-58 to I-60, Articles III-330 to III-372, Articles III-374 and III-375, Articles III-378 to III-381, Articles III-384 and III-385, Articles III-389 to III-392, Articles III-395 to III-410, Articles III-412 to III-415 and Articles III-427, III-433, IV-439 and IV-443 of the Treaty establishing a Constitution for Europe shall apply to this Treaty.

2.   Within the framework of this Treaty, the references to the Union and to the Constitution in the provisions referred to in paragraph 1 and those in the protocols annexed both to the Treaty establishing a Constitution for Europe and to this Treaty shall be taken, respectively, as references to the European Atomic Energy Community and to this Treaty.

3.   The provisions of the Treaty establishing a Constitution for Europe shall not derogate from the provisions of this Treaty."

ARTICLE 4
Chapters I, II and III of Title III of the EAEC Treaty shall be renumbered II, III and IV.

ARTICLE 5
1.   Article 3, Articles 107 to 132, Articles 136 to 143, Articles 146 to 156, Articles 158 to 163, Articles 165 to 170, Articles 173 and 173A, Article 175, Articles 177 to 179a, and Articles 180b, 181, 183, 183A, 190 and 204 of the EAEC Treaty shall be repealed.

2.   The Protocols previously annexed to the EAEC Treaty shall be repealed.

ARTICLE 6
The heading of Title IV of the EAEC Treaty "Financial provisions" shall be replaced by the heading: "Specific financial provisions".

ARTICLE 7
1.   In the third paragraph of Article 38 and the third paragraph of Article 82 of the EAEC Treaty the references to Articles 141 and 142 shall be replaced by references to Articles III-360 and III-361 respectively of the Constitution.

2.   In Article 171(2) and Article 176(3) of the EAEC Treaty the references to Article 183 shall be replaced by references to Article III-412 of the Constitution.

3.   In Article 172(4) of the EAEC Treaty the reference to Article 177(5) shall be replaced by a reference to Article III-404 of the Constitution.

4.   In Articles 38, 82, 96 and 98 of the EAEC Treaty the term "directive" shall be replaced by the term "European regulation".

5.   In the EAEC Treaty the term "decision" shall be replaced by "European decision" save in Articles 18, 20 and 23 and the first paragraph of Article 53 and in cases where a decision is taken by the Court of Justice of the European Union.

6.   In the EAEC Treaty the term "Court of Justice" shall be replaced by "Court of Justice of the European Union".

ARTICLE 8
Article 191 of the EAEC Treaty shall be replaced by the following:

"ARTICLE 191
The Community shall enjoy in the territories of the Member States such privileges and immunities as are necessary for the performance of its tasks, under the conditions laid down in the Protocol on the privileges and immunities of the European Union."

ARTICLE 9
Article 198 of the EAEC Treaty shall be replaced by the following:

"ARTICLE 198
Save as otherwise provided, the provisions of this Treaty shall apply to the European territories of the Member States and to the non-European territories under their jurisdiction. They shall also apply to the European territories for whose external relations a Member State is responsible.
The provisions of this Treaty shall apply to the Åland Islands with the derogations which were originally set out in the Treaty referred to in Article IV-437(2)(d) of the Treaty establishing a Constitution for Europe and which have been incorporated in the Protocol on the Treaties and Acts of Accession of the Kingdom of Denmark, Ireland and the United Kingdom of Great Britain and Northern Ireland, of the Hellenic Republic, of the Kingdom of Spain and the Portuguese Republic, and of the Republic of Austria, the Republic of Finland and the Kingdom of Sweden.
Notwithstanding the first, second and third paragraphs:
(a)   this Treaty shall not apply to the Faroe Islands or to Greenland;
(b)   this Treaty shall not apply to the Sovereign Base Areas of the United Kingdom of Great Britain and Northern Ireland in Cyprus;
(c)   this Treaty shall not apply to the overseas countries and territories having special relations with the United Kingdom of Great Britain and Northern Ireland which are not mentioned in the list in Annex II to the Treaty establishing a Constitution for Europe;
(d)   this Treaty shall apply to the Channel Islands and the Isle of Man only to the extent necessary to ensure the implementation of the arrangements for those islands originally set out in the Treaty referred to in Article IV-437(2)(a) of the Treaty establishing a Constitution for Europe and which have been incorporated in the Protocol on the Treaties and Acts of Accession of the Kingdom of Denmark, Ireland and the United Kingdom of Great Britain and Northern Ireland, of the Hellenic Republic, of the Kingdom of Spain and the Portuguese Republic, and of the Republic of Austria, the Republic of Finland and the Kingdom of Sweden."

ARTICLE 10
Article 206 of the EAEC Treaty shall be replaced by the following:

"ARTICLE 206
The Community may conclude with one or more States or international organisations agreements establishing an association involving reciprocal rights and obligations, common action and special procedures.
These agreements shall be concluded by the Council, acting unanimously after consulting the European Parliament.
Where such agreements call for amendments to this Treaty, these amendments shall first be adopted in accordance with the procedure laid down in Article IV-443 of the Treaty establishing a Constitution for Europe."

ARTICLE 11
In Article 225 of the EAEC Treaty, the second paragraph shall be replaced by the following:

"The Czech, Danish, English, Estonian, Finnish, Greek, Hungarian, Irish, Latvian, Lithuanian, Maltese, Polish, Portuguese, Slovak, Slovenian, Spanish and Swedish versions of the Treaty shall also be authentic."

ARTICLE 12
The revenue and expenditure of the European Atomic Energy Community, except for those of the Supply Agency and Joint Undertakings, shall be shown in the budget of the Union.

DECLARATIONS OF THE CONFERENCE

Descriptions have been added in brackets and in italics by the BMDF to aid the reader in identifying the subject of each Declaration.

* * * * *

DECLARATIONS

A. DECLARATIONS CONCERNING PROVISIONS OF THE CONSTITUTION

1. DECLARATION ON ARTICLE I-6

The Conference notes that Article I-6 reflects existing case law of the Court of Justice of the European Communities and of the Court of First Instance.

2. DECLARATION ON ARTICLE I-9(2)

The Conference agrees that the Union's accession to the European Convention on the Protection of Human Rights and Fundamental Freedoms should be arranged in such a way as to preserve the specific features of Union law. In this connection, the Conference notes the existence of a regular dialogue between the Court of Justice of the European Union and the European Court of Human Rights; such dialogue could be reinforced when the Union accedes to that Convention.

3. DECLARATION ON ARTICLES I-22, I-27 AND I-28

In choosing the persons called upon to hold the offices of President of the European Council, President of the Commission and Union Minister for Foreign Affairs, due account is to be taken of the need to respect the geographical and demographic diversity of the Union and its Member States.

4. DECLARATION ON ARTICLE I-24(7) CONCERNING THE EUROPEAN COUNCIL DECISION ON THE EXERCISE OF THE PRESIDENCY OF THE COUNCIL

The Conference declares that the European Council should begin preparing the European decision establishing the measures for applying the European decision of the European Council on the exercise of the Presidency of the Council as soon as the Treaty establishing a Constitution for Europe is signed and should give its political approval within six months. A draft European decision of the European Council, which will be adopted on the date of entry into force of the said Treaty, is set out below:

DRAFT EUROPEAN DECISION
OF THE EUROPEAN COUNCIL ON THE EXERCISE OF THE PRESIDENCY OF THE COUNCIL

ARTICLE 1

1. The Presidency of the Council, with the exception of the Foreign Affairs configuration, shall be held by pre-established groups of three Member States for a period of 18 months. The groups shall be made up on a basis of equal rotation among the Member States, taking into account their diversity and geographical balance within the Union.

2. Each member of the group shall in turn chair for a six-month period all configurations of the Council, with the exception of the Foreign Affairs configuration. The other members of the group shall assist the Chair in all its responsibilities on the basis of a common programme. Members of the team may decide alternative arrangements among themselves.

ARTICLE 2

The Committee of Permanent Representatives of the Governments of the Member States shall be chaired by a representative of the Member State chairing the General Affairs Council.

The Chair of the Political and Security Committee shall be held by a representative of the Union Minister for Foreign Affairs.

The chair of the preparatory bodies of the various Council configurations, with the exception of the Foreign Affairs configuration, shall fall to the member of the group chairing the relevant configuration, unless decided otherwise in accordance with Article 4.

ARTICLE 3

The General Affairs Council shall ensure consistency and continuity in the work of the different Council configurations in the framework of multiannual programmes in co-operation with the Commission. The Member States holding the Presidency shall take all necessary measures for the organisation and smooth operation of the Council's work, with the assistance of the General Secretariat of the Council.

ARTICLE 4

The Council shall adopt a European decision establishing the measures for the implementation of this decision.

5.   DECLARATION ON ARTICLE I-25

The Conference declares that the European decision relating to the implementation of Article I-25 will be adopted by the Council on the day the Treaty establishing a Constitution for Europe enters into force. The draft decision is set out below:

DRAFT EUROPEAN DECISION
OF THE COUNCIL RELATING TO THE IMPLEMENTATION OF ARTICLE I-25

THE COUNCIL OF THE EUROPEAN UNION,

Whereas:
(1)   Provisions should be adopted allowing for a smooth transition from the system for decision-making in the Council by a qualified majority as defined in the Treaty of Nice and set out in Article 2(2) of the Protocol on the transitional provisions relating to the institutions and bodies of the Union annexed to the Constitution, which will continue to apply until 31 October 2009, to the voting system provided for in Article I-25 of the Constitution, which will apply with effect from 1 November 2009.
(2)   It is recalled that it is the practice of the Council to devote every effort to strengthening the democratic legitimacy of decisions taken by a qualified majority.
(3)   It is judged appropriate to maintain this decision as long as is necessary to ensure smooth transition to the new voting system provided for in the Constitution,

HAS DECIDED AS FOLLOWS:

ARTICLE 1

If members of the Council, representing:
(a)   at least three quarters of the population, or
(b)   at least three quarters of the number of Member States
necessary to constitute a blocking minority resulting from the application of Article I-25(1), first subparagraph, or Article I-25(2), indicate their opposition to the Council adopting an act by a qualified majority, the Council shall discuss the issue.

ARTICLE 2

The Council shall, in the course of these discussions, do all in its power to reach, within a reasonable time and without prejudicing obligatory time limits laid down by Union law, a satisfactory solution to address concerns raised by the members of the Council referred to in Article 1.

ARTICLE 3

To this end, the President of the Council, with the assistance of the Commission and in compliance with the Rules of Procedure of the Council, shall undertake any initiative necessary to facilitate a wider basis of agreement in the Council. The members of the Council shall lend him or her their assistance.

ARTICLE 4

This decision shall take effect on 1 November 2009. It shall remain in force at least until 2014. Thereafter the Council may adopt a European decision repealing it.

6. DECLARATION ON ARTICLE I-26

The Conference considers that when the Commission no longer includes nationals of all Member States, the Commission should pay particular attention to the need to ensure full transparency in relations with all Member States. Accordingly, the Commission should liaise closely with all Member States, whether or not they have a national serving as member of the Commission, and in this context pay special attention to the need to share information and consult with all Member States.

The Conference also considers that the Commission should take all the necessary measures to ensure that political, social and economic realities in all Member States, including those which have no national serving as member of the Commission, are fully taken into account. These measures should include ensuring that the position of those Member States is addressed by appropriate organisational arrangements.

7. DECLARATION ON ARTICLE I-27

The Conference considers that, in accordance with the provisions of the Constitution, the European Parliament and the European Council are jointly responsible for the smooth running of the process leading to the election of the President of the European Commission. Prior to the decision of the European Council, representatives of the European Parliament and of the European Council will thus conduct the necessary consultations in the framework deemed the most appropriate. These consultations will focus on the backgrounds of the candidates for President of the Commission, taking account of the elections to the European Parliament, in accordance with Article I-27(1). The arrangements for such consultations may be determined, in due course, by common accord between the European Parliament and the European Council.

8. DECLARATION ON ARTICLE I-36

The Conference takes note of the Commission's intention to continue to consult experts appointed by the Member States in the preparation of draft delegated European regulations in the financial services area, in accordance with its established practice.

9. DECLARATION ON ARTICLES I-43 AND III-329

Without prejudice to the measures adopted by the Union to comply with its solidarity obligation towards a Member State which is the object of a terrorist attack or the victim of natural or man-made disaster, none of the provisions of Articles I-43 and III-329 of the Constitution is intended to affect the right of another Member State to choose the most appropriate means to comply with its own solidarity obligation towards that Member State.

10. DECLARATION ON ARTICLE I-51

The Conference declares that, whenever rules on protection of personal data to be adopted on the basis of Article I-51 could have direct implications for national security, due account will have to be taken of the specific characteristics of the matter. It recalls that the legislation presently applicable (see in particular Directive 95/46/EC) includes specific derogations in this regard.

11. DECLARATION ON ARTICLE I-57

The Union will take into account the particular situation of small-sized countries which maintain specific relations of proximity with it.

12. DECLARATION CONCERNING THE EXPLANATIONS RELATING TO THE CHARTER OF FUNDAMENTAL RIGHTS

The Conference takes note of the explanations relating to the Charter of Fundamental Rights prepared under the authority of the Praesidium of the Convention which drafted the Charter and updated under the responsibility of the Praesidium of the European Convention, as set out below.

EXPLANATIONS RELATING TO THE CHARTER OF FUNDAMENTAL RIGHTS

These explanations were originally prepared under the authority of the Praesidium of the Convention which drafted the Charter of Fundamental Rights of the European Union. They have been updated under the responsibility of the Praesidium of the European Convention, in the light of the drafting adjustments made to the text of the Charter by that Convention (notably to Articles 51 and 52 [Articles II-111 and II-112 of the Constitution]) and of further developments of Union law. Although they do not as such have the status of law, they are a valuable tool of interpretation intended to clarify the provisions of the Charter.

PREAMBLE

The peoples of Europe, in creating an ever closer union among them, are resolved to share a peaceful future based on common values.

Conscious of its spiritual and moral heritage, the Union is founded on the indivisible, universal values of human dignity, freedom, equality and solidarity; it is based on the principles of democracy and the rule of law. It places the individual at the heart of its activities, by establishing the citizenship of the Union and by creating an area of freedom, security and justice.

The Union contributes to the preservation and to the development of these common values while respecting the diversity of the cultures and traditions of the peoples of Europe as well as the national identities of the Member States and the organisation of their public authorities at national, regional and local levels; it seeks to promote balanced and sustainable development and ensures free movement of persons, services, goods and capital, and the freedom of establishment.

To this end, it is necessary to strengthen the protection of fundamental rights in the light of changes in society, social progress and scientific and technological developments by making those rights more visible in a Charter.

This Charter reaffirms, with due regard for the powers and tasks of the Union and the principle of subsidiarity, the rights as they result, in particular, from the constitutional traditions and international obligations common to the Member States, the European Convention for the Protection of Human Rights and Fundamental Freedoms, the Social Charters adopted by the Union and by the Council of Europe and the case law of the Court of Justice of the European Union and of the European Court of Human Rights. In this context the Charter will be interpreted by the courts of the Union and the Member States with due regard to the explanations prepared under the authority of the Praesidium of the Convention which drafted the Charter and updated under the responsibility of the Praesidium of the European Convention.

Enjoyment of these rights entails responsibilities and duties with regard to other persons, to the human community and to future generations.

The Union therefore recognises the rights, freedoms and principles set out hereafter.

TITLE I

DIGNITY

ARTICLE 1   [Article II-61 of the Constitution] *Human dignity*
Human dignity is inviolable. It must be respected and protected.

Explanation
The dignity of the human person is not only a fundamental right in itself but constitutes the real basis of fundamental rights. The 1948 Universal Declaration of Human Rights enshrined human dignity in its preamble: "Whereas recognition of the inherent dignity and of the equal and inalienable rights of all members of the human family is the foundation of freedom, justice and peace in the world." In its judgment of 9 October 2001 in case C-377/98 Netherlands v. European Parliament and Council, 2001 ECR 7079, at grounds No 70 - 77, the Court of Justice confirmed that a fundamental right to human dignity is part of Union law.
It results that none of the rights laid down in this Charter may be used to harm the dignity of another person, and that the dignity of the human person is part of the substance of the rights laid down in this Charter. It must therefore be respected, even where a right is restricted.

ARTICLE 2   [Article II-62 of the Constitution] *Right to life*
1.   Everyone has the right to life.

2.   No one shall be condemned to the death penalty, or executed.

Explanation
1.   Paragraph 1 of this Article is based on the first sentence of Article 2(1) of the ECHR, which reads as follows:
       "1.   Everyone's right to life shall be protected by law..."

2.   The second sentence of the provision, which referred to the death penalty, was superseded by the entry into force of Article 1 of Protocol No 6 to the ECHR, which reads as follows:
       "The death penalty shall be abolished. No-one shall be condemned to such penalty or executed."
       Article 2(2) of the Charter [Article II-62(2) of the Constitution] is based on that provision.

3.   The provisions of Article 2 of the Charter [Article II-62 of the Constitution] correspond to those of the above Articles of the ECHR and its Protocol. They have the same meaning and the same scope, in accordance with Article 52(3) of the Charter [Article II-112(3) of the Constitution]. Therefore, the "negative" definitions appearing in the ECHR must be regarded as also forming part of the Charter:
       (a)   Article 2(2) of the ECHR:
               "Deprivation of life shall not be regarded as inflicted in contravention of this article when it results from the use of force which is no more than absolutely necessary:
               (a)   in defence of any person from unlawful violence;
               (b)   in order to effect a lawful arrest or to prevent the escape of a person lawfully detained;
               (c)   in action lawfully taken for the purpose of quelling a riot or insurrection."
       (b)   Article 2 of Protocol No 6 to the ECHR:
               "A State may make provision in its law for the death penalty in respect of acts committed in time of war or of imminent threat of war; such penalty shall be applied only in the instances laid down in the law and in accordance with its provisions..."

ARTICLE 3   [Article II-63 of the Constitution] *Right to the integrity of the person*
1.   Everyone has the right to respect for his or her physical and mental integrity.

2.   In the fields of medicine and biology, the following must be respected in particular:
(a)   the free and informed consent of the person concerned, according to the procedures laid down by law;
(b)   the prohibition of eugenic practices, in particular those aiming at the selection of persons;
(c)   the prohibition on making the human body and its parts as such a source of financial gain;
(d)   the prohibition of the reproductive cloning of human beings.

Explanation
1.   In its judgment of 9 October 2001 in case C-377/98 Netherlands v. European Parliament and Council, 2001 ECR 7079, at grounds No 70, 78 - 80, the Court of Justice confirmed that a fundamental right to human integrity is part of Union law and encompasses, in the context of medicine and biology, the free and informed consent of the donor and recipient.

2.   The principles of Article 3 of the Charter [Article II-63 of the Constitution] are already included in the Convention on Human Rights and Biomedicine, adopted by the Council of Europe (ETS 164 and additional protocol ETS 168). The Charter does not set out to depart from those principles, and therefore prohibits only reproductive cloning. It neither authorises nor prohibits other forms of cloning. Thus it does not in any way prevent the legislature from prohibiting other forms of cloning.

3.   The reference to eugenic practices, in particular those aiming at the selection of persons, relates to possible situations in which selection programmes are organised and implemented, involving campaigns for sterilisation, forced pregnancy, compulsory ethnic marriage among others, all acts deemed to be international crimes in the Statute of the International Criminal Court adopted in Rome on 17 July 1998 (see its Article 7(1)(g)).

ARTICLE 4   [Article II-64 of the Constitution] *Prohibition of torture and inhuman or degrading treatment or punishment*
No one shall be subjected to torture or to inhuman or degrading treatment or punishment.

Explanation
The right in Article 4 [Article II-64 of the Constitution] is the right guaranteed by Article 3 of the ECHR, which has the same wording: "No one shall be subjected to torture or to inhuman or degrading treatment or punishment". By virtue of Article 52(3) of the Charter [Article II-112(3) of the Constitution], it therefore has the same meaning and the same scope as the ECHR Article.

ARTICLE 5   [Article II-65 of the Constitution] *Prohibition of slavery and forced labour*
1.   No one shall be held in slavery or servitude.

2.   No one shall be required to perform forced or compulsory labour.

3.   Trafficking in human beings is prohibited.

Explanation
1.   The right in Article 5(1) and (2) [Article II-65 of the Constitution] corresponds to Article 4(1) and (2) of the ECHR, which has the same wording. It therefore has the same meaning and scope as the ECHR Article, by virtue of Article 52(3) of the Charter [Article II-112(3) of the Constitution]. Consequently:
    –   no limitation may legitimately affect the right provided for in paragraph 1;
    –   in paragraph 2, "forced or compulsory labour" must be understood in the light of the "negative" definitions contained in Article 4(3) of the ECHR:
    "For the purpose of this article the term "forced or compulsory labour" shall not include:
    (a)   any work required to be done in the ordinary course of detention imposed according to the provisions of Article 5 of this Convention or during conditional release from such detention;
    (b)   any service of a military character or, in case of conscientious objectors in countries where they are recognised, service exacted instead of compulsory military service;
    (c)   any service exacted in case of an emergency or calamity threatening the life or well-being of the community;
    (d)   any work or service which forms part of normal civic obligations."

2.   Paragraph 3 stems directly from human dignity and takes account of recent developments in organised crime, such as the organisation of lucrative illegal immigration or sexual exploitation networks. The annex to the Europol Convention contains the following definition which refers to trafficking for the purpose of sexual exploitation: "traffic in human beings: means subjection of a person to the real and illegal sway of other persons by using violence or menaces or by abuse of authority or intrigue with a view to the exploitation of prostitution, forms of sexual exploitation and assault of minors or trade in abandoned children". Chapter VI of the Convention implementing the Schengen Agreement, which has been integrated into the Union's acquis, in which the United Kingdom and Ireland participate, contains the following wording in Article 27(1) which refers to illegal immigration networks: " The Contracting Parties undertake to impose appropriate penalties on any person who, for financial gain, assists or tries to assist an alien to enter or reside within the territory of one of the Contracting Parties in breach of that Contracting Party's laws on the entry and residence of aliens." On 19 July 2002, the Council adopted a framework decision on combating trafficking in human beings (OJ L 203/1) whose Article 1 defines in detail the offences concerning trafficking in human beings for the purposes of labour exploitation or sexual exploitation, which the Member States must make punishable by virtue of that framework decision.

TITLE II

FREEDOMS

ARTICLE 6   [Article II-66 of the Constitution] *Right to liberty and security*
Everyone has the right to liberty and security of person.

Explanation

The rights in Article 6 [Article II-66 of the Constitution] are the rights guaranteed by Article 5 of the ECHR, and in accordance with Article 52(3) of the Charter [Article II-112(3) of the Constitution], they have the same meaning and scope. Consequently, the limitations which may legitimately be imposed on them may not exceed those permitted by the ECHR, in the wording of Article 5:

"1.   Everyone has the right to liberty and security of person. No one shall be deprived of his liberty save in the following cases and in accordance with a procedure prescribed by law:

(a)   the lawful detention of a person after conviction by a competent court;

(b)   the lawful arrest or detention of a person for non-compliance with the lawful order of a court or in order to secure the fulfilment of any obligation prescribed by law;

(c)   the lawful arrest or detention of a person effected for the purpose of bringing him before the competent legal authority on reasonable suspicion of having committed an offence or when it is reasonably considered necessary to prevent his committing an offence or fleeing after having done so;

(d)   the detention of a minor by lawful order for the purpose of educational supervision or his lawful detention for the purpose of bringing him before the competent legal authority;

(e)   the lawful detention of persons for the prevention of the spreading of infectious diseases, of persons of unsound mind, alcoholics or drug addicts or vagrants;

(f)   the lawful arrest or detention of a person to prevent his effecting an unauthorised entry into the country or of a person against whom action is being taken with a view to deportation or extradition.

2.   Everyone who is arrested shall be informed promptly, in a language which he understands, of the reasons for his arrest and of any charge against him.

3.   Everyone arrested or detained in accordance with the provisions of paragraph 1.c of this article shall be brought promptly before a judge or other officer authorised by law to exercise judicial power and shall be entitled to trial within a reasonable time or to release pending trial. Release may be conditioned by guarantees to appear for trial.

4.   Everyone who is deprived of his liberty by arrest or detention shall be entitled to take proceedings by which the lawfulness of his detention shall be decided speedily by a court and his release ordered if the detention is not lawful.

5.   Everyone who has been the victim of arrest or detention in contravention of the provisions of this Article shall have an enforceable right to compensation."

The rights enshrined in Article 6 [Article II-66 of the Constitution] must be respected particularly when the European Parliament and the Council adopt laws and framework laws in the area of judicial co-operation in criminal matters, on the basis of Articles III-270, III-271 and III-273 of the Constitution, notably to define common minimum provisions as regards the categorisation of offences and punishments and certain aspects of procedural law.

ARTICLE 7   [Article II-67 of the Constitution] *Respect for private and family life*
Everyone has the right to respect for his or her private and family life, home and communications.

Explanation

The rights guaranteed in Article 7 [Article II-67 of the Constitution] correspond to those guaranteed by Article 8 of the ECHR. To take account of developments in technology the word "correspondence" has been replaced by "communications".

In accordance with Article 52(3) [Article II-112(3) of the Constitution], the meaning and scope of this right are the same as those of the corresponding article of the ECHR. Consequently, the limitations which may legitimately be imposed on this right are the same as those allowed by Article 8 of the ECHR:

"1.   Everyone has the right to respect for his private and family life, his home and his correspondence.

2.   There shall be no interference by a public authority with the exercise of this right except such as is in accordance with the law and is necessary in a democratic society in the interests of national security, public safety or the economic well-being of the country, for the prevention of disorder or crime, for the protection of health or morals, or for the protection of the rights and freedoms of others."

ARTICLE 8   [Article II-68 of the Constitution] *Protection of personal data*

1.   Everyone has the right to the protection of personal data concerning him or her.

2.   Such data must be processed fairly for specified purposes and on the basis of the consent of the person concerned or some other legitimate basis laid down by law. Everyone has the right of access to data which has been collected concerning him or her, and the right to have it rectified.

3.   Compliance with these rules shall be subject to control by an independent authority.

Explanation

This Article has been based on Article 286 of the Treaty establishing the European Community and Directive 95/46/EC of the European Parliament and of the Council on the protection of individuals with regard to the processing of personal data and on the free movement of such data (OJ L 281, 23.11.1995) as well as on Article 8 of the ECHR and on the Council of Europe Convention of 28 January 1981 for the Protection of Individuals with regard to Automatic Processing of Personal Data, which has been ratified by all the Member States. Article 286 EC Treaty is now replaced by Article I-51 of the Constitution. Reference is also made to Regulation No 45/2001 of the European Parliament and of the Council on the protection of individuals with regard to the processing of personal data by the Community institutions and bodies and on the free movement of such data (OJ L 8, 12.1.2001). The abovementioned Directive and Regulation contain conditions and limitations for the exercise of the right to the protection of personal data.

ARTICLE 9   [Article II-69 of the Constitution] *Right to marry and right to found a family*
The right to marry and the right to found a family shall be guaranteed in accordance with the national laws governing the exercise of these rights.

Explanation

This Article is based on Article 12 of the ECHR, which reads as follows: "Men and women of marriageable age have the right to marry and to found a family according to the national laws governing the exercising of this right." The wording of the Article has been modernised to cover cases in which national legislation recognises arrangements other than marriage for founding a family. This Article neither prohibits nor imposes the granting of the status of marriage to unions between people of the same sex. This right is thus similar to that afforded by the ECHR, but its scope may be wider when national legislation so provides.

ARTICLE 10   [Article II-70 of the Constitution] *Freedom of thought, conscience and religion*
1.   Everyone has the right to freedom of thought, conscience and religion. This right includes freedom to change religion or belief and freedom, either alone or in community with others and in public or in private, to manifest religion or belief, in worship, teaching, practice and observance.

2.   The right to conscientious objection is recognised, in accordance with the national laws governing the exercise of this right.

Explanation

The right guaranteed in paragraph 1 corresponds to the right guaranteed in Article 9 of the ECHR and, in accordance with Article 52(3) of the Charter [Article II-112(3) of the Constitution], has the same meaning and scope. Limitations must therefore respect Article 9(2) of the Convention, which reads as follows: "Freedom to manifest one's religion or beliefs shall be subject only to such limitations as are prescribed by law and are necessary in a democratic society in the interests of public safety, for the protection of public order, health or morals, or for the protection of the rights and freedoms of others."
The right guaranteed in paragraph 2 corresponds to national constitutional traditions and to the development of national legislation on this issue.

ARTICLE 11   [Article II-71 of the Constitution] *Freedom of expression and information*
1.   Everyone has the right to freedom of expression. This right shall include freedom to hold opinions and to receive and impart information and ideas without interference by public authority and regardless of frontiers.

2.   The freedom and pluralism of the media shall be respected.

Explanation

1.   Article 11 [Article II-71 of the Constitution] corresponds to Article 10 of the European Convention on Human Rights, which reads as follows:
"1.   Everyone has the right to freedom of expression. This right shall include freedom to hold opinions and to receive and impart information and ideas without interference by public authority and regardless of frontiers. This Article shall not prevent States from requiring the licensing of broadcasting, television or cinema enterprises.
2.   The exercise of these freedoms, since it carries with it duties and responsibilities, may be subject to such formalities, conditions, restrictions or penalties as are prescribed by law and are necessary in a democratic society, in the interests of national security, territorial integrity or public safety, for the prevention of disorder or crime, for the protection of health or morals, for the protection of the reputation or rights of others, for preventing the disclosure of information received in confidence, or for maintaining the authority and impartiality of the judiciary."
Pursuant to Article 52(3) of the Charter [Article II-112(3) of the Constitution], the meaning and scope of this right are the same as those guaranteed by the ECHR. The limitations which may be imposed on it may

therefore not exceed those provided for in Article 10(2) of the Convention, without prejudice to any restrictions which competition law of the Union may impose on Member States' right to introduce the licensing arrangements referred to in the third sentence of Article 10(1) of the ECHR.

2.   Paragraph 2 of this Article spells out the consequences of paragraph 1 regarding freedom of the media. It is based in particular on Court of Justice case law regarding television, particularly in case C-288/89 (judgment of 25 July 1991, Stichting Collectieve Antennevoorziening Gouda and others [1991] ECR I-4007), and on the Protocol on the system of public broadcasting in the Member States annexed to the EC Treaty and now to the Constitution, and on Council Directive 89/552/EC (particularly its seventeenth recital).

ARTICLE 12   [Article II-72 of the Constitution] *Freedom of assembly and of association*
1.   Everyone has the right to freedom of peaceful assembly and to freedom of association at all levels, in particular in political, trade union and civic matters, which implies the right of everyone to form and to join trade unions for the protection of his or her interests.

2.   Political parties at Union level contribute to expressing the political will of the citizens of the Union.

Explanation
Paragraph 1 of this Article corresponds to Article 11 of the ECHR, which reads as follows:
"1.   Everyone has the right to freedom of peaceful assembly and to freedom of association with others, including the right to form and to join trade unions for the protection of his interests.

2.   No restrictions shall be placed on the exercise of these rights other than such as are prescribed by law and are necessary in a democratic society in the interests of national security or public safety, for the prevention of disorder or crime, for the protection of health or morals or for the protection of the rights and freedoms of others. This article shall not prevent the imposition of lawful restrictions on the exercise of these rights by members of the armed forces, of the police or of the administration of the State."
The meaning of the provisions of paragraph 1 is the same as that of the ECHR, but their scope is wider since they apply at all levels including European level. In accordance with Article 52(3) of the Charter [Article II-112(3) of the Constitution], limitations on that right may not exceed those considered legitimate by virtue of Article 11(2) of the ECHR.
2.   This right is also based on Article 11 of the Community Charter of the Fundamental Social Rights of Workers.

3.   Paragraph 2 of this Article corresponds to Article I-46(4) of the Constitution.

ARTICLE 13   [Article II-73 of the Constitution] *Freedom of the arts and sciences*
The arts and scientific research shall be free of constraint. Academic freedom shall be respected.

Explanation
This right is deduced primarily from the right to freedom of thought and expression. It is to be exercised having regard to Article 1 [Article II-61 of the Constitution] and may be subject to the limitations authorised by Article 10 of the ECHR.

ARTICLE 14   [Article II-74 of the Constitution] *Right to education*
1.   Everyone has the right to education and to have access to vocational and continuing training.

2.   This right includes the possibility to receive free compulsory education.

3.   The freedom to found educational establishments with due respect for democratic principles and the right of parents to ensure the education and teaching of their children in conformity with their religious, philosophical and pedagogical convictions shall be respected, in accordance with the national laws governing the exercise of such freedom and right.

Explanation
1.   This Article is based on the common constitutional traditions of Member States and on Article 2 of the Protocol to the ECHR, which reads as follows:
        "No person shall be denied the right to education. In the exercise of any functions which it assumes in relation to education and to teaching, the State shall respect the right of parents to ensure such education and teaching in conformity with their own religious and philosophical convictions."
        It was considered useful to extend this article to access to vocational and continuing training (see point 15 of the Community Charter of the Fundamental Social Rights of Workers and Article 10 of the Social Charter) and to add the principle of free compulsory education. As it is worded, the latter principle merely implies that as regards compulsory education, each child has the possibility of

attending an establishment which offers free education. It does not require all establishments which provide education or vocational and continuing training, in particular private ones, to be free of charge. Nor does it exclude certain specific forms of education having to be paid for, if the State takes measures to grant financial compensation. Insofar as the Charter applies to the Union, this means that in its training policies the Union must respect free compulsory education, but this does not, of course, create new powers. Regarding the right of parents, it must be interpreted in conjunction with the provisions of Article 24 [Article II-84 of the Constitution].

2.   Freedom to found public or private educational establishments is guaranteed as one of the aspects of freedom to conduct a business but it is limited by respect for democratic principles and is exercised in accordance with the arrangements defined by national legislation.

ARTICLE 15   [Article II-75 of the Constitution] *Freedom to choose an occupation and right to engage in work*

1.   Everyone has the right to engage in work and to pursue a freely chosen or accepted occupation.

2.   Every citizen of the Union has the freedom to seek employment, to work, to exercise the right of establishment and to provide services in any Member State.

3.   Nationals of third countries who are authorised to work in the territories of the Member States are entitled to working conditions equivalent to those of citizens of the Union.

Explanation
Freedom to choose an occupation, as enshrined in Article 15(1) 1, is recognised in Court of Justice case law (see inter alia judgment of 14 May 1974, Case 4/73 Nold [1974] ECR 491, paragraphs 12 to 14 of the grounds; judgment of 13 December 1979, Case 44/79 Hauer [1979] ECR 3727; judgment of 8 October 1986, Case 234/85 Keller [1986] ECR 2897, paragraph 8 of the grounds).
This paragraph also draws upon Article 1(2) of the European Social Charter, which was signed on 18 October 1961 and has been ratified by all the Member States, and on point 4 of the Community Charter of the Fundamental Social Rights of Workers of 9 December 1989. The expression "working conditions" is to be understood in the sense of Article III-213 of the Constitution.
Paragraph 2 deals with the three freedoms guaranteed by Articles I-4 and III-133, III-137 and III-144 of the Constitution, namely freedom of movement for workers, freedom of establishment and freedom to provide services.
Paragraph 3 has been based on TEC Article 137(3), fourth indent, now replaced by Article III-210(1)(g) of the Constitution, and on Article 19(4) of the European Social Charter signed on 18 October 1961 and ratified by all the Member States. Article 52(2) of the Charter [Article II-112(2) of the Constitution] is therefore applicable. The question of recruitment of seamen having the nationality of third States for the crews of vessels flying the flag of a Member State of the Union is governed by Union law and national legislation and practice.

ARTICLE 16   [Article II-76 of the Constitution] *Freedom to conduct a business*
The freedom to conduct a business in accordance with Union law and national laws and practices is recognised.

Explanation
This Article is based on Court of Justice case law which has recognised freedom to exercise an economic or commercial activity (see judgments of 14 May 1974, Case 4/73 Nold [1974] ECR 491, paragraph 14 of the grounds, and of 27 September 1979, Case 230-78 SPA Eridiana and others [1979] ECR 2749, paragraphs 20 and 31 of the grounds) and freedom of contract (see inter alia Sukkerfabriken Nykøbing judgment, Case 151/78 [1979] ECR 1, paragraph 19 of the grounds, and judgment of 5 October 1999, C-240/97 Spain v. Commission, [1999] ECR I-6571, paragraph 99 of the grounds) and Article I-3(2) of the Constitution, which recognises free competition. Of course, this right is to be exercised with respect for Union law and national legislation. It may be subject to the limitations provided for in Article 52(1) of the Charter [Article II-112(1) of the Constitution].

ARTICLE 17   [Article II-77 of the Constitution] *Right to property*
1.   Everyone has the right to own, use, dispose of and bequeath his or her lawfully acquired possessions. No one may be deprived of his or her possessions, except in the public interest and in the cases and under the conditions provided for by law, subject to fair compensation being paid in good time for their loss. The use of property may be regulated by law insofar as is necessary for the general interest.

2.   Intellectual property shall be protected.

245

Explanation

This Article is based on Article 1 of the Protocol to the ECHR:

"Every natural or legal person is entitled to the peaceful enjoyment of his possessions. No one shall be deprived of his possessions except in the public interest and subject to the conditions provided for by law and by the general principles of international law.

The preceding provisions shall not, however, in any way impair the right of a State to enforce such laws as it deems necessary to control the use of property in accordance with the general interest or to secure the payment of taxes or other contributions or penalties."

This is a fundamental right common to all national constitutions. It has been recognised on numerous occasions by the case law of the Court of Justice, initially in the Hauer judgment (13 December 1979, ECR [1979] 3727). The wording has been updated but, in accordance with Article 52(3) [Article II-112(3) of the Constitution], the meaning and scope of the right are the same as those of the right guaranteed by the ECHR and the limitations may not exceed those provided for there.

Protection of intellectual property, one aspect of the right of property, is explicitly mentioned in paragraph 2 because of its growing importance and Community secondary legislation. Intellectual property covers not only literary and artistic property but also inter alia patent and trademark rights and associated rights. The guarantees laid down in paragraph 1 shall apply as appropriate to intellectual property.

ARTICLE 18   [Article II-78 of the Constitution] *Right to asylum*

The right to asylum shall be guaranteed with due respect for the rules of the Geneva Convention of 28 July 1951 and the Protocol of 31 January 1967 relating to the status of refugees and in accordance with the Constitution.

Explanation

The text of the Article has been based on TEC Article 63, now replaced by Article III-266 of the Constitution, which requires the Union to respect the Geneva Convention on refugees. Reference should be made to the Protocols relating to the United Kingdom and Ireland annexed to the [Treaty of Amsterdam] Constitution and to Denmark to determine the extent to which those Member States implement Union law in this area and the extent to which this Article is applicable to them. This Article is in line with the Protocol on Asylum annexed to the Constitution.

ARTICLE 19   [Article II-79 of the Constitution]   *Protection in the event of removal, expulsion or extradition*

1.   Collective expulsions are prohibited.

2.   No one may be removed, expelled or extradited to a State where there is a serious risk that he or she would be subjected to the death penalty, torture or other inhuman or degrading treatment or punishment.

Explanation

Paragraph 1 of this Article has the same meaning and scope as Article 4 of Protocol No 4 to the ECHR concerning collective expulsion. Its purpose is to guarantee that every decision is based on a specific examination and that no single measure can be taken to expel all persons having the nationality of a particular State (see also Article 13 of the Covenant on Civil and Political Rights).

Paragraph 2 incorporates the relevant case law from the European Court of Human Rights regarding Article 3 of the ECHR (see Ahmed v. Austria, judgment of 17 December 1996, [1996] ECR VI-2206 and Soering, judgment of 7 July 1989).

TITLE III

EQUALITY

ARTICLE 20   [Article II-80 of the Constitution] *Equality before the law*

Everyone is equal before the law.

Explanation

This Article corresponds to a general principle of law which is included in all European constitutions and has also been recognised by the Court of Justice as a basic principle of Community law (judgment of 13 November 1984, Case 283/83 Racke [1984] ECR 3791, judgment of 17 April 1997, Case 15/95 EARL [1997] ECR I–1961, and judgment of 13 April 2000, Case 292/97 Karlsson [2000] ECR 2737).

ARTICLE 21 [Article II-81 of the Constitution] *Non-discrimination*
1. Any discrimination based on any ground such as sex, race, colour, ethnic or social origin, genetic features, language, religion or belief, political or any other opinion, membership of a national minority, property, birth, disability, age or sexual orientation shall be prohibited.

2. Within the scope of application of the Constitution and without prejudice to any of its specific provisions, any discrimination on grounds of nationality shall be prohibited.

Explanation
Paragraph 1 draws on Article 13 of the EC Treaty, now replaced by Article III-124 of the Constitution, Article 14 of the ECHR and Article 11 of the Convention on Human Rights and Biomedicine as regards genetic heritage. Insofar as this corresponds to Article 14 of the ECHR, it applies in compliance with it.
There is no contradiction or incompatibility between paragraph 1 and Article III-124 of the Constitution which has a different scope and purpose: Article III-124 confers power on the Union to adopt legislative acts, including harmonisation of the Member States' laws and regulations, to combat certain forms of discrimination, listed exhaustively in that Article. Such legislation may cover action of Member State authorities (as well as relations between private individuals) in any area within the limits of the Union's powers. In contrast, the provision in paragraph 1 does not create any power to enact anti-discrimination laws in these areas of Member State or private action, nor does it lay down a sweeping ban of discrimination in such wide-ranging areas. Instead, it only addresses discriminations by the institutions and bodies of the Union themselves, when exercising powers conferred under other articles of Parts I and III of the Constitution, and by Member States only when they are implementing Union law. Paragraph 1 therefore does not alter the extent of powers granted under Article III-124 nor the interpretation given to that Article.
Paragraph 2 corresponds to Article I-4(2) of the Constitution and must be applied in compliance with that Article.

ARTICLE 22 [Article II-82 of the Constitution] *Cultural, religious and linguistic diversity*
The Union shall respect cultural, religious and linguistic diversity.

Explanation
This Article has been based on Article 6 of the Treaty on European Union and on Article 151(1) and (4) of the EC Treaty, now replaced by Article III-280(1) and (4) of the Constitution, concerning culture. Respect for cultural and linguistic diversity is now also laid down in Article I-3(3) of the Constitution. The Article is also inspired by Declaration No 11 to the Final Act of the Amsterdam Treaty on the status of churches and non-confessional organisations, now taken over in Article I-52 of the Constitution.

ARTICLE 23 [Article II-83 of the Constitution] *Equality between women and men*
Equality between women and men must be ensured in all areas, including employment, work and pay.
The principle of equality shall not prevent the maintenance or adoption of measures providing for specific advantages in favour of the under-represented sex.

Explanation
The first paragraph has been based on Articles 2 and 3(2) of the EC Treaty, now replaced by Articles I-3 and III-116 of the Constitution which impose the objective of promoting equality between men and women on the Union, and on Article 141(1) of the EC Treaty, now replaced by Article III-214(1) of the Constitution. It draws on Article 20 of the revised European Social Charter of 3 May 1996 and on point 16 of the Community Charter on the rights of workers.
It is also based on Article 141(3) of the EC Treaty, now replaced by Article III-214(3) of the Constitution, and Article 2(4) of Council Directive 76/207/EEC on the implementation of the principle of equal treatment for men and women as regards access to employment, vocational training and promotion, and working conditions.
The second paragraph takes over in shorter form Article III-214(4) of the Constitution which provides that the principle of equal treatment does not prevent the maintenance or adoption of measures providing for specific advantages in order to make it easier for the under-represented sex to pursue a vocational activity or to prevent or compensate for disadvantages in professional careers. In accordance with Article 52(2) [Article II-112(2) of the Constitution], the present paragraph does not amend Article III-214(4).

ARTICLE 24 [Article II-84 of the Constitution] *The rights of the child*
1. Children shall have the right to such protection and care as is necessary for their well-being. They may express their views freely. Such views shall be taken into consideration on matters which concern them in accordance with their age and maturity.

2. In all actions relating to children, whether taken by public authorities or private institutions, the child's best interests must be a primary consideration.

3.   Every child shall have the right to maintain on a regular basis a personal relationship and direct contact with both his or her parents, unless that is contrary to his or her interests.

Explanation
This Article is based on the New York Convention on the Rights of the Child signed on 20 November 1989 and ratified by all the Member States, particularly Articles 3, 9, 12 and 13 thereof.
Paragraph 3 takes account of the fact that, as part of the establishment of an area of freedom, security and justice, Union legislation on civil matters having cross-border implications, for which Article III-269 of the Constitution confers power, may include notably visiting rights ensuring that children can maintain on a regular basis a personal and direct contact with both his or her parents.

ARTICLE 25   [Article II-85 of the Constitution] *The rights of the elderly*
The Union recognises and respects the rights of the elderly to lead a life of dignity and independence and to participate in social and cultural life.

Explanation
This Article draws on Article 23 of the revised European Social Charter and Articles 24 and 25 of the Community Charter of the Fundamental Social Rights of Workers. Of course, participation in social and cultural life also covers participation in political life.

ARTICLE 26   [Article II-86 of the Constitution] *Integration of persons with disabilities*
The Union recognises and respects the right of persons with disabilities to benefit from measures designed to ensure their independence, social and occupational integration and participation in the life of the community.

Explanation
The principle set out in this Article is based on Article 15 of the European Social Charter and also draws on point 26 of the Community Charter of the Fundamental Social Rights of Workers.

TITLE IV

SOLIDARITY

ARTICLE 27   [Article II-87 of the Constitution] *Workers' right to information and consultation within the undertaking*
Workers or their representatives must, at the appropriate levels, be guaranteed information and consultation in good time in the cases and under the conditions provided for by Union law and national laws and practices.

Explanation
This Article appears in the revised European Social Charter (Article 21) and in the Community Charter on the rights of workers (points 17 and 18). It applies under the conditions laid down by Union law and by national laws. The reference to appropriate levels refers to the levels laid down by Union law or by national laws and practices, which might include the European level when Union legislation so provides. There is a considerable Union *acquis* in this field: Articles III-211 and III-212 of the Constitution, and Directives 2002/14/EC (general framework for informing and consulting employees in the European Community), 98/59/EC (collective redundancies), 2001/23/EC (transfers of undertakings) and 94/45/EC (European works councils).

ARTICLE 28   [Article II-88 of the Constitution] *Right of collective bargaining and action*
Workers and employers, or their respective organisations, have, in accordance with Union law and national laws and practices, the right to negotiate and conclude collective agreements at the appropriate levels and, in cases of conflicts of interest, to take collective action to defend their interests, including strike action.

Explanation
This Article is based on Article 6 of the European Social Charter and on the Community Charter of the Fundamental Social Rights of Workers (points 12 to 14). The right of collective action was recognised by the European Court of Human Rights as one of the elements of trade union rights laid down by Article 11 of the ECHR. As regards the appropriate levels at which collective negotiation might take place, see the explanation given for the above Article. The modalities and limits for the exercise of collective action, including strike action, come under national laws and practices, including the question of whether it may be carried out in parallel in several Member States.

ARTICLE 29   [Article II-89 of the Constitution] *Right of access to placement services*
Everyone has the right of access to a free placement service.

Explanation
This Article is based on Article 1(3) of the European Social Charter and point 13 of the Community Charter of the Fundamental Social Rights of Workers.

ARTICLE 30   [Article II-90 of the Constitution] *Protection in the event of unjustified dismissal*
Every worker has the right to protection against unjustified dismissal, in accordance with Union law and national laws and practices.

Explanation
This Article draws on Article 24 of the revised Social Charter. See also Directive 2001/23/EC on the safeguarding of employees' rights in the event of transfers of undertakings, and Directive 80/987/EEC on the protection of employees in the event of the insolvency of their employer, as amended by Directive 2002/74/EC.

ARTICLE 31   [Article II-91 of the Constitution] *Fair and just working conditions*
1.   Every worker has the right to working conditions which respect his or her health, safety and dignity.

2.   Every worker has the right to limitation of maximum working hours, to daily and weekly rest periods and to an annual period of paid leave.

Explanation
1.   Paragraph 1 of this Article is based on Directive 89/391/EEC on the introduction of measures to encourage improvements in the safety and health of workers at work. It also draws on Article 3 of the Social Charter and point 19 of the Community Charter on the rights of workers, and, as regards dignity at work, on Article 26 of the revised Social Charter. The expression "working conditions" must be understood in the sense of Article III-213 of the Constitution.
2.   Paragraph 2 is based on Directive 93/104/EC concerning certain aspects of the organisation of working time, Article 2 of the European Social Charter and point 8 of the Community Charter on the rights of workers.

ARTICLE 32   [Article II-92 of the Constitution] *Prohibition of child labour and protection of young people at work*
The employment of children is prohibited. The minimum age of admission to employment may not be lower than the minimum school-leaving age, without prejudice to such rules as may be more favourable to young people and except for limited derogations.
Young people admitted to work must have working conditions appropriate to their age and be protected against economic exploitation and any work likely to harm their safety, health or physical, mental, moral or social development or to interfere with their education.

Explanation
This Article is based on Directive 94/33/EC on the protection of young people at work, Article 7 of the European Social Charter and points 20 to 23 of the Community Charter of the Fundamental Social Rights of Workers.

ARTICLE 33   [Article II-93 of the Constitution] *Family and professional life*
1.   The family shall enjoy legal, economic and social protection.

2.   To reconcile family and professional life, everyone shall have the right to protection from dismissal for a reason connected with maternity and the right to paid maternity leave and to parental leave following the birth or adoption of a child.

Explanation
Article 33(1) [Article II-93 of the Constitution] is based on Article 16 of the European Social Charter. The second paragraph draws on Council Directive 92/85/EEC on the introduction of measures to encourage improvements in the safety and health at work of pregnant workers and workers who have recently given birth or are breastfeeding and Directive 96/34/EC on the framework agreement on parental leave concluded by UNICE, CEEP and the ETUC. It is also based on Article 8 (protection of maternity) of the European Social Charter and draws on Article 27 (right of workers with family responsibilities to equal opportunities and equal treatment) of the revised Social Charter. "Maternity" covers the period from conception to weaning.

ARTICLE 34 [Article II-94 of the Constitution] *Social security and social assistance*
1. The Union recognises and respects the entitlement to social security benefits and social services providing protection in cases such as maternity, illness, industrial accidents, dependency or old age, and in the case of loss of employment, in accordance with the rules laid down by Union law and national laws and practices.

2. Everyone residing and moving legally within the European Union is entitled to social security benefits and social advantages in accordance with Union law and national laws and practices.

3. In order to combat social exclusion and poverty, the Union recognises and respects the right to social and housing assistance so as to ensure a decent existence for all those who lack sufficient resources, in accordance with the rules laid down by Union law and national laws and practices.

Explanation
The principle set out in Article 34(1) [Article II-94 of the Constitution] is based on Articles 137 and 140 of the EC Treaty, now replaced by Articles III-210 and III-213 and on Article 12 of the European Social Charter and point 10 of the Community Charter on the rights of workers. The Union must respect it when exercising the powers conferred on it by Articles III-210 and III-213 of the Constitution. The reference to social services relates to cases in which such services have been introduced to provide certain advantages but does not imply that such services must be created where they do not exist. "Maternity" must be understood in the same sense as in the preceding Article.
Paragraph 2 is based on Articles 12(4) and 13(4) of the European Social Charter and point 2 of the Community Charter of the Fundamental Social Rights of Workers and reflects the rules arising from Regulation No 1408/71 and Regulation No 1612/68.
Paragraph 3 draws on Article 13 of the European Social Charter and Articles 30 and 31 of the revised Social Charter and point 10 of the Community Charter. The Union must respect it in the context of policies based on Article III-210 of the Constitution.

ARTICLE 35 [Article II-95 of the Constitution] *Health care*
Everyone has the right of access to preventive health care and the right to benefit from medical treatment under the conditions established by national laws and practices. A high level of human health protection shall be ensured in the definition and implementation of all Union policies and activities.

Explanation
The principles set out in this Article are based on Article 152 of the EC Treaty, now replaced by Article III-278 of the Constitution, and on Articles 11 and 13 of the European Social Charter. The second sentence of the Article takes over Article III-278(1).

ARTICLE 36 [Article II-96 of the Constitution] *Access to services of general economic interest*
The Union recognises and respects access to services of general economic interest as provided for in national laws and practices, in accordance with the Constitution, in order to promote the social and territorial cohesion of the Union.

Explanation
This Article is fully in line with Article III-122 of the Constitution and does not create any new right. It merely sets out the principle of respect by the Union for the access to services of general economic interest as provided for by national provisions, when those provisions are compatible with Union law.

ARTICLE 37 [Article II-97 of the Constitution] *Environmental protection*
A high level of environmental protection and the improvement of the quality of the environment must be integrated into the policies of the Union and ensured in accordance with the principle of sustainable development.

Explanation
The principles set out in this Article have been based on Articles 2, 6 and 174 of the EC Treaty, which have now been replaced by Articles I-3(3), III-119 and III-233 of the Constitution.
It also draws on the provisions of some national constitutions.

ARTICLE 38 [Article II-98 of the Constitution] *Consumer protection*
Union policies shall ensure a high level of consumer protection.

Explanation
The principles set out in this Article have been based on Article 153 of the EC Treaty, now replaced by Article III-235 of the Constitution.

TITLE V

CITIZENS' RIGHTS

ARTICLE 39   [Article II-99 of the Constitution] *Right to vote and to stand as a candidate at elections to the European Parliament*

1.   Every citizen of the Union has the right to vote and to stand as a candidate at elections to the European Parliament in the Member State in which he or she resides, under the same conditions as nationals of that State.

2.   Members of the European Parliament shall be elected by direct universal suffrage in a free and secret ballot.

Explanation

Article 39 [Article II-99 of the Constitution] applies under the conditions laid down in Parts I and III of the Constitution, in accordance with Article 52(2) of the Charter [Article II-112(2) of the Constitution]. Article 39(1) [Article II-99 of the Constitution] corresponds to the right guaranteed in Article I-10(2) of the Constitution (cf. also the legal base in Article III-126 for the adoption of detailed arrangements for the exercise of that right) and Article 39(2) [Article II-99 of the Constitution] corresponds to Article I-20(2) of the Constitution. Article 39(2) [Article II-99 of the Constitution] takes over the basic principles of the electoral system in a democratic State.

ARTICLE 40   [Article II-100 of the Constitution] *Right to vote and to stand as a candidate at municipal elections*

Every citizen of the Union has the right to vote and to stand as a candidate at municipal elections in the Member State in which he or she resides under the same conditions as nationals of that State.

Explanation

This Article corresponds to the right guaranteed by Article I-10(2) of the Constitution (cf. also the legal base in Article III-126 for the adoption of detailed arrangements for the exercise of that right). In accordance with Article 52(2) of the Charter [Article II-112(2) of the Constitution], it applies under the conditions set out in these Articles of Parts I and III of the Constitution.

ARTICLE 41   [Article II-101 of the Constitution] *Right to good administration*

1.   Every person has the right to have his or her affairs handled impartially, fairly and within a reasonable time by the institutions, bodies, offices and agencies of the Union.

2.   This right includes:
(a)   the right of every person to be heard, before any individual measure which would affect him or her adversely is taken;
(b)   the right of every person to have access to his or her file, while respecting the legitimate interests of confidentiality and of professional and business secrecy;
(c)   the obligation of the administration to give reasons for its decisions.

3.   Every person has the right to have the Union make good any damage caused by its institutions or by its servants in the performance of their duties, in accordance with the general principles common to the laws of the Member States.

4.   Every person may write to the institutions of the Union in one of the languages of the Constitution and must have an answer in the same language.

Explanation

Article 41 [Article II-101 of the Constitution] is based on the existence of the Union as subject to the rule of law whose characteristics were developed in the case law which enshrined inter alia good administration as a general principle of law (see inter alia Court of Justice judgment of 31 March 1992 in Case C-255/90 P, Burban [1992] ECR I-2253, and Court of First Instance judgments of 18 September 1995 in Case T-167/94 Nölle [1995] ECR II-2589, and 9 July 1999 in Case T-231/97 New Europe Consulting and others [1999] ECR II-2403). The wording for that right in the first two paragraphs results from the case law (Court of Justice judgment of 15 October 1987 in Case 222/86 Heylens [1987] ECR 4097, paragraph 15 of the grounds, judgment of 18 October 1989 in Case 374/87 Orkem [1989] ECR 3283, judgment of 21 November 1991 in Case C-269/90 TU München [1991] ECR I-5469, and Court of First Instance judgments of 6 December 1994 in Case T-450/93 Lisrestal [1994] ECR II-1177, 18 September 1995 in Case T-167/94 Nölle [1995] ECR II-258) and the wording regarding the obligation to give reasons comes from Article 253 of the EC Treaty, now replaced by Article I-38(2) of the Constitution (cf. also the legal base in Article III-398 of the Constitution for the adoption of legislation in the interest of an open, efficient and independent European administration).

Paragraph 3 reproduces the right now guaranteed by Article III-431 of the Constitution. Paragraph 4 reproduces the right now guaranteed by Articles I-10(2)(d) and III-129 of the Constitution. In accordance with Article 52(2) of the Charter [Article II-112(2) of the Constitution], those rights are to be applied under the conditions and within the limits defined by Part III of the Constitution.

The right to an effective remedy, which is an important aspect of this question, is guaranteed in Article 47 of this Charter [Article II-107 of the Constitution].

ARTICLE 42 [Article II-102 of the Constitution] *Right of access to documents*
Any citizen of the Union, and any natural or legal person residing or having its registered office in a Member State, has a right of access to documents of the institutions, bodies, offices and agencies of the Union, whatever their medium.

Explanation
The right guaranteed in this Article has been taken over from Article 255 of the EC Treaty, on the basis of which Regulation 1049/2001 has subsequently been adopted. The European Convention has extended this right to documents of institutions, bodies and agencies generally, regardless of their form, see Article I-50(3) of the Constitution. In accordance with Article 52(2) of the Charter [Article II-112(2) of the Constitution], the right of access to documents is exercised under the conditions and within the limits for which provision is made in Articles I-50(3) and III-399.

ARTICLE 43 [Article II-103 of the Constitution] *European Ombudsman*
Any citizen of the Union and any natural or legal person residing or having its registered office in a Member State has the right to refer to the European Ombudsman cases of maladministration in the activities of the institutions, bodies, offices or agencies of the Union, with the exception of the Court of Justice of the European Union acting in its judicial role.

Explanation
The right guaranteed in this Article is the right guaranteed by Articles I-10 and III-335 of the Constitution. In accordance with Article 52(2) of the Charter [Article II-112(2) of the Constitution], it applies under the conditions defined in these two Articles.

ARTICLE 44 [Article II-104 of the Constitution] *Right to petition*
Any citizen of the Union and any natural or legal person residing or having its registered office in a Member State has the right to petition the European Parliament.

Explanation
The right guaranteed in this Article is the right guaranteed by Articles I-10 and III-334 of the Constitution. In accordance with Article 52(2) of the Charter [Article II-112(2) of the Constitution], it applies under the conditions defined in these two Articles.

ARTICLE 45 [Article II-105 of the Constitution] *Freedom of movement and of residence*
1.   Every citizen of the Union has the right to move and reside freely within the territory of the Member States.

2.   Freedom of movement and residence may be granted, in accordance with the Constitution, to nationals of third countries legally resident in the territory of a Member State.

Explanation
The right guaranteed by paragraph 1 is the right guaranteed by Article I-10(2)(a) of the Constitution (cf. also the legal base in Article III-125; and the judgement of the Court of Justice of 17 September 2002, C-413/99 Baumbast, [2002] ECR 709). In accordance with Article 52(2) of the Charter [Article II-112(2) of the Constitution], it applies under the conditions and within the limits defined for which provision is made in Part III of the Constitution.

Paragraph 2 refers to the power granted to the Union by Articles III-265 to III-267 of the Constitution. Consequently, the granting of this right depends on the institutions exercising that power.

ARTICLE 46 [Article II-106 of the Constitution] *Diplomatic and consular protection*
Every citizen of the Union shall, in the territory of a third country in which the Member State of which he or she is a national is not represented, be entitled to protection by the diplomatic or consular authorities of any Member State, on the same conditions as the nationals of that Member State.

Explanation

The right guaranteed by this Article is the right guaranteed by Article I-10 of the Constitution; cf. also the legal base in Article III-127. In accordance with Article 52(2) of the Charter [Article II-112(2) of the Constitution], it applies under the conditions defined in these Articles.

TITLE VI

JUSTICE

ARTICLE 47   [Article II-107 of the Constitution] *Right to an effective remedy and to a fair trial*

Everyone whose rights and freedoms guaranteed by the law of the Union are violated has the right to an effective remedy before a tribunal in compliance with the conditions laid down in this Article.

Everyone is entitled to a fair and public hearing within a reasonable time by an independent and impartial tribunal previously established by law. Everyone shall have the possibility of being advised, defended and represented.

Legal aid shall be made available to those who lack sufficient resources insofar as such aid is necessary to ensure effective access to justice.

Explanation

The first paragraph is based on Article 13 of the ECHR:

"Everyone whose rights and freedoms as set forth in this Convention are violated shall have an effective remedy before a national authority notwithstanding that the violation has been committed by persons acting in an official capacity."

However, in Union law the protection is more extensive since it guarantees the right to an effective remedy before a court. The Court of Justice enshrined that right in its judgment of 15 May 1986 as a general principle of Union law (Case 222/84 Johnston [1986] ECR 1651; see also judgment of 15 October 1987, Case 222/86 Heylens [1987] ECR 4097 and judgment of 3 December 1992, Case C-97/91 Borelli [1992] ECR I-6313). According to the Court, that general principle of Union law also applies to the Member States when they are implementing Union law. The inclusion of this precedent in the Charter has not been intended to change the system of judicial review laid down by the Treaties, and particularly the rules relating to admissibility for direct actions before the Court of Justice of the European Union. The European Convention has considered the Union's system of judicial review including the rules on admissibility, and confirmed them while amending them as to certain aspects, as reflected in Articles III-353 to III-381 of the Constitution, and in particular in Article III-365(4). Article 47 [Article II-107 of the Constitution] applies to the institutions of the Union and of Member States when they are implementing Union law and does so for all rights guaranteed by Union law.

The second paragraph corresponds to Article 6(1) of the ECHR which reads as follows:

"In the determination of his civil rights and obligations or of any criminal charge against him, everyone is entitled to a fair and public hearing within a reasonable time by an independent and impartial tribunal established by law. Judgment shall be pronounced publicly but the press and public may be excluded from all or part of the trial in the interests of morals, public order or national security in a democratic society, where the interests of juveniles or the protection of the private life of the parties so require, or to the extent strictly necessary in the opinion of the court in special circumstances where publicity would prejudice the interests of justice."

In Union law, the right to a fair hearing is not confined to disputes relating to civil law rights and obligations. That is one of the consequences of the fact that the Union is a community based on the rule of law as stated by the Court in Case 294/83, "Les Verts" v. European Parliament (judgment of 23 April 1986, [1988] ECR 1339). Nevertheless, in all respects other than their scope, the guarantees afforded by the ECHR apply in a similar way to the Union.

With regard to the third paragraph, it should be noted that in accordance with the case law of the European Court of Human Rights, provision should be made for legal aid where the absence of such aid would make it impossible to ensure an effective remedy (ECHR Judgment of 9.10.1979, Airey, Series A, Volume 32, 11). There is also a system of legal assistance for cases before the Court of Justice of the European Union.

ARTICLE 48   [Article II-108 of the Constitution] *Presumption of innocence and right of defence*

1.   Everyone who has been charged shall be presumed innocent until proved guilty according to law.

2.   Respect for the rights of the defence of anyone who has been charged shall be guaranteed.

Explanation

Article 48 [Article II-108 of the Constitution] is the same as Article 6(2) and (3) of the ECHR, which reads as follows:

"2. Everyone charged with a criminal offence shall be presumed innocent until proved guilty according to law.

3. Everyone charged with a criminal offence has the following minimum rights:

(a) to be informed promptly, in a language which he understands and in detail, of the nature and cause of the accusation against him;

(b) to have adequate time and facilities for the preparation of his defence;

(c) to defend himself in person or through legal assistance of his own choosing or, if he has not sufficient means to pay for legal assistance, to be given it free when the interests of justice so require;

(d) to examine or have examined witnesses against him and to obtain the attendance and examination of witnesses on his behalf under the same conditions as witnesses against him;

(e) to have the free assistance of an interpreter if he cannot understand or speak the language used in court."

In accordance with Article 52(3) [Article II-112(3) of the Constitution], this right has the same meaning and scope as the right guaranteed by the ECHR.

ARTICLE 49 [Article II-109 of the Constitution] *Principles of legality and proportionality of criminal offences and penalties*

1. No one shall be held guilty of any criminal offence on account of any act or omission which did not constitute a criminal offence under national law or international law at the time when it was committed. Nor shall a heavier penalty be imposed than that which was applicable at the time the criminal offence was committed. If, subsequent to the commission of a criminal offence, the law provides for a lighter penalty, that penalty shall be applicable.

2. This Article shall not prejudice the trial and punishment of any person for any act or omission which, at the time when it was committed, was criminal according to the general principles recognised by the community of nations.

3. The severity of penalties must not be disproportionate to the criminal offence.

Explanation

This Article follows the traditional rule of the non-retroactivity of laws and criminal sanctions. There has been added the rule of the retroactivity of a more lenient penal law, which exists in a number of Member States and which features in Article 15 of the Covenant on Civil and Political Rights.

Article 7 of the ECHR is worded as follows:

"1. No one shall be held guilty of any criminal offence on account of any act or omission which did not constitute a criminal offence under national or international law at the time when it was committed. Nor shall a heavier penalty be imposed than the one that was applicable at the time the criminal offence was committed.

2. This Article shall not prejudice the trial and punishment of any person for any act or omission which, at the time when it was committed, was criminal according to the general principles of law recognised by civilised nations."

In paragraph 2, the reference to "civilised" nations has been deleted; this does not change the meaning of this paragraph, which refers to crimes against humanity in particular. In accordance with Article 52(3) [Article II-112(3) of the Constitution], the right guaranteed here therefore has the same meaning and scope as the right guaranteed by the ECHR.

Paragraph 3 states the general principle of proportionality between penalties and criminal offences which is enshrined in the common constitutional traditions of the Member States and in the case law of the Court of Justice of the Communities.

ARTICLE 50 [Article II-110 of the Constitution] *Right not to be tried or punished twice in criminal proceedings for the same criminal offence*

No one shall be liable to be tried or punished again in criminal proceedings for an offence for which he or she has already been finally acquitted or convicted within the Union in accordance with the law.

Explanation

Article 4 of Protocol No 7 to the ECHR reads as follows:

"1. No one shall be liable to be tried or punished again in criminal proceedings under the jurisdiction of the same State for an offence for which he has already been finally acquitted or convicted in accordance with the law and penal procedure of that State.

2. The provisions of the preceding paragraph shall not prevent the reopening of the case in accordance with the law and the penal procedure of the State concerned, if there is evidence of new or newly discovered facts, or if there has been a fundamental defect in the previous proceedings, which could affect the outcome of the case.

3. No derogation from this Article shall be made under Article 15 of the Convention."

The "non bis in idem" rule applies in Union law (see, among the many precedents, the judgment of 5 May 1966, Cases 18/65 and 35/65, Gutmann v. Commission [1966] ECR 103 and a recent case, the decision of the Court of First Instance of 20 April 1999, Joined Cases T-305/94 and others, Limburgse Vinyl Maatschappij NV v. Commission [1999] ECR II-931). The rule prohibiting cumulation refers to cumulation of two penalties of the same kind, that is to say criminal law penalties.

In accordance with Article 50 [Article II-110 of the Constitution], the "non bis in idem" rule applies not only within the jurisdiction of one State but also between the jurisdictions of several Member States. That corresponds to the *acquis* in Union law; see Articles 54 to 58 of the Schengen Convention and the judgment of the Court of Justice of 11 February 2003, C-187/01 Gözütok (not yet published), Article 7 of the Convention on the Protection of the European Communities' Financial Interests and Article 10 of the Convention on the fight against corruption. The very limited exceptions in those Conventions permitting the Member States to derogate from the "non bis in idem" rule are covered by the horizontal clause in Article 52(1) of the Charter [Article II-112(1) of the Constitution] concerning limitations. As regards the situations referred to by Article 4 of Protocol No 7, namely the application of the principle within the same Member State, the guaranteed right has the same meaning and the same scope as the corresponding right in the ECHR.

TITLE VII

GENERAL PROVISIONS GOVERNING THE INTERPRETATION AND APPLICATION OF THE CHARTER

ARTICLE 51   [Article II-111 of the Constitution] *Field of application*
1.   The provisions of this Charter are addressed to the institutions, bodies, offices and agencies of the Union with due regard for the principle of subsidiarity and to the Member States only when they are implementing Union law. They shall therefore respect the rights, observe the principles and promote the application thereof in accordance with their respective powers and respecting the limits of the powers of the Union as conferred on it in the other Parts of the Constitution.

2.   This Charter does not extend the field of application of Union law beyond the powers of the Union or establish any new power or task for the Union, or modify powers and tasks defined in the other Parts of the Constitution.

Explanation
The aim of Article 51 [Article II-111 of the Constitution] is to determine the scope of the Charter. It seeks to establish clearly that the Charter applies primarily to the institutions and bodies of the Union, in compliance with the principle of subsidiarity. This provision was drafted in keeping with Article 6(2) of the Treaty on European Union, which required the Union to respect fundamental rights, and with the mandate issued by Cologne European Council. The term "institutions" is enshrined in Part I of the Constitution. The expression "bodies, offices and agencies" is commonly used in the Constitution to refer to all the authorities set up by the Constitution or by secondary legislation (see, e.g., Articles I-50 or I-51 of the Constitution).

As regards the Member States, it follows unambiguously from the case law of the Court of Justice that the requirement to respect fundamental rights defined in a Union context is only binding on the Member States when they act in the scope of Union law (judgment of 13 July 1989, Case 5/88 Wachauf [1989] ECR 2609; judgment of 18 June 1991, ERT [1991] ECR I-2925); judgment of 18 December 1997 (C-309/96 Annibaldi [1997] ECR I-7493). The Court of Justice confirmed this case law in the following terms: "In addition, it should be remembered that the requirements flowing from the protection of fundamental rights in the Community legal order are also binding on Member States when they implement Community rules ..." (judgment of 13 April 2000, Case C-292/97, [2000] ECR 2737, paragraph 37 of the grounds). Of course this rule, as enshrined in this Charter, applies to the central authorities as well as to regional or local bodies, and to public organisations, when they are implementing Union law.

Paragraph 2, together with the second sentence of paragraph 1, confirms that the Charter may not have the effect of extending the competences and tasks which the other Parts of the Constitution confer on the Union. Explicit mention is made here of the logical consequences of the principle of subsidiarity and of the fact that the Union only has those powers which have been conferred upon it. The fundamental rights as guaranteed in the Union do not have any effect other than in the context of the powers determined by Parts I and III of the Constitution. Consequently, an obligation, pursuant to the second sentence of paragraph 1, for the Union's institutions to promote principles laid down in the Charter, may arise only within the limits of these same powers.

Paragraph 2 also confirms that the Charter may not have the effect of extending the field of application of Union law beyond the powers of the Union as established in the other Parts of the Constitution. The Court of Justice has already established this rule with respect to the fundamental rights recognised as part of Union law (judgment of 17 February 1998, C-249/96 Grant, 1998 ECR I-621, paragraph 45 of the grounds). In accordance with this rule, it goes without saying that the incorporation of the Charter into the Constitution cannot be understood as extending by itself the range of Member State action considered to be "implementation of Union law" (within the meaning of paragraph 1 and the above-mentioned case law).

ARTICLE 52 [Article II-112 of the Constitution] *Scope and interpretation of rights and principles*
1. Any limitation on the exercise of the rights and freedoms recognised by this Charter must be provided for by law and respect the essence of those rights and freedoms. Subject to the principle of proportionality, limitations may be made only if they are necessary and genuinely meet objectives of general interest recognised by the Union or the need to protect the rights and freedoms of others.

2. Rights recognised by this Charter for which provision is made in other Parts of the Constitution shall be exercised under the conditions and within the limits defined by these relevant Parts.

3. Insofar as this Charter contains rights which correspond to rights guaranteed by the Convention for the Protection of Human Rights and Fundamental Freedoms, the meaning and scope of those rights shall be the same as those laid down by the said Convention. This provision shall not prevent Union law providing more extensive protection.

4. Insofar as this Charter recognises fundamental rights as they result from the constitutional traditions common to the Member States, those rights shall be interpreted in harmony with those traditions.

5. The provisions of this Charter which contain principles may be implemented by legislative and executive acts taken by institutions, bodies, offices and agencies of the Union, and by acts of Member States when they are implementing Union law, in the exercise of their respective powers. They shall be judicially cognisable only in the interpretation of such acts and in the ruling on their legality.

6. Full account shall be taken of national laws and practices as specified in this Charter.

7. The explanations drawn up as a way of providing guidance in the interpretation of the Charter of Fundamental Rights shall be given due regard by the courts of the Union and of the Member States.

Explanation
The purpose of Article 52 [Article II-112 of the Constitution] is to set the scope of the rights and principles of the Charter, and to lay down rules for their interpretation. Paragraph 1 deals with the arrangements for the limitation of rights. The wording is based on the case law of the Court of Justice: "... it is well established in the case law of the Court that restrictions may be imposed on the exercise of fundamental rights, in particular in the context of a common organisation of the market, provided that those restrictions in fact correspond to objectives of general interest pursued by the Community and do not constitute, with regard to the aim pursued, disproportionate and unreasonable interference undermining the very substance of those rights" (judgment of 13 April 2000, Case C-292/97, paragraph 45 of the grounds). The reference to general interests recognised by the Union covers both the objectives mentioned in Article I-2 of the Constitution and other interests protected by specific provisions of the Constitution such as Articles I-5(1), III-133(3), III-154 and III-436.
Paragraph 2 refers to rights which were already expressly guaranteed in the Treaty establishing the European Community and have been recognised in the Charter, and which are now found in other Parts of the Constitution (notably the rights derived from Union citizenship). It clarifies that such rights remain subject to the conditions and limits applicable to the Union law on which they are based, and for which provision is now made in Parts I and III of the Constitution. The Charter does not alter the system of rights conferred by the EC Treaty and now taken over by Parts I and III of the Constitution.
Paragraph 3 is intended to ensure the necessary consistency between the Charter and the ECHR by establishing the rule that, insofar as the rights in the present Charter also correspond to rights guaranteed by the ECHR, the meaning and scope of those rights, including authorised limitations, are the same as those laid down by the ECHR. This means in particular that the legislator, in laying down limitations to those rights, must comply with the same standards as are fixed by the detailed limitation arrangements laid down in the ECHR, which are thus made applicable for the rights covered by this paragraph, without thereby adversely affecting the autonomy of Union law and of that of the Court of Justice of the European Union.
The reference to the ECHR covers both the Convention and the Protocols to it. The meaning and the scope of the guaranteed rights are determined not only by the text of those instruments, but also by the case law of the European Court of Human Rights and by the Court of Justice of the European Union. The last sentence of the paragraph is designed to allow the Union to guarantee more extensive protection. In any event, the level of protection afforded by the Charter may never be lower than that guaranteed by the ECHR.
The Charter does not affect the possibilities of Member States to avail themselves of Article 15 ECHR, allowing derogations from ECHR rights in the event of war or of other public dangers threatening the life of the nation, when they take action in the areas of national defence in the event of war and of the maintenance

of law and order, in accordance with their responsibilities recognised in Articles I-5 (1), III-131, III-262 of the Constitution.

The list of rights which may at the present stage, without precluding developments in the law, legislation and the Treaties, be regarded as corresponding to rights in the ECHR within the meaning of the present paragraph is given hereafter. It does not include rights additional to those in the ECHR.

1.   Articles of the Charter where both the meaning and the scope are the same as the corresponding Articles of the ECHR:
–   Article 2 [Article II-62 of the Constitution] corresponds to Article 2 of the ECHR
–   Article 4 [Article II-64 of the Constitution] corresponds to Article 3 of the ECHR
–   Article 5(1) and (2) [Article II-65 of the Constitution] correspond to Article 4 of the ECHR
–   Article 6 [Article II-66 of the Constitution] corresponds to Article 5 of the ECHR
–   Article 7 [Article II-67 of the Constitution] corresponds to Article 8 of the ECHR
–   Article 10(1) [Article II-70 of the Constitution] corresponds to Article 9 of the ECHR
–   Article 11 [Article II-71 of the Constitution] corresponds to Article 10 of the ECHR without prejudice to any restrictions which Union law may impose on Member States' right to introduce the licensing arrangements referred to in the third sentence of Article 10(1) of the ECHR
–   Article 17 [Article II-77 of the Constitution] corresponds to Article 1 of the Protocol to the ECHR
–   Article 19(1) [Article II-79 of the Constitution] corresponds to Article 4 of Protocol No 4
–   Article 19(2) [Article II-79 of the Constitution] corresponds to Article 3 of the ECHR as interpreted by the European Court of Human Rights
–   Article 48 [Article II-108 of the Constitution] corresponds to Article 6(2) and(3) of the ECHR
–   Article 49(1) (with the exception of the last sentence) and (2) [Article II-109 of the Constitution] correspond to Article 7 of the ECHR

2.   Articles where the meaning is the same as the corresponding Articles of the ECHR, but where the scope is wider:
–   Article 9 [Article II-69 of the Constitution] covers the same field as Article 12 of the ECHR, but its scope may be extended to other forms of marriage if these are established by national legislation
–   Article 12(1) [Article II-72 of the Constitution] corresponds to Article 11 of the ECHR, but its scope is extended to European Union level
–   Article 14(1) [Article II-74 of the Constitution] corresponds to Article 2 of the Protocol to the ECHR, but its scope is extended to cover access to vocational and continuing training
–   Article 14(3) [Article II-74 of the Constitution] corresponds to Article 2 of the Protocol to the ECHR as regards the rights of parents
–   Article 47(2) and (3) [Article II-107 of the Constitution] correspond to Article 6(1) of the ECHR, but the limitation to the determination of civil rights and obligations or criminal charges does not apply as regards Union law and its implementation
–   Article 50 [Article II-110 of the Constitution] corresponds to Article 4 of Protocol No 7 to the ECHR, but its scope is extended to European Union level between the Courts of the Member States.
–   Finally, citizens of the European Union may not be considered as aliens in the scope of the application of Union law, because of the prohibition of any discrimination on grounds of nationality. The limitations provided for by Article 16 of the ECHR as regards the rights of aliens therefore do not apply to them in this context.

The rule of interpretation contained in paragraph 4 has been based on the wording of Article 6(2) of the Treaty on European Union (cf. now the wording of Article I-9(3) of the Constitution) and takes due account of the approach to common constitutional traditions followed by the Court of Justice (e.g., judgment of 13 December 1979, Case 44/79 Hauer [1979] ECR 3727; judgment of 18 May 1982, Case 155/79, AM&S, [1982] ECR 1575). Under that rule, rather than following a rigid approach of "a lowest common denominator", the Charter rights concerned should be interpreted in a way offering a high standard of protection which is adequate for the law of the Union and in harmony with the common constitutional traditions.

Paragraph 5 clarifies the distinction between "rights" and "principles" set out in the Charter. According to that distinction, subjective rights shall be respected, whereas principles shall be observed (Article 51 (1)) [Article II-111 of the Constitution]. Principles may be implemented through legislative or executive acts (adopted by the Union in accordance with its powers, and by the Member States only when they implement Union law); accordingly, they become significant for the Courts only when such acts are interpreted or reviewed. They do not however give rise to direct claims for positive action by the Union's institutions or Member States authorities. This is consistent both with case law of the Court of Justice (Cf. notably case law on the "precautionary principle" in Article 174 (2) TEC (replaced by Article III-233 of the Constitution): judgment of the CFI of 11 September 2002, T-13/99, Pfizer vs. Council, with numerous references to earlier case law; and a series of judgments on Article 33 (ex-39) on the principles of agricultural law, e.g. judgment of the Court of Justice C- 265/85, Van den Berg, 1987 ECR 1155: scrutiny of the principle of market stabilisation and of reasonable expectations) and with the approach of the Member States' constitutional systems to "principles" particularly in the field of social law. For illustration, examples for principles recognised in the Charter include e.g. Articles 25, 26 and 37 [Articles II-85, II-86 and II-97 of the Constitution]. In some cases, an Article of the Charter may contain both elements of a right and of a principle, e.g. Articles 23, 33 and 34 [Articles II-83, II-93 and II-94 of the Constitution].

Paragraph 6 refers to the various Articles in the Charter which, in the spirit of subsidiarity, make reference to national laws and practices.

ARTICLE 53   [Article II-113 of the Constitution] *Level of protection*

Nothing in this Charter shall be interpreted as restricting or adversely affecting human rights and fundamental freedoms as recognised, in their respective fields of application, by Union law and international law and by international agreements to which the Union or all the Member States are party, including the European Convention for the Protection of Human Rights and Fundamental Freedoms, and by the Member States' constitutions.

Explanation

This provision is intended to maintain the level of protection currently afforded within their respective scope by Union law, national law and international law. Owing to its importance, mention is made of the ECHR.

ARTICLE 54   [Article II-114 of the Constitution] *Prohibition of abuse of rights*

Nothing in this Charter shall be interpreted as implying any right to engage in any activity or to perform any act aimed at the destruction of any of the rights and freedoms recognised in this Charter or at their limitation to a greater extent than is provided for herein.

Explanation

This Article corresponds to Article 17 of the ECHR:

"Nothing in this Convention may be interpreted as implying for any State, group or person any right to engage in any activity or perform any act aimed at the destruction of any of the rights and freedoms set forth herein or at their limitation to a greater extent than is provided for in the Convention."

13.   DECLARATION ON ARTICLE III-116

The Conference agrees that, in its general efforts to eliminate inequalities between women and men, the Union will aim in its different policies to combat all kinds of domestic violence. The Member States should take all necessary measures to prevent and punish these criminal acts and to support and protect the victims.

14.   DECLARATION ON ARTICLES III-136 AND III-267

The Conference considers that in the event that a draft European law or framework law based on Article III-267(2) would affect fundamental aspects of the social security system of a Member State, including its scope, cost or financial structure, or would affect the financial balance of that system as set out in Article III-136(2), the interests of that Member State will be duly taken into account.

15.   DECLARATION ON ARTICLES III-160 AND III-322

The Conference recalls that the respect for fundamental rights and freedoms implies, in particular, that proper attention is given to the protection and observance of the due process rights of the individuals or entities concerned. For this purpose and in order to guarantee a thorough judicial review of European decisions subjecting an individual or entity to restrictive measures, such decisions must be based on clear and distinct criteria. These criteria should be tailored to the specifics of each restrictive measure.

16.   DECLARATION ON ARTICLE III-167(2)(C)

The Conference notes that Article III-167(2)(c) shall be interpreted in accordance with the existing case law of the Court of Justice of the European Communities and of the Court of First Instance regarding the applicability of the provisions to aid granted to certain areas of the Federal Republic of Germany affected by the former division of Germany.

17.   DECLARATION ON ARTICLE III-184

With regard to Article III-184, the Conference confirms that raising growth potential and securing sound budgetary positions are the two pillars of the economic and fiscal policy of the Union and the Member States. The Stability and Growth Pact is an important tool to achieve these goals.

The Conference reaffirms its commitment to the provisions concerning the Stability and Growth Pact as the framework for the co-ordination of budgetary policies in the Member States.

The Conference confirms that a rule-based system is the best guarantee for commitments to be enforced and for all Member States to be treated equally.

Within this framework, the Conference also reaffirms its commitment to the goals of the Lisbon Strategy: job creation, structural reforms, and social cohesion.

The Union aims at achieving balanced economic growth and price stability. Economic and budgetary policies thus need to set the right priorities towards economic reforms, innovation, competitiveness and strengthening of private investment and consumption in phases of weak economic growth. This should be reflected in the orientations of budgetary decisions at the national and Union level in particular through restructuring of public revenue and expenditure while respecting budgetary discipline in accordance with the Constitution and the Stability and Growth Pact.

Budgetary and economic challenges facing the Member States underline the importance of sound budgetary policy throughout the economic cycle.

The Conference agrees that Member States should use periods of economic recovery actively to consolidate public finances and improve their budgetary positions. The objective is to gradually achieve a budgetary surplus in good times which creates the necessary room to accommodate economic downturns and thus contribute to the long-term sustainability of public finances.

The Member States look forward to possible proposals of the Commission as well as further contributions of Member States with regard to strengthening and clarifying the implementation of the Stability and Growth Pact. The Member States will take all necessary measures to raise the growth potential of their economies. Improved economic policy co-ordination could support this objective. This Declaration does not prejudge the future debate on the Stability and Growth Pact.

18.   DECLARATION ON ARTICLE III-213

The Conference confirms that the policies described in Article III-213 fall essentially within the competence of the Member States. Measures to provide encouragement and promote co-ordination to be taken at Union level in accordance with this Article shall be of a complementary nature. They shall serve to strengthen co-operation between Member States and not to harmonise national systems. The guarantees and practices existing in each Member State as regards the responsibility of the social partners will not be affected.

This Declaration is without prejudice to the provisions of the Constitution conferring competence on the Union, including in social matters.

19.   DECLARATION ON ARTICLE III-220

The Conference considers that the reference in Article III-220 to island regions can include island States in their entirety, subject to the necessary criteria being met.

20.   DECLARATION ON ARTICLE III-243

The Conference notes that the provisions of Article III-243 shall be applied in accordance with the current practice. The terms "such measures are required in order to compensate for the economic disadvantages caused by the division of Germany to the economy of certain areas of the Federal Republic affected by that division" shall be interpreted in accordance with the existing case law of the Court of Justice of the European Communities and of the Court of First Instance.

21. DECLARATION ON ARTICLE III-248

The Conference agrees that the Union's action in the area of research and technological development will pay due respect to the fundamental orientations and choices of the research policies of the Member States.

22. DECLARATION ON ARTICLE III-256

The Conference believes that Article III-256 does not affect the right of the Member States to take the necessary measures to ensure their energy supply under the conditions provided for in Article III-131.

23. DECLARATION ON ARTICLE III-273(1), SECOND SUBPARAGRAPH

The Conference considers that the European laws referred to in the second subparagraph of Article III-273(1) should take into account national rules and practices relating to the initiation of criminal investigations.

24. DECLARATION ON ARTICLE III-296

The Conference declares that, as soon as the Treaty establishing a Constitution for Europe is signed, the Secretary-General of the Council, High Representative for the common foreign and security policy, the Commission and the Member States should begin preparatory work on the European External Action Service.

25. DECLARATION ON ARTICLE III-325 CONCERNING THE NEGOTIATION AND CONCLUSION OF INTERNATIONAL AGREEMENTS BY MEMBER STATES RELATING TO THE AREA OF FREEDOM, SECURITY AND JUSTICE

The Conference confirms that Member States may negotiate and conclude agreements with third countries or international organisations in the areas covered by Sections 3, 4 and 5 of Chapter IV of Title III of Part III of the Treaty establishing a Constitution for Europe insofar as such agreements comply with Union law.

26. DECLARATION ON ARTICLE III-402(4)

Article III-402(4) of the Constitution provides that where no European law of the Council establishing a new financial framework has been adopted by the end of the previous financial framework, the ceilings and other provisions corresponding to the last year of that framework shall be extended until such time as that law is adopted.

The Conference states that if no European law of the Council establishing a new financial framework has been adopted by the end of 2006 and where the Treaty of Accession of 16 April 2003 provides for a phasing-in period for the allocation of appropriations to the new Member States ending in 2006, the allocation of funds as from 2007 will be established on the basis of the same criteria being applied for all Member States.

27. DECLARATION ON ARTICLE III-419

The Conference declares that Member States may indicate, when they make a request to establish enhanced co-operation, if they intend already at that stage to make use of Article III-422 providing for the extension of qualified majority voting or to have recourse to the ordinary legislative procedure.

28. DECLARATION ON ARTICLE IV-440(7)

The High Contracting Parties agree that the European Council, pursuant to Article IV-440(7), will take a European decision leading to the modification of the status of Mayotte with regard to the Union in order to make this territory an outermost region within the meaning of Article IV-440(2) and Article III-424, when the French authorities notify the European Council and the Commission that the evolution currently underway in the internal status of the island so allows.

29. DECLARATION ON ARTICLE IV-448(2)

The Conference considers that the possibility of producing translations of the Treaty establishing a Constitution for Europe in the languages mentioned in Article IV-448(2) contributes to fulfilling the objective of respecting the Union's rich cultural and linguistic diversity as set forth in the fourth subparagraph of Article I-3(3) of that Treaty. In this context, the Conference confirms the attachment of the Union to the cultural diversity of Europe and the special attention it will continue to pay to these and other languages.

The Conference recommends that those Member States wishing to avail themselves of the possibility recognised in Article IV-448(2) communicate to the Council, within six months from the date of the signature of that Treaty, the language or languages into which translations of that Treaty will be made.

30. DECLARATION ON THE RATIFICATION OF THE TREATY ESTABLISHING A CONSTITUTION FOR EUROPE

The Conference notes that if, two years after the signature of the Treaty establishing a Constitution for Europe, four fifths of the Member States have ratified it and one or more Member States have encountered difficulties in proceeding with ratification, the matter will be referred to the European Council.

B. DECLARATIONS CONCERNING PROTOCOLS ANNEXED TO THE CONSTITUTION

DECLARATIONS
CONCERNING THE PROTOCOL ON THE TREATIES AND ACTS OF ACCESSION OF THE KINGDOM OF DENMARK, IRELAND AND THE UNITED KINGDOM OF GREAT BRITAIN AND NORTHERN IRELAND, OF THE HELLENIC REPUBLIC, OF THE KINGDOM OF SPAIN AND THE PORTUGUESE REPUBLIC, AND OF THE REPUBLIC OF AUSTRIA, THE REPUBLIC OF FINLAND AND THE KINGDOM OF SWEDEN

31. DECLARATION ON THE ÅLAND ISLANDS

The Conference acknowledges that the regime applicable to the Åland islands, referred to in Article IV-440(5), is established taking into account the special status that these islands enjoy under international law.
To that end, the Conference stresses that specific provisions have been included in Section 5 of Title V of the Protocol on the Treaties and Acts of Accession of the Kingdom of Denmark, Ireland and the United Kingdom of Great Britain and Northern Ireland, of the Hellenic Republic, of the Kingdom of Spain and the Portuguese Republic, and of the Republic of Austria, the Republic of Finland and the Kingdom of Sweden.

32. DECLARATION ON THE SAMI PEOPLE

Having regard to Articles 60 and 61 of the Protocol on the Treaties and Acts of Accession of the Kingdom of Denmark, Ireland and the United Kingdom of Great Britain and Northern Ireland, of the Hellenic Republic, of the Kingdom of Spain and the Portuguese Republic, and of the Republic of Austria, the Republic of Finland and the Kingdom of Sweden, the Conference recognises the obligations and commitments of Sweden and Finland with regard to the Sami people under national and international law.
The Conference notes that Sweden and Finland are committed to preserving and developing the means of livelihood, language, culture and way of life of the Sami people and considers that traditional Sami culture and livelihood depend on primary economic activities, such as reindeer husbandry in the traditional areas of Sami settlement.
To that end, the Conference stresses that specific provisions have been included in Section 6 of Title V of the Protocol on the Treaties and Acts of Accession of the Kingdom of Denmark, Ireland and the United Kingdom of Great Britain and Northern Ireland, of the Hellenic Republic, of the Kingdom of Spain and the Portuguese Republic, and of the Republic of Austria, the Republic of Finland and the Kingdom of Sweden.

DECLARATIONS
CONCERNING THE PROTOCOL ON THE TREATY AND THE ACT OF ACCESSION OF THE CZECH REPUBLIC, THE REPUBLIC OF ESTONIA, THE REPUBLIC OF CYPRUS, THE REPUBLIC OF LATVIA, THE REPUBLIC OF LITHUANIA, THE REPUBLIC OF HUNGARY, THE REPUBLIC OF MALTA, THE REPUBLIC OF POLAND, THE REPUBLIC OF SLOVENIA AND THE SLOVAK REPUBLIC

33. DECLARATION ON THE SOVEREIGN BASE AREAS OF THE UNITED KINGDOM OF GREAT BRITAIN AND NORTHERN IRELAND IN CYPRUS

THE CONFERENCE,

Recalling that the Joint Declaration on the Sovereign Base Areas of the United Kingdom of Great Britain and Northern Ireland in Cyprus annexed to the Final Act of the Treaty concerning the Accession of the United Kingdom to the European Communities provided that the arrangements applicable to relations between the European Economic Community and the Sovereign Base Areas will be defined within the context of any agreement between the Community and the Republic of Cyprus,

Taking account of the provisions concerning the Sovereign Base Areas set out in the Treaty concerning the Establishment of the Republic of Cyprus (hereinafter referred to as the "Treaty of Establishment") and the associated Exchanges of Notes dated 16 August 1960,

Noting the Exchange of Notes between the Government of the United Kingdom and the Government of the Republic of Cyprus concerning the administration of the Sovereign Base Areas, dated 16 August 1960, and the attached Declaration by the United Kingdom Government that one of the main objects to be achieved is the protection of the interests of those resident or working in the Sovereign Base Areas, and considering in this context that the said persons should have, to the extent possible, the same treatment as those resident or working in the Republic of Cyprus;

Noting further the provisions of the Treaty of Establishment regarding customs arrangements between the Sovereign Base Areas and the Republic of Cyprus and in particular those of Annex F to the said Treaty;

Noting also the commitment of the United Kingdom not to create customs posts or other frontier barriers between the Sovereign Base Areas and the Republic of Cyprus and the arrangements made pursuant to the Treaty of Establishment whereby the authorities of the Republic of Cyprus administer a wide range of public services in the Sovereign Base Areas, including in the fields of agriculture, customs and taxation;

Confirming that the accession of the Republic of Cyprus to the Union should not affect the rights and obligations of the parties to the Treaty of Establishment;

Recognising therefore the need to apply certain provisions of the Constitution and acts of the Union to the Sovereign Base Areas and to make special arrangements regarding the implementation of these provisions in the Sovereign Base Areas;

Points out that specific provisions to that end have been included in Title III of Part Two of the Protocol on the Treaty and Act of Accession of the Czech Republic, the Republic of Estonia, the Republic of Cyprus, the Republic of Latvia, the Republic of Lithuania, the Republic of Hungary, the Republic of Malta, the Republic of Poland, the Republic of Slovenia and the Slovak Republic.

34. DECLARATION BY THE COMMISSION ON THE SOVEREIGN BASE AREAS OF THE UNITED KINGDOM OF GREAT BRITAIN AND NORTHERN IRELAND IN CYPRUS

The Commission confirms its understanding that the provisions of Union law applicable to the Sovereign Base Areas pursuant to Title III of Part Two of the Protocol on the Treaty and Act of Accession of the Czech Republic, the Republic of Estonia, the Republic of Cyprus, the Republic of Latvia, the Republic of Lithuania, the Republic of Hungary, the Republic of Malta, the Republic of Poland, the Republic of Slovenia and the Slovak Republic include:

(a) Council Regulation (EC) No 3448/93 of 6 December 1993 laying down the trade arrangements applicable to certain goods resulting from the processing of agricultural products;

(b) Council Regulation (EC) No 1260/1999 of 21 June 1999 laying down general provisions on the Structural Funds, to the extent required by Council Regulation (EC) No 1257/1999 of 17 May 1999 on support for rural development from the European Agricultural Guidance and Guarantee Fund (EAGGF) for the purpose of financing rural development measures in the Sovereign Base Areas under the EAGGF Guarantee Section.

35. DECLARATION ON THE IGNALINA NUCLEAR POWER PLANT IN LITHUANIA

THE CONFERENCE,

Declaring the Union's willingness to continue to provide adequate additional assistance to Lithuania's decommissioning effort also after Lithuania's accession to the Union for the period until 2006 and beyond and noting that Lithuania, bearing in mind this expression of Union solidarity, has committed to close Unit 1 of the Ignalina Nuclear Power Plant before 2005 and Unit 2 by 2009;

Recognising that the decommissioning of the Ignalina Nuclear Power Plant with two 1500 MW RBMK-type reactor units inherited from the former Soviet Union is of an unprecedented nature and represents for Lithuania an exceptional financial burden not commensurate with the size and economic strength of the country and that this decommissioning will continue beyond the current Financial Perspective as defined by the Interinstitutional Agreement of 6 May 1999;

Noting the need to adopt implementing provisions for the additional Union assistance to address the consequences of the closure and the decommissioning of the Ignalina Nuclear Power Plant;

Noting that Lithuania will pay due attention to the needs of the regions most affected by the closure of the Ignalina Nuclear Power Plant in its use of Union assistance;

Declaring that certain measures that will be supported through public aid shall be considered as compatible with the internal market, such as the decommissioning of the Ignalina Nuclear Power Plant, and the environmental upgrading in line with the *acquis* and modernisation of conventional electricity production capacity needed to replace the two Ignalina Nuclear Power Plant reactors after their closure,

Points out that specific provisions to that end have been included in Title IV of Part Two of the Protocol on the Treaty and Act of Accession of the Czech Republic, the Republic of Estonia, the Republic of Cyprus, the Republic of Latvia, the Republic of Lithuania, the Republic of Hungary, the Republic of Malta, the Republic of Poland, the Republic of Slovenia and the Slovak Republic.

36. DECLARATION ON THE TRANSIT OF PERSONS BY LAND BETWEEN THE REGION OF KALININGRAD AND OTHER PARTS OF THE RUSSIAN FEDERATION

THE CONFERENCE,

Considering the particular situation of the Kaliningrad region of the Russian Federation in the context of the Union's enlargement;

Recognising the obligations and commitments of Lithuania with regard to the *acquis* establishing an area of freedom, security and justice;

Noting, in particular, that Lithuania shall fully apply and implement the Union *acquis* regarding the list of countries whose nationals must be in possession of visas when crossing the external borders and those whose nationals are exempt from that requirement as well the Union *acquis* regarding the uniform format for a visa as from accession at the latest;

Recognising that the transit of persons by land between the region of Kaliningrad and other parts of the Russian Federation through Union territory is a matter concerning the Union as a whole and should be treated as such and must not entail any unfavourable consequence for Lithuania;

Considering the decision to be taken by the Council to remove controls at internal borders after it has verified that the necessary conditions to that effect have been met;

Determined to assist Lithuania in fulfilling the conditions for full participation in the Schengen area without internal frontiers as soon as possible,

Points out that specific provisions to that end have been included in Title V of Part Two of the Protocol on the Treaty and Act of Accession of the Czech Republic, the Republic of Estonia, the Republic of Cyprus, the Republic of Latvia, the Republic of Lithuania, the Republic of Hungary, the Republic of Malta, the Republic of Poland, the Republic of Slovenia and the Slovak Republic.

264

37. DECLARATION ON UNIT 1 AND UNIT 2 OF THE BOHUNICE V1 NUCLEAR POWER PLANT IN SLOVAKIA

THE CONFERENCE,

Noting Slovakia's commitment to close Unit 1 and Unit 2 of the Bohunice V1 Nuclear Power Plant at the end of 2006 and 2008 respectively and declaring the Union's willingness to continue to provide financial aid until 2006 in continuation of the pre-accession aid planned under the Phare programme in support of Slovakia's decommissioning effort;

Noting the need to adopt implementing provisions regarding continued Union assistance;

Points out that specific provisions to that end have been included in Title IX of Part Two of the Protocol on the Treaty and Act of Accession of the Czech Republic, the Republic of Estonia, the Republic of Cyprus, the Republic of Latvia, the Republic of Lithuania, the Republic of Hungary, the Republic of Malta, the Republic of Poland, the Republic of Slovenia and the Slovak Republic.

38. DECLARATION ON CYPRUS

THE CONFERENCE,

Reaffirming its commitment to a comprehensive settlement of the Cyprus problem, consistent with relevant United Nations Security Council Resolutions, and its strong support for the efforts of the United Nations Secretary General to that end;

Considering that such a comprehensive settlement to the Cyprus problem has not yet been reached;

Considering that it is, therefore, necessary to provide for the suspension of the application of the *acquis* in those areas of the Republic of Cyprus in which the Government of the Republic of Cyprus does not exercise effective control;

Considering that, in the event of a solution to the Cyprus problem, this suspension will be lifted;

Considering that the Union is ready to accommodate the terms of such a settlement in line with the principles on which the Union is founded;

Considering that it is necessary to provide for the terms under which the relevant provisions of Union law will apply to the line between the abovementioned areas and both those areas in which the Government of the Republic of Cyprus exercises effective control and the Eastern Sovereign Base Area of the United Kingdom of Great Britain and Northern Ireland;

Desiring that the accession of Cyprus to the Union shall benefit all Cypriot citizens and promote civil peace and reconciliation;

Considering, therefore, that nothing in Title X of Part Two of the Protocol on the Treaty and Act of Accession of the Czech Republic, the Republic of Estonia, the Republic of Cyprus, the Republic of Latvia, the Republic of Lithuania, the Republic of Hungary, the Republic of Malta, the Republic of Poland, the Republic of Slovenia and the Slovak Republic shall preclude measures with this end in view;

Considering that such measures shall not affect the application of the *acquis* under the conditions set out in the that Protocol in any other part of the Republic of Cyprus;

Points out that specific provisions to that end have been included in Title X of Part Two of the Protocol on the Treaty and Act of Accession of the Czech Republic, the Republic of Estonia, the Republic of Cyprus, the Republic of Latvia, the Republic of Lithuania, the Republic of Hungary, the Republic of Malta, the Republic of Poland, the Republic of Slovenia and the Slovak Republic.

39. DECLARATION CONCERNING THE PROTOCOL ON THE POSITION OF DENMARK

The Conference notes that with respect to legal acts to be adopted by the Council acting alone or jointly with the European Parliament and containing provisions applicable to Denmark as well as provisions not applicable to Denmark because they have a legal basis to which Part I of the Protocol on the position of Denmark applies, Denmark declares that it will not use its voting right to prevent the adoption of the provisions which are not applicable to Denmark.

Furthermore, the Conference notes that on the basis of the Declaration by the Conference on Articles I-43 and III-329 of the Constitution, Denmark declares that Danish participation in actions or legal acts pursuant to Articles I-43 and III-329 will take place in accordance with Part I and Part II of the Protocol on the position of Denmark.

40. DECLARATION CONCERNING THE PROTOCOL ON THE TRANSITIONAL PROVISIONS RELATING TO THE INSTITUTIONS AND BODIES OF THE UNION

The common position which will be taken by the Member States at the conferences on the accession to the Union of Romania and/or Bulgaria regarding the allocation of seats in the European Parliament and the weighting of votes in the European Council and the Council will be as follows.

1.   If the accession to the Union of Romania and/or Bulgaria takes place before the entry into force of the European Council Decision referred to in Article I-20(2), the allocation of seats in the European Parliament throughout the 2004-2009 parliamentary term will be in accordance with the following table for a Union of 27 Member States.

MEMBER STATES	SEATS IN THE EP
Germany	99
United Kingdom	78
France	78
Italy	78
Spain	54
Poland	54
Romania	35
Netherlands	27
Greece	24
Czech Republic	24
Belgium	24
Hungary	24
Portugal	24
Sweden	19
Bulgaria	18
Austria	18
Slovakia	14
Denmark	14
Finland	14
Ireland	13
Lithuania	13
Latvia	9
Slovenia	7
Estonia	6
Cyprus	6
Luxembourg	6
Malta	5
TOTAL	**785**

The Treaty of Accession to the Union will therefore, by way of derogation from Article I-20(2) of the Constitution, stipulate that the number of members of the European Parliament may temporarily exceed 750 for the remainder of the 2004 to 2009 Parliamentary term.

2.   In Article 2(2) of the Protocol on the transitional provisions relating to the institutions and bodies of the Union, the weighting of the votes of Romania and Bulgaria in the European Council and the Council will be set at 14 and 10 respectively.

3.   At the time of each accession, the threshold referred to in the Protocol on the transitional provisions relating to the institutions and bodies of the Union will be calculated according to Article 2(3) of that Protocol.

41. DECLARATION CONCERNING ITALY

The Conference notes that the Protocol on Italy annexed in 1957 to the Treaty establishing the European Economic Community, as amended upon adoption of the Treaty on European Union, stated that:

"THE HIGH CONTRACTING PARTIES,

DESIRING to settle certain particular problems relating to Italy,

HAVE AGREED upon the following provisions, which shall be annexed to this Treaty:

THE MEMBER STATES OF THE COMMUNITY

TAKE NOTE of the fact that the Italian Government is carrying out a ten-year programme of economic expansion designed to rectify the disequilibria in the structure of the Italian economy, in particular by providing an infrastructure for the less developed areas in Southern Italy and in the Italian islands and by creating new jobs in order to eliminate unemployment;

RECALL that the principles and objectives of this programme of the Italian Government have been considered and approved by organisations for international co-operation of which the Member States are members;

RECOGNISE that it is in their common interest that the objectives of the Italian programme should be attained;

AGREE, in order to facilitate the accomplishment of this task by the Italian Government, to recommend to the institutions of the Community that they should employ all the methods and procedures provided in this Treaty and, in particular, make appropriate use of the resources of the European Investment Bank and the European Social Fund;

ARE OF THE OPINION that the institutions of the Community should, in applying this Treaty, take account of the sustained effort to be made by the Italian economy in the coming years and of the desirability of avoiding dangerous stresses in particular within the balance of payments or the level of employment, which might jeopardise the application of this Treaty in Italy;

RECOGNISE that in the event of Articles 109h and 109i being applied it will be necessary to take care that any measures required of the Italian Government do not prejudice the completion of its programme for economic expansion and for raising the standard of living of the population."

DECLARATIONS
BY MEMBER STATES

42. DECLARATION BY THE KINGDOM OF THE NETHERLANDS ON ARTICLE I-55

The Kingdom of the Netherlands will agree to a European decision as referred to in Article I-55(4) once a revision of the European law referred to in Article I-54(3) has provided the Netherlands with a satisfactory solution for its excessive negative net payment position vis-à-vis the Union budget.

43. DECLARATION BY THE KINGDOM OF THE NETHERLANDS ON ARTICLE IV-440

The Kingdom of the Netherlands declares that an initiative for a European decision, as referred to in Article IV-440(7) aimed at amending the status of the Netherlands Antilles and/or Aruba with regard to the Union, will be submitted only on the basis of a decision taken in conformity with the Charter for the Kingdom of the Netherlands.

44. DECLARATION BY THE FEDERAL REPUBLIC OF GERMANY, IRELAND, THE REPUBLIC OF HUNGARY, THE REPUBLIC OF AUSTRIA AND THE KINGDOM OF SWEDEN

Germany, Ireland, Hungary, Austria and Sweden note that the core provisions of the Treaty establishing the European Atomic Energy Community have not been substantially amended since its entry into force and need to be brought up to date. They therefore support the idea of a Conference of the Representatives of the Governments of the Member States, which should be convened as soon as possible.

45. DECLARATION BY THE KINGDOM OF SPAIN AND THE UNITED KINGDOM OF GREAT BRITAIN AND NORTHERN IRELAND

The Treaty establishing the Constitution applies to Gibraltar as a European territory for whose external relations a Member State is responsible. This shall not imply changes in the respective positions of the Member States concerned.

46. DECLARATION BY THE UNITED KINGDOM OF GREAT BRITAIN AND NORTHERN IRELAND ON THE DEFINITION OF THE TERM "NATIONALS"

In respect of the Treaty establishing a Constitution for Europe and the Treaty establishing the European Atomic Energy Community, and in any of the acts deriving from those Treaties or continued in force by those Treaties, the United Kingdom reiterates the Declaration it made on 31 December 1982 on the definition of the term "nationals" with the exception that the reference to "British Dependent Territories Citizens" shall be read as meaning "British overseas territories citizens".

47. DECLARATION BY THE KINGDOM OF SPAIN ON THE DEFINITION OF THE TERM "NATIONALS"

Spain notes that, under Article I-10 of the Constitution, every national of a Member State shall be a citizen of the Union. Spain also notes that, under the current state of European integration reflected in the Constitution, only nationals of Member States are entitled to the specific rights of European citizenship unless Union law expressly provides otherwise. In that respect, Spain notes, finally, that under Articles I-20 and I-46 of the Treaty, the European Parliament currently represents the citizens of the Union.

48. DECLARATION BY THE UNITED KINGDOM OF GREAT BRITAIN AND NORTHERN IRELAND ON THE FRANCHISE FOR ELECTIONS TO THE EUROPEAN PARLIAMENT

The United Kingdom notes that Article I-20 and other provisions of the Treaty establishing a Constitution for Europe are not intended to change the basis for the franchise for elections to the European Parliament.

49. DECLARATION BY THE KINGDOM OF BELGIUM ON NATIONAL PARLIAMENTS

Belgium wishes to make clear that, in accordance with its constitutional law, not only the Chamber of Representatives and Senate of the Federal Parliament but also the parliamentary assemblies of the Communities and the Regions act, in terms of the competences exercised by the Union, as components of the national parliamentary system or chambers of the national Parliament.

50. DECLARATION BY THE REPUBLIC OF LATVIA AND THE REPUBLIC OF HUNGARY ON THE SPELLING OF THE NAME OF THE SINGLE CURRENCY IN THE TREATY ESTABLISHING A CONSTITUTION FOR EUROPE

Without prejudice to the unified spelling of the name of the single currency of the European Union referred to in the Treaty establishing a Constitution for Europe as displayed on the banknotes and on the coins, Latvia and Hungary declare that the spelling of the name of the single currency, including its derivatives as applied throughout the Latvian and Hungarian text of the Treaty establishing a Constitution for Europe, has no effect on the existing rules of the Latvian and the Hungarian languages.

TABLES OF EQUIVALENCES
AND GENERAL INDEX

Tables of Equivalences

This fourteen-page subject index, prepared by the BMDF, covers the four parts of the Treaty, the Protocols and Declarations and the Additional Papers.

TABLES OF EQUIVALENCES

These two sets of Tables of Equivalences have been prepared by the BMDF in order to assist the reader in tracing individual articles from earlier treaties to the Treaty establishing the Constitution.

The numbering system used in the treaties has been changed twice; firstly by the Treaty of Amsterdam in 1997 and now by the Treaty establishing the Constitution. The original numbering of the Treaties was used up to and including the Maastricht Treaty. In 1997, the numbering system was revised and simplified by the Treaty of Amsterdam. The numbering of the Articles has been changed again by the Treaty establishing the Constitution, since this Treaty replaces the existing treaties and has fundamentally changed the order and structure of the articles.

TABLES FROM THE TEU AND TEC TO THE CONSTITUTION

The first set of Tables show the numbering of the Articles from the Maastricht Treaty to the revised numbering of the Constitution.

Column One *shows the numbering system and the articles as they stood after the Treaty of Maastricht.*

Column Two *shows the amended and new numbers of the Articles of the Treaties, as adjusted by the Treaty of Amsterdam and subsequent Articles introduced by the Treaty of Nice.* **The order of the articles in the Tables is taken from this numbering system.**

Column Three *shows the original Article number in the Treaty establishing the Constitution.*

Column Four *shows the revised numbering system of the Constitution, after the IGC in June 2004, where it was agreed by the Heads of Government that the numbering system should be consecutive throughout the new Constitutional Treaty.*

Original Number (Maastricht)	Amended Number (Amsterdam/Nice)	Original Number (Constitution)	Revised Number (Constitution)
The Treaty on European Union			
Title I:	*Title I*		
Common Provisions			
Article A	Article 1	- *deleted* -	- *deleted* -
Article B	Article 2	Article I-3	Article I-3
Article C	Article 3	Article I-18, III-193	Article I-19, III-292
Article D	Article 4	Article I-20	Article I-21
Article E	Article 5	- *deleted* -	- *deleted* -
Article F	Article 6: Art. 6(1)	Article I-2	Article I-2
	Art. 6(2)	Article I-7	Article I-9
	Art. 6(3)	Article I-5	Article I-5
	Article 7	Article I-58	Article I-59
Title II:	*Title II*		
Treaty establishing the European Community			
Article G	Article 8	- *deleted* -	- *deleted* -
Title III:	*Title III*		
Steel and Coal Community			
Article H	Article 9	- *deleted* -	- *deleted* -

Original Number (Maastricht)	Amended Number (Amsterdam/Nice)	Original Number (Constitution)	Revised Number (Constitution)
Title IV: *Atomic Power Community*	*Title IV*		
Article I	Article 10	*- deleted -*	*- deleted -*
Title V: *Foreign and Security Policy*	*Title V*		
Article J	*- repealed -*		-
Article J.1 (1, 2)	Article 11 (1)	Articles III-193, III-195	Articles III-292, III-294
Article J.1 (4)	Article 11(2)	Article I-15	Article I-16
Article J.1 (3)	Article 12	Article III-195	Article III-294
Article J.3 (1)	Article 13	Article III-196	Article III-295
Article J.8 (1, 2)	Article 13	*- deleted -*	*- deleted -*
Article J.3 (3-7)	Article 14	Article III-198	Article III-297
Article J.2 (2)	Article 15	Article III-199	Article III-298
Article J.2 (1)	Article 16	*- deleted -*	*- deleted -*
Article J.4 (2, 3)	Article 17(1)	Article I-15	Article I-16
Article J.4 (1, 4)	Article 17: Art 17(2)	Article III-210	Article III-309
Article J.4 (5, 6)	Article 17(4, 5)	*- deleted -*	*- deleted -*
Article J.5 (1-3)	Article 18: Art 18(5)	Article III-203	Article III-302
Article J.5 (4)	Article 19	Article III-206	Article III-305
Article J.2 (3)	Article 19 (1)	*- deleted -*	*- deleted -*
Article J.6	Article 20	Article III-207	Article III-306
Article J.10	Article 20	*- deleted -*	*- deleted -*
Article J.7	Article 21	Article III-205	Article III-304
Article J.8 (3, 4)	Article 22	Article III-200	Article III-299
Article J.3 (2)	Article 23	Article III-201	Article III-300
	Article 24	Articles III-204, III-225	Articles III-303, III-323
Article J.8 (5)	Article 25	Article III-208	Article III-307
	Article 26	*- deleted -*	*- deleted -*
Article J.9	Article 27	*- deleted -*	*- deleted -*
	Article 27.a	*- deleted -*	*- deleted -*
	Article 27.b	*- deleted -*	*- deleted -*
	Article 27.c	Article III-325	Article III-419
	Article 27.d	*- deleted -*	*- deleted -*
	Article 27.e	Article III-326(2)	Article III-420(2)
Article J.11 (1, 2)	Article 28	Article III-215	Article III-313
Title VI: *Justice and Home Affairs*	*Title VI*		
Article K	*- repealed -*		-
Article K.1	Article 29	Articles III-158, III-168	Articles III-257, III-267
Article K.2	Article 30: Art. 30(1)	Article III-176	Article III-275
	Art. 30(2)	Article III-177	Article III-276
Article K.3	Article 31: Art. 31(1)	Article III-171	Article III-270
	Art. 31(1)(e)	Article III-168	Article III-267
	Art. 31(2)	Article III-174	Article III-273
	Article 32	Article III-178	Article III-277
Article K.2 (2)	Article 33	Article III-163	Article III-262
Article K.3 (1)	Article 34 (1)	*- deleted -*	*- deleted -*
Article K.4 (3)	Article 34	*- deleted -*	*- deleted -*
	Article 35	*- deleted -*	*- deleted -*
	Article 35(5)	Article III-283	Article III-377
Article K.4 (1, 2)	Article 36	Article III-162	Article III-261
Article K.5	Article 37	*- deleted -*	*- deleted -*
	Article 38	*- deleted -*	*- deleted -*
Article K.6	Article 39	*- deleted -*	*- deleted -*
	Article 40	*- deleted -*	*- deleted -*

Original Number (Maastricht)	Amended Number (Amsterdam/Nice)	Original Number (Constitution)	Revised Number (Constitution)
Article K.7	Article 40	- deleted -	- deleted -
	Article 40.a	- deleted -	- deleted -
	Article 40.b	- deleted -	- deleted -
Article K.8	Article 41	- deleted -	- deleted -
Article K.9	Article 42	- deleted -	- deleted -
	Title VII: Enhanced Co-operation		
	Article 43: - 43(a)-(d)	Article I-43	Article I-44
	Art. 43(e)	Articles I-43, III-322	Articles I-44, III-416
	Art. 43(f)-(g)	Article I-43	Article I-44
	Art. 43(h)	Articles I-43, III-323	Articles I-44, III-417
	Article 43.a	Article I-43	Article I-44
	Article 43.b	Articles I-43, III-324	Articles I-44, III-418
	Article 44	Articles I-43, III-323	Articles I-44, III-417
	Article 44.a	Articles I-43, III-327	Articles I-44, III-421
	Article 45	Articles I-43, III-329	Articles I-44, III-423
Title VII: Final Provisions	*Title VIII*		
Article L	Article 46 : - 46(a)-(d)	- deleted -	- deleted -
	Art 46(e)	Article III-276	Article III-371
	Art 46(f)	Article III-209	Article III-308
Article M	Article 47	Article III-209	Article III-308
Article N	Article 48	Article IV-7	Article IV-443
Article O	Article 49	Article I-57	Article I-58
Article P	Article 50	- deleted -	- deleted -
Article Q	Article 51	Article IV-7c	Article IV-446
Article R	Article 52	Article IV-8	Article IV-447
Article S	Article 53	Article IV-10	Article IV-448

The Treaty establishing the European Community

Original Number (Maastricht)	Number in TEC (Amsterdam/Nice)	Original Number (Constitution)	Revised Number (Constitution)
Part One: Principles	*Part One*		
Article 1	Article 1	- deleted -	- deleted -
Article 2	Article 2	Article I-3	Article I-3
Article 3	Article 3: Art. 3(1)(c)	Article I-4	Article I-4
	Art. 3(2)	Article III-2	Article III-116
Article 3a	Article 4	Article III-69	Article III-177
Article 3b	Article 5	Article I-9	Article I-11
	Article 6	Article III-4	Article III-119
Article 4	Article 7	Articles I-18, I-31	Articles I-19, I-32
Article 4a	Article 8	Article I-29	Article I-30
Article 4b	Article 9	- deleted -	- deleted -
Article 5	Article 10	Article I-5	Article I-5
	Article 11	Article I-43	Article I-44
	Article 11.a	Article III-326(1)	Article III-420(1)
Article 6	Article 12	Articles I-4, III-7	Articles I-4, III-123
	Article 13	Article III-8	Article III-124

Original Number (Maastricht)	Amended Number (Amsterdam/Nice)	Original Number (Constitution)	Revised Number (Constitution)
Article 7	*- repealed -*	-	-
Article 7a	Article 14	Articles I-13, III-14	Articles I-14, III-130
Article 7b	*- repealed -*	-	-
Article 7b (para 2)	Article 14 (3)	*- deleted -*	*- deleted -*
Article 7c	Article 15	Articles I-13, III-14	Articles I-14, III-130
	Article 16	Article III-6	Article III-122
Part Two: Citizenship	*Part Two*		
Article 8	Article 17	Article I-8(2)	Article I-10(2)
Article 8a	Article 18	Articles I-8(2a), III-9	Articles I-10(2a), III-125
Article 8b	Article 19	Articles I-8(2b), III-10	Articles I-10(2b), III-126
Article 8c	Article 20	Articles I-8(2c), III-11	Articles I-10(2c), III-127
Article 8d	Article 21	Articles I-8(2d), III-12	Articles I-10(2d), III-128
Article 8e	Article 22	Article III-13	Article III-129
Part Three: *Community Policies*	*Part Three*		
Title I: *Free Movement of Goods*	*Title I*		
Article 9	Article 23	Article III-36(1)&(2)	Article III-151(1)&(2)
Article 10 (para 1)	Article 24	Article III-37(3)	Article III-151(3)
Article 10 (para 2)	*- repealed -*	-	-
Article 11	*- repealed -*	-	-
Chapter 1: *Customs Union* *Section 1:* *Customs Duties*	*Chapter 1*		
Article 12	Article 25	Article III-38(4)	Article III-151(4)
Articles 13 – 17	*- repealed -*	-	-
Section 2: *Common customs tariff*			
Articles 18 – 27			
Article 28	Article 26	Article III-39(5)	Article III-151(5)
Article 29	Article 27	Article III-40(6)	Article III-151(6)
Chapter 2: *Quantitative Restrictions*	*Chapter 2*		
Article 30	Article 28	Article III-42	Article III-153
Articles 31 – 33	*- repealed -*	-	-
Article 34 (para 1)	Article 29	Article III-42	Article III-153
Article 34 (para 2)	*- repealed -*	-	-
Article 35	*- repealed -*	-	-
Article 36	Article 30	Article III-43	Article III-154
Article 37 (para 1, 2, 4)	Article 31 (para 1, 2, 3)	Article III-44	Article III-155
Article 37 (para 3, 5, 6)	*- repealed -*	-	-
Title II: Agriculture	*Title II*		
Article 38	Article 32	Article III-122	Article III-226
Article 39	Article 33	Article III-123	Article III-227
Article 40 (para 1)	*- repealed -*	-	-
Article 40 (para 2, 3, 4)	Article 34 (para. 1, 2, 3)	Article III-124	Article III-228
Article 41	Article 35	Article III-125	Article III-229
Article 42	Article 36	Article III-126	Article III-230
Article 43	Article 37	Articles I-13, III-127	Articles I-14, III-231
Articles 44 – 45	*- repealed -*	-	-
Article 46	Article 38	Article III-128	Article III-232

Original Number (Maastricht)	Amended Number (Amsterdam/Nice)	Original Number (Constitution)	Revised Number (Constitution)
Article 47	- repealed -	-	-
Title III: **Free Movement of Persons, Services and Capital**	**Title III**		
Chapter 1: Workers	**Chapter 1**		
Article 48	Article 39	Article III-18	Article III-133
Article 49	Article 40	Article III-19	Article III-134
Article 50	Article 41	Article III-20	Article III-135
Article 51	Article 42	Article III-21	Article III-136
Chapter 2: **Right of Establishment**	**Chapter 2**		
Article 52	Article 43	Article III-22	Article III-137
Article 53	- repealed -	-	-
Article 54 (para 1)	- repealed -	-	-
Article 54 (Para 2, 3)	Article 44 (para 1,2)	Article III-23	Article III-138
Article 55	Article 45	Article III-24	Article III-139
Article 56	Article 46	Article III-25	Article III-140
Article 57	Article 47	Article III-26	Article III-141
Article 58	Article 48	Article III-27	Article III-142
Chapter 3: Services	**Chapter 3**		
Article 59	Article 49	Article III-29	Article III-144
Article 60	Article 50	Article III-30	Article III-145
Article 61	Article 51	Article III-31	Article III-146
Article 62	- repealed -	-	-
Article 63 (para 1)	- repealed -	-	-
Article 63 (para 2, 3)	Article 52 (para 1, 2)	Article III-32	Article III-147
Article 64	Article 53	Article III-33	Article III-148
Article 65	Article 54	Article III-34	Article III-149
Article 66	Article 55	Article III-35	Article III-150
Chapter 4: **Capital and Payments**	**Chapter 4**		
Articles 67 – 73a	- repealed -	-	-
Article 73b	Article 56	Article III-45	Article III-156
Article 73c	Article 57	Article III-46	Article III-157
Article 73d	Article 58	Article III-47	Article III-158
Article 73e	- repealed -	-	-
Article 73f	Article 59	Article III-48	Article III-159
Article 73g	Article 60	Article III-49	- deleted -
Article 73h	- repealed -	-	-
Title IIIa **Visas, Asylum and Immigration**	**Title IV**		
(*Introduced by Amsterdam*)	Article 61	Articles I-13, I-41, III-158	Articles I-14, I-42, III-257
	Article 62	Articles I-13, III-166(1)-(2)	Articles I-14, III-265(1)-(2)
	Article 63 :	Article I-13	Article I-14
	Art. 63(1)-(2)	Article III-167	Article III-266
	Art. 63(3)-(4)	Article III-168(2a)(2b)	Article III-267(2a)(2b)
	Article 64 :	Article I-13	Article I-14
	Art. 64(1)	Articles III-163, III-166(3)	Articles III-262, III-265(3)

Original Number (Maastricht)	Amended Number (Amsterdam/Nice)	Original Number (Constitution)	Revised Number (Constitution)
	Article 64(2)	Article III-167(3)	Article III-266(3)
	Article 65	Article III-170	Article III-269
	Article 66	Article III-164	Article III-263
	Article 67	- deleted -	- deleted -
	Article 68	- deleted -	- deleted -
	Article 69	- deleted -	- deleted -
Title IV: Transport	**Title V**		
Article 74	Article 70	Article III-133	Article III-236(1)
Article 75 (para 1, 3)	Article 71 (para 1, 2)	Article III-134	Article III-236(2)-(3)
Article 75 (para 2)	- repealed -	-	-
Article 76	Article 72	Article III-135	Article III-237
Article 77	Article 73	Article III-136	Article III-238
Article 78	Article 74	Article III-137	Article III-239
Article 79	Article 75	Article III-138	Article III-240
Article 80	Article 76	Article III-139	Article III-241
Article 81	Article 77	Article III-140	Article III-242
Article 82	Article 78	Article III-141	Article III-243
Article 83	Article 79	Article III-142	Article III-244
Article 84	Article 80	Article III-143	Article III-245
Title V: Common Rules	**Title VI**		
Chapter 1: Competition	**Chapter 1**		
Section 1: Undertakings	**Section 1**		
Article 85	Article 81	Article III-50	Article III-161
Article 86	Article 82	Article III-51	Article III-162
Article 87	Article 83	Article III-52	Article III-163
Article 88	Article 84	Article III-53	Article III-164
Article 89	Article 85	Article III-54	Article III-165
Article 90	Article 86	Article III-55	Article III-166
Section 2: Dumping	- repealed -	-	-
Article 91	- repealed -	-	-
Section 3: Aids	**Section 2**		
Article 92	Article 87	Article III-56	Article III-167
Article 93	Article 88	Article III-57	Article III-168
Article 94	Article 89	Article III-58	Article III-169
Chapter 2: Tax	**Chapter 2**		
Article 95	Article 90	Article III-59	Article III-170(1)
Article 96	Article 91	Article III-60	Article III-170(2)
Article 97	- repealed -	-	-
Article 98	Article 92	Article III-61	Article III-170(3)
Article 99	Article 93	Article III-62	Article III-171
Chapter 3: Approximation of Laws	**Chapter 3**		
Article 100	Article 94	Article III-65a	Article III-173
Article 100a	Article 95	Articles I-13, III-65	Articles I-14, III-172
Articles 100b-100d	- repealed -	-	-
Article 101	Article 96	Article III-66	Article III-174
Article 102	Article 97	Article III-67	Article III-175

Original Number (Maastricht)	Amended Number (Amsterdam/Nice)	Original Number (Constitution)	Revised Number (Constitution)
Title VI: EMU	*Title VII*		
Chapter 1: Economic Policy	*Chapter 1*		
Article 102a	Article 98	Article III-70	Article III-178
Article 103	Article 99	Article III-71	Article III-179
Article 103a	Article 100	Article III-72	Article III-180
Article 104	Article 101	Article III-73	Article III-181
Article 104a	Article 102	Article III-74	Article III-182
Article 104b	Article 103	Article III-75	Article III-183
Article 104c	Article 104	Article III-76	Article III-184
Chapter 2: Monetary Policy	*Chapter 2*		
Article 105	Article 105	Articles I-29, III-77	Articles I-30, III-185
Article 105a	Article 106	Article III-78	Article III-186
Article 106	Article 107	Articles I-29, III-79	Articles I-30, III-187
Article 107	Article 108	Article III-80	Article III-188
Article 108	Article 109	Article III-81	Article III-189
Article 108a	Article 110	Article III-82	Article III-190
Article 109	Article 111	Article III-228	Article III-326
Chapter 3: Institutions	*Chapter 3*	*Chapter 3*	*Chapter 3*
Article 109a	Article 112	Article III-289a	Article III-382
Article 109b	Article 113	Article III-289b	Article III-383
Article 109c	Article 114 :		
	Art. 114(1)	*- deleted -*	*- deleted -*
	Art. 114(2)-(4)	Article III-86	Article III-192
Article 109d	Article 115	Article III-87	Article III-193
Chapter 4: Transition	*Chapter 4*		
Article 109e	Article 116	*- deleted -*	*- deleted -*
Article 109f	Article 117 :		
	Art 117(1), (3)-(9)	*- deleted -*	*- deleted -*
	Art 117(2)	Article III-93	Article III-199
Article 109g	Article 118	*- deleted -*	*- deleted -*
Article 109h	Article 119	Article III-95	Article III-201
Article 109i	Article 120	Article III-96	Article III-202
Article 109j	Article 121	Article III-92	Article III-198
Article 109k	Article 122	Articles III-91, III-92	Articles III-197, III-198
Article 109*l*	Article 123 :		
	Art. 123(1)-(2)	*- deleted -*	*- deleted -*
	Art. 123(3)	Article III-93	Article III-199
	Art. 123(4)	Article III-83	Article III-191
	Art. 123(5)	Article III-92	Article III-198
Article 109m	Article 124(1)	Article III-94	Article III-200
Title VIa: Employment	*Title VIII*		
(*Introduced by Amsterdam*)	Article 125	Article III-97	Article III-203
	Article 126	Article III-98	Article III-204
	Article 127	Article III-99	Article III-205
	Article 128	Article III-100	Article III-206
	Article 129	Article III-101	Article III-207
	Article 130	Article III-102	Article III-208
Title VII: Commercial Policy	*Title IX*		
Article 110	Article 131	Article III-216	Article III-314

Original Number (Maastricht)	Amended Number (Amsterdam/Nice)	Original Number (Constitution)	Revised Number (Constitution)
Article 111	(*repealed by Maastricht Treaty*)	-	-
Article 112	Article 132	- *deleted* -	- *deleted* -
Article 113	Article 133	Article III-217	Article III-315
Article 114	(*repealed by Maastricht Treaty*)		-
Article 115	Article 134	- *deleted* -	- *deleted* -
Article 116	(*repealed by Maastricht Treaty*)	-	-
Title VIIa: Customs (*Introduced by Amsterdam*)	*Title X* Article 135	Article III-41	Article III-152
Title VIII: Social Policy	*Title XI*		
Chapter 1: Social Provisions	*Chapter 1*		
Article 117	Article 136	Article III-103	Article III-209
Article 118	Article 137	Articles I-13, III-104	Articles I-14, III-210
Article 118a	Article 138	Articles I-47, III-105	Articles I-48, III-211
Article 118b	Article 139	Article III-106	Article III-212
Article 118c	Article 140	Article III-107	Article III-213
Article 119	Article 141	Article III-108	Article III-214
Article 119a	Article 142	Article III-109	Article III-215
Article 120	Article 143	Article III-110	Article III-216
Article 121	Article 144	Article III-111	Article III-217
Article 122	Article 145	Article III-112	Article III-218
Chapter 2: Social Fund	*Chapter 2*		
Article 123	Article 146	Article III-113	Article III-219(1)
Article 124	Article 147	Article III-114	Article III-219(2)
Article 125	Article 148	Article III-115	Article III-219(3)
Chapter 3: Education, Vocational Training and Youth	*Chapter 3*		
Article 126	Article 149	Articles I-16, III-182	Articles I-17, III-282
Article 127	Article 150	Article III-183	Article III-283
Title IX: Culture	*Title XII*		
Article 128	Article 151	Articles I-16, III-181	Articles I-17, III-280
Title X: Public Health	*Title XIII*		
Article 129	Article 152	Articles I-13, I-16, III-179	Articles I-14, I-17, III-278
Title XI: Consumer Protection	*Title XIV*		
Article 129a	Article 153	Articles I-13, III-132	Articles I-14, III-235
	Article 153(2)	Article III-5	Article III-120
Title XII: Trans-European Networks	*Title XV*		
Article 129b	Article 154	Articles I-13, III-144	Articles I-14, III-246
Article 129c	Article 155	Article III-145(1), (3), (4)	Article III-247(1), (3), (4)
Article 129d	Article 156	Article III-145(2)	Article III-247(2)

Original Number (Maastricht)	Amended Number (Amsterdam/Nice)	Original Number (Constitution)	Revised Number (Constitution)
Title XIII: Industry	**Title XVI**		
Article 130	Article 157	Articles I-16, III-180	Articles I-17, III-279
Title XIV: Economic and Social Cohesion	**Title XVII**		
Article 130a	Article 158	Article III-116	Article III-220
Article 130b	Article 159	Articles I-13, III-117	Articles I-14, III-221
Article 130c	Article 160	Article III-118	Article III-222
Article 130d	Article 161	Article III-119	Article III-223
Article 130e	Article 162	Article III-120	Article III-224
Title XV: Research	**Title XVIII**		
Article 130f	Article 163	Article III-146	Article III-248
Article 130g	Article 164	Article III-147	Article III-249
Article 130h	Article 165	Article III-148	Article III-250
Article 130i	Article 166	Article III-149	Article III-251
Article 130j	Article 167	Article III-150	Article III-252(1)
Article 130k	Article 168	Article III-151	Article III-252(2)
Article 130l	Article 169	Article III-152	Article III-252(3)
Article 130m	Article 170	Article III-153	Article III-252(4)
Article 130n	Article 171	Article III-154	Article III-253
Article 130o	Article 172 (1)	Article III-154	Article III-253
	Article 172(2)	Article III-150	Article III-252(1)
Article 130p	Article 173	Article III-156	Article III-255
Article 130q	(repealed by Maastricht Treaty)		-
Title XVI: Environment	**Title XIX**		
Article 130r	Article 174	Articles I-13, III-129	Articles I-14, III-233
Article 130s	Article 175	Article III-130(1)-(5)	Article III-234(1)-(5)
Article 130t	Article 176	Article III-130(6)	Article III-234(6)
Title XVII: Development Co-operation	**Title XX**		
Article 130u	Article 177	Article III-218	Article III-316
Article 130v	Article 178	- deleted -	- deleted -
Article 130w	Article 179	Article III-219	Article III-317
Article 130x	Article 180	Article III-220	Article III-318
Article 130y	Article 181	Articles III-219, III-220	Articles III-317, III-318
	Title XXI: Economic, financial and technical co-operation with third countries		
	Article 181.a	Article III-221	Article III-319
Part Four: Overseas Countries and Territories	**Part Four**		
Article 131	Article 182	Article III-186	Article III-286
Article 132	Article 183	Article III-187	Article III-287
Article 133	Article 184	Article III-188	Article III-288
Article 134	Article 185	Article III-189	Article III-289

Original Number (Maastricht)	Amended Number (Amsterdam/Nice)	Original Number (Constitution)	Revised Number (Constitution)
Article 135	Article 186	Article III-190	Article III-290
Article 136	Article 187	Article III-191	Article III-291
Article 136a	Article 188	Article III-186(1)	Article III-286(1)
Part Five: Institutions	*Part Five*		
Title I: Governing Provisions	*Title I*		
Chapter 1: Institutions	*Chapter 1*		
Section 1: European Parliament	*Section 1*		
Article 137	Article 189	*- deleted -*	*- deleted -*
Article 138	Article 190	Article III-232	Article III-330
Article 138a	Article 191	Article III-233	Article III-331
Article 138b	Article 192	Article III-234	Article III-332
Article 138c	Article 193	Article III-235	Article III-333
Article 138d	Article 194	Article III-236	Article III-334
Article 138e	Article 195	Articles I-48, III-237	Articles I-49, III-335
Article 139	Article 196	Article III-238	Article III-336
Article 140	Article 197	Article III-239(1)	Article III-337
Article 141	Article 198	Article III-240	Article III-338
Article 142	Article 199	Article III-241	Article III-339
Article 143	Article 200	Article III-239(3)	Article III-337(3)
Article 144	Article 201	Article III-243	Article III-340
Section 2: Council	*Section 2*		
Article 145	Article 202	Articles I-22(1), I-35, I-36	Articles I-23(1), I-36, I-37
Article 146	Article 203	Articles I-22(2), III-245	Articles I-23(2), III-342
Article 147	Article 204	Article III-245	Article III-342
Article 148	Article 205	Article I-22(3), Article III-246(2)-(3)	Article I-23(3), Article III-343(2)-(3)
Article 149	*(repealed by Maastricht Treaty)*	-	-
Article 150	Article 206	Article III-246(1)	Article III-343(1)
Article 151	Article 207	Article III-247	Article III-344
Article 152	Article 208	Article III-248	Article III-345
Article 153	Article 209	Article III-249	Article III-346
Article 154	Article 210	Article III-306	Article III-400
Section 3: Commission	*Section 3*		
Article 155	Article 211	*- deleted -*	*- deleted -*
Article 156	Article 212	Article III-256	Article III-352
Article 157	Article 213(1)	Article III-250	*- deleted -*
	Article 213(2)	Article III-251	Article III-347
Article 158 (para. 1, 2)	Article 214 (1)(2)	Article III-250	*- deleted -*
Article 158 (para. 3)	*- repealed -*	-	-
Article 159	Article 215	Article III-252	Article III-348
Article 160	Article 216	Article III-253	Article III-349
Article 161	Article 217	Article III-254	Article III-350
Article 162	Article 218	Article III-256	Article III-352
	Art. 218(1)	Article III-303	Article III-397
Article 163	Article 219	Article III-255	Article III-351

Original Number (Maastricht)	Amended Number (Amsterdam/Nice)	Original Number (Constitution)	Revised Number (Constitution)
Section 4:	**Section 4**		
Court of Justice			
Article 164	Article 220	Article I-28(1)	Article I-29(1)
Article 165	Article 221	Articles I-28(2), III-258	Articles I-29(2), III-353
Article 166	Article 222	Articles I-28(2), III-259	Articles I-29(2), III-354
Article 167	Article 223	Article III-260	Article III-355
Article 168	Article 224	Article III-261	Article III-356
Article 168a	Article 225	Article III-263	Article III-358
	Article 225.a	Article III-264	Article III-359
Article 169	Article 226	Article III-265	Article III-360
Article 170	Article 227	Article III-266	Article III-361
Article 171	Article 228	Article III-267	Article III-362
Article 172	Article 229	Article III-268	Article III-363
	Article 229.a	Article III-269	Article III-364
Article 173	Article 230	Article III-270	Article III-365
Article 174	Article 231	Article III-271	Article III-366
Article 175	Article 232	Article III-272	Article III-367
Article 176	Article 233	Article III-273	Article III-368
Article 177	Article 234	Articles I-28(3), III-274	Articles I-29(3), III-369
Article 178	Article 235	Article III-275	Article III-370
Article 179	Article 236	Article III-277	Article III-372
Article 180	Article 237	Article III-278	Article III-373
Article 181	Article 238	Article III-279	Article III-374
Article 182	Article 239	Article III-280	Article III-375(3)
Article 183	Article 240	Article III-281	Article III-375(1)
Article 184	Article 241	Article III-285	Article III-378
Article 185	Article 242	Article III-286	Article III-379(1)
Article 186	Article 243	Article III-287	Article III-379(2)
Article 187	Article 244	Article III-288	Article III-380
Article 188	Article 245	Article III-289	Article III-381
Section 5:	**Section 5**		
Court of Auditors			
Article 188a	Article 246	Article I-30	Article I-31
Article 188b	Article 247	Articles I-30, III-291	Articles I-31, III-385
	Art. 247(8)	Article III-306	Article III-400
Article 188c	Article 248	Article III-290	Article III-384
Chapter 2:	**Chapter 2**		
Common Provisions			
Article 189	Article 249	Article I-32	Article I-33
Article 189a	Article 250	Article III-301	Article III-395
Article 189b (para 1 -7)	Article 251 (para 1-7)	Article III-302	Article III-396
Article 189b (para 8)	*- repealed -*	-	-
Article 189c	Article 252	*- deleted -*	*- deleted -*
Article 190	Article 253	Article I-37	Article I-38
Article 191	Article 254	Article I-38	Article I-39
	Article 255	Articles I-49, III-305	Articles I-50, III-399
Article 192	Article 256	Article III-307	Article III-401
Chapter 3:	**Chapter 3**		
Economic and Social			
Committee			
Article 193	Article 257	Article I-31	Article I-32
Article 194	Article 258	Articles I-31, III-295	Articles I-32, III-389
Article 195	Article 259	Articles I-31, III-296	Articles I-32, III-390
Article 196	Article 260	Articles I-31, III-297	Articles I-32, III-391
Article 197	Article 261	Article I-31	Article I-32
Article 198	Article 262	Articles I-31, III-298	Articles I-32, III-392

Original Number (Maastricht)	Amended Number (Amsterdam/Nice)	Original Number (Constitution)	Revised Number (Constitution)
Chapter 4:	**Chapter 4**		
Committee of the Regions			
Article 198a	Article 263	Articles I-31, III-292	Articles I-32, III-386
Article 198b	Article 264	Articles I-31, III-293	Articles I-32, III-387
Article 198c	Article 265	Articles I-31, III-294	Articles I-32, III-388
Chapter 5:	**Chapter 5**		
European Investment Bank			
Article 198d	Article 266	Article III-299	Article III-393
Article 198e	Article 267	Article III-300	Article III-394
Title II:	**Title II**		
Financial Provisions			
Article 199	Article 268	Article I-52(1)	Article I-53(1)
Article 200	- repealed -	Articles I-52(5), I-53	-
Article 201	Article 269	Article I-52	Articles I-53(5), I-54
Article 201a	Article 270		Article I-53
Article 202	Article 271	Articles I-52(3), III-312	Articles I-53(3), III-406
Article 203	Article 272:		
	Art. 272(1)	Articles I-52, I-55, III-309	Articles I-53, I-56, III-403
	Art. 272(2)-(10)	Articles I-52, III-309	Articles I-53, III-404
Article 204	Article 273	Articles I-52, III-311	Articles I-53, III-405
Article 205	Article 274	Articles I-52(6), III-313	Articles I-53(6), III-407
Article 205a	Article 275	Articles I-52, III-314	Articles I-53, III-408
Article 206	Article 276	Articles I-52, III-315	Articles I-53, III-409
Article 206a	- repealed -	-	-
Article 207	Article 277	Articles I-52, III-316	Articles I-53, III-410
Article 208	Article 278	Articles I-52, III-317	Articles I-53, III-411
Article 209	Article 279	Articles I-52, III-318	Articles I-53, III-412
Article 209a	Article 280	Articles I-52(7), III-321	Articles I-53(7), III-415
Part Six:	**Part Six**		
General Provisions			
Article 210	Article 281	- deleted -	- deleted -
Article 211	Article 282	Article III-332	Article III-426
	Article 283	Article III-333	Article III-427
Article 213	Article 284	Article III-334	Article III-428
	Article 285	Article III-335	Article III-429
	Article 286	Article I-50	Article I-51
Article 214	Article 287	Article III-336	Article III-430
Article 215	Article 288	Article III-337	Article III-431
Article 216	Article 289	Article III-368	Article III-432
Article 217	Article 290	Article III-339	Article III-433
	Article 291	Article III-340	Article III-434
Article 219	Article 292	Article III-284	Article III-375(2)
Article 220	Article 293	- deleted -	- deleted -
Article 221	Article 294	Article III-28	Article III-143

Original Number (Maastricht)	Amended Number (Amsterdam/Nice)	Original Number (Constitution)	Revised Number (Constitution)
Article 222	Article 295	Article III-331	Article III-425
Article 223	Article 296	Article III-342	Article III-436
Article 224	Article 297	Article III-16	Article III-131
Article 225	Article 298	Article III-17	Article III-132
Article 226	- repealed -		-
Article 227	Article 299	Articles III-330, IV-4	Articles III-424, IV-440
Article 228	Article 300	Articles I-56, III-204, Article III-227	Articles I-57, III-303, Article III-325
	Art. 300(7)	Article III-225	Article III-323
Article 228a	Article 301	Article III-224	Article III-322
Article 229	Article 302	Article III-229(1)	Article III-327(1)
Article 230	Article 303	Article III-229(1)	Article III-327(1)
Article 231	Article 304	Article III-229(1)	Article III-327(1)
Article 232	Article 305	- deleted -	- deleted -
Article 233	Article 306	Article IV-5	Article IV-441
Article 234	Article 307	Article III-341	Article III-435
Article 235	Article 308	Article I-17	Article I-18
	Article 309	- deleted -	- deleted -
Article 237	(repealed by Maastricht Treaty)		-
Article 238	Article 310	Article III-226	Article III-324
Article 239	Article 311	Article IV-6	Article IV-442
Article 240	Article 312	Article IV-7c	Article IV-446
Heading: Setting up of the Institutions	- deleted -		-
Articles 241 - 246	- repealed -		-
Final Provisions	*Final Provisions*		
Article 247	Article 313	Article IV-8	Article IV-447
Article 248	Article 314	Article IV-10	Article IV-448

TABLES COMPARING THE ORIGINAL AND REVISED NUMBERING

IN THE CONSTITUTION

The following tables have been prepared by the BMDF to show the comparatives between the original numbering system used for the Articles in the draft texts of the Treaty establishing a Constitution for Europe and the revised numbering system of the final text.

Original Numbers	Revised Numbers	Original Numbers	Revised Numbers
Part I: Text of the Constitution			
Article I-1	Article I-1	Article I-35	Article I-36
Article I-2	Article I-2	Article I-36	Article I-37
Article I-3	Article I-3	Article I-37	Article I-38
Article I-4	Article I-4	Article I-38	Article I-39
Article I-5	Article I-5	Article I-39	Article I-40
Article I-5a	Article I-6	Article I-40	Article I-41
Article I-6	Article I-7	Article I-41	Article I-42
Article I-6a	Article I-8	Article I-42	Article I-43
Article I-7	Article I-9	Article I-43	Article I-44
Article I-8	Article I-10	Article I-44	Article I-45
Article I-9	Article I-11	Article I-45	Article I-46
Article I-10	-	Article I-46	Article I-47
Article I-11	Article I-12	Article I-47	Article I-48
Article I-12	Article I-13	Article I-48	Article I-49
Article I-13	Article I-14	Article I-49	Article I-50
Article I-14	Article I-15	Article I-50	Article I-51
Article I-15	Article I-16	Article I-51	Article I-52
Article I-16	Article I-17	Article I-52	Article I-53
Article I-17	Article I-18	Article I-53	Article I-54
Article I-18	Article I-19	Article I-54	Article I-55
Article I-19	Article I-20	Article I-55	Article I-56
Article I-20	Article I-21	Article I-56	Article I-57
Article I-21	Article I-22	Article I-57	Article I-58
Article I-22	Article I-23	Article I-58	Article I-59
Article I-23	Article I-24	Article I-59	Article I-60
Article I-24	Article I-25		
Article I-25	Article I-26		
Article I-26	Article I-27	**Part II: Charter of Fundamental Rights**	
Article I-27	Article I-28		
Article I-28	Article I-29	Article II-1	Article II-61
Article I-29	Article I-30	Article II-2	Article II-62
Article I-30	Article I-31	Article II-3	Article II-63
Article I-31	Article I-32	Article II-4	Article II-64
Article I-32	Article I-33	Article II-5	Article II-65
Article I-33	Article I-34	Article II-6	Article II-66
Article I-34	Article I-35	Article II-7	Article II-67

Original Numbers	Revised Numbers
Article II-8	Article II-68
Article II-9	Article II-69
Article II-10	Article II-70
Article II-11	Article II-71
Article II-12	Article II-72
Article II-13	Article II-73
Article II-14	Article II-74
Article II-15	Article II-75
Article II-16	Article II-76
Article II-17	Article II-77
Article II-18	Article II-78
Article II-19	Article II-79
Article II-20	Article II-80
Article II-21	Article II-81
Article II-22	Article II-82
Article II-23	Article II-83
Article II-24	Article II-84
Article II-25	Article II-85
Article II-26	Article II-86
Article II-27	Article II-87
Article II-28	Article II-88
Article II-29	Article II-89
Article II-30	Article II-90
Article II-31	Article II-91
Article II-32	Article II-92
Article II-33	Article II-93
Article II-34	Article II-94
Article II-35	Article II-95
Article II-36	Article II-96
Article II-37	Article II-97
Article II-38	Article II-98
Article II-39	Article II-99
Article II-40	Article II-100
Article II-41	Article II-101
Article II-42	Article II-102
Article II-43	Article II-103
Article II-44	Article II-104
Article II-45	Article II-105
Article II-46	Article II-106
Article II-47	Article II-107
Article II-48	Article II-108
Article II-49	Article II-109
Article II-50	Article II-110
Article II-51	Article II-111
Article II-52	Article II-112
Article II-53	Article II-113

Original Numbers	Revised Numbers
Article II-54	Article II-114

Part III: Policies and Functioning of the Union

Original Numbers	Revised Numbers
Article III-1	Article III-115
Article III-2	Article III-116
Article III-2a	Article III-117
Article III-3	Article III-118
Article III-4	Article III-119
Article III-5	Article III-120
Article III-5a	Article III-121
Article III-6	Article III-122
Article III-7	Article III-123
Article III-8	Article III-124
Article III-9	Article III-125
Article III-10	Article III-126
Article III-11	Article III-127
Article III-12	Article III-128
Article III-13	Article III-129
Articles III-14/15	Article III-130
Article III-16	Article III-131
Article III-17	Article III-132
Article III-18	Article III-133
Article III-19	Article III-134
Article III-20	Article III-135
Article III-21	Article III-136
Article III-22	Article III-137
Article III-23	Article III-138
Article III-24	Article III-139
Article III-25	Article III-140
Article III-26	Article III-141
Article III-27	Article III-142
Article III-28	Article III-143
Article III-29	Article III-144
Article III-30	Article III-145
Article III-31	Article III-146
Article III-32	Article III-147
Article III-33	Article III-148
Article III-34	Article III-149
Article III-35	Article III-150
Articles III-36 - 40	Article III-151
Article III-41	Article III-152
Article III-42	Article III-152
Article III-43	Article III-153
Article III-44	Article III-154

Original Numbers	Revised Numbers	Original Numbers	Revised Numbers
Article III-45	Article III-155	Article III-93	Article III-199
Article III-46	Article III-156	Article III-94	Article III-200
Article III-47	Article III-157	Article III-95	Article III-201
Article III-48	Article III-158	Article III-96	Article III-202
Article III-49	Article III-159	Article III-97	Article III-203
Article III-50	Article III-160	Article III-98	Article III-204
Article III-51	Article III-161	Article III-99	Article III-205
Article III-52	Article III-162	Article III-100	Article III-206
Article III-53	Article III-163	Article III-101	Article III-207
Article III-54	Article III-164	Article III-102	Article III-208
Article III-55	Article III-165	Article III-103	Article III-209
Article III-56	Article III-166	Article III-104	Article III-210
Article III-57	Article III-167	Article III-105	Article III-211
Article III-58	Article III-168	Article III-106	Article III-212
Article III-59/60/61	Article III-169	Article III-107	Article III-213
Article III-62	Article III-170	Article III-108	Article III-214
Article III-63	Article III-171	Article III-109	Article III-215
Article III-64	-	Article III-110	Article III-216
Article III-65	Article III-172	Article III-111	Article III-217
Article III-65a	Article III-173	Article III-112	Article III-218
Article III-66	Article III-174	Article III-113 - 115	Article III-219
Article III-67	Article III-175	Article III-116	Article III-220
Article III-68	Article III-176	Article III-117	Article III-221
Article III-69	Article III-177	Article III-118	Article III-222
Article III-70	Article III-178	Article III-119	Article III-223
Article III-71	Article III-179	Article III-120	Article III-224
Article III-72	Article III-180	Article III-121	Article III-225
Article III-73	Article III-181	Article III-122	Article III-226
Article III-74	Article III-182	Article III-123	Article III-227
Article III-75	Article III-183	Article III-124	Article III-228
Article III-76	Article III-184	Article III-125	Article III-229
Article III-77	Article III-185	Article III-126	Article III-230
Article III-78	Article III-186	Article III-127	Article III-231
Article III-79	Article III-187	Article III-128	Article III-232
Article III-80	Article III-188	Article III-129	Article III-233
Article III-81	Article III-189	Article III-130/131	Article III-234
Article III-82	Article III-190	Article III-132	Article III-235
Article III-83	Article III-191	Article III-133/134	Article III-236
Article III-84	-	Article III-135	Article III-237
Article III-85	-	Article III-136	Article III-238
Article III-86	Article III-192	Article III-137	Article III-239
Article III-87	Article III-193	Article III-138	Article III-240
Article III-88	Article III-194	Article III-139	Article III-241
Article III-89	Article III-195	Article III-140	Article III-242
Article III-90	Article III-196	Article III-141	Article III-243
Article III-91	Article III-197	Article III-142	Article III-244
Article III-92	Article III-198	Article III-143	Article III-245

Original Numbers	Revised Numbers	Original Numbers	Revised Numbers
Article III-144	Article III-246	Article III-193	Article III-292
Article III-145	Article III-247	Article III-194	Article III-293
Article III-146	Article III-248	Article III-195	Article III-294
Article III-147	Article III-249	Article III-196	Article III-295
Article III-148	Article III-250	Article III-197	Article III-296
Article III-149	Article III-251	Article III-198	Article III-297
Article III-150 - 153	Article III-252	Article III-199	Article III-298
Article III-154	Article III-253	Article III-200	Article III-299
Article III-155	Article III-254	Article III-201	Article III-300
Article III-156	Article III-255	Article III-202	Article III-301
Article III-157	Article III-256	Article III-203	Article III-302
Article III-158	Article III-257	Article III-204	Article III-303
Article III-159	Article III-258	Article III-205	Article III-304
Article III-160	Article III-259	Article III-206	Article III-305
Article III-161	Article III-260	Article III-207	Article III-306
Article III-162	Article III-261	Article III-208	Article III-307
Article III-163	Article III-262	Article III-209	Article III-308
Article III-164	Article III-263	Article III-210	Article III-309
Article III-165	Article III-264	Article III-211	Article III-310
Article III-166	Article III-265	Article III-212	Article III-311
Article III-167	Article III-266	Article III-213	Article III-312
Article III-168	Article III-267	Article III-214	-
Article III-169	Article III-268	Article III-215	Article III-313
Article III-170	Article III-269	Article III-216	Article III-314
Article III-171	Article III-270	Article III-217	Article III-315
Article III-172	Article III-271	Article III-218	Article III-316
Article III-173	Article III-272	Article III-219	Article III-317
Article III-174	Article III-273	Article III-220	Article III-318
Article III-175	Article III-274	Article III-221	Article III-319
Article III-176	Article III-275	Article III-222	Article III-320
Article III-177	Article III-276	Article III-223	Article III-321
Article III-178	Article III-277	Article III-224	Article III-322
Article III-179	Article III-278	Article III-225	Article III-323
Article III-180	Article III-279	Article III-226	Article III-324
Article III-181	Article III-280	Article III-227	Article III-325
Article III-181a	Article III-281	Article III-228	Article III-326
Article III-182	Article III-282	Article III-229	Article III-327
Article III-183	Article III-283	Article III-230	Article III-328
Article III-184	Article III-284	Article III-231	Article III-329
Article III-185	Article III-285	Article III-232	Article III-330
Article III-186	Article III-286	Article III-233	Article III-331
Article III-187	Article III-287	Article III-234	Article III-332
Article III-188	Article III-288	Article III-235	Article III-333
Article III-189	Article III-289	Article III-236	Article III-334
Article III-190	Article III-290	Article III-237	Article III-335
Article III-191	Article III-291	Article III-238	Article III-336
Article III-192	-	Article III-239/242	Article III-337

Original Numbers	Revised Numbers	Original Numbers	Revised Numbers
Article III-240	Article III-338	Article III-289b	Article III-384
Article III-241	Article III-339	Article III-290	Article III-385
Article III-242	-	Article III-291	Article III-386
Article III-243	Article III-340	Article III-292	Article III-387
Article III-244	Article III-341	Article III-293	Article III-388
Article III-245	Article III-342	Article III-294	Article III-389
Article III-246	Article III-343	Article III-295	Article III-390
Article III-247	Article III-344	Article III-296	Article III-391
Article III-248	Article III-345	Article III-297	Article III-392
Article III-249	Article III-346	Article III-298	Article III-393
Article III-250	Article III-347	Article III-299	Article III-394
Article III-251	Article III-348	Article III-300	Article III-395
Article III-252	Article III-349	Article III-301	Article III-396
Article III-253	Article III-350	Article III-302	Article III-397
Article III-254	Article III-351	Article III-303	Article III-398
Article III-255	Article III-352	Article III-304	Article III-399
Article III-256/257	Article III-353	Article III-305	Article III-400
Article III-258	Article III-354	Article III-306	Article III-401
Article III-259	Article III-355	Article III-307	Article III-402
Article III-260	Article III-356	Article III-308	Article III-403
Article III-261	Article III-357	Article III-309	Article III-404
Article III-262	Article III-358	Article III-310	Article III-405
Article III-263	Article III-359	Article III-311	Article III-406
Article III-264	Article III-360	Article III-312	Article III-407
Article III-265	Article III-361	Article III-313	Article III-408
Article III-266	Article III-362	Article III-314	Article III-409
Article III-267	Article III-363	Article III-315	Article III-410
Article III-268	Article III-364	Article III-316	Article III-411
Article III-269	Article III-365	Article III-317	Article III-412
Article III-270	Article III-366	Article III-318	Article III-413
Article III-271	Article III-367	Article III-319	Article III-414
Article III-272	Article III-368	Article III-320	Article III-415
Article III-273	Article III-369	Article III-321	Article III-416
Article III-274	Article III-370	Article III-322	Article III-417
Article III-275	Article III-371	Article III-323	Article III-418
Article III-276	Article III-372	Article III-324	Article III-419
Article III-277	Article III-373	Article III-325	Article III-420
Article III-278	Article III-374	Article III-326	Article III-421
Article III-279	Article III-375	Article III-327	Article III-422
Article III-281/280/284	Article III-376	Article III-328	-
Article III-282	Article III-377	Article III-329	Article III-423
Article III-283	Article III-378	Article III-330	Article III-424
Article III-285	Article III-379	Article III-331	Article III-425
Article III-286/287	Article III-380	Article III-332	Article III-426
Article III-288	Article III-381	Article III-333	Article III-427
Article III-289	Article III-382	Article III-334	Article III-428
Article III-289a	Article III-383	Article III-335	Article III-429

Original Numbers	Revised Numbers	Original Numbers	Revised Numbers
Article III-336	Article III-430		
Article III-337	Article III-431		
Article III-338	Article III-432		
Article III-339	Article III-433		
Article III-340	Article III-434		
Article III-341	Article III-435		
Article III-342	Article III-436		

Part IV: General and Final Provisions

Article IV-1	-
Article IV-2	Article IV-437
Article IV-3	Article IV-438
Article IV-3a	Article IV-439
Article IV-4	Article IV-440
Article IV-5	Article IV-441
Article IV-6	Article IV-442
Article IV-7	Article IV-443
Article IV-7a	Article IV-444
Article IV-7b	Article IV-445
Article IV-7c	Article IV-446
Article IV-8	Article IV-447
Article IV-9	-
Article IV-10	Article IV-448

GENERAL INDEX

The General Index covers the four Parts of the Treaty and the Protocols and Declarations, and is intended to be a guide to the more important areas.

The references refer to the Part-Article (and paragraph) number and page number. Protocols and Declarations have page references.

Protocols and Declarations are referred to where relevant under the appropriate headings. There are detailed indexes to the Protocols and Declarations on pages 125 and 233.

	Part-Article	Page
Religion:		
- Animal welfare	III-121	31
- General	I-52	19
Repeal of earlier treaties	IV-437	113
Resources (financial) - *see also Own resources*	I-54	20
Restrictive measures on relations with third countries	III-322	87
Right of initiative to introduce proposals for legislation:		
- Commission	I-26(2)	11
- Common foreign and security policy	III-293(2), III-299	79, 80
- Freedom, security and justice	III-264	67
Rights of Citizens:		
- Fundamental rights	II-99	28
- General provisions	I-9	6
Right to strike	II-88	26
Role of National Parliaments in the European Union	Protocol no. 1	127
Rules on competition	III-161 *et. seq.*	39

S

	Part-Article	Page
Schengen *acquis*	Protocol no. 17	209
Scope:		
- Charter of Fundamental Rights	II-111 to II-112	29
- Treaty	IV-440	114
Seat of the Institutions	III-432, Protocol no. 6	111, 159
Services of general economic interest:		
- Competition	III-166	40
- Fundamental right	II-96	27
- General provisions	III-122	31
- State aid	III-167	41
- Transport	III-238	62
Shared competences	I-14	8
Sincere co-operation	I-5(2)	6
Social and territorial cohesion:		
- Declaration on island states	Declaration no. 19	258
- General provisions	II-220 to III-221	57 - 58
- Enhanced co-operation	III-416	109
- Services of general economic interest	III-122	31
Social partners (management and labour):		
- Employment	III-203 *et seq.*	53 - 54
- General provisions	I-48	19
- Social Policy	III-209 to III-212	55 - 56
- Social Protection Committee	III-217	57
Social Policy:		
- Areas and fields included in social policy	III-210	55
- Commission's role in co-ordination	III-213	56
- Declaration no. 18	-	258
- Equal pay	III-214	56
- European Social Fund	III-219	57
- Objectives	III-209	55
- Shared competence	I-14(2)	8
- Social partners	III-211 to III-212	56
- Social Protection Committee	III-217	57
Social security:		
- *'Barber Protocol'* on pension fund limits	Protocol no. 28	222
- Commission's role in co-ordination	III-213	56
- Documentation	III-125(2)	32
- Freedom of movement of workers	III-136	34
- Fundamental right	II-94	27
- Member States' rights	III-210(5)(a)	56
- Social policy	III—210(1)(c)	55

BRITISH MANAGEMENT DATA FOUNDATION

The British Management Data Foundation (BMDF) was formed in 1979. It is non-profit making and limited by guarantee.

It is an independent body supported by a wide range of major British companies and is concerned with matters affecting global competitiveness of its member companies to whom it gives independent advice and data.

The companies and organisations supporting the BMDF do not have an overall corporate view. They represent many differing interests and viewpoints. This, however, is one of the strengths of the BMDF and enables issues to be considered from a wide perspective.

The aim of all BMDF activities is to achieve a better understanding of current core issues so as to enable more informed decision-making.

Activities include review meetings and the issue of data and information on a wide range of current matters of importance to industry.
